COMMUNITY MENTAL HEALTH AND BEHAVIORAL-ECOL-OGY: a handbook of theory, research, and practice, ed. by Abraham M. Jeger and Robert S. Slotnick. Plenum, 1982. 510p index 82-13122. 37.50 ISBN 0-306-40850-3. CIP

As a whole, this book constitutes the best single collection of work on applied social ecology in a major human service area. It contains over 25 articles on the principles of what the editors refer to as the "behavioral-ecological perspective" and its applications to community mental health issues and problems. The editors have arranged the works in a clear and orderly way, moving from a consideration of the basic principles of behavioral ecology to an examination of specific programs that have attempted to use these principles to solve community mental health problems. The contributors represent a nice balance of academics, program consultants and evaluators, and mental health practitioners. Of particular note are some fine offerings on specific prevention projects and some provocative readings that reconsider common notions of professionalism, paraprofessionalism, ethics, and the role of mental health centers in the community. For those not so well versed in the theoretical foundations of human ecology, however, this reviewer recommends Urie Bronfenbrenner's *The Ecology of Human Development* (CHOICE, Nov. 1979) as a primer or as a companion resource. An appendix lists 97 professional societies, journals, newsletters, clearinghouses, and organizations that provide useful information on community mental health issues and behavioral ecology. A major contribution to the field of community mental health and an essential resource for libraries serving social work, psychology, or other human service students.

Community Mental Health and Behavioral-Ecology

A HANDBOOK OF THEORY, RESEARCH, AND PRACTICE

Edited by
ABRAHAM M. JEGER
and
ROBERT S. SLOTNICK

New York Institute of Technology at Old Westbury
Old Westbury, New York

454026

PLENUM PRESS · NEW YORK AND LONDON

Library of Congress Cataloging in Publication Data

Main entry under title:

Community mental health and behavioral-ecology.

Includes bibliographical references and indexes.
1. Community mental health services. 2. Behavior modification. 3. Social structure—
Therapeutic use. I. Jeger, Abraham M., 1952 –   . II. Slotnick, Robert S. 1940 –
         . [DNLM: 1. Behavior. 2. Environment. 3. Community psychiatry. WM 30.6
C734]
RA790.C68117 1982   362.2   82-13122
ISBN 0-306-40850-3

© 1982 Plenum Press, New York
A Division of Plenum Publishing Corporation
233 Spring Street, New York, N.Y. 10013

Printed in the United States of America

Community
Mental Health and
Behavioral-Ecology

A HANDBOOK OF THEORY, RESEARCH, AND PRACTICE

To
ROCHELLE, DEBBIE, and STEVEN JEGER
to
ANN SLOTNICK — IRVINGS
and to the memory of
DAVID SLOTNICK

Contributors

George J. Allen, Department of Psychology, University of Connecticut, Storrs, Connecticut

Robert P. Archer, Florida Mental Health Institute, 13301 N. 30th St., Tampa, Florida

Jeffrey R. Bedell, Florida Mental Health Institute, 13301 N. 30th St., Tampa, Florida

David E. Biegel, School of Social Work, University of Pittsburgh, Pittsburgh, Pennsylvania

Harold Braithwaite, Department of Psychology, University of South Carolina, Columbia, South Carolina

Jack M. Chinsky, Department of Psychology, University of Connecticut, Storrs, Connecticut

Joseph A. Durlak, Applied Psychology Program, Water Tower Campus, Loyola University, 10 East Pearson St., Chicago, Illinois

Thad Eckman, Clinical Research Center, Camarillo-Neuropsychiatric Institute (UCLA), Box A, Camarillo, California

Eileen D. Edmunson, Florida Mental Health Institute, 13301 N. 30th St., Tampa, Florida

Leo R. Eilbert, Human Resources Development Center, New York Institute of Technology, Old Westbury, New York

Henry Eilbirt, Bernard M. Baruch College, School of Business and Public Administration, New York, New York

Maurice J. Elias, Psychology Department, Livingston College, Rutgers University, New Brunswick, New Jersey

Stephen B. Fawcett, Community Technology Project, Center for Public Affairs, University of Kansas, Lawrence, Kansas

Esther O. Fergus, Psychology Department, Michigan State University, East Lansing, Michigan

R. Kay Fletcher, Community Technology Project, Center for Public Affairs, University of Kansas, Lawrence, Kansas

Steven Friedman, Downstate Medical Center, Brooklyn, New York

Howard L. Garber, Rehabilitation Research and Training Center in Mental Retardation, University of Wisconsin, Madison, Wisconsin

William H. Goodson, Jr., 303 Williams Avenue, S.W., Suite 931, Huntsville, Alabama

Richard E. Gordon, Department of Psychiatry, University of Florida, Gainesville, Florida

Steven B. Gordon, Behavior Therapy Associates, Somerset, New Jersey

Rick Heber, Rehabilitation Research and Training Center in Mental Retardation, University of Wisconsin, Madison, Wisconsin

Paulette Hines, UMDNJ-Rutgers Medical School, Rutgers Community Mental Health Center, Piscataway, New Jersey

Robert A. Hoffnung, Elizabeth General Hospital, Community Mental Health Center, Elizabeth, New Jersey

Leonard A. Jason, Psychology Department, DePaul University, Chicago, Illinois

Abraham M. Jeger, Human Resources Development Center, New York Institute of Technology, Old Westbury, New York

Judith A. Jurmann, Psychology Department, St. John's University, Jamaica, New York

Dawne Kimbrell, Department of Psychology, University of South Carolina, Columbia, South Carolina

Martin B. Koretzky, Veterans Administration Hospital, Northport, New York

Julie M. Kuehnel, Clinical Research Center, Camarillo-Neuropsychiatric Institute (UCLA), Box A, Camarillo, California

Timothy G. Kuehnel, Clinical Research Center, Camarillo-Neuropsychiatric Institute (UCLA), Box A, Camarillo, California

Stephen W. Larcen, United Social and Mental Health Services, Inc., 51 Westcott Road, Danielson, Connecticut

Stanley Lehmann, Department of Psychology, New York University, New York, New York

Sonne Lemke, Social Ecology Laboratory, Geriatric Research, Education, and Clinical Center, Veterans Administration and Stanford University Medical Center, Palo Alto, California

Robert P. Liberman, Clinical Research Center, Camarillo-Neuropsychiatric Institute (UCLA), Box A, Camarillo, California

George Livingston, Department of Psychology, University of South Carolina, Columbia, South Carolina

Francis Matese, Psychology Department, DePaul University, Chicago, Illinois

R. Mark Mathews, Department of Psychology, University of Hawaii, Hilo, Hawaii

Alfred McAlister, Harvard University School of Public Health, Boston, Massachusetts

Gary McClure, Department of Psychology, Georgia Southern College, Statesboro, Georgia

Rudolf H. Moos, Social Ecology Laboratory, Geriatric Research, Education, and Clinical Center, Veterans Administration and Stanford University Medical Center, Palo Alto, California

deRossett Myers, Jr., Department of Psychology, University of South Carolina, Columbia, South Carolina

Arthur J. Naparstek, University of Southern California, Washington Public Affairs Center, Washington, D.C.

Louise Merola Nielsen, Community Technology Project, Center for Public Affairs, University of Kansas, Lawrence, Kansas

N. Dickon Reppucci, Psychology Department, University of Virginia, Charlottesville, Virginia

Todd Risley, Department of Human Development, University of Kansas, Lawrence, Kansas

Jeffrey Rosenstein, Clinical Research Center, Camarillo-Neuropsychiatric Institute (UCLA), Box A, Camarillo, California

J. Terry Saunders, Offenders Aid and Restoration of the United States, 409 East High St., Charlottesville, Virginia

Matthew Schure, Human Resources Development Center, New York Institute of Technology, Old Westbury, New York

Tom Seekins, Community Technology Project, Center for Public Affairs, University of Kansas, Lawrence, Kansas

Susan I. Shorr, Psychology Department, DePaul University, Chicago, Illinois

Robert S. Slotnick, Human Resources Development Center, New York Institute of Technology, Old Westbury, New York

Kenneth R. Suckerman, UMDNJ-Rutgers Medical School, Piscataway, New Jersey

H. Augustus Taylor, Elizabeth General Hospital, Community Mental Health Center, Elizabeth, New Jersey

Louis G. Tornatzky, National Science Foundation, Division of Policy Research and Analysis, 1800 G St., N.W., Washington, D.C.

A. Jack Turner, 303 Williams Avenue, S.W., Suite 931, Huntsville, Alabama

Sandra Twardosz, Department of Child and Family Studies, College of Home Economics, University of Tennessee, Knoxville, Tennessee

Issac Tylim, Elizabeth General Hospital, Community Mental Health Center, Elizabeth, New Jersey

John C. Wadsworth, Department of Psychology, University of South Carolina, Columbia, South Carolina

Abraham Wandersman, Department of Psychology, University of South Carolina, Columbia, South Carolina

Paula L. Whang, Community Technology Project, Center for Public Affairs, University of Kansas, Lawrence, Kansas

Preface

This volume is addressed to professionals and students in community mental health—including researchers, clinicians, administrators, educators, and students in relevant specialities within the fields of psychology, psychiatry, social work, public health, and nursing. The intent of this book is to serve as a practical resource for professionals and also as a didactic text for students. In addition, the volume seeks to make a theoretical contribution to the field by presenting, for the first time in book form, a behavioral-ecological perspective in community mental health.

We present behavioral-ecology as an emerging perspective that is concerned with the *interdependence* of people, behavior, and their sociophysical environments. Behavioral-ecology attributes mental health problems to *transactions* between persons and their settings, rather than to causes rooted exclusively within individuals *or* environments. In this volume we advance the notion of behavioral-ecology as an integration of two broad perspectives—*behavioral* approaches as derived from the individual psychology of learning, and *ecological* approaches as encompassing the study of communities, environments, and social systems. Through the programs brought together in this book we are arguing for a merging of these two areas for purposes of advancing theory, research, and practice in community mental health.

To enhance its pedagogic utility and resource value, we have organized the volume around several unique features. First, the emphasis of the book is on major *current* topics in community mental health. Second, in Part I we devote three chapters to the conceptualization, values, and knowledge bases informing behavioral-ecology in order to provide the context for the entire volume. Third, most chapters are project oriented, with contributors describing, evaluating, and discussing their own innovative research/intervention programs. We have selected these projects as "exemplars" of behavioral-ecology in action. Fourth, we have included introductory comments in each part. They complement the presentations by placing the chapters within the behavioral-ecological framework, providing an overview of the relevant literature and issues pertaining to the part topics, and contributing to the integrative thread of the volume. Finally, an appendix listing resources in community mental health and behavioral-ecology is included.

The book has eight parts, comprising a total of 27 chapters. Each part is devoted to projects in a major current area of community mental health. An editorial introduction precedes each part.

In Part I three chapters by the editors provide the orientation for the entire volume. Chapter 1 consists of a conceptual overview of behavioral-ecology as well as a historical analysis of the community mental health movement. In Chapter 2, the values informing behavioral-ecological interventions are explicated; Chapter 3 reviews the major streams of theory, research, and practice that contribute to a knowledge base for behavioral-ecology.

Part II contains descriptions and evaluations of three "model" programs that reflect behavioral-ecological alternatives to institutionalization for acute and chronic psychiatric clients: namely, the Behavior Analysis and Modification (BAM) Project by Liberman *et al.* (Chapter 4), the Community Lodge by Tornatzky and Fergus (Chapter 5), and the Community Network Development (CND) Project by Edmunson *et al.* (Chapter 6). The chapters on the BAM and the Lodge also describe the national dissemination of these innovative programs.

Part III presents examples of consultation programs as fulfilling the mandate of community mental health for the provision of "indirect" service and expanding mental health personpower. In Chapter 7, Twardosz and Risley describe their work on behavioral-ecological consultation to day care centers; in Chapter 8 Suckerman and his colleagues focus on school-based behavioral consultation to teachers and parents. Reppucci and Saunders (Chapter 9) report on a longitudinal research effort employing behavioral consultation to change an entire institution for juvenile offenders. In Chapter 10 Friedman describes the use of social climate assessment within a consultation context to stimulate change in mental health treatment environments.

In Part IV several "exemplary" prevention programs are reviewed. Elias *et al.* (Chapter 11) describe a research/intervention program based on training problem-solving skills to school children as a vehicle for primary prevention. An environmental enrichment program aimed at preventing cultural-familial mental retardation is the subject of Chapter 12 by Garber and Heber. Matese *et al.* (Chapter 13) discuss their programs to facilitate transitions to parenthood within a crisis intervention con-

text. Finally, McAlister (Chapter 14) considers the role of the media coupled with community support systems to promote physical and mental
health as exemplified by the Stanford and North Karelia (Finland) Heart
Disease Prevention programs.

A relatively new topic, social support networks, is the focus of Part
V. Following a conceptual chapter by Schure *et al.* outlining the compatibility of self-help/professional collaboration and behavioral-ecology
(Chapter 15), Fawcett and his colleagues (Chapter 16) review their Community Technology Project, whereby they have developed, implemented,
evaluated, and disseminated various behavioral technologies with community self-help organizations. In Chapter 17, Biegel and Naparstek discuss the Neighborhood and Family Services Project within the context of
their community mental health empowerment model. The social ecology
of natural supports in single-resident occupancy (SRO) hotels is the focus of Lehmann's (Chapter 18) research-oriented chapter.

Part VI is devoted to program evaluation as facilitating community
accountability. In Chapter 19 Goodson and Turner report on the evaluation of a behaviorally oriented community mental health center. Moos
and Lemke (Chapter 20) describe their Multiphasic Environmental Assessment Procedure (MEAP), a comprehensive assessment package that
taps physcial and architectural resources, policy and program resources,
resident and staff resources, and social-environmental resources of a specific program or setting. Wandersman *et al.* (Chapter 21) describe a case
study in the evaluation of a citizen advisory board of a community mental health center. In Chapter 22 Jeger and McClure use a behavioral consultation program to a psychiatric center to demonstrate the comple-
mentarity of experimental evaluation and process analysis. Finally,
Eilbert and Eilbirt (Chapter 23) offer a structural framework for conceptualizing ethical issues in behavioral-ecological practice by considering
the major contexts for ethical enigmas and dilemmas along the entire
temporal sequence of interventions.

Part VII considers the education of mental health personnel at various levels. Chapter 24 by Tornatzky describes the Ecological Psychology
Doctoral Training Program at Michigan State University over a 10-year
period, from the standpoint of its goal to train social systems interventionists. Durlak (Chapter 25) provides guidelines for training paraprofessional mental health workers and discusses the issues pertaining to the
larger paraprofessional movement. Hoffnung *et al.* (Chapter 26) demonstrate the use of the Community Mental Health Ideology Scale as a
guide for in-service staff training.

Finally, in Part VIII the editors address the question, Where do we
go from here? They take the reader on a fantasy trip to future commu-

nity *resource* centers, as distinct from current community *mental health* centers.

The Appendix provides a listing of resources in the general area of community mental health as well as behavioral-ecology. These include journals, newsletters, professional societies, organizations, clearinghouses, and informal networks.

We hope this book will serve as a catalyst for the further development of the behavioral-ecological perspective in community mental health. Furthermore, we hope that in some small way we have stimulated ideas for specific programs that will contribute to the enhancement of mental health in our communities.

ABRAHAM M. JEGER
ROBERT S. SLOTNICK

Acknowledgments

It is gratifying to extend acknowledgment to the many persons who contributed to this book. First and foremost we express our sincere appreciation to our able contributors. Their work has not only made this book possible, but their innovative projects have enhanced community mental health research and practice.

Our own behavioral-ecological "thinking" was influenced by leading professionals/scholars in the fields of behavior modification, social ecology, community psychology, and community mental health. Many of our ideas build upon earlier contributions by Len Krasner, Seymour Sarason, Jim Kelly, Julian Rappaport, Rudolf Moos, Todd Risley, Ralph Catalano, Harold Proshansky, Roger Barker, and Dan Stokols.

On a more personal level, the support of colleagues, friends, and family members throughout the course of editing this book was most valuable. Our colleagues at the New York Institute of Technology, especially Matt Schure and Tom Burke, provided a supportive environment to carry on our day-to-day work. Friends and family members who provided emotional support which allowed us to persevere in this endeavor include Shia, Eugenia, and Meyer Jeger; Ference and Bertha Gross; and Yitz Grossman (especially for his diversionary humor).

We appreciate the staff assistance and material resources provided by the New York Institute of Technology that made this work possible. Special thanks are due to President Alexander Schure and Provost David G. Salten of the New York Institute of Technology for their support in establishing the Long Island Self-Help Clearinghouse and Self-Help Action Center, Inc., which provided the setting for our community mental health activities. Staff members who helped assist us in our work include Audrey Leif, Lorraine Purrificato, Elise Chavis, K. H. Lateef, and Susan Spieler.

Finally, we are appreciative of the expertise and professionalism of the staff of Plenum Press, who were a pleasure to work with in all phases of the project.

Contents

Chapter 4

The Behavioral Analysis and Modification Project for Community Mental Health: From Conception to Dissemination 95

Robert Paul Liberman, Timothy G. Kuehnel, Julie M. Kuehnel, Thad Eckman, and Jeffrey Rosenstein

Chapter 5

Innovation and Diffusion in Mental Health: The Community Lodge 113

Louis G. Tornatzky and Esther O. Fergus

Chapter 6

Integrating Skill Building and Peer Support in Mental Health Treatment: The
Early Intervention and Community Network Development Projects

Eileen D. Edmunson, Jeffrey R. Bedell, Robert P. Archer, and
Richard E. Gordon

Chapter 7

Behavioral-Ecological Consultation to Day Care Centers

Sandra Twardosz and Todd Risley

Chapter 11

*A Multilevel Behavioral-Preventive School Program: Process, Problems, and
Potential*   203

Maurice J. Elias, Jack M. Chinsky, Stephen W. Larcen, and
George J. Allen

Chapter 12

Prevention of Cultural-Familial Mental Retardation   217

Howard L. Garber and Rick Heber

Chapter 13

Behavioral and Community Interventions during Transition to Parenthood   231

Francis Matese, Susan I. Shorr, and Leonard A. Jason

Chapter 16

Designing Behavioral Technologies with Community Self-Help Organizations .. 281

Stephen B. Fawcett, R. Kay Fletcher, R. Mark Mathews, Paula L.
Whang, Tom Seekins, and Louise Merola Nielsen

Chapter 17

*The Neighborhood and Family Services Project: An Empowerment Model Linking
Clergy, Agency Professionals, and Community Residents* 303

David E. Biegel and Arthur J. Naparstek

Chapter 18

The Social Ecology of Natural Supports 319

Stanley Lehmann

PART VI.   EVALUATION AND COMMUNITY
                ACCOUNTABILITY 335

Chapter 19

Evaluating a Behavioral Community Mental Health Center 343

W. H. Goodson, Jr., and A. Jack Turner

Chapter 20

Rudolf H. Moos and Sonne Lemke

Chapter 21

Abraham Wandersman, Dawne Kimbrell, John C. Wadsworth,
deRossett Myers, Jr., George Livingston, and Harold Braithwaite

Chapter 22

Abraham M. Jeger and Gary McClure

Chapter 23

A Structural Framework for Conceptualizing Ethical Issues in Behavioral-Ecological Practice 403

Leo R. Eilbert and Henry Eilbirt

PART VII. MENTAL HEALTH PERSONPOWER: EDUCATION AND TRAINING 423

I
Behavioral-Ecology

CONCEPTUALIZATION, VALUES, AND KNOWLEDGE BASES

The world we have made as a result of the level of thinking we have done thus far creates problems that we can't solve at the same level as the level we created them at. (Albert Einstein; cited by Ulrich, 1980, p. 2.)

Introduction

What is mental health? What constitutes a mental health problem? What is meant by "positive" mental health? When does a person become an appropriate target of intervention? Where should services be offered? By whom? What interventions are most appropriate? And, can mental health problems be prevented? Answers to these, and related, questions are tied to one's perspective of mental health. Although different historical eras have approached these questions differently (see Gottesfeld, 1979; Mehr, 1980; Szasz, 1971; Ullmann & Krasner, 1975; Zilboorg & Henry, 1941), contemporary mental health practice is characterized by a plethora of concepts and practices—all operating concurrently and tied to different ideological perspectives.

In this part the editors provide the foundation and integrating thread for the thesis of this volume—namely, that the emerging behavioral-ecological perspective should provide a conceptual framework to guide the development of a data base for community mental health practice. Specifically, the chapters in this part present a formulation of

1

behavioral-ecology as an alternative to existing models of mental health. They consider the general features of a behavioral-ecological perspective (Chapter 1), the values guiding behavioral-ecological interventions (Chapter 2), and behavioral-ecological knowledge bases for community mental health practice (Chapter 3). As a backdrop against which to discuss our conceptualization of behavioral-ecology, we present an overview of the major contemporary models of mental health.

Five major models of "psychopathology" have guided mental health practice in recent years: (1) biological/medical; (2) psychodynamic/intrapsychic; (3) behavioral/learning; (4) humanistic, and (5) social/sociocultural (Burgess & Lazare, 1976; Catalano, 1979; Gottesfeld, 1979; Mehr, 1980; Ullmann & Krasner, 1975). We turn now to the defining characteristics of each.

The *biological* model views mental health problems as rooted in physiological structures. These might include disorders of the brain and central nervous system, biochemical and biophysical disturbances, or genetic anomalies. People experiencing psychological distress are said to be "sick" and suffering from an "illness" like any other. "Abnormal" behavior is seen as qualitatively different from "normal" behavior, as it is a symptom of an underlying disease (just as fever may be symptomatic of an underlying virus or bacteria). This view emerged as an alternative to those of earlier historical periods in which people manifesting "bizarre" behavior were seen as possessed by demons and as victims of sin (see Foucault, 1967).

Following a diagnosis of the illness as established by the Diagnostic and Statistical Manual of the American Psychiatric Association (DSM III), a variety of medical treatments are offered to patients. They range from chemotherapy to electroconvulsive therapy to psychosurgery. Depending on the treatment, it is offered in psychiatric hospitals, outpatient clinics, or private therapy offices.

Like the biological model, the *psychodynamic* approach as developed by Freud also looks "inside" the person to determine causes for his/her symptoms. However, rather than focusing on physical disturbance, such psychological determinants as unconscious conflicts, early deprivation, and fixations at psychosexual stages are seen as sources of mental illness. The focus of treatment, usually one-to-one psychotherapy, is on restructuring the "abnormal personality" by providing "insight" into the causes of problems. This model maintains the medical analogy, as it still views "mental illness" as a symptom of some underlying cause. Furthermore, it uses such medical nomenclature as doctor, patient, diagnosis, treatment, prognosis, and cure. (Indeed, early psychoanalytic training centers required their applicants to have medical degrees.) In seeking to resolve underlying conflicts, unconscious motivations are explored by the therapist through such techniques as free association, dream interpretation, and transference analysis.

Behavioral approaches view mental health problems as maladaptive behaviors acquired through *learning*, that is, experience with the environment. Maladaptive behavior is acquired through the same learning processes as "normal" behavior—namely, classical conditioning, operant conditioning, observational learning (modeling/imitation), and cognitive learning (see the first section of Chapter 3 for a more elaborate review). According to this view there is no such thing as "mental illness," and people with faulty learning are not considered "sick."

The goal of interventions within a behavioral framework is an "educational" one; that is, to unlearn maladaptive habits and acquire new adaptive responses. This goal is pursued through procedures based on the same learning principles that are said to have contributed to the development of the inappropriate behaviors in the first place—classical and operant conditioning, and so on. The focus is on changing overt behavior and training in self-control skills so that the individual becomes more competent in exchanges with other people (and the environment).

Whereas the behavioral approach is clearly an alternative to the "medical" model (based either on biological or intrapsychic views of etiology), the style of service delivery remained, for the most part, parallel to the medical orientation (Rappaport & Chinsky, 1974). That is, most behavioral interventionists in mental health saw themselves as providing "therapy" (albeit behavior therapy), practiced in institutional and clinic or office settings, and offered services on a one-to-one or small-group level.

Humanistic approaches (e.g., Rogers's self theory) tend to see the source of psychological distress in terms of alienation from the "self." Through such treatment models as client-centered therapy (Rogers) the therapist takes a nondirective stance in exploring with the client his/her self (e.g., discrepancies between one's real and ideal self) in a climate of total acceptance. By being empathic and creating a climate of "unconditional positive regard," the goal of clients' actualization of their potential for autonomy, authenticity, and spontaneity is facilitated. The vehicle for service delivery is individual or group counseling.

Finally, the *sociocultural* viewpoint has its roots in sociology as well as social and community psychiatry. It tends to view mental illness as a social problem rather than just an individual problem. Such factors as socioeconomic status, race, educational level, housing conditions, and so on are seen as related to individual stress. Interventions seek to change the social systems of which a person is part—for example, by advocating for better housing, more employment opportunities (see Brenner, 1973), and elimination of racism and sexism.

Thus, like the behavioral model, the sociocultural approach looks at the external environment instead of inside the person to explain mental health problems. However, whereas the behavioral viewpoint has generally restricted its concerns to the immediate situation, the sociocultural view has focused on the macroenvironment. As such, interventions derived from the sociocultural model call for large-scale social change, whereas most behavioral interventions have focused on changing individuals in order to help them adjust to the existing social system.

An approach that focuses on individual *behavior* (as does the behavioral model) while taking into account the larger society (as does the social model) is reflected in our behavioral-ecological perspective. Rather than looking exclusively at individuals *or* environments as sources of mental health problems, behavioral-ecology focuses on the *transaction* between persons and their settings. Thus behavioral-ecology is an alternative to approaches that tend to blame individuals for their problems (e.g., biological or psychological deficits) as well as to those that blame the environment (e.g., cultural deprivation).

The salient features of behavioral-ecology are presented in Chapter 1, followed by a general and historical background of the community mental health movement. Next, the limitations of community mental health practice are discussed. These problems of implementation are attributed to the domination of community mental health centers by the medical model (with its biological and intrapsychic emphasis). It is our argument in Chapter 1 that a behavioral-ecological perspective can potentially meet the limitations inherent in current community mental health practice.

In the second chapter, the editors consider the values guiding community mental health interventions at the individual, community, and societal levels: promoting individual competence, enhancing the psychological sense of community, and supporting cultural diversity, respectively. These values are essential components of behavioral-ecology, which we characterize as a merging of ethics and practice. Thus it is our contention that professionals guided by behavioral-ecological thinking are likely to develop ethical interventions.

Finally, in Chapter 3 we discuss four major streams of theory, research, and practice that contribute to a knowledge base for behavioral-ecological interventions in community mental health: behavioral community technology; bioecological analogies; environment-and-behavior field (i.e., environmental and ecological psychology); and networks. These streams are not mutually exclusive; nor are they exhaustive. We feel that a synthesis of these areas will translate into programs based on a view of individuals in their broader societal contexts. Such programs will integrate behavioral skill training, social support, and influences of the physical environment to foster competent individuals and create autonomous living and learning environments. In the course of empowering people and catalyzing the self-help capacities of communities, behavioral-ecological programs should be stimulating for professional and non-professional staff. All behavioral-ecological interventions are characterized by a commitment to evaluation in order to maintain community accountability. The projects represented in this volume exemplify behavioral-ecological practice.

References

Brenner, M. H. *Mental illness and the economy*. Cambridge: Harvard University Press, 1973.

Burgess, A. W., & Lazare, A. *Community mental health: Target populations*. Englewood Cliffs, N.J.: Prentice-Hall, 1976.

Catalano, R. *Health, behavior, and community: An ecological perspective*. Elmsford, N.Y.: Pergamon Press, 1979.

Foucault, M. *Madness and civilization*. New York: Mentor Books, 1967.

Gottesfeld, H. *Abnormal psychology: A community mental health perspective*. Chicago: SRA, 1979.

Mehr, J. *Human services: Concepts and intervention strategies*. Boston: Allyn & Bacon, 1980.

Rappaport, J., & Chinsky, J. M. Models for delivery of service from a historical and conceptual perspective. *Professional Psychology*, 1974, *5*, 42–50.

Szasz, T. J. *The manufacture of madness*. New York: Dell Books, 1971.

Ullmann, L. P., & Krasner, L. *A psychological approach to abnormal behavior*. Englewood Cliffs, N.J.: Prentice-Hall, 1975.

Ulrich, R. E. The use of behavior modification strategies to increase the probability of attendance at evening chapel through the use of food contingent reinforcement at the Life Line Mission, San Francisco, California. *Behaviorists for Social Action Journal*, 1980, *2* (2), 1–2.

Zilboorg, G., & Henry, G. W. *A history of medical psychology*. New York: W. W. Norton, 1941.

1

Community Mental Health
Toward a Behavioral-Ecological Perspective

ABRAHAM M. JEGER AND ROBERT S. SLOTNICK

Behavioral-ecology represents a perspective on people and their environments, one that guides theory, research, and practice in the behavioral sciences. It is an evolving orientation that is characterized by a general set of assumptions, principles, and values, rather than a single theory or set of specific methods. In this volume we develop the behavioral-ecological perspective as a conceptual framework for community mental health. The framework is offered to guide the development of a knowledge base for community mental health interventions.

At the most general level, as an orientation to community mental health, behavioral-ecology focuses on the individual in his/her broader social context. Our notion of behavioral-ecology reflects a coalescence of two broad perspectives—"behavioral" approaches as derived from a psychology of the individual, and "ecological" approaches as encompassing the study of communities, environments, and social systems. Behavioral-ecology draws on relevant streams from both of these broad areas (see Chapter 3).

It is interesting to note that both the behavioral and ecological orientations represent alternatives to the medical model described in the "Introduction" to this part. Furthermore, their increasing popularity during the 1960s and 1970s parallels the growth of community mental

ABRAHAM M. JEGER AND ROBERT S. SLOTNICK • Human Resources Development Center, New York Institute of Technology, Old Westbury, New York 11568.

7

health as a movement. Finally, the behavioral and ecological approaches developed independently of each other as well as of the community mental health movement. Through the programs brought together in this volume, we argue for a merging of these two areas for purposes of advancing community mental health theory, research, and practice.

The primary purpose of this chapter is to present an overview of behavioral-ecology that will provide the orienting theme for the entire volume. The major argument advanced in this volume is that the behavioral-ecological perspective in community mental health holds much promise as exemplified by the projects, programs, and research that are brought together in this book.

In addition, this chapter presents a historical overview of the community mental health movement as well as a discussion of its limitations. The chapter concludes with a statement on how behavioral-ecology, though not a panacea, provides a perspective that can potentially help overcome some of the problems in community mental health practice.

Behavioral-Ecology: An Emerging Perspective

In this section we consider three major aspects of the emerging behavioral-ecological perspective for community mental health. First, we present an overview of the orienting features of behavioral-ecology. Second, we examine the values of behavioral-ecology that inform action. Next, we show how behavioral-ecology provides guidelines for community mental health interventions, and give examples of such interventions.

General Features of the Behavioral-Ecological Perspective

Both the behavioral and ecological components of behavioral-ecology constitute alternatives to a disease model that relies on "person-centered" casual explanations of mental health problems. However, rather than attribute behavior exclusively to "external" environmental influences, behavioral-ecology considers the reciprocal influences between people and their settings. We shall consider those salient features of the behavioral and ecological approaches that contribute to an integrated behavioral-ecological perspective.

Following the behavioral model, a major feature of behavioral-ecology lies in its focus on overt behavior. This aspect translates into the requirement that mental health goals be defined in behavioral (i.e., measurable) terms. Behavioral psychology emphasizes that behavior is learned through experience with the environment. It encompasses learning through association, reinforcing and punishing consequences, and modeling/imitation (Krasner, 1971). In addition, the role of cognitive factors in learning is incorporated into behavior modification approaches (e.g., Goldfried & Davison, 1976, Mahoney, 1977; Meichenbaum, 1977). Furthermore, according to this social learning model, an individual's self-efficacy or competence is formed and defined by his/her ability to influence the environment (Krasner, 1976).

Unique contributions of behavior modification make it especially compatible with community mental health. Its focus on situational influences on behavior advanced the psychological analysis of individual behavior. Behavior modification techniques (e.g., contingency management) are relatively straightforward and can be taught to paraprofessionals and natural socializing agents (e.g., parents, teachers) in short periods of time. Another feature of behavior modification is the "indirect" service roles taken on by professionals—that is, consultants to and supervisors of "mediators" who implement behavior change strategies with target clients (e.g., Tharp & Wetzel, 1969). Finally, an overarching dimension of the behavioral approach is the commitment to empirically derived intervention strategies and to the incorporation of evaluation into behavior modification programs. The above features were emphasized in the early attempts to develop a behavioral conceptualization of community mental health (Gambrill, 1975; Levy, 1976; MacDonald, Hedberg, & Campbell, 1974; Meyers, Craighead, & Meyers, 1974).

In recent years, the environmental focus of behavior modification has led to extensions of behavioral techniques (particularly those derived from operant conditioning) to larger-scale community problems. The growing number of research/intervention programs in this area has led to the emergence of a new speciality area, referred to as behavioral community technology (Fawcett, Mathews, & Fletcher, 1980) or behavioral community psychology (e.g., Glenwick & Jason, 1980).

The general aim of behavioral community technology is to promote mental health and facilitate community development. As such, it contributes the behavioral technology stream to our behavioral-ecological perspective.

Ecology in the biological sciences is generally defined as the study of functional relationships between organisms and their environments. Similarly, in the behavioral sciences ecological approaches focus on interdependencies among environments, people, and behavior (Willems, 1974, 1977). The focus is on natural settings, molar behaviors, and reciprocal influence processes between people and their environments. That is, people act on their environments, just as environments influence people. Both the social and physical (natural and built) aspects of environments are incorporated into an ecological viewpoint. Interventions carried out within an ecological framework are usually system centered rather than person centered. Thus ecological interventions are likely to include environmental design and modification, political and social action, and institutional change activities.

More specifically, ecology views linkages between persons and their environments as forming an integrated whole, with all parts being interdependent. A change in any part of the person–environment transactional unit influences change in other parts. Therefore, community mental health professionals must be especially sensitive to the "unintended" consequences of their interventions, since short-term gains may produce long-term harm (see Kelly, 1968; Willems, 1977). Thus ecology sensitizes us to anticipate unintended consequences of interventions, and requires a long-term time perspective for analyzing person–environment transactions.

In combining the behavioral and ecological streams, behavioral-ecology approaches individual behavior as part of a dynamic person–environment interplay. The environment is not merely a static background for individual behavior; it constitutes a continuous flux, providing the context within which to view behavior. As well as considering environmental influences on behavior, behavioral-ecology emphasizes the capacities of individuals to design their environments. Unilateral cause–effect relations are superseded by a more holistic person–environment transactional view.

It follows from the *transactional* emphasis of behavioral–ecology that there are neither good nor bad persons nor good nor bad environments. Instead, the notion of person–environment "fit" (e.g., Holahan, Wilcox, Spearly, & Campbell, 1979; Insel, 1980; Rappaport, 1977), a major premise of ecology, is more appropriate. That is, there exists either congruence or incongruence (i.e., mismatch) between individuals and environments. Environments are characterized by the *demands* they make on individuals and the *resources* they provide. Likewise, individuals bring their own demands and resources to specific environments. The extent of person–environment congruence is based on "how well these demands and resources coincide" (Insel, 1980, p. 65). Person–environment congruence is achieved if the nature of environmental structure and support "fits" the needs and abilities of individuals. For example, environments providing high levels of challenge and high support are likely to yield optimal adaptations. On the other hand, environments providing low levels of challenge and excessive support tend to result in dependence behaviors. Thus ecology is concerned with maximizing fit (and reducing discord) between people and their environments.

Following the view that the unit of analysis in behavioral-ecology should be person–environment transactions, adaptation is a phenomenon of major interest. Adaptation is the way people cope with the environmental stressors that they encounter and create. In addition to looking at the environmental sources of coping abilities, behavioral-ecology considers individual competence (behavioral skills), which may be required to engage in optimally adaptive responses to environmental stress. To promote individual competence, the three major variables of adaptation discussed by White (1974; see Chapter 2, this volume)—access to information, satisfactory internal organization, and autonomy—need to be considered by behavioral-ecology.

Thus a concern with effective coping, rather than just maladjustment or pathology, is a defining attribute of behavioral-ecology. Furthermore, in considering coping the interdependence between individual behavior and social settings is emphasized. According to Kelly (1968), an early proponent of an ecological view in community mental health, adaptive coping behaviors mediate between the characteristics of social settings and of individual personality.

Values of the Behavioral-Ecological Perspective

In contrast to most mental health models whose interventions are guided by an implicit value system, a major feature of behavioral-ecology is that values are an integral part of the perspective. In our view, behavioral-ecology represents a *merging of ethics and practice*, as it espouses relatively specific values to inform action. In Chapter 2 we discuss three values that guide behavioral-ecological interventions—promoting individual competence, enhancing the psychological sense of community, and supporting cultural diversity. A brief overview of these values is presented here.

Individual-level community mental health interventions should aim to provide learning opportunities to consumers that will increase their ability to influence their environments (i.e., promote competence). Behavioral training to facilitate coping with stress, developing social skills, and improving general problem-solving capacities are compatible with this value. As Rappaport (1980) cautions, however, competence should not become a substitute label for psychotherapy, which maintains a hierarchical doctor–patient relation. Furthermore, experts should not offer canned behavioral packages to teach specific skills under the guise of competence training. Instead, the broader community context within which competence training takes place must be considered, since the community provides the meaning system and values of what constitutes adaptive behavior.

The second value, enhancing the "psychological sense of community" (PSC; Sarason, 1974), suggests that behavioral-ecological interventions should strengthen communities by promoting a sense of
belongingness and mutuality among residents. Individuals should be interdependent with their communities to the mutual benefit of both. PSC
redefines mental health problems as a *community* responsibility rather
than exclusively a *professional* responsibility. Behavioral-ecological interventions should therefore seek to foster "competent communities"
(Iscoe, 1974) by building on their existing strengths and enhancing their
resourcefulness.

Finally, promoting cultural diversity (e.g., Rappaport, 1977) is a value that follows from behavioral-ecology because of its recognition of the
differential adaptive capacities associated with different cultures. It suggests that interventions be guided by a commitment to promote alternatives to traditional ideologies that use a single standard of competence
(i.e., social Darwinism) as the criterion for gaining access to psychological and material resources. The notion of person–environment fit should
be informed by the value of promoting pluralism on a societal level.
Strengthening what Berger and Neuhaus (1977) have referred to as mediating structures—family, church, neighborhood, ethnic/racial subcul-
tures—is a means of promoting pluralism.

The "pursuit of paradox" (Rappaport, 1980) is the unifying thread
of these values. Professionals working within a behavioral-ecological
framework should advocate the development of diverse, often paradoxical (i.e., contradictory), solutions to specific mental health problems. This
underlying value follows from behavioral–ecology's analysis of mental
health problems as rooted in divergent sources.

Guidelines for Community Mental Health Practice

Behavioral-ecological interventions in mental health seek to optimize the congruence between persons and environments. Interventions
can be directed toward changing individuals, changing environments, or
both. Irrespective of the level of intervention (individual or system), behavioral-ecology calls for programs aimed at competence enhancement
rather than deficit remediation. That is, in contrast to a medical or public
health model that espouses "treatment" of "mental illness" or prevention of disease, behavioral-ecological interventions seek to optimize human development by enhancing individuals' coping and mastery skills to
increase self-efficacy and self-esteem and/or by enhancing organizational and community strengths so that quality of life is improved (McClure,
Cannon, Allen, Belton, Connor, D'Ascoli, Stone, Sullivan, & McClure,
1980).

Individual-level interventions might include programs seeking to facilitate adaptation to such normal life transitions as retirement or parenting (see Chapter 13 for an example of a parent support group). Individual-level interventions also include behavioral skill training and personal problem-solving training. Environmental interventions include the enhancement of natural caregivers (parents, teachers, neighbors) and the establishment of artificial networks when deemed necessary (e.g., self-help groups). Systems-level interventions are exemplified by designing autonomous living environments as alternatives to institutional settings (e.g., the Community Lodge, see Chapter 5). For interventions aimed at enhancing natural support networks or developing alternative support systems, see Edmunson *et al.*'s Community Network Development Project (Chapter 6) as well as those reviewed by Schure, *et al.* (Chapter 15).

The premise underlying these behavioral-ecological interventions is that people are viewed as resources, and problems are seen as opportunities for competence development. Thus these programs seek to build on existing individual and community strengths. The focus on personal support networks follows from the view that an individual's social support system is the "processive link" between the environment and mental health (Holahan *et al.*, 1979).

Another class of environmental interventions to which behavioral-ecology calls attention is the modification of physical aspects of environments. Such interventions are derived from the environmental psychology stream of behavioral-ecology (see Chapter 3, the section on "Environment-and-Behavior Field"). Consideration is given both to the built and the natural components of physical environments (e.g., space manipulation, noise and density modification), as emphasized by the recent reports of the Task Force on Environmental Assessment of the National Council of Community Mental Health Centers (Monahan & Vaux, 1980; Wittman & Arch, 1980).

Furthermore, the behavioral-ecological approach emphasizes incorporation of an evaluation design into all intervention programs. As such, it represents a merging of research and service, in contrast to traditional mental health models that tend to separate research and clinical practice. The nature of evaluation design and assessment criteria will vary depending on local conditions. A major characteristic of such evaluation is that program participants are involved in all phases of the evaluation process (see Part VI).

In terms of evaluation, the work of Moos and his colleagues at the Stanford University Laboratory of Social Ecology (e.g., Moos, 1974; Chapter 20, this volume), in which they developed a series of "social climate" scales to measure 10 different environments (e.g., psychiatric wards, community mental health programs, classrooms, groups), is especially relevant. These instruments have been employed to catalyze change in numerous environments, indicating their utility for merging evaluation and change (see Chapter 10). This conceptualization of environmental domains contributed to an understanding of the relation between dimensions of social environments and individual and group functions (Moos, 1980).

Finally, the behavioral-ecological perspective calls for broader mental health roles. In contrast to the traditional focus on direct service provision by professionals (e.g., individual and group psychotherapy), behavioral-ecologists are more likely to function as consultants, trainers, program designers, catalysts, participant/conceptualizers, resource linkers, mediators, and evaluators. In carrying out these roles community mental health professionals are seen as operating within a "seeking-mode" style of service delivery, in contrast to the more traditional "waiting mode" (Rappaport & Chinsky, 1974). That is, rather than take a passive stance and wait for individuals to bring their problems to the mental health agency, behavioral-ecologists are actively engaged in collaborating with local communities to foster their mental health resources by building on their existing strengths.

Concerning the funding of mental health programs, we agree with Rappaport's (1977) suggestion that programs should be federally financed but locally designed in keeping with the culturally diverse character of neighborhoods. Each community would develop new programs relative to its own unique needs and sensitive to the concerns that local conditions dictate.

Summary

Behavioral-ecology is concerned with person–environment transactions in understanding mental health problems and guiding interventions. This view is an alternative to looking exclusively "inside" persons (as do the biological and intrapsychic models) or exclusively at the external environment (as does the sociocultural model). By assuming a reciprocal influence process between people and their environments, behavioral-ecological interventions can focus on individuals, environments, or both. Individual-level or one-to-one helping is reconceptualized as training for competence enhancement that will increase individuals' access to environmental resources and facilitate their design of environments in accordance with their own values and goals. Environmental interventions include modification of the social environment through strengthening natural support systems or designing alternative supports, as well as changing aspects of the physical environment that influence mental health.

Our view of behavioral-ecology represents a merging of the process focus associated with ecological approaches and the psychotechnology focus of behavior modification. Whereas behavior modification offers a technology of change derived from a psychology of the individual, ecology provides guidelines for larger-scale interventions in natural community settings (as opposed to closed institutions or private office settings). As an integrated framework, behavioral-ecology analyzes problems at multiple levels and sensitizes community mental health professionals to anticipate many "unintended" consequences of behavioral interventions. As we shall discuss in Chapter 3, the knowledge base for behavioral-ecological practice is interdisciplinary. It derives from such areas as behavioral community technology, bioecology, social ecology, environmental psychology, ecological psychology, and network analysis, among others. It is our contention that interventions guided by a behavioral-ecological framework as exemplified by projects described in this volume constitute a viable means to fulfill the mandates of community mental health.

The Community Mental Health Movement: An Overview

A review of the conceptions of community mental health during its infancy (e.g., Goldston, 1965) as well as adolescence (e.g., Langsley, 1977) points to a great diversity. Conceptions run the gamut from a focus on treating individual mental health problems in local communities (as opposed to state hospitals) and incorporating community resources for such services, to a focus on community-level interventions to prevent "mental illness" and promote positive mental health. Inherent in the various definitions is the view of community mental health as both a philosophy and a methodology. As a philosophy it has its roots in the fields of social psychiatry and public health, which recognized the iatrogenic effects of institutionalization, redefined "mental illness" as a social problem, advocated alternatives to hospitalization, and called for community change for purposes of preventing mental health problems. As a methodology, community mental health refers to specific programs that sought to translate this ideology into practice. Such operational definitions of community mental health *practice* come from federal legislation that defined and redefined the mandates of agencies labeled community mental health *centers*—beginning with the Community Mental Health Centers Act of 1963 and through to the Mental Health Systems Act of 1980.

We shall refer to the community mental health "movement" as encompassing both its ideological and practical features. In this section we present an overview of this movement from World War II to the present. In addition, we consider some of the difficulties encountered by the movement.

Historical Evolution

Before World War II, public mental health services were primarily the responsibility of state and local governments. The increased demand for psychiatric services during World War II prompted the federal government into a new role in the mental health field. With the passage of the National Mental Health Act of 1946, which led to the establishment of the National Institute of Mental Health (NIMH), mental health became a target for public policy. (For a discussion of the prewar antecedents to community mental health, see Rossi, 1962.)

A decade after the war Congress passed the Mental Health Study Act (1955), which established the Joint Commission on Mental Illness and Health "to survey the resources and to make recommendations for combating mental illness in the United States." *Action for Mental Health,* the final report of the Joint Commission (1961), recommended (1) intensive care of acute mental illness in community-based clinics, each to serve a population of 50,000; (2) improving care of chronic mental patients by reducing the size of state hospitals; (3) developing aftercare and rehabilitation services; and (4) initiating consultation programs to community caregivers in order to educate the public and expand the mental health personpower. The Joint Commission suggested that the federal government bear the financial burden in supporting the recommended mental health programs.

The final report of the Joint Commission was studied extensively by governmental agencies. It led to President Kennedy's message to Congress on a national policy toward mental illness and mental retardation on February 3, 1963. In that historic address, marking the first time that a president focused on the topic, he called for a "bold new approach" to mental health problems. This approach was to focus on the prevention of mental illness rather than just treatment. For prevention to be achieved the president called for "the general strengthening of our fundamental community, social welfare, and educational programs which can do much to eliminate or correct the harsh environmental conditions which often are associated with mental retardation and mental illness." These words clearly represent a recognition of the broader social context in which human problems are developed and maintained.

The president went on to propose a "new type of health facility": the "comprehensive community mental health center." The Community Mental Health Centers Act (Public Law 88-164) was passed in October 1963, allocating construction funds, and an amendment followed in 1965 providing staffing grants. To be eligible for federal funding, centers were mandated to provide five "essential" services: (1) inpatient (for short-term stays); (2) outpatient; (3) partial hospitalization (i.e., day and/or night hospitals); (4) emergency care (i.e., 24-hour crisis services); and (5) consultation (i.e., indirect service) and community education (i.e., prevention). In order for a center to be considered "comprehensive," five *additional* services were required: (1) diagnostic; (2) rehabilitation; (3) precare and aftercare; (4) training; and (5) research and evaluation. The initial plan called for the establishment of 2,000 centers by 1980, each serving local "catchment" areas of approximately 100,000 people. (As of this writing, about 600 federally funded centers are operating in the United States.)

The Community Mental Health Centers Amendments of 1975 (Public Law 94-63) redefined the notion of a comprehensive community mental health center from the five minimum and five optional services to a mandated set of 12 services. They include the five originally established as "essential" plus seven *additional* services: (1) special services for children (diagnosis, treatment, liaison, and follow-up); (2) special services for the elderly; (3) preinstitutional screening and alternative treatment (as pertains to the courts and other public agencies); (4) follow-up for persons discharged from state mental hospitals; (5) transitional living facilities (i.e., halfway houses); (6) alcoholism services (prevention, treatment, and rehabilitation); and (7) drug abuse services (prevention, treatment, and rehabilitation). In addition to expanding the mandated number of services, the 1975 amendments also obligated centers to allocate 2% of their operating budgets for program evaluation.

The mandated delivery of these 12 services was modified in the Community Mental Health Extension Act of 1978 (Public Law 95-622). Specifically, new centers were required to provide six services (inpatient, outpatient, emergency, screening, follow-up of discharged inpatients, and consultation/education), and were allowed to phase in gradually the remaining six of the 12 services over their initial 3 years of operation (i.e., partial hospitalization, children's services, elderly services, transitional halfway houses, alcohol abuse, and drug abuse services).

The *Final Report* of the President's Commission on Mental Health (1978), established by President Carter, provided the basis for the Mental Health Systems Act of 1980 (Public Law 96-398). This legislation extended the Community Mental Health Centers Act through 1981. In addition, it authorized the following *new* federal programs (for which local governments and nonprofit agencies may apply) beginning fiscal year 1982: support services for the chronically mentally ill; projects for "priority populations" (such as elderly and minorities); health care centers (i.e., to establish mental health services in walk-in health care centers); programs for severely disturbed children, adolescents, and their families; mental illness prevention; and rape services. In addition, the act directed the National Institute of Mental Health to establish a new office for prevention in order to determine "national priorities" for the areas of mental illness prevention and mental health promotion. Also, the act established an "associate director for minority concerns" in the National Institute of Mental Health. Finally, the act authorized grants for "advocacy" for the rights of the mentally ill, and recommended a model mental health patients' "bill of rights" for voluntary adoption by states.

In considering all the various provisions for services mandated by legislation during the past 17 years, we can convey the spirit of the community mental health movement. The 10 characteristics delineated by Bloom (1977) as differentiating community mental health from "traditional" clinical practice can serve to identify both the ideological and operational aspects of the movement:

- First, as opposed to institutional (i.e., mental hospital) practice, the community provides the practice setting.
- Second, rather than an individual patient, a total population or community is the target; hence the term "catchment area" to define a given center's area of responsibility.
- A third feature concerns the type of service delivered, that is, offering preventive services rather than just treatment.
- Continuity of care among the components of a comprehensive system of services constitutes the fourth dimension.
- The emphasis on indirect services, that is, consultation, is the fifth characteristic.
- A sixth characteristic lies in the area of clinical innovations— brief psychotherapy and crisis intervention.
- The emphasis on systematic planning for services by considering the demographics of a population, specifying unmet needs, and identifying "high-risk" groups represents a seventh characteristic.
- Utilizing new personpower resources, especially nonprofessional mental health workers, constitutes the eight dimension.
- The ninth dimension is defined in terms of the community control concept which holds that consumers should play central roles in establishing service priorities and evaluating programs.

• Finally, the tenth characteristic identifies community mental health as seeking environmental causes of human distress, in contrast to the traditional "intrapsychic" emphasis.

Although a majority of community mental health workers might agree that these characteristics reflect the orientation of community mental health, there is much less agreement on the emphasis of these concepts in practice. We turn to a discussion of the limitations of community mental health.

Limitations of Community Mental Health: Problems of Implementation

Since their very inception, community mental health centers have encountered problems in achieving their goals. The view taken here is that the major technical limitations of community mental health are tied to their underlying conceptual framework—the medical model of mental health problems. From the outset mental health centers relied on a disease model of human problems and were intended to be dominated by the medical profession (which espouses chemotherapy and psychotherapy as its major intervention strategies). As President Kennedy stated in 1963, "we need a new health facility, one which will return mental health care to the mainstream of American medicine, and at the same time upgrade mental health services." Therein lies the inherent contradiction. As it turned out, relying on a medical model proved too narrow for a "bold new approach" to treatment and prevention. Although Kennedy is not to be blamed for this orientation, his recommendation indeed reflects the professional climate during which the Community Mental Health Centers Act was passed.

Albee (1980) considers some of the ramifications of adopting the two major streams of the disease model—namely, those exemplified by the "organic" psychiatrist and the "analytic" psychiatrist. These ramifications include the requirement that only "expert" professionals (e.g., psychiatrists, psychologists, social workers) are competent to render mental health services; the demand that clients be provided with a psychiatric diagnosis, a label that itself has damaging consequences; the emphasis on "one-to-one patchwork symptom reduction" as the preferred mode of helping; and the tendency to divert attention from the societal origins of mental health problems, thereby ignoring the need for larger-scale social and environmental changes.

How has adherence to a disease model limited the accomplishment of community mental health goals? To answer this question we shall take a brief look at some of the limitations of community mental health centers in the following six areas: (1) deinstitutionalization; (2) consultation/education; (3) paraprofessional utilization; (4) citizen participation; (5) evaluation and community accountability; and (6) the catchment-area concept.

A major limitation of community mental health has been its inability to meet the goal of supplanting state hospitals (Brown, 1980; Chu & Trotter, 1974; Sarason, 1974). A primary objective of community mental health centers was to reduce admissions to state hospitals by offering community-based alternatives. However, with the exception of specific catchment areas, overall admissions and readmissions to state hospitals have increased consistently since the establishment of community mental health centers (Brown, 1980). Indeed, many centers used the state hospital as "dumping grounds for the poor and chronically ill" (Chu & Trotter, 1974, p. 33). Furthermore, the lack of appropriate day treatment and other community support programs for deinstitutionalized state hospital patients pointed to the inability of community mental health centers to provide the necessary continuity of care for this client group. Thus community mental health centers may be seen as partially responsible for the problems associated with dumping unprepared chronic psychiatric patients into unprepared communities, with no follow-up care (see Slotnick & Jeger, 1978). The lack of community support services has no doubt contributed to the recidivism rates of discharged state hospital patients.

Sarason (1974) captures another aspect of the relation between community mental health centers and state hospitals:

> The community mental health center virtually guarantees the continued existence of the state hospital even though its initial rationale was opposed to that of the state hospital! It could hardly have been otherwise because these centers were conceived within the same traditions of professional practice and theory—the same nomenclature, administrative hierarchical structure, professional preciousness, and professional responsibility—that are the basis for the state hospitals. (pp. 190–191)

The prevailing disease model is said to be the underlying cause of community mental health centers' contribution to the "maintenance" of state hospitals.

Even with only nontraditional services mandated—consultation as an indirect service and community education as prevention—extreme limitations were apparent. Statistical data available from the NIMH for an average week in January 1970 showed an average of only 6.6% of total staff time spent in consultation/education (Taube, 1971). More recent data for the 5-year period 1973–1977 showed consultation/education services to account for only 4.1% of staff time in all federally funded community mental health centers (NIMH, 1978). Furthermore, a 33% decline is apparent over the course of this period, from a high of 4.8% in 1973 to 3.2% in 1977. Of these amounts, case-oriented consultation received the majority of staff time.

Snow and Newton (1976) argue that despite President Kennedy's call for prevention, consultation/education was given low priority by center staff because it was never intended to be emphasized in the federal legislation. They show that the primary consultation/education mandate was to extend the availability of direct (i.e., clinical) services, rather than change social institutions. Since centers were dominated by the medical model, consultation/education programs aimed at social problems would represent "the greatest degree of change from a medical entity" (Snow & Newton, 1976, p. 582). This point is in line with empirical data obtained by Mazade (1974), which indicate that the *type* of consultation offered (e.g., case centered vs. program centered) is related to the organizational affiliation of community mental health centers. That is, case-centered consultation was the likely focus in hospital-affiliated centers, whereas program-centered consultation was emphasized in autonomous, community-based centers.

Another aspect of community mental health that has been criticized is the use of nonprofessional personpower. Whereas the incorporation of nonprofessional workers into the mental health system would appear to accomplish the dual purpose of meeting the mental health personpower shortage (e.g., Albee, 1959) as well as providing opportunities for indigenous people to develop human service careers (e.g., Pearl & Riessman, 1965), the emergence of such personnel into the traditionally professional-dominated mental health arena resulted in unprecedented conflicts.

According to Bloom (1977), "the most vexing problem regarding mental health personnel is the new type of worker—the so-called paraprofessional" (p. 222). One class of problems centers around their low salaries, low position in the hierarchy, and general lack of a career ladder or lattice. The other major problem is a developing "new segregation," whereby Black nonprofessionals are assigned to serve Black clients, and welfare mothers serve other welfare mothers, whereas White professionals serve middle-class clients.

Again, these difficulties, associated with the obvious resistance of professionals to accepting new mental health personpower, can be linked to the prevailing medical model. As Chu and Trotter (1974) conclude, "the major difficulty in the development of paraprofessional careers is that they must be implemented within a hierarchical structure dominated by the medical profession" (p. 63). This point is compatible with Albee's (1980) view that the illness model

> restricts the field of therapy to a small elite band by setting artificially high nonfunctional educational criteria for helpers. If one works directly with "sick patients" then one must have prestigious training and high status. (p. 221)

Another area of difficulty concerns the mandate of citizen involvement in community mental health program planning. Lack of specific guidelines as to how to incorporate consumer input into a center's functioning has resulted in an insignificant participation of community members. The discretionary policies adopted by the professional staff at each center have generally limited consumer involvement. Rappaport (1977) points out that although most efforts at influencing community control of community mental health services were directed toward people in the lower socioeconomic classes, it may be a myth to assume that middle-class people are already playing a role. Where so-called community advisory boards did exist, they were largely composed of "elite" citizens as opposed to consumers.

Related to the issue of community participation is the notion of accountability and evaluation. The lack of an initial mandate for evaluating community mental health center programs is a major point of criticism. Later, in 1969, when 1% of the operating budget was to be appropriated for evaluation, Chu and Trotter (1974) attributed many difficulties to the fact that the NIMH had contracted out the evaluative studies (as opposed to developing program evaluation units *within* the centers). Equally disturbing is that the information that was generated did not translate into programmatic changes within centers. The 1975 legislation mandating community involvement in the evaluation process represents the first systematic step toward community accountability.

The relationship between accountability and community control is perhaps best expressed by Rappaport (1977):

> Community control as accountability does not necessarily infer that local people run the service, but that experts are the employees of the local people who are the consumers. . . . The consumers would judge effectiveness and decide on continuation of the service, expansion or reorientation of the policy and programs. One does not need to know how to help others resolve a crisis to be able to decide that that is a worthwhile service and to later evaluate if it has been helpful to one's community. . . . This is community control as accountability. *It has never been fully tested.* (emphasis added) (p. 302)

Finally, we point to the limitations associated with defining "community" in terms of populations residing within geographically targeted catchment areas. This practice has often resulted in cutting into existing "natural" communities and possibly damaging (and certainly not capitalizing on) existing support systems (see Giordano & Giordano, 1976). It may also have acted as an impediment to voicing service needs on the part of community residents. That is, by mandating the same services for all catchment areas no provisions were made for taking into account the unique needs of particular communities. As Chu and Trotter (1974) put it, "perhaps the most damaging consequence of the disease analogy is that it seriously impedes alternative and innovative service programs" (p. 56).

Conclusion

To meet the limitations we have discussed, the community mental health movement requires an alternative conceptualization to the medical model. Such a conceptualization should translate into programs that: provide appropriate community supports for deinstitutionalized psychiatric clients; promote consultation and prevention activities; provide for the meaningful engagement of nonprofessional mental health workers; promote program evaluation and community accountability; and offer vehicles for citizen involvement in community mental health center operations. We contend that the behavioral-ecological perspective presented at the outset of this chapter provides one such alternative conceptualization.

The programs selected for inclusion in this book were guided by (or are compatible with) a behavioral-ecological viewpoint. They are examples of innovative interventions that, if disseminated on a large scale, can significantly contribute to overcoming the problems in achieving community mental health center goals. For example, the behaviorally oriented Oxnard Day Treatment Center (Chapter 4) and the Community Network Development Project (Chapter 6) provide alternative support systems that have been successful in maintaining chronic mental health clients in the community. Twardosz and Risley's work (Chapter 7) on behavioral-ecological consultation to day care centers constitutes an alternative to traditional clinical consultation, with implications for expanding mental health personpower and for avoiding the labeling of individual children as deviant. The program described by Reppucci and Saunders (Chapter 9) reflects the role of behavioral consultants as institutional change agents. Behavioral-ecological approaches to prevention are reflected in programs that offer early environmental enrichment to "high-risk" children (Chapter 12), personal problem-solving education in the schools (Chapter 11), and media training in self-control for entire communities (Chapter 14). Tornatzky (Chapter 24) describes a doctoral training program in "ecological psychology" aimed at training social systems interventionists; Durlak (Chapter 25) discusses vehicles for the optimal utilization of nonprofessionals in community mental health. In terms of community accountability, the entire Huntsville (Alabama) community mental health center operates along a data-guided behavior modification approach (Chapter 19). The Multiphasic Environmental Assessment Procedure described by Moos and Lemke (Chapter 20) is a program evaluation package compatible with behavioral-ecology. Finally, Wandersman et al. (Chapter 21) consider citizen participation in community mental health centers by assessing the role of the advisory boards.

This chapter presented an overview of an emerging behavioral-ecological perspective. We argued that behavioral-ecology can provide community mental health with a conceptual framework to guide the development of interventions that will facilitate the accomplishment of community mental health center goals. It does so by focusing on person–environment transactions, and by suggesting interventions that seek to optimize the congruence between people and their environments.

References

Albee, G. W. *Mental health manpower trends.* New York: Basic Books, 1959.

Albee, G. W. A competency model to replace the defect model. In M. S. Gibbs, J. R. Lachenmeyer, & J. Sigal (Eds.), *Community psychology: Theoretical and empirical perspectives.* New York: Gardner Press, 1980.

Berger, P. L., & Neuhaus, R. J. *To empower people: The role of mediating structures in public policy.* Washington, D.C.: American Enterprise Institute for Public Policy Research, 1977.

Bloom, B. L. *Community mental health: A general introduction.* Monterey, Calif.: Brooks/Cole, 1977.

Brown, P. Social implications of deinstitutionalization. *Journal of Community Psychology,* 1980, *8,* 314–322.

Chu, F., & Trotter, S. *The madness establishment.* New York: Grossman, 1974.

Fawcett, S. B., Mathews, R. M., & Fletcher, R. K. Some promising dimensions for behavioral community technology. *Journal of Applied Behavior Analysis,* 1980, *13,* 505–518.

Gambrill, E. D. Role of behavior modification in community mental health. *Community Mental Health Journal,* 1975, *11,* 307–315.

Giordano, J., & Giordano, G. P. Ethnicity and community mental health: A review of the literature. *Community Mental Health Review,* 1976, *1*(1), 4–14.

Glenwick, D., & Jason, L. (Eds.). *Behavioral community psychology: Progress and prospects.* New York: Praeger, 1980.

Goldfried, M. R., & Davison, G. C. *Clinical behavior therapy.* New York: Holt, Rinehart & Winston, 1976.

Goldston, S. E. (Ed.). *Concepts of community psychiatry: A framework for training* (DHEW PHS Publication No. 1319). Washington, D.C.: U.S. Government Printing Office, 1965.

Holahan, C. J., Wilcox, B. L., Spearly, J. L., & Campbell, M. D. The ecological perspective in community mental health. *Community Mental Health Review*, 1979, *4*(2), 1; 3–8.

Insel, P. M. Social climate of mental health. *Community Mental Health Journal*, 1980, *16*, 62–78.

Iscoe, I. Community psychology and the competent community. *American Psychologist*, 1974, *29*, 607–613.

Joint Commission on Mental Illness and Health. *Action for mental health*. New York: Basic Books, 1961.

Kelly, J. G. Toward an ecological conception of preventive interventions. In J. W. Carter, Jr. (Ed.), *Research contributions from psychology to community mental health*. New York: Behavioral Publications, 1968.

Krasner, L. Behavior therapy. *Annual Review of Psychology*, 1971, *22*, 483–532.

Krasner, L. Behavior modification: Ethical issues and future trends. In H. Leitenberg (Ed.), *Handbook of behavior modification and behavior therapy*. Englewood Cliffs, N.J.: Prentice-Hall, 1976.

Langsley, D. G. Community health: A review of the literature. In W. E. Barton & C. J. Sanborn (Eds.), *An assessment of the community mental health movement*. Lexington, Mass.: Lexington Books, 1977.

Levy, R. L. Behavior therapy techniques as a fulfillment of community mental health ideology. *Community Mental Health Journal*, 1976, *12*, 415–421.

MacDonald, K. R., Hedberg, A. G., & Campbell, L. M. A behavioral revolution in community mental health. *Community Mental Health Journal*, 1974, *10*, 228–235.

Mahoney, M. J. Reflections on the cognitive learning trend in psychotherapy. *American Psychologist*, 1977, *32*, 5–13.

Mazade, N. A. Consultation and education practice and organizational structure in ten community mental health centers. *Hospital and Community Psychiatry*, 1974, *25*, 673–675.

McClure, L., Cannon, D., Allen, S., Belton, E., Connor, P., D'Ascoli, C., Stone, P., Sullivan, B., & McClure, G. Community psychology concepts and research base. *American Psychologist*, 1980, *35*, 1000–1011.

Meichenbaum, D. H. *Cognitive-behavior modification*. New York: Plenum Press, 1977.

Meyers, A. W., Craighead, W. E., & Meyers, H. H. A behavioral-preventive approach to community mental health. *American Journal of Community Psychology*, 1974, *2*, 275–285.

Monahan, J., & Vaux, A. Task Force report: The macroenvironment and community mental health. *Community Mental Health Journal*, 1980, *16*, 14–26.

Moos, R. H. *Evaluating treatment environments: A social ecological approach*. New York: Wiley, 1974.

Moos, R. H. Major features of a social ecological perspective. In R. S. Slotnick, A. M. Jeger, & E. J. Trickett (Eds.), *Social ecology in community psychology*. Special issue, APA Division of Community Psychology Newsletter, Summer 1980.

National Institute of Mental Health. Provisional data on federally funded community mental health centers, 1976–1977. Rockville, Md.: Author, 1978.

Pearl, A., & Riessman, F. *New careers for the poor*. New York: Free Press, 1965.

President's Commission on Mental Health. *Final report*. Washington, D.C.: U.S. Government Printing Office, 1978.

Rappaport, J. *Community psychology: Values, research, and action*. New York: Holt, Rinehart & Winston, 1977.

Rappaport, J. *In praise of paradox*. Presidential Address, Division of Community Psychology, meeting of the American Psychological Association, Montreal, September 1980.

Rappaport, J., & Chinsky, J. M. Models for delivery of service from a historical and conceptual perspective. *Professional Psychology*, 1974, *5*, 42–50.

Rossi, A. M. Some pre–World War II antecedents of community mental health theory and practice. *Mental Hygiene*, 1962, *46*, 78–93.

Sarason, S. B. *The psychological sense of community: Prospects for a community psychology.* San Francisco: Jossey-Bass, 1974.

Slotnick, R. S., & Jeger, A. M. *Barriers to deinstitutionalization: Social systems influences on environmental design interventions.* Paper presented at the meeting of the American Psychological Association, Toronto, August 1978.

Snow, D. L., & Newton, P. M. Task, social structure, and social process in the community mental health center movement. *American Psychologist*, 1976, *31*, 582–594.

Taube, C. A. *Consultation and education services, community mental health centers: January 1970* (Statistical Note 43). Rockville, Md.: National Institute of Mental Health, 1971.

Tharp, R. G., & Wetzel, R. J. *Behavior modification in the natural environment.* New York: Academic Press, 1969.

White, R. W. Strategies of adaptation: An attempt at systematic description. In G. V. Coelho, D. A. Hamburg, & J. E. Adams (Eds.), *Coping and adaptation.* New York: Basic Books, 1974.

Willems, E. P. Behavioral technology and behavioral ecology. *Journal of Applied Behavior Analysis*, 1974, *7*, 151–165.

Willems, E. P. Behavioral ecology. In D. Stokols (Ed.), *Perspectives on environment and behavior: Theory, research, and applications.* New York: Plenum Press, 1977.

Wittman, F. D., & Arch, M. Task Force report: Sociophysical settings and mental health. *Community Mental Health Journal*, 1980, *16*, 45–61.

2

Guiding Values of Behavioral-Ecological Interventions

The Merging of Ethics and Practice

ABRAHAM M. JEGER AND ROBERT S. SLOTNICK

It is generally believed that values influence mental health practice in relatively subtle ways. As a result, value systems guiding mental health interventions usually remain implicit. All too often ethics and values are considered abstract underpinnings of mental health programs—something theoreticians and scholars need to attend to, but not daily practitioners. In our view, ethics and values are an integral part of the behavioral-ecological perspective advanced in this volume (see also similar statements by such earlier advocates of an ecological paradigm in the health and human service field as Moos & Insel, 1974; Rappaport, 1977; Willems, 1977). That is, an essential feature of the behavioral-ecological perspective is its emphasis on the *merging of ethics and practice*. Such a merging goes beyond the requirement of making explicit the values guiding behavioral-ecological interventions in community mental health. It suggests that *specific* values should guide practitioners in planning, imple-

ABRAHAM M. JEGER AND ROBERT S. SLOTNICK • Human Resources Development Center, New York Institute of Technology, Old Westbury, New York 11568.

menting, and evaluating interventions—if such interventions are to constitute ethical practice from the standpoint of our behavioral-ecological perspective.

The behavioral-ecological projects described in this volume show these values in action. What is more, we feel that these projects constitute ethical mental health practice for the populations they are dealing with.

In this chapter we shall make explicit three general values guiding behavioral-ecological interventions in community mental health: (1) promoting individual competence; (2) enhancing the psychological sense of community; and (3) supporting cultural diversity. These values correspond to three levels of intervention—individual, organizational/ community, and societal, respectively. Although these values may be agreed on by most professionals espousing a behavioral-ecological perspective, there is less agreement concerning which specific interventions are optimal. As Sarason (1974) notes, "agreement on values is easier to reach than agreement about the appropriateness of value-derived actions" (pp. 268–269).

Promoting Individual Competence

A major value guiding individual-level interventions is that they aim to enhance personal competence. Behavioral-ecological interventions should seek to strengthen an individual's coping skills and ability to encounter potentially stressful life events. Interventions uniquely derived from the behavior modification stream of behavioral-ecology include technologies for promoting individual competence through training in social skills, assertiveness, problem solving, anxiety reduction, and so on.

Krasner (1976), an early proponent of behavior modification, suggested the following notion of helping at the individual level:

> The goal of helping individuals is to enable them to learn how to control, influence, or design their own environment. Implicit in this is a value judgement that individual freedom is a desirable goal and that the more an individual is able to affect his environment, the greater is his freedom. (p. 646)

According to Krasner this value is derived directly from the social learning or behavioral model of human behavior.

This value is compatible with White's (1959,1974) notion of competence and adaptation. According to White (1959), competence refers to the ability of individuals to influence their environments, and is characterized by a "feeling of efficacy." White emphasizes the psychological drive to master and control one's environment, rather than obtaining pleasure exclusively from the reduction of tension (as suggested by Freud's motivation theory). Aspects of competence are manifested in people's need for exploration, for curiosity, for variety of sensory stimulation, and for engaging in information processing.

In addition, White (1974) considers strategies of adaptation, which refers to a striving toward acceptable compromise between total triumph and total surrender to the environment. He sees all behavior as attempts at adaptation in the course of an individual's transaction with his/her environment. That is, even simple behaviors taken for granted cannot be accomplished in purely habitual or mechanical ways. Such daily concerns as what clothes to put on, what errands to run, how to schedule one's work, how to interact with one's children, and so on all call upon various strategies of adaptation. The environment always presents a challenge and poses demands that require novel and creative behaviors.

White (1974) considers three major variables of adaptive behavior: (1) information; (2) internal organization; and (3) autonomy. The first refers to securing optimal information about the environment so as not to overload or underload the information channel. The second variable refers to maintaining satisfactory internal organization, since such internal conditions as anxiety or physical illness stand in the way of exerting an impact on the environment. Finally, adaptive behavior requires autonomy—that freedom of action be maintained, and that individuals design their environment so that initiatives for action remain in their own hands rather than succumbing to external pressures for behaving in certain ways. Behavioral-ecological interventions need to consider these variables of adaptation when designing programs to promote individual competence.

Our view of competence is likewise compatible with Albee's (1980) competence model as an alternative to the "mental defect" or "sickness" model. Albee sees human problems as resulting from an interaction between environmental stress and competence (i.e., one's ability to cope with stress). A competence model is an alternative to the view that mental illness is an illness like any other. It does not view human problems as rooted exclusively within individuals. Instead, it is concerned with problems-in-living created by the damaging forces of society, which fail to prepare individuals for competent adaptation.

A competence model requires alternative settings and staff to deal with human problems. Albee calls for "social intervention centers," whose primary staff would be made up of people holding bachelor's degrees working as educators. The aim of these centers would be to build on the strengths of individuals and families. Individuals would be trained to manage stress in order to improve their adaptive capacities.

Strengthening families would serve a preventive function by increasing the social support systems in society.

In promoting competence, community mental health interventions need to foster individual autonomy and independence rather than reinforce a state of dependence. Skinner (1975), in an article aptly entitled "The Ethics of Helping People," calls attention to the fact that too much helping is detrimental to the development of individual skills. As he states, "by giving too much help, we postpone the acquisition of effective behavior and perpetuate the need for help. The effect is crucial in the very profession of helping—in counseling and psychotherapy" (p. 624). Thus helping people by doing things for them and "teaching them too much" is not likely to lead to learning. Skinner also calls attention to contingencies of reinforcement operating on a societal level, for example, the welfare system, which tends to increase dependence and to incapacitate individuals rather than provide them with the opportunities to earn rewards through development of individual competence by participating in society.

Skinner's analysis is compatible with Ryan's (1971) critique of centralized human service systems as the "giving enemy"—"the agent of public service who gives us what we have to have, but seems to be against us" (p. 274). This "enemy" is antithetical to developing individual competence that will promote personal freedom.

A primary goal, then, of competence training is to foster "resourceful" individuals. This notion is parallel to Lehmann's (1971) concept of positive mental health—namely, that the "utilization of resources" (as opposed to absence of symptoms) constitutes an index of mental health. The competent individual is characterized as an activated client/consumer who takes primary responsibility for the maintenance and enhancement of his/her own positive mental health.

Finally, we wish to stress that the acquisition of individual behavioral skills requires linkage to a larger meaning system, that is, the goals and values of the larger community. It is impossible to talk about personal competence without considering the larger cultural and community context within which the person behaves. The community provides the context, cohesion, and sense of meaning that influence what will be considered adaptive behavior. That is why community mental health professionals know they cannot export canned behavioral packages without considering the context within which the behavioral skills are to be acquired and later utilized. There are many different ways of achieving similar outcomes, just as one can acquire information and skills through formal traditional schooling, alternative schools, independent studies, and on-the-job training. Thus both community and personal characteristics must be considered when conducting therapeutic programs to enhance individual competence.

Enhancing the Psychological Sense of Community

Another guiding value of behavioral-ecological interventions concerns the interface between individual and community needs—the value of enhancing one's "psychological sense of community" (PSC; Sarason, 1974). As Sarason states:

> The perception of similarity to others, an acknowledged interdependence with others, a willingness to maintain this interdependence by giving to or doing for others what one expects from them, the feeling that one is part of a larger dependable and stable structure—these are some of the ingredients of the psychological sense of community. You know when you have it and when you don't. It is not without conflict or changes in its strength. . . . It is one of the major bases for self-definition and the judging of external events. The psychological sense of community is not a mystery to the person who experiences it. It is a mystery to those who do not experience it but hunger for it. (p. 157)

Sarason sees the destruction of PSC as a major problem in contemporary society, evidenced by the prevalence of popular articles and books dealing with loneliness, alienation, and rootlessness.

Sarason discusses additional features of PSC. He points out that PSC goes beyond considering the number of people one knows, as it emphasizes the immediately available network of relationships on a daily basis. Within such a network of relationships, individual needs for intimacy, diversity, usefulness, and belongingness can be expressed. This sense of identification with one's community helps individuals overcome the feelings of alienation, anomie, and isolation prevalent in contemporary community life.

The sense of mutuality and reciprocity that characterizes PSC is linked with a sense of purpose that transcends both selfish "individualism" and irresponsible "group interest." Attempts at promoting PSC should aim to integrate individuals and their communities in mutually productive ways. That will often require a compromise between individual needs and group or community goals. Sarason states that this feature of PSC shares a common theme with Skinner's (1948) *Walden Two* and (1971) *Beyond Freedom and Dignity*—namely,

> that the welfare of the community must take precedence over that of individual, because it is only through a shared sense of community that the creative potential of the individual and the community will reach expression. (Sarason, 1974, pp. 158–159)

Finally, PSC is not a fixed state but an evolving process that is always in flux. Indeed, Sarason considers PSC a "transient experience" that is generally preceded and followed by tensions and threats to the sense of community.

Sarason discusses some barriers to PSC, that behavioral-ecological interventions seeking to promote it must consider. All too often, agreements on program values do not translate into concurrence on action. Lack of mechanisms to handle disagreements leads to the dilution of PSC even in settings with the best of intentions. Furthermore, many settings designed to provide helping services become absorbed in a "production ethic," (i.e., the mere recruiting of more clients) that is incompatible with PSC. In addition, the tendency of most new settings to define human problems as being exclusively in the professional domain (professionalism) leads to gaps between the demand for services and their availability. Likewise, lack of relations between a new service setting and existing agencies or with the community of which it is a part results in diminished PSC. Finally, a major barrier to PSC results from overvaluing individual or community goals at the expense of each other, without recognition of their complementary nature.

How does PSC guide behavioral-ecological interventions? According to Sarason, PSC, as an overarching, value-informing action, provides the basis for evaluating institutional and community change as well as suggesting a framework for creating new settings. It does so by raising a question that behavioral-ecological interventionists must ask: What is a community? The answer should center on whether a particular intervention contributes to the presence or absence of PSC as a central feature of the community or setting. In a sense, PSC can function as a dependent measure in judging the effects of community changes.

In community mental health, the effects on PSC of segregating individuals into special classes, residential institutions, mental hospitals, and so on need to be considered. Sarason argues that such institutions lead to a destruction of PSC for both the individuals segregated and the service providers (professional and nonprofessional) alike. Thus interventions guided by PSC as a value will seek to develop alternatives to such institutions. These alternatives should aim to restore PSC among clients as well as employees (see Chapter 9, this volume). Sarason takes the further position that the very existence of such institutions constitutes a barrier to the development of interventions that will promote PSC, and should therefore be challenged.

PSC also calls attention to the nonpsychological factors that need to be considered when defining a community. For example, the destructive influence of highway construction on PSC is rarely observed if one views a community exclusively in psychological terms. That is, psychologists generally do not see how our modern highway system has, over a long period, contributed to the deterioration of public transportation in the central city which, in turn, has reduced the psychological sense of community among major subgroups of residents—particularly the elderly, youth, and the poor. Sarason points out that the community mental health movement viewed the community in narrow, catchment-area terms and "directed attention away from *community* in its geo-political, social, and psychological interrelationships" (p. 11).

What is ultimately required is that mental health problems be redefined as a *community* responsibility as opposed to their current conceptualization as almost exclusively a *professional* responsibility. Professionals who are socialized to find differences, tend to create programs that remove those who are "different" (e.g., the mentally ill) into settings controlled by professionals. Solutions to mental health problems will require creating new resources that can only be made possible by redefining such problems as a community responsibility.

Fostering the Competent Community

A value compatible with promoting PSC is that of fostering the "competent community."

> The development of the competent community involves the provision and utilization of resources in a geographical or psychological community so that the members of the community may make reasoned decisions about issues confronting them, leading to the most competent coping with these problems. Coping is stressed rather than adjustment, in keeping with a positive, activist point of view. . . . Success of coping with one type of problem should broaden the repertoire of skills of the community and enhance its possibilities of more effective coping with other problems that arise. (Iscoe, 1974, pp. 608–609)

The powerlessness of lower-socioeconomic groups and of mental patients lies both at the individual and community levels. Their limited resources are a function of their restricted opportunity structure (labor roles, welfare, etc.) as well as of the psychological and behavioral limitations of individuals with feelings of powerlessness. Furthermore, as Iscoe points out, the lack of integration within less competent communities minimizes opportunities for communication of the few successes that are achieved. Such lack of integration follows from the relative absence of resources to mobilize the community, as well as the shortage of individuals who possess the necessary leadership and organizational skills to activate community residents.

To foster competent communities it is necessary that communities contain small-scale settings that provide opportunities for participation (see the review of Barker's research in the next chapter). Furthermore, residents will have to learn to take advantage of opportunities for participation in community affairs and thereby influence the delivery of human services as well as of other facets of community life. Considering that because of a prior history of nonparticipation the poor lack the knowhow of utilizing power, our position is that it becomes the ethical obligation of community mental health professionals to educate their constituents to advocate and problem-solve for themselves (see Briscoe, Hoffman, & Bailey, 1975, for a program with promising implications for such training.) Community enhancement for purposes of promoting the competent community is accomplished by providing environmental resources and opportunities whereby more people will be able to engage in a broader array of behaviors, or to choose from a greater number of alternatives—thereby increasing their freedom. Thus we have the beginnings of a notion of "environmental repertoire" parallel to the individualistic notion of a behavioral repertoire.

We see a positive reciprocal relationship between PSC and the competent community. Settings characterized by PSC are likely to foster the competent community. That is, the existence of a mutually satisfying interdependence among residents is conducive to the development of individual and community competence. Likewise, competence at the community level is likely to contribute to the promotion of PSC. The reciprocal relationship is exemplified by Sarason's (1974) statement on the impact of highway construction on PSC. Lacking the power to affect the construction of highways through the community led to a weakening of the decision-making abilities of its members (i.e., reduced competence) and decreased PSC. In turn, the dilution of PSC led to further reduction of community competence.

Supporting Cultural Diversity

Cultural diversity as a value guiding behavioral-ecological interventions follows from behavioral-ecology as a perspective of human behavior. On a societal level, cultural diversity suggests that it is advantageous to support multiple cultures because of their differential adaptive capacities in a broad range of environments.

Anthropologists have defined culture as an organizing concept that explains the underlying patterns of people's daily activities (e.g., Netting, 1977). Culture is viewed as a system composed of such subsystems as religion, kinship, politics, social structure, and so on. Different social groups may be distinguished on the basis of their salient cultural features. The field of *cultural ecology* within anthropology is concerned with relationships between a culture and the larger environment of which it is a part, or how culture is used as means of adaptation to the environment.

Ecologically oriented anthropologists (e.g., Geertz, 1966; Netting, 1965, 1977; Steward, 1955) have long considered culture as part of a large, comprehensive network of relationships—the ecosystem. The ecological approach in anthropology is concerned with determining relationships between the natural physical environment and cultural processes (Geertz, 1966). Behavioral reactions to environmental processes are mediated by cultural processes. These transactions are expressed as cyclical forces where the environment shapes culture, culture guides behavior, behavior modifies the environment, and so on. Similarly, Lehmann (1975), an ecologically oriented community psychologist, emphasizes the development of social customs as collective behavioral adaptations to environmental changes. Thus distinctions between the natural and the social environment have been blurred, with social and cultural norms representing perhaps the most important features of the person-made environment. Culture mediates the transaction between individuals and their environments. Therefore, to a large extent, culture determines the adaptive capacities of individuals and groups. We agree with Lehmann (1975) that "for the behavioral scientist today, human ecology is largely social ecology" (p. 489).

Cultural diversity as a value guiding behavioral-ecological interventions begins with the assumption that desirable differences exist between individuals and cultures. Everyone is said to benefit from living in a culturally diverse and pluralistic society. The adaptive capacities of individuals and communities are enhanced by interacting with members of culturally diverse groups.

How does this value translate into community mental health interventions? To answer the question we draw on Rappaport's (1977) analysis of cultural diversity as a value integral to the ecological paradigm in community psychology. Rappaport points to two basic dimensions as characterizing all human service models—an *economic policy dimension*, and a *cultural value dimension.* He goes on to distinguish between the *conservative* and *liberal* positions within both of these dimensions:

> The conservative economic position favors individual responsibility as opposed to societal responsibility for economic welfare. The liberal economic position favors societal economic responsibility. With regard to cultural values, the liberal, while "tolerating" differences (e.g. one should not discriminate because of them), seeks a unified society with one standard by which all people can be fairly judged. Each person has a right to private beliefs, but

judgments of competence, and therefore, employment and educational opportunity, must be based on the same standards for all. More important, the liberal tends to support a system in which the federal government helps everyone to adapt to the prevailing culture. The conservative on the cultural value dimension is much more inclined to support diversity, believing one's own values are better, but differences among local communities, cultures, and people are a fact of life not to be tampered with by "big government." (p. 23–24)

The essential features of these dimensions are summarized in Table 1. The values of the ecological perspective endorse interventions that approximate a synthesis of the *liberal economic* and the *conservative cultural* dimensions. That is, whereas it supports federal provision of resources, the ecological orientation calls for local community determination of resource utilization. Furthermore, it advocates supporting diverse programs in diverse communities that will maintain and amplify cultural differences.

Operationally, ecological interventions that follow from the above values aim to build on community strengths rather than seeking out those in need of mental health or other human services. Ecological interventions begin by finding individuals (e.g., informal community leaders, natural helpers) with the potential for strengthening their own communities.

Table 1. Values of Human Service Models[a]

Political positions	Dimensions of human services	
	Economic policy	Cultural value
Conservative	Individual responsibility	Supports diversity[b] and differential community life styles
	No federal support of social welfare	
		No government tampering[b]
Liberal	Societal economic[b] responsibility	Seeks unified society with one standard
	Supports social welfare[b] programs	Government should help people conform to prevailing culture

[a]Originally derived, based on Rappaport (1977), pp. 23–24.
[b]Values of ecological perspective.

The kind of *accountability* that the ecological perspective demands is, in essence, "community control" of human services. It does not imply that services must necessarily be delivered by local people; local communities may "import" *technical expertise* to deliver services, if they do not possess the requisite skills. Technical expertise should not be confused with accountability. As long as experts who provide services are seen as serving the local people—who decide on community priorities and evaluate the utility of services—accountability can be achieved (Rappaport, 1977).

The community entry points that facilitate seeking out such individuals are likewise suggested by the ecological perspective. As Labarta, Steele, and Trickett (1980) indicate the ecological perspective sensitizes one to the relative utility of various community support structures. That is, community support structures that facilitate entry for purposes of ecological interventions will differ as a function of ethnic composition. For example, religious institutions are more significant as entry points in Afro-American communities; families in Hispanic communities; and synagogues or social service agencies in Jewish communities.

Kurtines and Escovar (1980) point to the relevance of an ecological view of monoculturalism/biculturalism for community mental health. They state that when two cultures meet in the same territorial space, their interdependencies need to be worked out. Three outcomes are possible: assimilation, polarization, or biculturation. Biculturalism is viewed as compatible with the value of cultural plurality. Kurtines and Escovar point to research that found a poor fit among individuals who were inappropriately monocultural in a bicultural context. On the other hand, better adjustment of bicultural individuals in bicultural settings has been empirically determined. Promoting biculturation, then, is compatible with the guiding value that ecological interventions support cultural diversity.

Strengthening Mediating Structures

A major vehicle through which behavioral-ecological interventions can contribute to the promotion of cultural diversity is through programs aimed at strengthening "mediating structures." According to Berger and Neuhaus (1977), mediating structures are "those institutions standing between the individual in his private sphere and the large institutions of public life" (p. 2). Berger and Neuhaus focus on four mediating structures—neighborhood, family, church, and voluntary association—as providing the connection between the individual and the larger society. Mediating structures are crucial for fostering meaning and identity in one's private life, as well as for reducing alienation associated with the more distant "megastructures," including government, big labor, education, and other modern bureaucracies. Mediating structures are considered "people-sized institutions" and are said to constitute "the value-generating and value-maintaining agencies in society" (p. 6).

Berger and Neuhaus call for a public policy that will "empower" mediating structures for purposes of sustaining pluralism. For example, rather than government taking over the functions of families, the role of the family as an institution needs to be recognized and utilized in planning social programs. Such a public policy would recognize children's rights within the context of the family—one of which should be the right to a strong family—and would caution against the trend to substitute state childcare without the mediation of families. Berger and Neuhaus point to education as an area where the state has already disenfranchised families. They recommend the voucher approach for both day care and education as an antidote to the monopolistic tendencies of the state. If individuals were provided with vouchers that they could cash in at any school (which would later be reimbursed by the state), a greater diversity of educational opportunities would result, as would improved quality of education because of accountability by community control.

Likewise, to deny funding to social service agencies because of religious affiliation will result in a state monopoly over values. Separation of church and state should apply only to rule out favoritism toward any particular religious denomination. On the neighborhood level, diversity should be encouraged through allowing local residents to determine the values by which they want to live. To have national uniform standards imposed under the guise of protecting individual liberties translates into the undermining of local communal rights. Pluralism on a societal level can be maintained by recognizing the rights of communities to uphold their respective values. Otherwise, erosion of local neighborhoods will lead to "massification" of society, with options for individual identities greatly diminished. As Berger and Neuhaus (1977) conclude:

> *Liberation is not escape from particularity but discovery of the particularity that fits.* Elected particularities may include life style, ideology, friendships, place of residence, and so forth. Inherited particularities may include race, economic circumstances, region, religion, and in most cases, politics. Pluralism means the lively interaction among inherited particularities and through election, the evolution of new particularities. The goal of public policy in a pluralistic society is to sustain as many particularities as possible, in the hope that most people will accept, discover, or devise one that fits. (emphasis in original) (pp. 43–44)

By strengthening mediating structures pluralism will be supported and thereby individuals will be more empowered, as more options on which to establish personal identities and meaning in life will be available.

In a similar vein, Newbrough (1980) calls upon community psychologists and mental health professionals to stimulate the development of a "participating society." He suggests that individuals would be empowered through opportunities to participate in local communities. Newbrough argues that such participation would be facilitated if professionals devoted more attention to strengthening the mediating structures discussed by Berger and Neuhaus. This notion of a participating society through enhancement of mediating structures is an essential aspect of supporting cultural diversity as a value guiding behavioral-ecological interventions.

Finally, we wish to emphasize that as societal changes make traditional mediating structures (e.g., church, family) less viable for significant segments of the population, behavioral-ecological interventions should seek to facilitate the development of alternative structures in the *natural environment* capable of providing parallel social supports. That is, when traditional mediating structures cannot be strengthened, the behavioral-ecological perspective suggests such alternatives as self-help groups for specific problems (see Chapter 15), autonomous living environments for psychiatric patients (see Chapter 5), peer supports for deinstitutionalized mental patients (see Chapters 6, 18), as well as day care centers, senior citizens centers, single-parent networks, and community resource centers.

If professionals are to have the incentive to design interventions that will strengthen natural support systems, they will need to operate out of a base that encourages such activities. Presently, universities and grass-roots community organizations are more likely settings for such activities than are traditional mental health and human service agencies. To encourage such interventions, it may be necessary to build into the reward structure the reinforcement of such activities. For example, the government might subsidize 5% of staff time to engage in the strengthening of natural support systems while working out of health and human service agencies bases.

Conclusion

We have discussed three major values guiding behavioral-ecological interventions: promoting individual competence; enhancing the psychological sense of community; and supporting cultural diversity. The common thread among these values is expressed in Rappaport (1980), where he uses the notion of paradox to explore relationships between the roots of social problems and solutions. Because of the tendency to apply convergent solutions to divergent problems, it is axiomatic that "today's solution *must* be tomorrow's problem." Because of the dialectical roots of human problems—that is, their multiple and contradictory origins—solutions will need to rely on divergent thinking. Rappaport suggests that *pursuit of paradox* is paradigmatic for identifying the dialectical forces on which to base divergent solutions to mental health and social problems.

Guided by an underlying notion of the pursuit of paradox in analyzing mental health problems, the process of empowerment makes possible diverse solutions. Such solutions suggest valuing multiple standards of competence, collaborating with local communities in planning and implementing interventions, and promoting pluralism by strengthening mediating structures. In essence, then, the pursuit of paradox is a central theme of the values guiding behavioral-ecological interventions.

Although it may not be stated explicitly, we believe the programs reported in this volume exemplify these values in action. For example, in their consultation to day care centers Twardosz and Risley (Chapter 7) carried out organizational and environmental modification. This behavioral-ecological consultation resulted in child behavior change (e.g., less disruption) while avoiding the personal blame and "labeling" frequently associated with individually oriented behavior modification. Similarly, Liberman *et al.*'s (Chapter 4) Behavior Analysis and Modification Project offered behavioral skill training to promote independent living among psychiatric clients of a day treatment center operating within a token economy. This project built on existing individual strengths while providing a structure that recognized the limitations of this population. Likewise, Goodson and Turner's (Chapter 19) project at the Huntsville (Alabama) community mental health center incorporated a system of behavioral performance contracting to promote accountability at all staff levels. This was accomplished by incorporating incentives to motivate staff (something that civil service systems guided by uniformity cannot employ). Equally innovative was the Community Lodge (Chapter 5), an autonomous living environment for psychiatric clients. This program was based on a recognition of their right to be different, which does not contradict the right of access to psychological and material resources. Finally, the Community Network Development Project (Chapter 6) combined behavioral skill training with peer support networks among former psychiatric inpatients. In this way, training for competence within the context of an enhanced psychological sense of community was accomplished.

Finally, in contrast to usual treatments of values and ethics that relegate these concerns to the end of a volume or chapter, our strategy has been to present them at the outset—before offering the details of the knowledge bases for behavioral-ecological interventions. We emphasize that the guiding values for behavioral-ecological practice are based on the premise that ethics and practice cannot be separated. Furthermore, we call attention to the significance of understanding interventions in community mental health and the values underlying such interventions within a larger cultural context. As Sarason (1974) puts it:

> Before we indulge our tendencies to develop formulas and techniques (to become absorbed with technical-engineering issues) in our endeavor to effect change, we need to understand better how the nature of our culture produced a situation we wish to change. (p. 276)

The need for such understanding calls for articulating the guiding values at the outset.

References

Albee, G. W. A competency model to replace the defect model. In M. S. Gibbs, J. R. Lachenmeyer, & J. Sigal (Eds.), *Community psychology: Theoretical and empirical perspectives.* New York: Gardner Press, 1980.

Berger, P. L., & Neuhaus, R. J. *To empower people: The role of mediating structures in public policy.* Washington, D.C.: American Enterprise Institute for Public Policy Research, 1977.

Briscoe, R. V., Hoffman, D. B., & Bailey, J. S. Behavioral community psychology: Training a community board to problem solve. *Journal of Applied Behavior Analysis*, 1975, *8*, 157–168.

Geertz, C. *Agricultural involution: The processes of ecological change in Indonesia.* Berkeley: University of California Press, 1966.

Iscoe, I. Community psychology and the competent community. *American Psychologist*, 1974, *29*, 607–613.

Krasner, L. Behavior modification: Ethical issues and future trends. In H. Leitenberg (Ed.), *Handbook of behavior modification and behavior therapy.* Englewood Cliffs, N.J.: Prentice-Hall, 1976.

Kurtines, W., & Escovar, L. A. Culture, acculturation, biculturation and community psychology. In R. S. Slotnick, A. M. Jeger, & E. J. Trickett (Eds.), *Social ecology in community psychology*. Special issue, APA Division of Community Psychology Newsletter, Summer 1980.

Labarta, M. M., Steele, R. E., & Trickett, E. J. Community psychology and cultural diversity: The ecological analogy as metaphor. In R. S. Slotnick, A. M. Jeger, & E. J. Trickett (Eds.), *Social ecology in community psychology*. Special issue, APA Division of Community Psychology Newsletter, Summer 1980.

Lehmann, S. Community and psychology and community psychology. *American Psychologist*, 1971, *26*, 554–560.

Lehmann, S. Ecology, psychology, and evaluation. In M. Guttentag & E. L. Struening (Eds.), *Handbook of program evaluation.* Beverly Hills, Calif.: Sage, 1975.

Moos, R. H., & Insel, P. M. (Eds.) *Issues in social ecology.* Palo Alto, Calif.: National Press Books, 1974.

Netting, R. A trial model of cultural ecology. *Anthropological Quarterly,* 1965, *38,* 81–96.

Netting, R. *Cultural ecology.* Menlo Park, Calif.: Cummings, 1977.

Newbrough, J. R. Community psychology and the public interest. *American Journal of Community Psychology,* 1980, *8,* 1–17.

Rappaport, J. *Community psychology: Values, research, and action.* New York: Holt, Rinehart & Winston, 1977.

Rappaport, J. *Education, training, and dealing with the contingent future.* Unpublished manuscript, Department of Psychology, University of Illinois at Urbana-Champaign, 1978.

Rappaport, J. *In praise of paradox.* Presidential Address, Division of Community Psychology, meeting of the American Psychological Association, Montreal, September 1980.

Ryan, W. *Blaming the victim.* New York: Random House, 1971.

Sarason, S. B. *The psychological sense of community: Prospects for a community psychology.* San Francisco: Jossey-Bass, 1974.

Skinner, B. F. *Walden two.* New York: Macmillan, 1948.

Skinner, B. F. *Beyond freedom and dignity.* New York: Alfred A. Knopf, 1971.

Skinner, B. F. The ethics of helping people. *Criminal Law Bulletin,* 1975, *11,* 623–636.

Steward, J. *Theory of culture change.* Urbana: University of Illinois Press, 1955.

White, R. W. Motivation reconsidered: The concept of competence. *Psychological Review,* 1959, *66,* 297–333.

White, R. W. Strategies of adaptation: An attempt at systematic description. In G. V. Coelho, D. A. Hamburg, & J. E. Adams (Eds.), *Coping and adaptation.* New York: Basic Books, 1974.

Willems, E. P. Behavioral ecology. In D. Stokols (Ed.), *Perspectives on environment and behavior: Theory, research, and applications.* New York: Plenum Press, 1977.

3

Streams of Behavioral-Ecology

A Knowledge Base for Community Mental Health Practice

ABRAHAM M. JEGER AND ROBERT S. SLOTNICK

As an orientation to community mental health, behavioral-ecology is best characterized as an emerging perspective, one that draws on diverse bodies of knowledge. At the most general level, it is concerned with the *interdependence* among people, their behavior, and their sociophysical environments. Behavioral-ecology focuses on the *transaction* between persons and their settings, rather than viewing mental health problems as rooted exclusively within individuals *or* environments. More specifically, our notion of behavioral-ecology represents a merging of two broad perspectives—"behavioral" approaches as derived from the individual psychology of learning, and "ecological" approaches as encompassing the study of communities, environments, and social systems.

In this chapter we shall review the major streams comprising the behavioral-ecological perspective. We shall seek to integrate selected areas of theory, research, and practice that contribute to a knowledge

ABRAHAM M. JEGER AND ROBERT S. SLOTNICK • Human Resources Development Center, New York Institute of Technology, Old Westbury, New York 11568.

base for behavioral-ecological interventions in community mental health.

We have organized these diverse streams into (1) behavioral community technology; (2) bioecological analogies; (3) environment-and-behavior field; and (4) networks and social support. The first stream reflects the area within behavior modification that contributes the "behavioral" features of behavioral-ecology; the remaining three reflect areas contributing to the "ecological" features of behavioral-ecology. These streams are not distinct or mutually exclusive but have, to some extent, influenced each other in the course of their respective development. It is the thesis of this chapter (and the volume) that these streams are coalescing to form a broad knowledge base for behavioral-ecological practice in community mental health.

Behavioral Community Technology

The behavioral components of the behavioral-ecological perspective are derived primarily from the behavioral community technology stream. As defined by Fawcett, Mathews, and Fletcher (1980), behavioral community technology is concerned with the application of "behavioral principles to the analysis and solution of problems in open community settings. . . and developing the capacities of communities to achieve their own goals" (p. 505). It will become apparent from our discussion that this area is compatible with what others have referred to as behavioral community psychology (e.g., Briscoe, Hoffman, & Bailey, 1975; Glenwick & Jason, 1980; Jason, 1977; Martin & Osborne, 1980a; Nietzel, Winett, MacDonald, & Davidson, 1977). We shall employ the term "behavioral community technology" because of its relative clarity and more circumscribed nature.

Behavior Modification: An Overview

The behavior modification/therapy movement has been dubbed by Levis (1970) the "fourth therapeutic revolution." (Pinel, Freud, and community mental health represent the first, second, and third, respectively.) Bootzin (1975) uses the terms behavior "modification" and behavior "therapy" to refer to the "application of learning and other experimentally derived psychological principles to behavior change" (p. 1). Others, however, distinguish between behavior modification and behavior therapy. For example, according to Redd, Porterfield, and Anderson (1979),

> behavior modification refers to the application of behavior principles to many human situations, including child rearing, education, psychotherapy, vocational

preparation, business, and social movements. *Behavior therapy* is a special case of behavior modification and refers to the application of these principles to psychological problems, disturbances, and disorders in adults and children. (p. 8)

We shall employ the term "behavior modification" because its inclusiveness renders it more compatible with our perspective of community mental health. Behavior modification developed parallel to, but independent of, community mental health during the same period (the 1960s). Indeed, like community mental health, it developed, in part, as a reaction to the limitations of traditional psychotherapeutic approaches to mental health problems (see Ullmann & Krasner, 1975). Behavior modification/therapy offered scientifically derived principles from the psychology of learning as an alternative for dealing with individual problems. As we shall see, it was not until the 1970s that these two areas began to interface.

In their recent texts, Kazdin (1980) and Rimm and Masters (1979) hold that the following major characteristics of behavior modification/therapy distinguish it from more traditional approaches: (1) an emphasis on overt behavior rather than on any underlying disease entity as a cause; (2) that abnormal or maladaptive behaviors are acquired through the same learning processes as "normal" behaviors; (3) that maladaptive behaviors can be modified through applications of learning techniques; (4) that specific and clearly defined treatment goals be employed in therapy; and (5) that emphasis be placed on the evaluation of treatment and on obtaining empirical support for behavioral techniques.

What major types of learning provide the data base for behavior modification/therapy? In a historical review, Krasner (1971) notes that as many as 15 streams of research and application merged to form the uneasy alliance known as behavior modification or behavior therapy. However, three major streams appear to have characterized behavior modification in the 1960s: (1) operant conditioning; (2) classical conditioning; and (3) observational learning/modeling. Jeger (1979) refers to these three areas as "classic" streams, and identifies two additional "emerging" streams that developed during the 1970s: (4) cognitive behavior therapy, and (5) behavioral community technology.

Operant conditioning has its source in Thorndike's law of effect formulated at the turn of the century: Behavior is strengthened when followed by a "satisfying state of affairs" and weakened when followed by an "annoying state of affairs." Subsequently, Skinner (1938) emphasizes behavior as a function of its environmental consequences. The systematic extension of reinforcement (i.e., operant) techniques to the modification of human behavior came to be known as applied behavior analysis (e.g. Baer, Wolf, & Risley, 1968). It began with applications to individual clinical problems (Fuller, 1949) and broadened to include larger-scale applications to entire psychiatric wards via token economies (Atthowe & Krasner, 1968; Ayllon & Azrin, 1968; Schaefer & Martin, 1966). Other behavioral techniques that have their roots in the operant stream include extinction, satiation, timeout, response cost, overcorrection, shaping, prompting, and contracting. Although it cannot be said that these techniques are within the exclusive domain of behavior modification, their widespread use in recent years can be attributed largely to their behaviorally oriented advocates.

The *classical conditioning* stream, with its roots in the work of Pavlov, emphasizes the law of association (i.e., that learning occurs from repeated pairings of conditioned and unconditioned stimuli). Originally basing their work on Hullian learning theory, workers within this stream focused on reflexive behaviors. Most notably, Wolpe's (1958) method of systematic desensitization was geared toward the treatment of phobias and anxieties. Techniques derived from this stream include variations of relaxation training, aversion therapy, and covert sensitization.

Observational learning is derived from the work of Bandura (1969, 1977; Bandura & Walters, 1963), who emphasized the role of modeling per se (irrespective of external reinforcement) in learning. Numerous variations of the modeling paradigm (e.g., covert modeling, participant modeling) have been used to alleviate different kinds of fears and anxieties as well as to teach alternative behaviors. In general, the unique contribution of modeling procedures over the two earlier streams lies in their focus on vicarious learning processes.

Cognitive behavior therapy broadens the conceptualization of learning principles by introducing cognitive variables as determinants of behavior. Mahoney (1977) delineates four supporting hypotheses of this cognitive learning perspective: (1) that humans respond primarily to cognitive representations of their environments rather than to the environment per se; (2) that cognitive representations are functionally related to the processes and parameters of learning; (3) that most human learning is cognitively mediated; and (4) that thoughts, feelings, and behavior are causally interactive.

Some specific techniques employed by cognitive behavior therapists (e.g., Goldfried & Goldfried, 1975; Mahoney, 1977; Meichenbaum, 1977) include variations of Ellis's (1962) rational-emotive therapy—that is, the therapist challenges irrational beliefs of clients ("I must be loved and approved by everyone"). Additional techniques include cognitive tactics used by Beck (1976) in his approach to the treatment of depression—cognitive monitoring, disattribution, reality testing, and so on.

Behavioral community technology represents an extension of behavior modification (particularly techniques derived from operant conditioning) to larger-scale community problems. As opposed to earlier behavior modification that was largely confined to therapy offices and such institutions as mental hospitals, the behavioral community approach is unique in its emphasis on interventions in the natural environment. Its concern with problems and populations that go beyond the traditional domain of "mental health" makes it especially compatible with a behavioral-ecological perspective of community mental health.

A major limitation of behavior modification is that although it recognizes the role of the environment in determining behavior, it "attempts to reshape the individual rather than the environment, when dealing with human suffering and dissatisfaction" (Beit-Hallahmi, 1974, p. 127). Although behavior modification employed a conceptualization of human problems different from that of traditional psychodynamic approaches, the style of delivering service remained parallel to that of traditional clinical psychologists and psychiatrists. That is, carrying out behavior therapy in private offices on a one-to-one or group basis and attempting to remedy individuals' "deficits" in order to facilitate their adjustment to existing social structures characterizes the majority of behavioral interventions. Furthermore, as Nietzel *et al.* (1977) point out,

> while behavioral methods have been shown to produce change in highly controlled, well-funded demonstration projects, their application for the most part has not been organized around system-level interventions that attempt to be preventive in nature. (p. 4)

The emergence of behavioral community technology (or behavioral community psychology) represents an initial step toward meeting these limitations.

Applications of Behavioral Community Technology

According to Fawcett *et al.* (1980), three classes of procedures are most frequently employed by behavioral community technologists: (1) instructional technologies; (2) behavior management methods; and (3) environmental design techniques. Behavioral *instructional technologies*, which incorporate such teaching methods as behavioral specification, modeling, and feedback, have been applied to such community-relevant behaviors as peer teaching, parenting, childcare, and problem solving. *Behavior management* methods, which make use of contingent incentives, have been applied to job finding, energy conservation, promoting dental care, increasing participation in senior center programs, and increasing attendance of welfare recipients at self-help meetings. *Environmental design* procedures, which seek to modify the physical environment to facilitate behavior change, have been applied to day care centers (see Chapter 7).

Whereas Fawcett *et al.* (1980) organize the field in terms of technologies, in a review of behavioral community "psychology" Jason and Glenwick (1980a) delineate the area along five levels of intervention: individual, group, organizational, community, and societal. *Individual-level* applications include behavioral programs aimed at preventing speech anxiety, enhancing intellectual development among children from low-socioeconomic backgrounds, and reducing students' disruptive behavior in classrooms. *Group-level* applications include projects involving entire classes of elementary school children to improve their problem-solving skills (see Chapter 11, this volume), behaviorally based curricula for classrooms to prevent smoking, obesity, and poor nutrition as a means of heart disease prevention, and development of a comprehensive community-reinforcement program for alcoholics. *Organizational-level* applications include conversion of an institution for delinquents into community-oriented token economy cottages (see Chapter 9) and the development of Achievement Place, a behaviorally oriented halfway house for delinquent youth. *Community-level* applications include the employment of behavioral skills and media instruction to reduce smoking and promote exercise and positive nutrition to prevent heart disease (see Chapter 14) as well as an increasing number of behavioral interventions aimed at reducing littering, conserving energy, reducing crime, reducing air pollution, promoting recycling, and increasing carpooling and bus ridership. Finally, as examples of *societal-level* applications, Jason and Glenwick point to the use of incentives in legislation designed to reduce overpopulation. They also point to other larger-scale legal actions (e.g., school desegregation) that, although not designed by behavioral psychologists, clearly contain behavioral components. They call upon behavioral community psychologists to direct their attention toward influencing "socio-political power blocks" in order to effect larger-scale societal change. The Behaviorists for Social Action group (an interest group within the Association for Behavior Analysis, International), which examines social problems from a behavioral-analytic viewpoint (e.g., poverty, racism, sexism), represents a step in this direction, with implications for social change applications.

Two major features of the above projects are worth noting. First, the basic operant methodology remains as the overarching framework for community interventions. As Martin and Osborne (1980b) emphasize in connection with their definition of behavioral community psychology:

> Projects in behavioral community psychology focus on problems relatively new to the behavior modifier. . . . But we see nothing conceptually unique here. Baselines of human behavior, either singly, collectively, or in terms of their otucomes, are recorded. Change procedures are put in and withdrawn,

results are presented in terms of individuals behaving individually or collectively, procedures are operationally described, and functional relations are sought among antecedent and consequent events (i.e., stimuli) as they relate to responses. (p. 8)

Second, most of the projects are characterized by their "technological" focus, whereby procedures are clearly specified and "packaged"—increasing their replicability.

Thus behavioral community technology/psychology combines some of the innovations associated with the community mental health movement—use of nonprofessionals; broadening the roles of mental health professionals to those of program designer, trainer, and consultant; an emphasis on program evaluation and accountability—with the adoption of a behavior modification approach to operationalize these innovative trends. Behavioral community projects were implemented at three time points: primary, secondary, or tertiary. They varied in the type of behavioral strategies employed—including those derived from classical and operant conditioning as well as applications of modeling and cognitive restructuring. Furthermore, populations to which interventions were directed included children, adolescents, adults, and elderly. In terms of primary prevention efforts, behavioral interventions have sought to prevent the onset of specific disorders (phobias, anxieties, smoking); to prevent behavioral problems among "high-risk" children (e.g., those of schizophrenic or alcoholic parents); to enhance coping during milestone transitions (school entrance, marriage); and to build general competences and strengths.

Overcoming Problems of Implementation. Fawcett *et al.* (1980) identify several major problems pertaining to the large-scale adoption of behavioral community technologies. In many instances, the costs (e.g., of cash incentives, equipment, professional time) are prohibitive. At other times, fixed behavioral packages are too inflexible for adaptation to varying local conditions. Furthermore, adoption of a technology often ceases upon the departure of the program designer.

Since all these implementation problems are tied to the lack of fit between a behavioral technology and the social context within which it is applied, Fawcett *et al.* (1980) call for a "contextually appropriate behavioral technology." As an analogy, they use the notion of "appropriate" and "intermediate" agricultural technologies designed for underdeveloped countries. "Appropriate" refers to a technology's compatibility with a community's social context, and "intermediate" refers to a technology's cost being in the moderate range—between the expensive high technology of developed countries and the inexpensive, ineffective, low technologies of underdeveloped countries. Extending this analogy, they identify seven relevant characteristics for contextually appropriate behavioral community technologies: (1) effective, (2) inexpensive, (3) decentralized, (4) flexible, (5) sustainable, (6) simple, and (7) compatible.

Effective technologies are those that are "observably" superior to those previously in place. A technology is considered *inexpensive* if it can be absorbed by 1 month's discretionary funds of the average not-for-profit community agency. *Decentralized* technologies are those that can be applied on a small scale (i.e., neighborhood level) to increase consumer involvement in the design and implementation of programs. The design of *flexible* technologies that permit local adaptation may require presenting alternative problem-solving methods and inviting participants to select and modify the procedures as they see fit. This approach is an alternative to presenting a finished product as the only means of dealing with a problem. Technologies are said to be *sustainable* if they are based on local resources, which are more easily renewed than outside grant funding. *Simple* technologies are those that consider the reading level of potential users, among other characteristics bearing on ability for dealing with complexity. Finally, *compatible* technologies are those that consider the values and culture of local communities. Again, involvement of potential consumers is likely to enhance the compatibility of a technology.

It is self-evident that behavioral community technologists adhering to these criteria are more likely to design interventions that are in line with the guiding values of behavioral-ecological interventions discussed in the previous chapter. Furthermore, their interventions will have a better chance at overcoming some of the implementation problems outlined by Fawcett *et al.* (1980).

Limitations and Future Directions. Although behavioral community technology holds much promise if it moves toward adoption of these characteristics, Fawcett *et al.* (1980) point to possible limitations "inherent" in a behavioral approach to community problems. First, a behavioral technology may be insufficient because social problems often require knowledge from multiple disciplines for their solution. Furthermore, exclusive reliance on a behavioral technology may result in confining the problems sought to those for which behavioral solutions fit. That is, behavioral technology may be more appropriate for convergent problems (i.e., those for which scientists and practitioners can converge on "the" answer) than for divergent problems (i.e., those for which solutions are conflicting, based on opposite values, or may be "intractable"). (Recall Rappaport's views on the paradoxical nature of social problems discussed at the end of Chapter 2.) Finally, behavioral technology may be limited to producing change at the "micro" levels of society (individual, group, and organization) without changing the structure and function of social systems. Such "macro" changes require efforts aimed at the redistribution of power and resources within society.

Similar limitations of behavioral community "psychology" are identified by Nietzel *et al.* (1977), who argue that "the behavioral paradigm has been victimized by its own provincialism" (p. 354), and go on to point out that

> the conceptual narrowness of many behaviorists has prevented them from considering the functional relationships between the social systems in which they participate and the official designation of certain populations as problems, deviants, or victims. The ultimate danger of such theoretical sterility is that the behavioral paradigm will become as entrenched in institutionalized forms of service delivery and person-blaming ideologies as the ideologies it sought to replace. (p. 354)

Rappaport (1977) argues that although behavior modification is useful for changing individual behavior, "it may actually be a distraction when thinking about community behavior" (p. 89). He goes on to consider the frequently neglected question of "who controls the reinforcers":

> It is one thing to talk about a "community" setting its own contingencies, but quite another to change *who* in the community makes such decisions. This is simply a restatement of the need to distribute power more equitably and has little to do with behaviorism. It is reasonable to expect that those now in power are likely to continue to be in power unless that issue is dealt with directly. This is a question of social values, not of technology. . . . The socially marginal people who are now expected to conform to the status quo are not likely to be given power to set their own "schedules of reinforcement" or choose their own "desirable" behavior simply because behavior modification has shown that systematic distribution of material resources is obviously important as a means of behavior control. If anything, this is likely to increase the control of those already in power. . . . Because the principles are based on an analysis of individual behavior they may be misleading as a basis on which to understand the behavior of a community. (pp. 89–90)

Conclusion

Most of the interventions in the behavioral community area are one-sided. They generally reflect the extension of behavior modification (usually operant procedures) to significant community problems. They do not reflect an interplay or incorporation of interdisciplinary community change procedures with behavioral procedures for influencing social systems. Many community-level applications, as reviewed by Jason and Glenwick (1980a), seem to constitute individual change procedures in the natural community environment rather than being truly community-*level* interventions. Staging raffles to promote recycling and employing prompting to reduce energy consumption are hardly going to have a large-scale effect without considering such systems issues as the economics of energy distribution and people's pride and identification with their communities.

To meet the deficiencies of behavior modification for community change, Nietzel *et al.* (1977) recommend three "paradigm expansions": that behaviorally oriented professionals be committed as advocates for the populations they serve in order to effect community change; that interdisciplinary knowledge bases be incorporated into the paradigm including contributions from economics, political science, sociology, and other areas of psychology beyond learning theory; and that behaviorists adopt a more "expansive" view of community service within which professionals serve as program planners, consultants, and trainers rather than as direct service providers.

Concerning behavioral community psychology projects pertaining to mental health, Jason (1977) indicates that they are primarily focused on pathology and/or the prevention of "illness." He emphasizes the need for behavioral community psychology interventions to refocus their orientation from "mental disorders to mental health." This goal will require that we go beyond the application of a *behavioral* technology to community problems to develop a new *behavioral community* technology.

We contend that as behavioral community technology merges with other streams discussed in this chapter, the confluence will contribute to more effective behavioral-ecological interventions. Some of the limitations inherent in the one-sided extension of behavior modification to community mental health problems will then become more tractable. Conceived as part of a broader behavioral-ecological technology, both the goals of intervention and the style of delivery will be different from the straight behavioral applications to community settings. This broader orientation is essential if behavior modification is to contribute to building a psychological sense of community, a future direction discussed by Jason and Glenwick (1980b) as well as by Nietzel *et al.* (1977).

Bioecological Analogies

This section considers analogies from the field of biological ecology and their applications as a stream in our behavioral-ecological perspective. It draws primarily from the work of James Kelly (1966, 1968, 1970, 1979; Trickett, Kelly, & Todd, 1972), one of the first and foremost advocates for an ecological orientation in community mental health.

Conceptualization and Principles

As a guide to community mental health professionals for identifying problems, generating alternative solutions, facilitating their implementation, and evaluating their effectiveness Kelly (1968; Trickett *et al.*, 1972) delineates four principles derived from bioecology: (1) interdependence; (2) cycling of resources; (3) adaptation; and (4) succession.

The *principle of interdependence* emphasizes that a change in any unit of the ecosystem (i.e., community) will effect changes in other components. This ecosystem axiom predicates the reciprocity between structures and functions. The principle of interdependence sensitizes community mental health professionals to the reality that so-called unintended consequences of interventions are *not* mere side effects. Indeed they are often predictable events associated with "intended" interventions, and need to be anticipated. If one is not attuned to this ecological feature of communities there is greater risk of designing solutions that later create their own problems.

The *principle of cycling resources* is based on concerns in biological ecology with the utilization and replacement of energy forms (i.e., in food chains). In human environments the concern is with developing and utilizing new resources as personal and organizational requirements change.

The *principle of adaptation* defines adaptation as the relative diversity of environments in which organisms can survive. In human societies environmental constancy leads to a specialized adaptive capacity, whereas environmental uncertainty increases one's "niche breadth" (i.e., generalized adaptation).

The *principle of succession* calls attention to observations in biology that the activities through which organisms exploit their habitats will, over time, make them unfavorable for their own survival. Thus destruction of natural communities, unintended consequences of interventions, and continuous environmental changes will lead to species changes that, in turn, will result in a new "species–environment gestalt." A long-term perspective is therefore needed for planning and assessing interventions as well as for understanding their unintended consequences.

In his more recent writing Kelly (1979) builds on the bioecological analogy to emphasize the processes of interventions that follow from ecological premises. According to Kelly, process is necessary to mediate between the method and content of the intervention and the desired change. He offers a series of guidelines for defining process in community interventions that rest on the notion of the "dignity of problem solving"—that problem solving is an opportunity and that operating within a problem-solving perspective is energizing. He suggests a set of three preliminary guidelines defining process, with particular focus on managing "entry" in communities: (1) creating resources for ourselves; (2) expressing competences in diverse settings; and (3) committing time and energy. Briefly, the first guideline calls upon ecologically oriented practitioners and researchers to begin by generating a social support system for themselves. As Kelly points out, the reward structure of mental health agencies and of universities all too often encourages "solitary activities," a fact whose significance is further enhanced by the increasing observations of "burnout" in the helping professions (e.g., Cherniss, 1980). The second guideline calls attention to the role of the entry process in assessing the setting to determine ways in which competences can be expressed as well as to provide opportunities for new competences to develop in the course of entry. The third guideline emphasizes that committing extra time and energy is especially crucial during the entry phase in order to make it possible "to take advantage of the unplanned and natural opportunities that occur as the new working relationship unfolds" (1979, p. 254). Kelly discusses the implications of these three guidelines for community interventions with both responsive settings (those whose resources are overtly available) and resistant settings (those characterized as having "latent resources").

Applications

The bioecological analogies can serve as a backdrop against which to discuss major concerns of community mental health. For example, Mann (1978) demonstrates the relevance of the principle of interdependence for understanding a problem associated with deinstitutionalization—namely, discharging patients without integrating them into the social structure of the natural community through new roles. Thus, as we point out elsewhere (Slotnick & Jeger, 1978; Slotnick, Jeger, & Cantor, 1978), the primary barriers to deinstitutionalization are systemic in nature (e.g., union fears of job losses, community fears of declining property values). Cognizance of the interdependence principle would have predicted these problems, but they were largely ignored because of a preoccupation with individual-level analyses (e.g., lack of patient skills). Similarly, the cycling-of-resources principle suggests that new community resources need to be developed for discharged residents (to maintain their independent living), for hospital staff (to work in open settings), and for communities (to integrate these new residents). Likewise, the principle of adaptation would have predicted that the "specialized" adaptive capacity required for living or working in the institution would be maladaptive in the open community. The principle of succession points to the need for long-term interventions given the changing nature of communities—particularly evident in the case of long-term hospitalized patients who enter a new world upon discharge: Relatives, friends, and neighbors may have moved; the ethnic and religious composition of the community may have changed; and such physical features as stores, buildings, and landmarks may have been altered.

Kelly and his colleagues have also devoted considerable attention to the implications of ecological principles for developing prevention programs. For example, in a now classic chapter, Trickett *et al.* (1972) show how the ecological approach to planning prevention programs in the high school calls for redeveloping the high school environment rather than attempting to prevent a specific disorder (depression, alcohol abuse, delinquency). They offer general guidelines for designing preventive interventions:

> (1) interventions will deal directly with local conditions; (2) they will derive from a longitudinal assessment of the social organization; (3) they will focus upon expected effects of a change program upon members of the setting; and (4) they will include a variety of potential interventions. The ecological principles [previously] presented . . . are assumed to be relevant for affecting change of individuals in a locale because of these properties. The noise of the environment is trapped within the ecological perspective and then utilized. Effects of interventions are anticipated and mechanisms are created to reduce negative effects and actualize positive effects. (p. 389)

In line with the guiding values of behavioral-ecology that we presented in Chapter 2, Trickett *et al.* emphasize that a concern with long-term effects, attempts to anticipate side effects, and sensitivity to the requirements of local conditions are necessary for *community accountability*.

In extending the bioecological paradigm to community research, Trickett, Kelly, and Vincent (1982) emphasize the view of research as an "evolutionary process," thereby underlining the importance of adapting the research process to the community. This view is based on the value that in the course of research, community resources should be enhanced rather than depleted. As Munoz, Snowden, and Kelly (1979) observe, "community research would ideally combine the value of helping people to achieve psychological well-being with the value of empirically evaluating results" (p. 3). Munoz *et al.* offer three guidelines to help community research programs satisfy these values: (1) Each step of an intervention should include empirical tests; (2) a collaborative relation with the community should be employed; and (3) the *process* of implementation should receive special attention. They emphasize community participation in all phases of the research or intervention—including formulation and planning, implementation, and the monitoring of long-term effects. Trickett *et al.* further emphasize the use of multiple assessments, appropriate to the community setting.

An example of the bioecological approach to research aimed at knowledge building is Kelly's (1980) research study of proactive leaders, that is, citizens who initiate community change. The goal of the research is to answer such questions as how present resources can be better utilized and how new resources can be identified. Kelly draws on the ecological analogy to generate hypotheses about the interface among characteristics of proactive leaders, the nature of the setting within which they operate, and the conditions of the change process. That is, he considers person–environment hypotheses pertaining to responsive and resistant settings, proactive citizens of high and low status, and "patient" and "zealous" conditions of the change process. He considers the following potential ecological consequences associated with maladaptive conditions that need to be prevented: High-social-status persons working in responsive settings are prone to "elitism"; low-social-status persons working in responsive environments are prone to "co-optation"; high-social-status persons working in resistant environments are prone to "cynicism"; and low-social-status persons working in resistant environments are prone to alienation.

The major goal of proactive work is to identify, manage, conserve, and exchange resources—including money, policies, persons, settings, and ideas. The proactive role involves stimulating resource exchange that will contribute to the evolution of the setting and strengthen its adaptive capacities. Research on proactive leaders follows directly from ecology's ethical prescriptions—namely, that resources be channeled to preserve a natural resource and endangered species: the proactive citizen. Results of such ecological research will thus be used to meet an ethical obligation of empowering natural resources.

Conclusion

Although we have restricted our discussion of the bioecological analogy to the work of Kelly and his colleagues in the field of community psychology, human ecologists in the fields of sociology (e.g., Dunham, 1937; Faris & Dunham, 1939; Park, 1934; Park & Burgess, 1926) and anthropology (e.g., Geertz, 1966; Netting, 1965, 1977; Steward, 1955) have long looked at biology as a source for theoretical models. In our view, the bioecology stream as developed in the field of community psychology is most relevant to the perspective of contemporary community mental health advanced in this volume. For a more detailed discussion of the biological basis of the ecological paradigm in the fields of criminology, public health, and psychopathology, see Catalano's (1979) erudite treatment of the topic. A general comparison of ecology in the biological and social sciences is presented by Richerson (1977). Finally, the relation between culturally and genetically determined behaviors and their influence on individual adaptation is considered by Richerson and Boyd (1980).

Environment-and-Behavior Field

The "environment-and-behavior" field is an emerging stream in behavioral-ecology. According to Stokols (1977), the environment-and-behavior field represents the coalescence of ecological psychology and environmental psychology. Ecological psychology refers primarily to the work of Barker and his colleagues from 1947 to 1972 at the Midwest Psychological Field Station (e.g., Barker, 1968; Barker & Gump, 1964; Barker & Schoggen, 1973; Barker & Wright, 1955; Barker & Associates, 1978). Environmental psychology, on the other hand, is reflected in the work of diverse investigators in different parts of the country (e.g., Altman, 1975; Ittleson, Proshansky, Rivlin, & Winkel, 1974; Proshansky & Altman, 1979; Proshansky, Ittleson, & Rivlin, 1970).

Ecological Psychology

Barker's research in ecological psychology has been incorporated into most accounts of the ecological perspective in community psychology and community mental health (e.g., Holahan, Wilcox, Spearly, & Campell, 1979; Kelly, 1968; Lehmann, 1975; Mann, 1978; Rappaport, 1977; Weinstein & Frankel, 1974). The following elucidation of ecological psychology is based largely on Barker's (1978) recent statement on the field.

Conceptualization. According to Barker (1978), a major question characterizing his research is: "To what degree are people and to what degree are locales sources of behavior attributes?" (pp. 285–286). This problem became a central theme in his research following observations that the behavior of different persons changes in parallel patterns as they move between different locales. These locales, identified by Barker as "behavioral settings," constitute the basic environmental units in ecological psychology. They are small-scale social systems characterized by relatively standard behavior patterns irrespective of the types of persons participating in them—for example, churches, restaurants, drugstores, lectures, basketball games, third-grade music classes, and city council meetings. Barker sees behavior settings as interdependent, dynamic, and homeostatic entities in semistable equilibrium—with people as their essential component. Given the significance of people in managing behavior settings and providing satisfying opportunities to others involved in the setting, the view of the environment as merely "stable, reliable ground for action" has been challenged by Barker.

Barker considers two major directions of research on behavior settings: (1) inward—to examine the relationship between behavior settings and their human components (e.g., how people select the behavior settings in which they allow themselves to be incorporated and how they influence behavior-setting programs), and (2) outward—to examine the relationship of behavior settings to institutions and communities. Most of Barker's research in the first area has focused on the influence of the number of inhabitants in a setting on behavior. This research has led to the development of "manning theory," and to the distinction between undermanned and overmanned environments. Undermanned environments have too few people relative to the number of behavior settings; overmanned environments have too many people relative to the number of available behavior settings. For example, research in high schools (Barker & Gump, 1964) found that compared to students in overmanned schools, those in undermanned schools participated in a greater diversity of behavior settings, held more responsible positions, and felt more involved. On a larger societal level, Barker noted, we seem to be moving from scarcity of human components in behavior settings to redundancy. When we were a nation of undermanned behavior settings, people were more likely to derive satisfaction and feel competent in these settings—in line with undermanning theory, which associates undermanned settings with hard work, versatility, responsibility, self-confidence, and mutual support.

As for influences on behavior settings from *outside* their boundaries, Barker points to his research on five classes of institutions: government, schools, businesses, churches, and voluntary associations. Specifically, Barker and his colleagues examined the relationship between the size of institutions (as measured by the number of their members) and the "manning of their component behavior setting." They found that in large institutions the constituent behavior settings are generally overmanned, whereas in small institutions they are generally undermanned. These researchers raise the question whether large, consolidated schools necessarily have to contain overmanned behavior settings rather than incorporate smaller, undermanned behavior settings, which were found to be more optimal. That is, it may be possible to combine the usual benefits of larger institutions (e.g., greater variety of opportunity) with those of smaller institutions—namely, greater tendency for participation, and hence, enhanced competence and self-esteem. Barker points to the fact that more dropouts come from large schools than from small schools. Thus the efficiency obtained from consolidation generates problems that, in the long run, are exported to other institutions (such as the criminal justice and mental health systems).

Applications. Although most early accounts of Barker's contribution to an ecological view of community mental health (e.g., Kelly, 1968; Weinstein & Frankel, 1974) emphasize ecological psychology's focus on naturalistic observation, Rappaport (1977) considers the implications of undermanning theory for the psychological sense of community. Research on organizations that encourage participation among their members contributes to the knowledge base for developing interventions to enhance this sense of community. Rappaport shows how undermanning extends beyond discrete settings to the ultimate purpose of ecological interventions—"to involve local members of a community in the control of their own social institutions" (p. 145).

The relevance of ecological psychology for our broader behavioral-ecological perspective will no doubt increase as ecological psychologists turn their attention to some of the additional directions outlined by Wicker (1979). For example, Wicker points to increasing concern with service settings, an interest in the life cycle of settings (how they are created, maintained, and adapt to changes), and consideration of linkages among behavior settings (including interpersonal links, shared clientele, economic dependencies, flow of information, and flow of goods and services). More generally, Wicker points to increasing concern with "optimal" manning (rather than just over- or undermanning) and with the development of technologies to enhance human environments.

As for individual-level interventions, "knowledge of a community's behavior settings should be a strong weapon in the armory of those professionals who counsel individual persons" (Barker, 1978, p. 287). Indeed, ecological psychology has been incorporated into Bechtel's (1979) approach to "therapy." He employs the notion of "behavioral range" (the ecological psychology technique of listing the behavior settings with which an individual has contact on a daily basis as well as over the span of a year) as the basis for diagnosis and treatment. The roles of clients in these settings are analyzed along the dimension of performer (i.e., leader) versus nonperformer (inactive participant). A goal of treatment may be to engage the client in more settings and/or to increase (or decrease) the client's participation within particular settings. The behavioral range thus serves both as a pre- and a posttreatment measure.

Finally, we wish to link the philosophical position of ecological psychology to the values considered in Chapter 2. In his discussion of participation in behavior settings, Gump (1971) states that "experience in these settings is life. If the quality of experience is good, life expands; if it is bad, life diminishes" (p. 34). This important point reflects the value underlying ecological psychology's research on behavior settings—that participation is worthwhile irrespective of its relationship to some outcome variable (such as personality change or post-high school success). As such, this value is compatible with the values guiding community mental health interventions from a behavioral-ecological perspective.

Barker (1978) concludes that the contribution of ecological psychology lies in its specification of how the interdependence of people and settings can enhance citizen empowerment.

> The pressure of population, of technology, and efficiency against opportunities for people to be significant may be as great threats to survival as the pressure of population against food. The former threats are as salient, or more so, in "advanced" as in underdeveloped countries. The assertion that large, manpower-efficient, technically superior enterprises inevitably produce a better product more cheaply requires searching investigation. (p. 295)

Environmental Psychology

According to Proshansky and Altman (1979), the field of environmental psychology has its roots in research on psychiatric-ward design dating to the late 1950s and early 1960s (e.g., Osmond, 1957; Sommer & Osmond, 1961). The term "environmental psychology" has replaced such earlier terms as "architectural psychology" and "man–environment relations." Environmental psychology is defined as a field "concerned with establishing and understanding the relationship between human behavior and experience and the *physical environment*" (Proshansky & Altman, 1979, p. 4). Although environmental psychology is concerned with the mutual influences of people and the *built* environment, it should be emphasized that the social and psychological aspects of physical space are integral parts of the definition. As Proshansky and Altman put it:

> It is axiomatic that physical spaces and places are also social, psychological, and cultural spaces and places. In effect, these physical settings are defined by the social realities we identify as communities, playgrounds, housing developments, hospitals, transportation systems, courthouses, and, on a smaller scale, as bedrooms, hospital wards, classrooms, bathrooms, diners, hotel suites, operating rooms, treehouses, secretarial work spaces, and bus stops. (p. 4)

In a very general sense, then, environmental psychology can be seen as focusing on reciprocal influences between persons and their environment and, as such, is compatible with the behavioral-ecological perspective.

Conceptualization. Stokols (1977) emphasizes environmental psychology's concern with the roles of such psychological processes as perception, cognition, and learning as mediators of environment–behavior relationships. Thus he sees environmental psychology as a complement to Barker's ecological psychology, which tends to "downplay the role of individual differences in mediating the relationship between the structure of the setting and the responses of its occupants" (Stokols, 1977, p. 12). That is, such questions as the types of individuals who are most likely to be affected by undermanning and overmanning have hardly been addressed by ecological psychologists.

In an earlier article, Proshansky (1976) discusses the characteristics of environmental psychology. The first concerns the "absolute integrity of person/physical setting events," that is, only the real world, as opposed to the laboratory is the appropriate focus of study for environmental psychologists. This requirement calls for studying individuals in their natural contexts, observing persons and settings extensively over long periods, and involving subjects (i.e., community residents) in the research process. Environmental psychology is concerned with the processes involved in people's adaptation to the physical world and the influence of the physical world on internal psychological processes, for example, the relation of place identity to development of self-identity and self-esteem.

Furthermore, Proshansky considers *context orientation* in the analysis of environmental psychology problems. This term refers to the social and cultural aspects of physical settings that must be considered when studying person–environment relations. For example, analyzing children's use of a playground with a particular design and equipment in a given setting "requires us to consider who runs the playground, what rules are set, how it is governed, how it relates to the immediately surrounding area, of what broader institutional context it is a part of, and so on" (Proshansky, 1976, p. 309). Thus a conceptual analysis takes into account the social, organizational, and cultural factors defining a physical setting and attempts to conceptually link these to behavior in that setting.

Proshansky (1976) maintains that environmental psychology discards the physical-science, laboratory model of research, since it seeks to go beyond simple cause-and-effect relationships usually tested by manipulating single variables in isolated laboratory conditions. It is seen as an alternative to imposing experimental controls to determine the usual relationships of dependent and independent variables. Proshansky and Altman (1979) further stated that in environmental psychology "all applied research is basic research and all basic research is applied research" (p. 14). Thus environmental psychology rejects the traditional distinction between pure and applied research. Such a distinction is only relevant for a principle-oriented behavioral science, which argues that general principles must first be established before one can consider applying them to problems. Environmental psychology, on the other hand, is problem focused rather than principle focused.

Environmental psychology's problem-focused orientation is said to be an organizing principle of the field, which follows from its commitment to contribute to the solution of applied human problems. This orientation is also linked with environmental psychology's holistic approach, as well as its focus on the natural setting. The research process must not distort the natural process of person–environment transactions. Thus observation and description are the primary research tools. It also follows that flexible as well as multiple research methodologies are required. They are made possible by the interdisciplinary nature of the field, which incorporates theories and research methodologies from such areas as sociology, anthropology, architecture, urban planning, political science, geography, and design. Finally, environmental psychology is viewed as a sociohistorical behavioral science in that knowledge established today will be less relevant in the future as the context changes.

Stokols (1977) organizes the research streams in environmental psychology along three major categories of human transactions with the environment: (1) orientation, (2) operation, and (3) evaluation. *Orientation* refers to processes by which people perceive where they are, what will happen, and decide what to do. Research on environmental perception, cognitive mapping, and social climate assessment focuses on these processes. *Operation* refers to processes by which people act on and are influenced by their environment. Research on operation processes includes work on behavioral and psychological effects of noise, crowding, and pollution. *Evaluation* refers to assessment of one's effectiveness in the environment in terms of obtaining goals, and the adequacy of the environment for future goal attainment. Evaluation processes are reflected in research on environmental assessment which seeks to determine the health and social consequences of environmental changes.

In considering future directions of environmental psychology, Proshansky and Altman (1979) stress problems associated with the physical environment, the intensification of urban life, and the acceleration of our technological existence. They suggest that the potential contribution of environmental psychology might lie in its new way of looking at problems—namely, consideration of the unintended consequences of technological and other changes associated with the built and natural environment. They are optimistic about the contributions of environmental psychology, given the increasing opportunities for individuals and citizens to obtain information about their physical environments and to participate in changing these environments.

On the other hand, in considering the future of environmental psychology, Taylor (1980) takes a different view:

> The past decade has witnessed a precipitous decline in concern over environmental problems. Perhaps, as Dubos prophesied, we have adapted all too well to pollution, crime, crowding, and litter. Instances of dramatic environmental hazard (Three Mile Island, Love Canal) are viewed as rare, chance events, rather than as symptoms of a pervasive and deep seated conundrum. (p. 15)

Thus, Taylor is less optimistic that society will embrace the concerns of environmental psychology as priority human problems requiring major allocation of resources.

Applications. The application of environmental psychology to mental health research and practice is reflected in various projects. For example, Spivack (1969) urges that the design of mental health centers contain clearly designated "behavior settings" to guide appropriate place-dependent behavior. These would be an alternative to "vaguely designated" room types, such as hospital dayrooms and corridors. The latter, though flexible, are said to resemble hotel lobbies and train stations, which have no specific behavioral prescription and are a catchall for random behavior.

Early work by Ittelson, Rivlin, and Proshansky (1970) employed "behavioral maps" to relate patient behavior to specific physical locations in psychiatric wards. Social interaction among psychiatric patients has been related to bedroom occupancy (Ittleson, Proshansky, & Rivlin, 1970) and to dayroom seating arrangements (Holahan, 1972). Improved social behavior as a function of ward remodeling was demonstrated by Holahan's project (1976, 1979a,b).

Concerning the broader architectural aspects involved in designing mental health treatment environments, we point to the recent report on "Sociophysical Settings and Mental Health" by a task force of the National Council of Community Mental Health Centers (Wittman & Arch, 1980). In general, physical settings should encourage socializing and self-expression and be aesthetically pleasing. Wittman and Arch differentiate between two major features of the physical environment that all treatment programs should consider. One involves the need for personal space and discretion for its use (e.g., private sleeping quarters); the other involves such design features as natural and artificial lighting, acoustics (see also Spivack, 1969; Wheeler, 1964), size of rooms, temperature control, use of colors, and furnishings. The latter dimensions are crucial for maintaining a social climate most conducive to positive mental health. Finally, Wittman and Arch introduce the notion of a physical design *process* for community mental health centers, whereby local residents, including client groups, work with mental health and design professionals to locate facilities and redesign them to meet program needs.

The contributions of environmental psychology to realizing the above goals will no doubt be significant. For example, environmental psychology can contribute to the goal of privacy in mental health treatment settings by specifying "what kind of privacy, for what kind of setting, with what kind of individuals attempting to achieve what kind of purposes" (Proshansky, 1976, p. 308). Framing such research questions is deemed the appropriate analytic task since research on privacy from other perspectives has failed to identify underlying personality attributes that would appropriately characterize this phenomenon.

In the National Council of Community Mental Health Centers' task force report on the macroenvironment (Monahan & Vaux, 1980), two aspects of the physical environment that have received research attention from environmental psychologists, noise and crowding, were considered in terms of their mental health implications. At least under certain circumstances both of these variables were found to have negative effects on social, cognitive, and affective behaviors (e.g., decrease affiliation, impair academic performance, and depress mood). Monahan and Vaux recommend that community mental health workers consider these variables for mounting prevention programs. For example, rather than offer clinical treatment for persons experiencing noise-related stress, community mental health staff should work toward reducing noise in the community by advocating insulation of homes and schools and better zoning standards.

A Synthesis: Human–Environment Optimization

According to Stokols (1977), human–environment optimization (HEO) is a core thread in the interface between environmental and ecological psychology, or the environment-and-behavior field. This integrated environment-and-behavior field is characterized by the merging of ecological psychology's systems emphasis on adaptation and equilibrium processes with environmental psychology's concern with intrapersonal processes, contemporary community problems, and incorporation of interdisciplinary strategies for analyzing and solving these problems.

The processes of HEO are "the ways in which individuals and groups rationally guide their transactions with the environment in accord with specified goals and plans" (Stokols, 1977, p. 25). These processes are said to reflect "the active role taken by people in perceiving, shaping, and evaluating their surroundings according to their needs, as well as the reciprocal impact of the environment on people" (p. 25). Stokols distinguishes between the concept of optimization and earlier notions of behavior–environment fit. The latter emphasize environmental influences that are responsible for maintaining typical behavior patterns, and imply a quasistationary equilibrium (e.g., Barker's concept of "behavior–milieu synomorphy"—the correspondence between behavior settings and characteristic group activity). Optimization is both goal and design oriented; as such it is a more dynamic process. This is also so because of the inclusion of psychological dimensions derived from environmental psychology, which view individuals as active agents in designing their environments who thereby contribute to their behavior settings being in flux.

Stokols (1977) calls for research: (1) to ascertain relevant dimensions along which people attempt to optimize their environments; (2) to develop appropriate assessment criteria for measuring optimization process and outcome; and (3) to translate empirical information into guidelines for environmental design. Such research is exemplified in Wandersman's Neighborhood Participation Project (Wandersman, 1978, 1979; Wandersman & Giamartino, 1980) on individual and community factors that influence participation in block associations. (*Optimizing Environments* was the theme of the 11th annual meeting of the Environmental Design Research Association. The proceedings were edited by Stough and Wandersman, 1980.)

Recognizing that many people may not *want* to participate in settings and programs (Wandersman, 1978), it should be emphasized that although the behavioral-ecological perspective respects such individual preferences, it stresses that community mental health programs (1) provide the *option* for participation, and (2) allow informed choices for nonparticipation. The latter suggests that it is the responsibility of program administrators to ensure that people have the knowhow to participate; mere awareness of opportunity is hardly of value. To the extent that large segments of our society lack *participation skills,* their so-called choice of nonparticipation clearly cannot be considered informed. Participation of citizens on a community mental health center's advisory board is examined in Chapter 21 of this volume; training board members to problem-solve has been considered by Briscoe *et al.* (1975).

As a stream in our behavioral-ecological perspective, HEO is relevant both from practical and conceptual vantage points. Practically, the nature of most behavioral-ecological interventions is such that they engage participants in the process of planning programs and services to meet their needs. For example, Wandersman (1978) emphasizes "user participation" (consumer, client, resident, etc.) as a strategy for optimizing environments—since participation increases the feeling of control over an environment and is likely to yield greater individual satisfaction with a setting. Conceptually, HEO is congruent with the guiding value of behavioral-ecological interventions—that is, to enhance individual and community participation in the operation (if not control) of their living environments. Optimization is based on the ecological view, which assumes a natural tendency for people to play active roles in designing their environments.

Networks and Social Support

Two major types of networks are considered here as contributing to a behavioral-ecological perspective in community mental health: (1) individual social networks, and (2) interorganizational resource exchange networks. Social networks among individual community residents are considered from the vantage point of their serving as a social support system. Interorganizational networks, as exemplified by "resource exchange networks" a la Sarason and his colleagues (Sarason & Lorentz, 1979; Sarason, Carroll, Maton, Cohen, & Lorentz, 1977), are considered from the standpoint of their relevance in meeting the needs for agency coordination by establishment of linkages among various mental health and human service programs in the community.

Individual Social Networks

In recent years community mental health professionals have begun to direct their attention to informal helping networks in the community as potential sources of individual social support. Such networks were considered both in terms of their implications for treatment as well as within a preventive context to assist individuals in encountering numerous life stressors and developmental transitions.

Conceptualizations. Caplan (1974), whose work was a major impetus for the community mental health movement in the United States, defines *support systems* as:

> continuing social aggregates that provide individuals with opportunities for feedback about themselves and for validations of their expectations about others. . . . People have a variety of specific needs that demand satisfaction through enduring interpersonal relationships. . . . Most people develop and maintain a sense of well-being by involving themselves in a range of relationships in their lives that in toto satisfy these specific needs. (pp. 4–5)

Based on studying networks within the context of social support, Hirsch (1979) offers the following definitions:

> In its most inclusive sense, the social network is defined as the set of all others with whom one has social interactions. Social network may be used in a more restricted manner to refer only to the set of presently significant others with whom one has social interactions. (p. 264)

What are some of the social support systems to which mental health professionals have recently directed their attention? In his analysis of "lay treatment networks" in the mental health field, Gottlieb (1976) distinguishes among four major informal helping systems: (1) *self-help groups,* made up of people sharing a common need or problem; (2) *social network,* consisting of an individual's "primary group members" (e.g., extended family); (3) *community gatekeepers,* which include family physicians, clergy, teachers, and so on; and (4) *neighborhood-based support systems,* composed of block association leaders, PTA organizers, opinion leaders, and "natural neighbors" (e.g., Collins & Pancoast, 1976). More recently, Mitchell and Trickett (1980) suggest that the support systems of individuals tend to cut across any formal demarcations (such as the above). As such, they employ the notion of social networks to examine the "total social field within which the individual is embedded" (p. 28).

Heller (1979) employs the term "network" to emphasize the reciprocal nature of social support. Tolsdorf (1976) arranges network dimensions into three categories: (1) structure; (2) content; and (3) function. *Structural* variables include size and adjacent density. Adjacent density refers to the number of dyadic linkages in a network proportional to the number of linkages possible, given the size of a network. *Content* variables define the nature of the relationship around which network linkages are formed—such as primary kin, economics, recreation, or politics. Relationships that contain linkages in more than one content area are defined as "multiplex" in contrast to those formed around a single content area, which are defined as "uniplex." Multiplex relationships are seen as more powerful and important. *Function* variables refer to the nature of the transactions between network members—for example, providing support, advice, or feedback.

Behavioral scientists have examined these variables in their research on the role of social networks in moderating life stress. Reviews of major studies on the effects of social support on mental health can be found in Chapter 18 (this volume), Heller (1979), and Mitchell and Trickett (1980). Our major purpose in this section is to consider the potential applications of network analysis to community mental health interventions.

Applications. In considering such applications, we shall present one model of network analysis that is compatible with the behavioral-ecological perspective. Politser (1980) developed a statistical decision-theoretic model of social network analysis based on the "logic of support-seeking behavior." Essentially, he considered the potential effects of network size (and density) from the standpoint of an individual's expectation as to whether broadening the number of individuals in one's network (or strengthening their intensity) will yield benefits in the form of increased support that outweigh the costs associated with new stressors created by the demands of the new (or intense) relationships. Thus individuals strive to maximize support through their social networks by attempting to reach some hypothetical "optimal" network size (i.e., one that will provide a reasonable balance between the costs and benefits of new relationships), which constitutes an alternative to the bigger-is-better assumption about the value of network size.

Following the premise that "with increasing network size, the potential for benefits and the potential for costs increase simultaneously" (Politser, 1980, p. 78), four possible adaptational outcomes can be derived from a calculation of the expected net values (i.e., benefits minus the costs associated with various network sizes): (1) social adaptiveness, (2) social withdrawal; (3) social insatiability; and (4) social ambivalence. In the first case, it is possible for the person to achieve an optimal balance between "loneliness" and feeling "overwhelmed" based on a relatively well-defined notion of his/her "ideal" network size. Reaching this state of social adaptation depends on an appropriate combination of individual skills and environmental opportunities. The second situation, social withdrawal, will be preferred by individuals for whom the risk of demands associated with new supports yields a negative net value when network size exceeds zero. Here, interventions should focus on promoting individual skills (e.g., through behavior modification) to facilitate adaptation by being able to deal with the demands of social support. Social insatiability, the third situation, occurs when an individual's need to affiliate (i.e., seek support) is so great that he/she continuously "expects" to benefit from increased network size even to the point when the network will be more demanding than supportive. Unlike the previous cases, no optimally balanced state exists. The suggested intervention is on the network level; that is, attempts should be made to reduce the demands of the network and/or to increase its supportiveness. The fourth condition, social ambivalence, is characterized by a conflict in which the person vacillates between increasing and decreasing network size (to deal with loneliness and thwart feeling overwhelmed, respectively). Because of their ambivalence, an intermediate network size may be the worst possible state for such individuals. Both individual- and network-level interventions are suggested here in order to increase the person's responsiveness to social support (and/or ability to handle social demands) as well as to make the network more supportive (and/or less demanding).

Similarly, Politser considers the potentially dual effects of network density. Close-knit networks may provide support or may create excessive stress (through pressure to enforce norms); thereby they may either contribute to social adaptation or help create the less optimal conditions we have described.

Politser concludes that this model

> suggests a rational basis for some forms of seemingly irrational behavior. Here the origins of certain forms of loneliness, conflict and psychosocial distress are viewed as logical consequences of the interaction of the individual with the network. To whatever extent this is true, clinical approaches that challenge the logic of illness may be doomed to frustration. At least for the social predicaments described, the model suggests that a concerted attack upon the processes giving rise to them is likely to be more productive than an attack upon the rationality of the client behavior itself. (p. 84)

Finally, Politser looks at research with individuals who underwent such transitions as divorce or retirement that was conducted to test some empirical predictions of the model. Politser reports that preliminary findings support the model, at least as applied to people in crisis.

More broadly Mitchell and Trickett (1980) discuss the implications of network concepts for community mental health policy and practice in the following five areas: (1) individual and family interventions; (2) paraprofessional training; (3) evaluation and planning; (4) community needs and resource assessment; and (5) strengthening natural helping networks.

Examples of interventions in the first area include the work on family network therapy (e.g., Speck & Rueveni, 1969), as well as skill training to help an individual communicate with network members. In terms of paraprofessional training, it is suggested that programs move beyond the development of interpersonal helping and counseling skills to training paraprofessionals to help mental health clients establish networks as well as to link the clients with existing community resources. Concerning community assessment, Mitchell and Trickett suggest examining network patterns across different groups and neighborhoods in order to identify problem areas (e.g., high-risk groups) as well as community strengths and resources. For example, if church membership is discovered to be a frequent link in a community, then clergy may be a logical starting point for developing programs (see Chapter 17, this volume, for a collaborative program with clergy). Finally, professionals are called upon to identify and enhance the skills of informal community leaders by offering information and support within a consulting relationship. Mitchell and Trickett conclude that "the concept of social network as a mediator of social support provides a conceptual orientation for a reemphasis on the community component of community mental health centers" (pp. 42–43).

Thus community mental health professionals need to pay closer attention to research developments in social network analysis from numerous disciplines including psychology, sociology, anthropology, political science, and mathematics. Understanding individual networks will enhance behavioral-ecological interventions that seek to identify support networks in a community and to strengthen their further development as well as to create alternative supports to natural structures (e.g., self-help groups, neighborhood helpers, and community education programs in lieu of traditional family and religious supports). The latter is necessary if natural support networks are absent or if there is an incongruence between an individual and his/her natural support system.

Indeed, Turkat (1980) holds that the "creation of social networks will be one of the most difficult challenges for the future of community mental health" (p. 101). To meet this challenge parallel individual- and community-level interventions will be required—that is, designing environmental opportunities for the creation of new support systems (by employing community organization strategies) as well as conducting social skill training so that individuals learn to maintain their new network relationships. This effort will call for a unique combination of the "behavioral" (i.e., for skill training) and "ecological" (i.e., for environmental design) features of behavioral-ecology. The Community Network Development Project for psychiatric patients described in Chapter 6 of this volume is one such behavioral-ecological intervention. Other projects that exemplify professional collaboration with community residents for developing new support networks or interfacing with existing, informal help-giving systems are reviewed by Jeger, Slotnick, and Schure (1982) and in Chapter 15 of this volume.

Concerning societal implications of social networks, Granovetter (1973) discusses an interesting example of the relevance of social network analysis for community resource mobilization. He points to the destruction of Boston's West End Italian community because of its inability to organize against "urban renewal," despite West End's socially cohesive structure. Granovetter's thesis is that although *strong* ties existed among many small-group segments of the community, there were insufficient *weak* ties to link these small, cohesive groups with one another to permit communitywide mobilization. Indeed, another community, Charlestown, was successful in organizing against Boston's urban renewal plan because it contained a "rich organizational life" that allowed the formation of weak ties to bridge the smaller groups with strong ties. Thus special environmental conditions are necessary if weak ties are to develop. This point underlines the limitation of earlier network analyses that restricted their focus to strong ties.

The significance of weak ties in linking micro-macro levels of analysis suggests an interesting paradox in sociological theory, one we deem compatible with a behavioral-ecological perspective:

> Such linkage generates paradoxes: weak ties, often denounced as generative of alienation are seen here as indispensable to individuals' opportunities and to their integration into communities; strong ties, leading to cohesion, lead to overall fragmentation. Paradoxes are a welcome antidote to theories which explain everything all too neatly. (Granovetter, 1973, p. 1378)

Granovetter points to the limitation of considering only the strength of ties in micro-macro linkage. He calls upon future network analysis to examine the contents of network interactions as well as the influence of such variables as demography, coalition structure, and mobility in a community on the development of micro-macro linkages.

As a stream in behavioral-ecology, social networks have implications for various areas of community mental health practice. These include employing network concept to promote individual competence and social support; to strengthen natural helping networks; to devise "artificial" networks (e.g., self-help groups); and to catalyze community resource mobilization.

Interorganizational Resource Exchange Networks

Interorganizational networks are distinguished from individual networks in that the unit of analysis is an agency rather than an individual. Our major purpose in this subsection is to consider one type of interagency network—the "resource exchange network" (REN; Sarason & Lorentz, 1979; Sarason *et al.,* 1977)—as being especially compatible with a behavioral-ecological viewpoint.

Conceptualization. Sarason and his colleagues (1977) began thinking in terms of networks because of several observations. First, they noted the "unprecedented interrelatedness" in our society within and between settings and institutions (recall Kelly's bioecological principle of interdependence). The failure of human service agencies to recognize the fact of "limited resources" and their constant competition for a share of limited funding for personnel and capital are critical causes of the diminished psychological sense of community (Sarason, 1974).

As a partial response to this situation, Sarason and other individuals from various educational and human service settings formed linkages to exchange resources in barter style. As the number of participants increased, a greater diversity of institutions and resources became accessible and eventually a REN (the Essex Network) evolved. With the walls of agencies permeated, the effects of the REN included expansion of agency resources as well as satisfaction of individual needs for support and sense of community. Opportunities for personal and professional growth of mental health service providers are valued as much as the growth of clients of those services (Sarason, 1972). Thus the rationale of the REN is based on the fact of limited resources coupled with the value of the psychological sense of community as informing action. The REN philosophy capitalizes on the interface between the individual and the organization and thereby enhances both.

According to Sarason and Lorentz (1979), the ideal REN is

> a voluntary, loose association of heterogeneous individuals willing to consider ways whereby each is willing to give and get needed resources from others, to seek to increase the number and diversity of participants, to place no restrictions on the substance of foci of exchanges, and to resist putting considerations of exchange and planning under the pressures of funding and the calendar. (p. 178)

Although recognizing that most RENs do not operate at this ideal, we emphasize several salient features of RENs that are compatible with this definition. RENs provide opportunities for redefining oneself and others as resources. Rather than dwell on deficits, the nature of REN transactions builds on strengths, thereby serving a capacity-building and empowerment function in addition to improving service. The operating base of a REN is generally *between* agencies rather that *within* an agency. However, unlike federations, coalitions, and coordinating councils, which are comprised of member organizations and are major vehicles of interorganizational relations, RENs are composed of individuals who are also members of organizations but are not necessarily official representatives. As such, RENs are loose, informal, and voluntary, with no formal decision-making structure or director; instead they use a "leader-coordinator," who functions more as a facilitator than as a conventional leader. His/her special abilities should include scanning the environment for resources, matchmaking, and sensitivity to interrelatedness. For example, the leader-coordinator should be able to see the possible connection among the needs of children, youth, and the elderly for its resource linkage potential—for example, the utilization of teen-agers and elderly in childcare for the mutual benefit of all three groups.

Furthermore, the REN rationale has larger-scale societal implications. Sarason and Lorentz (1979) propose the establishment of a "resource exchange ombudsman" at the local, state, and federal levels.

These ombudspersons would deal with problems of service (i.e., resource) coordination in the public sector. Their role would parallel that of the leader-coordinator in a REN:

> In the most general terms, the ombudsman responsibility concerns the ways in which agencies define and utilize resources, the ways in which they can share resources, how informal networks among agencies can be developed to increase resource exchange, and identification of the barriers that prevent public agencies from locating and utilizing existing community networks with which some form of resource exchange would be mutually enhancing. (p. 257)

The ombudsperson is likened to the Scandinavian "citizen protector" in that he/she would have no formal decision-making power; any changes resulting from his/her activities would be, in essence, entirely voluntary.

Implications. The relevance of interorganizational networks for community mental health programs is obvious when we consider the need for coordination between agencies. For example, the requirement of "continuity of care" in the transition of psychiatric clients from hospital to community and the need for interagency collaboration in maintaining the institutionalized clients in the community cannot be overemphasized. As cited by the Comptroller General of the United States in a report focusing on the plight of mental patients in the communities, "at least 135 federal programs administered by 11 major departments and agencies of the government affect the mentally ill" (U.S. General Accounting Office, 1977, p. viii). Coordination among federal, state, and local agencies engaged in the implementation of deinstitutionalization programs is crucial for alleviating diffusion of responsibility at the expense of psychiatric clients. The need for coordination is equally critical once we move from treatment to prevention programs. That is, for any successful prevention effort community mental health centers need to establish linkages with such organizations as social service agencies, schools, day care centers, and juvenile justice systems, to name but a few.

RENs bear directly as a stream in our behavioral-ecological perspective. First, as we pointed out, an ecological analysis of human services would sensitize mental health professionals to the conditions that led Sarason *et al.* (1977) to establish a REN. Furthermore, the establishment of RENs is seen as an "ecological" response to such conditions (i.e., RENs are an ecological intervention). To the extent that RENs attempt to redefine and redistribute resources, they are compatible with aspects of the ecological perspective emphasized by Kelly's principle of cycling of resources. RENs also represent face-to-face support settings in which the kinds of positive experiences associated with participation in undermanned settings (as identified by Barker's research in ecological psychology) can be realized.

Furthermore, we see RENs in yet broader terms—namely, as a *delivery system*, providing vehicles for planning and implementing other ecologically oriented programs (e.g., mutual support networks among individuals, school-based prevention programs). In this regard, the broader roles of professionals such as consultant, trainer, catalyst, and resource person are encouraged by interventions emanating from a REN rationale. Through such professional roles, RENs can stimulate collaborative activities between formal agencies and natural support networks and self-help organizations (Gottlieb, in press; Jeger *et al.*, 1982) for the purpose of enhancing the psychological sense of community among the participating citizens and professionals.

The importance of interorganizational relations in community interventions is apparent from an example cited by Koenig (1980). He points to a failure in the interorganizational relations system of a community in adjusting to a new antipoverty agency. The mandate of this agency was to stimulate economic development through local planning and by catalyzing collaboration among existing agencies. The agency's lack of knowledge about how the existing agencies could work together coupled with the insufficient time for establishing such interorganizational linkages before utilization of funds placed the new agency in a double bind (i.e., alienating the local community and spending the money without its participation, or alienating government by not spending the money) that led to its demise. Citizen participation cannot be achieved by a mere mandate; time is required for its natural evolution if an ecologically sound balance is to be achieved within a given community.

Finally, at the larger community and societal levels it is our hope that realization of the present shortcomings in the mental health delivery system—especially those stemming from lack of cooperation, competition for limited resources, diminished psychological sense of community or burnout among service providers, and general lack of coordination among the multitude of groups, agencies, and bureaucracies that play a role in delivering mental health services to individual clients—will give way to the establishment of resource exchange ombudspersons at the local, state, and federal levels as suggested by Sarason and Lorentz (1979).

Synthesis: Toward a Merging of Streams

This chapter calls for the confluence of several major streams to form a knowledge base for behavioral-ecological interventions in community mental health. As is apparent from a review of these areas, they share many common assumptions, which makes for a special compatibility. For example, both behavior modification and bioecology are concerned with the relationship between environment and behavior, although they each view the environment differently. As Willems (1974) and Studer (1978) have argued, these two approaches can complement each other, and the combined strengths of each can lead to a more powerful perspective. Behavioral community technology is explicit, rigorous, and empirically grounded. Bioecology is concerned with the *context* of interventions. By combining the two we can hope for an "ecobehavioral" technology that is concerned with the culture of the setting, committed to multiple measures and data sources to ascertain "unintended" consequences, and that takes a long-term perspective. Interventions should go beyond attempts to modify single dimensions and should instead encompass multiple levels (individual and community).

Furthermore, we contend that a synthesis of behavior modification's skill-training and content/package orientation with bioecology's process focus is more likely to lead to *true* adoption of mental health programs. In distinguishing between *manifest* and *true* adoption of demonstration projects, Rappaport, Seidman, and Davidson (1979) use the notion of *essence*. The essence of a program, which is necessary for true adoption refers to "the essential rules of the game that govern relationships among program participants as well as the spirit, ideology, values, and goals of the original project" (p. 102). They point to the widespread adoption of token economy programs to illustrate the notion of essence:

> Anyone familiar with the Ayllon and Azrin (1968) book on token economies and with the large number of behavior modification units of state hospitals, which it and other similar demonstration projects helped to create, will know that something is amiss. While the words are the same, somehow, what goes on in settings labeled behavior modification is often so different in intangible ways (words like excitement, expectation, and atmosphere come to mind) as to be very different from the original, although they may be objectively the same. Certainly such units have been widely adopted, in the jargon of dissemination research, but have they really been adopted if they lost their essence? We are not speaking here of simply sloppy or incorrect programming, although that is part of the problem, but rather of the elements of a human service program that are impossible to quantify or to put into program manuals. (p. 104)

Thus, packaged programs should not be "parachuted" into organizations or communities without taking into account their fit with local conditions. Process variables need to be considered along with the behavioral content. In larger-scale community interventions, in which the modification of settings is a primary goal, we suggest the notion of *behavioral markers* to guide and demarcate major turning points and/or accomplishments within the more complex process of community change.

What is needed is a refinement of methodologies of *behavioral process monitoring* in the natural environment.

Contributions from behavioral technology can provide the methodologies and analytic change procedures and thus meet the operational limitations of ecological concepts as guides to interventions (Lehmann, 1980). In a discussion of the integration of ecological analysis and behavior analysis, Risley (1977) states that the *internal* ecology of behavior analysis is its insistence on *experimental analysis.* He goes on to assert that ecological analysis of behavior (i.e., naturalistic observation) alone is not sufficient; instead, it is experimental *interventions* that will lead to methods for changing society. Experimental analysis of environments (i.e., environmental modification) will lead to ecological *procedures*—not merely the ecological analysis of behavior.

Examples of Syntheses

The merging of ecology with the other streams discussed in this chapter will contribute to "exemplars" (i.e., paradigmatic research/intervention programs), the lack of which constitutes another limitation of ecology as a paradigm (Price, 1980). Some of the projects in this volume are beginning steps toward such a merging. Many of the projects are explicit attempts to integrate behavior modification with some ecological stream; others are exclusively "behavioral" or "ecological," and we are suggesting their contribution to an integrated perspective. For example, the Community Network Development Project for psychiatric patients (Chapter 6) draws on both the behavioral and network streams. Likewise, Twardosz and Risley's consultation program to day care centers (Chapter 7) draws on the behavioral and ecological streams. (See Rogers-Warren & Warren, 1977 for more extensive discussions on the interface between behavior analysis and ecological analysis.)

The interface between behavior modification and streams of the environment-and-behavior field is reflected in Krasner's (1980) conceptualization of environmental design, which is compatible with our notion of behavioral-ecology. The merging of a behavioral approach with physical environment concerns is reflected in Cohen and Filipczak's (1971) early efforts with a residential "learning environment" for youthful offenders. Guided by a "behavioral architecture" perspective, the entire facility incorporated a behavioral approach to design. (This synthesis is reflected in the Foreword by R. Buckminster Fuller *and* B. F. Skinner to their 1971 book.) Colman's (1971) work on psychiatric wards likewise reflects attempts to integrate physical design with behavioral principles. Recent work by Ribes (1980) reflects a merging of environmental psychology and applied behavior analysis to housing design. He employed behavioral measurement techniques to evaluate the effects of physical space of houses and cities on behavior. Community mental health centers would benefit by drawing explicitly on a synthesis of these two streams in designing facilities and developing programs.

An interface between a concern with the physical setting and the network stream is reflected in the National Council of Community Mental Health Centers' task force report on *Sociophysical Settings and Mental Health* (Wittman & Arch, 1980). Specifically, the impact of physical rearrangements on social relationships was addressed. As Wittman and Arch note, "moves also result in social dislocations. It is most unlikely that a social network could be transferred as a whole from one setting to another" (p. 48). Thus changes in physical settings can result in the uprooting of an individual's social network. Indeed, the Community Lodge Program described by Tornatzky and Fergus (Chapter 5) has taken this problem into account: By discharging an entire cohort of patients, their support system is not disrupted. On a larger scale, Lehmann (1975) points to the unanticipated consequences of moving ghetto dwellers into high-rise apartments. Such transfers are likely to lead to a breakdown of existing natural support networks and a weakening of adaptive behaviors among many residents.

The work of Moos (1974, 1975, 1976; Moos & Insel, 1974) in the area of "social ecology" represents an interface between the bioecological and environment-and-behavior streams. In discussing the practical applications of social ecology, Moos (1976) suggests both individual- and community-level interventions. For example, he calls for an Environmental Status Examination (ESE) to describe an individual's "ecological niche" (family, work, or other social settings) to complement the usual Mental Status Examinations in clinical treatment settings. Furthermore, he calls for enhancing "environmental competence" through development of educational curricula to teach people how to create and select their environments (including educational, social, work, and service settings). For example, individuals wishing to become more assertive might select environments that reward assertiveness. The recent work of Jason and his colleagues (e.g., Jason & Smith, 1980) on the "behavioral-ecological matchmaker" (BEM) is another example of this approach. Rather than changing individual behavior through direct clinical interventions, the BEM role was exemplified by matching individuals manifesting low rates of sharing behaviors with groups where sharing is the norm. Moos (1976) calls for environmental pluralism, whereby numerous alternative environments are created to provide options for different groups of individuals with different needs at different points in their life cycle.

Behavioral-Ecological Research Paradigms

Although we have emphasized the merging of research and service as a major feature of the behavioral-ecological perspective, there is a need to distinguish between research directed toward knowledge building, and evaluation as an ongoing process built into intervention programs. Behavioral-ecological inquiries whose primary purpose is knowledge building include research by Edwards and Kelly (1980) and Munoz *et al.* (1979). Such research aims to identify major strategies that will guide interventions to promote individual and community competence. Once behavioral-ecological programs are implemented, there is an ongoing need for evaluation both for purposes of accountability to the community and for providing continuous feedback in order to modify and enhance the interventions.

It follows from the behavioral-ecological perspective that there is no single research paradigm—encompassing a specific methodology, research design, assessment procedure, and process/outcome measures—for which knowledge building and evaluations are required. Instead, a *multiparadigmatic* (Susskind & Klein, 1982) approach is recommended.

The relevant research paradigms include those derived from behavior modification (especially the operant stream): single-subject designs, multiple baselines, reversal designs, and so on. The major outcome criteria employed by this paradigm are overt behavioral changes—skill acquisition, reduced energy use, increased sharing behaviors. Intervention strategies can be disseminated and built into ongoing community interventions. The community self-help technologies developed by Fawcett and his colleagues at the University of Kansas largely rely on such methodologies (see Chapter 16).

Another major research paradigm appropriate for behavioral-ecology is Fairweather's (1967) experimental social innovation (ESI). This model calls for employing an experimental methodology with pre-, post-, and follow-up assessments of an experimental group. As for controls, this approach suggests that existing intervention programs (rather than no-treatment groups) serve as a comparison against which to evaluate experimentally new social innovations. Thus "true" experimental designs employing traditional between-group statistical comparisons are integral to ESI. The prototype for ESI is the development and evaluation of the Community Lodge, a community-based alternative to psychiatric hospitalization for chronic schizophrenics (see Chapter 5, this volume). Once an innovation is evaluated, this model also calls for disseminating the innovation to impel wider adoptions. The innovation process is then likewise experimentally evaluated (see Chapter 5, this volume). This methodology is the basis of the doctoral training program in ecological psychology at Michigan State University founded by Fairweather (see Davidson, 1980; Tornatzky Chapter 24, this volume).

The work of Moos and his colleagues (e.g., Moos, 1974, 1976) at the Social Ecology Laboratory at Stanford University Medical Center represents another relevant stream for research and evaluation. This work focused on the development of environmental assessment strategies for purposes of both clarifying dimensions of environments and their relation to individual behavior, as well as designing instruments for assessing and catalyzing change in numerous social environments. Moos and his colleagues developed a series of "social climate" scales to measure the perceived environment (by both clients and staff) of such settings as psychiatric wards, community psychiatric programs, classrooms, dormitories, families, work settings, and sheltered care environments. Most recently, the area of environmental assessment was broadened to encompass the salient architectural features of environments, policy and program factors, and personal characteristics (e.g., the aggregate characteristics of setting's inhabitants and participants) (see Chapter 20).

Another compatible research paradigm is derived from Kelly's (1980) bioecological analogies (discussed earlier). Briefly, this approach emphasizes research as a collaborative process between the research team and community residents. Participants should be involved in all phases of the research. Bioecological research employs multiple assessments, obtains measures over long-term periods, and anticipates unintended consequences. The value underlying this research is the enhancement of community resources.

Several other research/evaluation approaches are relevant. Lehmann (1975) points to the relevance of epidemiology, social area analysis, ethology, and ethnomethodology for ecological evaluation. Finally, Levine's (1974) "adversary model," which draws on legal rules of evidence, and Sarason's model based on "disciplined observation" (e.g., Sarason, 1974) are likewise relevant to a multiparadigmatic approach to behavioral-ecological research and evaluation.

Future Directions

We call for a broadening of streams that will contribute to wider knowledge bases for guiding interventions. A broader behavioral-ecological perspective will need to incorporate the "social" paradigm, as exemplified in the work of Goffman (1961), Scheff (1966), and Sarbin (1969), who focused on "labeling" and "roles" in mental health. Also relevant is the work of early human ecologists such as McKenzie (1926) and Dunham (1937) who focused on economic factors and their relation to mental health. Indeed, Catalano (1979) suggests a merging of these two paradigms with the learning paradigm to form a "new, more holistic, paradigm" (p. 175). Whereas Catalano is primarily concerned with incorporating concepts from economics and sociology to generate assumptions (i.e., a paradigm) that will yield a better understanding of the etiology of abnormal behavior, our focus has been on the utility of behavioral-ecology as a *perspective* guiding community mental health interventions, and, as such, we view behavioral-ecology as preparadigmatic (i.e., a perspective).

Some of the recent concerns with the economic environment and its relation to mental health are likely to translate into intervention guides. Specifically, the recent task force report on *The Macroenvironment and Community Mental Health* by the National Council of Community Mental Health Centers (Monahan & Vaux, 1980) focused on three aspects of the economic environment: (1) economic status; (2) unemployment; and (3) economic change.

The relationships between social class and psychological disorder have been confirmed through epidemiological research (e.g., Dohrenwend & Dohrenwend, 1969). Unemployment was likely to be associated with self-dissatisfaction and, in some studies, with suicide. Brenner (1973, 1976) found an inverse relation between economic prosperity and admissions to mental hospitals, crime, alcohol abuse, and suicide. This finding was cited by the task force as evidence for a relation between mental health and economic change. Monahan and Vaux (1980) suggest that mental health professionals participate in "environmental impact assessments" to consider the social costs associated with economic policies. In addition, they suggest the development of prevention programs in anticipation of social stress brought on by predictable economic trends. For example, through individually or media-based "anticipatory guidance," people can be psychologically prepared to deal with economic downturns or unemployment.

Sudden spurts in economic growth can have negative consequences on physical and social ecology—for example, disruption of natural communities. Although hardly explored, the mental health stressors associated with such public health crises as Three Mile Island (see Schaar, 1979) and Love Canal constitute another area of particular relevance to a behavioral-ecological perspective of community mental health.

Perhaps by broadening our perspective through the inclusion of these streams, we can meet Sarason's recent (1980) challenge for social ecology to confront the issue of "social order." That is, consideration of societal stratification, distribution of resources, and other political-economic factors is integral to a more complete ecology of behavior. As Sarason (1980) puts it:

> The most exciting and challenging feature of ecology: the recognition that whom we study and where are parts of a larger system or setting which, if we ignore, can lead us to conclusions that at best may be misleading and at worst harmful. (p. 4)

References

Altman, J. *The environment and social behavior.* Monterey, Calif.: Brooks/Cole, 1975.

Atthowe, J. M., Jr., & Krasner, L. A preliminary report on the application of contingent reinforcement procedures (token economy) on a "chronic" psychiatric ward. *Journal of Abnormal Psychology,* 1968, *73,* 37–43.

Ayllon, T., & Azrin, N. H. *The token economy: A motivational system for therapy and rehabilitation.* New York: Appleton, 1968.

Baer, D. M., Wolf, M. M., & Risley, T. R. Some current dimensions of applied behavior analysis. *Journal of Applied Behavior Analysis,* 1968, *1,* 91–97.

Bandura, A. *Principles of behavior modification.* New York: Holt, Rinehart & Winston, 1969.

Bandura, A. *Social learning theory.* Englewood Cliffs, N.J.: Prentice-Hall, 1977.

Bandura, A., & Walters, R. H. *Social learning and personality development.* New York: Holt, Rinehart & Winston, 1963.

Barker, R. G. *Ecological psychology: Concepts and methods for studying the environment of human behavior.* Stanford, Calif.: Stanford University Press, 1968.

Barker, R. G. Return trip, 1977. In R. G. Barker & Associates (Eds.), *Habitats, environments, and human behavior.* San Francisco: Jossey-Bass, 1978.

Barker, R. G., & Gump, P. V. (Eds.). *Big school, small school.* Stanford, Calif.: Stanford University Press, 1964.

Barker, R. G., & Schoggen, P. *Qualities of community life: Methods of measuring environment and behavior applied to an American and an English town.* San Francisco: Jossey-Bass, 1973.

Barker, R. G., & Wright, H. F. *Midwest and its children.* New York: Harper & Row, 1955.

Barker, R. G., & Associates (Eds.). *Habitats, environments, and human behavior.* San Francisco: Jossey-Bass, 1978.

Bechtel, R. B. *The use of ecological psychology techniques in therapy.* Tucson: Environmental Research and Development Foundation, 1979.

Beck, A. T. *Cognitive therapy and the emotional disorders.* New York: International Universities Press, 1976.

Beit-Hallahmi, B. Salvation and its vicissitudes: Clinical psychology and political values. *American Psychologist,* 1974, *29,* 124–129.

Bootzin, R. R. *Behavior modification and therapy: An introduction.* Cambridge, Mass.: Winthrop, 1975.

Brenner, M. H. *Mental illness and the economy.* Cambridge: Harvard University Press, 1973.

Brenner, M. H. *Estimating the social costs of economic policy: Implications for mental and physical health and criminal aggression* (Report to the Congressional Research Service of the Library of Congress and the Joint Economic Committee of Congress). Washington, D.C.: U.S. Government Printing Office, 1976.

Briscoe, R. V., Hoffman, D. B., & Bailey, J. S. Behavioral community psychology: Training a community board to problem solve. *Journal of Applied Behavior Analysis,* 1975, *8,* 157–168.

Caplan, G. *Support systems and community mental health.* New York: Human Sciences Press, 1974.

Catalano, R. *Health, behavior, and community: An ecological perspective*. Elmsford, N.Y.: Pergamon Press, 1979.

Cherniss, C. *Staff burnout: Job stress in the human services*. Beverly Hills, Calif.: Sage, 1980.

Cohen, H. L., & Filipczak, J. *A new learning environment*. San Francisco: Jossey-Bass, 1971.

Collins, A. H., & Pancoast, D. L. *Natural helping networks*. Washington, D.C.: National Association of Social Workers, 1976.

Colman, A. D. *The planned environment in psychiatric treatment: A manual for ward design*. Springfield, Ill.: Charles C Thomas, 1971.

Davidson, W. S. Ecological doctoral education: The ecological psychology program at Michigan State University. In R. S. Slotnick, A. M. Jeger, & E. J. Trickett (Eds.), *Social ecology in community psychology*. Special issue, APA Division of Community Psychology Newsletter, Summer 1980.

Dohrenwend, B. P., & Dohrenwend, B. S. *Social status and psychological disorder: A causal inquiry*. New York: Wiley-Interscience, 1969.

Dunham, H. W. The ecology of the functional psychoses in Chicago. *American Sociological Review*, 1937, *2*, 467–479.

Edwards, D. W., & Kelly, J. G. Coping and adaptation: A longitudinal study. *American Journal of Community Psychology*, 1980, *8*, 203–215.

Ellis, A. *Reason and emotion in psychotherapy*. New York: Lyle Stuart, 1962.

Fairweather, G. W. *Methods for experimental social innovation*. New York: Wiley, 1967.

Faris, R. E. L., & Dunham, H. W. *Mental disorders in urban areas*. Chicago: University of Chicago Press, 1939.

Fawcett, S. B., Mathews, R. M., & Fletcher, R. K. Some promising dimensions for behavioral community technology. *Journal of Applied Behavior Analysis*, 1980, *13*, 505–518.

Fuller, P. R. Operant conditioning of a vegetative human organism. *American Journal of Psychology*, 1949, *62*, 587–590.

Geertz, C. *Agricultural involution: The processes of ecological change in Indonesia*. Berkeley: University of California Press, 1966.

Glenwick, D. S., & Jason, L. A. (Eds). *Behavioral community psychology: Progress and prospects*. New York: Praeger, 1980.

Goffman, E. *Asylums*. Garden City, N.Y.: Anchor Books, 1961.

Goldfried, M. R., & Goldfried, A. P. Cognitive change methods. In F. H. Kanfer & A. P. Goldstein (Eds.), *Helping people change*. Elmsford, N.Y.: Pergamon Press, 1975.

Gottlieb, B. H. Lay influences on the utilization and provision of health services: A review. *Canadian Psychological Review*, 1976, *17*, 126–136.

Gottlieb, B. H. Opportunities for collaboration with informal support systems. In S. Cooper & W. F. Hodges (Eds.), *The field of mental health consultation*. New York: Human Sciences Press, in press.

Granovetter, M. S. The strength of weak ties. *American Journal of Sociology*, 1973, *78*, 1360–1380.

Gump, P. V. The behavior setting: A promising unit for environmental designers. *Landscape Architecture*, 1971, *61*, 130–134.

Heller, K. The effects of social support: Prevention and treatment implications. In A. P. Goldstein & F. H. Kanfer (Eds.), *Maximizing treatment gains: Transfer enhancement in psychotherapy*. New York: Academic Press, 1979.

Hirsch, B. J. Psychological dimensions of social networks: A multimethod analysis. *American Journal of Community Psychology*, 1979, *7*, 263–277.

Holahan, C. J. Seating patterns and patient behavior in an experimental dayroom. *Journal of Abnormal Psychology*, 1972, *80*, 115–124.

Holahan, C. J. Environmental change in a psychiatric setting: A social system analysis. *Human Relations*, 1976, *29*, 153–166.

Holahan, C. J. Redesigning physical environments to enhance social interactions. In R. F.

Munoz, L. R. Snowden, & J. G. Kelly (Eds.), *Social and psychological research in community settings*. San Francisco: Jossey-Bass, 1979.(a)

Holahan, C. J. Environmental psychology in psychiatric hospital settings. In D. Canter & S. Canter (Eds.), *Designing for therapeutic environments*. New York: Wiley, 1979.(b)

Holahan, C. J., Wilcox, B. L., Spearly, J. L., & Campbell, M. D. The ecological perspective in community mental health. *Community Mental Health Review*, 1979, *4*, 1, 3–8.

Ittleson, W. H., Proshansky, H. M., & Rivlin, L. G. A study of bedroom use on two psychiatric wards. *Hospital and community psychiatry*, 1970, *21*, 25–28.

Ittleson, W. H., Rivlin, L. G., & Proshansky, H. M. The use of behavioral maps in environmental psychology. In H. M. Proshansky, W. H. Ittleson, & L. G. Rivlin (Eds.), *Environmental psychology: Man and his physical setting*. New York: Holt, Rinehart & Winston, 1970.

Ittleson, W. H., Proshansky, H. M., Rivlin, L. G., & Winkel, G. H. *An introduction to environmental psychology*. New York: Holt, Rinehart & Winston, 1974.

Jason, L. A. Behavioral community psychology: Conceptualizations and applications. *Journal of Community Psychology*, 1977, *5*, 302–312.

Jason, L. A., & Glenwick, D. S. An overview of behavioral community psychology. In D. S. Glenwick & L. A. Jason (Eds.), *Behavioral community psychology: Progress and prospects*. New York: Praeger, 1980.(a)

Jason, L. A., & Glenwick, D. S. Future directions: A critical look at the behavioral community approach. In D. S. Glenwick & L. A. Jason (Eds.), *Behavioral community psychology: Progress and prospects*. New York: Praeger, 1980.(b)

Jason, L. A., & Smith, T. The behavioral ecological matchmaker. *Teaching of Psychology*, 1980, *7*, 116–117.

Jeger, A. M. Behavior theories and their appliactions. In L. D. Hankoff & B. Einsidler (Eds.), *Suicide: Theory and clinical aspects*. Littleton, Mass.: PSG Publishing Co., 1979.

Jeger, A. M., Slotnick, R. S., & Schure, M. Towards a "self-help/professional collaborative perspective" in mental health. In D. E. Biegel & A. J. Naparstek (Eds.), *Community support systems and mental health: Research, practice, and policy*. New York: Springer, 1982.

Kazdin, A. E. *Behavior modification in applied settings*. Homewood, Ill.: Dorsey Press, 1980.

Kelly, J. G. Ecological constraints on mental health services. *American Psychologist*, 1966, *21*, 535–539.

Kelly, J. G. Toward a ecological conception of preventive interventions. In J. W. Carter, Jr. (Ed.), *Research contributions from psychology to community mental health*. New York: Behavioral Publications, 1968.

Kelly, J. G. The quest for valid preventive interventions. In C. D. Spielberger (Ed.), *Current topics in clinical and community psychology* (Vol. 2). New York: Academic Press, 1970.

Kelly, J. G. 'Tain't what you do, it's the way that you do it. *American Journal of Community Psychology*, 1979, *7*, 244–261.

Kelly, J. G. *Ecological theorems and citizen participation: Methods and process*. Paper presented at the annual meeting of the American Psychological Association, Montreal, September 1980.

Koenig, R., Jr. *The interorganizational network as a system: Toward a conceptual framework*. Unpublished manuscript, School of Business Administration, Temple University, 1980.

Krasner, L. Behavior therapy. *Annual Review of Psychology*, 1971, *22*, 483–532.

Krasner, L. Environmental design in perspective: Theoretical model, general principles, and historical context. In L. Krasner (Ed.), *Environmental design and human behavior*. Elmsford, N.Y.: Pergamon Press, 1980.

Lehmann, S. Psychology, ecology, and community: A setting for evaluative research. In M. Guttentag & E. L. Struening (Eds.), *Handbook of evaluation research* (Vol. 1). Beverly Hills, Calif.: Sage, 1975.

Lehmann, S. Community psychology and social ecology: A commentary from the New York University Program. In R. S. Slotnick, A. M. Jeger, & E. J. Trickett (Eds.), *Social ecology in community psychology.* Special issue, APA Division of Community Psychology Newsletter, Summer 1980.

Levine, M. Scientific method and the adversary model: Some preliminary thoughts. *American Psychologist,* 1974, *29,* 661–677.

Levis, D. J. (Ed.). *Learning approaches to therapeutic behavior change.* Chicago: Aldine, 1970.

Mahoney, M. J. Reflections on the cognitive learning trend in psychotherapy. *American Psychologist,* 1977, *32,* 5–13.

Mann, P. A. *Community psychology: Concepts and applications.* New York: Free Press, 1978.

Martin, G. L., & Osborne, J. G. (Eds.). *Helping in the community: Behavioral applications.* New York: Plenum Press, 1980.(a)

Martin, G. L., & Osborne, J. G. Introduction: Behavior modification in the community. In G. L. Martin & J. G. Osborne (Eds.), *Helping in the community: Behavioral applications.* New York: Plenum Press, 1980.(b)

McKenzie, R. The ecological approach to the study of the human community. In R. E. Park & E. Burgess (Eds.), *The city.* Chicago: University of Chicago Press, 1926.

Meichenbaum, D. H. *Cognitive-behavior modification.* New York: Plenum Press, 1977.

Mitchell, R. E., & Trickett, E. J. Task Force report: Social networks as mediators of social support. *Community Mental Health Journal,* 1980, *16,* 27–44.

Monahan, J., & Vaux, A. Task Force report: The macroenvironment and community mental health. *Community Mental Health Journal,* 1980, *16,* 14–26.

Moos, R. H. *Evaluating treatment environments: A social ecological approach.* New York: Wiley, 1974.

Moos, R. H. *Evaluating correctional and community settings.* New York: Wiley, 1975.

Moos, R. H. Evaluating and changing community settings. *American Journal of Community Psychology,* 1976, *4,* 313–326.

Moos, R. H., & Insel, P. M. (Eds.). *Issues in social ecology.* Palo Alto, Calif.: National Press Books, 1974.

Munoz, R. F., Snowden, L. R., & Kelly, J. G. Research-oriented interventions in natural settings. In R. F. Munoz, L. R. Snowden, & J. G. Kelly (Eds.), *Social and psychological research in community settings.* San Francisco: Jossey-Bass, 1979.

Netting, R. M. A trial model of cultural ecology. *Anthropological Quarterly,* 1965, *38,* 81–96.

Netting, R. M. *Cultural ecology.* Menlo Park, Calif.: Cummings, 1977.

Nietzel, M. T., Winett, R. A., MacDonald, M., & Davidson, W. S. *Behavioral approaches to community psychology.* Elmsford, N.Y.: Pergamon Press, 1977.

Osmond, H. Function as the basis of psychiatric ward design. *Mental Hospitals,* 1957, *8,* 23–30.

Park, R. E. Human ecology. *American Journal of Sociology,* 1934, *42,* 1–15.

Park, R. E., & Burgess, E. (Eds.). *The city.* Chicago: University of Chicago Press, 1926.

Politser, P. E. Network analysis and the logic of social support. In R. H. Price & P. E. Politser (Eds.), *Evaluation and action in the social environment.* New York: Academic Press, 1980.

Price, R. H. Reflections on education in social ecology: Building a disciplinary matrix. In R. S. Slotnick, A. M. Jeger, & E. J. Trickett (Eds.), *Social ecology in community psychology.* Special issue, APA Division of Community Psychology Newsletter, Summer 1980.

Proshansky, H. M. Environmental psychology and the real world. *American Psychologist,* 1976, *31,* 303–310.

Proshansky, H. M., Ittleson, W., & Rivlin, L. (Eds.). *Environmental psychology: Man and his physical setting.* New York: Holt, Rinehart & Winston, 1970.

Proshansky, H. M., & Altman, J. Overview of the field. In W. P. White (Ed.), *Resources in environment and behavior.* Washington, D.C.: American Psychological Association, 1979.

Rappaport, J. *Community psychology: Values, research, and action.* New York: Holt, Rinehart & Winston, 1977.

Rappaport, J., Seidman, E., & Davidson, W. S., II. Demonstration research and manifest versus true adoption: The natural history of a research project to divert adolescents from the legal system. In R. F. Munoz, L. R. Snowden, & J. G. Kelly (Eds.), *Social and psychological research in community settings.* San Francisco: Jossey-Bass, 1979.

Redd, W. H., Porterfield, A. L., & Anderson, B. L. *Behavior modification: Behavioral approaches to human problems.* New York: Random House, 1979.

Ribes, E. Some measurement scales for public housing and urban development. In G. L. Martin & J. G. Osborne (Eds.), *Helping in the community.* New York: Plenum Press, 1980.

Richerson, P. J. Ecology and human ecology: A comparison of theories in the biological and social sciences. *American Ethnologist,* 1977, *4,* 1–26.

Richerson, P. J., & Boyd, R. The evolutionary ecology of humans: Two approaches. In R. S. Slotnick, A. M. Jeger, & E. J. Trickett (Eds.), *Social ecology in community psychology.* Special issue, APA Division of Community Psychology Newsletter, Summer 1980.

Rimm, D. C., & Masters, J. C. *Behavior therapy: Techniques and empirical findings.* New York: Academic Press, 1979.

Risley, T. R. The ecology of applied behavior analysis. In A. Rogers-Warren & S. F. Warren (Eds.), *Ecological perspectives in behavior analysis.* Baltimore: University Park Press, 1977.

Rogers-Warren, A., & Warren, S. F. *Ecological perspectives in behavior analysis.* Baltimore: University Park Press, 1977.

Sarason, S. B. *The creation of settings and the future societies.* San Francisco: Jossey-Bass, 1972.

Sarason, S. B. *The psychological sense of community: Prospects for a community psychology.* San Francisco: Jossey-Bass, 1974.

Sarason, S. B. Psychologists and the social order. In R. S. Slotnick, A. M. Jeger, & E. J. Trickett (Eds.), *Social ecology in community psychology.* Special issue, APA Division of Community Psychology Newsletter, Summer 1980.

Sarason, S. B., & Lorentz, E. *The challenge of the resource exchange network.* San Francisco: Jossey-Bass, 1979.

Sarason, S. B., Carroll, C. F., Maton, K., Cohen, S., & Lorentz, E. *Human services and resource networks.* San Francisco: Jossey-Bass, 1977.

Sarbin, T. R. Schizophrenic thinking: A role theoretical analysis. *Journal of Personality,* 1969, *37,* 190–206.

Schaar, K. Measuring mental health fallout: Studies pursue psychological effects of TMI. *APA Monitor,* December 1979, 1, 12.

Schaefer, H., & Martin, P. Behavior therapy for "apathy" of hospitalized schizophrenics. *Psychological Reports,* 1966, *19,* 1147–1158.

Scheff, T. J. *Being mentally ill: A sociological theory.* Chicago: Aldine, 1966.

Slotnick, R. S., & Jeger, A. M. *Barriers to deinstitutionalization: Social systems influences on environmental design interventions.* Paper presented at the meeting of the American Psychological Association, Toronto, August 1978.

Slotnick, R. S., Jeger, A. M., & Cantor, A. *The interface between organization and community: A behavioral-systems impact study.* Paper presented at the meeting of the Association for the Advancement of Behavior Therapy, Chicago, November 1978.

Skinner, B. F. *The behavior of organisms: An experimental analysis.* New York: Appleton-Century-Crofts, 1938.

Sommer, R., & Osmond, H. Symptoms of intitutional care. *Social Problems,* 1961, *8,* 254.

Speck, R., & Rueveni, U. Network therapy: A developing concept. *Family Process,* 1969, *8,* 182–191.

Spivack, M. *Psychological implications of mental health center architecture.* Paper presented at the annual meeting of the New England Psychological Association, Boston 1969.

Steward, J. *Theory of culture change.* Urbana: University of Illinois Press, 1955.

Stokols, D. Origins and directions of environment-behavioral research. In D. Stokols (Ed.), *Perspectives on environment and behavior: Theory, research, and applications.* New York: Plenum Press, 1977.

Stough, R. R., & Wandersman, A. (Eds.). *Optimizing environments: Research, practice, and policy.* Washington, D.C.: Environmental Design Research Association, 1980.

Studer, R. G. The design and management of environment-behavior systems. Paper presented at the conference, "Conditions of Life in the Future and Consequences for Education," Technische Universität Berlin, Berlin, Germany, November 1978.

Susskind, E. C., & Klein, D. C. (Eds.). *Knowledge building in community psychology.* Book in preparation, 1982.

Taylor, R. B. Comments on environmental psychology: New trends in theory and research on people-in-settings. *Population and Environmental Psychology Newsletter,* Spring 1980, pp. 13–14.

Tolsdorf, C. C. Social networks, support and coping: An exploratory study. *Family Process,* 1976, *15,* 407–417.

Trickett, E. J., Kelly, J. G., & Todd, D. The social environment of the high school. In S. E. Golann & C. Eisdorfer (Eds.), *Handbook of community mental health.* New York: Appleton-Century-Crofts, 1972.

Trickett, E. J., Kelly, J. G., & Vincent, T. Inquiry and community psychology: An ecological paradigm. In E. C. Susskind & D. C. Klein (Eds.), *Knowledge building in community psychology.* Book in preparation, 1982.

Turkat, D. Social networks: Theory and practice. *Journal of Community Psychology,* 1980, *8,* 99–109.

Ullmann, L. P., & Krasner, L. *A psychological approach to abnormal behavior.* Englewood Cliffs, N.J.: Prentice-Hall, 1975.

U.S. General Accounting Office. *Returning the mentally disabled to the community: Government needs to do more.* Washington, D.C.: Author, 1977.

Wandersman, A. *Participation: A strategy of human environment optimization.* Paper presented at the annual meeting of the American Psychological Association, Toronto, August 1978.

Wandersman, A. User participation in planning environments: A Conceptual framework. *Environment and Behavior,* 1979, *11,* 465–482.

Wandersman, A., & Giamartino, G. A. Community and individual difference characteristics as influences on initial participation. *American Journal of Community Psychology,* 1980, *8,* 217–228.

Weinstein, M., & Frankel, M. Ecological and psychological approaches to community psychology. *American Journal of Community Psychology,* 1974, *2,* 43–52.

Wheeler, T. Architectural considerations in planning for community mental health centers. *American Journal of Public Health,* 1964, *54,* 1987–1995.

Wicker, A. W. Ecological psychology: Some recent and prospective developments. *American Psychologist,* 1979, *34,* 755–765.

Willems, E. P. Behavioral technology and behavioral ecology. *Journal of Applied Behavior Analysis,* 1974, *7,* 151–165.

Wittman, F. D., & Arch, M. Task Force report: Sociophysical settings and mental health. *Community Mental Health Journal,* 1980, *16,* 45–61.

Wolpe, J. *Psychotherapy by reciprocal inhibition.* Stanford, Calif.: Standford University Press, 1958.

II
Community Alternatives to Institutionalization

Convalescent hospitals accelerate the process of dying by obscuring the difference between death and living death; correctional institutions prepare individuals for a new career in crime; mental hospitals recycle the ingredients of madness; and training schools for the mentally retarded neither train nor school except for a cattle-like, custodial existence. (Sarason, 1974, pp. 175–176)

Introduction

The chapters in Part II describe the development and evaluation of three innovative programs designed as alternatives to hospitalization for psychiatric clients. In the first two cases, the national dissemination of the programs is also emphasized.

The development of community treatment programs as alternatives to state hospitals was a primary mandate of community mental health centers. Two major populations are targets of community alternatives: clients who were never institutionalized or for only brief periods; and long-term residents of state hospitals who are being deinstitutionalized (e.g., chronic schizophrenics). A central issue pertaining to both of these groups is continuity of care—between hospital and community, and between various community agencies.

For the nonchronic population, "residential" treatment since the passage of the Community Mental Health Centers Act has moved increasingly in the direction of short-term stays. Such was the case for general hospitals, VA hospitals, state hospitals, and especially community mental health centers. Riessman, Rabkin, and Struening (1977) found evidence for the earlier reconstitution of patients subjected to brief hospitalization (3 to 60 days) relative to longer stays; however, when considering the long-term effects (1- to 2-year follow-ups), the groups were comparable. The authors suggest the need for aggressive aftercare to maintain clients in the community. Although aftercare appears to be particularly critical for short-stay clients, aftercare services were not one of the five "essential" services (see Chapter 1) mandated by the original (1963) legislation. It was not until the list of essential services was expanded to 12 in the 1975 amendments that follow-up of discharged clients and provision of "transitional" services became mandatory. The new legislation was largely a response to the revolving-door (e.g., Putten, 1977) aspect of inpatient units. That is, although the resident population declined in mental hospitals, admissions and readmissions were greatly increasing (Brown, 1980; Chu & Trotter, 1974).

As for chronic populations or those institutionalized in state hospitals for uninterrupted periods of several years or more, the problems of community treatment have been rather unique. This group is comprised of typical "back-ward" residents who have lost basic skills necessary for independent living. Legislative mandates to deinstitutionalize and treat patients in the community resulted in the "dumping" of these unprepared chronic residents largely into various unaccepting locales (e.g., Brown, 1980; Lamb, 1979a; Scull, 1976). The places they were asked to reside in included many large hotels and "adult homes" that with their populations of several hundred resembled miniinstitutions (e.g., Bassuk & Gerson, 1978). An alternative is needed that would include community preparation of clients, adequate placement, and concerted follow-up, all within a coordinated, continuity-of-care framework.

Furthermore, concerning the deinstitutionalization of long-stay patients, the empirical basis for such policies (as they are being implemented) is still being questioned. For example, although such factors as the availability of phenothiazines to maintain clients in the community and the changing conceptions of institutional influences (e.g., Goffman, 1961) are generally used to support such policies, Scull (1976) cogently argues that the recent impetus for the "decarceration of the mentally ill" is tied to the notion that

> the availability of welfare programs has rendered the social control functions
> of incarcerating the mentally ill much less salient . . . other forms of social
> control have become equally functional. (p. 174)

He considers the primary significance of the alternative arguments "to be their value as ideological camouflage" (p. 212).

Whatever the rationale for the original policy, the current state of affairs is best described in the conclusion of U.S. General Accounting Office (1977):

> Mentally disabled persons have been released from public institutions without (1) adequate community-based facilities and services being arranged for and (2) an effective management system to make sure that only those needing inpatient or residential care were placed in public institutions and that persons released were appropriately placed and received needed services. (p. 172)

It may very well be, as Gottesfeld (1976) concludes following his review of data on alternatives to hospitalization, "that funded programs for psychotics must be on a continual basis" (p. 9) and are needed indefinitely. It remains for future research to determine the relative efficacy of various community alternatives (e.g., foster care vs. halfway houses; behavioral vs. milieu day treatment programs).

Although the search for nonhospital utopias has hardly begun, barriers to deinstitutionalization and pressures for maintaining the status quo of state hospitals abound. Elsewhere we (Slotnick & Jeger, 1978; Slotnick, Jeger, & Cantor, 1978) have identified five levels of barriers: (1) *individual/family* (e.g., increased burden on families); (2) *organizational* (e.g., civil service union pressures, resistance from state-hospital-supported vendors); (3) *community* (e.g., fears of declining property values in areas concentrated with discharged psychiatric clients, interference of local business by loitering clients, zoning ordinances that preclude establishment of group-living arrangements for discharged clients); (4) *institutional* (e.g., third-party reimbursements favoring inpatient care, the criminal justice system's reliance on state hospitals to "treat" the criminally insane); and (5) *societal* (e.g., acceptance of a disease model that perpetuates the need for a hospital structure).

We conclude in this work that the central factor impeding deinstitutionalization is the very existence of state hospitals. Similarly, Rappaport (1977) argues that as long as mental hospitals "are available as an option they will be used" (p. 273). It is this option that, in our view, activates and organizes the major barriers at all five levels. Unless viable alternatives to hospitals can be found—soon—the barriers will only strengthen. We believe that endorsement of a behavioral-ecological viewpoint is a step in the direction of finding such alternatives.

What types of alternatives to inpatient treatment have been developed in recent years? Ulmer and Franks (1973) consider three categories of programs and settings, corresponding to differential levels of clients' social competence: halfway houses, day treatment centers, and outpatient clinics. Halfway houses usually serve as transitional facilities between hospitals and independent living. Length of stay, types of programs, staff composition and roles, and general effectiveness vary greatly (Colten, 1978; Cometa, Morrison, & Ziskoven, 1979). Day treatment centers, for at least several hours daily, offer a diverse range of therapeutic activities. As Moscowitz (1980) points out, day centers likewise vary in terms of their treatment goals, administrative affiliations, staff, patients, specific treatments offered, and effectiveness. Outpatient clinics, which similarly vary along these dimensions, offer individual and/or small-group treatment typically limited to one or two short sessions per week. Treatments might include interventions from the growing field of crisis intervention (e.g., Moos, 1976), encompassing programs for specialized target populations (schizophrenics, suicidal, widowed, divorced, etc.). Importantly, programs at any of these three levels constitute alternatives to hospitalization for previously institutionalized clients as well as for those never hospitalized.

The chapters in this part describe programs at one or more of the three levels that are especially compatible with a behavioral-ecological perspective. Chapter 4 presents an overview of the Behavior Analysis and Modification (BAM) Project from its conception through dissemination. This project focuses on individual- and group-level behavioral strategies applied across a full range of community mental health services (e.g., outpatient, day treatment, and consultation/education). The aim of the behavioral programs developed and evaluated by BAM Project staff is to promote individual social competence.

BAM research staff served as consultants and trainers to staff who adopted their behavioral packages. In keeping with the behavioral contents of the packages, behavioral methods of training were employed. In addition, peer learning among adopting staff members was built into the learning process.

Although the clinical techniques are primarily behavioral, Liberman *et al.* were particularly sensitive to the "ecology" of the community mental health center in which the techniques were developed and evaluated. They were likewise sensitive to systems issues in selecting community mental health centers across the country to disseminate their innovative treatment and training materials. They developed and disseminated not merely isolated or discrete techniques, but an entire *program*. As such, social and political factors, especially when entering new systems, were considered by the staff. Thus *context* considerations proved significant in the success of both the development and diffusion stages of the BAM Project. Finally, in their dissemination efforts Liberman and his team operated within the context of action-oriented change agents.

Similarly, Tornatzky and Fergus (Chapter 5) report on the development and dissemination of the Community Lodge, a supportive posthospital environment for chronic schizophrenics. The Lodge facilitated continuity of treatment between hospital and community. Rather than serving as a transitional facility, however, the Lodge was created to serve as a permanent, autonomous living environment for psychiatric patients. Following vocational and social skill development and the formation of cohesive groups in the hospital, patients were discharged as a cohort into a community-based home, which they administered with minimal staff supervision. Once evaluated as a "demonstration" project, following Fairweather's (1967) model of "experimental social innovation," the Lodge was disseminated nationally to interested hospitals. In turn, the innovation-diffusion process was likewise subjected to experimental evaluation. The context for the chapter is the literature on changing mental health bureaucracies through various strategies aimed at influencing their adoption of innovative programs.

Achieving adoption for the Lodge was more difficult than in the BAM Project. Whereas Liberman *et al.* were disseminating individually oriented *behavioral programs*, Tornatzky and his colleagues were disseminating an *ecological intervention*—one that called for *structural changes in the style of service delivery*. Furthermore, the target institutions (e.g., state hospitals) are generally more resistant to change than are community mental health centers, which were the targets of the BAM Project. As an ecological intervention the Lodge represents a more systems-level social change effort.

Finally, Edmunson and her colleagues (Chapter 6) integrate behavioral and ecological strategies in their Early Intervention and Community Network Development (CND) projects. Beginning with a short-term inpatient behavioral program aimed at skill training (the last several weeks of which are conducted as a peer-managed token economy), upon their release patients are integrated into a network of peer supports. Staff serve as resource persons, program designers, and evaluators. They may offer crisis intervention and function as backup supports—all within the context of the designed patient networks. The CND Project eases the transition from hospital to community, increases community tenure, and reduces dependence on professional mental health agencies.

In contrast to the BAM Project, which relies primarily on professional staff to offer clinical behavioral treatment, CND staff are largely paraprofessionals. Furthermore, the style of service delivery has shifted in that the natural strengths of patients are capitalized on within a peer support context to enhance community living and prevent rehospitalization. In addition, CND represents a step beyond the Lodge in that it is based in the *natural environment* and the open community, rather than in a particular residential setting. In this regard CND clients are even more integrated into their communities. Like the BAM Project and the Lodge, the CND Project has been extensively evaluated and plans are under way to pursue a similar innovation-diffusion effort.

These projects were chosen as exemplars of behavioral-ecological interventions with psychiatric populations. Other community-alternative projects compatible with a behavioral-ecological perspective include Stein and Test's (1979) Training in Community Living Program, an alternative to acute hospitalization; Spruce House, a community-based "operant learning environment" for psychotic adults (Henderson, 1971); Achievement Place, a community-based behavioral program for youth (Phillips, 1968); Project Re-Ed (Hobbs, 1979), a reeducation program for "emotionally disturbed children" based on ecological and behavioral principles; and McGee's (1974) community-based Suicide and Crisis Intervention Service. Additional compatible projects can be found in Jeger (1980), Lamb (1979b), Luber (1979), and Stein (1979).

References

Bassuk, E. L., & Gerson, S. Deinstitutionalization and mental health services. *Scientific American*, 1978, *238*, 46–53.

Brown, P. Social implications of deinstitutionalization. *Journal of Community Psychology*, 1980, *8*, 314–322.

Chu, F., & Trotter, S. *The madness establishment.* New York: Grossman, 1974.

Colten, S. I. Community residential treatment strategies. *Community Mental Health Review*, 1978, *3*(1), 16–21.

Cometa, M. S., Morrison, J. K., & Ziskoven, M. Halfway to where?: A critique of research on psychiatric halfway houses. *Journal of Community Psychology*, 1979, *7*, 23–7.

Fairweather, G. W. *Methods for experimental social innovation.* New York: Wiley, 1967.

Goffman, E. *Asylums.* Garden City, N.Y.: Anchor Books, 1961.

Gottesfeld, H. Alternatives to psychiatric hospitalization. *Community Mental Health Review*, 1976, *1*(1), 4–10.

Henderson, J. D. A community-based operant learning environment. I. Overview. In R. D. Rubin, H. Fensterheim, A. A. Lazarus, & C. M. Franks (Eds.), *Advances in behavior therapy.* New York: Academic Press, 1971.

Hobbs, N. *Helping disturbed children and their families: Project Re-Ed twenty years later.* Nashville, Tenn.: Center for the Study of Families and Children, Vanderbilt University, 1979.

Jeger, A. M. Community mental health and environmental design. In L. Krasner (Ed.), *Environmental design and human behavior: A psychology of the individual in society.* Elmsford, N.Y.: Pergamon Press, 1980.

Lamb, H. R. Roots of neglect of the long-term mentally ill. *Psychiatry*, 1979, *42*, 201–207. (a)

Lamb, H. R. (Ed.). *Alternatives to acute hospitalization.* San Francisco: Jossey-Bass, 1979. (b)

Luber, R. F. (Ed.). *Partial hospitalization: A current perspective.* New York: Plenum Press, 1979.

McGee, R. K. *Crisis intervention in the community.* Baltimore, Md.: University Park Press, 1974.

Moos, R. H. (Ed.). *Human adaptation: Coping with life crises.* Lexington, Mass.: D. C. Heath, 1976.

Moscowitz, I. S. The effectiveness of day hospital treatment: A review. *Journal of Community Psychology*, 1980, *8*, 155–164.

Phillips, E. L. Achievement Place: Token reinforcement procedures in a home style rehabilitation setting for pre-delinquent boys. *Journal of Applied Behavior Analysis*, 1968, *1*, 213–223.

Putten, T. V. *The rising hospitalization rate of psychiatric patients.* Paper presented at the meeting of the American Psychiatric Association, Toronto, May 1977.

Rappaport, J. *Community psychology: Values, research, and action.* New York: Holt, Rinehart & Winston, 1977.

Riessman, C. K., Rabkin, J. G., & Struening, E. L. Brief versus standard psychiatric hospitalization: A critical review of the literature. *Community Mental Health Review*, 1977, *2*, 1–10.

Sarason, S. B. *The psychological sense of community: Prospects for a community psychology.* San Francisco: Jossey-Bass, 1974.

Scull, A. T. The decarceration of the mentally ill: A critical view. *Politics and Society*, 1976, *6*, 123–172.

Slotnick, R. S., & Jeger, A. M. *Barriers to deinstitutionalization: Social systems influences on environmental design interventions.* Paper presented at the meeting of the American Psychological Association, Toronto, August 1978.

Slotnick, R. S., Jeger, A. M., & Cantor, A. *The interface between organization and community: A behavioral-systems impact study.* Paper presented at the meeting of the Association for the Advancement of Behavior Therapy, Chicago, November 1978.

Stein, L. I. (Ed.). *Community support systems for the long-term patient.* San Francisco: Jossey-Bass, 1979.

Stein, L. I., & Test, M. A. From the hospital to the community: A shift in the primary locus of care. In H. R. Lamb (Ed.), *Alternatives to acute hospitalization.* San Francisco: Jossey-Bass, 1979.

Ulmer, R. A., & Franks, C. M. A proposed integration of independent mental health facilities into behaviorally oriented social training programs. *Psychological Reports*, 1973, *32*, 95–104.

U.S. General Accounting Office. *Returning the mentally disabled to the community: Government needs to do more.* Washington, D.C.: Author, 1977.

4

The Behavioral Analysis and Modification Project for Community Mental Health

From Conception to Dissemination

ROBERT PAUL LIBERMAN, TIMOTHY G. KUEHNEL,
JULIE M. KUEHNEL, THAD ECKMAN, AND
JEFFREY ROSENSTEIN

The confluence of two innovative streams in psychology and psychiatry —the delivery of mental health services through comprehensive, community-based centers, and the development of behavioral analysis and therapy—led to an applied research project aimed at demonstrating the applicability of behavioral approaches to the needs of clients and clinicians in a typical community mental health center (CMHC). The Behavior Analysis and Modification (BAM) Project in CMHCs began slowly in 1970 with the building of a clinical-research foundation in the Ox-

ROBERT PAUL LIBERMAN, TIMOTHY G. KUEHNEL, JULIE M. KUEHNEL, THAD ECKMAN, AND JEFFREY ROSENSTEIN ● Clinical Research Center, Camarillo-Neuropsychiatric Institute (UCLA), Box A, Camarillo, California 93010.
The work reported in this chapter was supported by NIMH Research Grant MH 26207 from the Mental Health Services Research and Development Branch. The opinions stated in this chapter are those of the authors and do not reflect the official policy of the NIMH, the Ventura County Mental Health Department, or the Regents of the University of California.

nard, California CMHC; accelerated during 1972–1975 when an NIMH research grant permitted the establishment and evaluation of systematic behavior therapies; and concluded in 1975–1979 with dissemination of six of the therapeutic methods that were experimentally validated to 40 other CMHCs across the nation. This chapter summarizes the procedures and results of the 9-year BAM Project.

After gaining the interest and support of NIMH staff in the promising prospects of harnessing the behavioristic horse to the community mental health cart through a series of conferences, the senior author sought a receptive CMHC in California to conduct the project. California was chosen because of its freedom from constraining psychiatric traditions and its openness to innovations. The choice of a specific CMHC involved social system considerations. For the greatest likelihood of successful innovation, the CMHC had to be open to new clinical leadership and ideology; be small enough to permit the senior author to train and influence the staff through face-to-face contacts; and offer support for the work by the administrative power structure. After a statewide search, the CMHC in Oxnard was selected, with a rural-urban and Anglo-Chicano mixed catchment population of 150,000.

The first 2 years of groundbreaking required the senior author to demonstrate his own competence as a clinician and behavior therapist with a wide variety of patients and problems. By becoming one of the clinical staff, taking on difficult cases, leading clinical conferences, identifying with the staff's hopes and goals, forming a mutually respectful bond with the agency director, helping to solve everyday administrative as well as clinical problems, and serving as a model and reinforcer of the staff's fledgling efforts at behavior therapy, the senior author gradually formed a climate that would support the more intensive training and research to come. These social and political factors, which contribute to the success or failure of a demonstration project, weigh much more heavily in the outcome than does the therapeutic use of behavioral techniques per se.

Behavioral Analysis and Therapy at the Oxnard CMHC: The First 5 Years

Clinically meaningful treatment methods were adapted, developed, and evaluated during the course of the BAM Project at the Oxnard CMHC. The project's objectives for the first 5 years were to introduce and evaluate behavioral approaches to the spectrum of clinical problems that are encountered in a typical comprehensive CMHC. Outpatient, day hospital, inpatient, and consultation and education services evolved from a behavioral, social learning framework and were evaluated by clinically useful and convenient means of assessment. Applications of behavioral learning principles were used with a wide range of problems including chronic schizophrenia, marital conflict, anxiety and depression, life crises, conduct disorders of children and adolescents, child abuse, psychosomatic illnesses, and academic underachievement of schoolchildren. Examples of studies carried out during this demonstration project are briefly reviewed in this chapter. More detailed descriptions of the project and its programs can be found elsewhere (J. M. Kuehnel & Kuehnel, 1978; Liberman & Bryan, 1977; Liberman, DeRisi, King, & Eckman, 1974; Liberman, King, & DeRisi, 1976).

Staff Training

The development of a behavioral approach for patient care in a CMHC required reorientation of both staff and patients. Behavioral innovation produced discomforts and resistances that had to be overcome in both groups. The patients and staff had to be convinced that the new techniques could be effective despite their apparent simplicity. Patients as well as staff had to depend less on vague, subjective views of improvement and more on their own data-based assessment of the extent of progress. Both staff and patients had to learn to set short-term, objective, attainable clinical goals rather than long-range, global, and ambiguously idealistic goals.

The discomfort associated with innovation was reduced at the Oxnard CMHC by intensive training of the 25-member, interdisciplinary staff along the following four levels:

1. There was formal training in behavioral principles and techniques at a 3-hour weekly seminar and through a self-paced sequence of readings.
2. The clinicians received individual supervision from the BAM Project staff on their case loads and community consultations.
3. The clinical staff engaged in their own behavioral self-management projects as a way of learning experientially.
4. The BAM Project staff conducted individual and group sessions with patients using various behavior therapies while the clinical staff observed, participated as cotherapists, and finally assumed primary therapeutic responsibility. Eventually they were able to use behavioral methods autonomously with only periodic supervision, positive feedback, and consultation from the project staff.

Behavioral Goal Setting

A basic innovation in the operation of the day hospital and outpatient services involved implementing a Behavioral Progress Record (Liberman, King, & DeRisi, 1976). All information necessary for a patient's monthly program was displayed on this single-page progress note, which could be placed in the clinical chart or posted on clipboards in the nursing office. Short-term goals were prepared and reviewed weekly by the day treatment therapist together with the client and family members. Goals generally focused on areas of social, family, and vocational functioning since their achievement facilitated the patient's reintegration into the community. Setting goals required the therapist to assess current assets and deficits and to reinforce small increments of behavior change on a week-to-week basis. Goal setting was the most personal of the services offered at the day hospital since it led to highly individualized treatment plans. Because the patients and their relatives shared in the goal setting, they came to understand their treatment and progress in a direct, tangible way.

For program evaluation purposes, the number of goals set and completed in the day hospital was tallied at the end of each month. The results were sent to the administrators of the mental health agency and were posted in the day hospital office. For a 2-year period an average of 2.5 goals were set for each patient each week, with monthly attainment rates ranging from 66% to 88%. Other research documented that simply setting specific goals and regularly monitoring them enhanced therapeutic outcomes.

Day Hospital Programs

The day hospital had an average census of 35 patients and a staff of seven nurses and psychiatric technicians, an occupational therapist, and a psychologist and psychiatrist who both worked half-time. Most of the patients were from lower to lower-middle social classes, and about 25% were Chicano or Black. The patients ranged from 15 to 75 years old, with a majority in the 22 to 55 range. Over half were acutely or chronically psychotic and were receiving phenothiazines or lithium.

Credit Incentive System. The first behavioral intervention at the day hospital was the introduction of a token economy that used credit cards as the medium of exchange. Patients earned credits by arriving promptly at the center, completing treatment goals, participating in therapeutic activities, cooking lunch, washing dishes, and serving as a monitor or staff aide. Patients spent credits on lunch, coffee, drug prescriptions, time off from the center, and individual time with therapists and the psychiatrist. Each patient received a credit card that was functional for 1 week. A number on the card, representing credits, was punched when the patient earned credits by performing therapeutic or maintenance activities. The same number was overpunched by a larger die when the patient paid for a reinforcer, such as lunch or coffee. The credit cards, collected at the end of the week, served as permanent products of earnings and payments, which the clinic secretary computed and summarized on a weekly basis. The totals were used to give feedback to the staff and patients at a weekly planning meeting.

When credits were dispensed, they were accompanied by praise and social recognition from the staff and other patients. The liberal use of social reinforcement more closely approximated the natural environment of the patients and made it possible gradually to phase patients off the credit system as they prepared for discharge. Controlled experiments at the Oxnard day hospital documented the value of the credit system and, more importantly, the systematic provision of social reinforcement in maintaining high performance levels among the patients (Liberman, Fearn, & DeRisi, 1977).

Educational Workshops. The central part of the Oxnard day hospital program consisted of educational workshops designed to teach groups of patients community survival and adaptation skills. The workshops were highly structured and kept the patients busily scheduled and engaged in constructive activities. Workshops were offered in consumerism and personal finance, personal effectiveness, grooming, use of public agencies, recreation and social opportunities, transportation, and vocational preparedness. Each workshop had a set of instructional objectives, lesson plans, and a built-in evaluation of attendance, spontaneous participation, and completion of homework assignments. Data from the record keeping were used to reevaluate and revamp the workshops at 10-week intervals.

A systematic evaluation of the workshop model was conducted using a time-sampling method of assessing the social participation of patients (Liberman *et al.*, 1974). Randomly chosen samples of patients from the Oxnard day hospital and from a day hospital using eclectic milieu therapy in an adjacent city were observed four times each day during a 2-week period just before and 6 months after the implementation of the workshop format at Oxnard. Following the introduction of workshops at the Oxnard day hospital, the social participation of patients doubled over the baseline period, whereas nonsocial, isolate behaviors decreased by one-half. While workshops were in progress, the level of social participation of Oxnard patients was significantly higher than that in the comparison setting. Staff–patient interaction also increased significantly from 30.5% to 64.8% of time-sampled observations of staff behavior at Oxnard, but not in the comparison day center.

To evaluate the progress of individual patients, a clinical experiment was conducted using goal attainment scaling to compare the outcome of patients undergoing behavior therapy at the Oxnard day hospital with a cohort of patients receiving eclectic milieu therapy at the comparison day hospital. This formal evaluation was done on every third admission to each day hospital, with 3-, 6-, and 24-month follow-ups, with a total of 56 patients participating. Goal attainment was greater for the Oxnard patients at the 3-month follow-up, and the differences between the groups increased to statistical significance at 6- and 24-month follow-ups (Austin, Liberman, King, & DeRisi, 1976).

As a further evaluation of the specificity of behavioral techniques in the improvement shown by Oxnard patients, 15 randomly chosen patients served as their own controls in time-series, experimental analyses of their treatment. Repeated measures were taken for up to 8 months on such target behaviors as rational versus delusional speech, social interaction, prevocational tasks, and phobias. Twelve of the patients showed marked improvement of 50% or more from the baseline periods as a result of such interventions as desensitization, social reinforcement, covert sensitization, and credit rewards (Liberman, King, & DeRisi, 1976).

Outpatient Programs

For reasons of efficiency and cost, the BAM Project staff decided to introduce behavioral methods into therapy groups for outpatients since the CMHC's clinicians were faced with overwhelming demands for services. Structured therapy groups were developed and empirically evaluated for such problems as anxiety and depression, life crises, adolescent behavioral disorders, and marital conflict. In each of the groups a package of therapeutic procedures, centering on training in personal effectiveness (Liberman, King, DeRisi, & McCann, 1975), was used to promote the learning of adaptive social and emotional behavior.

Training in Personal Effectiveness. Since competence in social relationships appears to mediate successful community adjustment as well as to mitigate symptoms, the staff at the Oxnard CMHC emphasized methods that aid the learning and relearning of social skills. The personal effectiveness approach starts with goal setting and progresses through behavioral rehearsal, modeling more appropriate ways of expressing feelings and communicating information and desires, positive feedback and coaching, and "homework assignments" to carry out in real life what has been practiced in the clinic (Liberman, King, DeRisi, & McCann, 1975).

As patients practice communicating to parents, spouses, friends, coworkers, and service people in public agencies and stores, nonverbal emotional expressiveness is targeted for improvement, such as eye contact, facial expression, posture, gestures, and vocal tone, loudness, pacing, and fluency. Other levels of interpersonal communication are also developed, such as verbal content, connotative meaning, timing, and reciprocity.

In an evaluation of training in personal effectiveness, patients and observers reported that 80% of 100 consecutively rehearsed scenes were successfully performed in community and home settings (King, Liberman, Roberts, & Bryan, 1977). Ratings of videotapes by trained observers indicated that schizophrenic as well as neurotic patients can significantly improve their nonverbal components of affect and social competence (Wallace, Nelson, Liberman, Aitchison, Lukoff, Elder, & Ferris, 1980).

Marital Therapy. A nine-session format for time-limited marital therapy was developed to improve communication of positive and negative feelings between marital partners (Liberman, Wheeler, DeVisser, Kuehnel, & Kuehnel, 1980). Homework was assigned to the couples in the form of practicing the communication exercises demonstrated and rehearsed in the sessions. Each spouse was also expected to note the occurrence of pleasing acts and statements made by the partner each day and to record these. In sharing the entries from each other's diaries and reporting these at the weekly group meeting, the couples gained greater awareness of reciprocity and were reinforced for increasing the frequency of pleasing interchanges. Couples also learned to distribute their recreational time more equitably within such dimensions as doing things apart from one's spouse, within the marital dyad, with other couples, and with the family. A final intervention was the development of contingency contracts wherein each partner agreed to carry out certain responsibilities in exhange for desired privileges.

An outcome study was conducted comparing this behavioral marital therapy with a more nondirective, insight-oriented marital therapy. Data were collected on several levels, including blind ratings of videotaped marital interactions during problem-solving discussions before and after the group session; direct coding of smiling at, looking at, and touching each other during the sessions; marital adjustment questionnaires; and client satisfaction. Results showed marked superiority of the behavioral format in both the videotaped and "live" codes of spousal interaction (Liberman, Levine, Wheeler, Sanders, & Wallace, 1976).

Anxiety and Depression Management. Anxiety and depression were the chief complaints of over 16% of the patients at the CMHC. Two groups of 10 patients each, which were led by the same cotherapists, were compared for their outcomes on symptom checklists; completion of homework assignments dealing with interpersonal relationships; verbal dysfluencies as an index of anxiety; and goal attainment scaling. One group was led in a nondirective, supportive manner. The members in the behavioral group were given training in deep muscle relaxation and imagery-based self-control for use in anxiety management, as well as training in behavioral rehearsal of problematic interpersonal situations with modeling and feedback. Comparisons at the time of termination, after 10 weekly sessions, and at 6-month follow-up indicated marked superiority for the behavior therapy group on all measures.

Consultation and Education Programs

At the Oxnard CMHC behavioral principles were flexibly applied to the development of indirect services for parents, schools, community workers, a probation department group home for delinquent boys (Liberman, Ferris, Selgado, & Selgado, 1975), and operators of community care facilities for expatients (DeRisi, Myron, & Goding, 1975). One such service was the Parent Workshop in Child Management, held for small groups of 6 to 12 parents who sought help for their children's behavioral and emotional problems. Typical problems included disruptiveness, restlessness, and hyperactivity; fears; disobedience and lack of discipline; aggression; tantrums; crying; shyness; lack of self-confidence; and bed-wetting. Parents of problem children referred from schools, social agencies, and by the parents themselves were offered the Parent Workshop as a first line of service for the children. The workshops, consisting of nine weekly meetings, including readings in social learning principles, observing and graphing behavior, pinpointing and reinforcing desirable behaviors, token economy, and contingency contracts. Role playing with feedback was used to give parents practice in improving their relationships with their children. For example, parents were taught to praise their children's desirable behavior by looking and smiling at the child, using a positive gesture or pat in close proximity, and verbalizing approval within 5 seconds of the occurrence of the behavior.

Parents' conceptual knowledge of child management principles before and after the workshops improved an average of 34%. Role-playing evaluations before and after the workshops indicated a 100% improvement among parents in using praise for positive behavior and ignoring or using mild social punishment for disruptive behavior. Seventy-five percent reported significant behavioral improvement in at least one of their children. In follow-up telephone calls 2 months to 1 year after the completion of the Workshop, 65% of the parents reported that they were still using behavioral techniques successfully.

Conclusions

The research and development project at the Oxnard CMHC provided evidence that well-structured behavioral programs can contribute to the realization of the laudable but ambiguous ideology of community mental health. Through careful training and supervision of clinical staff and paraprofessionals, improvements were achieved in day hospital and outpatient services, in child psychiatry, and with other indirect services. The methods, developed at a typical and comprehensive CMHC, were practical, convenient, and relevant as well as demonstrably effective.

Dissemination of Behavioral Analysis and Therapy: The Next 4 Years

The BAM Project had accomplished its objectives to develop, implement, adapt, and evaluate a series of behavioral treatment programs for use in a typical, full-service CMHC. The feasibility, economy, and clinical value of these innovative mental health programs were clearly established; however, despite over 80 publications, 4 films, 5 books, over 60 convention presentations, and thousands of requests for reprints, the innovative clinical programs were not being systematically implemented by more than a few CMHCs across the country. The failure of traditional strategies for diffusing information provided an excellent opportunity for a study of improving the process by which clinical innovations are effectively disseminated to mental health practitioners.

A thorough review of the available literature on transfer of knowledge, consultation, strategies for disseminating innovations, continuing education programs, and therapist training techniques revealed that a large number of variables determine the adoption of clinical innovations. These variables include characteristics of the innovation, the transfer process, the organization in which changes or new methods are needed, and the individual practitioners (Havelock, 1969; HIRI & NIMH, 1976; T. G. Kuehnel & Kuehnel, in press). Interpersonal modes of communicating clinical innovations to potential practitioners appeared to be more effective than print media or continuing education programs (Fairweather, Sanders, & Tornatzky, 1974; Roberts & Larsen, 1971). Although several methods for engaging in interpersonal communication existed, an action-oriented change agent who serves as a conveyor of knowledge about the clinical innovation and assists the potential users in their adoption of it had been demonstrated to be the most viable model available (Larsen, Norris, & Knoll, 1976; see also Chapter 5, this volume).

Renewal of the BAM Project research grant by the NIMH challenged the staff to develop an effective interpersonal approach to the dissemination of the behavioral-clinical innovations from the Oxnard CMHC to a representative sample of 40 CMHCs across the United States. Approximately 1,000 staff members from these CMHCs participated as therapist-trainees in the dissemination project. Their background characteristics and education are reported in Table 1. CMHCs in the dissemination project employed from 25 to 80 staff members and treated an average of 2,200 different clients per year.

The clinical experience of the CMHC staff members varied from 0 to 33 years, with a median of 3.8 years. The relative youth (median age = 31.6) and inexperience of the therapist-trainees is consistent with the brief history of CMHCs—most CMHCs in the current study had been in existence for less than 8 years. Pointing to the great need for the

Table 1. Demographic and Educational Characteristics of 386 Staff Members from the Final 18 CMHCs Participating in the Dissemination Project

	N	Percentage
Sex		
Male	166	43
Female	220	57
Completed systematic training in discipline		
Yes	175	46.4
No	202	53.6
Completed continuing education courses		
Yes	213	55.6
No	170	44.4
License or credential		
Yes	197	51.8
No	183	48.2
Type of license or credential		
Social work	60	32.8
Nursing	49	26.8
Psychology	29	15.8
Occupational therapy or vocational rehabilitation	17	9.3
Medicine	8	4.4
Other	20	10.9

Table 1. (Continued)

	N	Percentage
Education		
High School	7	1.8
AA	13	3.4
BA, BS	103	26.7
MA, MS	70	18.1
MSW	99	25.6
PhD, EdD	30	7.8
MD	9	2.3
Other	2	0.5
Not reported	53	13.7
Discipline		
Social work	145	38.4
Psychology	118	31.2
Nursing	53	14.0
Education	22	5.8
Occupational therapy	12	3.2
Psychiatry	10	2.6
Other	18	4.8
Function		
Therapist	305	79.4
Clinical service personnel	37	9.6
Administrator	26	6.8
Staff trainer	7	1.8
Clerical	1	0.3
Other	8	2.1

training offered by the BAM Project, a survey of 40 CMHCs in our sample indicated that 44% of staff members had not completed any formal continuing education courses. Furthermore, only 40% had completed any systematic postgraduate training beyond their degree program in their discipline. In view of these two facts it was very interesting that 58% of the staff members indicated that they had no access to a systematic inservice training program in their work environment.

The BAM dissemination strategy involved four components: (1) development of training procedures; (2) development of specific selection and entry procedures for participating CMHCs to facilitate their cooperation, training, and implementation; (3) on-site visitation for further consultation, orientation, demonstration, and first-stage training of the behavioral treatment packages; and (4) structured, systematic in-service training over a 3-month period.

Six of the most popular and empirically successful programs from the Oxnard CMHC were chosen and packaged for dissemination: Personal Effectiveness or social skills training, Parent Workshops, Marital Therapy, Contingency Contracting, Educational Workshops, and Evaluation Strategies for Clinicians. Each package or module contained a written instructional manual for each trainee; explicit directions for conducting the training that emphasized exercises for acquiring skills; and audiovisual materials demonstrating the use of the techniques.

Development of Selection and Entry Procedures

To be included in the dissemination project, CMHCs had to demonstrate administrative and staff support for the training. To assist in the process of making an informed decision regarding participation, printed brochures describing the goals and process of the dissemination project as well as the content of the training packages were provided to each center that expressed initial interest. If the administrator of the center was still interested after reviewing this brochure, he/she was asked to complete a detailed questionnaire about the center that included his/her endorsement. Likewise, the majority of the staff had to respond positively to a detailed questionnaire concerned with their commitment to and interest in receiving the training and consultation provided by the BAM Project. Both of these questionnaires contained behaviorally specific questions designed to shape the expectations and performance of CMHC staff in directions that were known to facilitate adoption of innovations. For example, rather than asking the administrator in general terms if he/she would cooperate with our efforts, a series of discrete questions were asked that defined the cooperative behaviors required to maximize the likelihood of adoption.

After reviewing the initial questionnaires for the presence of facilitating factors, the BAM staff selected those CMHCs determined by a telephone contact to be still interested and that had a sufficiently accurate understanding of the dissemination process. At this point, a liaison or coordinator at the center was selected to interact with the BAM staff before the on-site workshop. Telephone contacts were used to give the liaison an overview of the workshop and to enhance the likelihood of his/her advocacy of the program. Typically, this liaison became an internal "champion" who actively advocated and supported the program. In order to facilitate his/her efforts, each coordinator received a "Coordinator's Guide" that outlined specifically the steps and timelines to follow to ensure that the training process ran smoothly. Typically, by the time two members of the BAM staff arrived at the CMHC to inaugurate the training with a 2-day workshop, the coordinator was very familiar with the fine points of the dissemination plan.

On-Site Training and Consultation

The on-site workshop had four primary goals. The first was to further facilitate BAM's entry into the CMHC with all levels of staff. This goal was accomplished by informal meetings with the administrators, the designated center coordinator, and with as many of the staff as possible who would be participating in the training program. These meetings built rapport by answering questions and by allaying any fears or misconceptions.

A second goal of the on-site workshop was to provide participants with some initial training in behavior therapy by using the Personal Effectiveness training package. This package was selected because it exemplified the behavior analysis and therapy model repeated in the other five packages. Also, Personal Effectiveness training had high appeal to the therapist-trainees because of its flexibility and applicability to clients with a wide range of social and emotional problems.

A third goal was to provide staff with an introduction and overview of the five other modules. In this way enthusiasm was generated for upcoming in-service sessions, and staff members who were to serve as peer tutors for these sessions were given an opportunity to choose the area of most interest to them.

Finally, the on-site workshop attempted to gain staff commitment to continuing in the remaining training and to provide data regarding their satisfaction with and use of the training packages.

The content of the dissemination was a series of behaviorally oriented, clinical intervention packages, and the training process used during the on-site workshop was also behaviorally oriented. Action-oriented training procedures were used to help therapist-trainees to acquire clinical skills. The specific training techniques used were *goal setting, modeling, behavioral rehearsal, immediate performance feedback,* and *homework assignments.* At the conclusion of the on-site visit each CMHC therapist-trainee *contracted* with the BAM Project to: (1) complete all reading assignments; (2) attend six biweekly training sessions; (3) return all training materials; and (4) provide a 10-dollar "good-faith" contingency deposit to be returned upon completion of the training program.

Systematic Inservice Training

Six staff members at each local CMHC were selected to serve as peer tutors for the six training packages that the BAM Project sent to each CMHC on a biweekly basis. Each peer tutor was provided with a detailed training guide for the training session he/she was to lead. These on-site peer tutors were not required to be experts in these content areas but instead served to keep the training session on task and to facilitate the rehearsal activities during the session. They were also responsible for distributing and collecting the data and training materials for each of these packages and contacting the BAM Project if any problems or questions developed. These in-service tutors often became advocates for their training packages.

Adoption of Disseminated Innovations

The acceptability and feasibility of the training program itself were important to evaluate since a great deal of time and effort was demanded of all participants. The program spanned a 14-week period and participants were required to read a lengthy and detailed treatment procedures manual every 2 weeks, attend biweekly in-service training sessions, apply newly learned techniques with clients on their case load, and complete a great many tests, questionnaires, and self-report measures. One measure of acceptability was the extent to which individuals participated in the training program.

In the final 18 CMHCs,[1] a total of 562 staff members completed the preintervention data packet and attended the initial 2-day on-site training and program orientation session with an expectation to participate in the full training program. Approximately 26% of all participants completed the full program, attending the in-service training sessions for all six training packages. Slightly more than 66% completed four or more modules. The overall level of participation reflected reasonably good acceptance of the training program, particularly in light of the influences of vacations, clinical emergencies, administrative changes in operation of the CMHC, variations in case loads, and personal and professional preferences for one treatment technique over another.

The most meaningful measure of adoption of the techniques that were disseminated was the extent to which the treatment procedures were put into practice by the therapist-trainees. Utilization of the procedures was assessed 3 months after the on-site workshop. Implementation on a *programmatic level* indicated that (1) staff members integrated the modules into the CMHC's operation; and (2) the techniques that comprised those modules were described as an integral part of the clinical program. The latter represented the most stringent criterion for adoption.

[1]For ease of discussion and illustration, only data obtained from the final 18 centers will be discussed in this chapter. Centers 1 to 22 received a slightly modified training program.

Sixty-seven percent of the CMHCs used one or more module *programmatically*, with 28% using three or more modules.

In 78% of the CMHCs, a significant number of therapist-trainees established *therapy groups* that utilized the specific treatment procedures contained in one or more module. In terms of *individual therapy* practice, almost 90% of the CMHCs reported considerable numbers of staff utilizing procedures from one or more of the training packages. In 50% of the CMHCs, therapists were putting into practice procedures from three or more of the modules. The most popular treatment package, judging by utilization, was training in Personal Effectiveness, adopted by 44% of the CMHCs on a programwide basis and by a considerable number of individual therapists in over 60% of the CMHCs. The Parent Workshop was next more popular among the modules in terms of adoption. When asked how much they attributed their use of behavioral procedures to the BAM training effort, 72% to 94% of CMHC clinicians reported "major" or "moderate" influence by BAM for five of the six treatment packages. The increase in utilization of behavioral assessment and therapy procedures in the final 18 CMHCs from before to 3 months after the BAM training was statistically significant at the $p < 0.001$ level for all modules except Educational Workshops, which showed an increase significant at the $p < 0.025$ level.

Acquisition of Knowledge in Behavioral Analysis and Therapy

An attempt was made to evaluate the increase in knowledge of behavioral therapy among therapist-trainees as an outcome of the training by the BAM Project (see Table 2). Questionnaires tapping cognitive mastery of the basic principles and clinical applications of behavior therapy showed statistically significant rises from pre- to posttraining periods ($p < 0.001$). A scale measuring favorable attitudes toward behavioral approaches also showed statistically significant increases as a result of the BAM training. Regarding the specificity of the BAM training, a Community Mental Health Ideology Scale showed no pre- to posttraining changes; thus it is unlikely that the increases in knowledge and utilization of behavior therapy were a function of a nonspecific Hawthorne or halo effect. Results are presented for participants who completed training at the on-site workshop and inservice sessions on four or more of the disseminated training "packages."

Conclusions

The favorable adoption and utilization by CMHC programs, group and individual therapists of the behavior therapy packages offered by

Table 2. Preintervention versus Postintervention Mean Scores and Standard Deviations on Measures of Knowledge of Behavior Therapy, Community Mental Health Ideology, and Behavioral Counseling Ideology

		Pre	Post	*p*
General content mastery				
Clinical Application Subscale	*Mean*	22.80	24.60	.0001
	SD	4.28	4.52	
Basic Principles Subscale	*Mean*	16.23	18.52	.0001
	SD	5.19	4.91	
Total score	*Mean*	38.97	43.10	.0001
	SD	8.37	8.76	
Community mental health				
Ideology Scale	*Mean*	214.25	216.44	.1500
	SD	22.13	29.97	
Behavioral counseling				
Ideology Scale	*Mean*	67.84	72.09	.0001
	SD	11.52	10.04	

the BAM Project training provides evidence that action-oriented consultants using a behaviorally based training program can effectively disseminate clinical innovations. The amount of adoption of the behavior therapy modules is significant in view of the low levels of adoption produced earlier by traditional methods of dissemination. Traditional methods included journal articles, films, books, and presentations at conventions. The relative youth and inexperience of CMHC staff members and their lack of access to systematic, in-service training and continuing education programs appear to highlight a need to increase the dissemination of clinical innovations to this group through the use of methods similar to those employed by the BAM Project.

Summary

The planting of behavioral analysis and therapy took root in a typical and comprehensive CMHC in Oxnard, California, and led to the actualization of community mental health goals. Through careful training of clinical staff, improvements were achieved in day hospital, outpatient, and consultation and education services. The behavioral methods used were found more effective than more traditional approaches and were also practical and relevant to a wide range of clients and problems. Having survived the rigors of a CMHC mandate to provide treatment services rather than training and research, the behavioral strategies were found appropriate and welcomed by other CMHCs around the country. A structured dissemination program employing systematic behavioral training methods resulted in large-scale adoption, utilization, and improved knowledge of behavioral methods in 1,000 CMHC staff members around the United States.

ACKNOWLEDGMENTS

The authors wish to acknowledge the participation of the following individuals, whose creative contributions led to the success of the BAM Project: William DeRisi, Larry King, Nancy Austin, Jan Levine, Robert Aitchison, Johnnie Roberts, Nancy Sanders, Gayle McDowell, Vikki Smith, Eugenie Wheeler, Ann Hanson, Edwin Bryan, Ramon Rocha, Frank Dell, Janet Kohlmeier, Rose Baca, and Kris Grude. The encouragement provided by Dr. Rafael Canton, former director of the Ventura Mental Health Department, was indispensable to the BAM Project staff.

References

Austin, N., Liberman, R. P., King, L., & DeRisi, W. J. A comparative evaluation of two day hospitals: Goal Attainment Scaling of behavior therapy vs. milieu therapy. *Journal of Nervous and Mental Diseases*, 1976, *163*, 253–261.

DeRisi, W. J., Myron, M., & Goding, M. A workshop to train community-care staff to use behavior modification techniques. *Hospital and Community Psychiatry*, 1975, *26*, 636–641.

Fairweather, G. W., Sanders, D. H., & Tornatzky, L. G. *Creating change in mental health organizations.* New York: Pergamon Press, 1974.

Havelock, R. G. *Planning for innovation through dissemination and utilization of knowledge.* Ann Arbor, Michigan: Center for Research on Utilization of Scientific Knowledge, University of Michigan, 1969.

Human Interaction Research Institute and National Institute of Mental Health. *Putting knowledge to use: A distillation of the literature regarding knowledge transfer and change.* Los Angeles: Human Interaction Institute, 1976.

King, L. W., Liberman, R. P., Roberts, J., & Bryan, E. Personal effectiveness: A structured therapy for improving social and emotional skills. *European Journal of Behavioral Analysis and Modification*, 1977, *2*, 82–91.

Kuehnel, J. M., & Kuehnel, T. G. Community mental health. In R. P. Liberman (Ed.), *Behavior therapy in psychiatry* (Vol. 1, No. 2 of *Psychiatric clinics of North America*). Philadelphia: W. B. Saunders, 1978.

Kuehnel, T. G., & Kuehnel, J. M. Mental health consultation: An educative approach. In W. Hodges & S. Cooper (Eds.), *The field of mental health consultation.* New York: Human Sciences Press, in press.

Larsen, J. K., Norris, E. L., & Knoll, J. *Consultation and its outcome: Community mental health centers.* Palo Alto, Calif.: American Institutes for Research, 1976.

Liberman, R. P., & Bryan, E. Behavior therapy in a community mental health center. *American Journal of Psychiatry*, 1977, *134*, 401–406.

Liberman, R. P., DeRisi, W. J., King, L. W., & Eckman, T. A. Behavioral measurement in a community mental health center. In P. O. Davidson, F. W. Clark, & L. A. Hamerlynck (Eds.), *Evaluating behavioral programs in community, residential, and school settings.* Champaign, Ill.: Research Press, 1974.

Liberman, R. P., Ferris, C., Selgado, P., & Selgado, J. Replication of Achievement Place in California. *Journal of Applied Behavior Analysis*, 1975, *8*, 287–299.

Liberman, R. P., King, L. W., DeRisi, W. J., & McCann, M. *Personal effectiveness: Guiding people to assert themselves and improve their social skills.* Champaign, Ill.: Research Press, 1975.

Liberman, R. P., King, L. W., & DeRisi, W. J. Behavior analysis and therapy in community mental health. In H. Leitenberg (Ed.), *Handbook of behavior modification and behavior therapy.* Englewood Cliffs, N.J.: Prentice-Hall, 1976.

Liberman, R. P., Levine, J., Wheeler, E., Sanders, N., & Wallace, C. J. Marital therapy in groups: Behavioral vs. interactional formats. *Acta Psychiatrica Scandinavica*, 1976, Suppl. 226.

Liberman, R. P., Fearn, C. H., & DeRisi, W. J. The credit incentive system: Motivating the participation of patients in a day hospital. *British Journal of Social and Clinical Psychology*, 1977, *16*, 85–94.

Liberman, R. P., De Visser, L., Wheller, G., Kuehnel, J., & Kuehnel, T. *Handbook of Marital Therapy: A Positive Approach to Helping Troubled Relationships.* New York: Plenum Press, 1980

Roberts, A. O. H., & Larsen, J. K. *Effective use of mental health research information.* Palo Alto, Calif.: American Institutes for Research, 1971.

Wallace, C. J., Nelson, C. J., Liberman, R. P., Aitchison, R. A., Lukoff, D., Elder, J. P., & Ferris, C. A review and critique of social skills training with schizophrenic patients. *Schizophrenia Bulletin*, 1980, *6*, 42–63.

5

Innovation and Diffusion in Mental Health

The Community Lodge

LOUIS G. TORNATZKY AND ESTHER O. FERGUS

An implicit assumption of this volume is that community research will necessarily lead to the revitalization of mental health bureaucracies. Unfortunately, there is an emerging consensus that such an assumption is at best overoptimistic (Lynn, 1978), and that the utilization and dissemination of mental health research is the weakest link in the change process.

We wish to develop an overview of change processes in mental health bureaucracies that has particular relevance for issues of research utilization and dissemination. A parallel intent is to induce selective euthanasia to some overblown areas of social science that deal with change and innovation. In keeping with Kuhn's (1962) statements on the elegance of paradigmatic research, we become somewhat overwhelmed when confronted with 103 "generalizations" (Rogers & Shoemaker, 1971), 52 "propositions" (Rogers & Agarwala-Rogers, 1976) or 178 "general principles" (Zaltman & Duncan, 1977) dealing with the innovation

LOUIS G. TORNATZKY • National Science Foundation, Division of Policy Research and Analysis, 1800 G St., N.W., Washington, D.C. 20550. ESTHER O. FERGUS • Psychology Department, Michigan State University, East Lansing, Michigan 48823. The views expressed here should not be construed as indicating official policy of either the National Science Foundation or Michigan State University but are entirely those of the authors.

process. Unifying concepts that number into the hundreds are not unifying concepts. To develop a set of concepts about change that have *action* relevance we ought to concentrate our efforts on those variables that can be *changed*, rather than on those that can merely be described.

We should first note that bureaucracies are composed of *individuals*, who in turn are involved in *group processes* relative to a specific *programmatic innovation*. Backdrop variables are those personal and organizational *incentives* that "motivate" changing or not changing. These four elements—individuals, group processes, programmatic innovations, and incentives—encompass most of the variance in change situations.

A Conceptual Overview

Most of the change efforts in which we become involved as community researchers are located in the setting of public service bureaucracies. To be sure, "bureaucracies" is no misnomer. Most of them, either by intent or by historical accident, are patterned along the features of the classical bureaucracy as outlined by Weber (1947) nearly a hundred years ago.

Bureaucrats look at the world as a rationalizable place and feel that the best way to accomplish things is to make tasks as predictable, repeatable, and nonidiosyncratic as possible. A first assumption is that tasks can be subdivided in ways allowing *specialization*. Correspondingly, if one assumes that a well-established knowledge base exists, one can rely on the principle of *merit* to determine job allocations and promotions. One can also establish *rules* to coordinate activities and a *hierarchical* decision-making structure to augment coordination. Finally, in order to prevent individual differences and human frailties from intruding on task accomplishment, bureaucracies must be as *formal* as possible in their processes of communication. That is the ideal system of bureaucracy; but is it the actual one?

Thanks to such well-known studies as the Hawthorne research (Roethlisberger & Dickson, 1947), we know that even those organizations that attempt to follow the classical model often deviate significantly from it. This "irrationality" is particularly apparent in public service bureaucracies: There is a great deal of interpersonal interaction, informality, and de facto deviation from a strict authority structure. However, to the extent that public service organizations *define themselves* as bureaucracies, as most of them do, they will strive to emulate the classical model. Thus bureaucracies will always be moving to eliminate sources of uncertainty from their task environment (Thompson, 1967). They will always be inclined to create more rules, procedures, and unbending structures. The point of all this, and it is *one of the givens of this analysis, is that the mental health organizations that we are trying to change are not structured for change.*

In recent years a number of organizational theorists (Galbraith, 1973; Lawrence & Lorsch, 1967; Litwak, 1961; Perrow, 1972) have advocated a contingency model of organizational functioning. Their advice consists of an organizational analog to the clinical nostrum of different strokes for different folks. In short, the nature of a successful and effective organization depends on the nature of the task and task environment that the organization is trying to address. If, for example, the task is highly predictable, uniform, and repeatable, it would be best accomplished in a bureaucratic way. However, if the task confronting the organization is highly unpredictable and nonuniform, it would be better handled by organizational processes that are more flexible, open, or "human relations" oriented. This general theory has important implications for the problems of dissemination and planned change.

If we can assume that *any change process involves a significant degree of uncertainty, then any change effort must include strategies for dealing with the by-products of uncertainty.* Initially, we must decide which of the four elements—individuals, innovations, group processes, and incentives—are the proper targets for these strategies.

Individuals and Innovations: An Overworked 50% of the Variance

The Question of Individuals. Concerning the role of individuals in the change process, we would suggest that much of the innovation literature has constituted an overabundance of descriptive, sophisticated labeling. Rogers and Shoemaker (1971)—a classic reference in the field—cite 2,297 studies relative to their 103 generalizations about the diffusion of innovations. Of these 2,297 citations, 1,365 deal with personal, economic, educational, and attitudinal characteristics of *individual* participants. Thus we learn that early adopters are different from late adopters, that opinion leaders are different from non-opinion leaders, and so on. In other words, 60% of the literature cited in this prominent volume on dissemination deals with variables that are primarily descriptive, and over which we as members of a democratic society have no legitimate control[1] in the context of a change intervention.

What does this literature on the individual characteristics of innovators contribute to a conceptual understanding of innovation strategies?

---

[1] One could, of course, argue that reform and renewal would proceed more rapidly in a society in which the public bureaucracies are staffed by the smarter and the better. Unfortunately, defining "better" and "smarter" leads to Orwellian contradictions.

We learn that some people are harder to change than others. Perhaps, however, we could more profitably concentrate on developing *intervention* strategies that will deal with these individual differences, rather than continuing to catalog them.

Characteristics of Innovations. A great deal of attention has been devoted as well to defining characteristics of innovations, their "individual differences," if you will, and to using these variables in predicting the success of change efforts. To return to Rogers and Shoemaker (1971), there are another 72 references here regarding the relative advantage, compatibility, complexity, and observability of new ideas and innovations and the influence these aspects might have on eventual dissemination and adoption. Similarly, Zaltman and Duncan (1977) caution change agents to be attuned to the relative advantage, compatibility, diffusibility, complexity, and so on of a proposed change. Havelock (1971) likewise discusses characteristics of innovations and their implications for adoption.

What are the policy implications of this line of research? If we pursue the logic that some innovations are more adoptable than others, then we will make choices using that criterion to determine what needs to be disseminated. Change efforts will be supported and funded on the basis of the "diffusibility/adoptability" of the innovation. But is that what changing bureaucratic systems should be about?

We assume that efforts to change mental health bureaucracies should be oriented toward making them provide more effective client services. We cannot assume that all "innovations" are equivalent, and there are emerging data (Chalupsky & Coles, 1977) to indicate that the relationship between program innovation *per se* and program impact on clients is, at best, moot. We ought to make decisions about whether or not to disseminate innovations on the basis of whether or not they *work*, rather than on their "diffusibility/adoptability."

Similarly, we should not make recommendations that well-evaluated innovations should be *adapted* to make them more compatible, less complex, less threatening, and so on. Calsyn, Tornatzky, and Dittmar (1977) argue that we adapt innovations at our peril; we can no longer assume that an adapted innovation will have the same impact on clients as did the initial prototype. A body of empirical research (Hall & Loucks, 1977) seems to support this view.

Incentives: A Neglected 25% of the Variance

Motivation is a slippery concept and is, perhaps, the most neglected area of research in understanding bureaucratic change behavior and in learning what influences bureaucrats to adopt innovations. In short, what incentives—personal, organizational, positive, and negative—can influence the mental health system to change? One extremely important yet neglected area is the relationship between financial incentives and change in public service bureaucracies. Much of our literature on dissemination of innovation is based on studies of *profit-making* organizations. However, public bureaucracies cannot in the remotest sense be considered subject to the constraints of a market economy (Pincus, 1976). Most of them function as de facto monopolies, often with no clear performance expectations applied to them. If profit does not motivate bureaucrats' behavior, what does? There is some reason to believe that bureaucracies move to further aggrandize their own resource pools, in the form of staff and money. There are observational data to indicate that changes in federal and state funding patterns are responded to with changes in federal and state program priorities. In short, at a very gross level, financial incentives are being used to enhance innovation and change in public service bureaucracies, yet these incentives are not tied to *specific* innovations.

Unfortunately, there is a dearth of literature on these processes. At the very least, we should pursue longitudinal, correlational studies attempting to track changes in funding patterns with changes in bureaucratic "innovative" behavior. Perhaps in the distant future we might consider experimentally using financial incentives to foster specific innovation and change.

Organizational Change Processes: An Important 25% of the Variance

The central theme of the conceptual framework we have discussed is that most social change situations inevitably involve the creation of *uncertainty* in target organizations. To paraphrase a classic, the management of innovation (Burns & Stalker, 1961) really is the problem of change. What organizational processes need to be mobilized to deal with the uncertainty produced by change situations?

One recurrent finding in the organization literature is the relationship between participative decision making and the proclivity to change (Burns & Stalker, 1961; Havelock & Havelock, 1973). This fact would argue for experimentally evaluating change strategies that would enhance participation and, it would be hoped, increase the adoption of evaluated innovations. The implication is that the need for such interaction is likely enhanced in situations of increased uncertainty and anxiety. Data on the importance of site visits to exemplary programs (Fleischer, 1979; Glaser & Ross, 1971) also reinforce this notion in a more tangible way.

Much of the organizational development literature has relevance for problems of innovation adoption. Its emphasis on group confrontation, communication openness, shared decision making, and so on (Argyris, 1972; Bennis, 1966) can be seen as providing examples of techniques designed to facilitate organizations' attempts to deal with the uncertainty of change. Zaltman and Duncan's (1977) discussion of "reeducative" and "persuasive" strategies is quite congruent with an uncertainty-reduction conceptualization, and Havelock's (1971) central concept of "linkages"— the intensification of interpersonal and interorganizational contact—is also quite compatible.

The organizational intervention and organization development studies do have one glaring weakness. Much of this literature has been descriptive and anecdotal. We need to embark on a comparative, experimental strategy, examining the relative effectiveness of intervention techniques in producing innovation adoption. The work of Larsen, Norris, and Droll (1976) and the BAM Project described in Chapter 4 (this volume) are excellent examples of what might be needed. We would again urge that a conceptualization such as the *management of uncertainty* might provide a meaningful focus for further work. As implied in some of the literature discussed by Zaltman and Duncan (1977), we might discover that participative-facilitative techniques are more important in the early stages of change intervention than in the later stages.

To lend persuasion to the notion of a comparative-experimental strategy to sort out change interventions and to illustrate the uncertainty-reduction function of change strategies, we shall examine one particular innovation-diffusion project. For several years we have been involved in a research program designed both to disseminate an innovative mental health program and to gather experimental data on the change processes involved. What follows is a historical overview of this attempt to undertake and systematically evaluate a set of change tactics. We shall begin by describing the innovation, namely, the Community Lodge.

Disseminating the Community Lodge

Development of the Model Innovation

During the early research that led to the development of the Lodge program, Fairweather and his associates (Fairweather, 1964) initially had a simple objective: to see whether an autonomous group of psychiatric patients could be developed to function so as to reinforce each other's nondeviant behavior. A corollary objective was to discover whether such a cohesive group could enhance postdischarge productivity and reduce recidivism. The initial programmatic response to these objectives was an in-hospital ward that was designed to replace the typical staff-dominated system with a patient-peer-dominated one. Operationally, a large neuropsychiatric ward was divided into small groups of patients. A set of rules and procedures was established with four performance levels, or "step levels," each with increasing degrees of responsibility demanded from the patient, and each with increasing rewards or incentives for successful performance. The most innovative aspect of the program was that the patient group had the responsibility to make judgments about the step level performance of their peers, which in turn had implications for the level of incentive that was received. In addition, the patient group had significant responsibilities in dealing with personal problems, making plans for discharge, and so on.

This innovation was developed in the context of a true experiment. Patients were matched and then randomly assigned either to the experimental small-group treatment program or to a more traditional control ward. Longitudinal outcome data were gathered for both groups, including recidivism, posthospital employment, and personal-social adjustment. The results of this initial research were mixed. On the one hand, small-group ward patients did extremely well while working within the context of the small-group ward; on the other, most of the gains tended to dissipate over time following discharge. On balance, the data suggested that efforts should be concentrated on strengthening the supportiveness of the posthospital environment.

This perception led to the development of the Community Lodge Program itself (Fairweather, Sanders, Maynard, & Cressler, 1969). Briefly, the Community Lodge was akin to a kibbutz for the expatient. In the prototype model, 15 to 20 patients in a small-group ward were developed as a cohesive group and then discharged *as a unit* to a residential living and working facility. This facility was not designed to be transitional, but to function as a substitute family. Congruent with the notion of a living and working community, there was a heavy investment in self-government and a corresponding gradual withdrawal of staff intervention and control as the residents assumed more responsibilities. There was also a strong emphasis on work, with Lodge members creating their own business to bolster their economic well-being[2] and social status in the community.

---

[2] Those familiar with the subcultural norms of mental health workers will appreciate how aberrant the Lodge Program was. An anecdote may be helpful: The research team developed an index called the truck test to predict whether a hospital staff would adopt the program. If, during consultation, any of the staff expressed the remotest enthusiasm for performing such nonprofessional duties as driving a truck to get Lodge members to and from work, the hospital was awarded a positive prognosis.

Once again, the Lodge program was established as part of a true experiment that ran some 4 years. Patients were matched and then randomly assigned to the Community Lodge Program or to more traditional types of aftercare facilities.

The results of the Community Lodge experiment were startling. There were highly significant differences in recidivism and in community employment in favor of the experimental group as compared to the control group. The business operated by Lodge members (primarily custodial services) turned a profit of $52,000 in 3 years. Out of a painstaking process of program development and evaluation research, a viable innovation had been created. At this point the problem of dissemination of the findings appeared.

The First Dissemination Experiment

The first effort to study the dissemination of the Lodge innovation to mental hospitals was begun in 1967 in a project that lasted 4 years (Fairweather, Sanders, & Tornatzky, 1974). This research involved a two-stage experimental design that initially focused on a sample of 255 state and federal mental hospitals across the United States.

Phase 1: Approach and Persuasion. Phase 1 of this research initially involved approaching the hospitals and attempting to persuade them of the worth of the Lodge program. The research design was a 3 × 5 × 2 × 2 factorial experiment, which looked at four dimensions of interest relating to the change process. Two dimensions of the design were essentially demographic descriptors of the sample. The first reflected a comparison between state and federal hospitals. In addition, based on findings relating sophistication of staff to change (e.g., Rogers & Shoemaker, 1971), there was a comparison of urban versus rural hospitals. The notion here was that urban hospitals, being staffed by more worldly individuals, would be more likely to be receptive to change efforts and more capable of coping with the uncertainties engendered by the change process.

Two other factors were experimentally manipulated in Phase 1 of the study. Given the hierarchical nature of bureaucratic systems, one hypothesis was that an initial intervention directed toward individuals high in the organizational bureaucracy might yield a more direct route to change. In a sense, raw power might be able to override the inherent resistances to change. Therefore, on a random basis, our initial calls and contacts with the hospitals were directed toward one of five status levels, ranging from superintendent to nursing service.

Finally, a fourth factor concerned the modality of our initial intervention and is congruent with earlier observations about organizational processes and their relation to change. If more intensive, face-to-face human interactions facilitate change, the interventions that draw on these processes ought to be more effective. In order to test these notions hospitals were randomly assigned to one of three "persuasion" modalities. One-third of the hospitals were given the opportunity of receiving a written brochure describing the program; one-third were offered the possibility of an on-site workshop; and one-third were offered assistance in setting up a demonstration small-group ward program.

The outcomes of the research were instructive. There were no differences between urban and rural hospitals; nor were there any between state and VA hospitals. It also made no difference what level of the organizational hierarchy was initially approached—a somewhat counterintuitive finding.

Of considerable interest were our findings on persuasion modalities. We found that one can essentially discard persuasion attempts that do not rely on *face-to-face contact* between the change agent and members of the organization. Sending a brochure to a hospital was essentially useless in producing a commitment to change. Correspondingly, doing an on-site workshop was appreciably more effective. However, the response of the third group of hospitals—those in the demonstration ward condition—was the most interesting. It should be emphasized that an appreciable behavioral commitment was demanded from organizations in this condition. They were asked to engage in a consultation, to commit patients to a treatment regime, and actually to establish a pilot demonstration program for 90 days. Nearly three-fourths of the hospitals in the demonstration ward condition opted out immediately after initial telephone calls and letters. However, of the 25 hospitals that went ahead and actually set up the small-group demonstration program for 90 days, over half chose to receive consultation directed toward Lodge implementation.

Among the correlational data from Phase 1 of the 1967–1971 study, there was little to support the notion that money directly buys progress: Few of the measures of economic resources available to the sample of hospitals indicated a relationship between resources and change. Attitudinal acceptance of the program was also not strongly related to change.

We did find several bits of intriguing information regarding decision-making patterns. Several indicators of participative decision making were strongly related to the hospitals' willingness to make some commitment to change, and actually to move toward program implementation.

To the degree that there were shared decisions and discussions about the program, there was a corresponding likelihood that, in fact, some change would occur.

Phase 2: Implementation. Phase 2 of the study was directed toward a sample of 25 hospitals that had made some verbal commitment to Lodge adoption. The research design compared different types of technical assistance needed to move these hospitals from verbal commitment to actual implementation of the program. Hospitals were randomly assigned to one of two conditions: In one condition they received periodic on-site consultations; in the other they received a do-it-yourself training manual on how to set up the program. The intent was to equalize the cognitive, factual content of the two conditions while presenting one consultation option with a heavy emphasis on face-to-face interaction. The results were quite clear. With only one partial replicate of the Lodge actually established in the manual condition, this condition could be considered a write-off. In contrast, of those hospitals that received on-site consultation, approximately 40% eventually did set up a program that was a replicate of the Lodge prototype. In addition, most of the other hospitals in the condition made some progess toward implementation.

The Current Dissemination Experiment

In 1975 another comprehensive Lodge dissemination study was begun (Tornatzky, Fergus, Avellar, Fairweather, & Fleischer, 1980). This study, which is now concluded, was designed to focus on the implications of the correlational data from the previous dissemination study. Of particular interest were findings on the relationship between participative decision making and change. Fragmentary data had also pointed toward the necessity of having a cohesive adopting staff in order to achieve a successful implementation. All of these data suggested a research effort focusing on group process variables in the target hospitals.

The generic question that was addressed in the current research was whether specific techniques designed to enhance participative decision making, organizational openness, group cohesion, and so on could be harnessed to a dissemination effort designed to foster the adoption of a specific programmatic innovation—the Community Lodge. Whereas the previous study had found correlations between spontaneously occurring, participative decision making and change, we tried in this study to determine whether participation can be promoted "unspontaneously" by efforts of an outside change agent.

The current project (Tornatzky *et al.*, 1980) was another complex field experiment. Beginning with a sample of 108 state and VA hospitals, Phase 1 of the research once again focused on approaching and persuading the potential adopting hospitals to move toward change. This attempt yielded a 3 × 2 × 2 factorial experiment with all of the manipulations being attempts to enhance participative decision making and to foster the creation of a viable adopting group of staff within the hospital. For example, one manipulation involved varying the *number* of people that we contacted at initial entry. The notion was that if one could ipso facto avoid a unilateral gatekeeper at entry, one could subsequently avoid a unilateral decision as to whether or not the organization would adopt the program. Another set of manipulations was designed to foster the sense of "groupness" of the people who received our workshop presentation and brochure mailings. These involved the sharing of all correspondence to members of the workshop group with all other members of the group, asking the group members to adopt a group name, taking a kindergarten-style group picture at the workshop, and sending all workshop participants a certificate of workshop accomplishment. Although some of these manipulations may seem precious, there was clear reasoning behind them. As pointed out earlier, there are strong indications that an organization can facilitate a change process only if it has an *adopting group* that is highly participative, flexible, and open to new external events—or, as it is called in the organizational literature, a *boundary-spanning unit* (Thompson, 1967). Unfortunately, in hospitals and most human service agencies no such group usually exists before a change intervention. Therefore the consultant must attempt to *create* a participative, moderately cohesive group of potential adopters. Also, because the intervention must often be fairly brief, some rather novel manipulations are appropriate.

Phase 2 of the research was a more direct test of specific organizational development techniques. From our sample of 108 hospitals we emerged with 31 at the end of Phase 1 that had made some behavioral commitment to enter into a consultative relationship with us. All of these hospitals then received up to 8 days of consultation assistance, provided that they continued to move toward the goal of implementation. The experimental manipulation of Phase 2 involved using organizational development as an adjunct to task-oriented consultation. Half of the hospitals were provided consultation that was strictly task oriented and that focused on the mechanics of how to set up a Lodge program. For the other half, we condensed the task-oriented aspect of the consultation and spent an equivalent time on such organizational development activities as team development, sociometric analysis, internal restructuring of the adopting group, and participation in various organizational development games such as group paintings. As in the previously described experiments the overall intent was to further sharpen our change agent repertoire.

The Megastructure of Dissemination

We would like to close by making some summary observations about the dissemination business from the perspective of 9 years of involvement.

All of the research and development and dissemination activities that we have described have been done under the auspices of grant support, and by a relatively small group of researchers. Of course, much of what has sustained us over the years has been our own enthusiasm and belief in the Lodge program and our abiding fascination with the whole problem of change. Unfortunately, we do not feel that these are overly reliable commodities or incentives to support a long-term systematic effort of research, development, and dissemination (RD&D). Unfortunately again, at the federal and state levels there is currently no coherent effort to support, either organizationally or financially, the activities that have been described. Thus we arrive at the notion of *linkages* in the whole RD&D structure. The apparent coherence of the activities described here is not typical. Most social scientist who do develop a well-evaluated treatment program, such as the Lodge, do not involve themselves in dissemination activities. Another deficit of the current RD&D process is the absence of a relationship with the money allocation system for funding human service programs.

At the risk of being labeled midwestern chauvinists, we might also point out that excellent examples of such a closely linked RD&D network can be found in most of the land grant universities of the country. Agriculture is one of the most technologically sophisticated sectors of the economy, a testimonial to the structural relationships that the agricultural extension service and its associated universities have established. This type of RD&D operation has many features that workers in mental health should note. It has a centralized research and development apparatus, located in the university, for the creation and systematic evaluation of such innovations as new seed corns, hybrid tomatoes, picking machines, and the like. Coupled with this R&D effort is a comprehensive network of change agents working at the local level as agricultural extension agents. These individuals have become accepted and legitimate sources of information and innovation in agricultural communities.

The analogy to mental health, of course, is not quite so perfect as one might imagine. The organizational adoption of a fairly complex programmatic innovation such as the Community Lodge is not equivalent to the individual corn farmer trying a new fertilizing technique. However, the difficulties of promoting mental health innovation ought to give us pause and impel us to examine the processes involved. What is most clearly lacking is a *system* to facilitate innovation.

We have described how one research team has involved itself for the past several years in the process of change in the mental health system. As a result of this effort, we think we understand better what might be done to enhance this change process. We are not, however, Pollyannas when it comes to the feasibility of achieving change with any rapidity. Those with experience in the helping professions know that changing people is a very difficult undertaking. We ought to be aware of our own personal resistance to change and of the organizational constraints operating against it. It is not surprising that change is difficult; it is more surprising that change is possible at all.

During the context of our years of functioning as change agents, the members of our research team have come to be struck with the similarities of their lives to that of one of the more tragic figures in American literature: We sometimes refer to ourselves as the Willy Lomans of the mental health world. "Riding on a smile and a shoeshine,"[3] we leave the reader to cope with the difficulties of the change process.

References

Argyris, C. *Interpersonal competence and organizational effectiveness.* Homewood, Ill.: Dorsey Press, 1972.

Bennis, W. *Changing organizations.* New York: McGraw-Hill, 1966.

Burns, T., & Stalker, G. *The management of innovation.* London: Tavistock, 1961.

Calsyn, R. J., Tornatzky, L. G., & Dittmar, S. Incomplete adoption of an innovation: The case of goal attainment scaling. *Evaluation,* 1977, *4,* 127–134.

Chalupsky, A. B., & Coles, G. J. *The unfulfilled promise of educational innovation.* Paper presented at the annual meeting of the American Educational Research Association, New York, 1977.

Fairweather, G. W. *Social psychology in the treating of mental illness: An experimental approach.* New York: Wiley, 1964.

Fairweather, G. W., Sanders, D. H., Maynard, H., & Cressler, D. *Community life for the mentally ill.* Chicago: Aldine, 1969.

Fairweather, G. W., Sanders, D. H., & Tornatzky, L. G. *Creating change in mental health organizations.* New York: Pergamon Press, 1974.

Fleischer, M. *The effects of site visits on lodge adoption.* Unpublished doctoral dissertation, Michigan State University, 1979.

---

[3] Arthur Miller, *Death of a Salesman,* "Requiem."

Galbraith, J. *Designing complex organizations*. Reading, Mass.: Addison-Wesley, 1973.

Glaser, E. M., & Ross, H. L. *Increasing the utilization of applied research results*. Los Angeles: Human Interaction Research Institute, 1971.

Hall, G., & Loucks, S. F. A developmental model for determining whether the treatment is actually implemented. *American Educational Research Journal*, 1977, *14*, 263–276.

Havelock, R. G. *Planning for innovation through dissemination and utilization of knowledge*. Ann Arbor: Center for Research on Utilization of Scientific Knowledge, University of Michigan, 1969.

Havelock, R. G., & Havelock, M. *Educational innovation in the United States. Vol. 1. The national survey: The substance and the process*. Ann Arbor: University of Michigan, Institute for Social Research, 1973.

Kuhn, T. S. *The structure of scientific revolutions*. Chicago: University of Chicago Press, 1962.

Larsen, J. K., Norris, E. L., & Droll, J. *Consultation and its outcome: Community mental health centers*. Palo Alto, Calif.: American Institutes for Research, 1976.

Lawrence, P. R., & Lorsch, J. W. *Organization and environment*. Boston: Harvard Business School, 1967.

Litwak, E. Models of bureaucracy that permit conflict. *American Journal of Sociology*, 1961, *57*, 173–183.

Lynn, L. (Ed.). *Knowledge and policy: The uncertain connection*. Washington, D.C.: National Academy of Sciences, 1978.

Perrow, C. *Complex organizations: A critical essay*. Glenview, Ill.: Scott, Foresman, 1972.

Pincus, J. Incentives of innovation in the public schools. *Review of Educational Research*, 1976, *44*, 113–144.

Roethlisberger, F., & Dickson, W. *Management and the worker*. Cambridge: Harvard University Press, 1947.

Rogers, E., & Agarwala-Rogers, R. *Communication in organizations*. New York: Free Press, 1976.

Rogers, E., & Shoemaker, F. *Communication of innovations*. New York: Free Press, 1971.

Thompson, J. D. *Organizations in action*. New York: McGraw-Hill, 1967.

Tornatzky, L. G., Fergus, E., Avellar, J., Fairweather, G. W., & Fleischer, M. *Innovation and social process: A national experiment in implementing social technology*. Elmsford, N.Y.: Pergamon Press, 1980.

Weber, M. *The theory of social and economic organization* (A. M. Henderson & T. Parsons, Ed. and Trans.). New York: Oxford University Press, 1947.

Zaltman, G., & Duncan, R. *Strategies for planned change*. New York: Wiley, 1977.

6

Integrating Skill Building and Peer Support in Mental Health Treatment

The Early Intervention and Community Network Development Projects

EILEEN D. EDMUNSON, JEFFREY R. BEDELL, ROBERT P. ARCHER, AND RICHARD E. GORDON

The shortcomings of contemporary models of mental health treatment are evidenced by the poor quality of life (Ellsworth, Foster, Childers, Arthur, & Kroeker, 1968; Hogarty & Katz, 1971; Schooler, Goldberg, Boothe, & Cole, 1976) and the revolving-door recidivism (Bachrach, 1976) so frequently observed among mental health clients. If deinstitutionalization is to become a meaningful reality, new and creative models of treatment must be sought. In response to this need for innovation, the state of Florida founded the Florida Mental Health Institute (FMHI) in 1967. The FMHI is organized into demonstration projects, each of which addresses a statewide service need through an innovative program of service delivery. The programs are conceptualized

EILEEN D. EDMUNSON, JEFFREY R. BEDELL, AND ROBERT P. ARCHER • Florida Mental Health Institute, 13301 N. 30th St., Tampa, Florida 33612. RICHARD E. GORDON • Department of Psychiatry, University of Florida, Gainesville, Florida 32611.

and tested at the FMHI and are then disseminated into the state's mental health system. Emphasis is placed on the development of service models that (1) provide a continuum of residential, transitional, and community-based care, (2) efficiently utilize professional and paraprofessional personpower, and (3) provide alternatives to current treatment methods.

The two demonstration projects to be described in this chapter, the Early Intervention Project (EIP) and the Community Network Development (CND), Project, have been in operation at the FMHI for over 6 years. They are based on a unique conceptualization of adjustment and rehabilitation. In this chapter we shall describe this theoretical model of adjustment, the EIP and CND treatment programs, and the data supporting their effectiveness.

A Behavioral-Ecological Conceptualization of Adjustment

A model of the adjustment process as it was conceptualized in the development of the EIP and of CND is presented in Figure 1. According to this model, the ability to cope with the debilitating effects of stress is central to successful adjustment. When a problematic life event occurs, whether it is major, such as the loss of a job, or minor, such as the breakdown of a car, the individual's normal pattern of functioning is interrupted. The amount of stress the individual experiences as a result of any particular event depends on such factors as the nature of the event, the individual's personality structure, and past experience with similar problems. Whatever the nature or amount of stress experienced, the individual must make use of personal coping skills and knowledge to effect a resolution. This problem-solving phase involves several discrete steps. During the awareness step, the individual recognizes the problem and defines its nature. During the alternatives generation step, the individual generates and evaluates possible solutions. Finally, during the action step, the individual acts on his/her chosen plan. Adjustment can fail at several points in this process. The individual may be unable to define the problem in a rational and complete way, or he/she may not be able to identify appropriate action alternatives. Adjustment may also fail if the individual lacks the skills or knowledge to personally implement his/her solution or to ask for appropriate assistance.

Thus problem resolution and adjustment may fail as a result of skill deficits. The individual under stress must have an accurate assessment of the problem and its potential solutions and must also have the skills to implement a solution, either through his/her own efforts or through obtaining the help of others. If the individual's skills are not adequate to deal with the problem, or if the nature of the problem is such that external help is necessary for its solution, then the next factor in the adjustment process comes into play, namely, the individual's external resources and support systems.

As Figure 1 indicates, these external resources or supports fall into two broad categories: (1) natural support systems, and (2) professional support systems. The natural support system is composed of family, close friends, neighbors, coworkers, and other community groups or individuals. The professional support system is composed of individuals and agencies who exist specifically to provide counseling or social services. As indicated in the model, an individual may initially seek help from either of these sources, depending on past success or failure. The individual may be unable to obtain external aid for several reasons: (1) a natural or professional support system may be unavailable, (2) the individual may not seek assistance because he/she does not perceive the system as willing or able to help, and (3) the natural or professional support system, even when requested to intervene, may be unwilling or unable to respond.

Thus at least two factors are involved in successful resolution of problematic life events: (1) the adequacy of personal, social, and living skills, and (2) the adequacy of external resources and supports, whether natural or professional. Tolsdorf (1976) identifies several important differences in the coping processes and social support networks of psychiatric and nonpsychiatric populations. He compared two groups of hospitalized subjects: (1) recently admitted psychiatric clients, and (2) recently admitted medical clients with no psychiatric problems. When the nonpsychiatric group experienced stress, they first relied on their own strengths to cope and, if that was not sufficient, they turned to their support systems. In all cases, this strategy kept the stress situation manageable. However, the pattern of the psychiatric group was quite different:

> The psychiatric subjects experienced some significant life stress with which they attempted to cope by using their own defenses. When this strategy failed, they chose not to mobilize their networks, relying instead on their own resources which had already been shown to be inadequate. This resulted in more failure, higher anxiety, a drop in performance and self-esteem followed eventually by a psychotic episode. (p. 415)

Mental health clients' deficiencies in personal skills have been well documented (Anthony, 1979; Anthony & Margules, 1974; Lamb, 1976), as have differences in external support and resources. Pattison (1977) and Tolsdorf (1976) have found that mental health clients' social network is extremely small, predominantly composed of family members, and often perceived by the client as controlling and negative rather than supportive.

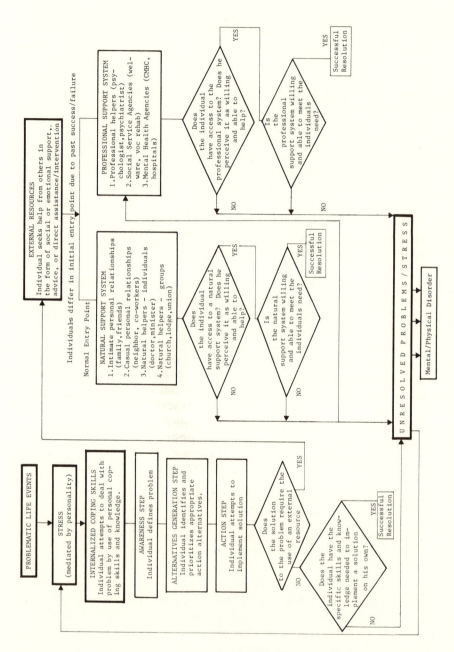

Figure 1. A behavioral-ecological conceptualization of adjustment.

When personal coping skills and the natural support system are not adequate, the mental health client must turn to the professional establishment. Unfortunately, this support system often fails to meet the client's needs as well. At the very best, the mental health client is doomed to the frustration of trying to get help from bureaucratic institutions that operate slowly, have confusing criteria for providing service, and do not coordinate with each other to meet clients' needs. This lack of integrated service delivery has been identified by the NIMH (Turner & TenHoors, 1978) as a major problem in serving the mental health population.

A comprehensive rehabilitation program should assist the mental health client in each step of the adjustment process. The EIP and CND programs provide clients with problem-solving and living skills and help them to develop and use natural and professional support systems.

The Early Intervention Project: Skill Building and Behavioral Management in a Short-Term Residential Setting

The EIP seeks to intervene early in the client's residential treatment experience, reducing the need for future and repeated hospitalization. Rather than simply providing a physical and pharmacological refuge from life stresses, the EIP involves clients in an active, time-limited treatment regimen designed to increase personal coping skills and independence. An intensive skill training program develops clients' skills in a variety of areas, and behavioral therapy techniques are used to reduce maladaptive behaviors.

Program Description

The EIP treats 16 male and 16 female clients with a staff of 21 mental health workers. All clients have had less than 4 months of previous hospitalization. Treatment lasts 9 weeks for all. Thus clients enter treatment with an exact knowledge of the length of hospital stay and a positive expectancy that change will occur relatively swiftly. Furthermore, EIP clients return to their home environments each weekend by operating on a 5-day, 4-night-per-week treatment schedule. This treatment structure minimizes the social disruption of hospitalization and provides clients with opportunities to practice new skills and behaviors in their home environment.

During residence on the EIP, all clients participate in structured skill building groups. These groups focus on the acquisition of positive adaptive skills rather than exploring individual failures and psychopathology.

Each psychoeducational skill building group (Bedell & Weathers, 1979) combines the didactic presentation of information with experiential exercises to facilitate skill acquisition and generalization. The client attends groups in the dual role of client and student. Participants are encouraged to take an active stance in asking questions, performing homework assignments, and relating the skill training to their own life situations. Skill training programs are designed with strong attention to behavioral and educational principles including sequential learning, immediate feedback, successive approximation, and stimulus and response generalization. Skill training groups are provided in a variety of functional skill areas. In the problem-solving skill group, clients are taught a four-step problem-solving process. In the problem recognition step, clients learn to accept responsibility for problems and to establish priorities for dealing with them. In the problem definition step, clients are taught to break down a problem into its component parts and to adopt a goal-oriented approach to finding a solution. In alternatives generation training, clients learn to apply six different methods of developing problem solutions; brainstorming, producing an idea checklist, minimizing hindering factors and maximizing helping factors, changing the frame of reference, solving analogous problems, and problem diagramming. In the decision process step, patients learn to evaluate alternative solutions and to select the best action plan.

Psychoeducational groups are also used to teach clients a broad range of personal and living skills including personal hygiene, nutrition, sexual awareness, relaxation, medication maintenance, communications, assertion, anxiety and depression management, leisure-time management, job seeking, and personal goal clarification.

The EIP also utilizes a token economy program (TEP) to identify and treat target behaviors of significance for each individual client. During the first 6 weeks of treatment, the TEP is managed by staff. During the last 3 weeks of EIP treatment, however, clients enter a *peer-managed* TEP (Bedell & Archer, 1980). Client groups meet daily to review each client's behavior during the previous day. Client self-reports of performance are reviewed by the peer group, and reinforcement points are awarded. Each client is responsible for a specific aspect of the peer-managed TEP. For example, clients are selected by their peers to conduct daily meetings, monitor group attendance, operate the unit store, and so on. Staff role in this special TEP is carefully limited to that of a "consultant" who responds to patients' requests for information. The peer-managed TEP has been designed to provide a transitional step between a traditional staff-managed TEP and client discharge to the community. It encourages clients to rely on their peers for support and feedback and decreases dependence on professional staff. The peer-managed TEP also serves as an excellent introduction to the type of community support program to be described later in this chapter.

Evaluation

Evaluation results support the effectiveness of the EIP in developing the living and coping skills of mental health clients. Specifically, the EIP has been shown to increase clients' expectancy that they will exercise more personal control over important reinforcers in their lives, and to reduce their disposition to perceive life situations as threatening (Archer, Bedell, & Amuso, 1980). Also, problem-solving skills (Bedell, Archer, & Marlowe, 1980) and the ability to manage depression were enhanced (Vagg, Archer, Bedell, & Leggett, 1982). Additional evaluations in progress suggest that communication skills are significantly strengthened, relaxation skills are learned, and more accurate sexual knowledge is acquired as a function of EIP treatment.

An evaluation of the peer-managed TEP demonstrated that it was as effective as a traditional staff-managed program in maintaining patients' performance of target behaviors. Furthermore, it was determined that the peer-managed TEP experience resulted in significant increases in clients' social adequacy and community adjustment potential (Bedell & Archer, 1980).

Community Network Development

The EIP teaches clients a broad range of new coping skills, thus increasing their ability to respond individually to problematic life events. However, environmental changes must also occur to support and maintain newly acquired behaviors. Furthermore, even when personal coping skills are adequately developed, the support of others is necessary for effective adjustment. The CND Project at the FMHI was developed to help clients improve the external support and resources available to them. In particular, CND attempts to foster the development of a peer support system whereby former mental health clients who reside in the community form a helping network and provide each other with emotional, instrumental, and recreational support in their daily lives. Through the CND network, members can practice new skills in a supportive environment and can develop a more extensive nonkin network. Although no program can force or guarantee the development of friendships and natural helping relationships, all decisions regarding

CND staffing patterns and program activities are made with the goal of encouraging peer support and self-determination.

Composition and Organization

The CND membership is composed of approximately 100 men and women from the ages of 18 to 45. All members have had mental health treatment, and close to 70% have been diagnosed as psychotic. The majority of CND members have had residential treatment in the EIP. Members of CND live in a variety of community settings including halfway houses, boarding homes, apartments, and family residences.

In order to facilitate interaction and communication among members, the CND network is subdivided into four geographic areas each containing from 20 to 40 individuals. Subdivision into smaller areas reduces transportation problems, facilitates contact between members, and allows each area to retain a sense of community identity. Although the network as a whole comes together monthly for planning and social activities, the area is the core component of the CND program.

Staffing Pattern and Roles

Within each area, a CND member is paid to act as a leader, activities organizer, and liaison with professional staff. The primary role of the client area manager (CAM) is to maintain contact with CND members. On a weekly basis, the CAM actively reaches out to members in his/her area, contacting them in person or by telephone. Members are encouraged to attend CND activities and to contact the CAM if they need support or assistance. Since most individuals who need social support are unlikely to seek it actively, CND's proactive stance involves many clients who otherwise would not participate.

Through regular contact with members, the CAM is able to identify current and potential problems in their lives. CAMs are encouraged to handle problems on their own and are given special training and resource manuals to aid them in making appropriate referrals and in dealing with crises. However, should the situation require more skill or knowledge than the CAM possesses professional staff are available for consultation or direct intervention at any point.

The CAM is also responsible for planning, organizing, and presiding over a weekly meeting in each area. Although these area meetings are predominantly social, when a member of the group requests the group's help with a personal problem, the CAM facilitates "goal planning"—a structured, problem-solving process whereby all group members help the individual develop an appropriate action plan to deal with his/her problem.

The overriding responsibility of the CAM is to stimulate as much involvement and interaction as possible among members. Because they are or have been mental health clients themselves, CAMs are able to develop a close rapport with other CND members and to serve as role models.

Professional staff in the CND network are referred to as staff area managers (SAMs). At this time, one SAM is assigned to work with each geographic area, although one SAM could supervise several areas depending on the size of the area and the strength of its CAMs and member leaders. The SAM has three major job responsibilities: (1) to supervise the activities of the CAM, (2) to intervene directly with members in situations that require the skills of a professional (e.g., crisis intervention), and (3) to link the CND program and its members to relevant community and professional resources. The SAM is responsible for hiring, training, and supervising the CAM's activities. The SAM and the CAM meet regularly to discuss interactions with members and work out details of upcoming area events. The SAM always attempts to work through the CAM and other group members, intervening only when members need help beyond the CAM's knowledge or expertise.

SAMs also act as a bridge to the professional service system, making professional and community services more available to members. SAMs maintain an up-to-date, comprehensive community resource file and act as advocates for members when they have difficulty obtaining needed services. They also link members to community and professional resources by acting as program or resource developers. For example, CND staff are currently cooperating with two other treatment programs to ensure that all 10 components of a community support system, as identified by the NIMH (Turner & TenHoors, 1978), are available and accessible to members. SAMs also respond to expressed needs of the CND membership. For example, several CND members who were living with their families asked staff to help them establish a cooperative apartment with a live-in peer manager.

Activities and Projects

CND activities provide regularly occurring, structured occasions when members can meet and socialize in a positively reinforcing atmosphere. Members in each of the four geographic areas hold a weekly area meeting; the evening's activity and location are chosen by the members. Most area meetings are social and recreational, involving outings to the movies, meals in restaurants, shopping excursions, covered-dish suppers, and so on. Typically, these activities are centered in the community rather than in a mental health setting, allowing members to get away from "client" status and to become aware of resources in their community. Occasionally, area meetings are used for problem solving with individual members or for fund raising to support social events. In the interval between area meetings, members are encouraged to contact each other to reinforce their social skills and aid group cohesion.

CND facilitates the adjustment process in several ways. First, it provides a supportive environment in which members can practice newly learned interpersonal and problem-solving skills. Secondly, through its structured area activities and outreach, CND fosters the development and maintenance of friendships and natural helping relationships. Finally, the professional staff, through crisis intervention, resource development, and active advocacy, link CND members to professional and community resources.

Evaluation

The traditional measure of a program's success is its ability to decrease the need for rehospitalization or other forms of mental health treatment. Gordon, Edmunson, Bedell, and Goldstein (1979) report a preliminary evaluation of CND's effectiveness. At the point of discharge from the EIP, 80 clients were randomly assigned either to CND or to a control group. Both groups received equivalent discharge planning, including referrals to their local mental health center. At a 10-month follow-up, one-half as many patients in the CND Project required rehospitalization compared to the control group (17.5% to 35%). The average total days of hospitalization for the CND patients was also lower (7.0 days for CND; 24.6 days for control). Finally, a significantly greater percentage of CND clients were able to function without any contact with the mental health system (52.5% for CND; 26% for control).

As important as these measures of outcome may be, however, the most direct measure of the CND Project's effectiveness is the increase in social and instrumental support that becomes available to members. A more thorough evaluation of this outcome is planned, but anecdotal reports suggest that the CND network is serving its intended role. CND members contact each other socially between organized meetings, and several have become roommates. Members have provided each other with emergency housing, transportation, assistance in moving, and other direct services. Most importantly, CAMs report numerous instances when members have been feeling depressed and have contacted other members just to "talk about how they feel" or "get their mind off their problems." It is precisely such spontaneous, flexible supports that the CND network ultimately seeks to engender.

A mutual aid network such as CND also has theoretical and programmatic advantages. The CND network is immediately available to clients following discharge, thus smoothing the transition from hospital to community life. For some clients CND acts as a bridge, supporting them while they develop or reestablish their own support system. However, CND can also provide a permanent support system to those clients who are unable to establish other community supports. Since the CND model is based on a network of peer support and friendship, members may continue to be a part of the CND support system indefinitely. Within other models of aftercare, either because of philosophy or a shortage of staff time, clients are often phased out of programs. By contrast, the more individuals who participate in the CND system, the greater the amount of support that is available to CND members. Furthermore, the type of support provided within a system such as CND cannot easily be duplicated by professional support systems. All too frequently the needs of mental health clients do not fit the working hours or job descriptions of mental health professionals. Through the development of friendships, members of the CND network are able to interact and to help each other in ways that typically would not be practical in other aftercare programs.

Conclusions

Adjustment, as conceptualized in this chapter, is a multidimensional process involving personal skills and social and professional support systems. In line with this conceptualization, the FMHI developed a sequential, integrated system of residential and community support services. During residential treatment, a modular skill building approach is used to enhance clients' problem-solving, psychosocial, and living skills. Peer management and a token economy are utilized to motivate performance and increase independence. On discharge, clients become part of a mutual aid network. Although other programs may employ one or more of these treatment components, the utility of combining these elements into an integrated system of treatment is underlined by the preliminary evaluation data that have been cited. Apparently, significant improvements in behavioral skills can be acquired in an intensive, time-limited residential treatment setting. When such enhancement of skills is coupled with supportive environmental changes, clients' tenure and independence in the community can be increased.

Furthermore, the treatment programs we have described utilize professional and paraprofessional personpower in potentially cost-effective ways. Within the EIP, professional staff have been utilized to develop detailed skill training modules. Paraprofessional staff are then taught to teach specific skill training groups so that the actual operation of the EIP may largely be carried out by paraprofessionals. The same process occurs in the peer-managed token economy. Again, considerable professional time was involved in establishing the point system and operation of the token economy. However, once in place, the actual operation of the economy requires only minimal professional supervision.

Programs such as CND also greatly expand the support and services that can be offered to clients under more traditional treatment models. Much of the direct contact and support in CND is provided by members who can be hired at considerably less cost than highly credentialed professionals. Since a mutual aid network capitalizes on natural helping among members, it increases the amount of support and services available to its members without additional programmatic cost. Professional staff function in the role of supervisors, resource developers, and advocates.

References

Anthony, W. A. *The principles of psychiatric rehabilitation.* Amherst, Mass.: Human Resource Development Press, 1979.

Anthony, W. A., & Margules, A. Towards improving the efficacy of psychiatric rehabilitation: A skills training approach. *Rehabilitation Psychology,* 1974, *21*(3), 101–105.

Archer, R. P., Bedell, J. R., & Amuso, K. Interrelationships and changes in locus of control and trait anxiety among residential psychiatric inpatients. *Social Behavior and Personality: An International Journal,* 1980, *8,* 161–165.

Bachrach, L. L. *National Institute of Mental Health, Deinstitutionalization: An analytical review and sociological perspective.* Washington, D.C.: U.S. Government Printing Office, 1976.

Bedell, J. R., & Archer, R. P. Peer managed token economies: Evaluation and description. *Journal of Clinical Psychology,* 1980, *36,* 716–722.

Bedell, J. R., & Weathers, L. R. A psycho-educational model for skill training: Therapist-facilitated and game-facilitated applications. In D. Upper & S. M. Ross (Eds.), *Annual review of behavior group therapy, 1979.* Champaign, Ill.: Research Press, 1979.

Bedell, J. R., Archer, R. P., & Marlowe, H. A. A description and evaluation of a problem solving skills training program. In D. Upper & S. M. Ross (Eds.), *Annual review of behavior group therapy,* (Vol. 2). Champaign, Ill.: Research Press, 1980.

Ellsworth, R. B., Foster, L., Childers, B., Arthur, G., & Kroeker, D. Hospital and community adjustment as perceived by psychiatric patients, their families, and staff. *Journal of Consulting and Clinical Psychology,* 1968, *32*(5) (Part 2, suppl.).

Gordon, R., Edmunson, E., Bedell, J., & Goldstein, N. Utilizing peer management and support to reduce rehospitalization of mental patients. *Journal of the Florida Medical Association*, 1979, *66*(9), 927–933.

Hogarty, G. E., & Katz, M. M. Norms of adjustment and social behavior. *Archives of General Psychiatry*, 1971, *25*, 470–480.

Lamb, H. R. An educational model for teaching living skills to long-term patients. *Hospital and Community Psychiatry*, 1976, *27*(12), 875–879.

Pattison, E. M. Clinical social systems intervention. *Psychiatry Digest*, 1977, *38*, 25–33.

Schooler, N. R., Goldberg, S. C., Boothe, H., & Cole, J. O. One year after discharge: Community adjustment of schizophrenic patients. *American Journal of Psychiatry*, 1976, *123*, 986–995.

Tolsdorf, C. Social networks, support and coping. *Pain Proceedings*, 1976, *15*, 407–417.

Turner, J. C., & TenHoors, W. The NIMH Community Support Program: Pilot approach to a needed social reform. *Schizophrenia Bulletin*, 1978, 319–344.

Vagg, P., Archer, R. P., Bedell, J. R., & Leggett, J. *A comparison of cognitive and behavioral treatments of depression.* Unpublished manuscript, 1982. (Available from the Florida Mental Health Institute, Tampa, Florida.)

III

Consultation as Indirect Service

Introduction

The four chapters in this part describe specific consultation projects. Indeed, consultation is an important feature of community mental health.

The purpose of the consultation mandate in community mental health is for professionals to provide "indirect" services that will expand mental health personpower. In general, consultation efforts are directed to schools, clergy, criminal justice settings, industry, and other human service agencies. By the mid-1970s, consultation had emerged as a distinct specialty in the mental health field (see Mannino, MacLennan, & Shore, 1975).

The classic typology of so-called mental health consultation was offered by one of its founders, Gerald Caplan (1963, 1970). He divides consultation activities into four major categories: (1) client-centered case consultation, in which the focus is on helping the consultee deal with a particular case or client; (2) program-centered administrative consultation, in which the major aim is to help the consultee in administering a treatment or prevention program; (3) consultee-centered case consultation, in which the primary goal is to help the consultees with problems in working with clients in general; and (4) consultee-centered administrative consultation, in which the goal of the consultant is to aid the consultee or consultee agency in planning, implementing, and maintaining mental health programs.

An alternative approach to classifying consultation activities is based largely on the consultant's orientation. This approach is exemplified by Dworkin and Dworkin (1975), who present a conceptual overview of four consultation models: (1) consultee centered; (2) group process; (3) social action; and (4) ecological.

Consultee-centered consultation, associated primarily with Caplan (1970), views the consultant as a professional expert whose target population is another professional caregiver. The goal of consultation is to increase skills, knowledge, and objectivity.

The group process model, largely identified with the work of Lippitt and his colleagues (e.g., Lippitt, Watson, & Westley, 1958), defines consultation as a relationship between a helper and a system or subsystem. The consultant serves as a participant-observer and functions as a facilitator in bringing about organizational changes and mobilizing internal resources.

Social action consultation, exemplified by the work of Alinsky (1969, 1972), characterizes the consultant's role as a community organizer and strategist. The target population consists of indigenous community leaders, and the goal is to facilitate a transfer of power in order to meet basic human needs.

In the ecological model, reflected in the work of Kelly (1966, 1970a, b), consultation is defined as a relationship between a professional team and an ecosystem. The consultant serves as a team member, functioning as a planner and researcher, with the goal of increasing the system's coping and adaptive mechanisms.

Against the background of previous typologies in the field, we introduce "behavioral-ecological" consultation to reflect a particular set of activities. These include consultants' application of behavioral techniques to provide indirect services to a consultee or consultee system (previously referred to as "behavioral consultation"—see Jeger, 1980); principles from the ecological streams discussed in Chapter 3; and a combination of strategies from the behavioral and ecological streams. In this regard, behavioral-ecological consultation shares some aspects of the consultation models discussed by Dworkin and Dworkin (1975). For example, the behavioral-ecological consultant is likely to function as part of a team with the consultee institution during the entire course of planning, implementing, and evaluating a program. Thus there are similarities with the participant-observer and researcher roles of the group process and ecological models. Following many "behavioral" consultation efforts (e.g., Jeger, 1977; Jeger & McClure, 1979, 1980; Keeley, Shemberg, & Ferber, 1973; King, Cotler, & Patterson, 1975; Suinn, 1974; Tharp & Wetzel, 1969), the consultant as behavioral-ecologist may train others to implement behavior change procedures (e.g., such direct interventionists as teachers and childcare workers).

Since behavioral-ecological consultation is often directed toward modifying larger social units (classrooms, wards, institutions), the influence of broader social systems must be considered. One major issue is the "system-entry" process, that is, the points in the power structure at which entry is initiated and progresses in the course of an evolving working relationship with a setting (e.g., Caplan, 1970; Glidewell, 1959; Levine, 1973; Mann, 1972; Northman, 1976; Sarason, Levine, Goldenberg, Cherlin, & Bennett, 1966; Schroeder & Miller, 1975). The significance associated with the entry phase in general is perhaps best captured by Northman (1976):

> The process of entry, while considerably less than half the fun, can appear to be something like ninety-eight percent of the work. One can be forgiven if goal substitution occurs and successful entry rather than program implementation or evaluation becomes an end in itself. (p. 2)

Key features of the entry process (such as initial contact, obtaining sanctions, and establishing fees) vary according to the consultant's base institution (Lekisch, 1976) as well as the consultee institution. Furthermore, although it has long been suggested that entry "at the top" is crucial (Glidewell, 1959), more often than not there are many tops, and "sanctions at one administrative level do not automatically transfer to other levels" (Schroeder & Miller, 1975, p. 184). For example, programs were jeopardized when consultants did not become aware how high the top really was (e.g., Friedman et al., 1975), or when "middle-level" staff were glossed over (e.g., Bolman, Halleck, Rice, & Ryan, 1969). Focusing specifically on behavioral consultation, Reppucci (1977) indicates that although support from staff at all levels is crucial for any innovation, it is "perhaps particularly so to a behavioral progam in which consistency, immediacy, contingency, and clarity are so important" (p. 596).

Another major issue concerns the potential of behavioral-ecological programs to persist following the consultant's departure. All too many innovations collapse when some key individual(s) depart from the scene (e.g., Miron, 1966). Overcoming this problem is crucial if any long-term effects are to result from a consultation effort. Ideally, the community mental health consultant should attempt to develop a program that continues after his/her departure and is flexible enough to adapt to the changing needs of the system as time goes on.

Finally, there is the issue of evaluation (see also Part VI). In their review of empirical research on the effects of consultation, Mannino and Shore (1975) identify three major evaluation targets or levels at which outcome measures were obtained: (1) *consultees*—changes in knowledge, skills, attitudes, and so on of the direct recipients of consultation; (2) *cli-*

ents—behavioral and attitudinal changes in clients served by consultees; and (3) *system*—changes in institutional structure or social environment. The latter category is especially relevant from a behavioral-ecological point of view since it encompasses interventions directed toward changing systems. Clearly, however, changes should be assessed at all three targets, although relatively few studies on consultation have done so (see Jeger, 1980). Furthermore, what is clearly needed are environmental assessment procedures that are sensitive to behavioral-ecological interventions and that are related to client outcome measures.

A promising direction in the field of environmental assessment is that taken by Moos (1974) and his colleagues at the Stanford Laboratory of Social Ecology. They developed a series of "social climate" scales to assess nine different environments, including treatment environments (wards and community psychiatric programs), educational environments (university residences and classrooms), total institutions (correctional settings and military companies), and community settings (work, group, and family environments). (See also Chapter 20, this volume, for a broader, multiphasic environmental assessment procedure.)

In Chapter 7, Twardosz and Risley review a series of sequential consultation efforts with child day care centers. At the most general level, they see the role of behavioral-ecological consultants as that of designers of environments (physical and social) that will maximize occasions for appropriate behaviors while minimizing occasions for inappropriate behaviors. Optimal day care centers strive to engage children with their teachers, peers, play materials, and so on. Twardosz and Risley sensitize consultants to the need for understanding the broader ecology of settings, even when offering *case* consultation. They emphasize that single, individual-level interventions cannot succeed if the larger context is not supportive. Their interventions constitute a synthesis of the behavioral and ecological features of behavioral-ecology in that they seek to integrate individual (i.e., behavioral) and organizational (i.e., ecological) change strategies.

In Chapter 8, Suckerman, Hines, and Gordon describe a multi-environment mental health consultation program. They offered parallel behavioral consultation to parents and teachers (of the same group of children) in order to facilitate consistency of transactions in the school and home settings. In addition, they sensitize mental health consultants to process issues relating to entry and implementation of behavioral consultation.

Reppucci and Saunders (Chapter 9) report on a long-term consultation effort with an institution for juvenile offenders. The goal of the consultation was explicitly to influence institutional change—that is, conversion of this state school into community-oriented, homelike cottages operating along behavioral (token economy) lines. The authors emphasize staff growth (personal and professional) as necessary for promoting positive institutional change. The chapter focuses on staff morale and perceived organizational climate as indicators of change.

Finally, Friedman (Chapter 10) reports on a series of exploratory case studies to demonstrate the use of consultation to promote self-evaluation in various mental health treatment environments. Specifically, he administered the Moos (1974) social climate scales in psychiatric day treatment and inpatient settings within a consultation context. He emphasized the utility of these instruments, particularly patient–staff discrepancies in the perceived environments, as catalysts for environmental change.

Additional behavioral-ecological consultation efforts have been carried out with schools (e.g., Jason, Ferone, & Anderegg, 1979), community support networks (e.g., Gottlieb, in press), and self-help organizations (e.g., Chapters 15, 16, this volume), among other settings (see Cooper & Hodges, in press).

References

Alinsky, S. *Reveille for radicals.* New York: Vintage Books, 1969.

Alinsky, S. *Rules for radicals.* New York: Random House, 1972.

Bolman, W. M., Halleck, S. L., Rice, D. G., & Ryan, M. L. An unintended side effect in a community psychiatric program. *Archives of General Psychiatry,* 1969, *20,* 508–513.

Caplan, G. Types of mental health consultation. *American Journal of Orthopsychiatry,* 1963, *33,* 470–481.

Caplan, G. *The theory and practice of mental health consultation.* New York: Basic Books, 1970.

Cooper, S., & Hodges, W. F. (Eds.). *The field of mental health consultation.* New York: Human Sciences Press, in press.

Dworkin, A. L., & Dworkin, E. P. A conceptual overview of selected consultation models. *American Journal of Community Psychology,* 1975, *3,* 151–159.

Friedman, R. M., Filipczak, J., & Reese, S. C. *Problems in initiating, implementing, and evaluating a large-scale behavioral program in the public schools.* Paper presented at the meeting of the Association for the Advancement of Behavior Therapy, San Francisco, December 1975.

Glidewell, J. C. The entry problem in consultation. *Journal of Social Issues,* 1959, *15,* 51–59.

Gottlieb, B. H. Opportunities for collaboration with informal support systems. In S. Cooper & W. F. Hodges (Eds.), *The field of mental health consultation.* New York: Human Sciences Press, in press.

Jason, L. A., Ferone, L., & Anderegg, T. Evaluating ecological, behavioral, and process consultation interventions. *Journal of School Psychology,* 1979 *17,* 103–115.

Jeger, A. M. The effects of a behavioral consultation program on consultees, clients, and the social environment (Doctoral dissertation, State University of New York at Stony Brook, 1977). *Dissertation Abstracts International,* 1977, *38,* 1405B. (University Microfilms No. 77-20, 019)

Jeger, A. M. Community mental health and environmental design. In L. Krasner (Ed.), *Environmental design and human behavior: A psychology of the individual in society.* Elmsford, N.Y.: Pergamon Press, 1980.

Jeger, A. M., & McClure, G. *Evaluation of a behavioral consultation program: Changes in consultees, clients, and the social environment.* Paper presented at the meeting of the Eastern Psychological Association, Philadelphia, April 1979.

Jeger, A. M., & McClure, G. The effects of a behavioral training program on non-professionals' endorsement of the "psychosocial" model. *Journal of Community Psychology,* 1980, *8,* 239–243.

Keeley, S. M., Shemberg, K. M., & Ferber, H. The training and use of undergraduates as behavior analysts in the consultative process. *Professional Psychology,* 1973, *4,* 59–63.

Kelly, J. G. Ecological constraints on mental health services. *American Psychologist,* 1966, *21,* 535–539.

Kelly, J. G. The quest for valid preventive interventions. In C. D. Spielberger (Ed.), *Current topics in clinical and community psychology* (Vol. 2). New York: Academic Press, 1970. (a)

Kelly, J. G. Antidotes for arrogance: Training for community psychology. *American Psychologist,* 1970, *25,* 524–531. (b)

King, L. W., Cotler, S. B., & Patterson, K. Behavior modification consultation in a Mexican-American school: A case study. *American Journal of Community Psychology,* 1975, *3,* 229–235.

Lekisch, H. A. *Consultants' contexts, priorities, and courses for action in long-term consultation.* Paper presented at the meeting of the American Psychological Association, Washington, D. C., September 1976.

Levine, M. Problems of entry in light of some postulates of practice in community psychology. In I. I. Goldenberg (Ed.), *The helping professions in a world of action.* Lexington, Mass.: Lexington Books, 1973.

Lippitt, R., Watson, J., & Westley, B. *The dynamics of planned change.* New York: Harcourt, Brace & World, 1958.

Mann, P. A. Accessibility and organizational power in the entry phase of mental health consultation. *Journal of Consulting and Clinical Psychology,* 1972, *38,* 315–318.

Mannino, F. V., & Shore, M. F. The effects of consultation. *American Journal of Community Psychology,* 1975, *3,* 1–21.

Mannino, F. V., MacLennan, B. W., & Shore, M. F. *The practice of mental health consultation.* Rockville, Md.: National Institute of Mental Health, 1975.

Miron, N. B. Behavior shaping and group nursing with severely retarded patients. In J. Fisher & R. Harris (Eds.), *Reinforcement theory in psychological treatment: A symposium* (Research Monograph No. 8). Sacramento: California Department of Mental Hygiene, 1966.

Moos, R. H. *Evaluating treatment environments: A social ecological approach.* New York: Wiley, 1974.

Northman, J. E. *Innovative programming in school mental health: Search for a methodology.* Paper presented at the meeting of the American Psychological Association, Washington, D. C., September 1976.

Reppucci, N. D. Implementation issues for the behavior modifier as institutional change agent. *Behavior Therapy,* 1977, *8,* 594–605.

Sarason, S. B., Levine, M., Goldenberg, I. I., Cherlin, D. L., & Bennett, E. M. *Psychology in community settings: Clinical, educational, vocational, and social aspects.* New York: Wiley, 1966.

Schroeder, C. S., & Miller, F. T. Entry patterns and strategies in consultation. *Professional Psychology,* 1975, *6,* 182–186.

Suinn, R. M. Training undergraduate students as community behavior modification consultants. *Journal of Counseling Psychology,* 1974, *21,* 71–77.

Tharp, R. G., & Wetzel, R. J., *Behavior modification in the natural environment.* New York: Academic Press, 1969.

7

Behavioral-Ecological Consultation to Day Care Centers

SANDRA TWARDOSZ AND TODD RISLEY

Day care centers serve many functions beyond providing supervision, care, and opportunities for normal development. They are remedial learning environments for disadvantaged children, havens for the abused and neglected, and placements for children with behavioral, physical, and mental handicaps (Guralnick, 1978; Zigler & Valentine, 1979). Sometimes it is assumed that children with special problems will benefit if they can simply participate in play and preacademic activities and interact with teachers and children. Most of them, however, clearly demand individual programs and more than the usual amount of adult attention. Some may even require placement in centers that are specifically designed for children with severe disorders.

SANDRA TWARDOSZ ● Department of Child and Family Studies, College of Home Economics, University of Tennessee, Knoxville, Tennessee 37996. TODD RISLEY ● Department of Human Development, University of Kansas, Lawrence, Kansas 66044. The material in this chapter is based on the research conducted by members of the Living Environments Group at the University of Kansas under the direction of Todd Risley and on the experience gained by Sandra Twardosz while consulting with the day care centers operated by Knoxville's Community Development Corporation as well as those operated by the Department of Child and Family Studies at the University of Tennessee.

Use of Behavior Modification in Day Care

Day care directors or teachers request assistance in designing behavior modification programs when individual problems do not respond to their customary teaching and disciplinary practices. Some of these problems are relatively mild and may only require that the teachers learn to differentially attend to and ignore specific behaviors. Others are much more serious. Excessive aggression or disruption, hyperactivity, refusal to interact with teachers or children, language delays or disorders, self-stimulation, and oppositional behavior are problems that require the consistent implementation of individually tailored procedures.

Behavior modification procedures have been developed for many of these individual problems. They require day care teachers to model, prompt, reinforce, ignore, or punish specific behaviors. For example, teachers at a university preschool used prompts, contingent attention, and training sessions to increase a cerebral palsied child's participation in large motor activities (Hardiman, Goetz, Reuter, & LeBlanc, 1975). Teachers in a community-based day care treatment center used overcorrection to decrease two boys' self-stimulation (Epstein, Doke, Sajwaj, Sorrell, & Rimmer, 1974). Because such procedures operate through the behavior of people in the child's environment, they may be called "personally mediated." (For a review of behavior modification in preschool and day care centers, see Risley & Twardosz, 1976.)

Of course, the successful implementation of any remedial procedure implies the existence of a support system—a well-organized day care center where teachers have time to interact with and teach the children, where children can participate in a wide variety of reinforcing activities, and where there are few disruptions. Even in such well-organized centers, however, it is difficult to maintain elaborate programs without additional resources; and *in poorly organized centers it is almost impossible to implement even the simplest individual program.* Teachers are too busy coping with group problems and disruptions, trying to care for the children's basic needs, or are simply not working. They will have neither the time nor the interest to assume additional responsibility.

A consultant may draw on a well-developed behavioral technology to help teachers with individual problems. However, teachers also have trouble managing the behavior of groups of children at specific times of the day. Children may be too noisy at lunch or get into fights while waiting to wash their hands. They may not pay attention during large-group activities or have trouble settling down for a nap. It is true that personally mediated behavior modification procedures have been applied to group as well as individual problems in day care. For example, Brown and Elliott (1965) reduced aggression in an entire class by instructing teachers to socially reinforce behavior incompatible with aggression. When children switched activity areas too frequently, Jacobsen, Bushell, and Risley (1969) required that they perform an academic task before switching. Again, the successful implementation of such procedures depends on a well-organized environment that is reinforcing for the children, where staff are in a position to interact frequently with them, and where cues from the environment do not conflict with the procedure. Herman and Tramontana (1971) provide a good illustration of this latter point. They found that instructions and token reinforcement decreased the disruptive behavior of a group of preschoolers during naptime in an experimental room. However, the procedures were more difficult to implement in the classroom because teachers and other children interacted with the target children. Of course, as soon as the contingency management procedures were discontinued, disruptions increased to their previous level. The difficulty with trying to implement personally mediated procedures with group behavior problems is that the presence of such problems usually indicates that a center is *not* well-organized and thus would not support those procedures.

Importance of the Day Care Environment

Anyone who wishes to implement behavioral procedures for either individual or group problems in a day care center must focus first on the ecology or environment of that center. It is the arrangement of the "impersonal" or setting variables of space, equipment, play materials, activity scheduling, staff assignments, and patterns of movement that distinguishes centers that operate smoothly from those that border on chaos. For individual problems, a consultant should be concerned about whether the environment will facilitate the implementation of a special procedure. However, for group problems, the consultant's first concern should be whether the day care environment can be organized so that the problem will rarely occur and, therefore, rarely require a special procedure. If teachers are having trouble managing the children's behavior while they wait in line, the consultant may be able to redesign the routine so that little or no time is spent waiting. The conditions that set the occasion for the development of the problem in the first place would thus be removed.

Krantz and Risley (1977), in a study that exemplifies this strategy, compared the effects of changing the setting conditions and using contingency management during teacher-directed activities. When the children's seating arrangements were crowded or when they were required to crowd around a teacher's demonstration, their visual attention to the teacher and educational materials was markedly reduced compared to a condition where they were spaced one or two feet apart. In the second experiment, visual attendance to a teacher or books throughout a story period was markedly lower when the academic session was preceded by a period of vigorous activity than when preceded by a rest period; transition times were longer and more disruptive following vigorous activities. When contingency management techniques were used to remediate the undesirable behaviors, they were shown to be no more effective than the favorable environmental conditions. These studies suggest that the setting or impersonal variables that may be contributing to the problem should be examined before personally mediated behavioral procedures are designed for group problems.

Anyone who has implemented behavioral procedures in a day care center has probably modified the ecology or organization of that setting to some extent. Perhaps a timeout room was built or work schedules rearranged so that a specific teacher could implement a procedure, or extra materials were provided for teaching a specific skill. Perhaps instructions were placed on the wall to remind teachers to perform procedures. For the well-managed day care centers that are run by experts in arranging environments for young children, such minor modifications may suffice; for others, such as the many custodial settings that lack such experts and where children spend much of their time waiting, a more comprehensive reorganization is necessary.

In the remainder of this chapter, we shall discuss some relationships between the day care environment and behavior. We shall then describe ways to arrange impersonal variables so that they set the occasion for appropriate behavior and support the implementation of individual intervention programs.

Engagement of Children with Their Environment

The primary goal of any change in day care organization is to increase children's appropriate engagement with their environment by increasing their opportunities to interact with play materials, peers, and caregivers. Many group behavior problems, especially for very young children, occur because there are few cues in the immediate environment for appropriate behavior and many cues for inappropriate behavior. For example, children who are waiting in line to play outside or eat lunch are in close proximity to a large number of unoccupied children who may be uncomfortable in their heavy clothes or hungry and sleepy. Crying, arguing, fighting, or leaving the line are common responses to this situation. Since adult attention may be one of the few reinforcers in the environment, reprimands may increase rather than decrease these behaviors. A vicious cycle of negative behavior quickly becomes the dominant mode of interaction and perpetuates itself as new staff and children observe and model their peers. In such cases, lack of opportunity for appropriate engagement *is* the problem, and if it occurs often throughout the day it can seriously interfere with the stated goals of most day care programs.

Providing opportunities for appropriate engagement is essential because children spend so much of their time in day care teaching each other how to behave and how to perform new skills (Devoney, Guralnick, & Rubin, 1974; Rubenstein & Howes, 1976). Opportunities to observe and model appropriate behavior are generally important for children and particularly important for the implementation of behavior modification procedures. For example, it will probably be easier to decrease a young child's excessive aggression by using timeout and teacher attention for appropriate behavior if that child can observe others asking or bargaining for toys and experience success with those methods (Baer & Wolf, 1970); whereas it will probably be more difficult to do so if the children at the center frequently use violence to solve problems.

High levels of appropriate engagement indicate that children find their environment reinforcing, particularly if teachers do not need to provide large amounts of social or token reinforcement for participation. If freeplay materials are reinforcing, one teacher can supervise a large group while others conduct small-group activities or intensive training sessions with one or a few children. Similarly, if a group of children are eating lunch and conversing happily, a teacher can devote some time to individual language training at the table.

Finally, the provision of a reinforcing environment will enhance the effect of timeout on those infrequent occasions when a punishment procedure is necessary (Plummer, Baer, & LeBlanc, 1978; Solnick, Rincover, & Peterson, 1977). Milder forms of timeout such as sit and watch (Porterfield, Herbert-Jackson, & Risley, 1976) will be effective and fewer children will need to be sent to a separate room or require more aversive and time-consuming procedures such as overcorrection. Teachers will be able to spend their time teaching and having fun with the children rather than punishing.

Children's appropriate engagement with their environment can be assessed with the Planned Activities (PLA) Check (Risley & Cataldo, 1974). This system simply requires that the consultant or observer know the daily activity schedule and the behaviors appropriate for each activity. Appropriate engagement during a large-group activity may include paying attention to the teacher or participating children; answering questions; singing, dancing, or reciting with the group; or helping the teacher with a demonstration. It may not include disruptive or aggressive behavior, talking out of turn, leaving the group to play with toys, or gazing aimlessly around the room.

At prespecified intervals the observer counts the number of children present in the activity and the number participating. The ratio obtained for that particular check can be compared with others taken at later points in the same activity or at other times of the day. A profile of appropriate engagement across the day provides information about what times or activities may require reorganization. For example, a PLA-Check may indicate that children's participation is highest during teacher-directed lessons or small-group activities, lower during indoor and outdoor freeplay, and lowest during transitions from lunch to nap and from large-group to indoor play.

While taking a PLA-Check, the observer may be struck by differences in the quality of the children's and teachers' behavior during periods of high and low engagement. These differences are most apparent when centers that have high or low levels of participation throughout the day are compared.

When children are provided with continuous opportunities to interact with play materials, peers, and teachers, they appear involved, animated, enthusiastic, and happy most of the time. Their teachers care for and interact with them in a friendly, affectionate way; they rarely scold, nag, or yell. Punishment is infrequent and mild. Although these teachers always seem to be in the right place at the right time, they do not look hurried or harried. To the casual observer their work may appear effortless.

Where there are few opportunities for engagement, children appear bored, uninvolved, and passive. Infants and toddlers cry frequently; older preschoolers damage materials and fight. Their teachers interact with them infrequently and the interaction that does occur is more often negative than positive in tone; there are frequent scoldings and even physical punishment. The disruptive, aggressive children receive most of the attention; those who follow instructions and play quietly are ignored. Teachers may either do as little work as possible or rush from problem to problem trying desperately to care for the children. They look very tired.

Such behaviors can serve as useful indicators of problems in addition to the PLA-Check. It is important to keep in mind that periods of low engagement, with their potential for setting the occasion for group problems and preventing the implementation of individual programs, are not a necessary part of day care. They occur because the environment is not organized to provide continuous opportunities for children to interact with play materials, peers, and teachers. The environment can provide these opportunities if careful consideration is given to the arrangement of space, equipment, materials, activity scheduling, teacher assignments, and the movement of children through activities.

Arranging the Environment for Engagement

The Physical Environment

One of the consultant's first concerns must be the arrangement of space, equipment, and materials so that they promote safety and set the occasion for appropriate behavior. The physical features prompt and reinforce children's behavior both directly and indirectly. For example, some toys such as a puzzle or jack-in-the-box provide immediate feedback when they are used correctly. Some equipment, such as a potty-chair designed to be placed on the floor rather than on the toilet, may prompt children to perform more of a self-help routine themselves. However, the physical features of a setting also affect the children indirectly by facilitating the teachers' performance.

Open Environment. One of the teacher's most important jobs is supervision. Teachers must always know where the children are and what they are doing, not only so they can ensure their safety but also so they can interact with, teach, and assist them contingent on their behavior. Supervision is easier in an open environment—a large area divided by low barriers such as bookshelves rather than by walls or floor-to-ceiling partitions. Such an environment allows supervision of children by teachers and of teachers by their supervisor without interfering with, for example, infants' or toddlers' sleep, or with toddlers' participation in small-group activities (Twardosz, Cataldo, & Risley, 1974). An open environment facilitates communication among teachers, permits them to assist each other quickly, and allows even very young children to walk independently from area to area.

The advantages of an open center can be easily appreciated if one imagines its opposite—the center comprised of a series of rooms arranged on either side of a corridor with a kitchen and bathroom down the hall. A series of rooms lends itself to permanent assignment of teachers and children to each one. This arrangement minimizes the necessity for communication and movement among rooms. Since room assignments are usually based on age, younger children miss opportunities to model the behavior of older children, and older children miss the chance to help care for and protect younger ones. If resources are scarce, each room will be poorly equipped, and teachers may hoard rather than share materials for fear of losing them. Children may have to be taken to the bathroom in groups, which probably means that a large portion of the day will be spent waiting for others to finish.

The consultant should begin the reorganization process by asking the teachers to substitute low barriers for walls or partitions. If walls cannot be removed, the tactics discussed in the remainder of this chapter, such as dividing a center into functional areas or assigning teachers to specific responsibilities, will still be applicable. It will just be a little more difficult to implement them. For example, transitions between areas will require very careful planning because a wall may separate areas. A teacher must be present on both sides of a wall before the transition begins so that children will be supervised continuously.

Functional Areas. After making the environment as open as possible, the consultant should consider how to divide the space into areas according to function. An infant center can be divided into eating, play, sleep, diapering, and receiving and departing areas. A center for 3- to 6-year-olds can be divided into housekeeping, large motor, manipulative, reading, large-group, eating, and bathroom areas. Hart (1978) suggests that a floor plan of the center be drawn and that different area arrangements be sketched in until a satisfactory one is found. The one chosen should minimize the amount of space to be covered during activity transitions, provide unimpeded traffic lanes, allow enough space for each activity, and require teachers to take the minimum number of steps to perform routine tasks. A convenient area plan in a center for older preschoolers would ensure that the large-group activity area did not block the bathroom entrance so that a child would not have to disturb the group to use the bathroom. The freeplay space would be divided so that children could engage in different types of play without interfering with each other. Such an arrangement would prevent fights, which can occur, for instance, when one child slides down a slide and into another's painstakingly constructed block castle.

After a center is divided into areas, the equipment and materials in those areas must be arranged to prompt appropriate and prevent inappropriate behavior. For example, the location of all necessary equipment and materials in the diapering area of an infant center makes it easier for teachers to get the job done and also helps prevent dangerous situations. Leaving a child unattended on a diaper table to hunt for a washcloth seems unthinkable; yet it occurs occasionally if all supplies are not readily available.

Most day care teachers feel that one of the primary advantages of attending a center is the opportunity for children to learn to play and get along with each other. A child who rarely takes advantage of this opportunity prompts concern or critical comment. If encouraging social play is a goal of the center, then teachers should select and arrange materials to set the occasion for this behavior (Quilitch & Risley, 1973; Updegraff & Herbst, 1933). A housekeeping or dress-up corner is a classic example of such an arrangement. In addition to providing opportunities for all the children, this area could support a behavior modification program for a withdrawn child. The situation would set the occasion for observing and engaging in interaction; teachers and peers could reinforce such successive approximations as playing near the area, responding to others' initiations, and taking a small role in their dramatic play.

Similarly, teachers may want the children to initiate interactions with them more frequently so they could use those occasions to prompt more elaborate language or shape other skills. Reasons for the children to initiate these interactions can be built into the environment (Hart & Risley, 1978). For example, at some centers teachers place individual plates of food on the table before calling the children to lunch. Although this practice may be convenient, it removes a natural opportunity for language since children do not need to ask for their food. If food is placed in serving bowls by the teacher's place at the table, there will be a reason for children to ask for it and a reminder to the teacher to wait for or prompt a request. When the child asks for the food the teacher can use that opportunity to prompt a more complete request or ask a question about how it was grown or prepared.

The importance of dividing a center into areas and furnishing them so that they set the occasion for appropriate behavior cannot be overemphasized. There are excellent sources on these topics in the early childhood education literature (e.g., Kritchevsky, Prescott, & Walling, 1969) and the environmental design literature (e.g., Seidel & Danford, 1979), as well as useful packaged technology for setting up infant and toddler day care centers (Herbert-Jackson, O'Brien, Porterfield, & Risley, 1977; O'Brien, Porterfield, Herbert-Jackson, & Risley, 1979).

Activity Schedules, Area Assignments, and Individual Movement of Children

Perhaps the most frequent cause of low levels of appropriate engagement in day care centers is the inadvertent programming of unnecessary waiting periods. They rob the scheduled activities of precious time and may set the occasion for unpleasant interaction. Waiting seems to result from two common methods of schedule preparation and teacher assignment. One method is characterized by a schedule of successive activities and the assignment of teachers to move with specific children through those activities. Sometimes a teacher is responsible for providing complete supervision, care, and teaching for the same group of children for weeks or months. One problem with this method is that children must wait for their entire group to finish an activity before they move to the next one. Those who finish first will have little to do and will not be the focus of the teacher's attention. This situation often sets the occasion for disruption, crying, and reprimands.

A second method is characterized by a schedule of activities and the assignment of teachers to the general task of helping each other care for the children. Although there is no planned division of responsibilities, teachers may divide them informally on a moment-by-moment basis. High levels of engagement rarely occur when this method is used because children must wait while teachers decide what will happen. Some teachers may assume very little responsibility; others may be overworked.

Fortunately, a third method used in many centers produces maximum engagement and little or no waiting. This method involves a schedule of overlapping or concurrent activities and the assignment of teachers to conduct those activities in specific areas of the center. Teachers are responsible for specific children only when they enter their area. Since activities overlap and occur concurrently, children can move individually from one to another when they are ready.

The efficiency of area assignments and individual movement of children was demonstrated by LeLaurin and Risley (1972), who compared the transition from lunch to bathroom to dressing room to nap in a center for 3- to 6-year-olds under two types of staff assignment. The "man-to-man defense" required each teacher to be responsible for the same group of children throughout the transition. Movement to the next area could not occur until the entire group was ready. During the "zone defense," all teachers were assigned initially to the lunch area but moved to other areas as soon as a child was ready. As children finished lunch, each moved individually through the other areas until all were on their cots. A greater number of children were appropriately engaged in each area and a smaller amount of time was required to complete the transition during the zone conditions.

The importance of allowing children to move individually was further highlighted in a study by Doke and Risley (1972) during an activities period. They demonstrated that a high level of engagement was maintained when there were enough materials for all the children and when another activity was ready as soon as a child finished with the first one.

The implementation of the zone defense method requires careful attention to the preparation of a daily schedule and to the assignment of teachers to areas so that children are never unsupervised. For detailed instructions, see Hart (1978), Herbert-Jackson *et al.* (1977), and O'Brien *et al.* (1979).

The most noticeable and welcomed change that may occur in a center after the teachers implement the zone defense method is a decrease in minor forms of disruptive behavior. An effect that is just as important but not quite as noticeable is an increase in opportunities for teaching and interacting individually with children. For example, since children can move from area to area when they are ready, teachers can stop them for a moment to ask a question, prompt and reinforce a behavior that the child needs to practice, or just give a hug or compliment.

Conclusion

Consideration of some of the relationships between the environment and behavior will allow a consultant to take a broader perspective on behavior problems and remedial programs in day care centers. Attention to some of the impersonal variables discussed in this chapter may help a consultant produce the desired result.

Immediate focus on the organization of the day care environment may be inappropriate in cases where a very serious problem or dangerous situation exists. Such a problem would require the design and implementation of a behavior modification program using whatever resources are available. Changes in the physical environment or teacher assignments can then be introduced to make it easier to maintain the program or to prevent the future occurrence of serious problems.

This chapter has been limited to a brief description of some ways to arrange physical features, schedules, and staff assignments in day care centers to promote appropriate engagement. Although these variables are extremely important, even their most optimal arrangement will not guarantee that children will receive good care or remedial programs, or that their teachers will interact with them. They simply make it easier for other aspects of good programs—the specification of objectives and procedures, training, supervision, and feedback—to be implemented and maintained.

ACKNOWLEDGMENTS

The cooperation of the teachers and administrators of the day care centers is deeply appreciated. The helpful comments of Mick Nordquist,

Dennis Russo, Cyndy Sappington, and Trish Damon during the preparation of the manuscript are also gratefully acknowledged.

References

Baer, D. M., & Wolf, M. M. The entry into natural communities of reinforcement. In R. Ulrich, T. Stachnik, & J. Mabry (Eds.), *Control of human behavior* (Vol. 2). Glenview, Ill.: Scott, Foresman, 1970.

Brown, P., & Elliott, R. Control of aggression in a nursery school class. *Journal of Experimental Child Psychology*, 1965, *2*, 103–107.

Devoney, C., Guralnick, M. J., & Rubin, H. Integrating handicapped and nonhandicapped preschool children: Effects on social play. *Childhood Education*, 1974, *50*, 360–364.

Doke, L. A., & Risley, T. R. The organization of day care environments: Required versus optional activities. *Journal of Applied Behavior Analysis*, 1972, *5*, 405–420.

Epstein, L. H., Doke, L. A., Sajwaj, T. E., Sorrell, S., & Rimmer, B. Generality and side-effects of overcorrection. *Journal of Applied Behavior Analysis*, 1974, *7*, 385–390.

Guralnick, M. J. (Ed.). *Early intervention and the integration of handicapped and nonhandicapped children.* Baltimore: University Park Press, 1978.

Hardiman, S. A., Goetz, E. M., Reuter, K. E., & LeBlanc, J. M. Primes, contingent attention, and training effects on a child's motor behavior. *Journal of Applied Behavior Analysis*, 1975, *8*, 399–409.

Hart, B. Organizing program implementation. In K. E. Allen, V. A. Holm, & R. L. Schiefelbusch (Eds.), *Early intervention: A team approach.* Baltimore: University Park Press, 1978.

Hart, B., & Risley, T. R. Promoting productive language through incidental teaching. *Education and Urban Society*, 1978, *10*, 407–429.

Herbert-Jackson, E., O'Brien, M., Porterfield, J., & Risley, T. R. *The infant center: A complete guide to organizing and managing infant day care.* Baltimore: University Park Press, 1977.

Herman, S. H., & Tramontana, J. Instructions and group versus individual reinforcement in modifying disruptive group behavior. *Journal of Applied Behavior Analysis*, 1971, *4*, 113–119.

Jacobsen, J. M., Bushell, D. B., Jr., & Risley, T. R. Switching requirements in a Head Start classroom. *Journal of Applied Behavior Analysis*, 1969, *2*, 43–47.

Krantz, P. J., & Risley, T. R. Behavioral ecology in the classroom. In K. D. O'Leary & S. G. O'Leary (Eds.), *Classroom management: The successful use of behavior modification* (2nd ed.). New York: Pergamon Press, 1977.

Kritchevsky, S., Prescott, E., & Walling, L. *Planning environments for young children: Physical space.* Washington, D.C.: National Association for the Education of Young Children, 1969.

LeLaurin, K., & Risley, T. R. The organization of day care environments: "Zone" versus "man-to-man" staff assignments. *Journal of Applied Behavior Analysis*, 1972, *5*, 225–232.

O'Brien, M., Porterfield, J., Herbert-Jackson, E., & Risley, T. R. *The toddler center: A practical guide to day care for one- and two-year-olds.* Baltimore: University Park Press, 1979.

Plummer, S., Baer, D. M., & LeBlanc, J. M. Functional considerations in the use of procedural timeout and an effective alternative. *Journal of Applied Behavior Analysis*, 1978, *11*, 689–705.

Porterfield, J. K., Herbert-Jackson, E., & Risley, T. R. Contingent observation: An effective and acceptable procedure for reducing disruptive behaviors of young children in group settings. *Journal of Applied Behavior Analysis*, 1976, *9*, 55–64.

Quilitch, H. R., & Risley, T. R. The effects of play materials on social play. *Journal of Applied Behavior Analysis*, 1973, *6*, 573–578.

Risley, T. R. & Cataldo, M. F. *Evaluation of planned activities: The PLA-check measure of classroom participation.* Lawrence, Kans.: Center for Applied Behavior Analysis, 1974.

Risley, T. R., & Twardosz, S. The preschool as a setting for behavorial intervention. In H. Leitenberg (Ed.), *Handbook of behavior modification and behavior therapy.* Englewood Cliffs, N.J.: Prentice-Hall, 1976.

Rubenstein, J., & Howes, C. The effects of peers on toddler interaction with mother and toys. *Child Development*, 1976, *47*, 597–605.

Seidel, A. D., & Danford, S. Environmental design: Research, theory, and application. *Proceedings of the 10th Annual Conference of the Environmental Design Research Association*, 1979.

Solnick, J. V., Rincover, A., & Peterson, C. R. Some determinants of the reinforcing and punishing effects of timeout. *Journal of Applied Behavior Analysis*, 1977, *10*, 415–424.

Twardosz, S., Cataldo, M. F., & Risley, T. R. Open environment design for infant and toddler day care. *Journal of Applied Behavior Analysis*, 1974, *7*, 529–546.

Updegraff, R., & Herbst, E. K. An experimental study of the social behavior stimulated in young children by certain play materials. *Journal of Genetic Psychology*, 1933, *42*, 372–391.

Zigler, E., & Valentine, J. (Eds.). *Project Head Start: A legacy of the war on poverty.* New York: The Free Press, 1979.

8

A Multienvironment School Mental Health Consultation

Behavioral Skill Training for Teachers and Parents

KENNETH R. SUCKERMAN, PAULETTE HINES, AND
STEVEN B. GORDON

The incidence rates for mental, emotional, and behavioral disorders in children far exceed the capacity for mental health professionals to engage in direct remedial action (O'Dell, 1974). Consequently, there are certain advantages to promoting both primary and secondary prevention in community schools. Schools are one of the few primary socialization systems that involve virtually all children. Evidence consistently suggests that to effect behavior change, the change agent must frequently be a part or become a part of the child's natural environment (Tharp & Wetzel, 1969). Clearly, teachers, who exist in significantly greater numbers than mental health professionals, are in a favorable position to facilitate healthy adjustment. The average child spends approximately 30 hours per week in the educational system. School staff have close proximity and easy access to the child, allowing for the identification of po-

KENNETH R. SUCKERMAN ● UMDNJ-Rutgers Medical School, Piscataway, New Jersey 00854. PAULETTE HINES ● UMDNJ-Rutgers Medical School, Rutgers Community Mental Health Center, Piscataway, New Jersey 08854. STEVEN B. GORDON ● Behavior Therapy Associates, Somerset, New Jersey 08873.

tential problems and early intervention. Therefore, prevention or remediation of childhood problems within the school environment is both logical and practical. At the same time, mental health services offered in the school environment tend to be less stigmatizing than outside referral and less expensive for the family, school, and community.

The ultimate aim of the mental health professional engaging in school consultation is to interact with caregivers within the school setting in such a way that they become better equipped to handle the current as well as future mental-health-related concerns of the child and adolescent populations with whom they work. These caregivers within the school environment may include administrators, teachers, classroom aides, guidance counselors, bus drivers, cafeteria workers, monitors, and school nurses.

Additionally, working in the child's natural environment inevitably must also involve the parents (Ross, 1972). O'Dell (1974) extensively reviews the needs and issues of parent training in behavior modification.

The behavioral approach lends itself well to mental health consultation in general and to school consultation in particular. The approach draws largely on learning theory principles and consequently emphasizes the use of multiple learning methods. Training is conducted in small, discrete steps that facilitate the trainee's learning and maximize his/her chances for successful performance. The extensive use of "hands-on" active processes works well with all populations. School personnel feel comfortable with the commonalities to their own instructional methods.

Consultees are taught a common conceptual base, language system, and approach to modifying behavior. In addition, well-specified operational definitions of target behaviors promote clear communication among all parties (consultant, teacher, parent, etc.). Objective evaluation of change follows as a natural extension from the specificity of behavioral goals. In fact, assessment remains an ongoing process within the behavioral model (Keefe, Kopel, & Gordon, 1978). Consequently, necessary and desirable program modifications can be identified and implemented thoughout the consultation, facilitating the likelihood of favorable results. The final program evaluation is merely the conclusive assessment conducted at the termination of the consultation process and follow-up.

The Present Project

In this chapter we shall describe a school mental health consultation conducted at a suburban New Jersey school system (school population of 10,000). Although the program provided for specific, behavioral intervention skill building for educators and parents, it was intended to result in positive behavior change in targeted children. Likewise, a generalization effect was expected to occur with the larger, nontargeted student population. Therefore, according to Caplan (1970), the program can be viewed as consultee-centered case consultation.

The school district's Special Education Department was granted special State Department of Education funds for a prototypical state-supported (Title VI) School-Community Competency Based Program for Handicapped Children. This program was designed to meet the needs that existed in special education for primary school children in low incidence categories (i.e., lower-range trainable, behavioral disorders, and severe communication disorders).

A self-contained classroom was created that served 15 children from the ages of 7 to 11 over 3 years. Since successful mainstreaming (i.e., gradually phasing children with special problems into regular classrooms) has obvious educational, social, and fiscal benefits, the concept is gaining widespread popularity in education. Accordingly, a primary goal of the program was to facilitate the mainstreaming of these severely problematic primary school children, who were unable to function in either normal or special classes.

Unfortunately, the teachers were ill prepared to deal with problems of the special child. In addition, many of these problems extended into the home as well. The project was designed to address these issues through two main features: the Competency Based Program, and Multienvironment Participation (school personnel and parents).

The Competency Based Program (Houston & Howsam, 1972) was developed as an alternative to traditional class placement, which is based on homogeneous diagnostic classification. There is general agreement that all children in the early stages of development manifest uneven developmental profiles. That is particularly true of children with handicapping conditions. Although it has been acknowledged by most authorities in special education that creating programs on the basis of categorical, diagnostic labels has little educational utility, to date, most public school programs still revolve around the classification–placement focus. But since classification *per se* cannot adequately provide the basis for educational programming, alternative models are needed.

The Title VI project made use of comprehensive assessment that provided detailed profiles of individual abilities in the cognitive, language, and emotional-social areas. From such an assessment, specific instructional objectives were identified for each child in each developmental area, thus providing a "competence-based" rather than a "categorically based" program. Such a profile for each child allowed individual objectives to be more easily defined. As a result, dimensions for the overall program evaluation were also defined.

The Special Education Department engaged two clinical psychologists (SBG and KRS) experienced in school consultation and the specific behavioral and education problems of special education students to provide the mental health consultation to the program. The consultants helped implement a concomitant program of Responsive Teaching and Responsive Parenting (Hall & Copeland, 1972).

Multienvironment Consultation

The multienvironment behavioral skill training aspect of the program grew out of the specific, stated needs of the district. The school system's representative addressed the problem that most of the educators and families lacked skills to bring about consistent, positive behavioral change in the problematic students. Therefore, all educators having contact with the students were invited to participate in Responsive Teaching, a behaviorally oriented teacher training program offered in 12 2-hour sessions. In addition to the teacher and the teacher aide of the competence-based class, participating school personnel included the school's principal, guidance counselor, supplemental instructor, three mainstream classroom teachers, and the district's Learning Disabilities Consultant, who also served as liaison between the school and the consultants.

In the Responsive Teaching groups, the participants were trained to (1) behaviorally define classroom problems; (2) observe and measure these behaviors; (3) systematically intervene to bring about desired changes in academic and social behaviors; and (4) verify the effectiveness of their interventions.

To meet the needs of the educators, the Responsive Teaching group met immediately after school. A part of each session was devoted to the presentation of basic behavioral concepts through the use of a transparency kit (Hall, 1973), supported with extensive use of videotapes, audiotapes, and films. Varied techniques of instruction included role playing, didactic instruction, small-group discussion, and self-scored quizzes.

Since "active" learning has always been shown to be superior to "passive" learning, the teaching of the behavioral skills was aided by having each participant complete a classroom behavior change project. This project enabled the consultees to have an actual, real-life experience in applying the newly acquired skills. After initial behavioral awareness each consultee was able to see the behavioral deficits or excesses that impeded the children's attainment of their established academic goals. Individual projects were developed to bring about positive behavior change. For example, one teacher's project focused on increasing the time a student attended to classwork. The teacher noted that the student frequently daydreamed, talked, and walked around the room, and reasoned that such behavior may be a main cause of his lack of academic progress. She elected to record his on-task behavior using a time sample method; she would record his activity precisely at each 15-minute interval. She found that the child initially attended to tasks on 42.6% of the time sample observations. Intervention included teacher's praise and token dispensing for attending behavior. Tokens were exchangeable for freeplay and for educational toys. This child's percentage of time attending increased to 89.3% in 1 week, and there was concomitant academic growth.

At each meeting the teachers shared their experiences with the group and planned their strategy for the next week. Group support appeared to encourage the teachers to use the Responsive Teaching approach with youngsters even when change did not occur overnight.

The second significant environment was the home. Since young children are still dependent on the family context for much of their social and emotional development, a sound program should include concomitant parental involvement. Therefore, in a parallel level of community participation, the consultation involved the children's parents in a behaviorally oriented parent training program, Responsive Parenting (Hall, 1973). This program was virtually identical to the teacher training program. The consultants' major goal was to help the children experience consistency between the school and home environments.

The Responsive Parenting group met evenings in the elementary school. Although an identical instructional format and materials were used, the meeting time and small-group environment facilitated the expression of shared frustrations and experiences and the awareness that, as parents, the participants' concerns with their children were not unique.

Thus a common conceptual base, language system, and approach to modifying behavior were used in the children's two significant environments. The commonalities of the teacher and parent programs were additionally designed to foster constructive communication among all parties. Just as the teachers developed classroom projects, the parents developed home projects designed to reduce undesirable behaviors and to build appropriate behaviors. For example, one mother decided to increase her son's appropriate play at home. She felt her son often handled toys inappropriately or did not play constructively with his brother. She used a time sample method of observations at 15-minute intervals. She included the problem period from 4:30 to 7:30 P.M. but excluded television-watching times, which were not problematic. Each day's record was the percentage of observations in which the child was engaged in appropriate play (i.e., using a toy or object for its express purpose).

The initial baseline was conducted over 6 days. At this time unobtrusive observations of the child's play behavior were made. His baseline percentage of appropriate play was 33.2%. Intervention was then initiated using social reinforcement in the form of verbal praise and light touching. The praise was extended at the time of observation for the first 3 weeks. In subsequent weeks the praise was extended to other times when appropriate play was also noted. The outcome was a steady increase to 71.5% appropriate play.

After 10 weeks of treatment and six group sessions, a functional assessment was made of the mother's intervention. For a single week, a second baseline was instituted when praise for appropriate play was discontinued. During this phase, appropriate play decreased slighty to 65.4%. Once social reinforcement was again provided, the rate of appropriate play increased to 75%.

During the 5-month period treatment the mother was able to generalize her skills, as evidenced by her design and implementation of another successful intervention program. In this case she used a timeout procedure; over 3 months, the child decreased his mean number of "sassing, making faces, and talking back" from a baseline of 12 per day to approximately 1 per day.

Evaluation

Over the course of the 3-year program, 15 children participated. In addition, eight families actively participated in Responsive Parenting and 15 educators participated in Responsive Teaching.

Evaluation was conducted in academic, language, and social-behavioral areas. Pretests were administered at the beginning of each school year and reassessed at the end of each year. The academic areas of reading, spelling, and mathematics were evaluated with the Wide Range Achievement Test (WRAT). Table 1 summarizes the academic success of the students who participated in the program. Since children participated for 1 to 3 years, academic success was defined as the number of years of academic progress on the WRAT as a function of the number of years participating. For example, 2 years progress over 2 years was considered average academic growth. Although each child had had consistent academic failure experiences throughout his/her previous school years, 12

Table 1. Distribution of Academic Success as Determined by Level of Attainment of Expected Academic Growth

	Level of expected academic growth		
	Deficient	Average	Surpasses
Number of children	3	6	6

of 15 students achieved average or superior academic growth during their involvement in the class.

Social-behavioral progress was assessed by having both teachers and parents complete the Walker Problem Behavior Checklist and the Louisville Behavior Checklist. Both scales were administered at the beginning and end of each academic year. Teachers and parents indicated decreases in acting out, in distractibility, in disturbed peer relations, and in immaturity.

The multienvironment approach also contributed positively to mainstreaming. Children whose parents participated in the program in addition to their educators were more successful in full placement into regular classes than were children whose parents did not participate (see Table 2). (For more complete assessment data, see Gordon, Suckerman, & Jackson, 1978.)

Discussion

Problems of Entry and Implementation

Most academic literature in behavioral consultation to schools gives the impression that implementation is both easy and straightforward, and that extensive knowledge of learning principles and techniques of

Table 2. Percentage of Children Attaining Various Levels of Mainstreaming by the Type of Parent Involvement in Responsive Parenting

Parent involvement in responsive parenting		Levels of mainstreaming	
		Partial	Returned to regular class[a]
Full and partial	(*n* = 11)	45%	55%
None	(*n* = 4)	75%	25%

[a]Includes children attending regular classes for all academic subjects and those who have "graduated" from the program.

behavior change is the only requirement for success (Bijou, 1970). More realistically, Reppucci and Saunders (1974) outline a host of problems that mental health practitioners face as they take their skills out of the laboratory and apply them to natural environments.

Our behavioral school consultation encountered numerous obstacles from politics, domain, tradition, and so on. The mental health professional is not always welcome, nor even invited without an inordinate investment of time and energy to educate and sell potential consultees on the consultation services available. Although we were invited by the school district, we had to make our services attractive to those educators to whom we directly provided services.

A problem of dual populations (Reppucci & Saunders, 1974) was evident as the consultants used intermediaries (educators and parents) to influence behavior change in the target population (children). In this way the intermediaries become ultimately responsible for executing the behavior change projects. Therefore, through second-order behavior modification, the behavior modifier influences the behavior of the target population by modifying the behavior of the intermediaries (Ayllon & Azrin, 1964).

Clear personal benefits were necessary in order to maintain strong interest on the part of all participants. All staff and parents were able to feel intrinsic satisfaction in their increased knowledge and skills. However, more concrete rewards seemed important to maintain morale, motivation, and willingness to devote the extra time required until the child's positive behavior change reached levels whose intrinsic rewards were sufficient to maintain program participation. The educators were offered credit toward salary increments, a statement of participation in their personnel file, and a handsome certificate. Although parents earned behavior management books, for the most part their rewards were less concrete. Participation won parents the opportunity to engage in regular small-group discussion, gave them the satisfaction of helping their children develop more desirable behavior, and afforded them a chance to participate actively in their children's education. And, of course, the parents gained an evening out.

Many educators naïvely view mental health programming as a detraction from the educational process and maintain that it is neither a defined nor appropriate part of their job function. Their union contracts may contain clauses that prohibit involuntarily drafting members to assume additional, nonteaching responsibilities. Educators may fear that involvement with a mental health consultant will reflect on their own professional or personal inadequacies; indeed, they may be hesitant to become involved even in less threatening, case-oriented consultation.

Mental health consultants are frequently plagued with the myth that their training, expertise, and interest lie solely in providing direct clinical treatment. Thus the structure for entry is often confusing to potential consultees. The mental health consultant must thoroughly delineate his/her role. That can often be accomplished with examples of past consultation experiences and a description of areas of expertise. In some states, school systems have special mental health personnel whose functions theoretically include consultation to nonmental-health staff. In reality, however, their functioning may be restricted largely to evaluation and classification of children with notable educational, social, behavioral, and emotional problems. An outside consultant may be extremely threatening and frustrating to the mental health professional already within the system who has been unable to develop such a program. Such factors can make the negotiation and coordination of outside consultant services cumbersome.

Moreover, there is a potential for confusion of the consultant's role. The consultant may be asked by the consultees to address issues outside the parameters of the task as initially defined by the person, often an administrator, who invited the consultant. Even if interested, supportive mental health staff employed by schools are seldom available to facilitate follow-through on mental health consultation. The consultant may be met with ambivalence from teachers and supportive staff because of their past experience in not having all of their needs immediately addressed.

Resentment may also result when a consultative relationship is forced on the consultee by a superior. Clearly, if a consultant is to succeed in the school setting, he/she must accept certain of its values. The union may modify not only the consultees' behavior, but the consultant's as well.

Conclusion

In spite of numerous obstacles, behavioral school consultation has proved highly successful in mental health service delivery. In the case we have described, the school has been able to continue without consultation services. The primary educators and parents have found intrinsic value in their own behavior change, leading to the maintenance of a consistent behavioral approach to dealing with both the targeted and generalized populations. In turn, the students continue to progress in both academic and social-emotional areas.

References

Ayllon, T., & Azrin, N. Reinforcement and instructions with mental patients. *Journal of the Experimental Analysis of Behavior*, 1964, *7*, 327–331.

Bijou, S. W. What psychology has to offer education now. *Journal of Applied Behavior Analysis*, 1970, *3*, 65–71.

Caplan, G. *The theory and practice of mental health consultation.* New York: Basic Books, 1970.

Gordon, S. B., Suckerman, K. R., & Jackson N. *Parallel behavioral child management training for parents and teachers: An evaluation of an integrative community-based model.* Paper presented at the meeting of the Association for the Advancement of Behavior Therapy, Chicago, December 1978.

Hall, R. V., & Copeland, R. E. The responsive teaching model: A first step in shaping school personnel as behavior modification specialists. In F. W. Clark, D. R. Evans, & L. A. Hamerlynck (Eds.), *Implementing behavioral programs for schools and clinics.* Champaign, Ill.: Research Press, 1972.

Hall, R. V. *Responsive teaching transparency kit.* Lawrence, Kansas: H&H Enterprises, 1973.

Houston, W. R., & Howsam, R. B. Change and challenge. In W. R. Houston & R. B. Howsam (Eds.), *Competency-based teacher education.* Chicago: Science Research Associates, 1972.

Keefe, F. J., Kopel, S. A., & Gordon, S. B. *A practical guide to behavioral assessment.* New York: Springer, 1978.

O'Dell, S. Training parents in behavior modification: A review. *Psychological Bulletin*, 1974, *81*, 418–433.

Reppucci, N. D., & Saunders, J. T. Social psychology of behavior modification: Problems of implementation in natural settings. *American Psychologist*, 1974, *29*, 649–660.

Ross, A. O. *Manual of child psychopathology.* New York: McGraw-Hill, 1972.

Tharp, R. G., & Wetzel, R. J. *Behavior modification in the natural environment.* New York: Academic Press, 1969.

9

Measures of Staff Morale and Organizational Environment as Indicators of Program Change in an Institution for Youthful Offenders

N. DICKON REPPUCCI AND J. TERRY SAUNDERS

With our growing experience in the area of behavioral treatment programs in human service organizations (e.g., mental hospitals, juvenile correctional facilities, schools), it has become apparent that a more ecological perspective (e.g., Reppucci, 1977; Willems, 1974), with its emphasis on understanding the complex interrelationships and interdependencies within and between person-behavior-environment systems, is necessary for the successful implementation of behavior modification programs in

N. DICKON REPPUCCI • Psychology Department, University of Virginia, Charlottesville, Virginia 22901. J. TERRY SAUNDERS Offenders Aid and Restoration of the United States, 409 East High St., Charlottesville, Virginia 22901. The authors express their appreciation for financial support from NIMH Small Grant No. 1 R03 MH-25 779-01.

these settings. In 1974, as an initial attempt to examine some major implementation issues that confront the change agent using behavior modification techniques in human service organizations, the authors, both behaviorally oriented community psychologists, wrote an article on the "Social Psychology of Behavior Modification: Problems of Implementation in Natural Settings." One of the issues we discussed was the Problem of Two Populations. In brief, we argued (1974) that the behavioral consultant can influence the behavior of the client population only by modifying the behavior of staff mediators. We further noted that consultants usually have little control over the most powerful contingencies of staff reinforcement—salaries, promotions, job security, and benefits. Yet staff are clearly a vital link in the service delivery chain within any human service organization. If a behavioral program affects them adversely, it is possible and perhaps even likely that the quality of care to residents will suffer as a consequence. To the degree that a behavioral program strengthens positive aspects of their work experience, both staff and residents should benefit. Nevertheless, the area of employee job satisfaction has been woefully ignored in human service organizations (Sarata, 1977; Sarata & Jeppesen, 1977).[1]

Most investigators have given priority to assessing changes among *residents* of institutions that have tried to improve their services. Although this bias is understandable, it has nevertheless severely limited our understanding of outcome with respect to various change strategies in various types of human service settings. Since staff are the primary caregivers in institutional settings, they are usually the primary implementers of program change. Thus their morale may be a crucial factor in determining the quality of services that reach the residents. In addition, because the tenure of staff usually exceeds that of most program consultants, an assessment of staff morale appears central to any prognosis regarding a new program's longevity or its receptiveness to future change efforts.

Sarason and his colleagues (Goldenberg, 1971; Reppucci, 1973; Sarason, Levine, Goldenberg, Cherlin, & Bennett, 1966) have stressed that one necessary ingredient of positive institutional change is the creation of a growth-producing and motivating environment for staff. Sarason (1974) uses the term "psychological sense of community,"

---

[1] This area, however, has been a central focus of psychologists in business and industry, who have consistently related job satisfaction and job design (e.g., Hackman & Lawler, 1971; Katz & Kahn, 1978; Porter, Lawler, & Hackman, 1975) to increased job performance. It seems paradoxical that in the human services, with their emphasis on human relationships and the usual lack of clear-cut criteria of success, there has been practically no attention paid to staff attitude and behavior.

whose achievement he views as the overarching goal of all intervention efforts. Although few social scientists or human service administrators would question the importance of developing a positive social climate in the organizational setting, relatively little research (with the exception of Moos, 1974, 1975, 1979a,b) or applied effort has been expended in this direction.

In this chapter we shall suggest that an important direction for behavioral and other intervention research in human service organizations is the study of changes that may occur as a result of the introduction of behavorial programs both in the organizational environment and in the morale of the indigenous staff who are called upon to implement the programs. We shall present data that pertain both to job satisfaction and to perceptions of job design and social climate by staff who were involved in a large-scale change project from 1970 to 1973 at the Connecticut School for Boys (CSB). At the time, CSB was Connecticut's only training school for adjudicated male delinquents aged 12 to 16. These data are part of an array of measures that were gathered during the course of the project to monitor outcome at the levels of resident, staff, and organization. (For a more detailed account, see Reppucci & Saunders, 1978.)

Project Description

The immediate stimulus for change at the CSB was a shooting incident in 1970 that involved a resident at the school. It prompted statewide headlines and a massive investigation of conditions at the school, which in turn led to administrative replacements and a gubernatorial commitment to change at the institution. A team psychological consultants from the Yale University Psycho-Educational Clinic, of which we were members, was brought in by the new superintendent to facilitate both a structural reorganization of the school and the development of a new rehabilitation program.

Although many changes occurred during the project's life span, for our present focus on staff job satisfaction two major dimensions of program development are essential. First, the new rehabilitation program was developed by *staff themselves* in a series of meetings involving all levels of staff who had any contact with residents. The consultants served as group leaders and information providers, but did not try to suggest how staff should go about building a rehabilitation program. As it happened, staff were greatly impressed with a behavioral model that was used at the Robert F. Kennedy Youth Center in Morgantown, West Virginia, and they developed their own token economy program. Being behavioral psychologists, the consultants were able to develop a staff training program focusing on the principles of this approach; but the initiative essentially came from staff.

Second, as a result of the staff meetings a structural reorganization was accomplished that gave primary decision-making responsibility for residents to *staff committees* in each residential cottage. These committees, called cottage counseling teams, were composed of all staff regularly assigned to each cottage, including cottage parents, teachers, social workers, and aftercare workers, and met on a weekly basis. The superintendent had the right to veto any decisions, but in 3 years he never vetoed a single one.

In emphasizing these staff-related aspects of program development, we simultaneously deemphasize a wide variety of other features, such as increased resident involvement in program planning and broader structural changes pertaining to organization across cottages (see, e.g., Dean & Reppucci, 1974; Reppucci & Saunders, 1978; Sarason, 1974). In short, staff decided on their own guiding philosophy and were given primary decision-making power.

Because the token economy program was begun with a volunteer staff on an experimental basis in two cottages out of six at the school, a direct comparison was possible between these token economy (TE) cottages and the other four, which we shall call benevolent custody (BC) cottages. The major difference between the TE and BC cottages was not in staff or decision-making structure within the cottages but in program. Representative staff were chosen from a large pool of volunteers to man the initial TE cottages. Every effort was made to ensure that the selected staff did not differ from the staff in the BC cottages. The BC cottages adopted a decision-making framework identical to the cottage counseling committees of the TE cottages; however, the staff of the BC cottages received no training in behavioral principles and thus did not work within a clearly articulated program framework such as a token economy. Each of the cottages housed 15 to 25 boys, who were assigned to the cottage at admission to the institution on a rotating basis with cottage population taken into account. Although this procedure was not truly random, no systematic bias in assignment patterns could be detected.

Using modified forms (Sarata, 1972) of both the Job Descriptive Index (JDI; a measure of staff job satisfaction) and the Hackman and Lawler (1971) Job Design Inventory (a measure of staff perceptions of their jobs), we compared the TE and BC cottages at two points, August 1971 and November 1972. At Time 1 (T_1) the TE cottages had been operating for 8 months. We hypothesized that if the program was being perceived as helpful and effective by the staff in the TE cottages, then their job satisfaction should be higher at this time than the job satisfaction of staff in the BC cottages. In addition, their perceptions of their jobs should be enhanced. At Time 2 (T_2) the staffs of the BC cottages had also been trained in behavioral principles, and these cottages had been operating with token economy programs for a minimum of 3 months. We hypothesized that at T_2, because of the change in program in the BC cottages, the staffs of these cottages would have increased their job satisfaction and changed their job perceptions positively from T_1. Moreover, there would be no statistically significant differences between TE and BC staff on the JDI or the Job Design Inventory.

A research assistant unknown to any of the staff administered the JDI and the Job Design Inventory as part of a larger questionnaire on job satisfaction to all employees of the training school. There was no reason for anyone to suspect that a comparison between TE and BC cottages was the focus of investigation. All staff were given time to complete the questionnaires during working hours. Names were requested, but confidentiality was assured.

Assessment Procedures and Results

Job Descriptive Index and Absenteeism

The JDI was developed by Smith and her colleagues (Smith, Kendall, & Hulin, 1969). The version used in the present study contained the original five subscales regarding satisfaction with work, supervision, pay, opportunity for promotion, and coworkers. An additional subscale pertaining to residents was added to try to assess this dimension, which is salient in human service organizations but absent in the usual industrial setting where the JDI has been employed in the past. Two subscales, pay and promotion, were eliminated from the analyses because no staff were officially promoted or received differential pay increases during this investigation.

At T_1 and T_2, a multivariate analysis of variance (MANOVA) was used to compare differences in means across all four subscales of the JDI between TE ($N = 13$) and BC ($N = 20$) staff.[2] At T_1 the MANOVA was statistically significant ($F = 3.12$, $p < .05$), as predicted. A univariate

---

[2] In this and other analyses, staff size was determined by the number of staff for whom we had complete data on all subscales of a given instrument at both T_1 and T_2. As a result, the Ns are greatly reduced.

analysis of the individual subscales revealed that most of this effect was accounted for by the extremely significant difference between groups on the supervision subscale ($F = 12.90$, $p < .01$). Although there were no other statistically significant findings, it should be noted that in all cases the TE group scored higher on each subscale than the BC group (see Table 1). At T_2, the MANOVA for all subscales was not statistically significant ($F = 1.70$, $p = 0.18$), again as predicted.

Following these analyses, a MANOVA for repeated measures on the JDI was performed in order to test for group by time interaction effects and time main effects. There were significant differences for both analyses ($F = 3.23$, $p < .05$; $F = 3.45$, $p < .05$, respectively). Univariate analyses indicated a group by time interaction effect for supervision ($F = 11.04$, $p < .01$) and a time main effect for work ($F = 5.51$, $p < .05$), supervision ($F = 6.27$, $p < .05$), and residents ($F = 3.87$, $p = .06$).

Table 1 shows that BC staff showed increases on all subscales, and that TE staff showed no regression toward the mean from T_1 to T_2 on three of the four subscales. There was some regression on the supervision subscale, but it was far less of a decrease than the comparable increase on this subscale by BC staff at T_2. Overall, it would appear that experience in the TE program had a positive effect on the job satisfaction of staff at CSB.

In order to provide convergent evidence for this change in morale, we also compared TE and BC staff on a behavioral index of job satisfaction, that is, absenteeism. Specifically, we compared records of absenteeism among staff who were in the initial two TE cottages with those of staff in the BC cottages for each of 3 years: 1969, the year before the beginning of the change project; 1970, the transition year before the actual start of the TE cottages; and 1971, the first year of operation for the two experimental TE cottages. Nineteen seventy-one was the only year in which we expected to find less absenteeism among TE staff than among BC staff.

Table 1. Means and Standard Deviations for Token Economy (TE) and Benevolent Custody (BC) Staff on Four Job Satisfaction Subscales of the Job Descriptive Inventory

| Subscale | TE ($N = 13$) | | | | BC ($N = 20$) | | | |
| | Time 1 | | Time 2 | | Time 1 | | Time 2 | |
	$\overline{X}$	SD	$\overline{X}$	SD	$\overline{X}$	SD	$\overline{X}$	SD
Work	26.92	3.64	27.92	4.54	24.80	5.63	28.10	5.24
Supervision	32.77	2.71	30.69	5.89	24.95	7.50	31.60	6.00
Coworkers	28.08	10.32	32.15	7.41	27.25	9.44	28.75	7.21
Residents	32.69	5.47	35.38	5.47	29.85	6.00	30.75	7.23

Our initial measure of absenteeism was simply the mean number of sick days taken by TE and BC staff per year. This measure was very gross and included many cases of actual and some cases of prolonged illness. It yielded no statistically significant differences in mean number of sick days between TE and BC staff for any of the 3 years in question. Therefore, we refined our measure of absenteeism to include *only single* sick days that occurred on either end of a weekend or a holiday; we called these "cheat days." (If a weekend or holiday was surrounded by one sick day on each side, we counted it as one cheat day. If a single day was followed or preceded by a weekend and more than one sick day, we did not count any as cheat days.) In comparing the two staffs on cheat days, we found the predicted results: no differences in 1969 and 1970, but a meaningful and statistically significant difference in 1971 when the program was operating. TE staff ($N = 19$) in 1971 had a mean of only .5 cheat days per staff member; BC staff ($N = 46$) had a mean of 1.8 cheat days per staff member ($t = 2.37$, $p = .02$). These data on absenteeism provide convergent support for the job satisfaction results, indicating that more positive morale tended to follow working in the TE program.

Job Design Inventory

Hackman and Lawler (1971) introduced the idea of operationally defining individual components of job enlargement. They defined specific aspects of work that can be manipulated to achieve enlargement, and they developed a job design inventory to measure them. The variables measured by this inventory (autonomy, variety, feedback, task identity, contact, and informal contact) specify the conditions under which jobs will facilitate internal motivation. They then demonstrated a positive relationship between these variables and motivation, satisfaction, and performance of telephone company workers, who showed a desire for the satisfaction of such higher-order needs as personal growth and feelings of worthwhile accomplishment.

Sarata (1972) adapted Hackman and Lawler's inventory for use with staff in human service institutions and added three new dimensions: participation, information, and learning. He then used this modified version to study satisfaction and performance among workers in three different types of centers for the retarded. He concluded that expanded responsibilities and activities encouraged hope and performance among institution staff and that the job design inventory accurately differentiated the various institutions.

Sarata's modified version was used in our investigation. The following nine dimensions were tapped:

- *Variety.* The degree to which a job requires employees to perform a wide range of operations and/or to use a variety of procedures.
- *Autonomy.* The opportunity for employees to have a say in scheduling their own work and in selecting the procedures they will use.
- *Task Idendity.* The extent to which employees are involved in most aspects of the programs provided for clients and/or are involved in projects from inception through completion, and therefore have the opportunity to see the results of their efforts.
- *Feedback.* The degree to which employees receive information concerning the adequacy of their performance.
- *Contact.* The extent to which the job requires employees to interact with other people.
- *Informal Contact.* The opportunities for the employees to meet and/or interact informally with other people, that is, to have non-work-related interactions while on the job.
- *Participation.* The extent to which employees take part in the planning of programs and in making decisions.
- *Information.* The extent to which the agency's policies, procedures, and decisions are explained and communicated to employees.
- *Learning.* The opportunity for employees to acquire added expertise and/or to become more informed about youth corrections. (Sarata, 1972, p. 12–13)

Each dimension was derived from a combination of two to four positively phrased descriptive sentences. Table 2 shows the items included with each. Staff were instructed to answer yes, no, or "?" according to how well the phrase described their own jobs. Positive answers were coded as 2, negative as 0, and "?" as 1, and totaled to obtain the variable's score. Since each variable is composed of a different number of items, absolute scores are not comparable. The variety and contact dimensions were eliminated because there was no reason to expect differences either between groups or over time; both of these dimensions were equivalent regardless of type of cottage.

At T_1 and T_2, a MANOVA was used to compare differences in means across the seven remaining dimensions of the Job Design Inventory between TE ($N = 14$) and BC ($N = 21$) staff. At T_1 the MANOVA was statistically significant ($F = 4.04$, $p < .01$), as predicted. A univariate analysis of the separate dimensions indicated that four dimensions were significantly different; task identity ($F = 19.58$, $p < .001$), feedback ($F = 4.36$, $p < .05$), participation ($F = 9.97$, $p < .01$); and information ($F = 8.25$, $p < .01$.) A fifth dimension, learning, approached

Table 2. Job Design Dimensions and Items Included within Each[a]

Dimension	Items
Variety	1. Allows me to do a number of different things (to be involved in different kinds of work or projects). 2. Involves a variety of responsibilities or procedures. 3. Is always changing.
Autonomy	1. Provides the freedom to do pretty much what I want on the job. 2. Includes planning and scheduling my own work. 3. Permits independent thinking and acting. 4. My supervisor gives me a say concerning what I am assigned to do.
Task identity	1. Involves doing a job from beginning to end (e.g., to work on a project from its planning until its completion or to work with a case or client from referral through termination). 2. Lets me finish what I start.
Feedback	1. Yields results I can see. 2. My supervisor tells me whether I am doing a good job or not.
Participation	1. Involves helping to plan future programs for the school. 2. Involves taking part in decisions about residents. 3. The supervisor asks for my ideas and opinions before making decisions. 4. My supervisor gives me a say in making plans and decisions.
Information	1. My supervisor tells me in advance of decisions that affect my work. 2. My supervisor keeps the staff informed about all the different parts or programs at the school. 3. My supervisor explains the reasons for the decisions and changes that are made.
Learning	1. Allows me to learn new techniques and approaches. 2. Provides me the opportunity to learn and grow. 3. Provides me the opportunity to learn more about youth corrections and about what other agencies are doing.
Contact	1. Involves working with people. 2. Includes working with other staff members on teams or in group projects.
Informal contact	1. Provides a chance to get to know many people. 2. Gives me a chance to meet and talk with most staff members. 3. Workers talk together informally.

[a] Adapted from Sarata (1972).

Table 3. Means and Standard Deviations for Token Economy (TE) and Benevolent Custody (BC) Staff on Seven Dimensions of the Job Design Inventory

| | TE ($N = 14$) | | | | BC ($N = 21$) | | | |
| | Time 1 | | Time 2 | | Time 1 | | Time 2 | |
Dimension	$\bar{X}$	SD	$\bar{X}$	SD	$\bar{X}$	SD	$\bar{X}$	SD
Autonomy	6.00	1.88	6.29	1.68	5.00	2.32	6.38	2.06
Task identity	3.50	0.76	3.71	0.61	2.14	0.96	3.10	1.18
Feedback	3.57	0.94	3.57	0.85	2.67	1.43	3.57	0.75
Participation	7.14	1.61	6.79	1.42	4.71	2.55	6.43	2.29
Information	5.21	1.25	4.86	2.21	3.19	2.42	4.76	1.41
Learning	5.29	1.44	5.43	1.02	4.43	1.33	5.43	0.98
Informal contact	4.50	1.87	5.79	1.48	4.67	1.46	5.71	0.64

significance ($F = 3.28$, $p < .08$). At T_2 the MANOVA for all dimensions was not significant ($F = 0.67$, $p = .70$), again as predicted.

Following these analyses, a MANOVA for repeated measures on the Job Design Inventory dimensions was performed in order to test for group by time interaction effects and time main effects. There was not a significant difference for the overall group by time analysis ($F = 1.44$; $p = .23$), although there were three significant group by time univariate analyses of the separate dimensions (feedback, $F = 4.21$, $p < .05$; participation, $F = 4.13$, $p = .05$; information $F = 5.30$, $p < .05$) and two that approached significance (autonomy, $F = 3.47$, $p < .08$; task identity, $F = 3.66$, $p < .07$).

The MANOVA for a time main effect was strongly significant ($F = 4.84$, $p < .01$). Five of the separate univariate analyses for time were significant (autonomy, $F = 10.72$, $p < .01$; task identity, $F = 12.07$, $p = .001$; feedback, $F = 6.33$, $p < .05$; learning, $F = 5.96$, $p < .05$; informal contact, $F = 17.18$, $p < .001$); the other two approached significance (participation, $F = 3.15$, $p < .09$; information, $F = 3.80$, $p < .06$).

Table 3, shows increases for BC staff on all seven dimensions, and slight regression toward the mean on only two of the dimensions for TE staff. These decreases were substantially less than the comparable increases on these dimensions by BC staff at T_2. Again it appears that experience in the TE program enhanced the staff's perception of their work.

Social Climate

Social climate refers to the attributes of a social setting that directly affect individual behavior. This focus on the treatment setting rather

Table 4. Means, Standard Deviations, and *F* Values for Token Economy (TE) and Benevolent Custody (BC) Staff on Seven Subscales of a Revised Social Climate Scale

	TE (N = 20)		BC (N = 22)		
Subscale	$\overline{X}$	SD	$\overline{X}$	SD	F
Spontaneity	7.70	1.56	5.46	2.13	14. 92[b]
Affiliation	9.05	0.89	7.41	1.82	13. 39[b]
Order	7.35	2.52	5.50	2.16	6. 58[a]
Insight	7.40	1.85	6.23	2.11	3. 63
Variety	5.45	1.79	6.09	1.54	1. 55
Clarity	8.80	1.67	5.55	2.22	28. 33[b]
Autonomy	7.50	1.64	6.14	1.89	6. 20[a]

[a] $p < .05$.
[b] $p < .001$.

than on the individual recipients of treatment provides another avenue for analyzing organizational perception. The concept, introduced by Moos (1968), has been studied extensively by Moos and his colleagues in several settings since that time (e.g., Moos, 1974, 1975, 1979a; Moos & Houts, 1968, 1970; Pierce, Trickett, & Moos, 1972). The measurement instrument has been continually refined over the years, but the version used in the present study was necessarily a modification of the early scale.

The questionnaire we used consisted of seven of the 12 original content subscales (spontaneity, affiliation, order, insight, variety, clarity, autonomy) of the Moos Social Climate Scale (Moos, 1968), modified for use at the CSB. It was administered in February 1972 to all staff and residents[3] at the CSB; thus there was no reason for anyone to suspect that a comparison between TE and BC cottages was the focus of investigation. All persons were instructed to fill in the questionnaire with their own cottage in mind. Twenty staff from the TE group and 22 from the BC group completed the questionnaire.

A MANOVA performed on the seven social climate subscales was statistically significant ($F = 5.03$, $p < .001$). Table 4 lists the means, standard deviations, and F values of the univariate analyses of variance. Only the insight and variety subscales failed to achieve significance.

---

[3] Thirty-six boys from the TE group and 38 boys from the BC group completed the social climate inventory; for the results, see Wilkinson and Reppucci (1973). Suffice it to say that on five of the seven subscales (spontaneity, order, insight, clarity, autonomy) the TE boys scored significantly higher than the BC boys.

These data strongly support the hypothesis that the social climate of the TE cottages was more positive on the measured dimensions than that of the BC cottages.

Discussion

We have sought to demonstrate that evaluation of behavioral and other change programs in human service organizations should concentrate both on organizational environments as perceived by staff and on staff morale, as well as on client change. If one accepts the proposition that staff perception, attitude, and behavior are important determinants of the type of service that can be rendered, then programs that affect these processes positively should have beneficial effects for both staff and clients.

Our data indicate that the staff working in the behavioral treatment program (TE) were clearly differentiated in a positive direction from staff working in the more traditional program (BC) within the same institution at T_1. Both the JDI and the Job Design Inventory were sensitive to change over time so that BC staff who scored low at T_1 demonstrated significant increases at T_2, when they were working in an environment similar to that of the TE staff. Equally importantly, the staff who remained within the TE program over the 14 months did not regress on either measure. This fact would argue against a Hawthorne effect, since the period between measurements was considerable and the amount of attention given to each cottage staff by consultants decreased significantly as the programs became more established. Finally, although there were significant differences at T_1 between the TE and BC staff, there were no differences between the two groups at T_2, when all staff were participants in the TE program. These results support the notion that the behavioral program brought about change as measured by staff perception of their own jobs and satisfaction with various aspects of these jobs. The morale factor is strengthened by the data on absenteeism, which demonstrate significant differences between the two groups on the cheat days measure. The organizational perceptions were reinforced by the differences on social climate that were obtained between the two groups at an entirely different period.

Moreover, specific aspects of job design, social climate, and job satisfaction were significantly higher among TE staff. The high information and feedback subscales of TE staff on the Job Design Inventory seem to indicate more clarity among this group about job responsibilities and job performance. Such clarity is a positive job attribute and is consistent with the reported difference on the Social Climate clarity subscale and the positive assessment of supervision on the JDI. The high autonomy subscale in job design is also consistent with the Social Climate data. Encouragement of independent action seems to have been a strong characteristic of the token economy. Participation, that is, active involvement in program planning, was also salient in the token economy, and was complemented by the TE staff's stronger feeling that they could see jobs through to completion (high task identity). The scores on informal contact (Job Design) and affiliation (Social Climate) were also complementary and positive.

Informal evidence from staff and residents supports the empirical findings and the hypothesis that the token economy contributed heavily to the results. Staff members of the TE group reported that the specification of contingencies had reduced personal biases and pressures and had defined appropriate responses for most situations. However, they did not feel a loss of autonomy in decision making but instead experienced an increase in personal responsibility through the increased participation in developing rehabilitation programs and in formulating general policy. The TE staff also said that they worried less about staff either not supporting them in front of residents or playing favorites with residents. (The boys in the TE cottages preferred the clear definition of goals, the terms of release, and the means for their achievement in the token economy.)

In focusing on client attributes and outcomes, most investigators of intervention programs have neglected the crucial relationships between the general enthusiasm of staff and the effectiveness of the program. The all too frequent finding of lack of program effectiveness (e.g., Lipton, Martinson, & Wilks, 1975) may well result from this neglect. Our emphasis on staff morale and staff perception of organizational environment goes well beyond polemics. By directing research concern to these characteristics, the program planner or evaluator obtains a much fuller appreciation of the possible benefits of a token economy or other intervention strategy. Only by understanding the contexts in which programs are implemented can we ever hope to understand why some programs succeed and others fail. Thus, although it is critical that we evaluate the recipients of treatment, it is equally critical that we evaluate the implementers and the setting of treatment. Such an ecological assessment should help to determine not only why different types of programs succeed or fail, but also why programs with the same label and treatment philosophy vary in their success rates.

References

Dean, C. W., & Reppucci, N. D. Juvenile correctional institutions. In D. Glaser (Ed.), *Handbook of criminology*. Chicago: Rand McNally, 1974.

Goldenberg, I. I. *Build me a mountain: Youth, poverty and the creation of new settings*. Cambridge, Mass.: M.I.T. Press, 1971.

Hackman, R., & Lawler, E. Employee reactions to job characteristics. *Journal of Applied Psychology Monograph*, 1971, *55*, 259–286.

Katz, D., & Kahn, R. *The social psychology of organizations* (2nd ed.). New York: Wiley, 1978.

Lipton, D., Martinson, R., & Wilks, J. *The effectiveness of correctional treatment: A survey of treatment evaluation studies*. New York: Praeger, 1975.

Moos, R. H. The assessment of the social climates of correctional institutions. *Journal on Research in Crime and Delinquency*, 1968, *5*, 174–188.

Moos, R. H. *Evaluating treatment environments: A social ecological approach*. New York: Wiley, 1974.

Moos, R. H. *Evaluating correctional and community settings*. New York: Wiley, 1975.

Moos, R. H. *Evaluating educational environments*. San Francisco: Jossey-Bass, 1979. (a)

Moos, R. H. Improving social settings by social climate measurement and feedback. In R. F. Munoz, L. R. Snowden, & J. G. Kelly (Eds.), *Social and psychological research in community settings*. San Francisco: Jossey-Bass, 1979. (b)

Moos, R. H., & Houts, P. S. Assessment of the social atmospheres of psychiatric wards. *Journal of Abnormal Psychology*, 1968, *23*, 595–604.

Moos, R. H., & Houts, P. S. Differential effects of the social atmosphere of psychiatric wards. *Human Relations*, 1970, *23*, 47–60.

Pierce, W. D., Trickett, E. J., & Moos, R. H. Changing ward atmosphere through staff discussion of the perceived ward environment. *Archives of General Psychiatry*, 1972, *26*, 35–41.

Porter, L., Lawler, E., & Hackman, R., *Behavior in organizations*. New York: McGraw-Hill, 1975.

Reppucci, N. D. The social psychology of institutional change: General principles for intervention. *American Journal of Community Psychology*, 1973, *1*, 330–341.

Reppucci, N. D. Implementation issues for the behavior modifier as institutional change agent. *Behavior Therapy*, 1977, *8*, 594–605.

Reppucci, N. D., & Saunders, J. T. Social psychology of behavior modification: Problems of implementation in natural settings. *American Psychologist*, 1974, *29*, 649–660.

Reppucci, N. D., & Saunders, J. T. Innovation and implementation in a state training school for adjucated delinquents. In R. Nelson & D. Yates (Eds.), *Innovation and implementation in public organizations*. Lexington, Mass.: D. C. Heath, 1978.

Sarason, S. B. *The psychological sense of community: Prospects for a community psychology*. San Francisco: Jossey-Bass, 1974.

Sarason, S. B., Levine, M., Goldenberg, I. I., Cherlin, D., & Bennett, E. *Psychology in community settings: Clinical, educational, vocational, social aspects*. New York: Wiley, 1966.

Sarata, B. P. V. *The job satisfactions of individuals working with the mentally retarded*. Unpublished doctoral dissertation, Yale University, 1972.

Sarata, B. P. V. Job characteristics, work satisfactions and task involvement as correlates of service delivery strategies. *American Journal of Community Psychology*, 1977, *5*, 99–110.

Sarata, B. P. V., & Jeppesen, J. Job design and staff satisfaction in human service settings. *American Journal of Community Psychology*, 1977, *5*, 229–236.

Smith, P., Kendall, L., & Hulin, C. *The measurement of satisfaction in work and retirement*. Chicago: Rand McNally, 1969.

Wilkinson, L., & Reppucci, N. D., Perceptions of social climate among participants in token economy and non–token economy cottages in a juvenile correctional institution. *American Journal of Community Psychology,* 1973, *1,* 36–43.

Willems, E. P. Behavioral technology and behavioral ecology. *Journal of Applied Behavior Analysis,* 1974, *7,* 151–165.

10

Consultation for Self-Evaluation

Social Climate Assessment as a Catalyst for Programmatic Change in Mental Health Treatment Environments

STEVEN FRIEDMAN

The purpose of this chapter is to illustrate the use of social climate assessment techniques within a consultation framework. The goal of such consultation to mental health treatment settings is to facilitate self-evaluation and programmatic changes on the part of the existing staff. The consultant educates the staff on the use of social climate assessment techniques that are highly economical, efficient, valuable to line staff, and incorporate clients' contributions.

Social Climate Assessment as a Catalyst for Change: An Overview of the Literature

A promising direction within the mental health evaluation field, one that has the potential of contributing to the assessment of program pro-

STEVEN FRIEDMAN ● Downstate Medical Center, Brooklyn, New York 11203.

cess and outcome as well as linking process–outcome evaluation, lies in the work of Moos and his colleagues at the Stanford University Laboratory of Social Ecology (Moos, 1973, 1974a,b,c; Moos & Houts, 1968; Pierce, Trickett, & Moos, 1972). They developed a pair of social climate scales to assess the environments of psychiatric treatment settings, namely, the Ward Atmosphere Scale (WAS) for inpatient wards, and the Community-Oriented Programs Environment Scale (COPES) for day hospitals, halfway houses, and so on. Briefly, the WAS and the COPES are conceptualized as measuring three broad environmental dimensions, each of which, in turn, consists of three or four subscales: involvement, support, and spontaneity (relationship dimensions); autonomy, practical orientation, personal problem orientation, and anger/aggression (personal growth dimensions); and order/organization, program clarity, and staff control (system maintenance dimensions). The social climate of a program is obtained by pooling the perceptions of respondents, that is, patients or staff (see the next section).

Since the development of the initial form of the WAS over 10 years ago, it has been used extensively in various research capacities (Moos & Houts, 1968). These studies (as well as those employing the more recent, parallel COPES) fall into three major categories: (1) measuring process; (2) assessing outcome; and (3) serving as a catalyst for change.

As a process measure, the WAS was found to differentiate systematically among wards practicing different treatment philosophies (Kish, 1971). In a more ambitious study, Price and Moos (1975) employed the WAS to develop a taxonomy of inpatient treatment environments. A cluster analysis of WAS data from 144 wards revealed six types of treatment programs: therapeutic community oriented, relationship oriented, action oriented, insight oriented, control oriented, and disturbed behavior oriented. Furthermore, the WAS was found to correlate with such objective criteria as dropout rate, release rate, and community tenure as well as patient satisfaction with the ward (Moos & Houts, 1970; Moos & Schwartz, 1972).

The WAS has also been employed as a dependent measure in outcome research to assess the social climate of experimental versus control programs. Mosher, Menn, and Matthews (1975) found more positive perceptions of social climate in a community-based home for schizophrenics than in a ward in a community mental health center. In addition, the WAS showed more favorable social climate in behaviorally oriented ward programs (i.e., token economies) than in comparison wards (Gripp & Magaro, 1971; Jeger & McClure, 1979; Milby, Pendergrass, & Clark, 1975).

Finally, the WAS was utilized as a catalyst for stimulating programmatic changes. The early study by Pierce *et al.* (1972) represents an exploratory effort in this regard. They provided staff of a general hospital psychiatric unit with feedback from WAS administration. Numerous changes resulted from these consultations, and a readministration of the WAS 2 months later revealed significant pre-post changes on several subscales (support, clarity, and insight). Similarly, Moos (1973) used the COPES in an adolescent residential treatment center to facilitate and evaluate changes in the social environment. The COPES guided interventions and was sensitive to pre-post changes over 6 months. Both staff and resident discrepancies between their perceptions of "real" and "ideal" treatment environments (as assessed by two parallel forms of the COPES) were reduced on most subscales.

More recently, the WAS was used in a psychiatric unit of a VA hospital to help staff redesign their treatment environment (Verinis & Flaherty, 1978). After 7 months, a readministration of the WAS showed changes in six subscales, corresponding to all the areas the authors attempted to modify: involvement, support, spontaneity, order/ organization, program clarity, and staff control. Thus the WAS is being recognized for its value in stimulating change rather than just serving as a measure of program social climate at a given point, as in the earlier process and outcome studies. In serving as a guide for designing interventions as well as a tool for monitoring the effects of changes, and, again, suggesting further interventions, the WAS is at the center of a "feedback loop" whereby it acts as a measure that links program process and program outcome.

In this chapter, I shall illustrate the use of the WAS and the COPES as vehicles for *self-evaluation*. The consultant emphasized patient–staff discrepancies in perceived social climate as data-based guides for program changes. Such use of social-ecological assessment can be incorporated into routine program evaluation and consultation efforts—in a manner that is economical (requiring only several hours of existing staff time), efficient (not requiring highly trained research specialists), valuable to line staff, and incorporates clients' contributions.

The Present Study: Case Applications

The study took place in an inner-city municipal psychiatric hospital, serving a catchment area of primarily poor and minority residents. The adult psychiatric hospital includes five acute inpatient units, one milieu treatment ward, two outpatient units, two day treatment centers for acute and chronic schizophrenics, as well as a separate day hospital for alcoholics. All units operate within an interdisciplinary staff model, including psychiatrists, psychologists, social workers, nurses, aides, activity therapists, and residents/interns in the various disciplines.

Measures and Procedure

The WAS and the COPES are parallel, 100-item instruments assessing patient- and staff-perceived psychosocial climate along a 2-point response mode (true or false). As we have seen, the WAS and the COPES tap three broad environmental dimensions, each with three or four subscales. The following is a description of all 10 subscales, grouped according to the three broader dimensions.

A. Relationship dimensions.
   1. Involvement: The extent of day-to-day social involvement of residents (e.g., "Patients put a lot of energy into what they do around here").
   2. Support: The extent to which residents are perceived as receiving support from other residents and staff (e.g., "Staff go out of their way to help patients").
   3. Spontaneity: The extent to which the program encourages expression of opinions and feelings (e.g., "Patients are encouraged to show their feelings").
B. Treatment program dimensions.
   4. Autonomy: The extent to which client independence is encouraged by the program (e.g., "Patients are expected to take leadership on the ward").
   5. Practical orientation: The extent to which planning for future release from the program is emphasized (e.g., "Patients must make plans before leaving the hospital").
   6. Personal problem orientation: The extent to which examination of problems with staff and patients is encouraged (e.g., "Patients tell each other of their personal problems").
   7. Anger and aggression: The extent to which the program allows residents to argue with each other and with staff (e.g., "Patients on this ward rarely argue").
C. System maintenance dimensions.
   8. Order and organization: The extent to which neatness and activity planning are emphasized (e.g., "Many patients look messy").
   9. Program clarity: The extent to which rules, procedures, and

goal expectations are clearly perceived (e.g., "Ward rules are clearly understood by the patients").

10. Staff control: The extent to which staff are perceived as determining rules to control residents (e.g., "Staff don't order the patients").

Each of the 10 subscales is generally tapped by 10 items (in some instances a few items are only fillers). To avoid a response set, each subscale has about half its items keyed positively and half negatively. Parallel forms exist for assessed "real" and "ideal" treatment environments. Extensive psychometric data have been provided by Moos (1974a, b, c).

As a psychologist on an acute inpatient ward, I offered to administer the WAS and the COPES to interested units and to provide consultation to facilitate enhancing the social climate of their treatment programs. In the next section I shall report on the data from the inpatient therapeutic community ward and the two day hospital programs. Staff and patients on the inpatient ward completed the WAS; staff and patients in the two day programs completed the COPES. I then conducted a workshop for staff or patient–staff groups to provide feedback. Feedback emphasized patient–staff discrepancies in perceptions of social climate, comparisons of their profiles to the normative sample for the WAS/COPES "real" and "ideal" forms, and the planning of interventions suggested by the data.

Findings and Discussion

The findings discussed here focus on the assessment of patient–staff discrepancies for purposes of catalyzing program changes. Figures 1 and 2 contain the patient and staff COPES profiles of the two day programs; Figure 3 contains the patient and staff WAS profiles of the inpatient therapeutic community ward.

Figure 1 shows a discrepancy in patient and staff perceptions of the day center for chronic schizophrenics, as their respective profiles are almost entirely nonoverlapping. With the exception of perceived staff control, patients consistently perceive the environment as more negative. Although normative data indicate more favorable environmental perceptions among staff, with their greater control of the environment, the discrepancies in this program are more marked—particularly on the relationship dimensions.

These findings formed the basis of discussions in initial staff workshops and later joint staff–patient workshops aimed at enhancing the re-

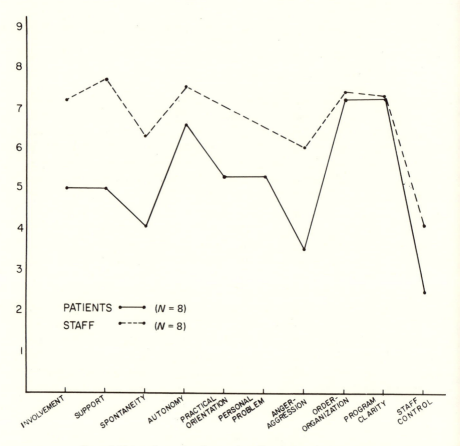

Figure 1. Comparison of patient and staff perceptions of day center.

lationship factors within the program. What emerged were "unspoken" significant differences among staff in their "treatment philosophies." These differences had never been openly discussed and were now identified as contributing to inconsistent behavior and rules on the part of staff. Participants felt that this inconsistency was responsible for patients' less than positive perceptions of social climate. Numerous changes were suggested based on these discussions. Although it is still too early to determine their full impact, changes are now being instituted and appear to have affected the social climate.

Findings from the alcohol day treatment center are presented in Figure 2. Like Figure 1, the patient and staff profiles are almost entirely nonoverlapping, with staff showing consistently more favorable perceptions of social climate. Unlike Figure 1, this profile indicates greater variability among subscales; yet patient and staff follow a parallel profile. Both patient and staff perceptions reveal a greater emphasis in the program on system maintenance dimensions than on relationship dimensions.

Feedback workshops focused on ways in which programmatic changes might accomplish the dual purpose of enhancing relationship factors in the environment while maintaining optimal order and structure. It was emphasized that relationship and structural factors can be balanced, rather than focusing on one at the expense of the other (Kohn, Jeger, & Koretzky, 1979). As of this writing, this program is undergoing many changes, partly as a result of the feedback provided by the COPES.

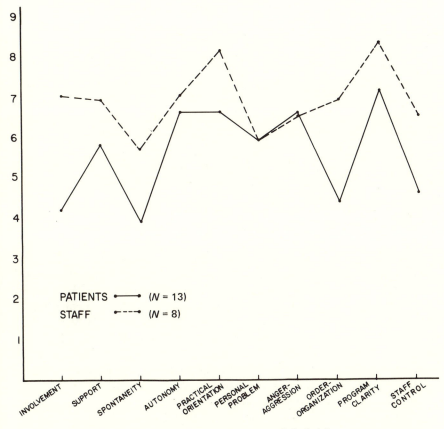

Figure 2. Comparison of patient and staff perceptions of alcohol day treatment center.

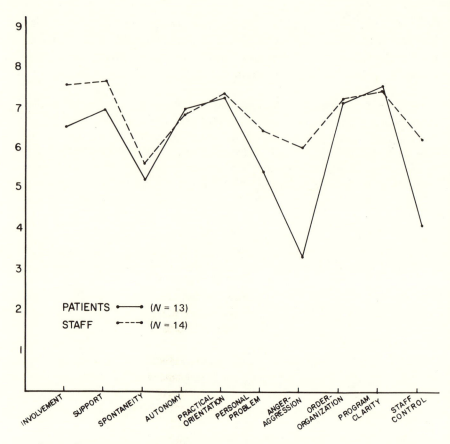

Figure 3. Comparison of patient and staff perceptions of therapeutic community ward.

Profiles of the WAS from the inpatient therapeutic community ward are presented in Figure 3. Both patient and staff perceptions are comparable and quite favorable across most subscales. The only major discrepancies emerge on the anger/aggression and staff control dimensions: In both cases, staff perceptions are higher. Patients' perception of low anger/aggression suggests that they perceive it as a "negative" dimension. This inference is consistent with their low perception of staff control, relative to staff (a finding inconsistent with the normative data). These discrepancies were stressed in the feedback sessions. Staff were surprised to learn that their perceptions of staff control were higher than in an acute inpatient ward in the same hospital. The appropriate expression of anger as part of the treatment environment was explored in the workshops with staff and patients.

These findings highlight the way in which the WAS and the COPES can be employed as self-evaluation tools to guide staff and patient input for programmatic changes. As well as providing a measure of social climate at a given time, the WAS and the COPES serve as catalysts for interventions that will enhance social climate. Future administrations of these scales at different times can be built in to monitor the impact of such interventions, thereby providing a "feedback loop" that can suggest additional program changes.

This chapter's emphasis on patient–staff discrepancies as a guide for planning interventions capitalizes on line staff and consumer input into the treatment and evaluation process. Furthermore, finer comparisons are possible by considering differential perceptions of various staff groups— for example, nursing personnel versus other professionals (Friedman, Jeger, & Slotnick, 1980). Finally, from the standpoint of time and economics in program evaluation, the WAS and the COPES have proved efficient. Relatively little time is required to administer, score, and interpret the social climate data, and highly trained technical researchers are not necessary.

ACKNOWLEDGMENTS

Thanks are due Drs. A. Alpert, R. Chaplan, E. Feigelson, R. Margolis, E. Twente, and D. Yamins for their support and cooperation in this study, as well as all staff and patients at Kings County Hospital who participated in this project.

References

Friedman, S., Jeger, A. M., & Slotnick, R. S. Psychosocial climate of a psychiatric ward: Differential perceptions of nursing personnel and other professionals. *American Journal of Community Psychology*, 1980, *5*, 613–615.

Gripp, R. F., & Magaro, P. A. A token economy program evaluation with untreated control ward comparison. *Behavior Research and Therapy*, 1971, *9*, 137–149.

Jeger, A. M., & McClure, G. *Evaluation of a behavioral consultation program: Changes in consultees, clients, and the social environment.* Paper presented at the meeting of the Eastern Psychological Association, Philadelphia, April 1979.

Kish, G. B. Evaluation of ward atmosphere. *Hospital and Community Psychiatry*, 1971, *22*, 159–161.

Kohn, M., Jeger, A. M., & Koretzky, M. B. Social-ecological assessment of environments: Toward a two-factor model. *American Journal of Community Psychology*, 1979, *7*, 481–495.

Milby, J. B., Pendergrass, P. E., & Clark, C. J. Token economy versus control ward: A comparison of staff and patient attitudes toward ward environment. *Behavior Therapy*, 1975, *6*, 22–29.

Moos, R. H. Changing the social milieus of psychiatric treatment settings. *Journal of Applied Behavioral Science*, 1973, *9*, 575–593.

Moos, R. H. *Evaluating treatment environments: A social ecological approach.* New York: Wiley, 1974. (a)

Moos, R. H. *Ward atmosphere scale manual.* Palo Alto, Calif.: Consulting Psychologists Press, 1974. (b)

Moos, R. H. *Community-oriented programs environment scale manual.* Palo Alto, Calif.: Consulting Psychologists Press, 1974. (c)

Moos, R. H., & Houts, P. S. The assessment of the social atmospheres of psychiatric wards. *Journal of Abnormal Psychology,* 1968, *73,* 595–604.

Moos, R. H., & Houts, P. Differential effects of the social atmosphere of psychiatric wards. *Human Relations,* 1970, *23,* 47–60.

Moos, R. H., & Schwartz, J. Treatment environment and treatment outcome. *Journal of Nervous and Mental Disease,* 1972, *154,* 264–275.

Mosher, L. R., Menn, A., & Matthews, S. M. Soteria: Evaluation of a home-based treatment for schizophrenia. *American Journal of Orthopsychiatry,* 1975, *45,* 455–467.

Pierce, W. D., Trickett, E. J., & Moos, R. H. Changing ward atmosphere through staff discussion of the perceived ward environment. *Archives of General Psychiatry,* 1972, *26,* 35–41.

Price, R. H., & Moos, R. H. Toward a taxonomy of inpatient treatment environments. *Journal of Abnormal Psychology,* 1975, *84,* 181–188.

Verinis, J. S., & Flaherty, J. A. Using the ward atmosphere scale to help change the treatment environment. *Hospital and Community Psychiatry,* 1978, *29,* 238–240.

IV
Prevention as Community Enhancement

Introduction

This part consists of four chapters that describe specific prevention projects that are compatible with our behavioral-ecological viewpoint.

As we saw in Chapter 1, a mandate of the original Community Mental Health Centers Act of 1963 was the prevention of "mental illness." Attempts to fulfill this mandate relied on Caplan's (1964) conceptualization of three types of prevention, derived from the field of public health: (1) *primary prevention,* which seeks to reduce the incidence of mental illness in the community; (2) *secondary prevention,* aimed at curtailing the effects of already visible problems through early identification and treatment; and (3) *tertiary prevention,* directed toward preventing the relapse or complication of already full-blown cases of mental illness.

As a "medical" concept, prevention implies knowledge of the causes of specific "disease" entities. As we pointed out in Chapter 1, this medical analogy was largely responsible for shortcomings in the implementation of the prevention mandate in community health centers. The conceptual fallacy of viewing the prevention of human problems as a logical extension of the "public health" model in medicine is elaborated on by Torrey (1974) in his provocatively entitled book, *The Death of Psychiatry.* Briefly, Torrey argues that translating broad social problems into disease terms in order to place them in the province of medicine represents the "psychiatrization of social problems," and that doing so "makes it more difficult to find real solutions to them" (p. 105).

A more recent approach to prevention is reflected in the work of Goldston (1977), who holds that

> the term "prevention" should be used solely to refer to actions which either (1) *anticipate* a disorder and/or (2) foster optimal health. Under these conditions the term "prevention" would be synonymous with primary prevention. (p. 27)

By "anticipate a disorder," Goldston is referring to programs aimed at reducing stress associated with such crisis situations as bereavement. Included in the aspect of fostering health are such activities as family-life education and parent education. Following this conceptualization, primary prevention is approached by "(1) strengthening individual capacities and/or decreasing individual vulnerabilities; (2) environmental modifications through planned social change" (p. 28). Rather than seeking to repair deficits, this approach attempts to identify individual and community strengths. This view is compatible with the behavioral-ecological approach to prevention as community enhancement that we are advancing in this part.

In a recent state-of-the-art discussion on prevention, Price, Bader, and Ketterer (1980) state that "the goal of prevention is now more broadly accepted than ever in the field of community mental health" (p. 10). They base their argument on a host of recent developments, including annual conferences on prevention, federal emphasis by the President's Commission on Mental Health, and the development of a Center for Prevention within the National Institute of Mental Health. They consider four major issues currently facing the field of prevention: (1) conceptualization; (2) practice methods; (3) policy; and (4) research/evaluation.

Conceptually, they point to two recent developments. The first is a gradual shift from a concern with "predisposing factors" to one with "precipitating factors." That is, instead of focusing on high-risk "populations," attention is being directed to high-risk "situations"—with stressful life events as the precipitating factors (e.g., divorce, death of a spouse). The second development is a shift from preventing specific disorders (e.g., schizophrenia, depression) to a more general concern with "health promotion." The latter is characterized by programs seeking to build competences and/or to foster positive mental health.

Concerning practice methods, Price *et al.* (1980) focus on the need for developing a knowledge base to guide preventive interventions. Since a great deal of this knowledge exists in fields other than prevention, Price *et al.* point to the need for systematizing this knowledge and disseminating it to prevention professionals. Perhaps such recent developments as the publication of two new journals in the field (*Journal of Prevention* and *Prevention in the Human Services*), the formation of the National Association of Prevention Professionals, the establishment of the Clearinghouse for Primary Prevention Programs (University of Vermont), and allocation of prevention funds through the Mental Health Systems Act of 1980 will help to accomplish this goal.

In the area of policy, Price *et al.* point to the relatively meager emphasis on prevention at the federal and state levels. As of 1979 only seven state departments of mental health had separate prevention units. At the federal level, an Office of Prevention within the National Institute of Mental Health was recently established. Over time, it is hoped that these advances will translate into local initiatives for prevention activities.

Finally, concerning research/evaluation, Price *et al.* point to the need for identifying key factors associated with individual health as well as for building ongoing evaluation into prevention programs. Relatively little effort has been directed to extending existing research methodologies to evaluation of prevention programs. Future efforts should address such issues as the specification of program targets, elements, and goals.

In his discussion of barriers to primary prevention, Goldston (1977) points to the lack of scientific evidence for the efficacy of prevention, the lack of a political constituency for primary prevention, the focus of professional mental health training on clinical skills, and general professional values favoring clinical endeavors over health promotion. Cherniss (1977) analyzes some organizational barriers to the development of successful primary prevention programs in community mental health centers. A major factor is that "the existence of direct treatment commitments works against preventive programming" (p. 137). The increasing demands for direct service become the priority and draw away resources. Similarly, using funding arrangements as a focal point, Landsberg and Hammer (1977) suggest that strong reliance on third-party reimbursement systems causes centers to emphasize inpatient care (since it is most often reimbursable) and neglect consultation and preventive activities.

Perhaps what is required for successful prevention, as Cherniss (1977) suggests, is a "new, totally separate institution" whose sole mission would be to engage in primary prevention activities. Ironically, Cherniss points to the medical delivery system as evidence for the viability of a separate institutional base for prevention:

> Although the medical care system in this country is a dubious model for community mental health, there is one feature we might do well to emulate in certain respects. In most instances, medical treatment and prevention are

conducted within different institutional contexts. Public health departments were created in order to advance and coordinate preventive health programs. Such departments generally eschew direct service and devote all their energies to the cause of prevention. Over time, public health has developed a distinctive professional and institutional identity which now is recognized and supported by most communities. (p. 139)

A similar conclusion that calls for the "structural segmentation" of treatment and prevention services is reached by Perlmutter (1974) based on an analysis of ideology, organizational theory, and professionalism in community mental health. Perlmutter recommended that prevention programs be designed as separate units and serve an entire city in order to have greater interaction with such institutions as employment services, education systems, and so on.

Interestingly, community mental health centers have hardly been the base for developing successful model projects in primary prevention. As Munoz (1976) observes in his review of prevention programs, "most well-designed preventive work has not come from mental health centers" (p. 11). He adds, however, that "once preventive programs are tested for effectiveness, community mental health centers could be an appropriate avenue for dissemination" (p. 11).

Although the projects described in this part were developed and evaluated using university centers as the working base, they could, as Munoz (1976) suggests, be disseminated for ongoing implementation out of consultation and education units in community mental health centers.

In Chapter 11, Elias and his colleagues present a series of school-based prevention programs that integrated behavioral and ecological elements. Their research program demonstrates the utility of an enhancement approach to primary prevention since their problem-solving curriculum was offered to *all* students, rather than directing intervention exclusively to "high-risk" students. Elias and his colleagues were particularly sensitive to the implementation issues inherent in behavioral-ecological interventions. They conclude that to strengthen the impact of primary prevention, school-based programs should attempt to incorporate additional community support systems.

Heber and Garber (Chapter 12) report on an extensive effort aimed at preventing cultural-familial retardation. A comprehensive environmental enrichment program was directed to a high-risk group of children immediately following birth. The project was conceptualized as a test of the social deprivation hypothesis and was carried out within an environmental-blame framework. Although these notions are not fully compatible with our perspective, aspects of the intervention indeed exemplify behavioral-ecological practice with this population. The results of Heber and Garber's experimentally evaluated program support the positive effects of early environmental enrichment. That gains achieved by the program began to erode as the children grew older is not surprising when one considers the children's natural environment and larger ecological context after termination of the formal intervention period. In order to maintain the initial progress, the support systems operating during the intervention need to be maintained for longer periods, before being *gradually* withdrawn when children can develop and maintain supports on their own. Unfortunately, school systems have yet to provide the kinds of environments that facilitate the maintenance of gains from early enrichment programs.

Chapter 13 depicts a crisis intervention approach within a prevention context. The underlying framework is the view of life transitions as crises. Specifically, Matese and colleagues draw on the behavioral and network streams of behavioral-ecology in developing primary prevention programs aimed at facilitating transitions to parenthood. They demonstrate their approach with two exploratory projects: (1) a behavioral training sequence for expectant parents, and (2) a support group for new parents.

Finally, McAlister (Chapter 14) considers the role of the media combined with community interventions (i.e., support groups) for prevention programming. The advantage of the media lies in its potential for large-scale dissemination of behavioral skills. Support groups provide the environmental context that facilitates individual use of media-based self-control training. MacAlister reviews a systematic research/intervention program demonstrating various combinations of media and community interventions that involve training in behavioral skills within the context of heart disease prevention.

Additional primary prevention projects compatible with a behavioral ecological perspective can be found in Price, Ketterer, Bader, and Monahan (1980), the volumes of the Vermont Conference Series on the *Primary Prevention of Psychopathology* (e.g., Forgays, 1978), Klein and Goldston (1977), Cowen (1980), and Munoz (1976).

References

Caplan, G. *Principles of preventive psychiatry.* New York: Basic Books, 1964.
Cherniss, C. Creating new consultation programs in community mental health centers: Analysis of a case study. *Community Mental Health Journal,* 1977, *13,* 133–141.
Cowen, E. L. The wooing of primary prevention. *American Journal of Community Psychology,* 1980, *8,* 258–284.

Forgays, D. G. (Ed.). *Primary prevention of psychopathology*. Vol. 2. *Environmental influences*. Hanover, N.H.: University Press of New England, 1978.

Goldston, S. E. Overview of primary prevention programming. In D. C. Klein & S. E. Goldston (Eds.), *Primary prevention: An idea whose time has come*. Rockville, Md.: National Institute of Mental Health, 1977.

Klein, D. C., & Goldston, S. E. (Eds.), *Primary prevention: An idea whose time has come*. Rockville, Md.: National Institute of Mental Health, 1977.

Landsberg, G., & Hammer, R. Possible programmatic consequences of community mental health center funding arrangements: Illustrations based on inpatient utilization data. *Community Mental Health Journal*, 1977, *13*, 63–67.

Munoz, R. F. The primary prevention of psychological problems. *Community Mental Health Review*, 1976 *1* (1), 5–15.

Perlmutter, F. Prevention and treatment: A strategy for survival. *Community Mental Health Journal*, 1974, *10*, 276–281.

Price, R. H., Bader, B. C., & Ketterer, R. F. Prevention in community mental health: The state of the art. In R. H. Price, R. F. Ketterer, B. C. Bader, & J. Monahan (Eds.), *Prevention in mental health: Research, policy and practice*. Beverly Hills, Calif.: Sage, 1980.

Price, R. H., Ketterer, R. F., Bader, B. C., & Monahan, J. (Eds.), *Prevention in mental health: Research, policy and practice*. Beverly Hills, Calif.: Sage, 1980.

Torrey, E. F. *The death of psychiatry*. New York: Penguin Books, 1974.

11

A Multilevel Behavioral-Preventive School Program

Process, Problems, and Potential

MAURICE J. ELIAS, JACK M. CHINSKY, STEPHEN W. LARCEN, AND GEORGE J. ALLEN

The emerging ecological paradigm is ideally suited for enhancing the social adaptation of children and preventing future behavioral or emotional difficulties. The particular formulation underlying the multilevel behavioral-preventive school program to be discussed is that of Kelly (Mills & Kelly, 1972; Trickett, Kelly, & Todd, 1972). In essence, Kelly recognizes the inseparability of behavior from the many contexts in which it occurs (i.e., social structural, organizational, group, and personal) and believes that the extent to which interventions affect these diverse contexts is proportional to the intensity, extent, and duration of desired effects that will be obtained.

Four primary ecological principles provide guidelines for planning, implementing, and evaluating community programs (Mills & Kelly, 1972). These concepts are essentially biological metaphors that are applied to social systems. First, people operate in contexts that are *interde-*

MAURICE J. ELIAS • Psychology Department, Livingston College, Rutgers University, New Brunswick, New Jersey 08903. JACK M. CHINSKY AND GEORGE J. ALLEN • Department of Psychology, University of Connecticut, Storrs, Connecticut 06268. STEPHEN W. LARCEN • United Social and Mental Health Services, Inc., 51 Westcott Road, Danielson, Connecticut, 06239.

pendent; an intervention in one system is likely to have "radiating effects" that affect other systems. Second, social systems are *adaptive* in that they seek to maintain a balance between their essential functions and stressful changes that threaten their equilibrium. The third principle is that, within a particular system, *access to resources* is stable over time. The final principle, called *dynamic equilibrium and succession,* suggests that social systems develop and change via environmental influences. (See Chapter 3, this volume, for a fuller discussion of the bioecological analogy.)

These principles suggest the necessity of having a theoretical model that guides decisions about when, where, and how to intervene in a social system and points out possible effects and side effects. Bower (1972) provides a concrete example of how these principles apply to interventions in school systems. Human adaptation is dependent on interactions with Key Integrative Social Systems (KISS) over time. The primary systems influencing child development are the pregnancy and birth health system, the family, peer play institutions, and the school; secondary influences come from economic and government institutions, religious organizations, and recreational media (Bower, 1972). Given Kelly's ecological orientation it becomes clear that the outcome of social enhancement and disability prevention efforts centered in the schools is dependent on the prior experience of children with KISSs; their current involvement with school, family, and peer systems; and the involvement of those systems with each other and with broader community influences.

An ecological overview provides a realistic framework within which to plan and evaluate intervention efforts. *The social ecology of human systems is highly dynamic,* and only by studying specific systems in detail can one determine the most advantageous points of intervention. Again, it is the goal of one's efforts, the nature of the systems involved, and the available resources that determine the scope of an intervention.

In this chapter we shall describe a long-term preventive mental health program in the schools, beginning with our first efforts and concluding with a summary of our most recent involvement. We shall then discuss this program and its implications from the ecological perspective.

A Multilevel Behavioral-Preventive School Program

The Program and Its Goals

Tolland is a rural community in northeastern Connecticut. Located near the University of Connecticut and also near industry and farmland, there are four schools in this predominantly white, lower-middle-class town. Our work has focused on the kindergarten to fourth-grade population. The goal of our research effort was twofold: to enhance the social well-being of the town's children, and to develop a *model* for school intervention programs that could be generalized to a variety of other settings.

The overall thrust of our initial program, which was begun in 1972, was to build on the strengths manifested by personnel within the system and to help the teachers, students, and parents to increase the skills essential for satisfying, productive social interaction. Three complementary strategies were employed at this stage.

Many investigators have experimented with teaching children specific skills that improve their ability to solve interpersonal problems (D'Zurilla & Goldfried, 1971; Spivack, Platt, & Shure, 1976). We expanded on this work to develop a curriculum on Social-Interpersonal Problem Solving (SPS) Training, which teachers used to instruct children to (1) clearly identify relevant social problems, (2) generate alternative solutions, (3) consider possible consequences of the alternatives, and (4) implement the best alternative. For a full description of this curriculum, see Allen, Chinsky, Larcen, Lochman, and Selinger (1976).

In light of documented evidence that socially withdrawn and isolated children are considerably at risk for later behavioral and emotional difficulty (Cowen, Pederson, Babigian, Izzo, & Trost, 1973), a Companionship Program for Socialization Training was developed to identify such children and work to integrate them into the mainstream of social life in school. Companionship programs, involving the pairing of a child with an older role model and also providing videotape modeling experiences for skill building, were formally pioneered in 1938 as part of the Cambridge-Somerville Youth Study (Powers & Witmer, 1951). Subsequent innovations in behavioral methodology (e.g., Ross, Ross, & Evans, 1971) seem to have greatly enhanced the effectiveness of these programs by specifically defining skills to be developed and systematically training companions to increase these skills in target children. We incorporated these improvements by training college-student companions to interact with socially isolated children on the playground. The efforts of the companions substantially raised the amount of time these children played appropriately with their peers.

Previous research outlined the key skills teachers require for successful management of disruptive classroom behaviors (e.g., observation; targeting; delineation and use of various reinforcers; modeling, shaping, and chaining new behaviors; contingency contracting; extinction, timeout, response cost, and stimulus change) (Allen *et al.*, 1976; Buckley & Walker, 1970). Our third program component, Classroom Management Training for Teachers, involved providing teachers with skills in these areas so that they could better control undesirable behavior in disruptive students. This program resulted in a dramatic decrease in the time such pupils were misbehaving.

The Tolland Project includes a number of separate research and program development efforts. Yet certain features have remained constant since 1972.

First, the program utilizes *collaborative consultation;* that is, it is responsive to the particular needs and circumstances of a given school and is fully owned by that school. University personnel act as teaching consultants and evaluators who build the skills of school personnel to maintain and upgrade the program over time. We view participating teachers as having expert knowledge about the children they work with and about specific environmental factors that could enhance any intervention. We view our own role as that of experts about general behavior change processes, and we seek to combine these two areas of expertise in designing and conducting all programs.

Second, the program has a *multilevel focus.* It recognizes the complex ecology of the school and attempts to address different service aspects with the three programs mentioned earlier, which correspond to primary, secondary, and tertiary levels of preventive programming (Allen *et al.,* 1976).

Third, the program is *behaviorally oriented,* and an "operant spirit" can be detected throughout it. Goals, objectives, and approaches are specified in detail, and all program participants are encouraged to become systematic interpersonal observers and problem solvers.

Rather than present detailed program descriptions available elsewhere (Allen *et al.,* 1976; Elias, 1979; Elias, Larcen, Zlotlow, & Chinsky, 1978; Larcen, 1980; McClure, Chinsky, & Larcen, 1978), the following sections will focus on the key program elements that are most relevant and transferable to other ecological settings.

Entry into the System

The typical plight of a community consultation team can be likened to that of an in-law. Once a stranger, the team now desires acceptance into the system, and wants to make some improvements in the system as well. Whether the family is initially cold and suspicious, open to persuasion, or warm and accepting is important, but the consultant team must work gradually to build its value in the culture of the system and not allow first impressions to dictate the course of events. The consultants must be clear about what they can offer and genuine in their concern for the system. Above all, initial contacts should be used to meet members of as many relevant groups as possible (e.g., administrators, teachers, secretaries, students, parents) so that the consultant team can help specify the explicit and implicit service needs of the system and present an integrated (and negotiable) proposal for consideration.

Because a major objective of our collaborative approach is to help build a school's capability for running a given set of programs once the consultants have departed, it is crucial that time be devoted to *participant-observation* of all aspects of systems functioning. Only after that has occurred and some understanding of the ecology of the setting has been obtained is the consultant team ready to make specific contracts with administrators, teachers, parents, and students. It is important to note that, just as there are in-laws who are never invited back after that first dinner, so there will be school systems that reject consultation efforts. It is far better to reach such an understanding early in the relationship, rather than after time and resources have been committed.

Building a Consultation Team

Although the complexities of the school consultation process are beyond the scope of this chapter, there are several important guidelines that are representative of the collaborative approach (cf. Allen *et al.*, 1976; Meyers, Parsons, & Martin, 1979). Contracts that are negotiated with a school vary in structure and flexibility, but *must* be clear about several key areas: (1) expectations of school personnel for the consultant team, (2) expectations of the consultant team for school personnel, and (3) explicit statements concerning evaluation issues, a topic we shall return to later.

In our experience, initial negotiations have been conducted by university faculty and graduate student project directors; the latter and selected undergraduate on-site project coordinators usually undertake the participant-observation. Once contracts have been arranged, the remainder of the team is assembled. The basic model is a *pyramid* structure that relies on highly motivated and well-prepared mental health paraprofessionals who perform on-site tasks in the schools. These nonprofessionals are usually undergraduates taking a field study course, but they can also be parents or school aides. Training is provided in the technique of collaborative consultation (Allen *et al.*, 1976) and in the specific assessment or programmatic task to be performed. All members of the consultant team, but particularly the project directors, are charged with building the skills of the organization and paving the way for program continuity with constant monitoring and refinement. Figure 1 summarizes the initial phases of the collaborative consultation process.

Not every school system is capable of hosting a multilevel intervention. What follows is an outline of the parameters the authors have found to be useful in such projects, because they can be flexibly adapted to suit the unique social ecology of the setting being consulted. Programs at each level are separate but highly complementary.

Level 1: Developing a Curriculum Program for Enhancing Children's Social Adaptation. The specific context of our curriculum programs has been social problem solving (SPS)—a set of adaptive cognitive-behavioral skills and expectancies found to be important mediators of social adjustment (Allen *et al.,* 1976; Elias *et al.,* 1978; Kaplan, 1975; Spivack *et al.,* 1976). Table 1 outlines these skills and expectancies. Curricula have been developed that incorporate many or all of these abilities for children from preschool age to adolescence and also for parents (cf. Allen *et al.,* 1976; Elias, 1979; McClure *et al.,* 1978; Spivack *et al.,* 1976). Most often, members of the consultant team train teachers, parents, or classroom aides in how to use and adapt SPS. Weekly group workshops are held in which

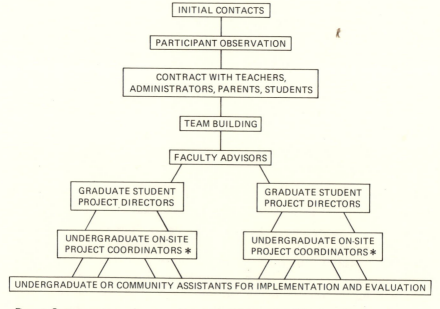

Figure 1. Systems entry and a pyramid team-building model. *These could also be nonprofessionals, such as parents, community volunteers, senior citizens, or peers.

Table 1. Cognitive-Behavioral Skills and Expectancies in Social Problem Solving[a]

Expectancies
1. Internal locus of control
2. Positive and realistic expectancy for successful outcome of situations
3. Generalized tendency to consider multiple alternatives and multiple plans when involved in problematic situations

Cognitive SPS skills
1. Understanding of problem situations
2. Understanding the motives, actions, and perspectives of individuals involved
3. Consideration of possible alternative means to goals and their consequences
4. Specific planning to match particular means to goals
5. Cognitive-behavioral problem resolution strategies

[a]Extensive information concerning these skills can be found in Elias *et al.* (1978).

the prior week's experiences are shared, difficulties resolved, and lesson plans outlined for the following week (Allen *et al.,* 1976). On-site team members provide further assistance as the need arises, but there is a conscious effort to make the pertinent workshop group into the nucleus of future program continuity.

Existing research is not conclusive regarding the most appropriate classroom or home formats for teaching SPS skills. Current evidence does point to a combination of experiential tasks (role playing, practice exercises, and games), guided discussion along with videotape materials, and teacher (or parent) modeling as most likely to have a positive effect, as long as the topics covered are *interpersonal* in nature (Elias, 1979; Spivack *et al.,* 1976). Specific formats for a program will also be dictated by the resources available to the consultant team and the school. Our experience has been that SPS programs are very inexpensive to initiate and even less expensive to maintain (Winans, Lincoln, Larcen, & Elias, 1979).

Level 2: Developing a Companion Program for Early Intervention with Potentially Maladaptive Behaviors. In contrast with Level 1 programs, which are usually administered on a nontargeted basis to entire classrooms or schools, these programs begin with defining target behaviors that indicate a child is at risk for future interpersonal difficulty. Our practice has been to focus on social isolation, but that is a matter to be decided among the consultant team, school personnel, and parents. Referrals can be made by teachers or others familiar with the child's behavior, or through behavioral observation, which can also be used to validate referrals and to define explicitly both the undesirable behaviors and the changes that will denote meaningful improvement.

Although undergraduates seem ideal for the role of companions, the role can also be filled by parents, interested adults, senior citizens, or peers (Cowen, 1973). The training process that seems most promising involves teaching the companions to perform behavioral analyses (Deibert & Harmon, 1970); to learn social reinforcement, modeling, and life-space intervention techniques; and, most importantly, to be empathic and convey understanding and concern through active listening (Allen *et al.*, 1976). Training should precede initial pairings with children, and weekly group meetings should be held to allow companions to share experiences and solve mutual problems.

Training techniques for companions can include specific readings, lectures, role play, and videotaped real-life or simulated companion-child interaction with discussion and feedback. Again, available resources determine the exact form a companion program will take. Such programs do tend to be well tolerated and highly cost effective from a school's point of view; much of the work is being conducted by the consultant team and the school receives direct benefits.

Level 3: Developing a Behavioral Management Program to Restore Children to the Social Mainstream. Whereas a school that implements the programs just described is primarily investing in its ecological future, the classroom management problems of the present often persist unabated. Perhaps the major task of the consultant team is to allow school personnel, in a nonthreatening way, to perceive the value of systematic training in behavior analysis and change techniques. In our experience, it is the problem children that often provide the basis for system entry and, subsequently, productive school–consultant relationships. These children become particularly visible during the participant-observation stage of the collaborative process; also visible are the skills school personnel employ to cope with disruptive behavior. It generally takes little probing and empathic discussion before the costs of the problem behaviors to the child, his/her peers, the teacher, and the school as a whole surface and consultation becomes welcomed.

From this point, various procedures can be employed. Target children can be selected, behaviors and expectancies to be weakened and strengthened can be outlined, skills to be taught to teachers can be specified, and the consultants can gather readings, plan small-group role play and practice exercises, and, if available, employ videotapes of teachers using the techniques as a valuable learning aid. An ongoing workshop format is again a useful training technique. A particular concern in this sort of program is to monitor teacher behavior over time to ensure that skills are being properly applied, and also to measure the radiating effects of training to nontarget children; thus important indexes are gained of the generalizability of training once consultant input ceases (Allen *et al.*, 1976; Kelly, 1971).

The Trilevel Intervention

The principal elements of our multilevel project are summarized in Table 2. Again, each level can be implemented independently, if that is all the school requires. A multilevel program is held together by the fit between the consultant team's interpersonal skills and a concerned and cooperative school. Nowhere is this relationship put to more of a test than during the evaluation phase of a program.

Building an Evaluation Component into Community Programs

A problem found in many community-action programs is a failure to evaluate the intervention adequately. We believe that any project worth trying out is also worth carefully evaluating. In open settings, however, evaluation is often difficult: It creates extra work for the direct service providers and raises staff anxieties about having their performance monitored. We found two guidelines particularly helpful in bal-

Table 2. Schemata of the Multilevel Behavioral-Preventive Intervention[a]

	Level 1	Level 2	Level 3
Level of preventive focus	Enhancement of social adaptation	Early intervention with high-risk children	Restoration of adequate behavioral functioning
Location of program	Classrooms	Peer interaction settings	classrooms
Primary target area	Interpersonal problem solving	Social interaction	Decreasing disruptive behaviors
Primary consultees	Teachers	Paraprofessionals	Teachers
Training format	Workshops	Seminars	Workshops
Program elements	SPS curriculum Videotapes Discussion Experiential	Companions Behavioral principles Videotapes Supervision	Behavior management Contracting Observation Behavioral principles
Primary outcome measure	Social problem solving cognitions	Social behavior	Classroom behavior

[a]Adapted from Allen *et al.* (1976).

ancing our need to investigate program effectiveness against the problems such evaluation creates.

First, a *theoretical model* specifies *what* an intervention is likely to change as well as *how* these changes should occur. By having a model of change, the evaluator can select measures that ought to reflect relevant outcomes and can gather such information in a cost-efficient manner. Evaluation in the absence of a model is haphazard and makes it difficult to determine the overall significance of any consequences created by the program.

Second, a complex intervention will have multiple effects within an ecological system that can reflect changes in self-perception, peer relationships, teacher attitudes, and behavior of all members of the system; thus assessment of these possible effects requires *multiple methods of measurement.* Clearly, an intervention that affects both the *self-reported perceptions* and the *behavior* of participants is preferable to a program that creates change in only one domain.

Our evaluation procedures have been tailored to the concerns of our consultation team and the specific schools with which we have worked. Their suitability for other situations depends on such factors as university involvement, theoretical research concerns, extent of continuity of contact with the consultees, and the particular contracts between the consultants and the school.

Only recently have we begun a concerted effort to create an evaluation component "owned" by the school. This component has taken the form of student and teacher program satisfaction surveys, a program planning questionnaire, and periodic classroom exercise worksheets to monitor the changes in children's SPS skills over time (Elias, 1979). School administrators are also being encouraged to collect and tabulate unobtrusive measures of behavior and systems change, such as referrals to the principal, bus complaints, recess and lunchtime incidents, and so on.

An Ecological Evaluation of the Multilevel Tolland Project

The Tolland Project fulfills some of Kelly's four ecological principles better than others. These differences raise important questions for university-based community psychologists. Table 3 provides an overview of the impact of the various interventions in the school system.

With regard to the social *adaptation* of students, we have found that each level of programming has been generally successful at achieving its respective primary goal: increasing SPS skills, socializing isolates, and modifying disruptive behaviors (Allen *et al.,* 1976; Elias, 1979; Larcen,

Table 3. Summary of Project Evaluation Results

Major assessments	Allen et al. (1976)			McClure et al. (1978)	Larcen (1980)	Elias (1979)
	Level 1	Level 2	Level 3			
1. Social problem solving cognitions	+[a]	n.a.	n.a.	+	+	+
2. In-class process indexes	0[b]	n.a.	0	n.a.[d]	n.a.	+
3. Child self-report	0	0	+	n.a.	0	0
4. Peer ratings	0	0	−[c]	n.a.	0	0
5. Teacher ratings	0	0	0	n.a.	0	+
6. Behavioral observation	n.a.	+	+	n.a.	n.a.	n.a.
7. Internal locus of control	+	n.a.	0	+	+	+
8. Analog situations	+	n.a.	n.a.	+	n.a.	+
9. Consumer benefits	+	+	+	n.a.	n.a.	+

[a]+ = positive impact.
[b]0 = nonsignificant impact.
[c]− = negative impact.
[d]n.a. = not assessed.

1980; McClure *et al.*, 1978). Follow-up studies have been emphasized only for the SPS program; results for the latter suggest that short-term gains are not meaningfully maintained without additional training input (Elias, 1979; McClure *et al.*, 1978). This fact, of course, makes intuitive sense; if our children received only one 6-week reading program in the hopes that gains would endure and the growth curve would continue to climb, then our children would be, for the most part, illiterate.

Closely related are the issues of *interdependence* and *cycling of resources.* At the individual level, we have not uncovered unambiguous evidence that target gains generalize to related areas (i.e., that cognitive change leads to behavioral change, or vice versa). We believe much additional work is required in the area of theory-based measurement before the interdependence of social adaptation abilities can be adequately defined *and* assessed.

At the systems level, we have attempted to work with the natural cycling of students through classes by building programs into the curriculum and training teachers as primary change agents. In order to evaluate the success of this strategy, we must note the operation of *succession* on the school system. When we began our work, open education was embraced as a promising and existing technique. Our most recent study was conducted in an atmosphere emphasizing basic, academic skills (Elias, 1979). However, many of the key trained teachers, supportive administrators, and guidance personnel have left the school system, and the outcome has been unevenness in program continuity. Nevertheless, SPS is taught to all third and fourth graders; some first and second graders are exposed to the training, but there is no continuity after fourth grade. Parent involvement was not continued, despite its empirical superiority over school-only SPS programming (Larcen, 1980). The classroom management program no longer operates and never meaningfully radiated to noninvolved classrooms, despite its empirical value and approval by teachers. Finally, the companion program has endured and is conducted primarily through the university and the school psychologist; however, it also has not significantly spread to other schools and provides little in the way of capacity building for prevention within the school culture.

In summary, the collaborative multilevel behavioral-preventive program we have developed has shown encouraging initial success and seems to be favorably received by school personnel, but still is not fully embedded into the fabric of community life, a life that involves multiple systems. Truly to enhance the social adaptation of the community, we would have to help all of the schools develop programs, particularly for SPS and socialization of at-risk children. The project would need community coordination and, of course, strong parental participation.

Such a task is difficult for community psychologists to accomplish, because their professional roles and training frequently result in their lacking the involvement, long-term commitment, and attachment to the intervention setting that its inhabitants possess (Cowen, 1973). As our consultant team has increasingly recognized our limitations, we have portrayed ourselves more as catalysts, researchers, and temporary, though concerned, visitors into the system rather than ongoing resources. It is perhaps the establishing of this relationship that leads the school to assimilate only that which they can reasonably hope to continue.

We do not wish to end on a pessimistic note, only one of cautious reflection. We believe that the creation of self-perpetuating, self-monitoring programs developed in particular communities by many participating members of those communities is a realistic aspiration. Furthermore, it is ecologically valid as a process that enhances social adaptation because it provides for the development of shared, articulated goals; in this case, we envision these goals as centering around providing children with a social and interpersonal environment in which they can maximize their individual capacities for competence and happiness. When the work of enhancing social adaptation ceases to be accomplished by "techniques" and "interventions," but instead becomes part of the fabric of community life, then genuine constructive ecological change may be said to have begun.

ACKNOWLEDGMENTS

The authors deeply appreciate the opportunity to have worked with Parker Memorial School and Hicks Memorial School in Tolland, Connecticut, and gratefully acknowledge the invaluable collaboration of many friends and colleagues over the years, particularly Andrew Winans, Robert Lincoln, Larry McClure, Susan Zlotlow, Larry Lavoie, Howard Selinger, John Lochman, Julian Rotter, and Reuben Baron. We also wish to thank Brenna Bry, Daniel Fishman, and Lawrence Pervin for their helpful review of earlier drafts of this chapter.

References

Allen, G. J., Chinsky, J. M., Larcen, S. W., Lochman, J. E., & Selinger, H. V. *Community psychology and the schools: A behaviorally oriented multi-level preventive approach.* Hillsdale, N.J.: Lawrence Erlbaum, 1976.

Bower, E. M. Education as a humanizing process and its relationship to other humanizing processes. In S. E. Golann & C. Eisdorfer (Eds.), *Handbook of community mental health*. New York: Appleton-Century-Crofts, 1972.

Buckley, N. K., & Walker, H. M. *Modifying classroom behavior*. Champaign, Ill.: Research Press, 1970.

Cowen, E. L. Social and community interventions. *Annual Review of Psychology*, 1973, *24*, 423–472.

Cowen, E. L., Pederson, A., Babigian, H., Izzo, L., & Trost, M. Long term follow-up of early detected vulnerable children. *Journal of Consulting and Clinical Psychology*, 1973, *41*, 438–446.

Deibert, A. N., & Harmon, A. J. *New tools for changing behavior*. Champaign, Ill.: Research Press, 1970.

D'Zurilla, T., J.,& Goldfried, M. R. Problem solving and behavior modification. *Journal of Abnormal Psychology*, 1971, *78*, 107–129.

Elias, M. J. *Promising strategies for enhancing children's social-cognitive and emotional development.* Paper presented at the meeting of the American Psychological Association, New York, September 1979.

Elias, M. J., Larcen, S. W., Zlotlow, S. F., & Chinsky, J. M. *An innovative measure of children's cognitions in problematic interpersonal situations.* Paper presented at the meeting of the American Psychological Association, Toronto, August 1978.

Kaplan, S. Adaptation, structure, and knowledge. In G. T. Moore & R. G. Golledge (Eds.), *Environmental knowing: Theories, perspectives, and models*. Stroudsburg, Pa.: Dowden, Hutchinson & Ross, 1975.

Kelly, J. G. The quest for valid preventive interventions. In G. Rosenblum (Ed.), *Issues in community psychology and preventive mental health*. New York: Behavioral Publications, 1971.

Larcen, S. W. *Enhancement of social problem solving skills through teacher and parent collaboration.* Unpublished doctoral dissertation, University of Connecticut, 1980.

McClure, L. F., Chinsky, J. M., & Larcen, S. W. Enhancing social problem-solving performance in an elementary school setting. *Journal of Educational Psychology*, 1978, *70*, 504–513.

Meyers, J., Parsons, R. D., & Martin, R. *Mental health consultation in the schools*. San Francisco: Jossey-Bass, 1979.

Mills, R. C., & Kelly, J. G. Cultural adaptations and ecological analogies: Analysis of three Mexican villages. In S. E. Golann & C. Eisdorfer (Eds.), *Handbook of community mental health*. New York: Appleton-Century-Crofts, 1972.

Powers, E. & Witmer, H. *An experiment in the prevention of delinquency: The Cambridge-Somerville Youth Study*. New York: Columbia University Press, 1951.

Ross, D. M., Ross, S. A., & Evans, T. A. The modification of extreme social withdrawal by modeling with guided participation. *Journal of Behavior Therapy and Experimental Psychiatry*, 1971, *2*, 273–279.

Spivack, G., Platt, J. J., & Shure, M. B. *The problem solving approach to adjustment: A guide to research and intervention*. San Francisco: Jossey-Bass, 1976.

Trickett, E. J., Kelly, J. G., & Todd, D. M. The social environment of the high school: Guidelines for individual change and organizational redevelopment. In S. E. Golann & C. Eisdorfer (Eds.), *Handbook of community mental health*. New York: Appleton-Century-Crofts, 1972.

Winans, A., Lincoln, R., Larcen, S., & Elias, M. *An elementary school primary prevention program.* Workshop presented at the meeting of the Connecticut Conference on Prevention: *An Idea Whose Time Has Come*, Hartford, Connecticut, April 1979.

12
Prevention of Cultural-Familial Mental Retardation

HOWARD L. GARBER AND RICK HEBER

Prevention—a term often associated simplistically with immunization against a specific disease—takes three major forms. The first and more widely known form is *primary prevention,* which is designed to incapacitate the disease-producing agent and therefore stop the anticipated occurrence of the disease. Immunization with vaccines is an example of this form of prevention. *Secondary prevention* has been defined as those activities undertaken to intervene after disease can be detected but before it is symptomatic. A third form, *tertiary prevention,* is defined as those activities undertaken to prevent the progression of symptomatic disease or illness (Report To The Congress, February 6, 1979). The definition of secondary prevention has been further refined to include (1) early diagnosis and prompt screening, and (2) disability limitation, or adequate treatment to arrest disease, stop further complications, and avert death (Report To The Congress, February 6, 1979). It is with primary and secondary prevention, and more specifically with the first aspect of secondary prevention, as it relates to mental retardation, that this chapter is concerned.

No easy way has been found to reduce the incidence of mental retardation. Some forms of mental retardation do lend themselves to spe-

HOWARD L. GARBER AND RICK HEBER • Rehabilitation Research and Training Center in Mental Retardation, University of Wisconsin, Madison, Wisconsin 53706. The research reported in this chapter was supported in part by Grant 16-P-56811 from the Social and Rehabilitation Service of the Department of Health, Education and Welfare.

cific treatments that can prevent or reduce the effect of the causative agents, as in the effects of rubella on the unborn infant or the accumulation of lead in the blood of the young developing infant. For the most part, however, there has been little success in preventing cultural-familial mental retardation (Clarke & Clarke, 1977).

The term "cultural-familial retardation" designates a certain kind of mild retardation (see Grossman, 1973; Heber, 1961). The term "mild mental retardation" is applied to an individual who has scored somewhere between 50 and 80 on a standardized IQ test with national norms. In actual practice the upper cutoff is 70 and is often accompanied by an impairment in adaptive behavior. There is some arbitrariness to the cutoff point and to the index of adaptive behavior. In any event, this category of mental retardation includes most—nearly 80%—of all those individuals who are ever identified as mentally retarded. Not only is it the largest category, it is also the most controversial, for at least two reasons. First, its origins are obscure because of its mildness. Whereas other forms of mental retardation have some etiologic referent (e.g., Down's syndrome, PKU), the origin of cultural-familial retardation rests on a statistical association between such epidemiologically derived referents as family IQs or cultural-group association. Second, there is an excess prevalence of low IQs in minority and low-socioeconomic population groups, and because of the nonspecific origins of this form of retardation the casual observer is led to judge the existence of retardation simply on the basis of those obvious characteristics displayed by these groups. However, neither the poverty nor the ignorance of health factors among these groups provides sufficient explanation for the high occurrence of low IQs among them. In fact, most persons in these groups score within the normal range of IQ, though showing features of other subgroup members who have been identified as mentally retarded.

A study of the origins of mild mental retardation is fundamental to any attempt at prevention. Those cases of mental retardation for which there are etiologic referents are disease syndromes that are now, in a majority of situations, fairly well understood. However, in mild mental retardation little research information has been available, and attempts to program health and social services for these individuals have therefore been relatively ineffective. One reason for this ineffectiveness is that most programs have allocated resources on the basis of the obvious but misleading characteristics of poverty and sociocultural background.

The Present Study

In an effort to understand the origins of cultural-familial mental retardation, we undertook an extensive epidemiologic investigation of one group that showed an extremely high prevalence of low IQs. This group was identified through United States Census Bureau statistics and data from the Milwaukee public schools. These data showed that in a set of inner-city census tracts that were extremely depressed by economic measures, there was also a very high rate of special-class (EMR, or educable mentally retarded) children. In fact, although containing less than 5% of the city's population, this grouping yielded nearly 33% of the EMR children. At this point we began to interview and test, door-to-door, all the residents with new live births in the area and at least one other child of age 6 (see Heber & Garber, 1975; Heber, Dever, & Conry, 1968). Among the findings from this extensive survey, and the most critical for the development of our hypothesis on how to *prevent* mild mental retardation, was the variable of maternal intelligence—which proved by far the best single predictor of the level and character of intellectual development in the offspring.

We separated mothers into two IQ groups of above and below 80 IQ. We thus found that less than half of the mothers, 45%, were responsible for nearly 80% of those children with IQs below 80. In addition, although it is generally acknowledged that severely disadvantaged children score lower on intelligence tests as they grow older, we found that actually there is a marked difference in the intellectual development of children from severely disadvantaged backgrounds as a function of their mothers' IQs. Figure 1 shows that children born to mothers with IQs above 80 (upper curve) remain in the normal IQ range with increasing age—in sharp contrast to the children born to mothers with below 80 IQ. As can be seen in the bottom curve of Figure 1, these children decline in IQ with increasing age until, at approximately 16 years old, their mean IQ approximates the mean maternal IQ, which is in the upper 60s. It appears, therefore, that although all of these families reside in the same physically disadvantaged environment, they can be differentiated by the IQ of the mother. It can also be seen that in the early years of development the mean IQ of the offspring of mothers with below 80 IQ is essentially in the normal range.

This analysis gave us some clues to the origins of mild mental retardation. It suggested that certain identifiable families living in poverty were producing children with retarded intellectual development at a greater rate than was the population at large; but that these children's IQs declined over time from the normal to a retarded level. Hence we hypothesized that if we could intervene in the lives of these families before this decline reached retarded IQ levels, it might be possible to mitigate the effects of whatever environmental forces were operating to depress intellectual performance.

These surveys convinced us that the very high prevalence of mental

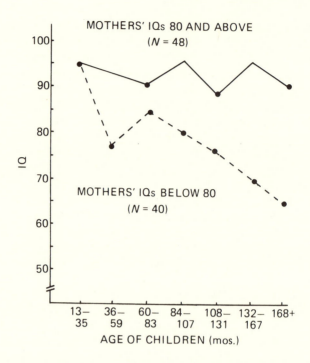

Figure 1. IQ development among children with mothers above and below 80 IQ.

retardation associated with the "slums" of American cities is not randomly distributed but, instead, is concentrated within individual families who can be identified on the basis of maternal intelligence. In other words, the source of the excessive prevalence of mental retardation appeared to us to be the retarded parent residing in the slum environment, rather than the environment itself in any general sense.

These population survey data have been taken by some to support the prevalence of hereditary determinants of "cultural-familial" mental retardation. However, our observations indicate that the mentally retarded mother residing in the slum does not transmit her retardation biologically but instead creates a social environment for her offspring that is distinctly different from that created by her next-door neighbor of normal intelligence.

Most importantly, these survey data suggested to us the feasibility of conducting the longitudinal, prospective research essential to a more adequate understanding of the determinants of the kind of retardation that perpetuates itself from parent to child in the economically deprived family. In other words, as a consequence of the survey data, we utilized maternal IQ as a tool for selection of a sample consisting of families with newborns, in the confidence that a substantial percentage would be identified as mentally retarded as they grew older. By screening all mothers of babies born in our survey area over nearly 2 years, we identified mothers of newborns with IQs less than 75. Forty of these mentally retarded mothers, each with a child from 3 to 6 months old, were assigned to either an experimental or a control group. There were no significant birth anomalies in any of the children, who were therefore normal at birth but according to our sampling statistics were at a 16 times greater risk for retardation.

Although our geographic study area was racially mixed, our sample was confined to black families because of the substantially lower mobility of the black population in that particular section of Milwaukee. Clearly, a longitudinal study would be seriously weakened if its test sample were decimated by attrition.

The 20 experimental families were entered into an intense rehabilitation program with two primary emphases: (1) education, vocational rehabilitation, and homemaking and childcare training for the mother; and (2) an intense, personalized intervention program for their newborns that began in the first few weeks of life. The objectives of this intervention were to displace the presumed negative factors in the social environment of the infant being reared in the slums by a retarded mother. We made an effort, thereby, to test the social deprivation hypothesis by attempting to stymie retardation in the normal offspring of these retarded mothers.

It was our contention that, should the experimental children reach school age and exhibit normal intelligence, we would know that it is indeed possible to prevent mental retardation from occurring at the present high frequency in this group. Should they exhibit a retarded level of functioning, we would at least know that their intensive exposure to learning experiences of the type we provided was not sufficient to displace their biosocial predispositions for intellectual functioning.

Family Rehabilitation Program

Initially, each experimental family was assigned one special teacher whose responsibility was to establish rapport, gain the family's confidence, and work with both the mother and the newborn in the home. Once the teacher had gained the mother's confidence, the infant began to attend our infant center every day from 9:00 A.M. to 4:00 P.M., 5 days a week, on a year-round basis. The mother began her own rehabilitation program when the child began participation in our infant intervention program.

One major objective of the maternal program was to change the manner in which the economically and intellectually disadvantaged mother interacted with her children, managed the home, and operated within the community. At the outset, a major obstacle was clearly the attitude of many of the mentally retarded mothers themselves: a mixture of hostility and suspicion toward social agencies, and a sense of both personal and economic despair. Through improved employment potential, increased earnings, and self-confidence, it was hoped that positive changes in the home environment would occur.

Over the course of the maternal rehabilitation program, the emphases changed. Initially, the focus was on the mother's vocational adjustment. Since a number of the families did not have a father who produced a stable income, occupational training and placement was of major importance. After formal vocational training and placement was completed, increased emphasis was given to remedial education as well as homemaking and childcare skills. As rapport was established with the parents, our staff was increasingly called upon by them to intervene and assist in internal family crises and, not uncommonly, in conflicts with the community.

The occupational training progam utilized two large, private nursing homes in Milwaukee. The nursing homes were chosen as a site for training because of the appropriate job skill areas they afforded, the availability of professional staff with some understanding of rehabilitation problems, and the employment opportunities available in nursing homes and other chronic care facilities. The basic remedial academic curriculum emphasized reading, writing, and arithmetic, or basic literacy training. In addition, the curriculum included childcare techniques, home economics, community-oriented social studies, interpersonal relations, and home management.

The experimental mothers showed some significant changes in behavior and attitude in dealing with their children. On experimental task measures of mother–child interaction, the experimental mothers encouraged communication between themselves and their children. They tended to use verbally informative behaviors as compared to the nontask-oriented physical behaviors shown by the control mothers (and by the experimental mothers at the beginning of the program). As we noted earlier, changes in the mother's attitude, self-confidence, employment, and her sensitivity to the needs of her family are very important and indicate an improvement in her ability to care for her family.

By every measure, the most effective component of our maternal program was the vocational one. We were successful in placing all mothers in employment where the family situation made doing so feasible. Their record of job stability and work performance has been distinctly superior to that of the control mothers. Among the mothers in both groups who are presently working, the experimental mothers are earning an average of 40 dollars per week more than the control mothers.

Our direct infant intervention program began shortly after the children reached the age of 3 months and continued until they entered public school. The general goal of our intervention program was to provide an environment and a set of experiences that would foster the acquisition of cognitive skills and allow each child to develop socially, emotionally, and physically. The program focused heavily on the development of language and cognitive skills and on maintaining a positive and responsive learning environment for the children.

The general intervention program is best characterized as having a cognitive-language orientation implemented through a planned environment utilizing informal prescriptive teaching techniques. By "informal prescriptive teaching," we mean that, in planning appropriate activities, each teacher would (1) make direct observation of the child's strengths, weaknesses, and preferences; (2) gear tasks and experiences specifically for this child; and (3) evaluate the effect of the task or experience on the child.

Most importantly, the program gave major emphasis to the social and emotional development of the children. Although language and cognitive development were the foundation, it was recognized that essential to making the system work was the child's desire to utilize these skills; in other words, the child's motivation. We attempted to develop achievement motivation by designing tasks and creating an atmosphere that would maximize interest and provide success experiences, ensure supportive and corrective feedback from responsive adults, and thus gradually increase the child's responsibility for task completion.

Assessment of Intervention

In order to assess the effects of this 6-year, comprehensive intervention in the natural environment of the infants and their retarded mothers, we undertook an ambitious schedule of measurements. It included medical evaluations, standardized and nonstandardized tests of general intelligence, experimental learning tasks, measures of mother–child interaction, and a variety of measures of language development.

Both the experimental and control subjects were on an identical measurement schedule that was keyed to each child's birth date, beginning at 6 months and carried out through age 6. The particular measure administered at a given session depended on the predetermined schedule of measures for that age level. Transformations of scores from a number of measures that have been administered at varying age levels showed that there was a sustained differential in performance in favor of the experimental children across the entire preschool program.

We began to test the children from both groups at 6 months old with the Gesell Developmental Schedules and then continued at 18 months with language assessment, and at 24 months with Cattell and Stanford-Binet tests and psychological learning tasks. When the children reached 30 months, we began our mother–child interaction assessment. A series of more sophisticated tests of language development began when the children were 36 months old.

Gesell data revealed the earliest differences in development between experimental and control infants. At 14 months the control group was already 3 to 4 months behind the experimental group. At 22 months the experimental group was 4½ to 6 months ahead of the control group on all four Gesell schedules, and the control group had fallen below Gesell norms on the adaptive and language schedules. In fact, the earliest divergence in performance was on the language schedules of the Gesell from 14 to 18 months. The language differential has continued and shows perhaps the most dramatic differences between the two groups. Figure 2 summarizes some of the more sophisticated measures of language development, such as tests of grammatical comprehension, sentence repetition, and morphology. We have tried to show that the difference in early language development was nearly twofold between groups. Each bar shows that the control group's performance level on any of the three tests was only a portion (about half) of the experimental group's performance at a particular age. The implications for school of this differential in preschool language performance are clear.

It is these same skills in language that we observed powerfully demonstrated in the mother–child interactions. It was the experimental child in the dyad who was mainly responsible for the strength of the interaction. In other words, the elicitation of the appropriate events for problem solving was done by the child, as were the prodding and shaping of the mother's verbal responses. In effect, the child supplanted the mother in the dyad as the educational engineer. No such changes occurred in the control mother–child dyads.

In experimental problem-solving tasks, the experimental children's performance was faster and more successful. They were enthusiastic and

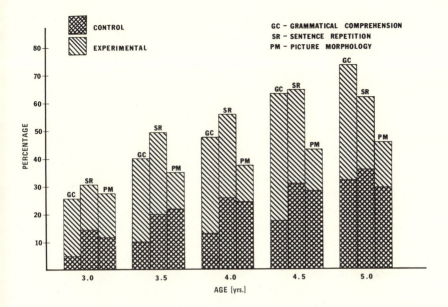

Figure 2. Comparative performance on language tests.

conscientious about the tasks, tending to use strategy behavior where appropriate. In marked contrast, the control children were unenthusiastic and relatively passive, tending to be uninterested and/or unable to develop appropriate problem-solving skills.

By the time the children entered the first year of school, there were substantial differences in their performance on IQ tests. Across the 6-year school program, on the Stanford-Binet, the mean IQ of the experimental group was about 123, compared to 94 for the control group. At 72 months the experimental group was at 121 and the control group at 87 on the Stanford-Binet. On the basis of these data we have been able to conclude that it is indeed possible to prevent this form of mental retardation.

We have continued to assess postintervention performance at roughly 1, 2, 3, and 4 years after school entry. One major question is, of course, the extent to which the gains of intervention will be maintained as time goes on. Based on data obtained to this point, at least, the WISC differential on the order of 20+ IQ points has been maintained over a 4-year follow-up to age 10. More striking as an index of the differential performance between the groups is the proportion of children who fall more than one standard deviation below test norms at successive age levels. Virtually no experimental children have tested below IQ 85, whereas for control children there has been a marked increase in low scores as age has increased. By age 10 nearly two-thirds of the group scored below 85 (Garber & Heber, 1981).

Discussion

How should these results be viewed thus far some 4 years after the conclusion of our family intervention? First, it is absolutely clear that our experimental children were extraordinarily well prepared to enter public school as compared with their less fortunate control peers. On virtually every behavioral measure experimental children were distinctly superior, and in a number of measures there was little or no overlap in performance between the groups.

As for our maternal intervention program, we were successful in the essential task of preparing the mothers for employment, which has proved reasonably stable. The mothers' stated aspirations for all of their children have been distinctly elevated as a result of their participation in the Milwaukee Project. But at the same time, we believe that we have been far less effective in changing each mother's social patterns, her ability to remain free of conflict with her community, and, most importantly, her modes of interacting with her children. Conflicts that we had been able to help resolve through crisis aid as part of intervention now continue unabated and have perhaps increased. We refer to social conflicts involving the mother within the family, those involving her friends outside the family, and those involving the police and other community agencies.

We have seen genuine problems of school adjustment emerge as well. With frequently poor communication between school and parent, simple problems are exaggerated to the detriment of the children. For example, notes are often sent home requesting a meeting and frequently our mothers do not respond; the public school teacher is thus led to believe the mother is not interested, rather than understanding that she may be unable to read or that the note's request is not clearly stated. On the mother's part, her unquestioning attitude of "schools know best" has led to placement decisions for the children with no parental input.

Observing the performance of our experimental children at the end of the preschool program, it was difficult to conceive of their ever dropping down to the performance level of the control group. Those of us who have participated in this experience witnessed a capacity for learning on the part of these children dramatically in excess of their epidemiologically based expectations. Now, however, some 4 years into follow-up, we are rapidly approaching the view that intervention and support for children reared with an intellectually inadequate parent and living in a disrupted family environment must continue throughout the child's school as well as preschool years. It has become evident that for some families there are parent–school incompatibilities and disrupted family living environments that act continually to erode the accomplishments of our intervention effort.

From our own research and that of others, it also appears that many families, although having in common many key indicator variables, are quite different in family process. Furthermore, although most of the children from these families respond favorably in a fairly similar fashion to preschool programs, the manner in which the benefits from such programs are sustained can differ widely in accordance with family situations, which can range from total family disruption to an approximation of our stereotype of the middle-class family. Therefore we continue to be cautious in interpreting our data because we are mindful that it is only a small portion of time and a small portion of the experiences in the lives of these families that we have influenced. Many years came before we entered their lives and many years are yet to come, especially for the youngest. We must be mindful that there is yet considerable room for all members of these families both to learn and unlearn appropriate and inappropriate behaviors. Nevertheless, our findings do nothing to inhibit the hope that it may indeed prove possible to prevent the high frequency of mental retardation among children reared by parents of limited intellectual competence under circumstances of severe economic deprivation.

How can the results of the Milwaukee Project described in this report be translated for use in a community mental health program concerned with prevention of mental retardation? Of first priority is the identification of families in need of help because of their at-risk status (Garber & Maykut, 1980). These families could, at least initially, be identified through the public schools. In school, the special-class or Exceptional Educational Needs (EEN) student from a seriously disadvantaged family can provide a telltale clue to a family in serious need of social services, who, furthermore, may have one or more children on the way to school with similar needs. Outreach in the public schools today is desperately needed since many of these families are either afraid of the schools, which they deem "authority," and/or are unaware of their responsibility in extending the educational process into the home. As information on the characteristics of such families is accumulated, a high-risk profile could be developed. This profile could then be used, for example, in a hospital setting to assign risk status, and, in effect, a priority-of-need status. This risk index would initiate a subsequent process for following by health and social services of the high-risk family. And, if ethical observers are selected, there need not be the fear associated with risk registries, as Firth (1952) suggests.

Second, as these families are identified and their needs assessed, the social service delivery should be comprehensive. By "comprehensive," we mean that the needs of all members of the family are considered, including home management and vocational needs, as well as child services; and that social service is not limited to "colorful, informative" brochures that illiterate parents cannot read. Service needs of these families also include the need for advocacy and help in obtaining access to social services. The Office of Human Development reported statistics in 1978 that indicate the majority of individuals seeking service are ultimately never served. An earlier report by the Rand Corporation with a similar commentary indicates that less than 3% of the national budget is devoted to prevention, screening, identification, and referral (Brewer & Kakalik, 1974). In other words, what the Rand Corporation reported in 1974, and OHD confirmed in 1978, is that what is actually a splendid system is not being fully utilized. There is neither effective service at the time of entry nor an attempt to follow through and adjust service to the evolving needs of the client. Treatment comes after the fact, if at all.

Third, schools must not only understand the unique problems that confront the children from such families, but must also—perhaps even more importantly—work toward eliminating the notion of irreversibility regarding disadvantaged children (e.g., see Rist, 1970). This attitude can blunt the effect of even the most ambitious programs. Indeed, the responsiveness of the families and the high performance levels obtained by the children in our program are testimony to both the desire and potential to achieve among many disadvantaged families. There is every reason to believe that mental retardation can be prevented and that the key is to reduce the factors that contribute to the elevation of risk. These include health problems, inability to manage the home and family, lack of vocational skills, limited employment opportunities, and the learning and social habits that impede academic success.

The results of the Milwaukee study demonstrate that the cornerstone of prevention is a screening and identification system that can pinpoint families in need. Although the present typical screening system is child oriented, we find that a *family screen* is more appropriate in the case of the child at risk for mental retardation. It must be remembered that these children are essentially normal through the early years of life. With no presenting symptoms, they may pass through the screen, though later they may well develop problems in school or in life. There are two aspects to screening: One is altruistic, the other a cost–benefit matter. In the first case, effective family screening can identify priority families—that is, those with the most urgent needs and therefore children at highest risk. In doing so, we can program services according to the range of needs of the disadvantaged population. Second, there are major cost–benefit implications if resources are not allocated according to the needs of individual target families. Money is being spent for services not used or needed by certain families while those families in greater need receive less than adequate levels of support. The result is less effective treatment, with greater demand for follow-up services.

Prevention remains a difficult issue. In medical prevention, vaccines have been developed that can in some cases immunize an individual against life-threatening forces for a lifetime. However, no comparable preventive measure appears possible for the ills that beset the seriously disadvantaged family with a retarded mother. After the rehabilitation program ends, there remain poverty, similarly disposed peers, poor schools, social services difficult to obtain, and the ignorance and suspicion that interferes with getting help with life's crises. The prevention of mental retardation requires a comprehensive, easily accessible, coordinated community health services program (see Aiken, Dewar, DiTomaso, Hage, & Zeitz, 1975). Such a program does not rely entirely on self-initiated diagnosis or on the obvious pathologies (medical or social), but through its screening system develops epidemiologic risk information on which preventive programming can be based. Furthermore, to the extent that service delivery can be facilitated, it is the responsibility of community health programs to improve both their services and the ability of those who will use these services to do so.

ACKNOWLEDGMENT

The authors wish to acknowledge the editorial assistance of Elena V. Reyes.

References

Aiken, M., Dewar, R., DiTomaso, N., Hage, J., & Zeitz, G. *Coordinating human services.* San Francisco: Jossey-Bass, 1975.

Brewer, G. D., & Kakalik, J. S. *Serving handicapped children: The road ahead* (Mimeograph). Santa Monica, Cal.: Rand Corporation, 1974.

Clarke, A. D. B., & Clarke, A. M. Prospects for prevention and amelioration of mental retardation: A guest editorial. *American Journal of Mental Deficiency,* 1977, *81,* 523–533.

Firth, R. Ethical absolutism and the ideal observer. *Philosophic Phenomenologic Research*, 1952, *12*, 317–345.

Garber, H. L., & Heber, R. The efficacy of early intervention with family rehabilitation. In M. J. Begab, H. C. Haywood, & H. L. Garber (Eds.), *Psychosocial influences in retarded performance*. Vol. II. *Strategies for improving competence*. Baltimore: University Park Press, 1981.

Garber, H. L., & Maykut, P. *Manual of technical assistance for the use of family rehabilitation programming as preventive therapy in high risk populations*. Madison: University of Wisconsin Press, 1980. (Monograph)

Grossman, H. J. (Ed.). *Manual on terminology and classification in mental retardation*. (Rev. ed.). Baltimore: Garamond/Pridemark Press, 1973.

Heber, R. *A manual on terminology and classification in mental retardation*. Washington, D.C.: American Association on Mental Deficiency, 1961.

Heber, R., & Garber, H. The Milwaukee Project: A study of the use of family intervention to prevent cultural-familial mental retardation. In B. Z. Friedlander, G. M. Sterritt, & G. E. Kirk (Eds.), *Exceptional infant*. Vol. III. *Assessment and intervention*. New York: Brunner/Mazel, 1975.

Heber, R., Dever, R., & Conry, J. The influence of environmental and genetic variables on intellectual development. In H. J. Prehm, L. A. Hamerlynck, & J. E. Crosson (Eds.), *Behavioral research in mental retardation*. Eugene: University of Oregon, 1968.

Report to the Congress (by the Comptroller General). *Early childhood and family development programs improve the quality of life for low-income families* (U.S. General Accounting Office, HRD-79-40). Washington, D.C.: U.S. Government Printing Office, 1979.

Rist, R. C. Student social class and teacher expectations: The self-fulfilling prophecy in ghetto education. *Harvard Educational Review*, 1970, *40*, 411–451.

13

Behavioral and Community Interventions during Transition to Parenthood

FRANCIS MATESE, SUSAN I. SHORR, AND
LEONARD A. JASON

When dealing with primary prevention interventions, behavioral-community practitioners can select classical conditioning, operant, modeling, or cognitive restructuring strategies either to (1) prevent the onset of specific disorders; (2) ensure that children from high-risk populations do not succumb to disorders; (3) strengthen competences to enable people to better withstand life stresses; or (4) help individuals cope with major transitions (Glenwick & Jason, 1980; Jason, 1980). Primary preventive interventions might also focus on using activist or consultative tactics to stimulate the formation of both formal or informal support groups in the community (Gottlieb, in press).

The community-oriented programs we shall discuss in this chapter illustrate preventive-transition and support group interventions. The first project was an operant skill training program for parents before the birth of their first child. The second project led to the evolution of a self-help group that served a social support function during early parenthood.

FRANCIS MATESE, SUSAN I. SHORR, AND LEONARD A. JASON ● Psychology Department, De Paul University, Chicago, Illinois 60604.

Parenthood as a Crisis or Transition

A central assumption of crisis theory, as articulated by Lindemann (1944) and Caplan (1964), is that crises are opportunities for growth or for regression. Based on a review of the literature, Taplin (1971) identifies five central components of crisis theory. First, during the normal maturational processes of life, individuals experience a succession of crisis events or stresses. Second, crises have the potential to cause personal disruption or strain if resolved in a maladaptive way. A third assumption is that crises are more accessible to amelioration at their peak. Fourth, assistance in resolving crises does not necessarily come from skilled professionals. Finally, the onset of a crisis usually involves identifiable external or internal precipitants. Psychological well-being might be thought of as the consequence of a history of successful crisis resolutions.

Theorists and researchers disagree as to whether the period of parenthood should be viewed as a crisis. Four theoretical models (i.e., systems, social-cultural, developmental-stage, and role transition) represent the alternative viewpoints.

A systems theory supports the notion that parenthood is a crisis that changes the established family equilibrium (Lidz, 1963). The birth of a child necessitates a shift in family roles as the nuclear family changes from a dyad to a triad (Donnor, 1972). In addition, differences in childrearing philosophies between generations may add stress to the family system (Gilberg, 1975). Loss of sleep, chronic exhaustion, confinement to the home, additional housework, decline in sexual response, and increased economic pressures are other changes that may upset the family equilibrium (Donnor, 1972). Data supportive of this theory have been collected by LeMasters (1957) and Dyer (1963), who found that the birth of the first child constitutes an "extensive" or "severe" crisis for many new parents.

Societal and cultural theories have also been used to support the notion of parenthood as a crisis (Crummette, 1975; Donnor, 1972; Gilberg, 1975; Rossi, 1968). The lack of preparatory education on parenting increases the chances that parents will be inadequately equipped to function in their new role. In addition, the romanticization of family life creates unrealistically high expectations for success and happiness. In reality, the new parent is frequently confronted with unanticipated demands and challenges that are likely to provoke anxiety. Furthermore, the mobility inherent in our present society limits a parent's access to an extended family, traditionally a major source of support for new parents (Gilberg, 1975).

Developmental theorists conceptualize parenthood as a predictable maturational crisis that signifies progression from one life stage to another (Benedek, 1959; Erikson, 1959; Hill, 1949). New parenthood is one of a succession of life stages, each of which requires adaptation so that further maturation can occur. The new role of parenthood is an especially difficult adjustment because of its abruptness and irrevocability (Rossi, 1968). Fatigue, lack of REM sleep, hormonal changes, mood shifts, and frequent crying are among the psychological and physical stresses of the postpartum period (Leifer, 1977).

A fourth, evolving theoretical position views the crisis perspective with its implied negative outcomes as an incongruous and restrictive approach to understanding new parenthood. For example, recent findings indicate that the gratifications of childrearing clearly outweigh the stresses (Hobbs, 1965; Hobbs & Cole, 1976; Meyerowitz & Feldman, 1966; Russell, 1974; Wandersman, 1978a). Viewing parenthood as a role transition rather than as a crisis emphasizes the gratifying as well as the stressful aspects of childrearing (Hirschowitz, 1976; Rossi, 1968; Silverman, 1976). The emphasis on coping in role transitions contrasts with the crisis perspective, which implies immobilization or regression. Given this life transition perspective, it is possible to conceptualize and formulate preventive interventions to facilitate coping behaviors among new parents. In devising such programs, investigators might borrow from the extensive literature on behavioral parent training.

Behavioral Parent Training

Considerable evidence indicates that behavioral principles can be effectively used in training parents to care for their children (Gelfand & Hartmann, 1968; Graziano, 1977; Tavormina, 1974; Tramontana, 1971; Ullmann & Krasner, 1965; Werry & Wollersheim, 1969). The advantages of using behavior modification include: (1) Parents unskilled in sophisticated therapy techniques can easily learn to implement behavior modification principles; (2) behavioral procedures can be taught to many parents at one time; (3) techniques can be taught in a short training period; (4) parents prefer a behavioral treatment model that stresses learning to a "sickness" orientation; and (5) the methods have been used effectively with a wide range of childhood disorders. Many behavioral practitioners strongly feel that, wittingly or unwittingly, parents use behavioral techniques to change or maintain their children's behavior. If that is true, it might be useful systematically to instruct parents to apply these principles consistenly and to decide explicitly which behaviors to develop in their children (Hawkins, 1972).

Training parents in groups has two clear advantages: (1) A greater number of parents can be provided services; and (2) groups engender both peer support and active discussion (Graziano, 1977). One of the first attempts at training groups of parents in behavioral principles was conducted by Pumroy (1965). Pumroy found that the experimental groups, who were provided lectures on behavior modification, learned the behavioral principles, and 10 of the 11 program families reported favorable changes at a 2-month follow-up. Walder, Cohen, Breiter, Datson, Hirsch, and Leibowitz (1969) and Hirsch and Walder (1969) successfully used didactic group training and individual consultation to increase knowledge of behavior modification principles and to reduce children's problem behaviors. Behavioral counseling has helped parents to become more confident, to show more favorable attitudes toward their children (Howard, 1970), and to reduce children's deviant behaviors (Walter & Gilmore, 1973). Finally, Jason and DiAmicis (1977) describe a successful behavioral training program for low-income parents that helped them learn a different set of childrearing skills and enhanced their feelings of self-worth and confidence.

In contrast to studies on training parents to deal with already existing child behavior problems, Sirbu, Cotler, and Jason (1978) focused on a nondeviant population—parents whose children were developing normally and who had expressed interest in learning behavioral child management techniques. The mothers were randomly divided into groups that received either a behavioral programmed text and weekly sessions, weekly behavioral group sessions, a behavioral text, or attention–placebo "rap sessions." All three training groups were significantly more effective than the attention–placebo group, suggesting that effective parent training is contingent on the clear and systematic presentation of behavior modification principles and not on the format in which these principles are delivered.

Although the evidence for the efficacy of behavioral parent training is convincing, there has been a preoccupation with youngsters with clear-cut dysfunctions as opposed to behavioral parent training before the onset of childhood difficulties. For example, a primary prevention intervention might focus on training parents in behavioral principles before the birth of their first child.

Behavioral Training before Childbirth

The primary prevention intervention focused on preparing parents for the transition to parenthood through instruction in behavioral principles. Through receiving training in behavioral skills that could be implemented with a nonverbal infant, parents were expected to adjust more successfully to the birth of their first child.

Participants in the comparison and behavioral training groups were first-time pregnant couples enrolled in two Lamaze birth classes. The comparison group received only Lamaze training, whereas the behavioral group received Lamaze instruction and training in behavioral principles. Both groups were pre- and posttested to assess their knowledge of behavioral principles. Following the birth of their child, the parents filled out a questionnaire that assessed how well they coped with the experience of having a child. The behavioral training group was provided four 45-minute sessions on behavioral principles and their application to infants and young children.

Program Description

The lectures in the behavioral training program were derived from Becker and Becker's (1974) *Successful Parenthood*. The first session consisted of explaining the basic principles of the behavioral approach and illustrating the use of various behavioral techniques. Differences between natural and learned reinforcers as well as social, token, and activity reinforcers were explicated. Parents were then instructed in ways to use these various reinforcers to accentuate desired behaviors. For example, the parents were told to get excited when using verbal praise. They were also instructed to use a variety of types of praise, to concentrate on rewarding behaviors as opposed to the entire child, to use activities of the day as rewards, and to warn or give a buffer before requiring their child to stop doing a favored activity. The advantages of positive reinforcement over negative reinforcement or punishment were also discussed. The session also stressed the importance of using cues or reminders to help keep a behavioral program consistent and to record regularly children's progress as a reward for the parents themselves.

The second session focused on the use of reinforcement and the administration of basic teaching principles. Although negative aspects of punishment were again discussed, during this session appropriate uses of punishment were also presented. For example, "don't signals" (such as, No, Don't, and Stop) were introduced as verbal cues that could be associated with punishers and thereby act as a substitute for punishers. In addition, alternatives to physical punishment, (e.g., withholding of rewards and response cost) were emphasized. In regard to basic teaching procedures, parents were instructed to plan goals, pick reinforcers, and divide the process into clearly defined behaviors. Techniques for "chaining" basic learning episodes into longer behavior sequences were also discussed. Illustrations were provided of the benefits of backward chaining. For example, in tying a shoe, the chain of behaviors is always strongest toward the final consequence; therefore completing the bow should be the first behavior established.

The final two sessions revolved around issues that might occur during a child's first 2 years of life. Parents were taught ways to meet the needs of their infants by (1) learning to anticipate needs by being aware of past behaviors; (2) learning to read their infants' signals before a problem occurred; and (3) teaching the infants to read their parents' signals through repeated and consistent associations. Consistency in feeding and sleeping, as well as helping the infants develop stable routines, were also discussed. Other major topics included establishing toilet training routines, encouraging exploration and play, reinforcing social interaction, dealing with aggressive behaviors, and teaching children how to use rules.

Evaluation

Although some parents enjoyed the behavioral training, others were more interested in the Lamaze part of the sessions. This fact suggests that some parents might need the presence of a child to be sufficiently motivated to participate in behavioral training. The parents seemed to be most interested in those sessions that dealt with toilet training and managing resistive and aggressive behaviors. As for program evaluation, the parents gained significantly more knowledge than the controls did about behavioral principles and their applications; however, there were no differences concerning their comfort in dealing with the actual birth of their child. The potential benefits of the intervention on parent and child behavior cannot be determined until more long-term follow-up data are available.

Support Groups for New Mothers

The second intervention involved the creation of a support group for mothers who had recently given birth to their first child. Since the transition to parenthood precipitates a significant narrowing of a couple's support networks (Duvall, 1971; White, 1974), it might be important to provide first-time parents access to support groups. Regrettably, there are few formal or informal resources that provide emotional support during the critical stage of new parenthood. Although pediatricians and nurses provide medical care and supervision, they are often unavailable for support or to answer many nonmedical questions about childcare. As a consequence, many mothers are forced to rely on their own resources during the early postpartum period.

In a comprehensive review, Cobb (1976) finds that social support mitigates the consequences of life stress in a variety of situations. Research also indicates that social support and parenting information are helpful during the early postpartum period. For example, mothers provided information on breast-feeding and social support from other breast-feeding mothers evidenced a better ability to breast-feed than mothers who had one or neither of these forms of assistance (Ladas, 1972; Silverman & Murrow, 1976). In another study, participation in a support group prompted new parents to increase the use of informal resources in their social support networks (McGuire & Gottlieb, 1979). Wandersman (1978b) reports that new parents reacted favorably to parenting groups that focused on explaining concepts in child development, optimizing family functioning, clarifying roles, and developing competence. These studies suggest that new parents can be provided with coping skills and support to ease the transition to parenthood. Given the importance of the first year of life for both parent and child, such programs may well help to establish strong, enduring parent–child relationships.

The intervention to be described was designed to provide support and coping skills for new mothers in order to ease their transition to the parent role. Five long-term goals were (1) to create a social network in order to reduce feelings of isolation; (2) to provide emotional support to the new mothers; (3) to help them comfortably assume a new identity as a parent; (4) to facilitate the achievement of a sense of competence as a parent; and (5) to help the mothers assume leadership roles within the program. Although a professional consultant stimulated the formation of the self-help group, the mothers assumed responsibility for conducting meetings and for generating program ideas.

Program Description

The project was conducted in the consultation and education department of a Chicago-based community mental health center. Mothers with children up to age 3 were recruited from Lamaze classes, maternity departments of local hospitals, diaper services, and local newspapers. After three initial open-house meetings, a core group of eight mothers began to attend biweekly group sessions. Babies, ranging from 2 to 10 months old, were brought along and served as a central focus of attention and conversation. In addition, three of the mothers had 2-year-olds who were also brought to meetings.

Group consensus was used to select the discussion topics for each meeting. Over the 5-month program, topics included coping with an infant's constant crying, dealing with feelings about breast-feeding and bottle feeding, adapting to changes in the marital relationship following childbirth, resolving feelings about leaving or returning to work, coping with postpartum blues, learning behavioral childcare skills, and finding ways to relate positively to in-laws. Although the consultant was specifically asked to answer some questions about childcare, the majority of the mothers' questions were directed to the group and answered by other group members.

With regard to group process, members easily self-disclosed personal feelings and were responded to with understanding and acceptance. Advice was commonly exchanged between newer and more experienced mothers. Over time, the focus of discussion shifted from the members' own experiences to several broader issues. For example, the mothers expressed feelings of anger toward society for viewing motherhood as a low-status job. Others expressed disappointment over the lack of preparation they had received before assuming their new roles. Still others raised concerns that it was no longer socially acceptable to remain home with an infant, since mothers are now expected to reenter the work force. There emerged a general consensus that the importance of childbearing is increasingly neglected in our contemporary society. The members seemed to find comfort and reassurance in the group's validation of their ideas and values.

Evaluation

All the members expressed positive feelings about their participation in the group. Their enthusiasm is possibly because the group provided a central focus in their lives and an important source of consensual validation. As a result of the group, many of the mothers formed new friendships that extended outside of group meetings. At this point, the mothers have taken the initiative to expand the breadth of the program for the upcoming year. For example, they are planning to (1) form new groups to be led by the experienced members; (2) allow new mothers to join the ongoing support groups; (3) launch evening workshops for fathers and mothers to discuss topics related to childbearing; and (4) set up a telephone system throughout the winter months (experienced mothers will call new mothers on a regular basis to offer support and guidance). This program is being planned collaboratively by the consultant and the group members. The upcoming programs will be formally evaluated to determine their effectiveness and cost efficiency.

Conclusion

The two community-oriented interventions described in this chapter suggest new roles for mental health professionals. In the first project, the behavioral-community practitioner adopted an educational approach to helping parents acquire requisite knowledge and skills to enhance development of their children after birth. A basic assumption in this approach was that establishing and strengthening parent skills would ultimately contribute to producing more stable and healthy children. In the second community intervention, a consultant helped create a self-help group for new mothers. The support group was designed to make the parenthood transition less disruptive and more productive. As the mothers gained confidence, they assumed more responsibility in planning future directions for the self-help group. In both interventions, the community-based professionals served as catalysts in the implementation of the programs.

Both studies should be perceived as exploratory. Future primary prevention parent training programs will need to document changes in parents' behaviors, assess long-term salutary alterations in parent–child interactions, and ensure random assignment of parents to treatment conditions. At this point, efforts are under way to better identify parents with requisite interests and motivation to participate in behavioral training before the birth of their first child. As for the self-help group, intensive evaluation is planned for the upcoming year. A wide assortment of criterion measures will be used to assess functioning of parents within the support network and those in a delayed control group. In addition, attempts will be made to assess short- and long-term attitudinal as well as behavioral changes in both fathers and children.

References

Becker, W. C., & Becker, J. C. *Successful parenthood.* Chicago: Follett, 1974.

Benedek, T. Parenthood as a developmental phase. *American Psychoanalytic Association*, 1959, *78*, 389–417.

Caplan, G. *Principles of preventive psychiatry.* New York: Basic Books, 1964.

Cobb, S. Social support as a moderator of life stress. *Psychosomatic Medicine*, 1976, *38*, 300–314.

Crummette, B. P. Transitions in motherhood. *Maternal Child Nursing Journal*, 1975, *4*, 65–73.

Donnor, G. Parenthood as a crisis: A role for the psychiatric nurse. *Perspectives in Psychiatric Care*, 1972, *10*, 84–87.

Duvall, E. *Family development.* New York: J. B. Lippincott, 1971.

Dyer, E. D. Parenthood as crisis: A re-study. *Marriage and Family Living*, 1963, *25*, 196–201.

Erikson, E. The problem of ego identity, identity, and the life cycle. *Psychological Issues*, 1959, *1*, 101–154.

Gelfand, D. M., & Hartmann, D. P. Behavior therapy with children: A review and evaluation of research methodology. *Psychological Bulletin,* 1968, *69,* 204–215.

Gilberg, A. L. The stress of parenting. *Child Psychiatry and Human Development,* 1975, *6,* 19–22.

Glenwick, D. S., & Jason, L. A. (Eds.). *Behavioral community psychology: Progress and prospects.* New York: Praeger, 1980.

Gottlieb, B. H. Opportunities for collaboration with informal support systems. In S. Cooper & W. F. Hodges (Eds.), *The field of mental health consultation,* in press.

Graziano, A. M. Parents as behavior therapists. In M. Hersen, R. M. Eisler, & P. M. Miller (Eds.), *Progress in behavior modification* (Vol. 4). New York: Academic Press, 1977.

Hawkins, R. P. It's time we taught the young to be good parents (and don't you wish we'd started a long time ago?). *Psychology Today,* 1972, *6,* 28–40.

Hill, R. *Families under stress.* New York: Harper & Bros., 1949.

Hirsch, I., & Walder, L. Training mothers in groups as reinforcement therapists for their own children. *Proceedings of the 77th Annual Convention of the American Psychological Association,* 1969, *4,* 561–562.

Hirschowitz, R. G. Groups to help people cope with the tasks of transition. In R. G. Hirschowitz & B. Levy (Eds.), *The changing mental health scene.* New York: Spectrum Press, 1976.

Hobbs, D. F. Parenthood as a crisis: A third study. *Journal of Marriage and the Family,* 1965, *27,* 367–372.

Hobbs, D. F., & Cole, S. P. Transition to parenthood: A decade replication. *Journal of Marriage and the Family,* 1976, *38,* 723–731.

Howard, O. F. *Teaching a class of parents as reinforcement therapists to treat their own children.* Paper presented at the meeting of the Southeastern Psychological Association, Louisville, Kentucky, April 1970.

Jason, L. A. Behavioral approaches to prevention in the schools. In R. H. Price, R. F. Ketterer, B. C. Bader, & J. Monahan, (Eds.), *Prevention in community mental health: Research, policy and practice* (Vol. I). New York: Sage, 1980.

Jason, L. A., & DeAmicis, L. An approach in providing preventive mental health services to low-income parents. *International Journal of Family Counseling,* 1977, *5,* 29–33.

Ladas, A. K. Information and social support as factors in the outcome of breastfeeding. *Journal of Applied Behavioral Science,* 1972, *8,* 110–114.

Leifer, M. Psychological changes accompanying pregnancy and motherhood. *Genetic Psychology Monographs,* 1977, *95,* 55–96.

LeMasters, E. E. Parenthood as crisis. *Marriage and Family Living,* 1957, *19,* 352–355.

Lidz, T. *The family and human adaptation.* New York: International Universities Press, 1963.

Lindemann, E. Symptomatology and the management of acute grief. *American Journal of Psychiatry,* 1944, *101,* 141–148.

McGuire, J. C., & Gottlieb, B. H. Social support groups among new parents: An experimental study in primary prevention. *Journal of Clinical Child Psychology,* 1979, *8,* 111–116.

Meyerowitz, J. H., & Feldman, H. Transition to parenthood. *Psychiatric Research Report,* 1966, *20,* 78–84.

Pumroy, D. K. *A new approach to treating parent-child problems.* Paper presented at the meeting of the American Psychological Association, Chicago, September 1965.

Rossi, A. S. Transition to parenthood. *Journal of Marriage and the Family,* 1968, *30,* 26–39.

Russell, C. S. Transition to parenthood: Problems and gratifications. *Journal of Marriage and the Family,* 1974, *36,* 294–301.

Silverman, P. R. Mutual help. In R. G. Hirschowitz & B. Levy (Eds.), *The changing mental health scene.* New York: Spectrum Press, 1976.

Silverman, P. R., & Murrow, H. G. Mutual help during critical role transitions. *Journal of Applied Behavioral Science,* 1976, *12,* 410–419.

Sirbu, W., Cotler, S., & Jason, L. Primary prevention: Teaching parents behavioral child rearing skills. *Family Therapy,* 1978, *5,* 136–170.

Taplin, J. R. Crisis theory: Critique and reformulation. *Community Mental Health Journal,* 1971, *7,* 13–23.

Tavormina, J. B. Basic models of parent counseling: A critical review. *Psychological Bulletin,* 1974, *81,* 827–835.

Tramontana, J. A review of research in behavior modification in the home and school. *Education Technology,* 1971, *11,* 61–64.

Ullmann, L. P., & Krasner, L. *Case studies in behavior modification.* New York: Holt, Rinehart & Winston, 1965.

Walder, L. O., Cohen, S. I., Breiter, D., Datson, P., Hirsch, I., & Leibowitz, J. Teaching behavioral principles to parents of disturbed children. In B. G. Guerney, Jr. (Ed.), *Psychotherapeutic agents: New roles for non-professionals, parents, and teachers.* New York: Holt, Rinehart & Winston, 1969.

Walter, H. I., & Gilmore, S. K. Placebo versus social learning effects in parent training procedures designed to alter the behavior of aggressive boys. *Behavior Therapy,* 1973, *4,* 361–377.

Wandersman, L. P. *Longitudinal changes in the adjustment to parenthood.* Paper presented at the meeting of the American Psychological Association, Toronto, 1978. (a)

Wandersman, L. P. Parenting groups to support the adjustment to parenthood. *Family Perspectives,* 1978, *12*(3), 117–128. (b)

Werry, J. S., & Wollersheim, J. P. Behavior therapy with children: A broad review. *American Academy of Child Psychiatry Journal,* 1969, *6,* 346–370.

White, R. W. Strategies of adaptation. In G. Coehlo, D. Hamburg, & J. Adams (Eds.), *Coping and adaptation.* New York: Basic Books, 1974.

14

Media and Community Organization for Prevention Programs

ALFRED MCALISTER

Mass media are believed by many to hold great promise as educators and agents of positive social influence. The seeming simplicity of an extensive mass media campaign and the larger number of persons reached make it an attractive alternative for cost-effective intervention in social problems arising out of individual behaviors (e.g., eating habits, tobacco and alcohol abuse, failure to use safety restraints in automobiles). However, most research on public service media makes them appear to be ineffective.

Analysis of the limitations of media influence and of the necessary supportive conditions for its effectiveness points toward the necessity of combining *media and community* intervention in order for substantial changes in complex personal habits to be achieved. Encouraging illustrations of that assertion are available, but further development and demonstration research is clearly needed.

ALFRED MCALISTER ● Harvard University School of Public Health, Boston, Massachusetts 02115. The author is grateful to the American Institutes for Research for their support in preparation of this chapter.

Effects of Mass Media: Overview of the Literature

Scientific theories concerning the effects of the mass media are varied and often contradictory. Some theorists believe that media are powerful influences on behavior; others consider their effects to be relatively insignificant concomitants of general economic and environmental conditions. Between these extreme positions, several general ideas about media effects are being articulated with considerable confidence.

McCombs and Shaw (1972) discuss and document what they call the "agenda-setting" function of mass media. The importance of issues and ideas tends to be judged by the amount of media coverage they receive. Thus what people think and talk about may be profoundly influenced by the content of newspapers and broadcasts, as well as entertainment programs or popular novels. Of course, the process also works the other way: Media tend to reflect their audiences' interests. The point is that talk and thought are known to be relatively easily evoked, but that significant changes in behavior or changes in firmly held attitudes are not so easily produced. In short, then, *media influence what people think and talk about.*

Simple choices are influenced by media, particularly choices among consumer goods for which a need already exists or can be easily created. Thus, for example, the sale of such items as beer can be profitably manipulated through television advertising. In a billion-dollar market, a .1% increase in share means a millon-dollar jump in revenues. Thus media are attractive to marketers even if their effects involve only a few percentage points. Media are considered worthwhile investments by political campaigners for the same reasons. However, the point here is that only very simple behavioral alternatives are influenced; that is, pulling one voting lever instead of another or picking one package off a shelf instead of another. To sum up, *media influence simple choices.*

The general relationship between a violent society and violent media is clearly reciprocal, and media may be more a reflector than a mold for culture. However, specific instances of violent or other unwanted behavior can almost certainly be attributed to mass media (Bandura, 1971). The epidemic of skyjacking that followed the widespread report of a successful airplane hijacking represents a particularly striking instance of the power of mass media. Even more striking was the beating and intimidation that occurred on a subway in New York shortly following the broadcast of a similar event in *The Incident.* It seems clear, then, that *media can have unwanted effects.*

Children seem especially susceptible to both advertising and violent models in the mass media (Liebert, Neale, & Davidson, 1973). Young children lack the critical faculties necessary to analyze intelligently the arguments and appeals used by commercial advertisers (Ward, Reale, & Levinson, 1972). They do not always understand the contexts and motives of televised violence and may imitate aggressive models indiscriminately (Liebert, 1972). On the positive side, programs such as "Sesame Street" appear to accelerate cognitive growth to some extent (Lesser, 1974). On the whole, *children appear to be more easily influenced than adults.*

Klapper (1960) and many others find the data concerning effects of intentional social action campaigns to be extremely disappointing. A recent example is O'Keefe's (1971) study of the effects of the antismoking spots that were broadcast about 10 years ago. His survey found that these public service announcements (PSAs) only rarely influenced decisions to stop smoking, though they occasionally were felt to support decisions that had already been made. Although they were widely believed to be effective, only a few individuals could be found who attributed change in behavior primarily to the antismoking spots. Another example is Robertson and Kelly's (1974) failure to show effects of television messages promoting safety belt use. Thus *public service media tend to appear ineffective.*

The preceding five generalizations are not encouraging to public and governmental interests considering the use of media to produce positive changes in behavior. The idea of solving important social and public health problems through the mass media would appear to be almost ludicrous. However, if their limitations are properly understood, television and other mass media can, in many circumstances, be combined with other interventions to become cost-effective instruments of social change.

Bandura (1969) explicitly distinguishes between *acquisition* and *performance* in his analysis of the effects of depicted action sequences. New words, ideas, simple actions, even complex sequences of behavior can be *acquired* from simple observation. But their *performance* depends on positive expectations and the presence of facilitating environmental conditions. This distinction highlights the importance of the immediate environment and the individual's perception of that environment in determining media effects. No matter how effectively they teach or preach, the behaviors that media recommend are not likely to be adopted unless environment and experience support the recommendation. Public service campaigns often attempt to promote changes that have immediate unpleasant consequences (e.g., stopping smoking) or that are pitted against strong social customs (e.g., moderating alcohol consumption). Thus it should be no surprise that their effects are small or nonexistent.

The most important aspect of environment and experience is *social support*, that is, the responses of other people to a person's decisions and actions. Most media effects tend to occur through multistep communication processes in which opinion leaders select and analyze messages for their circle of family, friends, and acquaintances (Rogers & Shoemaker, 1971). This important concept is also supported by research on schooling through media: Difficult material demands the assistance and support of a classroom teacher (Chu & Schramm, 1967). To be effective, a media campaign must accompany or engender a supportive social environment.

A second important aspect of environment is the existence of an effective *mechanism* for translating intention into action (Cartwright, 1971). For example, it does little good to advertise the benefits of a low-sodium diet unless salt-free foods are inexpensive and readily available. Urging people to stop smoking may be useless unless a specific plan of action is offered. In general, the effectiveness of a mass media campaign depends on the specificity of the behaviors it recommends and the presence of favorable opportunities to perform that behavior. Often extensive training in the skills of self-control may be needed to translate intentions into action (Thoresen & Mahoney, 1974).

Community Intervention

It is clear, then, that mass media cannot be expected to have much effect unless an environment supporting their content already exists or can be created. In a nonsupportive or ambiguous environment, media alone will have little or no effect on complex behaviors. This fact leads to the conclusion that community intervention beyond media is necessary for an ambitious social program to be effective.

Community interventions may take many forms, depending on the existing environmental conditions and the goal of the agency interested in bringing about change. In its simplest form, community intervention involves little more than an effort to *make recommended alternatives available*. For example, a media campaign aimed at increasing the consumption of low-sodium food must be accompanied by community interventions to ensure that such foods are available at the marketplace. A campaign for exercise such as bicycling will be greatly aided by the building of bicycle paths.

Another form of community intervention is the *organization of social support*. Rogers (1973) discusses this issue thoroughly in relation to the promotion of contraceptives in developing countries. One approach that this form of intervention can take is the recruitment and training of opinion leaders to spread a message. Existing organizations and institutions (schools, unions, etc.) may be recruited and adapted for this purpose. In some cases it may be necessary to develop an entirely new network of community support.

A more elaborate form of community intervention is the organization of social support into planned efforts to teach *self-help skills*. Organized groups dedicated to self-help and mutual support can be powerful agents of change, especially if their activities are guided and coordinated by well-produced mass media. An excellent example is the "radio forum" often employed in developing countries (Rogers & Shoemaker, 1971). Individuals seeking to learn, for example, the latest methods of farming gather to listen to radio instruction; following the broadcast they conduct a lengthy session of discussion and group problem solving. Much of the rapid development of postwar mainland China can probably be attributed to the leadership's skillful use of this procedure.

Another form of community intervention is *organization for political and economic power* (Zaltman, Kotler, & Kaufman, 1972). Voter groups, trade unions, and consumer boycotts fall into this category. Typically, all of the three forms of intervention we have looked at are combined, usually with leadership originating with a skilled community organizer. The question is what ingredients is one necessary to motivate widespread participation and the establishment of a solid network of local leadership. Organization and management of political parties is a particularly good model for this kind of activity.

Successful Media and Community Interventions

In light of the scope and complexity of the issues that must be considered in the development of effective media and community intervention, it is hardly surprising that few outstanding examples of effective efforts are available. Too many efforts have been doomed from the beginning by a naive approach and/or a lack of careful planning and analysis of the communication problem. However, even when the theories and principles discussed previously are creatively synthesized, an intervention may fail to show "success" because it has not been properly evaluated. The requirements of design and measurement for generating reliable conclusions about the effects of large-scale interventions are stringent (e.g., Cook & Campbell, 1976). Control sites or populations must be carefully selected to avoid biases that could make it impossible to draw correct inferences about effects. Goals on several levels must be specified and measured with precision and validity.

A number of interventions may be cited as indications of success in the application of media and/or community intervention (e.g., Bogartz & Ball, 1972; Douglass, Westley, & Chaffee, 1970; Mendelsohn, 1973; Mielke & Swinehart, 1976). But methodological weaknesses in the evaluations of these efforts range from the obvious to the esoteric (e.g.,

Cook, Appleton, Connor, Schaffer, Tamkin, & Weber, 1975), and very few strong conclusions can be drawn from them.

Fortunately, however, there are three well-researched interventions that do provide reliable information about the potential of media and community programs for positive social change. These three projects are exemplary in their utilization of sophisticated intervention procedures and rigorous evaluation methodology.

Stanford Three-Community Study

The Stanford Three-Community Study (Maccoby, Farquhar, Wood, & Alexander, 1977) was a large-scale field experiment designed to study the effects of mass media and face-to-face interventions on knowledge, attitudes, and behaviors relevant to the prevention of heart disease (e.g., eating habits, smoking). Three northern-California communities were selected for study. One received only annual surveying of a random sample of inhabitants. Another received surveying plus an intensive and sustained media campaign including virtually all media, carefully designed according to principles of social psychology. The third community received surveying, the media campaign, and a program of intensive face-to-face instruction for a random sample of two-thirds of those who exhibited high risk for heart disease (high blood pressure and cholesterol, smoking). This design allowed the assessment of the effects of the media campaign in a quasiexperimental form (i.e., without randomization) and the evaluation of the incremental effect of face-to-face intervention in both quasi- and "true" (randomized) experimental fashion. Both self-reports and physiological measurements (e.g., plasma cholesterol) were used to track these effects over 3 years.

The results were moderately encouraging. Media combined with surveying demonstrated a significant effect in comparison with surveying alone. This effect was in the form of changes in knowledge and attitudes and, more importantly, changes in means for blood pressure and cholesterol levels. Although these changes were fairly small (in the range of 5%), they were of a magnitude that, if sustained, could lead to corresponding changes in mortality and morbidity. Analysis of those changes indicated that they were because of alterations in diet, particularly fat and salt consumption. Simple and specific changes in that regard had been recommended by the media campaign and were easily accomplished in a favorable environment (e.g., margarine and low-fat milk were readily available and were becoming increasingly popular). Thus a moderately favorable result was achieved.

However, in other variables the media campaign alone produced no lasting change. As would be expected, these variables were characterized by personal difficulty and environmental resistance. For example, smoking cessation was recommended, and some specific guides for quitting were provided via media. But given the addictive qualities of tobacco and the lack of consistent environmental support for cessation, the media campaign was not effective. Increased exercise was promoted; but in an environment dominated by the automobile and supportive of the belief that physical exertion is undignified for nonathlete adults, no evidence of a change in activity patterns was detected.

Media alone may have had no effect on these more complex variables, but there was strong evidence that smoking behavior could be influenced by a combination of media and community intervention in the form of intensive face-to-face instruction. Among those receiving the face-to-face counseling there was a high rate of cessation (approximately 30% if the full sample is considered). This finding can be interpreted as a clear demonstration of the importance of social support and self-help skills, and it highlights the need for an integration of media and community intervention in order to maximize influence on complex and problematic behaviors.

North Karelia Study

The North Karelia Study (Puska, 1978) was a large-scale field experiment aimed at studying the reduction of heart disease through the implementation of a remarkably well-coordinated combination of media and community intervention. In eastern Finland the province of North Karelia, long noted for its prevalence of heart disease, asked the government to develop a program to reduce this problem. The neighboring province of Kuopio was selected as a comparison population, and a (still continuing) longitudinal study of cardiovascular mortality and morbidity, physiological risk factors, behavior, knowledge, and attitudes was conducted in both provinces through improved record keeping at hospitals and health centers, surveillance of food and tobacco consumption, and periodic examination and survey of random samples from both provinces.

Mass media were important elements in the campaign that was conducted in North Karelia. Radio and newspapers were the dominant media (television was not widely available in this rural area), although leaflets and posters were also extensively employed. A comprehensive program of community intervention was also conducted. The program was administered directly through the provincial health organization. Training programs were conducted that included influential members of voluntary organizations, journalists, and reporters, as well as opinion leaders nominated and recruited on the local level. In addition, changes in local health services were made in order to improve the detection and control of hypertension. Finally, modifications in the availability of foodstuffs were made by encouraging dairies to produce low-fat products, helping meat producers develop and market a special low-fat sausage, and increasing the production of vegetables in family and community gardens.

By comparing the two provinces' trends in physiological variables, self-reported behavior, attitudes and knowledge, as well as rates of mortality and morbidity, a meaningful assessment can be made of the effectiveness of the integrated intervention. Because the program was based in local communities, an extraordinary degree of awareness and support was generated. Data indicate that modest but meaningful changes in dietary and smoking habits were achieved and sustained (in the range of 10% to 20%). The drive to control hypertension was especially successful; the number of individuals on antihypertensive medication was greatly increased. In addition, there are preliminary indications that a reduction in mortality and morbidity due to strokes and heart disease may be attributed to the combined media and community intervention conducted in North Karelia.

United States–Finland Collaborative Study

McAlister (1976) performed a small-scale laboratory study in which one group of smokers was given direct counseling from an expert, and another (randomly assigned) group watched on closed circuit television. An untrained volunteer from the community acted as a leader and coordinator for the television-viewing group. The expert counselor often spoke through the camera to this group, thus also instructing them and their leader in the various suggestions and techniques that were being provided to the direct-counseling group. The two groups achieved very similar and sustained reductions in smoking rate and incidence (approximately 50% abstinence rate at a 6-month follow-up), comparable to the best results observed in intensive interventions. Similar results were obtained among several additional volunteer-led groups that were organized to view rough tapes of those sessions. These data are very encouraging because they suggest that the ability to widely disseminate effective counseling may be limited only by the number of volunteer-led, self-help groups that can be formed to view broadcasts similar to the programs used in this study.

Smoking Cessation Course on Television. Based on that notion, a comprehensive smoking cessation course was broadcast on Finnish television during February and March 1978, and intensive field activity was organized to encourage the formation of active viewing groups. The aims of the program were to assist adults who wished to stop smoking, and to increase general interest about the activities needed for reduction of smoking in the community. The television program was organized and conducted by the national public television network and the North Karelia Project. It consisted of seven sessions, each approximately 45 minutes long, over 1 month and featured a studio group of 10 voluntary smokers. The direct costs of producing and broadcasting the program were about $8,000, and about a week's work was required of two experienced cessation counselors.

The content of the program series represented an effort to combine the most successful group methods that had been used in previous work in Finland (Koskela, Bjorkqvist, Puska, Neittaanmaki, & jaSalonen, 1977) with new ideas and experiences arising out of research in the United States (McAlister, 1974). The program's most important aspect was its focus on preventing relapse rather than on achieving temporary change. This aim was accomplished through individual analysis of probable cause of relapse, development of specific plans for coping with those anticipated problems, and active practice of those coping skills. Relaxation and stress management exercises (e.g., Bernstein & Borkovec, 1973) were important tools, as were training in dietary self-control (e.g., Mahoney & Mahoney, 1976) and self-instruction (e.g., Mahoney, 1975).

Each program featured a group of 10 voluntary smokers (six men and four women, from 20 to 60 years old). Sessions were led by two experts from Finland (Pekka Puska and Kaj Koskela). Those leaders spoke both to the group, which thus received direct counseling, and to the camera, simultaneously giving remarks and advice to the viewing population. Each session was broadcast as it occurred, with minimal editing. The first session was preparatory and included instructions on recording and analyzing smoking behavior. In the second and third sessions the participants engaged in a brief session of rapid smoking (Lichtenstein, Birchler, Wahl, & Schmahl, 1973), which was modified to reduce the intensity and duration of stress on the pulmonary and cardiovascular systems. Instead of having the group smoke at a rate of one inhalation every 6 seconds over several sessions or until no more smoke could be tolerated, only one 10-minute session of puffing twice every 15 seconds was conducted. Viewers were told the procedure could be unsafe and were advised not to attempt it at home. From the second session on, a major effort was made to help each participant analyze and predict potential causes of relapse. Plans for avoiding or coping with such events and situations were developed, discussed, and practiced through mental rehearsal or role playing where appropriate. The latter sessions also included extensive instruction in dietary self-control and practice of stress management skills.

All but the last sessions were delayed broadcasts, timed so that the final, live session would reveal the 6-month follow-up experiences of the television group. The fact was announced only in the sixth session, and viewers were invited to write to the group leaders about their experiences or problems. During the last session many of those letters were read and commented on by the television leaders. Most of the television group stopped or greatly reduced smoking. By the last (6-month follow-up) session, six said they were still not smoking and three told of substantial reductions in smoking.

Community Organization. The program series was promoted throughout Finland, but in the province of North Karelia special community organization efforts were conducted. This intensified field activity was conducted through the established channels and networks of the ongoing North Karelia Project (Puska, 1974), which had been in operation for several years. The aim was to increase opportunities for individuals to view the television programs in an organized, supportive group environment. Personal letters, as well as the press and radio, provided extensive coverage and cooperation for the recruitment effort. Local health centers and community groups were contacted personally by staff from the project. Those who volunteered to help form and lead self-help groups received printed instructional and follow-up material. By the start of the program about 200 leaders had volunteered, or about one for every 300 to 400 smokers in the province.

The intensified field activity in North Karelia provided a natural experiment that allowed comparisons against other provinces in Finland where such local actions were not consistently organized.

Results. Results of the program obtained from national surveys, conducted 1 month before and one month after, show a nonsignificant decrease in the percentage of persons reporting some cessation. Internal analyses found that female heavy smokers reported a 6.3% decrease and male moderate smokers a 4.8% decrease, both significant at the .05 level of confidence.

Results from the panel study of older male smokers in North Karelia and Kuopio show effects of the intensified community activities that were conducted in North Karelia. Viewership and participation in that province were almost twice as frequent as in Kuopio. However, the percentages of actual reported success in the two provinces did not differ significantly either at the 1-month or the 6-month follow-up interval, perhaps because of the small sample sizes. Among those in the samples who reported that they viewed more than four programs and attempted cessation, 43% achieved temporary success and 27% maintained 6 months of nonsmoking.

We believe it can be reasonably estimated from our data that about 1% of the smokers in Finland achieved at least 6 months of cessation, at least partly as a result of the program series and the events surrounding it. That would translate into about 10,000 cases of sustained cessation. If our estimate is accurate, the results are unusually *cost effective*: About one dollar was spent for each 6-month success.

Discussion. Community activities seem to have increased participation, but the data that were collected did not make it possible to detect the unique effects of viewing context on the success of viewers. Comparing those who viewed in group settings with those who viewed alone or with minimal family involvement would be fruitless because of self-selection into those categories. However, we continue to believe that the creation of a supportive social environment is an essential accompaniment for any counseling that might be delivered through the mass media. What we do conclude from this experience is that much more needs to be learned about how such support can be effectively mobilized.

The method of delivering counseling described in this chapter can readily be extended from the problem of cigarette smoking to many other behavioral problems that often require counseling. The growing dissatisfaction with the efficacy of professional and institutional methods of delivering psychological and preventive medical services and, at the same time, the rapid emergence of self-help groups and peer counseling (Katz & Bender, 1976) may signal a need for change in the way that such services are delivered. Print and audiovisual treatment methods for such problems as weight reduction (Mahoney & Mahoney, 1976), phobias (Denholtz & Mann, 1975), and sexual dysfunctions (Lowe & Mikulas, 1975) are becoming increasingly common. Although most of these mediated treatment strategies have not been thoroughly evaluated, the results of the study reported here suggest that some audiovisual versions of counseling may be effective if supplemented by coordination and support from volunteer leaders or peer counselors.

If media-assisted self-help is indeed an effective way of providing behavioral counseling on a large scale, the role of the behavioral science professional may shift somewhat from direct provider of treatment toward media producer (e.g., Edwards & Penick, 1973) and community organizer (e.g., Reiff & Riessman, 1965). Rather than dealing with individuals in an institutional or office setting, the professional may deal with organizations and other natural aggregations of persons in the context of the total community (Iscoe, 1974) by providing instructional media, by facilitating the formation of self-help groups and recruiting peer counselors, and by providing consultative services. In this way, the efforts of each professional can be multiplied and the helping strategies developed in behavioral science can be efficiently delivered to the entire community.

Conclusion

The studies we have looked at confirm the views presented earlier on mass media effects in planned social education programs. Although most public service media tend to appear ineffective, these studies show that if the media are carefully designed and are supported by community intervention where necessary, a favorable impact may be possible. The following are some key points:

1. The translation of media recommendations into public action depends on their environmental and experiential consequences.
2. Social support is important, especially for difficult changes.
3. The environment must include an effective mechanism for translating intention into action.
4. Communication effectiveness may be markedly improved by employing the framework and theories of behavioral and social psychology.
5. The most effective approach is to combine media with comprehensive community intervention.
6. Rigorous design and measurement procedures must be employed for valid assessment of the effects of media and community intervention.

Despite these encouraging conclusions, there is still much to be learned about the nature of media and community interventions and how they can be most effectively conducted. There are many pressing social problems to which they may be applied, but few positive examples of their utility. Every effort to solve social problems through approaches of this sort should be conducted in a spirit of scientific exploration, seeking to expand our knowledge and understanding of the potentials and limitations of media and community intervention. That can be accomplished by ensuring that theory and research from the fields of communication and behavioral psychology are carefully considered in the intervention and that sophisticated design and measurement procedures are employed in its evaluation.

References

Bandura, A. *Principles of behavior modification.* New York: Holt, Rinehart & Winston, 1969.

Bandura, A. *Social learning theory.* Morristown, N.J.: General Learning Press, 1971.

Bernstein, D. A., & Borkovec, T. *Progressive relaxation training.* Champaign, Ill.: Research Press, 1973.

Bogartz, G. H., & Ball, S. *The second year of Sesame Street: A continuing evaluation.* Princeton, N.J.: Educational Testing Service, 1972.

Cartwright, D. Some principles of mass persuasion. In W. Schramm & D. F. Roberts (Eds.), *The process and effects of mass communication.* Urbana, Ill.: University of Illinois Press, 1971.

Chu, G. C., & Schramm, W. *Learning from television: What the research says.* Palo Alto, Calif.: Institute for Communication Research, Stanford University, 1967.

Cook, T. D., Appleton, H., Connor, R., Schaffer, A., Tamkin, G., & Weber, S. J. *"Sesame Street" revisited.* New York: Russell Sage Foundation, 1975.

Cook, T. D., & Campbell, D. T. The design and conduct of quasi-experiments and true experiments in field settings. In M. D. Dunnette (Ed.), *Handbook of industrial and organizational psychology.* Chicago: Rand McNally, 1976.

Denholtz, M. S., & Mann, E. G. Automated audiovisual treatment of phobias administered by nonprofessionals. *Journal of Behavior Therapy and Experimental Psychiatry,* 1975, *6,* 111–115.

Douglass, D. F., Westley, B. H., & Chaffee, S. H. An information campaign that changed community attitudes. *Journalism Quarterly,* 1970, *47,* 479–487.

Edwards, J. E., & Penick, E. C. Evaluating the use of television in community mental health education. *Hospital and Community Psychiatry,* 1973, *24,* 771–773.

Iscoe, I. Community psychology and the competent community. *American Psychologist,* 1974, *29,* 607–613.

Katz, A., & Bender, E. *The strength in us: Self-help groups in the modern world.* New York: New Directions, 1976.

Klapper, J. T. *The effects of mass communications.* Glencoe, Ill.: Free Press, 1960.

Koskela, K., Bjorkqvist, S., Puska, P., Neittaanmaki, L., & Jasalonen, J. Tupakasta vieroittamisryhmatoiminta osana Pohjois-Karjala projecktin tupakkaohjelmaa. *Hallinto ja Terveys,* 1977, *1,* 44.

Lesser, G. *Children and television: Lessons from "Sesame Street".* New York: Random House, 1974.

Lichtenstein, E., Birchler, F. R., Wahl, J. M., & Schmahl, D. P. Comparison of rapid smoking, warm smoky air, and attention placebo in the modification of smoking behavior. *Journal of Consulting and Clinical Psychology,* 1973, *40,* 92–98.

Liebert, R. M. Television and social learning: Some relationships between viewing violence and behaving aggressively. In J. P. Murray, E. A. Rubinstein, & G. A. Comstock (Eds.), *Television and social behavior* (Vol. 2). Washington, D.C.: U.S. Government Printing Office, 1972.

Liebert, R. M., Neale, J. M., & Davidson, E. S. *The early window: Effects of television on children and youth.* Elmsford, N.Y.: Pergamon Press, 1973.

Lowe, J. C., & Mikulas, W. L. Use of written material in learning self-control of premature ejaculation. *Psychological Reports*, 1975, *37*, 295–298.

Maccoby, N., Farquhar, J. W., Wood, P. D., & Alexander, J. Reducing the risk of cardiovascular disease: Effects of a community based campaign on knowledge and behavior. *Journal of Community Health*, 1977, *3*, 100–114.

Mahoney, M. *Cognitive behavior modification*. Boston: Ballinger, 1975.

Mahoney, M., & Mahoney, K. *Permanent weight control*. New York: Norton, 1976.

McAlister, A. Helping people quit smoking: Current progress. In A. Enelow & J. Henderson (Eds.), *Behavioral science applied to cardiovascular risk*. New York: American Heart Association, 1974.

McAlister, A. *Toward the mass communication of behavioral counseling*. Unpublished doctoral dissertation, Stanford University, 1976.

McCombs, M., & Shaw, D. The agenda setting function of mass media. *Public Opinion Quarterly*, 1972, *36*, 176.

Mendelsohn, H. Some reasons why information campaigns can succeed. *Public Opinion Quarterly*, 1973, *37*, 50.

Mielke, K., & Swinehart, J. *Evaluation of the "Feeling Good" television series*. New York: Children's Television Workshop, 1976.

O'Keefe, T. M. The anti-smoking commercials: A study of television's impact on behavior. *Public Opinion Quarterly*, 1971, *35*, 242–248.

Puska, P. *North Karelia project: A programme for community control of cardiovascular diseases* (Community Health Series A:1). Kuopio, Finland: University of Kuopio, 1974.

Puska, P. *The North Karelia Project: An example of health promotion in action*. Paper presented at the National Institute of Medicine Conference on Prevention, Washington, D.C., June 1978.

Reiff, R., & Riessman, F. The indigenous nonprofessional. *Community Mental Health Journal*, 1965, *1*. (Monograph)

Robertson, L. S., & Kelly, A. B. A controlled study of the effect of television messages on safety belt use. *American Journal of Public Health*, 1974, *64*, 1071.

Rogers, E. M. Mass media and interpersonal communication. In I. Pool, W. Schramm, & N. Maccoby (Eds.), *Handbook of communication*. Chicago: Rand McNally, 1973.

Rogers, E. M., & Shoemaker, F. F. *Communication of innovations: A cross-cultural approach*. New York: Free Press, 1971.

Thoresen, C. E., & Mahoney, M. J. *Behavioral self-control*. New York: Holt, Rinehart & Winston, 1974.

Ward, S., Reale, G., & Levinson, D. Children's perception, explanations and judgements of television advertising: A further exploration. In E. A. Rubinstein, J. P. Murray, & G. A. Comstock (Eds.), *Television and social behavior: Television in day-to-day life*. Washington, D.C.: U.S. Government Printing Office, 1972.

Zaltman, G., Kotler, P., & Kaufman, I. (Eds.). *Creating social change*. New York: Holt, Rinehart & Winston, 1972.

V
Social Support Networks

Introduction

The four chapters in this part review research/intervention programs focusing on support networks among diverse populations. As we saw in Chapter 3, networks are a major stream in behavioral-ecology. In recent years professionals have directed their attention to social support networks in conceptualizing mental health problems and in delivering services. The recognition is growing that support systems are significant in optimizing transactions between persons and their settings (Kelly, 1977). These support systems include "natural" helping networks (e.g., relatives, friends, neighbors) and "devised" social networks (e.g., self-help groups).

Gardner (1982) emphasizes the importance of social networks as major determinants of adaptation. According to Gardner, the network concept serves a "bridging" function between the individual/family level of analysis and the larger community/systems level. This notion parallels Granovetter's (1973) argument that social network analysis is a tool for linking "micro-level interactions to macro-level patterns" (p. 1360).

Gardner focuses on the reciprocal nature of networks to demonstrate the central functions of individual networks. One's network is considered a significant factor in determining the quality of one's interactions with the environment. One's ability to satisfy one's needs is facilitated by one's ability to satisfy the needs of others, since an expectation for reciprocity is thereby created. Need satisfaction is thus viewed as a rational process of "searching out" appropriate others and/or appropriate environments through one's network. Networks serve preventive mental health functions since they increase an individual's access to information, resources, and social support.

Following their comprehensive literature review and analysis of social network concepts, Mitchell and Trickett (1980) consider how social
network ideas can be translated into guidelines for community mental
health practice:

> Social network concepts can be applied in a variety of different ways,
> depending on one's ideological stance with regard to treatment versus pre-
> vention-oriented, and individual versus system-focused, interventions. Thus,
> one intervener may develop training in social skills, so that individuals would
> be more competent at developing networks; and another intervener might try
> to influence network structure by changing the social climate of a particular
> setting. Such decisions are dictated more by values than by empirical evi-
> dence. (p. 38)

We see both individual- and community-level interventions guided by
network concepts as compatible with the values of behavioral-ecology.
Self-help and mutual aid groups, as a special type of support network, have certain differences from professional helping and strong
compatibiity with behavioral-ecology. In contrast to the more informal
modalities of natural helping, self-help groups generally consist of people with a specific problem (e.g., alcoholism, drug abuse, child abuse)
who meet for mutual support. These groups are practical and task oriented, emphasizing self-reliance and skill mastery. Their leaders are
spontaneous and self-disclosing, and are chosen on the basis of having
mastered the common problem. Human problems are attributed to external environmental pressures, as opposed to the intrapersonal attributions
of traditional (i.e., psychodynamic) professional helping. Stuart (1977)
points to these dimensions as suggesting a special compatibility between
self-help and behavior modification. Given some shared assumptions,
there is greater potential for professional behavior modifiers to promote
self-help through various collaborative efforts with self-help organizations. Promoting self-help networks is likewise compatible with the ecological features of behavioral-ecology in that the existing strengths and
resources of individuals are capitalized on for purposes of providing mutual support.

In Chapter 15, Schure, Slotnick, and Jeger draw on their activities at
the Long Island Self-Help Clearinghouse, as well as numerous projects
reported in the literature, to exemplify self-help/professional collaboration that is compatible with behavioral-ecology. They discuss issues pertaining to five major areas of collaboration: information/referral,
consultation/education, self-help group development, natural helping
network enhancement, and research. In addition, they consider some

new directions for behavioral-ecological contributions to self-help/professional collaboration.

In Chapter 16 Fawcett and his colleagues review a programmatic series of consultation efforts between his campus-based Community Technology Project and various community self-help organizations. The project emphasizes the development, evaluation, and dissemination of behavioral-community technologies (usually in the form of procedural modules) in such areas as training nonprofessional counselors, developing skills exchanges, and carrying out social impact analyses. In all cases a collaborative approach to consultation with the local community is employed, with paraprofessionals and community residents serving as the primary change agents. Thus the methods of the project are behavioral technologies, whereas the specific contents span diverse community needs. Furthermore, the delivery system is sensitive to the ecological context in that local participants are engaged in all phases of technology development. The values underlying their range of activities include the promotion of individual and community competence and enhancement of the psychological sense of community.

Biegel and Naparstek (Chapter 17) describe their Neighborhood and Family Services Project and its underlying "community mental health empowerment model." The project is predicated on a set of assumptions that are especially compatible with the ecological features of behavioral-ecology—namely, a recognition that professional services are limited, that natural support systems must be strengthened, and that community-professional collaboration is necessary to stimulate linkages between professional and lay helping networks. In addition, explicit in their work is the concept of *neighborhood* as an active, organizing vehicle for citizen empowerment and mental health service delivery. More specifically, they emphasize that mental health services cannot be delivered *to* a neighborhood, but must be developed *with* a neighborhood. A major component of their project was the establishment of linkages among clergy, community helpers, and agency professionals. A process analysis of this component receives special attention in their chapter.

Finally, in Chapter 18 Lehmann reports on a research program that depicts the complexity of support networks among former psychiatric patients living in single-resident occupancy (SRO) hotels. The relationship of these networks to functional behavior and satisfaction points to the particular significance of relatively "undemanding" social networks for various psychiatric populations. The practical implications of this work lie in its message to professionals who interface with SROs as part of the increasing number of community support programs. Professionals should serve as facilitators and resource persons to allow for the preservation of the natural ecology of the setting—rather than take directive roles to influence "unnatural" social relationships among SRO hotel residents.

References

Gardner, J. M. *Community psychology: The left hand of the magician.* Manuscript in preparation, 1982.

Granovetter, M. S. The strength of weak ties. *American Journal of Sociology,* 1973, *78,* 1360–1380.

Kelly, J. G. *The ecology of social support systems: Footnotes to a theory.* Paper presented at the meeting of the American Psychological Association, San Francisco, August 1977.

Mitchell, R. E., & Trickett, E. J. Task Force report: Social networks as mediators of social support. *Community Mental Health Journal,* 1980, *16,* 27–44.

Stuart, R. B. Self-help group approach to self-management. In R. B. Stuart (Ed.), *Behavioral self-management.* New York: Brunner/Mazel, 1977.

15

Behavioral-Ecology and Self-Help/Professional Collaboration

MATTHEW SCHURE, ROBERT S. SLOTNICK, AND
ABRAHAM M. JEGER

With the growing interest among mental health professionals in the broad area of community supports (e.g., Biegel & Naparstek, 1982; Caplan, 1974), the self-help/mutual aid movement will take on increased significance in complementing professional mental health services. Although self-help groups and informal networks have existed throughout recorded social history, it was not until the 1970s that mental health professionals began to devote serious attention to these alternative forms of helping. Professional interest in self-help and natural helping networks is reflected in a host of developments including books, special journal issues, national and regional clearinghouses, and federal government initiatives (e.g., President's Commission on Mental Health, 1978).

The purpose of this chapter is to discuss the interface between behavioral-ecology[1] and the self-help movement. More specifically, we

[1] See Part I for detailed presentations of behavioral-ecology.

MATTHEW SCHURE, ROBERT S. SLOTNICK, AND ABRAHAM M. JEGER • Human Resources Development Center, New York Institute of Technology, Old Westbury, New York 11568.

shall consider the major contributions of behavioral-ecology to promoting collaboration between the self-help and professional communities. We shall draw on our experiences at the Long Island Self-Help Clearinghouse, a community service project of the New York Institute of Technology's Human Resources Development Center, as well as on other projects reported in the literature. As will become apparent, the overarching framework for the contributions of behavioral-ecology is an emerging "self-help/professional collaborative perspective" in mental health, which we have developed elsewhere (Jeger, Slotnick, & Schure, 1982).

The Self-Help Movement: An Overview

With origins in such established self-help groups as Alcoholics Anonymous and Recovery (for ex-mental patients), approximately one-half million groups exist for various problems and populations (Gartner & Riessman, 1977). Groups exist for the overweight, compulsive gamblers, the physically handicapped, people undergoing surgery, schizophrenics, abusive parents, widows, and so on. At the same time, mutual aid groups are forming for purposes of "enhancement"—for example, women's health collectives, parent centers, skill exchanges and bartering networks, cooperative day care centers, and advocacy programs for the poor and ethnic minorities.

Levy (1976) delineates five criteria as defining self-help groups: (1) purpose, (2) origin and sanction, (3) source of help, (4) composition, and (5) control. Briefly, the primary *purpose* of self-help groups is to provide help and support for their members. Their *origin and sanction* for existence rest with the members themselves, rather than an external agency. As to *sources of help*, the group relies primarily on its members' skills, knowledge, and concern. People who share a common problem or need form the *composition* of the group. Finally, *control* of structure and organizational format rests with members, who may seek professional assistance.

In addition to the attention given to self-help *groups*, mental health professionals are recognizing the roles of informal or natural helping *networks* (Collins & Pancoast, 1976; Gottlieb, in press). These involve neighborhood helpers who offer support, advise, and exchange information without any group or organizational sanctions. Although they are less structured and less visible than self-help groups, natural helping networks exist in every community in even greater numbers. Rather than refer exclusively to self-help *groups*, we shall use the term *self-help* in a more generic sense to include mutual aid through informal or natural helping. As such, it bears resemblance to Curry and Young's (1978) conceptual umbrella—"socially indigenous help"—which is said to encompass the numerous ways in which the "community cares for itself" through the different types of informal helping.

According to Silverman (1978), three major societal forces gave rise to the sudden surge of self-help groups: (1) professional failure, (2) technological advances, and (3) social change. *Professional failure* occurred when many physical and psychological conditions could not be alleviated through professional interventions (e.g., alcoholism, obesity, schizophrenia, child abuse). Many groups are responses to *advances in medicine and technology*, which alleviate acute illnesses but increase the number of persons with chronic difficulties; such groups include Make Today Count for cancer victims and others with terminal illness, Candlelighters for parents of children with cancer, and Mended Hearts for people who have had heart surgery. Finally, some groups have developed as a reaction to *social change*. The breakdown of traditional supports (e.g., extended families) for people undergoing "normal" life transitions (such as motherhood, divorce, and widowhood) has created a need for mutual aid groups. Similarly, societal changes have led to the increased bureaucratization of professional services, which, in turn, has led to their becoming less responsive and, at times, inadequate. Thus, as an alternative to professionals and out of a desire for community and affiliation, people are once again turning to each other for support (e.g., women's and men's "consciousness raising" groups).

Clearly, self-help groups are, in part, reactions to *failures* in natural support systems. Bankoff (1979) found that widowed persons turn to Naim (a self-help organization for Catholic widows and widowers) for social support that will compensate for inadequacies in their existing natural support networks. Similarly, Borkman (1979) reports unsupportiveness from the personal networks of self-helpers whom she studied— that is, groups of recovered alcoholics, ostomates, and stutterers.

The Self-Help/Professional Collaborative Perspective

Despite common assertions about the "antiprofessional" orientation of self-helpers, interfaces between the two systems appeared early in the development of the self-help movement. For example, Borman (1979a) identifies the founders and early supporters of 10 major self-help organizations, and concludes that "one can find, either in the forefront or behind the scenes, helpful health, social service, or religious professionals who see the limits of their disciplines' conventional domain" (p. 21). He emphasizes that in such major groups as Recovery, Inc. (for psychiatric patients), Parents Anonymous (for child abusers), and Integrity Groups, the founders were professionals.

Borman (1979a) discusses nine ways in which the roles of professionals who aligned themselves with self-help groups deviated from their conventional professional teachings and norms:

- Taking issue with the prevailing professional theories, particularly of psychotherapy
- Broadening their definitions of afflictions—that is, responding to the need to alleviate the stigma associated with mental illness
- Broadening the helping techniques—for example, recognition of the "helper therapy principle" (Riessman, 1965) that one is helped by helping others
- Focusing on such "neglected stages of conditions" as rehabilitation and aftercare
- Focusing on such neglected populations as alcoholics, drug addicts, schizophrenics, and child abusers
- Broadening the professional role—from "expert" to "collaborator"
- Acknowledging "new auspices" under which groups can form— for example, libraries instead of hospitals
- Modifying recruitment strategies—for example, media publicity rather than traditional referral and screening
- Offering mutual help without fees and attempting to be self-supporting (although such groups as Parents Anonymous and Epilepsy Self-Help have accepted governmental grants)

In an earlier article we (Jeger *et al.*, 1982) present an initial formulation of a self-help/professional collaborative perspective in mental health. We see a developing knowledge base for self-help/professional collaboration derived from an integration of "professional" and "experiential" knowledge. This distinction is also emphasized by Borkman (1976) based on her work with self-help groups.

Borkman suggests that professional knowledge is "acquired by discursive reasoning, observation, or reflection on information provided by others" (1976, p. 446). Established by a formal profession and transmitted through socialization into that profession, objective knowledge is derived from systematic data collection and analysis. In the mental health field, professionalism is associated with degrees, credentials, and certification. Experiential knowledge is acquired through personal experience and is "concrete, specific, and commonsensical." Borkman introduces the notion of experiential *expertise*, or the skills obtained through the application of experiential knowledge. Experiential expertise may serve as the basis for leadership in a self-help group.

Although Borkman's analysis of experiential knowledge is limited to self-help groups, it can be extended to informal or natural helping networks. Informal helpers likewise have their own experiential knowledge, which, over time, leads to the development and application of experiential expertise. Our integrated self-help/professional perspective draws on the experiential knowledge acquired by self-help groups as well as natural helpers.

A collaboration that synthesizes the experiential and professional knowledge bases results in a new data base, one that we have called "self-help/professional collaborative knowledge." Similarly, as experience with self-help/professional collaboration expands, there will develop "self-help/professional collaborative expertise." This increased expertise will be reflected in new roles of professionals vis-à-vis self-helpers as well as new roles for self-helpers vis-à-vis professionals.

Furthermore, we (Jeger *et al.*, 1982) delineate five major areas of self-help/professional collaboration: (1) information/referral; (2) consultation and education; (3) self-help group development; (4) natural helping network enhancement; and (5) research.

In the area of *information/referral*, professionals and self-help groups have engaged in mutual referrals of clients. Furthermore, national and regional clearinghouses were established to publish directories and newsletters on self-help, sponsor conferences, and generally contribute to raising awareness of self-help and mutual aid. The organizational base of information and referral services is crucial for their success (i.e., it should not conflict with resources for provision of direct clinical services).

As for *consultation and education*, professionals have interfaced with existing support groups. Their activities have included offering technical information and skill training workshops, developing resource materials, and designing educational curricula.

Self-help group development refers to the formation by professionals of new support groups for specific populations and/or problems. Professionals may or may not be formal members of such groups.

Natural helping network enhancement refers to the interface of professionals with informal community helping agents in order to strengthen their helping capacities as well as stimulate linkages with professional help-giving systems. Catalyzing informal support systems is a related activity that professionals have begun to engage in. A major goal of such activities is the promotion of community self-sufficiency.

Finally, professionals have begun to conduct *research* in the general area of self-help to an unprecedented extent. It has included research on the processes and outcomes of self-help groups and natural helping networks.

As a future direction for self-help/professional collaboration, we have pointed to Sarason's notion of "resource exchange networks" (RENs) (Sarason & Lorentz, 1979; Sarason, Carroll, Maton, Cohen, & Lorentz, 1977), or the exchange of personal and material resources in barter style as an alternative to the usual competition for limited capital and personnel funding among human service agencies. Professionals can (and have begun) to stimulate the development of RENs among individuals, self-help organizations, self-helpers, and professionals, as well as among professional organizations. "Leader-coordinators" of RENs who have the skills to scan the environment for resources and linkage potentials will need to be identified. For RENs to become more widespread and successful, professional agencies will need to overcome the "myth of unlimited resources" and learn to redefine problems as resources. (See Chapter 3 for a more detailed treatment of RENs.)

Contributions from Behavioral-Ecology

Information/Referral

Provision of information/referral for community residents, self-helpers, and professionals represents a new role for professionals. Such a role is compatible with the notion that behavioral-ecological-oriented community mental health professionals can provide "indirect" services, rather than devote their time exclusively to direct clinical services. Toward this end, national and regional clearinghouses have been established by professionals to integrate information on self-help/mutual aid groups (among other functions that will be described below). At least two regional clearinghouses have been established by professionals guided explicitly by a behavioral-ecological viewpoint—our own Long Island Self-Help Clearinghouse (Jeger *et al.*, 1982; Slotnick, Jeger, & Schure, 1980), and the Westchester Self-Help Clearinghouse developed by Borck (1979).

As part of our information/referral services at the Long Island Self-Help Clearinghouse, we maintain a telephone information service staffed by graduate and undergraduate students, who have answered several hundred requests during the first 2 years of operation. We sponsored a self-help conference on the theme of self-help/professional collaboration. It included workshops and a self-help fair, whereby representatives from self-help groups displayed information about their programs to professionals and community residents. Approximately 250 individuals living and/or working in the Long Island region participated in the conference events.

Another information/referral activity of our clearinghouse has been the publication of *People Helping People: Directory of Long Island Self-Help Organizations* (Schure, Leif, Slotnick, & Jeger, 1980). This directory was prepared in cooperation with the Suffolk Community Council (an umbrella agency of human service organizations in one of two Long Island counties), with input from the Nassau County Health and Welfare Council (their counterpart in the other Long Island county). An advisory board was formed that consisted of representatives from self-help groups and professional agencies, which guided the process from its proposal stage through completion, including input on funding. A local foundation (the Long Island Community Foundation) provided funds for the publication of 2,000 copies to be distributed free, as well as inclusion of an abridged version in the pocket directory of community services published by the Suffolk Community Council (of which 20,000 copies are distributed).

Our directory contains basic information of 167 autonomous self-help organizations. A unique feature is the inclusion of 77 human service agencies and 32 community hospitals that sponsor and/or refer clients to self-help groups. Thus we have given particular attention to self-help/professional collaboration.

Since most mental health professionals are not trained in the provision of information/referral services, specific resources need to be developed to guide professionals in such activities. Most recently, the National Self-Help Clearinghouse published *Developing a Directory of Self-Help Groups* as a practical guide to collecting and organizing self-help information, publishing, and disseminating directories on self-help. The Community Technology Project's manual, *Developing an Information and Referral Service* (see Chapter 16, this volume), is likewise a valuable resource to enhance such services (see Table 1).

Consultation and Education

Consultation and education is the area of greatest interface between behavioral-ecologists and the self-help movement. For example, an early project by L. K. Miller and Miller (1970) successfully employed reinforcement techniques to increase attendance at self-help meetings by welfare recipients. In an interesting study, Briscoe, Hoffman, and Bailey (1975) employed behavioral techniques in training members of a community board to problem-solve. As community self-help agents, citizen boards benefit from problem-solving skills that behavior analysts can offer. In the context of a "community consultation project," P. M. Miller (1978) offered training in assertion skills, interpersonal skills, relaxation,

Table 1. Behavioral-Ecology and the Emerging "Self-Help/Professional Collaborative Perspective"

Area of collaboration	Description	Issues	Representative projects
1. Information and referral (I & R)	Mutual referrals between self-helpers and professionals; preparing self-help directories; publishing newsletters; sponsoring conferences and self-help fairs; clearinghouse development to implement above and raise consciousness on self-help	Organizational base of I & R services; involving self-helpers in I & R activities; evaluating outcome data on types of groups or professional services cost-effective for problems	National and regional self-help clearinghouses; numerous community mental health centers; Community Technology Project—Fawcett *et al.* (Chapter 16, this volume)
2. Consultation and education	Consulting with existing groups by offering technical information and skill training/workshops; developing resource packages/materials; designing educational curricula	Reciprocity in consulting relation; involving self-helpers in planning, development, evaluation, and dissemination of resource materials and curricula	National and regional self-help clearinghouses; Community Technology Project—Fawcett *et al.* (Chapter 16, this volume); Levitz & Stunkard (1974); Miller (1978); Stuart (1977)
3. Self-help group development	Initiating new support groups for specific problems and/or populations	Maintaining group autonomy and avoiding cooptation; mutual respect for experiential and professional knowledge	Widow-to-Widow—Silverman (1970); Long Island Jewish Medical Center health-related groups; Azrin *et al.* (1975)
4. Natural helping network enhancement	Interfacing with informal community helpers to strengthen helping capacity; promoting horizontal and vertical linkages (see text)	Community "entry"; avoiding disrupting natural helping process; promoting community self-sufficiency	Community Network Development—Gordon *et al.* (1979); Neighborhood and Family Services Project—Biegel & Naparstek (Chapter 17, this

5. Research	Research on the processes and outcomes of self-help groups and natural helping within advocacy context (research *for* group, not *on* group) and providing feedback for groups	Involving self-helpers in all research phases; determining appropriate outcome measures and research designs	volume); Behavioral-Ecological Matchmakers—Jason & Smith (1980); Powell (1980)
			Self-Help Epilepsy Workshop and Self-Help Institute—Borman *et al.* (1980); Fremouw & Harmatz (1974); Gottlieb & Todd (1979); Levi (1979)
Future directions Resource Exchange Network (REN) Development	Stimulating development of RENs among individuals, self-help groups, self-helpers and professionals, and professional organizations	Overcoming "myth of unlimited resources"; developing "psychological sense of community"; redefining problems as resources; scanning environment for resources and linkages; indentifying "leader-coordinators"; efficiency vs. mutuality and informality; reinforcement of resource sharing; behavioral process monitoring	Essex Network—Sarason *et al.* (1977); United Way Network —Long Island, N.Y.; Minnesota Mutual-Help Council; Urban Brokerage Training Project—National Self-Help Clearinghouse, CUNY

and behavioral alternatives to alcohol abuse to staff of an Alcoholics Anonymous halfway house. As a result, participants requested that behavioral training be incorporated into the ongoing halfway house program.

Self-help groups for weight control have likewise interacted with professional behavior modifiers in order to enhance their programs. For example, Levitz and Stunkard (1974) added a behavior modification component to Take Off Pounds Sensibly (TOPS), the oldest weight management program. In a more ambitious project, Stuart (1977) developed 18 behavioral modules (Personal Action Plans), trained group leaders working with Weight Watchers in their use, and actively involved program participants in module discussion. Based on the success of this effort, Stuart suggests that a role for professionals vis-à-vis self-help groups is the development and evaluation of behavioral technologies, to be given to the self-help groups for dissemination to large numbers of people.

In our own work at the Long Island Self-Help Clearinghouse, we have consulted with a Youth Agency to establish youth resource groups around career exploration. We provided a framework whereby youth were engaged as community service interns in various field settings and met weekly with a youth worker to exchange information and provide mutual support for their career exploration activities. In the course of the program youth learned about different career possibilities while acquiring such skills as résumé writing, preparing for job interviews, and relating to adults in a work setting. Additionally, they learned more generic skills of networking to provide information and support for each other in these endeavors. At the end of the program, youth participants prepared a resource newsletter, a career resource file, and produced a videotape on different career themes.

Additional activities in the area of consultation and education fall into the category of resource development. Over several years, Fawcett and his colleagues (see Chapter 16) developed, evaluated, and disseminated behaviorally oriented "community education" materials as part of their Community Technology Project at the University of Kansas. The basic goal of this project is to enhance the capacities of local communities to help themselves and reduce their dependence on the formal help-giving systems. Written modules in the areas of self-help technologies, living skills, education, employment preparation, and community supports were developed in collaboration with staff members of a local neighborhood multipurpose center, Penn House.

At the National Self-Help Clearinghouse, resource materials on organizing self-help groups were prepared in the form of instructional guides (e.g., Bowles, 1978; Dory, 1979). Information contained in these comprehensive manuals ranges from finding a meeting place to group process skills. At our Long Island Clearinghouse, we developed materials for use by childcare workers in a community-run Mothers Center (Kohl & Marcus, 1979). They focused on developmental activities for enhancing cognitive, social, and motor functioning in children up to age 4. We also developed self-care modules for elderly community residents, focusing on their needs for medication (Marcus, 1979) and enhanced sensory functioning (Kohl, 1979).

Self-help-related course work has also been incorporated into the curricula designed for the preparation of professional and nonprofessional mental health workers. Influenced by our Long Island Clearinghouse, we offered graduate and undergraduate seminars on "self-help in the human services" at the New York Institute of Technology. As part of community mental health (and related) curricula, seminars of this nature constitute one vehicle for educating students in the practice of self-help/professional collaboration.

A major issue when consulting with self-help groups is the development of a truly collaborative relationship. Professionals and self-helpers alike need to be particularly sensitive to the processes inherent in sharing their respective technical skills. The self-helper should have the final choice as to whether and how to apply the professional knowledge offered. Professionals should not attempt to mold self-helpers in their style of delivering clinical skills. At the same time, self-helpers need to be ready to receive professional consultation, acknowledge and respect the utility of professional knowledge, and contribute to the mutuality and reciprocity that make possible a collaborative working relationship. Finally, in the area of resource development, wherever possible, self-helpers should be involved in all phases of production and evaluation. That will not only facilitate widespread dissemination of resources but will ensure that the materials are suited for use by group members—in terms of readability, writing style, use of jargon, and contents.

Self-Help Group Development

The initiation of new support groups is a major aspect of self-help/professional collaboration. A classic example is Silverman's (1970) widow-to-widow program at the Harvard Laboratory of Community Psychiatry. Since then numerous community mental health centers and human service agencies have sponsored support groups for widows. Given the crisis state that many widows experience, such groups serve preventive functions and are especially compatible with a behavioral-ecological perspective.

An example of a behavioral contribution to self-help group formation is the development of job-finding clubs by Azrin and his colleagues (e.g., Azrin, Flores, & Kaplan, 1975).

Another major trend is the development of hospital-based support groups for patients with chronic physical problems. For example, groups for people suffering from such chronic disabilities as diabetes, cancer, heart disease, and Diethystilbestrol-related (DES-related) disorders are part of a network of 18 self-help groups established at the Long Island Jewish Medical Center in our region (New Hyde Park, New York). In total, we have identified 32 hospitals on Long Island that sponsor groups and/or provide the setting for health-related mental health support groups (Schure *et al.*, 1980). Additional programs reflecting the interface between self-help and physical health are reviewed by Leif, Slotnick, and Jeger (in press).

Our own activities at the Long Island Self-Help Clearinghouse have included the development of a mutual aid group for drug abuse clients in conjunction with a methadone maintenance clinic, a support group for returning nursing students, several staff support groups for persons working in state-operated outpatient clinics, and groups for deinstitutionalized psychiatric clients residing in community-based adult homes.

Most recently, as a project of our Long Island Clearinghouse, Leif (1980) catalyzed a women's support network—WORTHE (Women Returning to Higher Education). It focuses on providing mutual support, exchanging resources, and sharing information that will enhance the women's career and educational experiences.

A major issue surrounding professionals' involvement in the initiation of self-help groups is the maintenance of the group's autonomy (Gartner & Riessman, 1977; Katz, 1979; Riessman, 1979). This issue is especially critical in agency-based support groups. The delicate line between collaboration and "co-optation" is apparent in the conflicts surrounding CanCervive, a self-help program sponsored by the American Cancer Society that ended in disarray (see Kleiman, Mantell, & Alexander, 1976). Related to the issue of autonomy is the need for both self-helpers and professionals to demonstrate mutual respect for each other's value systems and differential knowledge bases.

Professionals should not prematurely seek to impose their scientifically derived mental health technologies; instead, they should assist the self-helpers in determining when and how to incorporate the professional knowledge. To do so will require that the roles of mental health professionals be those of facilitator, resource person, and catalyst, rather than expert and provider of direct service, when initiating support groups. Such roles follow from a behavioral-ecological view of community mental health practice.

Natural Helping Network Enhancement

This area of collaboration refers to the interface between professionals and informal or natural helping networks, which tend to be less organized and less demarcated than self-help groups. The roles of professionals can range from initiating informal helping networks to enhancing existing networks.

An interesting illustration that is especially compatible with our perspective comes from the work of Jason and his colleagues at De Paul University and its affiliated community mental health center (e.g., Jason & Smith, 1980; Jason, Robson, & Lipshutz, 1980). They trained "behavioral-ecological matchmakers" (BEMs) to identify individuals or groups who seek behavioral change. Rather than intervene directly as a behavior modifier would, BEMs link these individuals and groups with existing natural networks or behavior settings that will facilitate desired changes.

For example, Jason *et al.* (1980) placed children manifesting low rates of sharing behaviors in triads of high sharers, and high sharers in triads of low sharers. Results showed a clear acceleration of sharing, including manifestations of sharing initiation among low sharers. Jason and Smith (1980) extended this approach to college students. Groups were formed of students manifesting specific target problems (e.g., studying, television watching, littering) and those who had successfully modified these problems. Following six brief meetings during which students exchanged their naturally developed strategies, significant changes resulted in many of the target behaviors.

Based on our activities at the Long Island Self-Help Clearinghouse, we were invited by our college, the New York Institute of Technology, to develop a self-help program for underprepared students. As a pilot project in an Introductory Psychology class, Slotnick, Jeger, and Schure (1981) organized networks of four students each who met every third class in lieu of the regular lecture. During the meeting students worked together studying course material and preparing for exams. Students were encouraged to contact each other outside of class as well for assistance. Compared to students enrolled in another section taught by the same instructor, the network class scored higher on several classroom social climate dimensions, scored higher on five of six tests, knew more students in the class by name, and met outside of class more frequently. In addition to improving academic skills, the networks provided opportunities for peer support and natural helping among students while humanizing the learning environment.

Libertoff (1979) reports on a project of the Washington County Youth Service Bureau (Montpelier, Vermont) that sought to capitalize on the strengths of the rural communities in providing help for runaway youth. In lieu of developing a central "runaway house" (typically an urban model), this agency identified and engaged natural helping families to offer temporary shelter and psychological support for runaway youth.

Norton, Morales, and Andrews (1980) report on the Neighborhood Self-Help Project, a joint effort of the Chicago Commons Association, the Taylor Institute for Policy Studies, and the University of Chicago's School of Social Service Administration. The purpose of this research/ intervention project was to identify natural helpers in a low-income ethnic neighborhood, strengthen their informal helping capacities, and stimulate linkages with formal service agencies. Initial results of the project demonstrate that horizontal linkages (ties among individual natural helpers) were strengthened. Vertical linkages (ties between natural helpers and professionals) were also strengthened, as staff roles included serving as educators, advisers, resource persons, and "matchmakers."

At the Florida Mental Health Institute (Tampa), Gordon and his colleagues (Gordon, Edmunson, Bedell, & Goldstein, 1979) have established the Community Network Development Project to improve the quality of community life for discharged psychiatric patients and to prevent their future rehospitalization. This project represents an application of a behavioral-ecological perspective to network development in that it integrates skill training and peer supports (for a detailed description, see Chapter 6, this volume).

In contrast, Biegel and Naparstek's Neighborhood and Family Services Project in Baltimore and Milwaukee (see Chapter 17) is based entirely on a process model as opposed to a program model.

Influenced by the ecological approach to primary prevention, Powell (1980) designed the Child and Family Neighborhood Program to strengthen parent's social networks. Mutual support groups of parents have been created to facilitate the exchange of instrumental and emotional support, to enhance their access to information and referral from extrafamilial sources, and to allow them to serve as role models in childrearing for each other (see also Chapter 13, this volume, on a support group for new mothers).

Additional programs that represent "professional partnerships" with natural helpers are described by Froland and Pancoast (1979).

Some of the autonomy issues that bear on self-help group development are likewise relevant to this type of collaboration. For example, careful specifications of the roles of each party need to be made at the outset. Professionals must guard against disrupting the natural network and against "professionalizing" their helping. Instead, professionals should be guided by the values of behavioral-ecology: that strengthening natural helping networks involves promoting their capacity to mobilize and redistribute human and material resources, as well as increasing the resourcefulness of individual natural helpers.

Although some of the projects we have cited report increased utilization of professional helping agencies, care must be taken not to encourage citizens to increase their dependence on professional agencies. That is, although we view the interface between professionals and natural helpers as positive, there exists the danger that citizens will gravitate to and come to overrely on the professional caregiving system. It is also important, however, that natural helpers learn to refer citizens to professional agencies when professional interventions seem warranted.

Research

Although behavioral-ecologists interfacing with the self-help movement have generally integrated a research/evaluation component into their activities, there are several interesting examples of projects conducted within a "pure research" context.

At the basic research level, the helper therapy principle (Riessman, 1965)—namely, that one is helped by helping others—gained some empirical support from the behavioral literature. Fremouw and Harmatz (1974) assigned speech-anxious college students to one of four conditions: (1) helper, (2) helpee, (3) latent helper, and (4) waiting-list control. Helpers were taught a standardized 5-hour behavioral program for speech anxiety—including relaxation training, self-control techniques, and public speaking skill building strategies. Helpers taught the same skills to subjects in Group 2—helpees—on a one-to-one basis as they progressed through training. Latent helpers, Group 3, were taught the entire package but did not teach it until later. Although significant reductions in speech anxiety were achieved for all three training groups, the extent of improvement was greater for Group 1, the helpers who taught the skills to the second group as they progressed in their own learning.

Self-help groups and natural helping networks have increasingly participated in research by professionals in various fields. Lieberman and Borman (1979) describe empirical studies on the processes and outcomes of such self-help groups as Mended Hearts (for heart surgery patients), widow groups, women's consciousness raising groups, and elderly mutual aid groups. Borkman (1979) reports on research concerning the relations between self-help groups and their natural social networks. Levy (1978) reports on a national survey of professionals' perceptions of major self-help groups. Gottlieb and Todd (1979) examined the nature of natural supports among single mothers. Finally, Froland and Pancoast (1979) studied various ways in which professional services are linked with informal helping networks in collaborative programs throughout the country.

Unfortunately, a great deal of this research evolved from a traditional research orientation, whereby self-helpers became subjects of professionally designed and executed research studies. The self-help/professional collaborative model calls for research that provides feedback to the self-help organization on its processes and outcomes. Borman's (1979b) "action anthropology" approach, which is sensitive to working *with* a subject group, has guided the research conducted at his Self-Help Institute (Northwestern University). This collaborative strategy merits attention by other researchers on self-help. Borman (1975) maintains that

> members of the (self-help) group should be involved in all phases of the research from the planning to the execution through the interpretation of findings. . . . Researchers should attempt to learn thoroughly the group's values and plan the total research process in a manner that respects and maintains the group's values. . . . Researchers should accept as a responsibility the training of group members in research in order to increase the capacity of self-helpers to solve their own problems. . . . All policy and operating decisions which might in any way be related to research being conducted should always be made by members of the group, not by the researchers. (pp. 274–275)

An example of the "action anthropology" approach to research that is compatible with behavioral-ecology is the ongoing national collaborative program between researchers at the Self-Help Institute and epilepsy self-help group participants (see Borman, Davies, & Droge, 1980). Through this effort, the collaborators are developing materials to facilitate the growth and development of epilepsy self-help groups, and at the same time forming a national information network.

The work of Levy and his colleagues (e.g., Levy, 1979; Wollert, Knight, & Levy, 1980) likewise reflects research that is compatible with a self-help/professional collaborative perspective. They studied the processes and activities of, among other self-help groups, Alcoholics Anonymous, Overeaters Anonymous, Make Today Count, Parents Anonymous, Take Off Pounds Sensibly, Emotions Anonymous, and Parents without Partners. A 28-item instrument of help-giving activities to be rated by members of self-help groups was developed by the research team (see Levy, 1979). It is a useful tool for monitoring group process over time by self-help group members. Also, in the course of their work, members of Levy's self-help research team served as organizational consultants to a chapter of Make Today Count, which resulted in improved group functioning (see Wollert *et al.*, 1980). Thus their research, carried out within a collaborative framework, was employed by the group for its own enhancement.

Conclusion

There is strong compatibility between behavioral-ecology and the self-help/professional collaborative perspective in mental health. The roles and activities of professionals vis-à-vis self-help groups are consistent with the essential features of the behavioral-ecological perspective developed in Part I. Practice in natural community settings is emphasized; a "strength-building" and enhancement orientation is espoused; research and service roles of professionals are merged; consultation roles are encouraged in lieu of direct service; and designing settings that contribute to a psychological sense of community remains an underlying value.

Furthermore, we feel that as more behavioral-ecologists interface with the self-help movement, they are likely to contribute to the further development of self-help/professional collaboration in the five areas we have reviewed. In addition, they are likely to contribute to the new directions of self-help/professional collaboration mentioned earlier in this chapter—that is, the enhancement of RENs.

The ecological stream of behavorial-ecology provides a perspective for understanding the larger social context within which individual mental health, human service, and educational institutions (which participate in RENs) operate. It calls attention to the "myth of unlimited resources," which all too often guides agency policy. Furthermore, it sensitizes professionals to the unintended consequences of mental health interventions (see Chapter 3). At the operational level of RENs, ecological principles are useful for facilitating the identification of "leader-coordinators" and for developing their abilities to scan the environment for resources and their linkage potential.

The behavioral stream of behavioral-ecology likewise offers some potential for enhancing REN operations. In a most general sense, behavioral skills are necessary to complement the "process"·orientation of most RENs as currently practiced. Behavioral strategies can be employed to shape objectives for a REN, to train leader-coordinators to identify resources, and to reinforce resource sharing among REN participants. The work of Jason and his colleagues (as reviewed earlier) in connection with applications of the BEM at the individual level can be extended to settings. That is, organizations high and low on specific resources can be identified and "matched" for purposes of forming a REN. Finally, behavior analysts can contribute their skills to documenting and evaluating RENs. By functioning as "participant/methodologists" (Jason, 1980), behavior analysts can conduct behavioral process monitoring through the use of multiple baseline research designs.

Although we have emphasized the contributions of behavioral-ecology to self-help, we believe behavioral-ecology and self-help have much to offer each other. Interfacing with self-help organizations within a collaborative framework will lead to the enhancement of behavioral-ecology as a perspective and of behavioral-ecologists as individuals.

ACKNOWLEDGMENTS

The authors acknowledge the support of the New York Institute of Technology in establishing the Long Island Self-Help Clearinghouse. Our experiences at the clearinghouse made possible the development of the ideas and projects presented in this chapter. Special thanks are due Dr. David Salten, executive vice-president and provost, and Dr. Alexander Schure, president, of the New York Institute of Technology, for their continued support.

References

Azrin, N. H., Flores, T., & Kaplan, S. J. Job finding club: A group-assisted program for obtaining employment. *Behavior Research and Therapy*, 1975, *13*, 17–27.

Bankoff, E. A. Widow groups as an alternative to informal social support groups. In M. A. Lieberman & L. D. Borman (Eds.), *Self-help groups for coping with crisis.* San Francisco: Jossey-Bass, 1979.

Biegel, D. E., & Naparstek, A. J. (Eds.), *Community support systems and mental health: Research, practice, and policy.* New York: Springer, 1982.

Borck, L. E. Personal communication, 1979.

Borkman, T. Experiential knowledge: A new concept for the analysis of self-help groups. *Social Service Review*, 1976, *50*, 445–456.

Borkman, T. *Mutual self-help groups: Strengthening the selectively unsupportive personal and community networks of their members.* Paper presented at the meeting of the American Public Health Association, New York, November 1979.

Borman, L. D. *Explorations in self-help and mutual aid.* Evanston, Ill.: Northwestern University Center for Urban Affairs, 1975.

Borman, L. D. Characteristics of development and growth. In M. A. Lieberman & L. D. Borman (Eds.), *Self-help groups for coping with crises.* San Francisco: Jossey-Bass, 1979. (a)

Borman, L. D. Action anthropology and the self-help/mutual-aid movement. In R. Hinshaw (Ed.), *Currents in anthropology: Essays in honor of Sol Tax.* Chicago: Aldine, 1979. (b)

Borman, L. D., Davies, J. & Droge, D. Self-help groups for persons with epilepsy. In B. P. Hermann (Ed.), *A multidisciplinary handbook of epilepsy.* Springfield, Ill.: Charles C Thomas, 1980.

Bowles, E. *Self-help groups: Perspectives and directions—An instructional guide for developing self-help mutual aid groups.* New York: New Careers Training Laboratory, CUNY Graduate Center, 1978.

Briscoe, R. V., Hoffman, D. B., & Bailey, J. S. Behavioral community psychology: Training a community board to problem solve. *Journal of Applied Behavior Analysis,* 1975, *8,* 157–168.

Caplan, G. *Support systems and community mental health.* New York: Human Sciences Press, 1974.

Collins, A. H., & Pancoast, D. L. *Natural helping networks.* Washington, D.C.: National Association of Social Workers, 1976.

Curry, R., & Young, R. D. *Social indigenous help: The community cares for itself.* Paper presented at the meeting of the American Psychological Association, Toronto, September 1978.

Dory, F. J. *Building self-help groups among older persons: A training curriculum to prepare organizers.* New York: New Careers Training Laboratory, CUNY Graduate Center, 1979.

Fremouw, W. J., & Harmatz, M. G. A helper model for behavioral treatment of speech anxiety. *Journal of Consulting and Clinical Psychology,* 1974, *43,* 652–660.

Froland, C., & Pancoast, D. L. (Eds.). *Networks for helping: Illustrations from research and practice.* Portland, Ore.: Portland State University, 1979.

Gartner, A., & Riessman, F. *Self-help in the human services.* San Francisco: Jossey-Bass, 1977.

Gordon, R., Edmunson, E., Bedell, J., & Goldstein, N. Utilizing peer management and support to reduce rehospitalization of mental patients. *Journal of the Florida Medical Association,* 1979, *66,* 927–933.

Gottlieb, B. H. Opportunities for collaboration with informal support systems. In S. Cooper & W. F. Hodges (Eds.), *The field of mental health consultation.* New York: Human Sciences Press, in press.

Gottlieb, B. H., & Todd, D. M. Characterizing and promoting social support in natural settings. In R. F. Munoz, L. R. Snowden, & J. G. Kelly (Eds.), *Social and psychological research in community settings.* San Francisco: Jossey-Bass, 1979.

Jason, L. A. Personal communication, May 1980.

Jason, L. A., Robson, S. D., & Lipshutz, S. A. Enhancing sharing behaviors through the use of naturalistic contingencies. *Journal of Community Psychology,* 1980, *8,* 237–244.

Jason, L. A., & Smith, T. The behavioral ecological matchmaker. *Teaching of Psychology,* 1980, *7,* 116–117.

Jeger, A. M., Slotnick, R. S., & Schure, M. Toward a "self-help/professional perspective" in mental health. In D. E. Biegel & A. J. Naparstek (Eds.), *Community support systems and mental health: Research, practice, and policy.* New York: Springer, 1982.

Katz, A. H. *A discussion of self-help groups: Haven in a professionalized world?* Paper presented at the Mediating Structures Project Conference on Professionalization, New York, May 1979.

Kleiman, M. A., Mantell, J. E., & Alexander, E. S. Collaboration and its discontents: The perils of partnership. *Journal of Applied Behavioral Science,* 1976, *12,* 403–410.

Kohl, G. J. *Self-help module on three senses: Vision, hearing, and taste.* Old Westbury, N.Y.: Long Island Self-Help Clearinghouse, New York Institute of Technology, 1979.

Kohl, G. J., & Marcus, C. R. *Suggested play activities to enhance the motor, language, and social skills in infants and preschoolers.* Old Westbury, N.Y.: Long Island Self-Help Clearinghouse, New York Institute of Technology, 1979.

Leif, A. Personal communication, January, 1980

Leif, A., Slotnick, R. S., & Jeger, A. M. Osteopathic medicine and the mutual-aid movement: Toward a collaborative perspective for self-health. *Osteopathic Annals,* in press.

Levitz, L. S., & Stunkard, A. J. A therapeutic coalition for obesity: Behavior modification and patient self-help. *American Journal of Psychiatry,* 1974, *131,* 423–427.

Levy, L. H. Self-help groups: Types and psychological processes. *Journal of Applied Behavioral Science,* 1976, *12,* 310–322.

Levy, L. H. Self-help groups viewed by mental health professionals: A survey and comments. *American Journal of Community Psychology*, 1978, *6*, 305–313.

Levy, L. H. Processes and activities in groups. In M. A. Lieberman & L. D. Borman (Eds.), *Self-help groups for coping with crisis*. San Francisco: Jossey-Bass, 1979.

Lieberman, M. A., & Borman, L. D. (Eds.). *Self-help groups for coping with crisis*. San Francisco: Jossey-Bass, 1979.

Libertoff, K. *Natural helping networks in rural youth and family services*. Paper presented at the meeting of the American Psychological Association, New York, September 1979.

Marcus, C. R. *You and your medications: Or how to become a better informed drug consumer*. Old Westbury, N.Y.: Long Island Self-Help Clearinghouse, New York Institute of Technology, 1979.

Miller, L. K., & Miller, O. Reinforcing self-help group activities of welfare recipients. *Journal of Applied Behavior Analysis*, 1970, *3*, 57–64.

Miller, P. M. Behavior modification and Alcoholics Anonymous: An unlikely combination. *Behavior Therapy*, 1978, *9*, 300–301.

Norton, D., Morales, J., & Andrews, E. *The neighborhood self-help project* (Occasional Paper No. 9). Chicago: School of Social Service Administration, University of Chicago, 1980.

Powell, D. R. *Strengthening parents' social networks: An ecological approach to primary prevention*. Paper presented at the meeting of the American Psychological Association, Montreal, September 1980.

President's Commission on Mental Health. *Final report*. Washington, D.C.: U.S. Government Printing Office, 1978.

Riessman, F. The helper therapy principle. *Social Work*, 1965, *10*, 27–32.

Riessman, F. *Self-help and the professional*. Keynote address presented at the conference on "The Self-Help Movement and Human Service Professionals: New Ways of Working Together," Long Island Self-Help Clearinghouse, New York Institute of Technology, Old Westbury, New York, January 1979.

Sarason, S. B., & Lorentz, E. *The challenge of the resource exchange network*. San Francisco: Jossey-Bass, 1979.

Sarason, S. B., Carroll, C. F., Maton, K., Cohen, S., & Lorentz, E. *Human services and resource networks*. San Francisco: Jossey-Bass, 1977.

Schure, M., Leif, A., Slotnick, R. S., & Jeger, A. M. *People helping people: A directory of Long Island self-help organizations*. Old Westbury, N.Y.: New York Institute of Technology Press, 1980.

Silverman, P. R. The widow as a caregiver in a program of preventive intervention with other widows. *Mental Hygiene*, 1970, *54*, 540–547.

Silverman, P. R. *Mutual help groups: A guide for mental health workers*. Rockville, Md.: National Institute of Mental Health, 1978.

Slotnick, R. S., Jeger, A. M., & Schure, M. *Self-help/professional collaboration: Catalyzing mutual support networks*. Paper presented at the meeting of the American Psychological Association, Montreal, September 1980.

Slotnick, R. S., Jeger, A. M., & Schure, M. Peer support networks in a large introductory psychology class. Paper presented at the meeting of the American Psychological Association, Los Angeles, August 1981.

Stuart, R. B. Self-help group approach to self-management. In R. B. Stuart (Ed.), *Behavioral self-management*. New York: Brunner/Mazel, 1977.

Wollert, R. W., Knight, B., & Levy, L. H. Make today count: A collaborative model for professionals and self-help groups. *Professional Psychology*, 1980, *11*, 130–138.

16

Designing Behavioral Technologies with Community Self-Help Organizations

STEPHEN B. FAWCETT, R. KAY FLETCHER, R. MARK
MATHEWS, PAULA L. WHANG, TOM SEEKINS, AND
LOUISE MEROLA NIELSEN

Attempts to bring about improvements in communities, or to enhance
the functioning and well-being of their individual members, are laden
with assumptions about the causes of problems and the mechanisms of
change. Similarly, several assumptions are implicit in a strategy to contribute to social change efforts through the development of behavioral
technologies for community self-help organizations. It is assumed that
the problems of living experienced by many individuals in society may
be a *function* of such fundamental social problems as poverty and power-

STEPHEN B. FAWCETT, R. KAY FLETCHER, PAULA L. WHANG, TOM SEEKINS,
AND LOUISE MEROLA NIELSEN ● Community Technology Project, Center for Public
Affairs, University of Kansas, Lawrence, Kansas 66045. R. MARK MATHEWS ●
Department of Psychology, University of Hawaii, Hilo, Hawaii 96720. Portions of this
research were supported by grants from the Kansas Board of Regents under Program
IMPACT, Title I of the Higher Education Act of 1965 and from the Kansas Adult
Education Office under 310 Projects for Staff Development and Special Demonstrations in
Adult Education.

lessness (Ryan, 1971a). If the causes lie outside the person in the broader social system, to treat problems of adjustment and coping individual by individual is to "blame the victim" for problems in society (Ryan, 1971b). Thus efforts to *prevent* problems of living in individuals might focus on improving the capacities of society's various community support groups to promote individual functioning and human fulfillment (Kessler & Albee, 1975).

The strategy of attempting to effect planned change through consultation with *community groups* reflects the belief that an individual's problems of living may be improved, or even prevented, by changing the person's environment (Kessler & Albee, 1975). Community service centers, neighborhood improvement associations, and other self-help organizations can contribute significantly to reducing stress and increasing social supports and strengths in the entire community (Rappaport, 1977). Accordingly, attempts to enhance the problem-solving and strength-building capacities of community self-help groups reflect a strategy for reducing the incidence of individuals' problems of living by improving the community's capacities to promote general welfare.

Consultation services are recognized as a promising approach to *multiplying* the effects of persons interested in facilitating such improvements (Bloom, 1977; Rogawski, 1979). The logic of consultation is that by providing technical assistance to potential change agents and change-facilitating organizations, large numbers of clients may be indirectly benefited by improvements in the helping abilities of caregivers. Indeed, the consultation and education services of community mental health centers are based on the idea of spreading effects by focusing efforts on the education of change agents and the design of more effective programs (Mannino & Shore, 1971). Thus consultation to community organizations and their members is recognized as a promising approach to remediating the many problems of living experienced by numerous community residents (Bard & Berkowitz, 1969; Libo & Griffith, 1966; Mannino & Shore, 1979; Scheidlinger, Struening, & Rabkin, 1970; Tharp & Wetzel, 1969).

Efforts to work through community *self-help* organizations, such as community service centers, neighborhood improvement associations, and other local self-help groups, reflect a belief that problems of living are often best handled by local support groups (Fawcett & Fletcher, 1977; Katz, 1970; Morris & Hess, 1975; Perlman & Jones, 1967). Such groups are often consumer initiated and peer oriented, providing assistance in coping with such life situations as poverty, unemployment, drug abuse, or alcoholism (Riessman, 1976). Such small-scale organizations are frequently understaffed (Barker & Gump, 1964), and, as such, provide opportunities for indigenous helpers to achieve success in leadership positions (Riessman, 1965b). Accordingly, community organizations may help reduce the incidence of psychiatric or behavior disorders by providing social supports, enhancing coping skills, and contributing to the self-esteem of their staff and clients (Hallowitz, 1968; Hallowitz & Riessman, 1967).

Behavioral technologies are designed in view of the demonstrated effectiveness of these methods in changing behavior in accordance with a group's goals (Baer, Wolf, & Risley, 1968; Wolf, 1978). The emphasis on *technology,* or a level of procedural detail that would permit a reader to use the procedures to produce similar results, is in recognition of the scope of the problems affecting community residents and the limited number of persons skilled in effective methods for solving community problems and enhancing community strengths. Such behavioral technologies for self-help groups might be particularly useful if they were designed to be inexpensive, decentralized, flexible, sustainable, simple, and compatible with existing customs, beliefs, and values (Fawcett, Mathews, & Fletcher, 1980).

The purpose of this chapter is to describe several examples of our Community Technology Project's efforts to effect improvements in the capacities of self-help organizations to assist their clients in various problems of living. By presenting several case histories of consultation with various community service centers and neighborhood improvement associations, we hope to illustrate a strategy for developing generalized methods for solving community problems through program-centered consultation with local groups. Finally, we shall discuss implications of designing behavioral technologies to build the strengths of communities.

Examples of Community Technology Building

We shall present several examples of consultation with community self-help organizations. These organizations include community service centers, neighborhood improvement associations, and community education programs. The behavioral methods used include instructional and behavior management techniques.

The examples represent attempts to collaborate with community self-help organizations in the design of behavioral technologies that might be usable by other similar community organizations. The selected case histories report technology-building efforts for several functions of community organizations noted by Hallowitz (1968):

1. Contributing to the improved functioning of neighborhood-based agencies

2. Informing residents of services available to them and how to make use of them
3. Increasing the competence of residents to cope with stressful situations
4. Fostering an attitude of service to others
5. Stimulating social and fraternal organizations to take an interest in community affairs
6. Supporting neighborhood organizations interested in community improvement
7. Assisting in the development of leadership in community councils

Case 1: Designing Methods to Teach Helping Skills to Low-Income Community Residents

The Community Technology Project has had a long and mutually rewarding history of collaboration with Penn House, a community service center located in a low-income neighborhood of east Lawrence, Kansas. Several years ago, Penn House requested assistance in teaching a variety of helping skills to the agency's low-income volunteer staff. It was agreed that the Community Technology Project would help develop, pilot test, evaluate, and make available to Penn House a series of modules designed to teach some identified helping skills.

Problem. Community service agencies such as Penn House provide a wide range of services to their clients (Kahn, 1976), including emergency food assistance, clothing assistance, assistance in paying for prescriptions, personal counseling, and information/referral to other agencies. Such services often require specialized knowledge and skills for the helper to be effective. If these skills are rare in any service agency, they are often noticeably absent in agencies staffed by volunteers. A practical and effective method of teaching these helping skills might build on the strengths of new volunteers and improve the services provided.

Learning Units and Training Procedures. In consultation with Penn House staff, a number of learning units were developed. Learning units were prepared for such helping skills as operating an emergency food room and obtaining, storing, and dispensing emergency clothing, and for such office management skills as greeting clients, taking telephone messages, and conducting client intake interviews.[1]

---

[1] These community technology modules and manuals are available from the Community Technology Project, Center for Public Affairs, University of Kansas, Lawrence, Kansas 66045.

Each learning unit consisted of a set of written instructions, a study guide, situational examples, practice situations, and a checklist that could be used to assess the learner's current skill level.[2] The content of each module was selected based on a review of the relevant literature and on interviews with expert service givers. The content identified in this collaborative process was presented to representatives of Penn House so that ultimate control over the skills to be taught remained with the neighborhood center.

The training procedures used to administer the learning modules involved the use of behavioral specifications, examples, and rationales. These were contained in the written instructions section of the module and were reviewed in the study guide and situational examples sections. In addition, the procedures provided practice in a series of role-playing situations, and practice was followed by feedback on the level of specified activities that were performed.[3]

Evaluation. Fawcett and Fletcher (1977) experimentally demonstrated that learning units could be prepared according to this format, and that such units were effective in teaching various helping skills to low-income volunteers. Mathews and Fawcett (1977) demonstrated that low-income volunteers could be trained to administer these learning units, and that trained teachers were more effective in teaching helping skills to low-income volunteers than were untrained teachers. In an experimental evaluation of the dissemination capability of these learning modules and training procedures, Mathews and Fawcett (1979a) demonstrated that these procedures could be administered successfully by nonprofessionals in other community centers who have no direct instructional contact with members of the project.

Dissemination. Field-tested learning units were organized in a helping skills curriculum at the neighborhood service center (Fawcett, Mathews, Fletcher, Morrow, & Stokes, 1976). During the initial implementation of the helping skills curriculum, eight low-income nonprofessional staff members of Penn House completed training in 85 helping skills learning units (Stokes, Mathews, & Fawcett, 1978). These and other new staff members at Penn House are contacted by approximately 650 clients per month. Thus it appears likely that the effects of this training in helping skills have been widespread.

A series of written manuals were prepared on various aspects of

---

[2] *Writing Instructional Packages: A Manual for Program Writers* by S. B. Fawcett and R. K. Fletcher.
[3] *Administering Instructional Packages: A Manual for Trainers* by R. M. Mathews and S. B. Fawcett.

helping skills involved in operating neighborhood service centers. Thus far, approximately 100 requests for manuals have been filled. In addition, low-income staff at Penn House have used these manuals to deliver workshops to change agents interested in forming neighborhood self-help organizations in other communities.

Implications. Behavioral methods for teaching helping skills may contribute to the capacities of residents to help each other, thus increasing the amount and quality of available assistance. In addition, such newly acquired skills may improve the coping abilities and self-esteem of low-income volunteer service givers (Riessman, 1965a). Thus consultation with neighborhood service centers on the design and implementation of helping skills training materials appears to be a promising approach to increasing the capacities of local communities to help themselves.

Case 2: Designing an Open Learning Center for Adult Learners

The Open Learning Center Program was developed jointly by the Community Technology Project and the East Central Kansas Action Network (ECKAN), the local CAP (Community Action Program) agency. The program was designed to address the acknowledged need for G.E.D. (General Educational Development Certificate) preparation for low-income adults. (The G.E.D. certificate is the nationally recognized equivalent of the high school diploma.) It was agreed that the project would collaborate with ECKAN on the development and evaluation of an individualized instructional program to prepare adults for the G.E.D. examination. It was further agreed that the resulting program should be administerable by the low-income nonprofessional staff of ECKAN so that the agency might not be dependent on assistance from the project.

Problem. A high school diploma, or G.E.D. certificate, is a prerequisite for many of the job training programs and semiskilled and skilled jobs available to adults. Thus many adults who have "dropped out" of the educational system perceive the attainment of the G.E.D. as a desirable and valuable goal. It was apparent, however, that many local adults were not participating in adult education programs. In Douglas County, Kansas, of some 7,000 persons without a high school diploma, only 150 were enrolled in an adult education program.

Open Learning Center and Peer-Teacher Training Program. The Open Learning Center Program was designed to meet the particular needs of low-income adult learners. ECKAN, the setting for the open learning center, was located near a low-income neighborhood and frequented by many of its residents. An adult education specialist and two peer-teachers operated the program. The peer-teachers were selected on the basis of their familiarity with the community and its residents. It was anticipated that the resulting social ties with students would help encourage the continued participation of their peers. The instructional program was self-paced (Keller, 1968), permitting flexible participation by students and individually determined rates of progress in the curriculum. Available support services, including transportation and childcare, removed some additional obstacles to participation.

A training program was developed to teach peer-teachers how to operate the program (Fletcher & Fawcett, 1978). In collaboration with the initial peer-teachers, a training manual was designed to teach such skills as interviewing applicants for the G.E.D. class, conducting placement tests, administering lesson materials, and making follow-up telephone calls to frequently absent students.[4] The training procedures included behavioral specifications, examples, rationales, practice, and feedback on performance of the specified peer-teacher activities.

Evaluation. Fletcher and Fawcett (1977) experimentally demonstrated the effectiveness of the peer-teacher training procedures in producing increases in the performance of the specified teaching activities. Ratings of the quality of teaching by relevant experts showed similar increases in such evaluative dimensions as helpfulness, competence, and overall satisfaction. In addition, attendance records for the first year of operation of the Open Learning Center showed that 60 people enrolled in the program, with 6 actually obtaining a G.E.D. certificate. The local adult education office and adult education specialist expressed satisfaction with the level of participation in the program and the number of G.E.D.s obtained by class members. These data and anecdotal evidence suggest that the program was effective in facilitating participation by low-income adult learners.

Dissemination. ECKAN's Open Learning Center is still in operation some 4 years after it began and 3 years after regular consultation from the Community Technology Project. The manual describing the Open Learning Center Program and used to prepare peer-teachers for their classroom duties has been disseminated to a number of potential program adopters.

Implications. The Community Technology Project's consultation with ECKAN and the local adult education office resulted in an educational program for low-income adult learners that could be administered by the indigenous nonprofessional staff of the service agency. Through skill training of local workers, the effects of the change agents were multi-

---

[4] *An Open Learning Center: Preparing Adult Learners for the High School Equivalency Exam* by R. K. Fletcher and S. B. Fawcett.

plied. In addition, the longevity of the program was significantly increased through special attention to making the program inexpensive, flexible, and compatible with available resources and existing program goals. Finally, the peer-teacher training procedures make it possible for local personnel to run the program with little dependence on outside resources.

Case 3: Developing an Information/Referral System for County Agencies

Under the auspices of Penn House, and in collaboration with the local county's council of social service agencies, the Community Technology Project developed an information/referral system for use by community residents working in social service agencies.

Problem. One service common to most community service centers, self-help organizations, and social service agencies is the offering of information about services provided in the community and of referrals to other helping agencies. However, it is equally common for these referral services to be provided unsystematically and for clients to be referred to agencies that can do nothing more than refer them to yet another agency. Before these program development efforts, high levels of inappropriate and unsuccessful referrals were noted in many of the social service agencies of Douglas County, Kansas. The local council of social service agencies identified information/referral as a top priority for improvement.

The Information/Referral System. The system involved the use of a social service directory, an interagency feedback procedure, and an information/referral training manual (Mathews & Fawcett, 1979c). The social service directory was based on information obtained in interviews with personnel from each of the 62 social service agencies in Douglas County that provide a direct social or community service. The directory consisted of Roladex file cards including an index of each of the 154 different services offered by local agencies, a separate card more fully describing each service offered or the problem that is handled, and a separate card listing demographic data about each agency offering a service. The feedback procedure involved the use of an interagency referral form that gave the referral agent information about the appropriateness and outcome of the referral. In addition, a staff training procedure was developed to teach the skills involved in effectively using the referral system. These procedures have been incorporated into a textbook (Mathews & Fawcett, 1981) designed to teach service givers the skills involved in using the information/referral system. The textbook also describes procedures by which others can set up information/referral systems in their own communities.

Evaluation. Mathews and Fawcett (1979b) experimentally analyzed the effects of the information/referral training procedure. The results showed that both the percentage of occurrence of specified referral behaviors and the proportion of referrals to an appropriate agency increased following training.

Dissemination. Each agency listed in the social service directory was contacted and informed of the availability of the referral system. A total of 15 local agencies completed training in the use of the referral system and adopted the program. Recently, the Community Resources Council, a United Way agency in Topeka, Kansas, contracted with the Community Technology Project to provide technical assistance in replicating the information/referral program in Topeka.

Implications. This information/referral system is an attempt to develop a technology designed to teach indigenous community service workers the skills involved in helping clients locate needed services. Insofar as these procedures help clients to do so, they extend the organization's capacities to serve and thereby increase the resources available for community improvement.

Case 4: Training Indigenous Staff of a Neighborhood Service Center in Nonprofessional Counseling and Problem-Solving Skills

In 1977, staff members at the Penn House neighborhood service center expressed a desire to learn counseling skills. In response to the staff requests, the Community Technology Project collaboratively developed and empirically tested the effectiveness of a set of counseling and problem-solving training procedures. In the first formal evaluation, with undergraduate college students acting as trainees, the procedures appeared effective in improving counseling performance, expert ratings of the quality of counseling skill, and client outcome (Borck, Fawcett, & Lichtenberg, 1979). Following this formative evaluation, the counseling training procedures were then ready to be further refined in formal evaluations with the low-neighborhood residents who served as staff members at Penn House.

Problem. Low-income people are an identified high-risk group for problems in living and are prime clientele for professional counselors. However, the monetary expense and growing unavailability of mental health professionals are obstacles to reaching low-income persons (Albee, 1967; Kaplan, Foyajian, & Meltzer, 1970). A self-help approach that encourages the use of indigenous low-income nonprofessionals as primary helpers to clientele with similar problems is consistent with a strength-building perspective on community change (Rappaport, 1977).

Counseling and Problem-Solving Skills Training Package. A manual designed to teach counseling and problem-solving skills was prepared (Borck & Fawcett, 1982b). Counseling skills trained included active listening, reflection statements, summarization statements, and question asking. A problem analysis format involving a discussion of the problem, alternatives, and consequences of alternatives was used to aid clients in solving their problems.

In consultation with Penn House staff, a number of changes in the training package were made to meet the needs of these trainees with less than a college education. For example, passages that were vague or too long were identified and revised with the assistance of house staff. In addition, these low-income counselor-trainees added many alternatives and consequences to the list of problems commonly experienced by low-income persons.

Evaluation. Whang, Fletcher, and Fawcett (1982) analyzed experimentally the effects of the training package on the counseling and problem-solving skills of these nonprofessional trainees. The results showed that the percentage of specified counseling behaviors increased following training as did the satisfaction ratings of clients.

Dissemination. The two Penn House staff members who are trained in the counseling skills will train staff of other community organizations as part of their CETA (Comprehensive Employment and Training Act) contracts. When available, the counseling manual (Borck & Fawcett, 1982) will allow for replication in other community self-help organizations. This community technology permits the training of counseling trainers, thus maximizing the effects of consultation with the indigenous staff of community organizations.

Implications. These counseling procedures were developed and evaluated under conditions that attempted to draw on the strengths of local self-help organizations and their indigenous staff members. The availability of effective self-help counseling and problem-solving procedures will help low-income residents to help each other and themselves using resources that exist in the local community.

Case 5: Designing a Community Faculty Program for County Residents

Currently, the Community Technology Project is developing a Community Faculty Program designed to link available persons knowledgeable in various living skills with persons interested in learning such skills. The program is being developed under the auspices of the Kansas Adult Education Office and in collaboration with the county adult education program and the Penn House neighborhood service center.

Problem. Based on a recent national survey, the Adult Performance Level Project concluded that 19% of all adults were incompetent, and 32% only marginally competent in the skills required to function effectively in modern society (Roth, 1976). Thus many adults appear deficient in such everyday living skills as balancing a checkbook, using bus schedules, interviewing for a job, or preparing nutritious meals. In response to a survey administered by the Community Technology Project, residents of Douglas County indicated the need for basic living skills and an interest in learning them.

Traditional modes of teaching adults appear incompatible with the needs of potential learners and with available agency resources. These factors include the lack of funds to hire trained teachers; many clients' previous, unfavorable experiences with traditional, lecture-style classroom learning; and such obstacles to regular attendance at standard classes as the absence of childcare and transportation. In addition, the identified living skills deficits cover a wider range of competence than could be expected in any one teacher. Furthermore, the varied educational levels of potential students preclude the acquisition or preparation of written materials suitable for all potential learners.

Community Faculty Program. The Community Faculty Program was designed to assist adults with a wide range of interests and abilities in learning everyday living skills. A coordinator located potential teachers based on contacts with experts from such broad knowledge areas as occupational knowledge, consumer economics, government and law, community resources, and health. The volunteer instructors who make up the community "faculty" might include employment service workers, bank clerks, legal aid lawyers, social service agency personnel, or county health department nurses.

Through advertisements at the adult education office, community organizations, and relevant service agencies, word of the availability may be spread to potential students. Since the program is designed to reflect an individual's strengths, a learner of one skill might serve as a teacher of another. Through volunteer involvement, apprenticeship-style instruction in living skills is made available to adult learners.

Evaluation, Dissemination, and Implications. As the program is currently being implemented, no evaluation data are yet available. Since the results appear promising, a description of the program will be prepared and its availability will be announced through state conferences and newsletters for adult educators and through the conventions and publications of relevant academic audiences. By providing instruction in various basic living skills, the program attempts to enhance the capacities of adults to function more effectively. By drawing on volunteers to provide instruction in the areas in which they are knowledgeable, the program recognizes and uses the community's existing strengths.

Case 6: Designing a Community Skills Exchange Program

Our collective experience with the clients of community organizations and other self-help groups underlined the fundamental inability of poor people to meet basic needs. The Community Technology Project, in collaboration with Penn House, sought to extend the resources available to residents of the low-income neighborhood of east Lawrence through the establishment of a barter system. The purpose of the Community Skills Exchange Program was to increase the cooperative exchanges of services and instruction among neighborhood residents.

Problem. The incidence of mutual help among neighbors appears to be an important indicator of the quality of community life. In many communities, mutual help is provided to residents on an informal basis through natural helping networks (Caplan, 1974).

For those residents who are not well integrated into a community, natural support systems may be of little value without additional mechanisms to enable individuals to find and use potentially available sources of help. In addition, potential helpers are often unaware of the needs of their neighbors. Furthermore, the needs of some persons in the network may be beyond the skills of their friends and immediate neighbors. Accordingly, it was reasoned that a skills exchange program providing information on community needs and skills would be helpful in extending the opportunities for mutual assistance.

The Community Skills Exchange Program. The Skills Exchange was designed to promote cooperative exchanges among neighbors by making such exchanges easier (Fletcher, Mathews, Roberts, & Fawcett, 1978). A credit "economy" was developed to ensure equity in the exchange of services and instruction. Skills were assigned credit values on the basis of the time required to perform the activity. For example, at base rate of 10 credits per work hour, a 2-hour plumbing job would cost 20 credits. Record-keeping materials allowed the storing of information on current requests and offers for skills and instruction. A trained coordinator maintained a logbook tracking each member's exchanges on an individual balance sheet.

In an effort to increase membership in the Skills Exchange and to promote exchanges among members, a list of currently available services and instruction was mailed periodically to members. In addition, a bulletin board posted outside the central clearinghouse provided a similar listing.

Evaluation. Evaluation of the Skills Exchange Program centered around two questions: whether the program allowed community residents to make exchanges successfully, and whether membership and activity within the program could be increased through outreach and publicity efforts. Informal evaluation suggested that the program components were effective in producing exchanges that were rated as highly satisfactory by consumers. Although no outreach or publicity efforts were very effective, the results suggested that the communitywide distribution of an informational brochure was an inexpensive and promising method of increasing membership (Fletcher *et al.*, 1978).

Dissemination. The capacity of the Skills Exchange Program to allow cooperative exchanges has been further demonstrated in the use of the program in a residence hall at the University of Kansas. In addition, a manual[5] describing the program has been distributed through the National Barter Project of VOLUNTEER: National Center for Citizen Involvement.

Implications. Through the practice of bartering, community residents may actually increase their resources, a condition that may lessen the stress from an inability to meet everyday needs. In addition, the social interaction aspects of cooperative activity might contribute to an increased sense of community and well-being for many individuals. Finally, the skills exchange may further the recognition of the collective strengths of local residents, thus contributing to a sense of community power.

Case 7: Developing a Speakers Bureau Program for Community Organizations

Penn House sought the assistance of the Community Technology Project in training its staff members to represent the community organization at speaking engagements with various civic, social, and fraternal organizations. Since some of the staff refused to speak because of their inexperience with and fear of public speaking, it was reasoned that a public speaking training program might enable new staff members to receive public recognition for representing the organization. The project agreed to develop such training procedures in collaboration with the initial learner-teachers.

Problem. Stimulating interest in community affairs among social and civic organizations is a function common to community organizations. Through such means as speakers bureaus, staff of self-help groups communicate their goals and activities to other community groups for pur-

---

[5] *The Skills Exchange* by R. K. Fletcher and S. B. Fawcett.

poses of sharing information, raising public issues, or seeking financial support. Successful participation in such public presentations may be an important source of self-esteem for low-income neighborhood residents. However, the probability of participation in community speakers bureaus, and the likelihood of reinforcement for participation, may be increased by training in public speaking skills.

Public Speaking Training Program. A Public Speaking training program[6] was developed to assist indigenous nonprofessional staff members of community organizations to represent their groups more effectively. Based on a review of the public speaking literature (e.g., Carnegie, 1971), a number of behaviors were selected for training including eye contact, gestures, and such opening and closing activities as greetings, topic introductions, and eye sweeps (Fawcett & Miller, 1975). A combination of procedures—including behavioral specifications, examples, rationales, study guides, practice, and feedback—was used to teach the selected public speaking activities.

Evaluation. Fawcett and Miller (1975) analyzed experimentally the effects of the training procedures on the public speaking activities of low-income nonprofessional speakers. The results showed marked increases following training in both observed rates of the targeted speaking behaviors and audience ratings of the quality of the presentation.

Dissemination. A manual describing these procedures has been distributed to numerous community leaders, academics, and community development specialists. Although the ultimate use of these manuals is difficult to determine, we are aware of at least one occasion in which the manual was used by a Chicano self-help organization in Topeka to create a speakers bureau with which to publicize their community's needs.

Implications. Insofar as the Public Speaking training program permits a broader range of community people to articulate the community's concerns, the resources for community involvement are enhanced. In addition, such community technologies may impact on the confidence and self-esteem of low-income volunteers in community organizations.

Case 8: Designing a Technology for Informing Community Residents about the Possible Consequences of Proposed Roadway Projects

In the fall of 1976, the East Lawrence Improvement Association asked the assistance of the Community Technology Project in its efforts to block the construction of a four-lane roadway through this low-in-

---

[6] An adaptation of these procedures is available, *Presenting Behavioral Research: A Public Speaking Manual for Researchers* by S. B. Fawcett.

come neighborhood. It was agreed that the project and the association would collaborate in developing a method for informing neighborhood residents about the possible consequences (both positive and negative) of the roadway.

Problem. Although decision makers are required to obtain citizens' views about building projects involving public funds such as proposed roadways and shopping malls (Francis, 1975; Kennard, 1976), the lack of relevant and easily understood information about the possible consequences of such projects is a major obstacle to citizen input (McCoy, 1975). A practical and unbiased method for informing residents about the possible consequences of a proposed project might promote knowledgeable debate and foster informed opinion.

Consequence Analysis Procedure. A consequence analysis guide was developed for citizen education about the possible effects of the planned roadway. Based on a review of the social and environmental impact assessment literature (Finsterbusch & Wolf, 1977) and interviews with representatives of the neighborhood association, city planners, and other experts, a list of 48 possible consequences of the roadway was prepared. Specific types of impacts (e.g., level of noise, time for travel to downtown) were grouped according to nine impact categories: economic, housing, transportation, safety, neighborhood unity and communication, recreation, community resources and services, community well-being, and environmental quality. Participants examined each possible consequence and rated whether the impact would be "favorable" or "unfavorable" and "large" or "small."

Evaluation. Sanford and Fawcett (1980) analyzed experimentally the effects of the consequence analysis procedure on residents' opinions about the favorability of the roadway project. The results showed that favorability ratings for the proposed roadway decreased following the use of the guide. In addition, ratings of the overall quality, knowledge, persuasiveness, and logic of the participants' verbal justifications of their opinions showed increases following the intervention.

Dissemination. A community impact analysis manual[7] detailing how other communities might design similar guides for educating their citizens about social and environmental impacts was prepared and disseminated to other interested communities.

Implications. Presumably, such methods for educating citizens about public projects that affect them might contribute to the capacities of neighborhood improvement associations to influence decisions affecting

---

[7] *Community Impact Analysis: Assessing the Possible Effects of Planned Environmental Change* by F. L. Sanford and S. B. Fawcett.

their communities. To the extent that the political participation of citizens can be enhanced by this educational technology, the citizens' power in controlling their local environment might be increased. Behavioral technologies for helping citizens prevent such shared negative impacts as an increase in traffic noise and the displacement of low-income families may reduce stress for large numbers of community residents. As such, they are compatible with efforts to reduce the incidence of problems of living by enhancing the power of community residents to control the quality of the local environment.

Case 9: Training Community Members to Chair Group Meetings

During its 13 years of operation, Penn House has relied on an executive board, composed of representative members of the low-income community and members of the staff, to direct the operation of the organization. The role of the chairperson at these meetings was crafted to provide an opportunity for indigenous helpers to achieve success in a position of leadership. This role rotates among the members so that, over a given period, each member of the executive board has the opportunity to act as chairperson. Although all of the members of the executive board were quite satisfied with this arrangement, the need for training of the chairperson had been discussed for some time. In November 1978, the Community Technology Project agreed to collaborate with the executive board in the development and use of a training procedure for chairing meetings.

Problem. Community boards have such purposes and responsibilities as sharing information, solving problems, and making decisions. Members of such groups sometimes lack the considerable skills needed to balance the need for decision making with full and equitable participation of all members. A practical and easy method of problem solving and discussion that creates opportunities for expanded participation by all members might result in a stronger group as well as wiser, more broadly espoused decisions.

Chairperson Training Procedure. Based on a review of the literature (e.g., Briscoe, Hoffman, & Bailey, 1975) and discussions with individuals who had been identified as conducting good meetings, 40 specific chairperson behaviors were identified under such categories as opening and closing meetings, leading discussions, and problem solving. These behaviors were taught using a combination of behavioral specifications, examples, rationales, study guides, practice, and feedback (Seekins, Mathews, & Fawcett, 1979).

Evaluation. Seekins *et al.* (1979) analyzed experimentally the effects of the chairperson training procedures on the activities of a low-income person serving as chairperson. The results showed marked increases in the level of chairperson behavior following training and increases in the percentage of agenda items for which closure was reached.

Dissemination. Although dissemination of these methods will await further refinement in the procedures, a manual[8] will be available for distribution of these chairperson training methods to other community organizations.

Implications. Insofar as these procedures increase the skills of the chairperson, they extend the community's resources for leadership. To the extent that the functioning of community groups may be improved by such behavioral technologies, the power of such organizations may be enhanced.

Discussion

These case histories of the design, evaluation, and subsequent use of community technologies illustrate a *collaborative* approach to consultation with community organizations. In the more traditional consultation process, the consultant bestows knowledge upon the consultee as in the "banking" concept of education (Freire, 1970). In contrast, this collaborative consultation approach emphasizes a dialogue in which the consultant presents material to consultees for their consideration. As the consultees present their own ideas about the suggestions, the consultant reconsiders the ideas first presented. Through this dialogue, community technologies are produced *with* community organizations. As a result of this coproduction process, local residents become critical of current conditions and committed to their improvement (Freire, 1970).

In the process of consulting with the various community self-help organizations, staff of the Community Technology Project provided information on alternative methods for solving problems and enhancing strengths, assistance in program planning, and support in program implementation (Feldman, 1979). To complement these contributions to community technology building, staff of self-help organizations provided information about actual consumer needs, feedback on the relevance of the consultants' recommendations, and support in implementing the procedures resulting from this coinvestigation. This collaborative consultation approach results in shared control of the design of the program and of its ultimate delivery (Feldman, 1979).

[8] *Chairing Meetings: A Manual for Community Leaders* by T. Seekins, R. M. Mathews, and S. B. Fawcett.

Broader participation in program design is consistent with Ryan's (1971a) recommendations for reorienting mental health services to produce increases in resources and power for low-income communities. Efforts should be made to increase the client's *resources* through improved information, training, and other services designed to promote independence and life satisfaction. As Table 1 suggests, the majority of the reported community technology-building efforts represent attempts to enhance available resources through information (e.g., Case 3), skill training (e.g., Case 4), or incentive procedures (e.g., Case 6).

Ryan (1971a) also recommends that actions be taken to increase the client's *power* in the community through community organizing, political, and public education activities. For example, efforts to teach people to chair community meetings (Case 9) represent attempts to design behavioral technologies to enhance the power of the community group and its members. Such resource-building and power-sharing technologies may help extend the ideological framework of community mental health from attention to treatment of an individual's dysfunction to development of the community's competence to promote human fulfillment.

Although efforts have been made to describe the characteristics of persons and groups who have competence (e.g., Iscoe, 1974), and necessary qualities for those who seek to build competence in communities (Kelly, 1971), paths to its creation remain elusive. This chapter shows the use of behavioral technologies to promote the capacities of staff of community organizations to improve the welfare of their clients. Through consultation with a number of community self-help organizations, various community problem-solving and strength-building technologies have been developed, evaluated, and implemented in the consultee's setting. Subsequently, these field-tested community technologies have been disseminated to other community organizations either by staff of the Community Technology Project or by members of the organization in which the technology was originally developed (Seekins and Fawcett, in press). Through consultation with a number of community groups, the impact of these methods has been spread to larger numbers of change agents, with the likely result that even greater numbers of clients have indirectly benefited. The emphasis on a *technology* for community improvement, providing sufficient detail for another change agent to replicate the effects achieved by the program designer, further contributes to the potential for spreading the impact of these community change efforts.

Although behavioral community technologies are promising in their potential for effecting improvements in the capacities of communities and their members, their sufficiency for remediating the fundamental problems of poverty and powerlessness is questionable (Fawcett,

Table 1. Some Behavioral Community Technologies and Their Functions

Project	Functions						
	Improving functioning of community agencies	Informing residents of available services and resources	Teaching coping skills	Fostering attitudes of service to others	Stimulating interest in community affairs	Supporting neighborhood improvement organizations	Assisting in the development of community leaders
Building community resources:							
1. Helping skills project	×		×	×	×		×
2. Peer-Teacher Training Project	×		×				×
3. Information/referral system project	×	×					
4. Counseling training project	×	×	×	×			×
5. Community Faculty Program		×	×	×	×		
6. Community Skills Exchange Project		×	×	×			
7. Public Speaking training project		×			×	×	×
Enhancing local power							
8. Environmental impact educational project						×	
9. Chairperson Training project					×	×	×

Mathews, & Fletcher, 1980). It appears that the major sources of human stress and distress often involve some form of excessive power such as environmental pollution, exploitation of underdeveloped countries, or the mistreatment of minority laborers (Kessler & Albee, 1975). Collaboration with community members in the coproduction of small-scale social improvements is only a modest step toward enhancing the resources and power of community groups and their clients. Hence the widespread realization of the competent community may await the discovery of more potent mechanisms for preventing the problems of living of many of society's members.

ACKNOWLEDGMENTS

Thanks are due our colleagues, Mike Musheno, Elaine Sharp, and John Wilson, for comments on an earlier version of this manuscript. We acknowledge our indebtedness to the people at Penn House for teaching us what we were able to learn about collaborative consultation with community organizations.

References

Albee, G. W. The relation of conceptual models to manpower needs. In E. L. Cowen, E. A. Gardner, & M. Zax (Eds.), *Emergent approaches to mental health problems.* New York: Appleton-Century-Crofts, 1967.

Baer, D. M., Wolf, M. M., & Risley, T. R. Some current dimensions of applied behavior analysis. *Journal of Applied Behavior Analysis,* 1968, *1,* 91–97.

Bard, M., & Berkowitz, B. A community psychology consultation program in police family crisis intervention: Preliminary impressions. *International Journal of Social Psychiatry,* 1969, *15,* 209–215.

Barker, R. G., & Gump, P. V. (Eds.). *Big school, small school: High school size and student behavior.* Stanford, Calif.: Stanford University Press, 1964.

Bloom, B. L. *Community mental health: A general introduction.* Monterey, Calif.: Brooks/Cole, 1977.

Borck, L., E. & Fawcett, S. B. *Learning counseling and problem-solving skills.* New York: Haworth Press, 1982.

Borck, L. E., Fawcett, S. B., & Lichtenberg, J. W. Training counseling and problem-solving with university students. *American Journal of Community Psychology,* 1982, *10*(2), 225–237.

Briscoe, R. V., Hoffman, D. B., & Bailey, J. S. Behavioral community psychology: Training a community board to problem solve. *Journal of Applied Behavior Analysis,* 1975, *8,* 157–168.

Caplan, G. *Support systems and community mental health.* New York: Behavioral Publications, 1974.

Carnegie, D. *How to develop self-confidence and influence people by public speaking.* New York: Pocket Books, 1971.

Fawcett, S. B., & Fletcher, R. K. Community applications of instructional technology: Training writers of instructional packages. *Journal of Applied Behavior Analysis*, 1977, *10*, 739–746.

Fawcett, S. B., & Miller, L. K. Training public-speaking behavior: An experimental analysis and social validation. *Journal of Applied Behavior Analysis*, 1975, *8*, 123–135.

Fawcett, S. B., Mathews, R. M., Fletcher, R. K., Morrow, R., & Stokes, T. F. Personalized instruction in the community: Teaching helping skills to low-income neighborhood residents. *Journal of Personalized instruction*, 1976, *1*, 86–90.

Fawcett, S. B., Mathews, R. M., & Fletcher, R. K. Some promising dimensions for behavioral community technology. *Journal of Applied Behavior Analysis*, 1980, *13*, 505–518.

Feldman R. E. Collaborative consultation: A process for joint professional-consumer development of primary prevention programs. *Journal of Community Psychology*, 1979, *7*, 118–128.

Fletcher, R. K., & Fawcett, S. B. *Community-based education: Behavioral training for peer-teachers.* Paper presented at the meeting of the American Psychological Association, San Francisco, August 1977.

Fletcher, R. K., & Fawcett, S. B. An open learning center for low-income adults. *Educational Technology*, 1978, *18*(11), 55–59.

Fletcher, R. K., Mathews, R. M., Roberts, T., & Fawcett, S. B. *The skills exchange: A community-based token economy.* Paper presented at the meeting of the American Psychological Association, Toronto, September 1978.

Finsterbusch, K., & Wolf, C. P. *Methodology of social impact assessment.* Stroudsburg, Pa.: Dowden, Hutchinson & Ross, 1977.

Francis, M. Urban impact assessment and community involvement. *Environment and Behavior*, 1975, *7*, 373–404.

Freire, P. *Pedagogy of the oppressed.* New York: Herder & Herder, 1970.

Hallowitz, E. The role of a neighborhood service center in community mental health. *American Journal of Orthopsychiatry*, 1968, *38*, 705–714.

Hallowitz, E., & Riessman, F. The role of the indigenous nonprofessional in a community mental health neighborhood service center. *American Journal of Orthopsychiatry*, 1967, *37*, 766–778.

Iscoe, I. Community psychology and the competent community. *American Psychologist*, 1974, *29*, 607–613.

Kahn, A. J. Service delivery at the neighborhood level: Experience, theory, and fads. *Social Service Review*, 1976, *50*(1), 23–56.

Kaplan, S. R., Boyajian, L. Z., & Meltzer, B. The role of the nonprofessional worker. In H. Grunebaum (Ed.), *The practice of community mental health.* Boston: Little, Brown, 1970.

Katz, A. H. Self-help organizations and volunteer participation in social welfare. *Social Work*, 1970, *15*(1), 51–60.

Keller, F. S. "Good-bye, teacher . . ." *Journal of Applied Behavior Analysis*, 1968, *1*, 79–89.

Kelly, J. G. Qualities for the community psychologist. *American Psychologist*, 1971, *26*, 897–903.

Kennard, B. Organization emphasis: Public's role is assessing technology. *Small Town*, 1976, *7*, 10.

Kessler, M., & Albee, G. W. Primary prevention. *Annual Review of Psychology*, 1975, *26*, 557–591.

Libo, L. M., & Griffith, C. R. Developing mental health programs in areas lacking professional facilities: The community consultation approach in New Mexico. *Community Mental Health Journal*, 1966, *2*, 163–169.

Mannino, F. V., & Shore, M. F. Consultation research in mental health and related fields: A critical review of the literature. *Public Health Monograph's*, 1971, *(79)*.

Mannino, F. V., & Shore, M. F. Evaluation of consultation: Problems and prospects. In A. S. Rogawski (Ed.), *Mental health consultations in community settings: New directions for mental health services.* San Francisco: Jossey-Bass, 1979.

Mathews, R. M., & Fawcett, S. B. Community applications of instructional technology: Training low-income proctors. *Journal of Applied Behavior Analysis,* 1977, *10,* 747–754.

Mathews, R. M., & Fawcett, S. B. Assessing dissemination capability: An evaluation of an exportable training program. *Behavior Modification,* 1979, *3,* 49–62. (a)

Mathews, R. M., & Fawcett, S. B. Community information systems: An analysis of an agency referral program. *Journal of Community Psychology,* 1979, *7,* 281–289. (b)

Mathews, R. M., & Fawcett, S. B. A community-based information and referral system. *Journal of the Community Development Society,* 1979, *10,* 13–25. (c)

Mathews, R. M., & Fawcett, S. B. *Matching clients and services: Information and referral.* Beverly Hills, Calif.: Sage Publications, 1981.

McCoy, C. R. The impact of an impact study. *Environment and Behavior,* 1975, *7,* 358–372.

Morris, D., & Hess, K. *Neighborhood power: The new localism.* Boston: Beacon Press, 1975.

Perlman, R., & Jones, D. *Neighborhood service centers.* Washington, D.C.: Office of Juvenile Delinquency and Youth Development, 1967.

Rappaport, J. *Community psychology: Values, research and action.* New York: Holt, Rinehart & Winston, 1977.

Reissman, F. The "helper" therapy principle. *Social Work,* 1965, *10*(2), 27–32. (a)

Reissman, F. The new community-based nonprofessional mental health aid. *Journal of Fort Logan Mental Health Center,* 1965, *3,* 87–100. (b)

Reissman, F. (Ed.). Special self-help issue. *Social Policy,* 1976, *7*(2).

Rogawski, A. S. New trends in consultation. In A. S. Rogawski (Ed.), *Mental health consultations in community settings: New directions for mental health services.* San Francisco: Jossey-Bass, 1979.

Roth, E. APL: A ferment in education. *American Education,* 1976, *12*(4), 6–9.

Ryan, W. Emotional disorder as a social problem: Implications for mental health programs. *American Journal of Orthopsychiatry,* 1971, *41,* 438–645. (a)

Ryan, W. *Blaming the victim.* New York: Random House, 1971. (b)

Sanford, F. L., & Fawcett, S. B. Consequence analysis: Its effects on verbal statements about an environmental project. *Journal of Applied Behavior Analysis,* 1980, *13,* 57–64.

Scheidlinger, S., Struening, E. L., & Rabkin, J. G. Evaluation of mental health consultation service in a ghetto area. *American Journal of Psychotherapy,* 1970, *23,* 485–493.

Seekins, T., & Fawcett, S. B. Planned diffusion of Social technologies for community groups. In S. Paine, T. Bellamy, & B. Wilcox (Eds.), *Human services that work: From innovation to standard practice.* Baltimore, Md.: Paul H. Brookes Publishing, in press.

Seekins, T., Mathews, R. M., & Fawcett, S. B. *Training members of a community organization to conduct meetings.* Paper presented at the meeting of the Association for Advancement of Behavior Therapy, San Francisco, December 1979.

Stokes, T. F., Mathews, R. M., & Fawcett, S. B. Promoting participation in a community-based educational system. *Journal of Personalized Instruction,* 1978, *3,* 29–31.

Tharp, R. G., & Wetzel, R. J. *Behavior modification in the natural environment.* New York: Academic Press, 1969.

Whang, P. L., Fletcher, R. K., & Fawcett, S. B. Training counseling skills: An experimental analysis and social validation. *Journal of Applied Behavior Analysis,* 1982.

Wolf, M. M. Social validity: The case for subjective measurement or how applied behavior analysis is finding its heart. *Journal of Applied Behavior Analysis,* 1978, *11,* 203–214.

17

The Neighborhood and Family Services Project

An Empowerment Model Linking Clergy, Agency Professionals, and Community Residents

DAVID E. BIEGEL AND ARTHUR J. NAPARSTEK

There is a growing realization today that mental health problems cannot be met by the services of professionals alone. The *Report to the President from the President's Commission on Mental Health* (1978) states that despite improvements in the current mental health service system, there are millions of Americans who remain unserved, underserved, or inappropriately served. Among those groups most underserved, as noted by the commission, are ethnic and racial minorities, the aged, and the urban poor. The commission specifically stresses the importance of community support systems (informal helping networks including friends, clergy, natural helpers, self-help groups, etc.) in meeting the needs of underserved populations and generally strengthening and maintaining the mental health of the citizenry.

This recognition of the importance of community support systems is, in itself, a breakthrough. The *Report* of the HEW Task Force on Implementation of the *Report to the President from the President's Commission on Mental*

DAVID E. BIEGEL ● School of Social Work, University of Pittsburgh, Pittsburgh, Pennsylvania 15260. ARTHUR J. NAPARSTEK ● University of Southern California, Washington Public Affairs Center, Washington, D.C. 20004. This research was supported in part by grant R01 MH 2653 from the Mental Health Services Development Branch, National Institute of Mental Health.

Health (1978) states that for the first time a prestigious national study group has afforded prominence to the role of non–mental health system supports in mental health. *People, Building Neighborhoods,* the final report to the president and Congress by the National Commission on Neighborhoods (1979), also emphasizes the role of community support systems in meeting mental health and human service needs. The commission recommends the development of a neighborhood-based approach to the delivery of services that would link community support systems and professional services.

Unfortunately, the growing recognition on the national level of the importance of community support systems has not as yet sufficiently filtered down to the community. Despite all the documentation, for example, of the important roles that the clergy, a major community support system element, can play in mental health prevention and treatment, there are few mental health programs that effectively utilize this important resource.

There have been difficulties in establishing linkages between lay helpers, such as the clergy, and professional networks. The mental health service delivery system suffers from problems of fragmentation, lack of coordination, and lack of access to services. These problems are reflected in the lack of communication and understanding between clergy and mental health and human service agencies. Too often clergy distrust agency professionals, most of whom they have never met, and too often agency professionals see the clergy solely as a source of financial resources for their clients.

In this chapter we shall present an empowerment model that addresses these issues by linking lay and professional helpers to improve service delivery at the neighborhood level. The model was developed through the University of Southern California's Washington Public Affairs Center's recently completed Neighborhood and Family Services Project (funded by the National Institute of Mental Health). We shall first present a general overview of the entire project and selected field experiences with the empowerment model. Next we shall discuss the role of the clergy in help seeking and receiving and review issues affecting the relationship between clergy and agency professionals. Finally, we shall focus on our field-tested demonstration projects linking clergy, community helpers, and agency professionals.

The Neighborhood and Family Services Project

The Neighborhood and Family Services Project is an action research and demonstration program. It was designed to: (1) mobilize ethnic neighborhoods around mental health issues; (2) develop model programs to overcome identified obstacles to effective service delivery; and (3) develop policy initiatives on the national, state, and local levels in support of neighborhood-based community mental health services.

Community Mental Health Empowerment Model

The project staff have conceptualized a *community mental health empowerment model* through which these goals have been addressed (Biegel & Sherman, 1979). The aim of the model is to enhance the unique existing strengths of communities and to utilize these strengths to overcome obstacles that prevent community residents from seeking and receiving help. In doing so, the model creates linkages between community and professional helping networks (see Figure 1).

Central to this model is the importance of neighborhood. The neighborhood is seen not only as a locus for service delivery but also as:

1. A support system and vehicle for the strengthening of networks, professional and lay
2. A basis for the development of mental health and human service programming
3. A means of citizen/client involvement
4. A basis for citizen empowerment in mental health

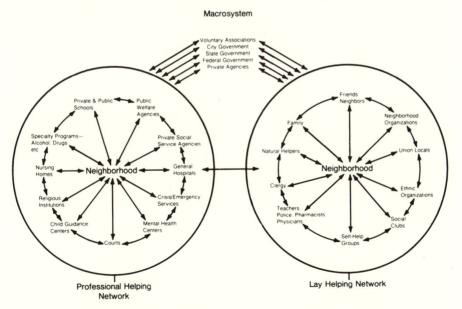

Figure 1. The community mental health empowerment model (Biegel & Sherman, 1979).

Such a view of neighborhood in the provision of mental health services helps to overcome such major problems in mental health service delivery as fragmentation, lack of accessibility, and lack of accountability of services.

The model is built on a set of assumptions that are well supported in the literature.

1. We live in a pluralistic society. Different groups of people solve problems, face crises, and seek help in various ways according to age, class, race, ethnicity, geographic factors, and so on. Social class and ethnicity are particularly important variables affecting attitudes toward and use of services; yet class and ethnic differences are often ignored by the service delivery system, which tends to be designed and operated on a monolithic, framework model.

2. Neighborhood and neighborhood attachment are a positive resource that can and should be used as a basis for mental health and human service delivery. People need to feel that daily life is being conducted at a manageable scale; in the urban setting such feelings occur largely within the neighborhood. Neighborhood has been used as a locus for service for some comprehensive mental health centers, but as little more. There are many strengths and helping resources in communities (friends, neighbors, family, clergy, schools, etc.). Professional services should be designed to strengthen these resources.

3. A sense of competence, self-esteem, and power is extremely important to the well-being of the community. Professional services should be designed to build competence and power for the community. That necessitates a radical change in the role of the community and in the role of the mental health and human service professional in the current service system.

4. The community, not agencies, needs to take primary responsibility for its own well-being. We need to rethink the role of professional services vis-à-vis the role of the local neighborhood in providing support to community members.

5. The mental health and human service systems need to become fully integrated, and such integration should involve all service delivery elements. Partnerships are needed among and between the lay and professional helping systems; these partnerships should include the community, private agency, and governmental sectors.

Project Description

The target areas for the project are Baltimore and Milwaukee. Both communities are stable, working-class areas with high concentrations of white ethnic population groups. The Milwaukee community is predominantly Polish; the Baltimore area contains Polish, German, Italian, Ukranian, Greek, and Lithuanian populations. White ethnic communities were chosen because of underutilization of professional services and evidence of strong, informal support systems (family, friends, clergy, ethnic clubs, neighbors, etc.) on which residents rely in times of stress.

The project in each city works through, and is directed by, a local community organization. In Baltimore we worked through an existing community umbrella group, the Southeast Community Organization (SECO). SECO formed the Neighborhood and Family Services Task Force to oversee the project in Baltimore. The task force, which plans and guides project activities, has 20 members and is broadly representative of the community. Its members are all community residents and are a mixture of community leaders, helpers, and others concerned with family-life issues in southeast Baltimore.

When the project began in Milwaukee, there was no community organization that represented the entire community. An intensive neighborhood organizing effort with concentration on the Catholic parishes, the area's most significant institutional resource, led to the formation of the South Community Organization (SCO). Now over 3 years old, SCO has over 20 members on its steering committee, all of whom are community leaders and helpers representing parishes, institutions, and ethnic organizations serving the community.

Parallel to the community groups' organizational process, professionals in each community were engaged to serve on a Professional Advisory Committee as a resource to the community groups. Unlike traditional models where consumers are brought in as advisers to existing programs, professionals were invited to be a part of a community-directed process. The professionals bring legitimacy, resources, and structures for programs if needed, but, more importantly, they have become active participants in the evolution of a community mental health process.

The first year of the project focused on collecting research data and organizing the community task forces and professional advisory committees. The focus of the research is on personal problems; where people go for help when they have these problems; how and when people make use of helping networks; what the obstacles are to seeking and/or receiving help; and how factors of ethnicity and community attachment intervene in the process of defining problems and utilizing helping networks.

The research methodology draws on three principal data sources:

1. *Community leader and helper survey*: 300 interviews of community leaders and helpers in each city, including clergy, human service

agency staff, natural helpers, neighborhood leaders, pharmacists, physicians, and school personnel serving the target area

2. *Community resident survey*: 250 interviews of a random sample of community residents in each city
3. *Statistical data*: census data, utilization of mental health services, and social indicator data—crime rates, welfare, health, and education statistics—utilized supportively

Community groups in each city were actively engaged in reviewing findings as they became available, in assessing needs, and then in determining mechanisms to address those needs. The following conclusions applicable to both Baltimore and Milwaukee grew out of a dynamic process of data review by community, agencies, and staff.

1. Family life and family breakdown are the focus of many interrelated problems for all the population groups.
2. A network of helping systems is needed to provide supports to the family whether that family is single, two-parent, or elderly. The present helping system is fragmented and therefore often inaccessible and not useful.
3. The fragmentation among helpers as well as between lay and professional helpers is a major obstacle to help seeking and leads to overemphasis on the values of pride and privacy.
4. People are not making use of the strengths within the community, and support system building needs to begin on a neighborhood level within the community itself.

Each city then began planning a series of demonstration projects to meet these identified needs. Although identified problems and needs in each city were similar, the strategies and priorities for demonstration programs proved quite unique.

A wide variety of demonstration projects were developed, of which seminars for clergy, agency, and community as well as brown-bag luncheons (see the following section) were a major component. The first project in Baltimore was a "Neighborhood and Family Day Picnic" attended by over 300 persons at which churches, community groups, and agencies distributed information about available family supports. The second project in Baltimore was the development of a Hotline run by community volunteers. Unlike professionally run hotlines, respondents serve as neighborhood advocates who will intervene directly (e.g., make calls) on behalf of callers, return the information, and provide follow-up support. Other activities include collaboration with the City

Health Department to establish a Health Education Center, and offering family workshops on coping with stress and related concerns.

In Milwaukee, the community organization sponsored a series of family communication workshops led by professionals and community facilitators. Mental health professionals had previously attempted to offer such a program but were unsuccessful because of a lack of community support. In this case, it was the community who initiated the project based on a need *they* had identified. Technical assistance in planning and conducting the workshops was provided by professionals. To date, over a dozen workshops, with over 500 community residents participating, have been held. In addition, presentations and skits are offered to various community gatherings as miniworkshops in family communication.

Other programs include "rap groups" for teen-agers and self-help groups for the separated, divorced, widowed, and agoraphobic. To date, four self-help groups, with over 150 members, have been formed. Many of the respondents who joined the self-help groups were ethnic, working-class women, a group that is hard to attract to organized self-help activities. In addition, an efficient referral directory was published and over 30,000 copies disseminated to community residents. Finally, a Senior Citizen Committee was formed—consisting of a coalition of groups and agencies seeking to publicize and coordinate services for the elderly.

Many of these programs are not unique and exist in other communities as well. What is perhaps most unique about the entire effort is that the project did not seek to "parachute" a standard "self-help" program into the communities, nor any *program* for that matter. Instead, guided by a conceptual framework (i.e., community mental health empowerment), the project catalyzed a *process* without prior knowledge of what specific activities might take place.

Role of the Clergy in Mental Health: An Overview

Various authors have stressed the helping role of clergy in community mental health (e.g., Caplan, 1974; Clinebell, 1970; Cumming & Harrington, 1963; Haugk, 1976; Larson, 1968; President's Commission, 1978; Veroff, Douvan, & Kulka, 1976). The importance of religious resources is recognized by the Joint Commission on Mental Illness and Health (1961), particularly in its final report, *Action for Mental Health,* in which it states that mentally troubled Americans turned most frequently to clergymen for help. McCann (1962), in one of a series of studies developed by the commission, examined the role of clergy in the use of mental health services. McCann found, through interviews with 160 individuals from one northeastern and one midwestern city, that although the majority of the respondents indicated a certain degree of independence in coping with their problems, they were more likely to seek help from a clergyman than from a psychiatrist. One-fifth or more of the respondents in the midwestern city had sought help from clergy, whereas none of the 160 respondents ever went to a psychiatrist, despite available psychiatric help.

Cumming and Harrington (1963) interviewed clergy from 59 churches and found that most of them were involved in counseling and making referrals of clients to other agencies. They also found that the clergyman, along with the physician, is the first contact made outside of the kinship and friendship circle during the onset of mental health problems. Larson (1968), using more than 1,800 cases, compared the counseling roles of clergy and psychiatrists and found that individuals who consulted a clergyman felt that they had received more help than did those who consulted a psychiatrist. Veroff et al. (1976) found more people (39%) who said that they would turn to clergy if they had a problem than to any other professional.

Religious personnel and institutions, by their very nature, seem to foster support and trust among individuals, families, and neighbors (Caplan, 1974). They are thus an important community resource that is underestimated and underutilized by community mental health agencies. "Churches and temples collectively represent a sleeping giant, a huge potential of barely tapped resources for fostering positive mental health" (Clinebell, 1970, p. 46).

The number of clergy in the United States is impressive: 393,826 ordained clergy of all faiths, including 235,189 affiliated with congregations. There are 328,657 separate congregations with an inclusive membership of 115,442,829 (Jacquet, 1972). The President's Commission on Mental Health (1978), notes that clergy and lay religious leaders are in daily, face-to-face contact with hundreds of thousands of persons who are experiencing periods of stress caused by illness, injury and accidents, death, separation or divorce, unemployment, and by other forms of loss and grief. Haugk (1976), reviewing contributions of churches and clergy to community mental health, calls local congregations "a therapeutic community" in which there are many opportunities for treatment and prevention. Haugk reports that Gurin, Hollingshead, and Redlich all found the psychiatric professions to be disproportionately preferred by those of higher education and income, whereas clergy were used about evenly by all income groups and by all educational groups. Haugk specifies numerous assets of clergy as help givers: They are geographically well located and distributed; they do not charge fees; they have personal relationships with many of their parishioners; they need not wait for people to come and talk with them—they are expected to call on people; there is little stigma attached to talking with a clergyman about problems; and they are principal "gatekeepers" in the helping system, uniquely positioned to pave the way to a referral because of their closeness to individuals in need and their professional authority.

Despite the numerous assets the clergy have to offer, the relationship between clergy and mental health professionals needs to be enhanced. The Community Support Systems Task Force of the President's Commission on Mental Health (1978) recommends that mechanisms be developed to "link the personnel and buildings owned by religious groups and institutions to community mental health centers and other social service agencies" (Vol. 2, p. 196). Research clearly pointed out that these necessary linkages are often hindered or blocked. Smith and Hobbs (1966) observe that the separation of mental health services from other human service organizations and agencies—such as the churches—has hindered the delivery of appropriate help to people in need.

Cumming and Harrington (1963) report considerable tension between clergy and mental health professionals. Whereas, clergy tended to make referrals of clients to mental health agencies, they did not receive appropriate referrals from mental health professionals. The authors cite insufficient personal contact between agency professionals and clergy as a cause of this tension:

> Social workers and psychiatrists who know a clergyman personally are more likely to exempt him from the stigma of "judgmental clergyman", and to consider him "professionalized" or "sophisticated" and thus to cooperate with him in the management of some clients. (p. 242)

This tension between clergy and mental health professionals has been aggravated by competition for so-called motivated clients. Clergy seemed to experience less tension in dealing with lawyers, doctors, and so on when there was no question of overlapping expertise. Clergy experienced role conflict, according to the authors, vis-à-vis their role as referrer rather than direct helper. They seemed unsure which clients to refer and not to refer, and how to refer without jeopardizing their role as a counselor. Their tension with human service professionals no doubt complicated this role conflict.

Larson (1968) reports significant disagreements between mental health professionals and clergy in their perception of each other's roles. In a study in which he sent psychiatrists and clergy six vignettes of persons experiencing varying degrees of emotional disturbances, Larson asked each respondent to assess the degree of mental illness, to specify the extent to which the respondent would become part of the therapeutic process, and to indicate to whom referrals ought to be made. In every instance, the psychiatrists were more likely to see the role of the clergy as referral agents only and to disagree significantly with the clergy's perception of their own role. In over 90% of the cases, psychiatrists were more likely to recommend psychiatric referral.

Our own research and field experience in Baltimore and Milwaukee confirms many of these same problems. Both clergy and agency professionals in our study reported that a considerable number of community residents in need came to them to discuss problems. There were considerable differences in sex, age, and marital status of the clients, however, with each group serving a different population. Problems of the clients tended to be similar, as were the helping actions of the clergy and agency professionals. There were considerable differences, however, in the reasons why clients came to each of the groups for help. The clergy stressed "trust," and the agency professionals "convenience/availability." Although both the clergy and the agency professionals made referrals, they made few referrals to each other.

There was also evidence that both clergy and agency professionals were unaware of problems and helping networks utilized by specific population groups. The clergy and agency professionals each thought that their own services were the most helpful in meeting needs of community residents, and each viewed the other group as much less helpful than their own. Apparently, then, clergy and agency professionals do not interact frequently and are not linked to each other. If they were, each group would tend to be less protective of their own expertise and more willing to see that other helping resources are also effective. In addition, linkages would allow each group to inform the other of community needs based on its areas of competence and experience. Professionals would learn more about lay helping resources, for example, and clergy more about professional helping resources.

Linking Clergy, Community, and Professional Helping Networks

Late in the fall of 1977, a young Lutheran minister from southeast Baltimore approached the SECO task force staff coordinator with an idea for a seminar to bring clergy and agency staff together. It was decided to form a Task Force Committee consisting of clergy, human service agency staff, and community residents.

A total of 12 persons were recruited for the committee—six clergy (four Catholic and two Protestant), five agency professionals, and one task force representative. Before the first meeting, project staff developed some planning strategies. First, it was decided that staff would contact a wide range of clergy before the first meeting of the committee in order to make sure that there was enough potential interest in a seminar among the clergy. No difficulty was anticipated in attracting agency staff to a seminar, since this type of activity is often a normal part of professional staff commitments. The clergy, it was felt, might be harder to reach. Before the first committee meeting, staff had made individual contact with over 20 clergy from the community—almost all of whom expressed considerable interest in the prospect of a seminar. This all but unanimous interest surprised us; we felt we had tapped a strong, unmet need.

The second strategy decided on by staff was to suggest to the committee that the seminar be cosponsored by as many different clergy and agency groups as possible to help ensure widespread "ownership" of the seminar, which should help attract participants. This strategy later proved a key factor in the seminar's success.

A total of three full committee meetings and one subcommittee planning meeting were actually held over 4 months to organize and structure the seminar, which was held in late April 1978. Attendance was excellent; no meeting had fewer than 10 persons present.

During the first planning meeting, the process seemed to represent a seminar in miniature. A number of clergy were meeting fellow clergy for the first time, and a number of agency professionals and clergy were interacting for the first time as well. Also, Catholic and Protestant clergy became acquainted. Relationships and linkages such as we hoped the seminar would encourage were beginning to form.

At the first two meetings, much time was spent discussing the focus and purpose of the seminar. At first the committee was inclined to an agenda that included skills training and the discussion of specific problems. This approach was later felt to be too ambitious for a first seminar, and gradually the focus shifted to an interchange of views and experience between clergy and agency professionals to foster understanding and cooperation.

From the beginning, it was the staff's "hidden agenda" that the seminar would be the first of an ongoing series. The committee members themselves decided on this goal at a very early stage in the planning process without any hints or pressure from the staff. It naturally emerged from the planning meetings that there were numerous topics that could not be covered in one seminar and that for ongoing linkages to be successfully established between clergy and human service agencies, a series of seminars or other activities was needed.

Also gradually emerging from the planning process was the realization that there were many natural helpers in the community—friends, neighbors, coworkers, bartenders, and so on (in fact, many of these natural helpers were interviewed in the research phase of the project). It was decided, later in the planning process, to widen the seminar to focus on clergy, agency, *and* community helpers.

The committee agreed to the staff's recommendations of cosponsorship, and cosponsorships were secured from about 10 clergy and agency organizations. Three separate mailings were sent to prospective seminar attendees, which included all clergy in southeast Baltimore, all Professional Advisory Committee agencies, selected other South East Human Service Agency staff, and selected guests. Personal contact was made by task force representatives to interest community helpers in attending.

Registrants were asked to preregister 2 weeks before the date of the seminar. By the preregistration deadline only 15 responses had been received—only one of which was from a clergyman. One week before the seminar, only 25 persons had preregistered. Staff began to worry that the seminar would be a failure, and the final planning committee meeting was held. Committee members took full responsibility at this point for personal recruiting efforts to increase preregistrations. Their efforts proved successful, and by the day of the seminar, over 60 persons had preregistered.

It was evident by this last meeting that committee members had taken "ownership" of the seminar. Decisions on steps to increase registration and on division of responsibilities for tasks were quickly made by committee members with little staff participation. A healthy tension developed between the Catholics and Protestants and between clergy and agency professionals, each not wanting to be embarrassed by a low turnout of their respective members.

The seminar was held in late April 1978, and 85 persons attended—32 clergy, 35 agency staff (representing 23 agencies), 15 community helpers, and three project staff. It was the largest turnout of clergy anyone could recall for any single event in southeast Baltimore. The day lasted from 8:30 A.M. to 3:00 P.M., with most of the time spent in small-group meetings. After welcoming remarks, a short skit was held, entitled "Family on the Rocks," that portrayed a family with multiple problems. Seminar participants were divided into small groups separately by clergy, agency, and community residents. Each group was charged to focus on the roles its members could play in helping the particular family and to discuss ways their group could work together more effectively. There followed a second small-group breakdown; this time each small group consisted of clergy, agency, and community representatives mixed together. The focus was now on ways that the three groups—clergy, agency, and community helpers—could work together better. Emphasis was placed on an examination of the strengths and weaknesses of each helping group.

Following these small-group discussions, there was a general session in which each group shared the high points of its small-group discussion. After lunch, a guest speaker emphasized the important roles that the clergy and agency each could play in the helping process. The day ended with a general discussion on the topic "Where Do We Go from Here?"

A sense of excitement seemed to fill the seminar room throughout the day. This impression was confirmed by written evaluations at the end of the day, in which 95% of the participants responding (42 respondents) rated the seminar as "good" or "excellent." Ninety-eight percent of the respondents stated that they would like to become involved again in similar activities.

The seminar was very successful and accomplished four main objectives.

First, approximately half the participants responding to the written evaluation form (20 individuals) volunteered to work on a committee to help plan possible future activities.

Second, participants succeeded in developing initial linkages with each other. For example, in comments at the end of the day, one nun, a parish school principal, said she came to the conference wanting to get help for two of her students, and had come away from the seminar with the names and telephone numbers of two specific agency helpers whom she had met.

Third, a "demystification" process took place. Several weeks after the seminar, a local pastor, a number of whose lay helpers had attended the seminar, remarked that his church helpers now felt much more confident as helpers. After the seminar, some of his lay helpers told him that they had previously thought that professionals had "all the answers," and that lay helpers had to be overly cautious about helping people because sometimes they might not know what to do. By interacting with professionals on an equal basis in a small group, they learned that professionals do not have all the answers either and are not omnipotent. This realization gave them encouragement and renewed energy; they learned that to help others one need not know everything all of the time.

Fourth, the seminar seemed to enhance helping groups' respect and understanding for the role of other helping groups. For example, a number of clergy remarked how surprised and pleased they were that so many community helpers appeared able to reach individuals who would not go to agencies for help. Similarly, a number of professionals who believed that professional "credentials" are necessary to help people in need went home questioning that belief.

As promised at the April seminar, in order to facilitate informal linkages, all participants were sent a list of names, telephone numbers, and affiliations of seminar attendees, as well as written suggestions from the participants for possible future activities. Soon after the seminar, an enlarged Planning Committee met to review the response to the April seminar and to plan future activities.

There were many varied suggestions for follow-up. A number of seminar participants suggested future half-day seminars to be held quarterly, an idea that the Planning Committee accepted. The committee felt, however, that additional activities also needed to be planned that would lead to more frequent interaction among the clergy, agency, and community helpers.

Melding the ideas of two committee members, it was decided that there should be monthly case study/brown-bag lunches, which would combine informal socializing with activities also having a substantive focus. The committee decided to utilize the Lancaster Case Study Method, developed by the Lancaster Theological Seminary, and to adapt it for use with an interdisciplinary group of helpers. The objective of the Lancaster approach is to develop and perfect a method of exchange among clergy around case material that will lead to sound understanding and effective decision making.

The brown-bag sessions were scheduled monthly from 12:00 to 2:00 P.M. and were open to clergy, agency, and community helpers. Participants were divided into mixed groups of about eight persons each, with each group to consider a different case. The cases were written and presented by a clergy, agency, or community helper, with one case presentation being made per group. Each case was written in advance by the presenter according to a supplied outline. Staff assisted community helpers in preparing their outlines. Before the start of the group discussion, the moderator described the process to be followed, the roles of presenter and group leader, and the time sequence (the Lancaster design was slightly modified to meet the project's purposes). The moderator emphasized that participants were not there to judge the "competence" of the presenters, but instead to seek alternative ways to help solve problems as indicated in the cases, to utilize the various kinds of expertise represented in each group, to consider workable solutions based on the specific information in the cases, and to explore the various community resources in southeast Baltimore available to help with the case problem.

Over the past several years, monthly seminars have been held and attended by approximately 25 to 60 persons per session. Feedback from participants after each session has been very positive, as has been the staff assessment of these sessions. The case study luncheons have achieved a number of goals.

First, because of the interdisciplinary mix of participants, including the specialized "common sense" of the untrained helpers, a holistic approach to problem solving has been developed by group participants. There has been a growing acceptance of the need for ongoing linkages among all helpers, lay and professional, to best meet community needs.

Second, knowledge of new and/or additional community resources in southeast Baltimore to meet identified needs was gained by group participants. The sheer number of helping resources makes it impossible even for experienced helpers to know where to refer people in need.

Third, the feedback individual helpers have received from their helping peers has led to a renewed sense of competence. For example, a young clergyman remarked that in his work he received feedback from many sources about the performance of his clerical duties—except in the area of counseling parishioners. Thus the feedback he received from the case study sessions on his counseling abilities was invaluable to him. Community helpers are often in the same isolated position, and several community helpers have also remarked how these sessions have similarly aided them.

Fourth, the sessions have protected helpers against "burnout" by allowing time to ventilate, to share frustrations and problems, and to develop expanded informal systems of social support.

Fifth, the sessions have helped to integrate new helpers into the community. Clergy and human service agency staff have high turnover rates, and these sessions have helped introduce new helpers to the community and its resources.

Sixth, the sessions have indicated areas of unmet need within the community and have stimulated the development of new services for those needs. For example, it became evident through a number of case study examples that youth problems were increasing and helpers were frustrated, uncertain how to respond. An all-day seminar was planned to focus on this issue, and over 80 helpers attended. Participants rated this seminar highly and formed a committee to pursue intervention suggestions made that day.

Conclusion

We have discussed the important role that clergy can play in the helping process and the obstacles that often prevent clergy and agencies from working together effectively. A model for overcoming these obstacles has been offered in the hope that it will stimulate others to try creative approaches to linking lay and professional helping networks. The model described is a process, not a program model. The specific mechanisms used to achieve linkages in southeast Baltimore may not be effective in New York, Chicago, or Los Angeles. The process, however, is universal in that it seeks to empower clergy, agency, and community helpers to identify resources, needs, and obstacles and to develop solutions that are relevant to their value frameworks and that will work in their particular communities.

References

Biegel, D., & Sherman, W. Neighborhood capacity building and mental health. In D. Gelfand & A. Kutzik (Eds.), *Ethnicity and aging.* New York: Springer, 1979.

Caplan, G. *Support systems and community mental health.* New York: Behavioral Publications, 1974.

Clinebell, H. J., Jr. The local church's contribution to positive mental health. In H. J. Clinebell (Ed.), *Community mental health: The role of the church and temple.* Nashville, Tenn.: Abingdon, 1970.

Cumming, E., & Harrington, C. Clergyman as counselor. *American Journal of Sociology,* 1963, *69,* 234–243.

Haugk, K. Unique contributions of churches and clergy to community mental health. *Community Mental Health Journal,* 1976, *12* (1), 20–28.

HEW Task Force on Implementation of the Report to the President from the President's Commission on Mental Health. *Report.* Washington, D.C.: Department of Health, Education and Welfare, 1978.

Jacquet, C. H., Jr. (Ed.). *Yearbook of American churches, 1972.* Nashville, Tenn.: Abingdon, 1972.

Joint Commission on Mental Illness and Health. *Action for mental health.* New York: Basic Books, 1961.

Larson, R. F. The clergyman's role in the therapeutic process: Disagreements between clergymen and psychiatrists. *Psychiatry,* 1968, *31,* 250–263.

McCann, R. *The churches and mental health* (Monograph Series No. 8). New York: Basic Books, 1962.

National Commission on Neighborhoods. *People, building neighborhoods.* Washington, D.C.: U.S. Government Printing Office, 1979.

President's Commission on Mental Health. *Report to the president from the President's Commission on Mental Health, 1978* (Vols. 1–4) (Thomas Bryant, Chairman). Washington, D.C.: U.S. Government Printing Office, 1978.

Smith, M. B., & Hobbs, N. The community and the community mental health center. *American Psychologist,* 1966, *21,* 499–509.

Veroff, J., Douvan, E., & Kulka, R. *Americans view their mental health.* Ann Arbor: Survey Research Center, University of Michigan, 1976.

18

The Social Ecology of Natural Supports

STANLEY LEHMANN

The behavioral sciences are currently undergoing what may be a paradigm shift (Kuhn, 1970). Systems approaches and ecological models are
replacing simple causal explanations with systems of reciprocal interdependences. The classic medical model, which has been criticized as inadequate for dealing with mental health issues, largely presumes unique
causes and may be inadequate for medicine as well. There is evidence
that stressful life events are closely related to disease processes (Holmes
& Masuda, 1974). External stressors, however, can be mediated by successful coping strategies (Felton, Brown, Lehmann, & Liberatos 1980;
Pearlin & Schooler, 1977). Social affiliation is a major coping resource
whether for hunting, warfare, or personal well-being. Recognition of the
importance of these factors for the understanding of behavior has stimulated new areas of research. One such area that is receiving a good deal
of attention is that of social networks and social supports: the variety of
social contacts that an individual maintains and their function in aiding
adaptation and adjustment.

This chapter takes a look at some of the ideas that have stimulated
interest in this area. Such ideas have a considerable history; the area is
broad and diverse and raises basic sociological and psychological issues.

STANLEY LEHMANN • Department of Psychology, New York University, New York,
New York 10003.

Data from a series of studies in welfare hotels in New York City will be presented with a view to understanding the nature and function of social networks and social supports. Although the populations studied are both distinctive and specialized, the data nevertheless help to develop an ecological perspective that can be applied to other populations and other conditions. Better-articulated information about social networks and how they operate as social supports may help to improve intervention and evaluation in community mental health.

Overview of the Literature

The Nature of Social Networks

It has long been a matter of conventional wisdom that relatives, friends, and neighbors make up a natural resource for most of us and one that is especially valuable in time of need. Major social theories have assumed the primacy of such groups for the welfare of the individual (Cooley, 1956) and as almost an inevitable basis for society itself (Simmel, 1949; Toennies, 1887/1957). Integration into a primary group has been cited as essential for a sense of self-unity (Mead, 1934) and lack of it as a prominent cause of suicide (Durkheim, 1897/1951). Natural supports have been celebrated in song (as in the Beatles' "I'll Get By with a Little Help from My Friends") and named as an important contribution to positive mental health (President's Commission, 1978). The concept of social ecology calls attention to the matrix of resources and demands that constitutes the functional environment of individuals. Viewing human behavior primarily as the mutual interaction between the individual and his/her environment is what distinguishes the ecological approach from the more traditional views of behavior. It is therefore no surprise that social support systems are receiving a great deal of attention from behavioral scientists who endorse an ecological point of view.

The intimate relationship between social networks and the dynamics of behavior has long been recognized, but the nature of the relationship has been subject to various interpretations. Embodied in the concept of urban ecology, the Chicago school of sociology (Park, 1967; Wirth, 1964) saw urban social patterns as closely tied to social forces that regulated urban behavior. An influential result of this concept was the social causation theory of mental illness promoted by the observed association between areas of social isolation in the city and the prevalence of mental disorder (Faris & Dunham, 1939). A more direct measure of social networks was introduced as sociometry (Moreno, 1934), and with it the idea of choice. The notion of affiliation patterns as a process of resource exchange was elaborated into social exchange theory (Blau, 1964; Homans, 1974; Thibaut & Kelley, 1959). A structuralist approach was introduced by the anthropologist Lévi-Strauss (1969) for the analysis of kinship patterns; it is not unrelated to the earlier work on communication patterns and influence in small groups and organizations (Bavelas, 1951; Leavitt, 1951). A number of these concepts have come together in studies of community power and influence (Boissevain, 1974; Boissevain & Mitchell, 1973; Mitchell, 1969).

Much of the research on social networks has concerned itself with the number of people in the network. Such studies tend to agree that the average person has from six to 10 intimate friends and a network of from 30 to 40 people who are seen regularly (Boissevain, 1974; Cubitt, 1973; Kapferer, 1973). On the other hand, a number of studies have found that schizophrenic patients have considerably smaller networks (Hammer, 1963–1964, 1973; Sokolovsky, Cohen, Berger, & Geiger, 1978; Tolsdorf, 1976). The implication seems to be that more is better. Other characteristics have differentiated the social networks of schizophrenics from those of nonschizophrenics, but there is little consistency from one study to another. The amount of interconnectedness or density of the social network is a common measure. Hammer (1963–1964) and Sokolovsky et al. (1978) report somewhat greater density in the networks of schizophrenics, but neither Cohen and Sokolovsky (1978) nor Tolsdorf (1976) report this finding. Pattison, de Francisco, Wood, Frazier, and Crowder (1975) reports both, finding that some schizophrenics are relatively isolated with sparse social networks, whereas others have small, dense networks largely made up of kin. Three of the studies (Cohen & Sokolovsky, 1978; Sokolovsky et al., 1978; Tolsdorf, 1976) agree that the people who make up the networks of schizophrenic patients tend to have fewer multiple functions in the network than people in networks of non-schizophrenics.

Community and Social Networks

These characteristics of social networks—number, density, and multiplicity of functions (generally referred to as "multiplexity" in the literature)—have figured in another important controversy. The concept of community has been linked to that of social networks. The traditional view of community is of a close-knit, localized group of people who perform multiple functions for one another—in contrast to urban social systems, which may be large but are generally more diffuse and more specialized. The change in social patterning has been represented as a decline of community and lamented as a psychological loss (Kenniston, 1965; Nisbet, 1969; Sarason, 1974; M. R. Stein, 1960). It is seen variously as a weakening of the social fabric, as an attenuation of moral and instrumental supports, and as creating a sense of alienation. A social forces theory of behavior is implicit in this point of view. Individuals have come adrift of their social anchor and become subject to the chaotic tides of social change. Social exchange theory, on the other hand, would see this change in social patterning as a response to changing demands and as possibly a more effective use of available resources. Thus the urban resident takes advantage of the broad array of available specialists and comes to adopt a social network that is relatively large. Inevitably it includes a number of people with individual functions who are not likely to know one another.

An urban social network that is relatively large but neither dense nor multiplex may represent an optimal adaptation to the urban environment, but there is seldom as much choice as this view implies. The urban poor have considerable need for support but customarily lack access to the resources and specialists they need. The ghetto resident will often retain a traditional social system with strong kinship ties not because it is more effective, but because conditions favoring the alternatives do not readily exist. Class, occupation, life style, sex, ethnicity, and so on will affect both the demands and the resources that are available and contribute to the nature of the social network that evolves (Coleman, 1975; Fischer, Jackson, Stueve, Gerson, Jones, & Baldassare, 1977; Parsons, 1968). The idea that the formal characteristics of social networks are subject to conditions imposed by social roles and social structures has been labeled the "choice constraint" model (Fischer et al., 1977). A test of this model on a sample of 985 males from Detroit showed that the formal characteristics of density and multiplexity influenced the quality of social relationships only in regard to neighborhood friends, who were chosen on the basis of proximity and convenience, but not in regard to childhood friends, friends from work, or formal affiliations or kin (Jackson, 1977). Social networks, like other ecological factors, will reflect the interplay among the context, individual needs, and competing resources.

The positive effects of social networks have been well documented in studies that demonstrate the benefits of social supports for women undergoing menopausal change (Coehlo, Hamburg, & Adams, 1974), adolescents making the change from high school to college (Hamburg & Adams, 1967), patients recovering from severe illness (Cassel, 1976; Coehlo et al., 1974; Kaplan, Cassel, & Gore, 1977), women coping with their first pregnancy (Carveth & Gottlieb, 1979; Nuckolls, Cassel, & Kaplan, 1972), recent widows (Maddison & Walker, 1967), and the rehabilitation of chronic psychiatric patients (Fairweather, Sanders, Maynard, & Cressler, 1969). The proliferation and success of self-help groups (see Chapter 15) also attests to the effectiveness of social supports. For the most part, however, social supports derive from the natural networks of friendship and kinship relationships.

Social Networks in Single-Resident Occupancy Hotels

Although social networks capable of performing supportive roles are nearly ubiquitous, most social network models suggest that they may not all be equally effective. Psychiatric patients, as observed earlier, have considerably smaller networks than most others, which is presumably disadvantageous. Difficulties in maintaining interpersonal relations appear to be characteristic of some psychiatric conditions (Gleser & Gottschalk, 1967; McCelland & Walt, 1968), and the isolating effects of custodial care undoubtedly exacerbate the problem. The lack of supportive relationships may contribute significantly to the high rate of rehospitalization (30% to 40% within 6 months: Anthony, Cohen, & Vitalo, 1978). In urban centers, large numbers of ex–psychiatric patients returned to the community end up in single-resident occupancy (SRO) hotels. These are privately owned hotels that have usually seen better days but remain in business mainly to collect welfare rent subsidies with a minimum of expenditures for maintenance. They are frequently located in commercial or transitional areas where there are few other local residents to complain about the sometimes erratic behavior of the hotel tenants. The estrangement of the expatients from society in general is thus maintained. Yet in spite of an environment that is high in stress and low in amenities, many of the hotel residents show a remarkable avoidance of rehospitalization. A small number of the hotels have some social service staff, but there is seldom sufficient time or staff for adequate therapeutic treatment. It has been suggested, however, that natural social networks in the hotels perform that therapeutic or supportive function (Cohen, Sichel, Berger, & Sokolovsky, 1975; Erickson & Eckert, 1977; Shapiro, 1971; Sokolovsky et al., 1975; Stephens, 1974, 1975).

The Initial Study

Our initial research endeavor was an attempt to document the relationship between social supports and well-being in an SRO hotel where 83% of the residents had psychiatric histories and 64% had been hospitalized for a year or longer. As a basis of comparison, we sought out two other SRO hotels. One of these had an elderly population with a median age of 72 (compared to 43 for the first hotel), but only 14% of the residents had psychiatric histories. A third hotel was chosen to be midway between the other two; it had a median age of 52 with 24% of the residents having psychiatric histories. Inevitably, there are socioeconomic differences among the hotels that correspond to the different population characteristics. In the elderly population, 74% of the residents had reached white-collar occupational levels or better as compared to 48% of their fathers. In the expsychiatric population, 48% of the residents had reached white-collar occupations or better but 52% of their fathers had reached these levels. In the third hotel, only 15% of the residents and 14% of their fathers had reached similar levels. The elderly residents had been upwardly mobile and had achieved a modest success in life, but not so much as to ensure a comfortable old age. The ex–psychiatric patients had not been able to manage any upward mobility and, in spite of their relative youth, only 10% were currently employed. Another indication of personality problems that characterize this population is that 63% had never married, as compared to slightly over one-third in the other two hotels. The residents of the third hotel represent an economically disadvantaged population that has shown little change in economic status.

Social supports were measured in two ways. A structured interview inquired about social contacts inside and outside of the hotel and an adaptation of the Family Environment Scale (Moos, 1975), was used to assess the hotel social environment. The scale was adapted in order to be appropriate for the subject population; the changes were minimal. However, only four subscales (cohesion, conflict, recreation, and organization) achieved satisfactory levels of reliability (alpha coefficients 0.63 to 0.73) and were retained. A fifth scale was devised to measure the perception of safety in the hotel, since casual conversation with the residents told us that this dimension was a crucial one in New York City. The scale, which was made to be equivalent to the format of the other scales, had an alpha reliability of 0.61. Several measures of life satisfaction were included but, since all correlated highly with each other, a simple 10-point rating ladder (Cantril, 1965) was employed as the criterion.

Identical measures were taken in all hotels and research was conducted simultaneously in all three. The data were analyzed by regressing life satisfaction on the social contact and hotel perception measures. Whereas social contacts account for only 5% of the variance in life satisfaction, positive perceptions of the social milieu of the hotel account for 20%. Differences among the hotels and perceptions of conflict and safety do not significantly influence life satisfaction. At first glance that would seem to indicate that social perceptions are more important to well-being than actual amount of social contact and that these relationships are stable across the considerable differences that exist among the hotels. A closer examination of the data, however, indicates that this interpretation is misleading.

When social contacts inside of the hotel and outside of the hotel are treated separately, a different picture emerges. The extent of outside contact is actually negatively related to life satisfaction. Although this relationship falls short of significance, it is sufficient to attenuate the overall relationship between social contact and satisfaction. Looking at the psychiatric portion of the sample separately from the nonpsychiatric portion furnishes additional information that helps to explain the results. The relationship between hotel social contacts and satisfaction is strongest for the nonpsychiatric residents. The relationship between perception of hotel social life and satisfaction is stronger for the expsychiatric residents. For these residents, outside social contacts are most detrimental. Since tenants with psychiatric histories can be expected to have greater difficulty with interpersonal relations, it follows that their perception of the goodness of their social life is more important than the actual amount of social contact.

The finding that social contacts within the hotel enhance the subjective well-being of the tenants was expected, but the discovery that outside contacts tend to be deleterious was unanticipated and more difficult to explain. Discussions with the residents of the hotels have fostered the impression that the preferred interpersonal relations are superficial and undemanding and that such interactions are characteristic of hotel social contacts but less so for outside contacts. These observations have been shared by Stephens (1974, 1975, 1976) in an in-depth anthropological study of SRO hotels in the midwest and have provided the basis for a recommendation that similar life styles may be optimal for some segments of the population (Felton, Lehmann, & Adler, 1981).

The Second Study

An ecological perspective should prepare us for diversity and specialization. The small, low-intensity social network encountered here is distinct from the traditional, in-depth community and from the large, loose urban networks. It appears to provide an effective support system for groups of ex–mental patients thrust into the urban community, the somewhat indigent elderly, and the chronic economically disadvantaged. These groups are far from identical but they seem to share a preference for a small, highly localized network of casual acquaintances. The preference is attributable not to the unavailability of other forms of social interaction but to the supportive advantage of the local network. Although the data support these conclusions, some of the reasoning remains conjectural. More needs to be known about the quality as well as the extent of the social relationships. It has been implicitly assumed that subjective satisfaction goes along with more effective functioning. Other than the gross observation that the expsychiatric population has a relatively low incidence of rehospitalization, functioning had not actually been measured. To overcome these limitations, a new study in another SRO hotel was initiated.

A hotel was chosen that had a majority of older residents with psychiatric histories. There was a full-time social service staff that provided a variety of therapy and activity groups and a lounge that offered additional opportunities for social activity. The median age of the residents was 58; the average stay in the hotel was almost 7 years. Nearly half had lived in other hotels before coming to this one. Half had never married and 40% had achieved white-collar occupational status or better as compared with only 26% of their fathers. They had an average of 12 years of education but 34% had had some college. In many respects these residents were roughly similar to the other residents we had studied, but they still represented the diversity of people that can be found in SRO hotels.

A structured interview was conducted with nearly a quarter of the residents, randomly selected. They were asked about their social contacts inside and outside of the hotel, and the quality of these relationships, from casual acquaintanceship to intimacy, was noted as well as extent. Life satisfaction was measured by the 10-point Cantril ladder and by the reported balance of positive and negative experiences over the past week (Bradburn, 1969). A new scale was devised to measure perceptions of cohesiveness, safety, and quality of social life in the hotel, using a Likert format. The residents' functional status was assessed with the Structured Clinical Interview (Burdock & Hardesty, 1968) and by cataloging their routine and recreational daily activities inside and outside of the hotel. Participation in activity and therapy groups was recorded.

The results of the study conform to the pattern of previous findings, but with valuable additional information provided by the new variables and more extensive measures. Scale reliabilities were substantially improved. Social support measures had alpha reliabilities of .82 to .89; hotel perception reliabilities were of the order of .86 and .87; the reliabilities of the functional measures varied from .76 to .82. Hotel supports have a well-documented relationship with most of the criteria that were used. Having diverse kinds of social relationships with other residents of the hotel accounted for sizable proportions of the variance in measures of subjective evaluation: 10% of the variance of reported global satisfaction; 11% of the variance in the evaluation-of-hotel social quality; and 27% of the variance in reported well-being as measured by the balance of positive and negative events experienced during the week. Hotel social contacts generally accounted for even more of the variance in most of the measures of day-to-day functioning. Although they did not account for a significant portion of the variance in routine daily activities, they did account for 17% of the variance in activities that can be considered self-enhancing such as attending class, reading books, working on a hobby, and so on, and 19% of the variance in hotel activities, such as the use of the lounge and planned group activities. They also accounted for 21% of the variance in the self-deprecation scale: the scale of the Structured Clinical Interview that is most sensitive to differences in behavior patterns. Better feelings toward the self and involvement in self-rewarding activities go along with greater social activity among residents. In contrast with hotel supports, such outside supports as contacts with friends and relatives outside of the hotel make negligible contributions to any of these criteria. There was a small negative relationship only between contact with relatives and satisfaction (1%) and well-being (4%).

Examination of the quality of social supports amply confirmed the assumption that casual, low-intensity relationships are allied with better effects than more intense relationships. Just being around others and indulging in casual conversation accounts for 27% of the variance in satisfaction and 29% of the variance in well-being. Evaluation of the quality of social life in the hotel is unrelated to any specific form of social relationship. Somewhat more involved relationships in which people do favors and the like for one another contribute significantly but modestly to satisfaction (6%) and well-being (8%). The more intense and demanding relationships of intimacy and affection make no significant contributions, and nurturance shows a negative association with satisfaction (3%). The functional criteria of self-enhancing activities, hotel activities, and the absence of self-deprecation each have 27% of their variance associated with recreational activities in which residents participate in various activities together. Intimacy in relationships contributes 5% of the variance of self-deprecation and affective relationships contribute a negative 3% to self-enhancing activities. Thus the more intense social relationships either make small negative contributions to the criteria or none at all.

This study was not designed to answer the causal questions of whether social supports lead to well-being or whether it is the other way around. It does, however, demonstrate that such general causal formulations are inappropriate. Specific forms of social relationships are associated with specific kinds of effects. In this population, hotel supports are related to both subjective well-being and better functioning whereas other forms of social support are not, although the data show that they occur with equal frequency. Furthermore, subjective well-being and functional behavior are only minimally related to one another with the exception of the self-deprecation measure, which, being subjective in itself, is related to the other subjective measures. Thus a support network can be related to positive subjective feelings but not contribute to functional behavior and, as we all know, effective functioning is not necessarily related to satisfaction. The quality of social relations appears to be equally specific. Casual relationships are associated with higher levels of functioning. The social network is part of an integral behavioral system that represents systematic ways of dealing with the environment. Recreational networks seem to be part of an active orientation, which correlates with higher levels of activity, and less involving relationships are associated with quieter forms of complacency and satisfaction. Recreational relationships actually contribute a negative 7% of the variance of satisfaction. Affective, intimate, and nurturant relationships were as common as the other forms of relating but did not perform the same functions as measured by the criteria employed, although the negative associations found in the previous samples were mostly absent. Since this population showed relatively little pathology as a whole on the Structured Clinical Interview, it is likely that the disability is comparatively well compensated and they are not as easily disturbed by more demanding relationships. Still it is clear that they respond better to the less demanding ones.

A comparison between residents with and without psychiatric histories generally replicates the results of the previous study. Both satisfaction and well-being are more closely associated with perceived hotel social quality than with the extent of hotel social supports for the expatient sample, whereas the reverse is so for residents without psychiatric histories. That the nonpsychiatric residents are mostly alcoholics undoubtedly complicates the picture. Their satisfaction and well-being are much more closely related to the hotel social network, which accounts for 27% and 43% of the variance, respectively, than that of the expatients where the contribution from hotel networks is small and not significant. On the other hand, hotel networks contribute 32% of the variance of perceived hotel social quality for the expatients but provide a negligible effect for the others. Thus it seems that the social networks influence the subjective evaluations of the expatients by providing a more positive social atmosphere in the hotel, which in turn leads to general satisfaction. The more socially inclined alcoholics appear to be responding more directly to social activity per se.

Networks as a Resource

The general pattern of results has been replicated in four different SRO hotels with a fair variety of residents. In-hotel supports tend to have a greater density or connectedness and to show a greater multiplicity of functions than outside networks. These properties probably enhance the effectiveness of the social network for this population, which has a restricted tolerance for social interactions and hence must make do with a smaller network.

In spite of the obvious importance of social contacts for the residents of these hotels, the actual level of social activity is quite low. Thus density and multiplexity mean something different for this population from what they may mean for a traditional rural community. Not only do these SRO residents not share the diffuse and specialized networks of other urban dwellers, but social relationships outside of their immediate environment are not generally facilitative. For apparently similar reasons, more intense and generally valued relationships of intimacy, affect, and nurturance do not provide the usual support. Although systematic investigations that would afford rigorous comparisons are simply not available, it is not likely that these characteristics are typical of the general population. On the other hand, social network characteristics that are typical for the general population may not exist and ecological variation may be the rule.

There is ample evidence that in-hotel social networks provide an important resource that contributes to the well-being and functioning of a sizable portion of those living in SRO hotels. By default, the hotels have become a major, though informal, social institution, serving as a neglected and largely unattended repository for the marginal and socially disadvantaged. As an inadvertent solution to a major social problem, SROs are problematic. They are considerably less expensive to the public and possibly more humane than the institutions they replace. Yet much of the general public, with reasonably good intentions, has decried the tawdry conditions of the buildings and the motley array of tenants, and advocates the elimination of SRO hotels. Even without such social pressure, the number of these hotels has decreased by over one-third within the past 5 years (*New York Times,* January 27, 1980). Ironically, the reason for their demise is the same as the reason for their existence: economic advantage. More profitable uses have now been found for this property.

The elimination of SRO hotels will not resolve the social problem. The hotels have existed and even thrived because they provide a social resource for a varied clientele who share an adaptation to adversity that makes effective use of a permissive and undemanding environment. Abolishing a resource without providing an alternative, like deinstitutionalization, which helped to spawn the SRO in the first place, simply changes the outward appearance of the problem and often eases it into someone else's backyard. Adequate solutions need to recognize that even unwanted situations must be functional to survive. In a very few of these hotels, such as the one just reported on, a small and dedicated group of social service workers is laboring to make them more habitable. Possibly, their most important functions are permitting these indigenous social networks to survive and encouraging them. Hospitalization tends to hinder the formation of natural social systems and may help to promote chronicity for this reason. The therapeutic community achieved some success by reversing this process. An alternative to, or an improvement on, the SRO hotel must concern itself with the preservation of those ingredients that foster indigenous support systems.

The specific findings of these studies are not meant to be readily generalized to other populations and other settings. Formation of small, dense, multiplex social networks and the avoidance of close personal relationships are not optimal strategies for everybody. These data clearly demonstrate that behavior must be understood as a coherent system. Neither number nor quality nor other specific characteristics of social relationships can serve as a universal criterion of goodness of fit. There is little doubt that social networks are important and necessary resources for most people, but the appropriate nature of the network will be determined by the needs and capacities of the individual and the facilities and limitations of the setting. The urban, suburban, or rural character of the setting, as well as age, sex, and economic status are clearly factors that will influence the nature of the social network, both singly and in combination. The study of SRO hotels has emphasized the importance of person–environment fit when dealing with the social environment. It also demonstrates the surprising amount of regularity that can be found in such systems.

The current emphasis on community support systems (L. I. Stein & Test, 1978; Turner & TenHoor, 1978) recognizes the need for continuing support for those with emotional and psychological handicaps but concentrates largely on professional networks. Without minimizing the importance of the professional contribution, it should be noted that friends, relatives, and associates are generally more important to the well-being of most of us. Edmunson *et al.* (Chapter 6), aware of that fact, are trying to develop peer supports in the community. To the extent that these are natural outgrowths of the needs and resources of a specialized community, they are likely to be serviceable and enduring. Jeger, Slotnick, and Schure (1982) suggest that both patients and professionals can profit by sharing mutual resource exchange networks. A clearer understanding of ecologically effective social systems can lead to interventions and innovations that have a better chance of producing the wanted results. This brief excursion into the affiliative networks of SRO hotels has shown that the natural development of support systems can take a variety of forms that are both adaptive and appropriate to the population and setting.

ACKNOWLEDGMENTS

I wish to acknowledge the indispensable cooperation of the staff of the Department of Psychiatry of Roosevelt Hospital in New York City, who provided the opportunity for this research. Special appreciation is due Dr. Kathleen Sullivan, staff psychologist, and the research assistants, Carol Huckabee and Mary Evers, who made the project possible.

References

Anthony, M. A., Cohen, M. R., & Vitalo, R. The measurement of rehabilitation outcome. *Schizophrenia Bulletin*, 1978, *4*, 365–398.
Bavelas, A. An experimental approach to organizational communication. *Personnel*, 1951, *27*, 366–371.
Blau, P. *Exchange and power in social life*. New York: Wiley, 1964.
Boissevain, J. *Friends of friends*. New York: St. Martin's Press, 1974.
Boissevain, J., & Mitchell, J. C. (Eds.). *Network analysis: Studies in human interaction*. The Hague: Mouton, 1973.
Bradburn, N. W. *The structure of psychological well-being*. Chicago: Aldine, 1969.
Burdock, E. I., & Hardesty, A. S. A psychological test for psychopathology. *Journal of Abnormal Psychology*, 1968, *73*, 62–69.
Cantril, H. *The patterns of human concerns*. New Brunswick, N.J.: Rutgers University Press, 1965.
Carveth, W. B., & Gottlieb, B. H. The role of primary group support in mediating stress: An empirical study of new mothers. *Canadian Journal of Behavioral Science*, 1979, *11*, 179–188.
Cassel, J. The contribution of the social environment to host resistance. *American Journal of Epidemiology*, 1976, *104*, 107–123.
Cobb, S. Social support as a moderator of life stress. *Psychosomatic Medicine*, 1976, *38*, 300–314.
Coelho, G., Hamburg, D. A., & Adams, J. E. *Coping and adaptation*. New York: Basic Books, 1974.

Cohen, C., & Sokolovsky, J. Schizophrenia and social networks: Ex-patients in the inner city. *Schizophrenia Bulletin,* 1978, *4,* 546–560.

Cohen, C. I., Sichel, W. R., Berger, D., & Sokolovsky, J. *Breaking the revolving door syndrome.* Paper presented at the annual meeting of the American Psychiatric Association, Anaheim, California, May 1975.

Coleman, J. S. Social structure and a theory of action. In P. Blau (Ed.), *Approaches to the study of social structure.* New York: Free Press, 1975.

Cooley, C. H. *Social organization.* Glencoe, Ill.: Free Press, 1956.

Cubitt, T. Network density among urban families. In J. Boissevain & J. C. Mitchell (Eds.), *Network analysis: Studies in human interaction.* The Hague: Mouton, 1973.

Durkheim, E. *Suicide.* Glencoe, Ill.: Free Press, 1951. (Originally published, 1897.)

Erickson, R. J., & Eckert, J. K. The elderly poor in downtown San Diego hotels. *Gerontologist,* 1977, *17,* 440–446.

Fairweather, G. W., Sanders, D. H., Maynard, H., & Cressler, D. L. *Community life for the mentally ill.* Chicago: Aldine, 1969.

Faris, R. E. L., & Dunham, H. W. *Mental disorders in urban areas: An ecological study of schizophrenia and other psychoses.* Chicago: University of Chicago Press, 1939.

Felton, B. J., Brown, P., Lehmann, S., & Liberatos, P. The coping function of sex role attitudes during marital disruption. *Journal of Health and Social Behavior,* 1980, *21*(3), 240–248.

Felton, B. J., Lehmann, S., & Adler, A. SRO hotels: Their validity as housing options for the elderly. In M. P. Lawton, & S. M. Hoover (Eds.), *Community housing choices for older Americans.* New York: Springer, 1981.

Fischer, C. S., Jackson, R. M., Stueve, C. A., Gerson, K., Jones, L. M., & Baldassare, M. *Networks and places: Social relations in an urban setting.* New York: Free Press, 1977.

Gleser, G. C., & Gottschalk, L. A. Personality characteristics of chronic schizophrenics in relationship to sex and current functioning. *Journal of Clinical Psychology,* 1967, *23,* 349–354.

Hamburg, D. A., & Adams, J. E. A perspective on coping behavior. *Archives of General Psychiatry,* 1967, *17,* 277–284.

Hammer, M. Influence of small social networks as factors on mental hospital admission. *Human organization,* 1963–1964, *22,* 243–251.

Hammer, M. Psychopathology and the structure of social networks. In M. Hammer & K. Salzinger (Eds.), *Psychopathology: Contributions from the social, behavioral and biological sciences.* New York: Wiley, 1973.

Holmes, T. H., & Masuda, M. Life change and illness susceptibility. In B. S. Dohrenwend & B. P. Dohrenwend (Eds.), *Stressful life events: Their nature and effects.* New York: Wiley, 1974.

Homans, G. C. *Social behavior.* New York: Harcourt, Brace & Jovanovich, 1974.

Jackson, R. M., Fisher, C. S., & Jones, L. M. The dimensions of social networks. In C. S. Fisher (Ed.), *Networks and places: Social relations in an urban setting.* New York: Free Press, 1977.

Jeger, A. M., Slotnick, R. S., & Schure, M. Towards a "self-help/professional collaborative" model of human service delivery. In D. E. Biegel & A. J. Naparstek (Eds.), *Community support systems and mental health: Research, practice, and policy.* New York: Springer, 1982.

Kapferer, B. Social network and conjugal role in urban Zambia. In J. Boissevain & J. C. Mitchell (Eds.), *Network analysis.* The Hague: Mouton, 1973.

Kaplan, B., Cassel, J., & Gore, S. Social support and health. *Medical Care,* 1977, *15,* 47–58.

Kenniston, K. *The uncommitted.* New York: Dell Books, 1965.

Kuhn, T. S. *The structure of scientific revolutions*. Chicago: University of Chicago Press, 1970.

Leavitt, H. J. Some effects of certain communication patterns on group performance. *Journal of Abnormal and Social Psychology*, 1951, *46*, 38–50.

Lévi-Strauss, C. *The elementary structures of kinship*. Boston: Beacon Press, 1969.

Maddison, D., & Walker, W. Factors affecting the outcome of conjugal bereavement. *British Journal of Psychiatry*, 1967, *113*, 1057–1067.

McCelland, D. C., & Walt, N. F. Sex role alienation in schizophrenia. *Journal of Abnormal Psychology*, 1968, *12*, 217–220.

Mead, G. H. Impulse to sociability. In C. Morris (Ed.), *Mind, self, and society*. Chicago: University of Chicago Press, 1934.

Mitchell, J. C. The concept and use of social networks. In J. C. Mitchell (Ed.), *Social networks in urban situations*. Manchester: University of Manchester Press, 1969.

Moos, R. H. *Evaluating correctional and community settings*. New York: Wiley, 1975.

Moreno, J. L. *Who shall survive?* Washington, D.C.: Nervous and Mental Disease Publishing Co., 1934.

Nisbet, R. A. *The quest for community*. New York: Oxford University Press, 1969.

Nuckolls, C. B., Cassel, J., & Kaplan, B. H. Psychosocial assets, life crisis and the prognosis of pregnancy. *American Journal of Epidemiology*, 1972, *95*, 431–441.

Park, R. E. *On social control and collective behavior: Selected papers*. Chicago: University of Chicago Press, 1967.

Parsons, T. *The structure of social action*. New York: Free Press, 1968.

Pattison, E. M., de Francisco, D., Wood, P., Frazier, H., & Crowder, J. A psychological kinship model for family therapy. *American Journal of Psychiatry*, 1975, *132*, 1246–1251.

Pearlin, L., & Schooler, C. The structure of coping. *Journal of Health and Social Behavior*, 1977, *18*, 1–32.

President's Commission on Mental Health. *Mental health in America, 1978*. Washington, D.C.: U.S. Government Printing Office, 1978.

Sarason, S. B. *The psychological sense of community*. San Francisco: Jossey-Bass, 1974.

Shapiro, J. H. *Communities of the alone: Working with single room occupants in the city*. New York: Association Press, 1971.

Simmel, G. The sociology of sociability. *American Journal of Sociology*, 1949, *55*, 254–261.

Sokolovsky, J., Cohen, C. I., Berger, D., & Geiger, J. Personal networks of ex-mental patients in a Manhattan SRO hotel. *Human Organization*, 1978, *37*, 5–51.

Stein, L. I., & Test, M. A. An alternative to mental hospital treatment. In L. I. Stein & M. A. Test (Eds.), *Alternatives to mental hospital treatment*. New York: Plenum Press, 1978.

Stein, M. R. *The eclipse of community*. New York: Harper & Row, 1960.

Stephens, J. Romance in the SRO: Relationships of elderly men and women in a slum hotel. *Gerontologist*, 1974, *14*, 279–282.

Stephens, J. Society of the alone: Freedom, privacy and utilization as dominant norms in the SRO. *Journal of Gerontology*, 1975, *30*, 230–235.

Stephens, J. *Loners, losers and lovers: A sociological study of the aged tenants in a slum hotel*. Seattle: University of Washington Press, 1976.

Thibaut, J., & Kelley, H. H. *The social psychology of groups*. New York: Wiley, 1959.

Toennies, F. *Community and society*. East Lansing: University of Michigan Press, 1957. (Originally published, 1887.)

Tolsdorf, C. C. Social networks, support and coping. *Family Process*, 1976, *15*, 407–418.

Turner, J. C., & TenHoor, W. J. The NIMH community support program: Pilot approach to a needed social reform. *Schizophrenia Bulletin*, 1978, *4*, 319–348.

Wirth, L. *On cities and social life: Selected papers*. Chicago: University of Chicago Press, 1964.

VI

Evaluation and Community Accountability

Introduction

The four chapters in this part present various approaches to evaluation and community accountability. They focus on specific case studies of community mental health center program evaluations, a particular comprehensive evaluation methodology, and a conceptual model of accountability to guide ethical practice. Here we shall consider the major types of evaluation and highlight some key issues in the emerging field of program evaluation in mental health.

Although clinical researchers have long been concerned with the evaluation of psychotherapy (e.g., Bergin & Strupp, 1970; Eysenck, 1952, 1966; Meltzoff & Kornreich, 1970), program evaluation or evaluation research as a distinct speciality is an outgrowth of the broader social and educational projects of the late 1960s and early 1970s (Glass, 1976). As funding and accrediting agencies increased their demands for accountability, the emphasis on evaluation permeated the mental health field. This emphasis is specifically reflected in community mental health centers: The 1975 Amendments (Public Law 94-63) required federally funded centers to allocate 2% of their operating funds to program evaluation.

Focusing on broadly based mental health programs, McLean (1974) identifies five major approaches to evaluation: (1) program structure; (2) program process; (3) program outcome; (4) cost analysis; and (5) systems analysis.

The evaluation of *program structure* is seen by McLean as "administrative" evaluation, since its major concern is with the resources allocated to a program. It includes such data as staff–client ratios, the nature of the clientele, and characteristics of the physical facilities. In general, information derived from such evaluations is descriptive. Although they do not bear directly on the effectiveness of a program, such data are especially useful to determine who is served and the extent of services provided relative to needs (Hammer, Landsberg, & Neigher, 1976).

Evaluation of *program process* is concerned with the entire course of intervention. It may consider such aspects as continuity of treatment and may incorporate analyses of case studies and treatment failures. Ellsworth (1975) points to the increased attention paid to documenting what is done to clients in mental health settings, as peer review and quality control committees have developed to examine client records. Many process studies (e.g., those that consider such variables as client satisfaction) do shed some light on outcome.

According to McLean, *outcome evaluation* is "the most fundamental and significant kind of evaluation data. It is the proof-in-the-pudding of all mental health programs" (p. 90). Two major classes of issues pertain to outcome evaluation: One is concerned with assessing change, the other with research design.

Evaluations of change have largely focused on client changes and have utilized self-reports, staff ratings, ratings of significant others, and overt, naturalistic behavior observations. Criteria have included symptom checklists, ratings of global functioning, changes in psychiatric traits, client satisfaction, and reduction of admissions to treatment facilities (McLean, 1974). Although client changes constitute the most frequent target in outcome assessment, in the case of such indirect service programs as consultation with community caregivers, training nonprofessionals, and community education, changes in consultees, trainees, and community residents are worthy goals in themselves even if they do not immediately translate into client changes (Jeger & McClure, 1980; see also Chapter 9).

In terms of demonstrating long-term impact of a program, the "timing" of evaluations is a major dilemma. As Wortman (1975) puts it, "the longer the period of evaluation, the more likely are systems feedback effects to alter and reduce its impact; and the shorter the period, the less likely the program will have sufficient time to achieve its goals" (p. 574). Thus there is a need for continuous assessment, measurement at several points, and long-term follow-ups.

Finally, the lack of standardization across outcome studies makes it increasingly difficult to arrive at empirically based decisions concerning the relative efficacy of programs. We believe that wherever possible, some standardized instrument should be incorporated.

In the area of research design, perhaps the key controversy centers around the utility of experimental designs. Clearly, from a methodological standpoint a treatment/intervention versus control group design with pre-post measures taken on both groups (i.e., a true experimental design —Campbell & Stanley, 1966) is ideal. Despite difficulties in assigning clients to control groups in natural settings, leading behavioral scientists have advocated the experimental model in evaluating social programs. Prototypical of this approach is Fairweather's (1967, 1972) model of "experimental social innovation," upon which the Community Lodge was evaluated (see Chapter 5). He suggests designing innovations and scientifically evaluating their effectiveness through experimental comparisons with already existing programs. This idea is consistent with Campbell's (1969) notion of the "experimenting society," whereby he recommends that an experimental methodology be used to evaluate social reform programs and that the data serve to guide social policy.

On the other hand, Weiss and Rein (1970) points to the limitations of experimental designs in evaluating broad-aim social programs from both practical and conceptual perspectives. For example, a major drawback of the experimental model lies in its inability to shed light on negative findings. That is, failure to obtain significant between-group mean differences allows for alternative interpretations to the apparent conclusion that the program had no positive impact. Unmeasured changes could have taken place, insensitive instruments could have been selected, or gains made by one segment of a population could have been canceled by a relatively unaffected segment. Furthermore, even in the case of positive findings, it is difficult to determine whether forces other than the program could be responsible for the effects because of the overwhelming number of uncontrolled factors. Also, the Hawthorne effect associated with any new innovation becomes almost impossible to control in a field experiment, leaving placebo factors as a possible explanation in simple experimental versus control group designs (Erickson, 1975). The use of additional control groups is rarely possible in the field.

Alternatives to experimental designs are necessary because they are predicated on the view that action programs are continuous, ongoing processes. Rather than one-shot measures to assess outcome, the comprehensive feedback models focus on a close monitoring of program process, incorporating historical and political analyses within a social systems framework (D'Augelli, 1976; Guttentag, 1971, 1973; Suchman, 1972; Weiss & Rein, 1970). The flavor of these alternative evaluation models is best captured by an excerpt from Weiss and Rein (1970):

> Evaluations of broad-aim programs should identify the forces which shaped the program, the nature of the opposition encountered, the reasons for suc-

cess or failure, and the program's unanticipated consequences. Then, in addition, the research might decide whether or not anticipated changes occurred. The issue in the evaluation of broad-aim programs is not "Does it work?" but "What happened?" (pp. 103–104)

The position of behavioral-ecology is that wherever possible, experimental designs should be employed: They ultimately yield more convincing data regarding cause-and-effect relationships and the differential effectiveness of two or more programs—data that are necessary for empirically rooted policies. However, realizing the limitations of experimental designs as well as the broader social context in which programs develop, process-type analyses are deemed essential if we are to arrive at an understanding of effects of the program and the social system on each other (Jeger, 1977). Thus behavioral-ecology emphasizes the complementary aspects of experimental and nonexperimental approaches to evaluation.

Cost analysis is becoming more critical given the limited allocation of resources to most social service programs. The impact of a program must be assessed relative to its direct and indirect costs (loss of productivity, etc.). Methods for cost accounting for primary prevention are provided by Dooley and Catalano (1977). Within behavioral programs, some cost–benefit analyses are beginning to appear (e.g., the token economy—Foreyt, Rockwood, Davis, Devousges, & Hollingsworth, 1975). Other aspects of mental health programs subjected to cost–benefit analyses include the effects of psychotherapy versus medication (Karon & Vandenbos, 1975), the use of psychologists versus psychiatrists (Karon & Vandenbos, 1976), and of professionals versus nonprofessional therapists (King, 1976). Clearly, cost analysis is not an alternative to the previous approaches but provides an additional focus.

As a model of program evaluation, McLean identifies *systems analysis* as a macrolevel analysis of a fairly large region for policy purposes. His example from the mental health field is the utilization of cumulative psychiatric case registers for determining statewide service needs.

We emphasize that for large-scale data banks to be meaningful, they must rely on local information. It is imperative that some standardized data be collected from all centers. In addition to serving mental health planners, a promising feature of systems analysis is that it may permit investigations of the many interacting factors related to outcome.

Several additional issues cut across all five types of evaluation. Evaluators should be sensitized to the need to involve clinicians (i.e., direct service staff) in data collection and to offer them feedback based on information collected. This approach will increase the likelihood of acceptable findings and result in program changes. There is nothing more frustrating to evaluators than when their data are not used to influence policy. Furthermore, evaluation data should be made available to catchment-area citizens and discussed at public forums.

Finally, Zusman and Bissonette (1973) recommend that evaluations be conducted early in a program's history "before vested interests have solidified and organizational inertia has set in" (p. 123). Resistance to change would make the entire evaluation effort futile regardless of how well it may be designed.

In Chapter 19 Goodson and Turner report on the evaluation of the Huntsville (Alabama) Mental Health Center, which operated along behavior modification lines. They emphasize the value of behavioral approaches in all service components of comprehensive community mental health centers because of their empirical features, which facilitate evaluation and accountability. A particularly unique feature of the center is the staff motivational system, in which incentives (pay increase, vacation time, etc.) contingent on behavioral job performance criteria are built into contracts. The authors also point to the need for behavioral programs (e.g., parent training) to be more sensitive to ethnic and cultural factors.

Moos and Lemke (Chapter 20) present their Multiphasic Environmental Assessment Procedure (MEAP), in which an instrument package taps various features of a setting including physical and architectural, policy and program, resident and staff, and social-environmental features. Although the MEAP was developed in the course of research on sheltered care environments, many of the dimensions are relevant to other health and human service settings. The authors emphasize the utility of the MEAP for catalyzing changes in programs. Specifically, the MEAP is useful in identifying problem areas, suggesting change strategies, and reassessing the setting to determine the effects of the change program.

In Chapter 21 Wandersman and his colleagues report on a project that focused on assessing the structure and functions of a citizen advisory committee (CAC) in one community mental health center. Guided by a systems perspective, the research compared assessments of the CAC by CAC members, representative staff members, and the center's board of directors. Furthermore, the authors report on the process of their study including such issues as perceived researchers' role, entry into the sytem, and utilization of findings. For example, the research team presented themselves as performing an assessment function, rather than program evaluation per se, but were somewhat misperceived by center administration. The significance of incorporating a process analysis to complement quantitative data in community research is underlined by the authors.

In Chapter 22 Jeger and McClure demonstrate the complementary use of an experimental evaluation and process analysis of a behavioral consultation program with a state psychiatric center. The experimental evaluation employed multilevel assessment procedures encompassing measures at three targets: consultees, clients, and the social environment. The process analysis focused on the effects of the system on the program as well as the programs's effects on the system.

Finally, in Chapter 23 Eilbert and Eilbirt present a structural framework for conceptualizing ethical issues in behavioral-ecological practice. They consider ethical issues pertaining to demand for mental health services, creation and allocation of supply of services, and quality of services along a five-stage temporal sequence of individual and community interventions—pre-client contact, initial assessment period, course of intervention, termination, and follow-up. In addition, underlying ethical enigmas pertaining to broader role relationships of professionals vis-à-vis clients, colleagues, and other professional systems are considered in the context of community accountability.

References

Bergin, A. E., & Strupp, H. H. New directions in psychotherapy research. *Journal of Abnormal Psychology*, 1970, *76*, 13–26.

Campbell, D. T. Reforms as experiments. *American Psychologist*, 1969, *24*, 409–429.

Campbell, D. T., & Stanley, J. C. *Experimental and quasi-experimental designs for research*. Chicago: Rand McNally, 1966.

D'Augelli, J. F. *Evaluation process: A model*. Paper presented at the meeting of the American Psychological Association, Washington, D.C., September 1976.

Dooley, C. D., & Catalano, R. Money and mental disorder: Toward behavioral cost acounting for primary prevention. *American Journal of Community Psychology*, 1977, *5*, 217–227.

Ellsworth, R. B. Consumer feedback in measuring the effectiveness of mental health programs. In E. L. Struening & M. Guttentag (Eds.), *Handbook of evaluation research* (Vol. 2). Beverly Hills, Calif.: Sage, 1975.

Erickson, R. C. Outcome studies in mental hospitals: A review. *Psychological Bulletin*, 1975, *82*, 519–540.

Eysenck, H. J. The effects of psychotherapy: An evaluation. *Journal of Consulting Psychology*, 1952, *16*, 319–324.

Eysenck, H. J. *The effects of psychotherapy*. New York: The International Science Press, 1966.

Fairweather, G. W. *Methods for experimental social innovation*. New York: Wiley, 1967.

Fairweather, G. W. *Social change: The challenge to survival*. Morristown, N.J.: General Learning Press, 1972.

Foreyt, J. P., Rockwood, C. E., Davis, J. C., Desvousges, W. H., & Hollingsworth, R. Benefit-cost analysis of a token economy program. *Professional Psychology*, 1975, *6*, 26–33.

Glass, G. V. (Ed.). *Evaluation studies review annual*. Beverly Hills, Calif.: Sage, 1976.

Guttentag, M. Models and methods in evaluation research. *Journal for the Theory of Social Behavior*, 1971, *1*, 75–95.

Guttentag, M. Subjectivity and its use in evaluation research. *Evaluation*, 1973, *1*, 60–75.

Hammer, R., Landsberg, G., & Neigher, W. (Eds.). *Program evaluation in community mental health centers*. New York: D&O Press, 1976.

Jeger, A. M. *The effects of a behavioral consultation program on consultees, clients, and the social environment*. Unpublished doctoral dissertation, State University of New York at Stony Brook, 1977.

Jeger, A. M., & McClure, G. The effects of a behavioral training program on non-professionals' endorsement of the "psychosocial" model. *Journal of Community Psychology*, 1980, *8*, 239–243.

Karon, B. P., & Vandenbos, G. R. Treatment costs of psychotherapy as compared to medication for schizophrenia. *Professional Psychology*, 1975, *6*, 293–298.

Karon, B. P., & Vandenbos, G. R. Cost/benefit analysis: Psychologist versus psychiatrist for schizophrenics. *Professional Psychology*, 1976, *7*, 107–111.

King, G. D. *Evaluation of training programs*. Paper presented at the meeting of the American Psychological Association, Washington, D.C., September 1976.

McLean, P. D. Evaluating community-based psychiatric services. In P. O. Davidson, F. W. Clark, & L. A. Hamerlynck (Eds.), *Evaluation of behavioral programs in community, residential, and school settings*. Champaign, Ill.: Research Press, 1974.

Meltzoff, J., & Kornreich, M. *Research in psychotherapy*. New York: Atherton, 1970.

Suchman, E. A. Action for what? A critique of evaluative research. In C. M. Weiss (Ed.), *Evaluating action programs: Readings in social action and education*. Boston: Allyn & Bacon, 1972.

Weiss, R. S., & Rein, M. The evaluation of broad-aim programs: Experimental design, its difficulties, and an alternative. *Administrative Science Quarterly*, 1970, *15*, 97–109.

Wortman, P. M. Evaluation research: A psychological perspective. *American Psychologist*, 1975, *5*, 562–575.

Zusman, J., & Bissonette, R. The case against evaluation (with some suggestions for improvement). *International Journal of Mental Health*, 1973, *2*, 111–125.

19

Evaluating a Behavioral Community Mental Health Center

W. H. GOODSON, JR., AND A. JACK TURNER

The model of service delivery developed and implemented in the Huntsville–Madison County (Alabama) Mental Health Center is based on two concomitant developments of the past 15 years: (1) an effort to transfer the bulk of mental health care to the community level, launched with the enactment of the Community Mental Health Centers Act of 1963, and (2) the evolution of behavior therapy as a less complex intervention strategy for mental health practice, with built-in accountability (Brown, Wienckowski, & Stolz, 1975). The purpose of this chapter is to describe and evaluate the major service programs of this center.

We decided to attempt an experiment unlike any other community mental health center at the time, namely, to determine whether applied learning (behavior modification) could be used successfully as the primary intervention model in a community mental health center. The literature contained reports of the successful use of behavior therapy in an ever-widening spectrum of clinical disorders. However, it appeared that the studies were coming from isolated, perhaps atypical, settings such as

W. H. GOODSON, JR., AND A. JACK TURNER ● 303 Williams Avenue, S. W., Suite 931, Huntsville, Alabama 35801.

universities and state hospitals (Ullmann & Krasner, 1965). If behavior modification could be used on a broad scale in a community mental health center, certain distinct advantages would result: (1) an accountable intervention strategy, (2) increased use of paraprofessionals and natural caregivers by virtue of the relative ease with which applied learning theory can be learned, and (3) improved continuity of care because of the objectivity of treatment goals and ease of communication regarding therapeutic plans.

Before the initiation of the project, the staff of the Huntsville–Madison County Mental Health Center were asking themselves such questions as: (1) What is the most efficient therapeutic model to use in a comprehensive mental health center? (2) How can paraprofessional staff be utilized maximally, given budget constraints? and (3) What of applied learning theory as an intervention model? These questions persisted while the center was in its formative stages. From 1970 to 1973, staff increased from 13 to 53 and the budget rose 250%. The task was to provide comprehensive mental health services to the 186,000 residents of Madison County over an area of 890 square miles. Such a mandate was not unlike that of hundreds of other community mental health centers. Most of them struggle with issues related to diverse intervention models, professional–paraprofessional relationships, and accountability (Harshbarger & Maley, 1974).

A research project (Behavior Modification Applied to a Community Mental Health Center) was funded beginning in June 1971, during the center's largest growth period. A federal staffing grant was also initiated in January 1971. The primary aim was to demonstrate that behavior modification could be successfully employed as an intervention model in a comprehensive community mental health center.

The specific hypotheses to be tested, and for which data were collected, were that behavior modification principles and procedures, when employed in a comprehensive community mental health center on a large scale, could result in:

1. Use of staff with significantly less formal education than usual for most mental health centers
2. Reduced admission and resident rates at the state hospital level
3. Stable therapy outcomes using these techniques measured by reduced readmission rates
4. Reduced therapy time needed to achieve goals
5. Successful outcomes in therapy when compared with other centers and positive changes over time within the same center

6. Successful use by other community caregivers
7. Acceptance by clients
8. Acceptance by professionals in the community

In the original design, it was hoped that there would be centers using other models that could be used as contrasts. However, direct comparisons became difficult, especially with regard to outcome indexes since very few centers had comparable data systems. This project has developed derivatives of the center's operations that have led to a unique emphasis on accountability. Program evaluation has a much higher priority than in most centers (Bolin & Kivens, 1974), which has yielded an enormous amount of data for comparison purposes, unfortunately missing from most other centers (Larsen & Sanderson, 1973). Thus comparative outcome data are limited to a few standard indexes.

Implementation of the Project

Training of Staff

The first goal was staff training in applied learning. The training ·components included:

1. Selection of key staff according to expertise in behavior therapy. It was thought that the heads of service units should have already-established interests and expertise in the field so that supervisees and paraprofessionals could have proper direction.
2. Didactic presentations by training staff. The principle investigator (Turner) conducted a 2-week initial training session for staff early in the project. Periodic updating of these sessions has been held for new employees via videotape.
3. Library materials.
4. Modeling of techniques and principles by more experienced staff. This was the first crucial step in the learning process for each new staff member. Live demonstrations and videotaped treatment sessions have been used.
5. Shaping of behaviors in new staff so that competences in use of the techniques are acquired. This aim has been achieved by a gradual increase in trainee activity, and fading of the trainer from the scene. In some instances, the "bug-in-ear" device, along with live video monitoring, has been used to shape therapists' behavior through immediate feedback.

6. Monitoring and feedback, accomplished through the following mechanisms:
   a. Direct observation of staff behavior when involved in therapeutic interventions. This mode of monitoring is prominent in those services (inpatient and day treatment) where the environment of therapy naturally lends itself to observation of staff by other staff.
   b. Scrutiny of clinical records to determine the therapists' skills in goal-setting, treatment planning, and intervention techniques. This has been the predominant mode of monitoring in outpatient service where direct observation is less likely.
   c. Consumer feedback. Questionnaires were completed by clients in outpatient service at the close of the intake interview and at termination of therapy. These results are immediately made available to the therapist and to the outpatient coordinator for analysis and feedback.

Implementation of Applied Learning Interventions in All Services

The selection of therapeutic interventions in mental health work is a complex matter. For our particular case, the following outlook has been adopted: (1) Where the literature clearly indicates a superior intervention for a given disorder, we are obligated to use that intervention, so long as it is available to us; (2) where the literature is unclear as to the most efficacious treatment for a given disorder, we use behavior therapy; and (3) every intervention, regardless of type, must be evaluated in an objective manner. In everyday practice, this approach leads to the use of nonbehavioral techniques, for example, chemotherapy in psychotic disorders and some depressive conditions. Even in these cases, behavioral treatment programs are the predominant strategy.

Direct Services. Inpatient services (IPS), day treatment services (DTS), aftercare services (ACS), and outpatient services (OPS) utilize behavioral interventions with clients. (The first three, serving a large number of psychotic clients, employ chemotherapy also.) From initial contact, clients are encouraged to formulate problems in behavioral terms. Client–therapist contracts are currently used to clarify mutual expectancies. Family members are often parties to these contracts, particularly in IPS, DTS, and ACS.

Treatment interventions run the gamut of behavioral techniques, including token economy (DTS), contingency contracting, relaxation training, desensitization, family contracting, assertive training, covert sensitization, parent training, implosion, and (rarely) aversive therapy. Reported studies have elaborated on OPS (Rinn & Tapp, 1973; Rinn & Vernon, 1975; Vernon & Turner, 1975), DTS (Turner & Owen, 1974), and ACS (Rinn, Bailey, Tapp, & Howard, 1974).

Indirect Services. Consultation and education service, with its high community visibility, has represented perhaps the severest test of community acceptance of behavior modification. In most areas, we have achieved a high degree of success. Programs included in this service range from television educational programs to short-term classes for the public to agency consultation programs. One of the functions with the community has been the training of natural caregivers in mental health technology. This endeavor was based on the premise that the largest payoff from personpower expenditures will occur if efforts are multiplied through other agents. Therefore, direct services have been deemphasized except for the more disturbed client. It is preferable to train parents to manage their children effectively rather than to "treat" them. It is preferable to train an agency worker to handle a client's behavior problem than to "treat" the client. Behavior modification has been woven into this training model via parent training courses (Rinn, Vernon, & Wise, 1975), marriage management courses (Turner, 1972), pastoral training, and agency training (Rinn & Goodson, 1973).

Procedures for Evaluation of Effectiveness

The overall goal of any mental health center could probably be stated as: to increase the probability of successful survival in society of those persons at risk for behavioral/mental disturbances. In order to evaluate the degree to which this goal is reached, a systems model was developed that included accountability at every level of center operations (Bolin & Kivens, 1974). This project in applied learning has generated a healthy respect for empiricism, which has found its way into both clinical and administrative matrices.

The empirical model is used in (1) overall center administration, (2) service components, (3) personnel performance evaluation, and (4) clinical intervention. In each of these areas the essential ingredients of empiricism are found, namely, goal setting, data collection, intervention, evaluation, and feedback. These steps are implemented in a systematic, cyclical manner. Thus the entire center is joined by interlocking and complementary goals, with feedback built into the administrative side via periodic evaluations (Turner & Pyfrom, 1979). In one sense the overall process of goal setting, monitoring, evaluation, and feedback can be conceptualized as a domino or ripple effect, in which the center as a whole determines its administrative and clinical goals on an annual basis. Once these goals are set, each succeeding level of the center refines them into more and more manageable behavioral tasks. For example, suppose that a clinical goal was to increase the number of new clients by 20% in the coming year. The next step or ripple would be for each of the two clinical departments (Adult, Child and Parent) to set goals to increase the number of new clients seen by 10% or more. If reached by the two departments the center would achieve a 20% increase. Once that department established that goal, the next step would be for its staff to establish procedures considered necessary to meet or exceed it. Following this step the next level of goal setting would be that of the individual staff member. Staff members would now divide up the behaviors necessary to ensure that the goal would be met. This part of the evaluation process is entitled "Catch a Fellow Worker Doing Something Good Today" and has been described in several publications (Turner & Goodson, 1976; Turner & Lee, 1976a,b). In many ways it is the "bottom line" of the process in that it is the individual staff member's behavior that directly affects clients and their families.

The following procedures are employed in this staff motivation system: On an annual basis, each staff member negotiates with his/her supervisor a written job contract. This contract has two parts. The first is a ranked list of job duties stated in readily measurable terms; the second is a criterion for evaluating performance of each job duty on a continuum from *unacceptable* to *far superior*. At the end of the evaluation period the staff member's performance of job duties is scored and converted to a "percentage of performance" rating. Job performance in the upper-90% range results in a maximum salary raise, with lesser salary raises going to lesser job performance. Scores slightly above the "unacceptable" level usually result in no pay increase; scores below "unacceptable" result in termination.

Thus the evaluation process filters down from the overall goals of the center to the individual staff member. The center is thereby able to obtain from each service component and each staff member contracts to reach measurable goals during an evaluation period. Data are kept on a systematic basis, and we are able to detect areas of strength and weakness. Attention is then directed to (1) maintaining successes, (2) modifying goals where indicated, and (3) modifying intervention strategies to meet old, new, and/or expanded goals. Care is taken so that goals of the different units of service delivery are complementary and not competing. In this way, the administrative flow of accountability (center to service component to staff) connects with consumer goals to help bring about increased survival skills.

Outcomes

Comprehensive supportive data are provided in documents published by the center (Turner & Goodson, 1976). Here we shall present the basic data for each hypothesis stated in the preceding section.

Hypothesis 1: That behavior modification will be utilized by a staff with significantly less formal education than usual for most mental health centers. The average number of years of postsecondary education by clinical staff in the years 1971, 1972, and 1973 was 4.1, 3.3, and 3.8, respectively. A comparison of outpatient staff with other mental health centers in 1971 reveals that the national average for professional workers was 67%, whereas we employed only 16% in this category. It would appear, then, that the staff of the center has less formal training than that of the average mental health center.

In an anonymous questionnaire completed by 37 clinical and administrative staff members in July 1974, an estimate of their use of behavior modification at the center was obtained. Over 80% of staff reported using behavior modification in over three-fourths of their work. One additional, somewhat surprising, finding was the percentage of staff reporting the use of behavioral techniques in their personal lives—94%.

Hypothesis 2: That the use of behavior modification could lead to reduced admission and resident rates at the state hospital level. Table 1 summarizes the comparative data covering our catchment area, the state of Alabama, and the nation; there seems to be little question about the effectiveness of our system in this area. Several points should be made: First, since many variables affect admission and resident rates, one can claim superiority of service only through such comparison figures. Second, it is questionable whether behavior therapy *per se* is a significant factor; most likely, the low rates are a product of a cohesive system of care and accountability (see above). Furthermore, the admission rates ap-

Table 1. State Hospital Admission and Resident Rate per 10,000 Population

	Resident rate[a]			Admission rate[b]		
Year	National	Alabama	Madison Co.	National	Alabama	Madison Co.
1971	15.1	17.1	7.6	20.3[c]	9.2	3.6
1972	13.4	14.0	5.7	19.0	8.8	1.5
1973	11.9	10.8	3.9	18.2	8.2	1.9

[a] Alabama State Department of Mental Health, Statistical Branch.
[b] Alabama State Department of Mental Health, Statistical Branch, *State trends in resident patients: State and county mental hospital inpatient services, 1971–73* (Statistical Note 113).
[c] Admissions are defined as admissions and readmissions, excluding transfers and/or returns from extended leave.

Table 2. Number of Therapy Sessions per Episode by Outcome (Outpatient)

	Outcome per episode			Sessions per episode		
Year	Much improved	Moderately improved	Unimproved	Center average	National average[c]	Regional average[c]
1971[a]	[d]	[d]	[d]	[d]	6.4	5.0
1972[b]	4.5	4.3	3.4	4.1	5.0	[d]
1973[b]	6.6	5.6	2.5	4.9	[d]	[d]

[a]U.S. Department of Health, Education and Welfare, National Institute of Mental Health Office of Program Planning and Evaluation, Biometry Branch, Survey and Reports Section, *Outpatient treatment services in federally funded community mental health centers—1971* (Statistical Note 94).
[b]Alabama State Department of Mental Health, Statistical Branch.
[c]CMHC with 600 to 1,199 annual outpatient episodes.
[d]Not available.

parently have reached a plateau, representing to us the limitations of resources in our community at this time.

Hypothesis 3: That the use of behavior modification could produce stable therapy outcomes that are measurable by reduced readmission rates. Data failed to confirm or refute this hypothesis. The complexity of interpreting readmission rates is reviewed elsewhere (Turner, 1979).

Hypothesis 4: That behavior modification can reduce therapy time required to achieve goal attainment. Although the data in Table 2 would appear to support this hypothesis if the center's averages are compared with the national averages, these two trends may be converging. They seem to be the same as the regional averages. An interpretation of the difference between them has to be very tentative and must await further information for the later years. The real significance of these data may be in the finding that those clients who stay in therapy longer profit more. The categories used to determine success by this center are typical of the behavioral approach in that we specify the behavior(s) to be modified, obtain a base rate, and measure behavior changes during and after therapy. Once that is done, all clients achieving 33% or less of their target behavior(s) as measured from their base rate are categorized as unimproved, those from 34% to 66% as moderately improved, and those from 67% to 100% as much improved.[1]

Another dimension of this hypothesis may be seen in length-of-stay data for partial and inpatient services. A comparison of trends between our center and national averages indicates reduced therapy time in these services. For example, in 1972, the average stays for national/our center in partial and inpatient were 36.9/33.4 and 20.0/12.5 days, respectively

[1] A more detailed description is available from the first author.

Table 3. Treatment Success at Termination (Outpatient)

Year	Unimproved	Moderately improved	Much improved
		Percentage	
1971	26	22	52
1972	24	22	54
1973	8	11	81

(Alabama Department of Mental Health, Statistical Branch, Molly Broome).

Hypothesis 5: That behavior modification can result in successful outcomes in therapy when compared to other centers and show positive changes over time within the same center. Table 3 shows that the changes were positive within the center. Although efforts to locate comparable data from similar sources were unsuccessful, the figures reported strongly suggest that the results obtained exceed the general findings reported in the professional literature.[2]

Hypothesis 6: That behavior modification can be successfully employed by community caregivers. Various types of community caregivers have been reached in specific training programs from 1971 to 1974: 642 parents, 291 public school teachers, 233 social agency staff, 52 health agency staff, and 23 ministers.[3] That says nothing, of course, about the "success" of the training; this hypothesis cannot be addressed as stated above.

Hypothesis 7: That clients will accept behavior modification therapy. A client satisfaction questionnaire has been administered at the end of 6 months post–therapy termination. Although the reply rate was only 35%, the sample did indicate an 85% level of client satisfaction. The questionnaire was designed to measure subjective goal attainment estimates, satisfaction with therapist, and likelihood of return to the center. An indirect indicator of client satisfaction has been the finding that self, family, or friend has ranked first and second as referral sources since 1972. That does not say that clients are satisfied with the approach, but they apparently have willingly come to the center on their own and have referred those close to them to this center when they had problems. A finding (Staples, Sloane, Whipple, Cristol, & Yorkston, 1975) that clients generally perceive behavior therapists as empathic is congruent with our experience.

[2] A detailed description of the procedure, logic, and supportive literature for the criteria used to determine treatment success is available from the first author.

[3] More detailed information on work with community caregivers is available on request.

Hypothesis 8: That professionals in the community will accept behavior modification. An anonymous questionnaire was distributed to the center's 21-member Professional Advisory Committee in July 1974. This committee is composed of five physicians, three university administrators, three public school officials, two judges, two social agency heads, one private psychologist, one government agency director, one hospital administrator, one minister, one practicing attorney, and one city government official. Of the 13 questionnaires returned, results indicated a high level of awareness and that use of behavior modification was equal to or better than other therapies. All respondents favored continuation of the project. These responses represent an estimate by professionals in the community; of course, the individuals are involved with the center.

Conclusions

The limited data presented here do not in themselves make a convincing case for the efficacy of behavior modification in a community mental health center. The many variables at work in such a complex setting mitigate the certainty of any conclusions. However, taken as a whole, the outcomes are of significance.

The system of accountability that has evolved has been important. Clear thinking about service goals yielded data that were useful in communicating to the public. Straightforward job descriptions and contingencies lent a clarity to staff expectancies that contributed to high performance. Any rigorous data system carries with it a burden of record keeping for staff; there are complaints from time to time. However, when we compare such complaints to those in other settings, there is a distinct difference: In our center, no one questions the *value* of the record keeping.

Another result of this project, difficult to pinpoint with clear data, has been an improvement in continuity of care. There are two indirect evidences: (1) Congruence in descriptive variables of clients in inpatient, day treatment, and aftercare services suggests that the same clients are accurately "tracked" through these separate service components; and (2) there is a low rate of readmission to inpatient service from the aftercare population. This group of clients, typically troublesome from the standpoint of continuity, often becomes lost in the service mill.

It is our subjective impression that the behavioral and empirical orientations have helped lead to this continuity. Several factors may have been responsible. First, client goals and treatment plans are clearly defined for each client in a "treatment planning sheet," which specifies

these plans and follows the client to the next service. We would speculate that there is less confusion among clients and staff, greater congruence between successive therapy experiences, and hence a greater chance
of the client's staying with us. Second, service goals in most cases clearly
specify that continuity (follow-up treatment) is the responsibility of the
prior service. In many settings, this area remains ambiguous. Our goal-
directed services leave little question, and we believe the result is staff
behaviors conducive to improved continuity.

There have also been some shortfalls with the project. One of these
has been a failure to implement a satisfactory program in the city school
system. The school system, with an enrollment of approximately 38,000
students in 1973–1974, is much larger than the county system (enrollment approximately 12,000). Although we realized an exceptional degree
of success in the county system, this fact is dimmed by the
unsatisfactory developments with the city. There were two important
factors in this failure. First, a change of school administration occurred
in mid-1971. When this project was being developed, the city school officials were most enthusiastic. Then the unexpected death of the superintendent began a series of staff changes that resulted in an
administration that had not been involved in the original planning. Second, there was a small group of vocal conservatives who, in November
1971, complained to the city school board about mental health interventions with students. Although most of the complaints raised by this
group were considered by us to be ill founded, and in spite of concilia-
tory efforts on our part, the result was a backlash by the school administration. We are now gradually recovering, but we have not been able
to affect the number of students originally intended in this project.

There was a failure to develop effective behavior modification programs with economically deprived families, as evidenced in two ways.
First, there was a lack of success in parent training within the Model
Cities area. The Positive Parent Training class was attempted in the
Model Neighborhood areas, but attendance was poor because of dropouts. We believe that the "middle-class verbal game" motif of the class
was ill suited for this group. Second, we have depended heavily on the
Satellite Operations Service, staffed by indigenous Black paraprofessionals with very little training, for service delivery to the poor. This particular staff did not adapt as quickly to the data-oriented, record-keeping
system that was required for successful behavioral interventions. This
fact may be an exception, then, to the general finding that paraprofessionals adapt quickly to the use of behavior modification.

There was a failure to demonstrate to our own satisfaction the stability, positive value, and generalization of changes brought about by

behavior therapy. The following questions remain unanswered: (1) Are behavioral improvements made during the intervention process permanent or relatively permanent? (2) Are the skills learned during the intervention process the kinds of skills that transfer to other problem situations in the lives of clients, and can this transfer be accomplished without additional professional intervention? (3) Do the problems resolved during successful therapy become replaced by desirable behaviors? That is, do the assumed natural consequences of success serve to maintain the success, or are there contingencies that serve to reestablish pathological patterns of behavior regardless of success in therapy for a given complaint at a given time?

Overall, we would judge the project as having affirmed the hypotheses. The senior staff (coordinators) have also registered their affirmation of the project, as well as the Citizens Advisory Committee, through signed resolutions. The deficiencies indicate a challenge yet unmet. With the baseline of success and acceptance that has been established in the community, these and other questions should be amenable to testing.

Indeed, the empirical framework in which we operate inevitably leads to the statement of unmet goals. Through the cyclic process of evaluation, new and better questions are continually being raised. Whether the problem relates to the city school system or client outcomes, the center operates under the assumption that it has the responsibility to evaluate effectiveness and rearrange contingencies for better results.

References

Bolin, D. C., & Kivens, L. Evaluation in a community mental health center: Huntsville, Alabama. *Evaluation*, 1974, *2*, 26–35.

Brown, B. S., Wienckowski, L. A., & Stolz, S. B. *Behavior modification: Perspective on a current issue* (DHEW Publication No. [ADM] 75–202). Washington, D.C.: U.S. Government Printing Office, 1975.

Broome, M. Alabama Department of Mental Health Statistical Branch. Personal Communication, June 1974

Harshbarger, D., & Maley, R. F. *Behavior analysis and systems analysis: An integrative approach to mental health programs.* Kalamazoo, Mich.: Behaviordelia, 1974.

Larsen, J. K., & Sanderson, B. A. *Source book of programs: Community mental health centers.* Palo Alto, Calif.: American Institutes for Research, 1973.

Rinn, R. C., & Goodson, W. H. *Consultation and education services: A model for community intervention.* Paper presented at the Workshop on Mental Health Consultation, New Orleans, November 1973.

Rinn, R. C., & Tapp, L. Behavior modification with outpatients in a community mental health center. *Journal of Behavior Therapy and Experimental Psychiatry*, 1973, *4*, 243–247.

Rinn, R. C., & Vernon, J. C. Process evaluation of outpatient treatment in a community mental health center. *Behavior Therapy and Experimental Psychiatry*, 1975, *6*, 5–11.

Rinn, R. C., Bailey, A., Tapp, L., & Howard, J. A comparison of aftercare programs: Preliminary report. *International Journal of Mental Health*, 1974, *3*, 153–159.

Rinn, R. C., Vernon, J. C., & Wise, M. J. Training parents of behaviorally disordered children in groups: A three-year program evaluation. *Behavior Therapy*, 1975, *6*, 378–387.

Staples, F. R., Sloane, R. B., Whipple, K., Cristol, A. H., & Yorkston, N. J. Differences between behavior therapists and psychotherapists. *Archives of General Psychiatry*, 1975, *32*, 1517–1524.

Turner, A. J. *Couple and group treatment of marital discord*. Unpublished manuscript, 1972.

Turner, A. J. Perspective on evaluation: Readmission rates to community mental health centers as a measure of program effectiveness. *Evaluation and the Health Professionals*, 1979, *1*(5), 20–31.

Turner, A. J., & Goodson, W. H. Catch a fellow worker doing something good today. *Journal of Mental Health Administration*, 1976, *4*, 17–21.

Turner, A. J., & Lee, W. Motivation through behavior modification. I. The job contract. *Health Services Manager*, 1976, *9*(9), 1–5. (a)

Turner, A. J., & Lee, W. Motivation through behavior modification. II. Evaluation. *Health Services Manager*, 1976, *9*(10), 1–4. (b)

Turner, A. J., & Owen, D. E. *A study of the effectiveness of a token economy in a partial hospitalization setting*. Paper presented at the 4th annual Southwestern Partial Hospitalization Conference, Dallas, November 1974.

Turner, A. J., & Pyfrom, C. H. A. *Evaluating a community mental health center*. Unpublished manuscript, 1979.

Ullmann, L. P., & Krasner, L. *Case studies in behavior modification*. New York: Holt, Rinehart & Winston, 1965.

Vernon, J. C., & Turner, A. J. *Behavior therapy with outpatients: A program evaluation*. Unpublished manuscript, 1975.

20
The Multiphasic Environmental Assessment Procedure
A Method for Comprehensively Evaluating Sheltered Care Settings

RUDOLF H. MOOS AND SONNE LEMKE

Congregate settings for older people have evolved in a somewhat hap-hazard manner to meet a variety of perceived needs. Among these are the need for physical security and social contact for isolated older peo-ple, the need for personal care for those whose ability to care for them-selves has declined, and the need for medical care for those with chronic physical or mental disabilities. Through such programs as Medicare and Medicaid legislation and the Federal Housing Acts, society has moved to take some responsibility for addressing these needs. This move has been accompanied by growing concern about regulating and improving condi-

Portions of the material included here were presented at the annual meeting of the Gerontological Society, Washington, D.C., November 1979.

RUDOLF H. MOOS AND SONNE LEMKE ● Social Ecology Laboratory, Geriatric Research, Education, and Clinical Center, Veterans Administration and Stanford University Medical Center, Palo Alto, California 94305. The work was supported by NIMH Grant MH28177 and by Veterans Administration Health Services Research and Development Service funds.

tions in these settings, studying their impact on residents, and planning better-quality housing for the future.

A necessary first step in such efforts is the articulation of a conceptual framework for organizing the myriad environmental variables and the development of instruments for assessing and describing settings. For example, environments can be viewed in terms of their physical characteristics, organizational structures, aggregate human characteristics, and social-environmental resources (Moos, 1976). Employing this general framework, we have developed the Multiphasic Environmental Assessment Procedure (MEAP), a comprehensive set of instruments for assessing sheltered care settings for the elderly. In this chapter we shall describe the four major parts of the MEAP, illustrate their use in comparing sheltered care settings, provide two examples of substantive issues that can be addressed using information from the MEAP, and note some of the practical applications of the procedure.

The Multiphasic Environmental Assessment Procedure

The MEAP assesses the environmental resources of sheltered care settings in terms of dimensions drawn from four conceptual domains: physical and architectural resources, policy and program resources, resident and staff resources, and social-environmental resources. These domains have been used to describe various settings and are four of the most important ways in which sheltered care facilities can be assessed (Moos, 1976, 1979). The MEAP thus represents an attempt to create a comprehensive, conceptually based environmental assessment procedure. The MEAP was developed with data obtained from sheltered care settings for the elderly, but we believe it is applicable, with minor modifications, to sheltered care settings serving other populations, such as retarded (Wandersman & Moos, 1981) or mentally ill people.

The MEAP consists of five instruments which can be used either separately or in conjunction.[1] In general, the content of the five instruments follows the conceptual organization of the four environmental domains just described.

Physical and Architectural Resources

The Physical and Architectural Features Checklist (PAF) assesses nine dimensions of the physical and architectural resources of a facility

[1] Copies of the MEAP, a *Handbook for Users*, a *Hand Scoring Booklet*, and a *Preliminary Manual* can be obtained from the authors.

(Moos & Lemke, 1980). The PAF covers questions about the facility's location, its external and internal physical features, and space allowances. Two of the dimensions focus on the presence of physical features that add convenience and special comfort (physical amenities) and foster social interactions and recreational activities (social-recreational aids). The next three PAF dimensions assess features of the physical environment that aid residents (especially those with impaired functional ability) in activities of daily living and in negotiating the facility environment (prosthetic aids, orientational aids, safety features). The next two subscales assess the extent to which the physical environment of the facility provides residents with potential flexibility in their activities (architectural choice, space availability). Finally, the PAF includes a dimension that measures the presence of features that make the setting more pleasant for staff (staff facilities), and one that reflects the degree of physical integration between the facility and the surrounding community (community accessibility).

Policy and Program Resources

The Policy and Program Information Form (POLIF) assesses 10 dimensions of the policy and programmatic resources of a facility (Lemke & Moos, 1980). The items cover the financial and entrance arrangements, the types of rooms or apartments available, the way in which the facility is organized, and the services provided for residents. The first three POLIF dimensions reflect how selective the facility is in admitting residents (selectivity) and the degree to which behavioral requirements are imposed on residents once they are in the facility (expectations for functioning, tolerance for deviance). The second set of POLIF dimensions taps the balance that exists between individual freedom and institutional order and continuity (policy clarity, policy choice, resident control, and provision for privacy), and the third set measures the provision of various services and activities within the facility (health services, daily living assistance, and social-recreational activities).

Resident and Staff Resources

The Resident and Staff Information Form (RESIF) includes six dimensions that tap the basic characteristics of the residents and staff in the facility. The dimensions measure such areas as the residents' social resources (educational and occupational background), the heterogeneity of the residents (in terms of such sociodemographic characteristics as age, ethnic background, and religion), and residents' functional abilities (how many residents can eat without help, can dress themselves, or can

go shopping on their own). The RESIF also evaluates the activity level of
the residents and the degree of their integration in the community (their
participation in activities outside the facility, such as attending religious
services and eating in a restaurant). A portion of the POLIF provides additional information concerning residents' use of the services provided
by the facility (utilization of health services, daily living assistance, and
social-recreational activities). For staff resources, the RESIF obtains information on staffing levels and includes a measure of staff richness that
focuses on the heterogeneity of staff, on staff training and turnover, and
on the contribution of volunteers.

Social-Environmental Resources

The Sheltered Care Environment Scale (SCES) assesses residents'
and staff members' perceptions of seven characteristics of a facility's social environment (Moos, Gauvain, Lemke, Max, & Mehren, 1979). The
subscales cover the quality of interpersonal relationships (cohesion, conflict), the opportunities for personal growth (independence, self-explora-
tion), and the mechanisms for system maintenance and change
(organization, resident influence, physical comfort).

The MEAP allows an evaluator to obtain data about a facility from
a variety of sources, including direct observations of relatively objective
physical characteristics (PAF), interviews of administrators and other
staff (POLIF, RESIF), tabulations of facility records (RESIF), and the residents' and staff members' own reports of the facility's social environment. The MEAP also includes a Rating Scale that covers evaluative
judgments by outside observers on four dimensions: Two tap physical
and architectural resources (physical attractiveness and environmental
diversity); the other two, resident and staff resources (resident functioning and staff functioning).

The current normative sample of 93 sheltered care settings, drawn
from five counties in California, is described elsewhere (Moos & Lemke,
1979), as are the conceptual and empirical criteria used in scale development. In brief, the initial sample is composed of 41 skilled nursing facilities (SNFs), 28 residential care facilities (RCs), and 24 apartment facilities
(APTs). The MEAP dimensions were constructed using a set of six conceptual and empirical criteria to guide the selection and retention of
items and their placement on particular dimensions or subscales: mean-
ingfulness, applicability, distribution, discrimination, and interrelatedness
of items, and independence of subscales.

The dimensions themselves are conceptual; each is unified by a
common functional implication for residents. The items represent oppor-

tunities or environmental "resources" for a given area of human functioning. For example, the existence of a residents' council offers residents a formal opportunity to participate in policy making and to experience a sense of efficacy, as do other items on the dimension of resident control. Such an institutional structure commonly arises out of a general philosophy about the older resident, which will also manifest itself in other ways. Information on the number of items in each subscale, internal consistencies and test–retest reliabilities, subscale intercorrelations, and means and standard deviations is given elsewhere (Moos & Lemke, 1979).

Comparing Sheltered Care Settings

The MEAP allows a program evaluator to obtain detailed descriptions of the architectural, policy, human aggregate, and social-environmental resources of a sheltered care facility. To illustrate the type of information that can be obtained from the MEAP, we shall present an example of the profiles of policy and program resources for two RCs (see Figure 1). Scores are expressed as standard scores (mean of 50 and standard deviation of 10) based on the norms for the subsample of RCs.

Both of these nonprofit facilities have about 100 residents. Facility 219 is one unit of a large rural facility offering several levels of care. Residents of this unit are all men, half of them less than 75 years old. In contrast, Facility 224 is located in an urban area, and its residents are predominantly women (80%) and 75 years of age or older (more than 80%). The level of functioning of residents is the same in these two facilities and above average for RCs. Over 85% of the residents in both facilities have lived there for more than a year.

Because it is a life-care facility, the program in Facility 219 is strongly oriented toward providing health care and assistance in daily living for its residents. Residents have access to a full range of medical services within the facility, including physicians, occupational therapists, and a medical clinic, as well as such services as legal advice and assistance with banking and laundry. Although there are few screening measures employed (low selectivity) and substantial services are offered, residents are expected to function relatively independently within this unit; prolonged illness or reduction in functioning may necessitate a move to another unit. Expectations about the behavior of residents and staff are transmitted through such formal institutional mechanisms as orientation for new residents and a regular newsletter (policy clarity). This facility offers many supportive services to residents but little free-

Standard Scores

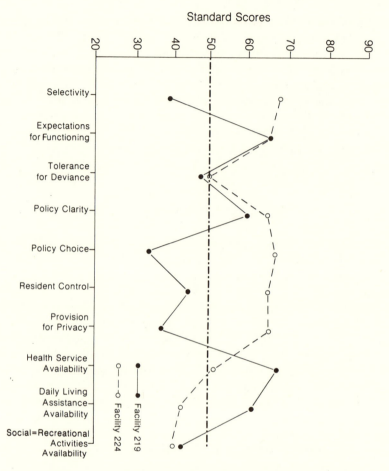

Figure 1. Policy and program resources profiles for two residential care facilities.

dom to individualize daily routines, few opportunities for input into the running of the unit, and little privacy (low policy choice, resident control, and provision for privacy).

In contrast, Facility 224 provides fewer supportive services but more freedom of choice and formal avenues by which residents can influence the operation of the facility. For example, there are regular house meetings and resident committees, and residents can participate in planning activities, dealing with complaints, setting meal times and visiting hours, and selecting new residents. Initial screening and requirements for continued residence are stricter than average. For example, this facility has a substantial entrance fee, a minimum age requirement, and a long waiting list. Residents have private apartments and enjoy a good deal of freedom in the use of their own rooms and in structuring their daily routine (high policy choice). Meal hours are flexible, as are times for getting up, going to bed, visiting, and being in the facility at night. In short, the facility imposes fewer institutional controls on residents but also offers them fewer supportive services.

These two facilities, licensed to provide comparable levels of care, set different tones by means of their policies. In both cases residents are expected to maintain a high level of independent functioning and to conform to certain standards of behavior. Rules and procedures are communicated to staff and residents systematically. Planned communal activities in both settings are somewhat less varied and frequent than in the average RC. Facility 219 provides richer services, but there is less individual freedom, resident control, and privacy. Facility 224 offers fewer services but imposes less institutional structure on residents' lives.

Information of this type can be useful to administrators and staff because it provides a comprehensive picture of how a setting is functioning. In addition, it can provide the basis for comparisons between facilities. Some relevant questions include: Does a new, modern-looking facility have more physical amenities, more safety features, or greater available space than a facility situated in an older building? Which facility has greater tolerance for deviant behavior, greater clarity of policies, and more policy choice and provision for privacy? Does a large facility with a high staff–resident ratio actually have clearer policies, more policy choice, more social-recreational activities, and a "richer" staff than a small, family-run, homelike facility with a low staff–resident ratio?

Exploring Environmental Domains and Their Impacts

The broad array of environmental features measured by the MEAP facilitates the exploration of relationships among domains of facility characteristics and of their potential impacts on resident functioning. Two substantive areas of our work illustrate these applications of the MEAP.

Environmental Choice and Control

Some of the characteristics frequently observed among the elderly, such as feelings of depression and helplessness and accelerated physical decline, may be attributable in part to their relative lack of environmental choice and control (Schulz, 1976; Schulz & Brenner, 1977). Residents in many sheltered care settings, particularly skilled nursing and interme-diate care facilities, exercise very little influence on their environment, spending most of their time in such passive behavior as sitting and do-ing nothing, watching television, or listening to the radio (Gottesman & Bourestom, 1974; Spasoff, Kraus, Beattie, Holden, Lawson, Rodenburg, & Woodcock, 1978). Austin and Kosberg (1976) found that most facili-ties did not have resident governing councils and did not allow residents to plan their own recreational activities or participate in selecting their roommates. Smith, Discenza, and Saxberg (1978) observed that adminis-trators exercised considerable control over all aspects of the policies and programs in 30 randomly selected proprietary long-term care facilities, that limited responsibilities were delegated to intermediate supervisors, and that residents were rarely included in the decision-making process.

These facts have led to explorations of the effects of increasing the degree of choice and control in sheltered care settings. Schulz (1976) found that the experimental introduction of predictable and controllable positive events (visits by college undergraduates) had a beneficial short-term influence on the morale and well-being of nursing home residents, but that there were no positive long-term effects attributable to the in-tervention (Schulz & Hanusa, 1978). Langer and Rodin (1976) found that a stable increase in choice and personal responsibility for self-care had positive effects on elderly residents' alertness, active participation, and general sense of well-being that persisted over an 18-month follow-up interval (Rodin & Langer, 1977). These results indicate that increases in control in institutional settings may be effective only when they are be-cause of stable factors that persist over time and underline the need to develop measures of the naturally existing levels of choice and control available to residents in different types of living settings (Krantz & Schulz, 1979).

We believe that the POLIF measures of policy choice and resident control help to meet this need. Personal control in institutional settings can be fostered in two major ways: by allowing residents to determine their daily routine, and by giving them responsibility for some aspects of facility programs and policies. Policy choice measures the extent to which the facility provides options from which residents can select indi-vidual patterns of daily living, whereas resident control assesses the amount of influence residents have in decision making and the extent of formal institutional structures that give residents a voice in running the facility (Lemke & Moos, 1980).

One of our studies focused on predicting the quality of the social environment and of resident functioning from information about envi-ronmental choice and control in combination with selected aggregate resident characteristics (social resources, functional ability, the proportion of women in the facility) (Moos, 1981). Residents with more social and functional resources and women residents were more likely to live in facilities high in choice and control, and these personal and environmental factors combined to create more cohesive, organized, independence-oriented social environments with relatively little conflict. These factors also enhanced resident activity levels and may have helped to reduce the turnover rate by contributing to resident satisfaction (as shown by higher cohesion). It should be noted that these sets of factors often mutually influence each other. For example, a cohesive resident population is more likely to be perceived as a social entity by administrators, and, as a social entity, it may be given a greater voice in running the facility. The turnover rate may be increased by resident dissatisfaction, but a higher turnover rate may also diminish the perceived need for resident input.

A combination of high choice and control in a facility with more women residents and residents with greater functional resources enhanced cohesion, organization, and observer-rated pleasantness beyond what would be expected from the relevant environmental and personal factors alone. This finding supports the idea that people with more personal resources are better able to take advantage of environmental opportunities (Carp, 1978–1979; Schulz & Hanusa, 1979). Conversely, those with fewer personal resources are less able to vary their behavior in response to environmental variations and are more constrained by environmental demands (Lawton & Nahemow, 1973).

Consistent with results obtained in other residential settings such as university student living groups (Moos, 1979), we found that women established somewhat more cohesive, organized, and pleasant environments and that the relative lack of environmental choice affected women more than men. Most of the elderly women currently living in sheltered care settings did not spend much of their lives working and are used to the flexibility of organizing their own pattern of everyday activities. The absence of such choices as when to get up, go to bed, bathe, and eat, and whether to do their own personal laundry may be especially salient to these women (Bennett & Eisdorfer, 1975). Furthermore, there is a high proportion of veterans among men who choose to live in sheltered care settings, especially in those settings that are mainly populated by other men. These men may not be as affected by a relative lack of choice, since they are familiar with structured military settings.

Recent evidence suggests that the effects of experimental manipulations may depend on the overall context in which they are conducted (Krantz & Schulz, 1979; Schulz & Hanusa, 1979). Thus one important implication of our results is that studies that attempt to increase choice and control in institutional settings need to consider not only the already existing opportunities for residents to exercise control, but the levels of other environmental and personal resources as well. For example, an increase in resident control in a setting populated by relatively poorly functioning residents who may not want more responsibility may not have beneficial effects. As Schulz and Hanusa (1979) note, it is also possible to experimentally increase elderly residents' expectations for choice and control beyond the level at which relevant behavioral opportunities exist in their living setting. Residents' personal competences and the stable environmental resources for exercising these competences must be considered in future experimental studies focused on increasing choice and control in institutional settings.

The Determinants of Social Climate

In another study we focused on the relationship between the social climate of a facility (as measured by the SCES) and the three other domains of environmental variables. We were interested in the reasons why the social environments of sheltered care settings differ so greatly and in the extent to which these differences are related to the physical and architectural characteristics of a facility, to its policies and procedures, to the types of residents in the setting, and to their level of functional ability. Feldman (1971) points out that certain characteristics of environments may conceptually and empirically "come before" others, that is, some aspects of environments may be causally dependent on others. In keeping with Feldman's logic, Figure 2 is a simplified model of the relationships among the four sets of characteristics of sheltered care facilities and of their relationship to the institutional context. The model is simplified because a unidirectional causal flow is depicted even though the four sets of factors can mutually influence each other.

The model suggests that the institutional context, that is, whether a setting is a skilled nursing facility (SNF), a residential care facility (RC), or an apartment setting (APT), can affect the social climate directly (RCs tend to have more cohesive and better-organized social environments than SNFs). Institutional context can also affect the social climate indirectly through its effect on architectural factors (the greater architectural choice and space availability in RCs than in SNFs may facilitate cohesion), on policy and program features (the greater selectivity and policy choice in RCs than in SNFs may enhance organization and resident influence), on staff attributes (RCs can obtain better-trained staff who help establish more cohesive settings), and on aggregate resident charac-

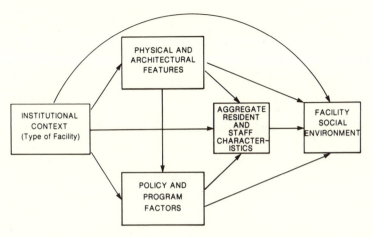

Figure 2. A model of the determinants of social environment in sheltered care settings.

teristics (RCs have more homogeneous and functionally able residents who develop more independence-oriented settings).

Physical and architectural features can affect social climate directly (more cohesive climates may develop in settings with more social-recreational aids) and indirectly, through their impact on program functioning (settings with more available space may facilitate resident activities and thereby increase resident influence). Physical features can also affect social climate indirectly through their influence on the types of residents and staff who decide to enter a setting (facilities characterized by better physical features may attract more socially competent residents who may promote a sense of cohesion and comfort). Similarly, organizational policies and aggregate resident and staff characteristics can influence social climate both directly and indirectly.

These hypotheses illustrate the framework presented in Figure 2. The underlying premise is that architectural, policy, and resident and staff factors influence the social environment of a setting and that they achieve their impact on resident behavior in part through the mediating effects of the social environment they help to create. We used data from the MEAP to explore this model by: (1) assessing the association between the institutional context (type of facility) and seven dimensions of the social environment; (2) determining the relation between these seven social climate dimensions and physical and architectural, policy and program, and resident and staff characteristics (holding constant or controlling for the type of facility); and (3) estimating the variation in the social environment that can be "explained" by the model and identifying the unique and shared influences attributable to each of the other sets of environmental variables (Moos & Igra, 1980).

The findings support the general idea that the type of facility, physical and architectural, policy and program, and resident and staff characteristics are important in influencing the social environment that emerges in a sheltered care setting. Three of the four sets of environmental variables had "effects" on social climate that were independent of the other sets (i.e., unique effects). In addition, some combinations of the four sets affected social climate more than each set taken by itself (i.e., shared effects). For example, we found that social environments high in cohesion, resident influence, and physical comfort are more likely to emerge in facilities with certain physical and architectural features: more physical amenities, better social-recreational aids, and more architectural choice and available space. These facilities also tend to be highly selective, to have more functionally able residents with high social resources, and to provide their residents more choice and control and a richer array of social-recreational activities. The emphasis on independence is also facilitated by these policy and aggregate resident factors, but it is somewhat less affected by physical and architectural features.

These findings provide some guidelines by which facility administrators and staff can understand the social environment likely to emerge in a sheltered care setting. However, since particular architectural, policy, or human aggregate characteristics do not inexorably lead to specific types of social environments, the relationships we found should not be construed rigidly. In fact, they may be used to help select facilities in which to intervene to create different social milieus than might normally develop. More heterogeneous residents with fewer social resources who live in settings with fewer physical amenities and little selectivity or policy choice tend to develop conflict-oriented environments. Administrators and staff might wish to intervene in such settings to help residents develop more activities and enhance their sense of community.

In this connection, it is important to note that the policy and program factors, which are probably most amenable to change, accounted for the largest proportions of unique and shared variance in most of the social-environmental dimensions. Holding other factors constant, an increase in environmental choice and control and in the richness of social-recreational activities should help to increase cohesion and independence, and possibly organization, resident influence, and physical comfort as well. The findings allow us to suggest the types of settings that may be most amenable to change and to identify the direction in which change is likely to occur.

The conceptual model is a first step toward identifying the unique influences of different domains of variables and developing a more coherent understanding of the interrelationships among the factors that affect the social environments of sheltered care settings. It also provides a useful framework to guide and interpret future studies. That researchers usually consider the important sets of factors separately from one another makes it difficult to interpret the results of prior studies. For example, a residential care setting that establishes a reality-oriented therapeutic program may have a different social environment than a comparable setting without such a program. But this difference may be attributable to architectural features (the first setting may have more social-recreational aids and space), to policy and program factors (there may be more policy clarity and resident control in the former facility), or to aggregate resident characteristics (the residents in the former facility may have higher functional abilities and activity levels).

Practical Utility of the MEAP

We have noted that the MEAP can be used to compare settings, to measure the stable levels of environmental choice and control in a facility, and to focus on the determinants of social climate and that each of these applications carries with it practical benefits. In addition, the MEAP can be used to facilitate and measure environmental change.

Every complex social group faces the challenge of maintaining the kind of open communication that will allow shared perceptions to develop and problem areas to be identified before they reach crisis proportions. In some sheltered care settings this difficulty is compounded by high staff turnover rates, staff alienation, and resident fatalism. Staff members can find themselves working in a "feedback vacuum"; they may be unable to effect change because they cannot identify problems and their potential solutions.

The MEAP is one means of filling this information vacuum. It summarizes residents' and staff members' perceptions of the setting and provides comparisons between the facility and others serving a similar function. The MEAP can serve as a focus for discussions among staff and administrators, possibly opening new lines of communication. Information about the facility environment can motivate responsible staff members to change the facility.

An incidental benefit of the MEAP is the exposure of staff to a differentiated framework for thinking about their programs and policies. Regardless of the changes that may follow the discussion of feedback, the MEAP can give staff a new vocabulary for construing and discussing their setting. Instead of locating their program in a one-dimensional space defined by "high quality" and "low quality," staff are encouraged to think in terms of a number of dimensions. This cognitive restructuring may facilitate program change, since it provides many different dimensions along which change can be instituted. The use of the MEAP may also prepare a facility for later change by encouraging staff to adopt the role of program designer and planner. Such indirect contributions help to ease an institution toward more flexible and responsive sheltered care programs.

Not only can the MEAP serve as an impetus for change, but it can be administered at two or more times to monitor a program of change. For example, to what extent do the policy and programmatic resources or the social climate of a sheltered care facility change when staff members participate in special training programs? Is the degree of change a function of the type or length of training? Does the redesign of a building to increase privacy have an effect on residents' activity level or on the social climate? Does the development of resident committees increase the residents' perception of their influence? The MEAP can be used to document the effects of such intervention efforts.

Conclusion

In this chapter we have sketched the broad outlines of a comprehensive environmental assessment procedure designed for use in congregate settings for older people, discussed the use of these instruments in feedback and change efforts, and given examples of how complex interrelationships among environmental dimensions can be analyzed. In these ways, the MEAP can facilitate efforts to address issues of vital social concern, such as defining and regulating quality of life in sheltered care settings and exploring the impact of settings on their residents. The MEAP can also serve as a useful model for applications to other community settings.

References

Austin, M. J., & Kosberg, J. I. Nursing home decision makers and the social service needs of residents. *Social Work in Health Care*, 1976, *1*, 447–455.
Bennett, R., & Eisdorfer, C. The institutional environment and behavior change. In S. Sherwood (Ed.), *Long-term care: A handbook for researchers, planners, and providers*. New York: Spectrum Press, 1975.
Carp, F. M. Effects of the living environment on activity and use of time. *International Journal of Aging and Human Development*, 1978–1979, *9*, 75–91.

Feldman, K. A. Measuring college environments: Some uses of path analysis. *American Educational Research Journal*, 1971, *8*, 51–70.

Gottesman, L. E., & Bourestom, N. C. Why nursing homes do what they do. *Gerontologist*, 1974, *14*, 501–506.

Krantz, D., & Schulz, R. Life crisis, control, and health outcomes: A model applied to cardiac rehabilitation and relocation of the elderly. In A. Baum & J. Singer (Eds.), *Advances in environmental psychology* (Vol. 2). Hillsdale, N.J.: Lawrence Erlbaum, 1979.

Langer, E. J., & Rodin, J. The effects of choice and enhanced personal responsibility for the aged: A field experiment in an institutional setting. *Journal of Personality and Social Psychology*, 1976, *34*, 191–198.

Lawton, M. P., & Nahemow, L. Ecology and the aging process. In C. Eisdorfer & M. P. Lawton (Eds.), *The psychology of adult development and aging*. Washington, D.C.: American Psychological Association, 1973.

Lemke, S., & Moos, R. H. Assessing the institutional policies of sheltered care settings. *Journal of Gerontology*, 1980, *35*, 96–107.

Moos, R. H. *The human context: Environmental determinants of behavior*. New York: Wiley-Interscience, 1976.

Moos, R. H. *Evaluating educational environments: Procedures, measures, findings, and policy implications*. San Francisco: Jossey-Bass, 1979.

Moos, R. H. Environmental choice and control in community care settings for older people. *Journal of Applied Social Psychology*, 1981, *11*, 23–43.

Moos, R. H., & Igra, A. Determinants of the social environments of sheltered care settings. *Journal of Health and Social Behavior*, 1980, *21*, 88–98.

Moos, R. H., & Lemke, S. *Multiphasic environmental assessment procedure (MEAP): Preliminary manual*. Palo Alto, Calif.: Social Ecology Laboratory, Stanford University and Veterans Administration Medical Center, 1979.

Moos, R. H., & Lemke, S. Assessing the physical and architectural features of sheltered care settings. *Journal of Gerontology*, 1980, *35*, 571–583.

Moos, R. H., Gauvain, M., Lemke, S., Max, W., & Mehren, B. Assessing the social environments of sheltered care settings. *Gerontologist*, 1979, *19*, 74–82.

Rodin, J., & Langer, E. Long-term effects of a control-relevant intervention with institutionalized aged. *Journal of Personality and Social Psychology*, 1977, *35*, 897–902.

Schulz, R. Effects of control and predictability on the physical and psychological well-being of the institutionalized aged. *Journal of Personality and Social Psychology*, 1976, *33*, 563–573.

Schulz, R., & Brenner, G. Relocation of the aged: A review and theoretical analysis. *Journal of Gerontology*, 1977, *32*, 323–333.

Schulz, R., & Hanusa, B. Long-term effects of control and predictability-enhancing interventions: Findings and ethical issues. *Journal of Personality and Social Psychology*, 1978, *36*, 1194–1201.

Schulz, R., & Hanusa, B. Environmental influences on the effectiveness of control and competence enhancing interventions. In L. C. Perlmutter & R. A. Monty (Eds.), *Choice and perceived control*. New York: Lawrence Erlbaum, 1979.

Smith, H. L., Discenza, R., & Saxberg, B. O. Administering long-term care services: A decision-making perspective. *Gerontologist*, 1978, *18*, 159–166.

Spasoff, R., Kraus, A. S., Beattie, E. J., Holden, D. E. W., Lawson, J. S., Rodenburg, M., & Woodcock, G. M. A longitudinal study of elderly residents of long-stay institutions. *Gerontologist*, 1978, *18*, 281–292.

Wandersman, A., & Moos, R. H. Evaluating sheltered living environments for retarded people. In C. Haywood & J. R. Newbrough (Eds.), *Living environments for mentally retarded persons*. Baltimore: University Park Press, 1981.

21
Assessing Citizen Participation in a Community Mental Health Center

ABRAHAM WANDERSMAN, DAWNE KIMBRELL,
JOHN C. WADSWORTH, DeROSSETT MYERS, JR.,
GEORGE LIVINGSTON, AND HAROLD BRAITHWAITE

Citizen participation in community mental health centers was instituted as a means of assuring interaction between a center and its particular community. The Community Mental Health Centers Act (1963; see Bloom, 1973) emphasized citizen participation as a crucial ingredient in a decentralized and citizen-responsive mental health system. Subsequent legislation mandates the establishment of citizen advisory or governing boards for community mental health centers that have specific functions in the operation of the centers and that are required to be representative of the populations the centers serve (Community Mental Health Centers Amendment of 1975). Ideally, citizen participation ensures that the community mental health center is accountable to the community.

ABRAHAM WANDERSMAN, DAWNE KIMBRELL, JOHN C. WADSWORTH, DeROSSETT MYERS, JR., GEORGE LIVINGSTON, AND HAROLD BRAITHWAITE. • Department of Psychology, University of South Carolina, Columbia, South Carolina 29208.

The enactment of legislation requiring citizen participation reflects the recent growth of citizen involvement and citizen action (including the consumer movement) in the United States (Langton, 1978). Legislative acts have mandated citizen participation in many government agencies, including the Department of Energy, the Environmental Protection Agency, and the Food and Drug Administration, and in such local agencies and institutions as community mental health centers and public schools. Many view citizen participation as a panacea whose benefits include decreasing citizen alienation, improving the quality and responsiveness of services, and increasing citizens' self-worth and feelings of efficacy. Citizen participation has caught the imagination of the public, grabbed the attention of agency administrators, and is being investigated by social science researchers. Yet the role of citizen participation in community mental health centers is often ambiguous; administrators as well as citizens are often puzzled by citizen participation and disappointed in its performance.

In our research, we are developing a conceptual framework of citizen participation in community mental health centers and are investigating citizen participation in a community mental health center guided by the framework. Major issues include: Who participates? What is the relationship between the citizen advisory committee and the staff and the board of the center? Why is it so difficult for citizen participation to work?

Literature reviews and research articles often omit a description of what happens in the process of performing research. In our research, we found an important interplay between the research process and the phenomenon of participation. In this chapter we shall briefly describe the formal aspects of the project. We shall then discuss several issues that arose in the research process that deepen our understanding of citizen participation and of the results of our questionnaire study.

Background

The research project grew out of a graduate psychology seminar on "Research on Citizen Participation." Early in the semester, a leader of the citizen advisory committee (CAC) of a local community mental health center suggested to the course instructor (Wandersman) that the class investigate the CAC as a case study of citizen participation. She suggested that an assessment of the CAC would provide the class with some real-life issues to focus on and simultaneously provide the CAC with some useful information about its structure and functioning and about ways of improving the recruitment and retention of members. The class and the instructor accepted the offer.

The CAC is part of a large community mental health center with a staff of 100. The Board of Directors has 15 members, appointed by the governor, and has policy-making and operational authority for the center. Although the board is made up of citizens from the catchment area, it has not been demographically representative of the community. The board created the CAC to develop a link between the center and the community and to increase the responsiveness and visibility of the center to the community. The first charter of the CAC states: "The purpose of this Committee shall be to advise the Board of Directors of the [name of the center] with respect to the operation of the Center." At the time of the study, the CAC was approximately 3 years old and the center approximately 12.

The issue placed before us was the role of citizen participation in the CAC, and we had few constraints on which aspects to focus on. Our first task was to find out more about citizen participation in community mental health centers in general and about this particular CAC. To familiarize ourselves with the issues, we reviewed the available literature and attended meetings of the CAC and several of its subcommittees. Since we wanted the study to be relevant to the CAC, we invited the chairperson of the CAC to attend our class sessions where we discussed the literature and the salient issues about citizen participation. She attended several sessions but provided little structure, saying that almost anything we would find was likely to be useful.

We had originally intended to survey only the CAC members because the original invitation came from that group, and because, as a class performing an unpaid service, our resources in time and money were limited. However, the literature review, framework discussions, and our meetings with members of the CAC convinced us of the need to have a fairly broad focus (systems perspective) and to get additional assessments of the CAC from the staff and board as well as from members of the CAC. Therefore, several months after the class began, we decided to assess the views of the staff, the board, and the CAC and to make direct comparisons among the three groups.

The Content of the Study

Literature Review and Framework

Our literature review revealed many important issues that can only be touched on here. Statements of the goals of citizen participation in mental health are diverse, including (1) conservative objectives that would maintain the current mental health structure such as the use of citizens for fund raising and public relations activities (Kupst, Reidda, & McGee, 1975) and the education of citizens about mental health services (Hunt, 1973, 1977), (2) less conservative goals aimed at improving the system to make it more accountable and responsive to community needs such as the examination and evaluation of existing services and the recommendation of changes (Hunt, 1977; Kupst *et al.*, 1975), and (3) citizen empowerment goals where citizens have control over services and program development (Nassi, 1978; Ruiz & Behrens, 1973).

Several case studies show that members of citizen groups have attended meetings and participated at a reasonable level (e.g., Greer & Greer, 1979; Morrison & Cometa, 1979; Smith, Morrison, & Brown, 1979). For example, in one setting a citizen advisory group achieved a 77% implementation rate in recommended changes in the mental health delivery system, including an increase in public education about available services, the development of a community needs assessment procedure, the development of an educational program about mental illness, and the establishment of preventive outreach programs in the community (Smith, *et al.*, 1979). However, the majority of studies indicate that most citizen groups have had trouble in achieving an adequate level of basic functioning. Many citizen groups have been found to be confused or unaware about what they were expected to do (Health Policy Advisory Center, 1972; Hunt, 1972; New, Hessler, & Cater, 1973), to have poor attendance at meetings (Carifi & Zinober, 1979; Hunt, 1972, 1973), a high rate of turnover (Hunt, 1972, 1973), and sporadic meetings coupled with a general apathy (Chu & Trotter, 1974).

The studies we reviewed ranged widely in scope, sampling, and methodology. Empirical evidence was spotty, and there was no systematic attempt to unify the issues either empirically or conceptually. In short, we needed a conceptual framework that would map the important issues and help us to systematize and assess the literature.

In developing a framework we were guided by two previous frameworks of citizen participation (user participation in planning environments—Wandersman, 1979; citizen participation in community organizations—Wandersman, 1981). Our preliminary framework of citizen participation in community mental health centers has four major components:

1. *External environment*: involves the relationships of the citizen group of the center with such external factors as the staff and director of the center and the community

2. *Organizational characteristics of the citizen group*: involves the goals, structure, and process characteristics of the group
3. *Individual characteristics of the citizens who participate*: involves the characteristics of the citizens (e.g., demographics, personality) and the reasons why they join
4. *Effects of the citizen group*: involves several levels of effects and evaluations by several groups; we are interested in the effects of the group on the functioning and programs of the center, on the community's relationships with the center, and on the participants themselves, and we also feel that it is important to have assessments of the group by several relevant bodies such as the staff of the center, the clients of the center, and the community, as well as by the participating citizens

Interrelationships among components are also stressed in the framework.

Questionnaires were developed to assess the external relationships of the CAC (e.g., its relationships with staff, board, and community), the organizational characteristics (e.g., its structure and functions), the effects of the CAC, and the individual characteristics of members of the CAC (e.g., demographics). The staff and board questionnaires had similar items, but some questions were omitted.

Results of the Study

Questionnaires were mailed to all members of the CAC, all members of the Board of Directors, and a sample of staff members. Twenty-three CAC members (60%) returned the questionnaire; almost 70% had been members for 1 year or less. Seventeen staff members (77%) responded; six were unit chiefs and 11 were service providers. Finally, seven board members (50%) returned the questionnaire.

External Relationships. Most CAC members (77%) felt that the community was largely unaware of the CAC, and 86% said it was important to make the community more aware. Both the board (100% of respondents) and the staff (94% of respondents) agreed that increasing public awareness of the CAC was very important.

The relationships between the CAC and the board and between the CAC and the staff were rated by respondents as either positive, neutral, or negative. In general, most CAC members viewed their external relationships as either positive or neutral (see Table 1). The CAC evaluated its relationships with the board and the staff more positively than either of these groups rated theirs with the CAC.

Specific elements of these relationships were examined (e.g., Table 2), and differences as well as some similarities were found in how the

Table 1. External Relationships

A. Committee and board relationship

	Committee responses	Board responses
Positive	58%	14%
Neutral	42%	57%
Negative	0%	29%

B. Committee and staff relationship

	Committee responses	Staff responses
Positive	55%	17%
Neutral	30%	67%
Negative	15%	17%

board, the staff, and the CAC view the CAC. As for whether the CAC had access to information held by the board, had early involvement in developing policies and programs, received feedback from the board, or had an impact on policies or on service delivery, CAC members were much less likely to respond positively than board members. There was more agreement between the CAC and the staff, although staff members reported less open communication channels. Almost all of the CAC members reported that they had little impact on policies and service de-

Table 2. Perceptions of Interrelationships

	CAC's view of relationship with board	CAC's view of relationship with center staff & director	Board's view of relationship with CAC	Staff's view of relationship with CAC
1. Access to information	45%	45%	100%	46%
2. Early involvement in developing policies and programs	5%	27%	33%	27%
3. Receives feedback from board on recommendations	33%	a	67%	a
4. Impact on policies and the delivery of service	11%	20%	67%	50%
5. Open communication channels	35%	57%	83%	17%

aNot asked of staff.

livery, whereas a majority of the board and staff reported that the CAC did have an impact.

In the CAC questionnaires, approximately one-third of the respondents were consistently dissatisfied with the role of the CAC, its relationship with the staff and the board, and the amount of its impact. Thus there was a sizable block of dissatisfied members. In order to improve relations with the center staff, CAC members suggested that the director attend more meetings, that all parties work on better communication, and that the director and staff call on the CAC more often for assistance.

In summary, CAC members viewed the general relationships between the CAC and the board and between the CAC and the staff as positive, whereas board and staff members were more likely to rate these relationships as neutral or negative. As for support for CAC activities, most CAC and staff members felt that it was lacking; the board tended to report that the CAC did receive such support.

Organizational Characteristics. What are the important functions of the CAC? The literature indicates that the functions of citizen groups are often vague, which can lead to frustration.

The four functions of the CAC that received the most endorsements are listed in Table 3. All three groups see meeting community mental health needs as either the first or second most important function. However, each of the three groups rated a different function as most important, and there was also a lack of agreement within each group. Seeing that community mental health needs are met was viewed as most important by the largest number of CAC members. Board members gave the most support to the function of advising the board about center policies and programs; the majority of staff felt that increasing public awareness

Table 3. The Most Important Functions or Purposes of the Committee

	Percentage responding		
	CAC	Board	Staff
1. Seeing that community mental health needs are met	47%	29%	20%
2. Increasing public awareness and support for the center	35%	14%	53%
3. Advising Board of Directors regarding center policies and programs	8%	43%	7%
4. Assisting Center in developing and promoting prevention programs	8%	14%	13%
5. Other	—	—	7%

and support for the center was most important. Thus the CAC seems to view itself as representing the community; the board sees the CAC as advising the board; and the staff sees the CAC as increasing support for the center and thus for the staff.

The CAC members said that its chairperson most often generated issues and options for the CAC; next were the members themselves, and then the staff liaison person. Those viewed as never having input were clients, the community, and the Board of Directors. Consonant with this perception is the fact that CAC members indicated that they wanted more input from clients, staff at the center, and the community, in that order. Board members felt that the most input should come from the CAC chairperson, the staff liaison, the director of the center, and the board, in that order. The staff members' priorities were that the clients, the community, CAC members, and the staff of the center should provide the most input into issues for the CAC.

The majority (76%) of committee members were satisfied with the way the committee was structured (with subcommittees or task forces for different service areas). Eighty-six percent were satisfied with the leadership of the committee.

In summary, there was disagreement about the major functions of the CAC, suggesting a lack of clarity about its purposes. There is clearly a need for the CAC to work with the board and the staff in defining its functions. The CAC cannot achieve such a definition alone, since it needs access to information as well as support from the board and the staff in order to function. CAC members were satisfied with the leadership of the CAC and with its structure. CAC members and staff members felt that the CAC should have more input from clients, the community, and staff.

Individual Characteristics. CAC respondents were predominantly white middleclass professionals and managers. Fifty-seven percent of the respondents were female. Ninety percent were white, and the median age was 40 years. Eighty percent were employed in professional and managerial positions, and 97% had attended at least some college (43% had graduate degrees). The CAC members had also had previous experience related to mental health or to advisory committees. Fifty-nine percent worked or had previously worked in mental health or other human service fields (e.g., medicine, rehabilitation, social services). Almost 68% had served on other citizen advisory boards or committees and 95% had been involved in other community groups.

Effects of CAC Activities. According to CAC members, the major accomplishments of the CAC were recognition of staff and volunteers for outstanding service, review of the center plan of operations, and working for improved services. However, 56% of the members felt that there were things the committee should be and was not presently doing. Concerning the degree of impact the CAC had had thus far on the development of center programs and policies, 23% were satisfied, 52% were neutral, and 24% were dissatisfied. CAC respondents felt that there were no negative impacts on the center from their activities. Staff members felt that the CAC's activities had had a moderate number of positive outcomes and no negative outcomes, and that the CAC's major accomplishments were in having affected policy, improved services, and made the center more responsive to the community. The board respondents likewise reported moderate positive outcomes and no negative outcomes.

CAC members were asked about the costs and benefits of working on the CAC. The cost most often reported (64% of the respondents) was the amount of time it took; the next most reported cost (50%) was frustration from not making progress. The most important personal benefits included increased knowledge of mental health issues and techniques, a sense of contribution and helpfulness, and satisfaction in providing a useful service to the community. Sixty-three percent of the members said that their involvement and satisfaction would increase if they had more influence on center operations.

In summary, one of the primary goals of this study was to obtain information that might improve the functioning of the CAC and the retention of members. The results show that there was some disagreement about the CAC's functions and purposes. CAC members were not satisfied with the amount of information and access to staff they received, nor with the CAC's impact on the operation of the center. CAC members were primarily white middle-class, active in community affairs, and not demographically representative of the community at large, although they recognized the need for more community involvement.

The Research Process Can Be Informative

The results of our study, appear to confirm a number of key assertions made in the literature about citizen participation in community mental health centers. In this section, we shall discuss several insights we gained into the phenomenon of citizen participation; the section is not intended as a "how-to" (or a "how-not-to") for field research in community mental health.

Our Role

Our first task was to define our role and our objectives for ourselves, for the CAC, and eventually for the center administration. We saw our role as one of assessment (i.e., description) rather than advocacy or program evaluation: that is, to obtain information about the functioning of the committee. We were entering the situation by invitation of the CAC as a class performing systematic research on citizen participation. A lack of prior knowledge about this particular CAC ruled against our acting as intervenors or advocates. Furthermore, a program evaluation role would have required an invitation and active participation by the center director and the board. Program evaluation has more political implications than our role was intended to have and might have engendered resistance (Cowen & Gesten, 1980).

The role we chose was one of academically oriented psychologists who would systematically assess the CAC. We would attempt a twofold contribution. First, we wanted to provide the CAC useful information concerning its functioning and the problem of turnover, including a report that would be brief, informative, and readable; in addition, we would offer assistance in usefully applying the results. Second, we wanted to add a systematic study to the literature on citizen participation in community mental health centers and disseminate the results to professionals and researchers.

Informal discussions revealed that the leader of the CAC and a staff administrator viewed our role differently. In recounting her initial interest in having us do the study, the CAC leader said that the CAC needed a chance to sit back and assess goals and directions. She then expressed frustration about what she saw as the CAC's major problem: that the center did not know how to use it, and did not provide guidance. She hoped that an outside group would see this problem and be able to deal with it better. She added that she thought we were probably favorably disposed toward the concept of participation and would be sympathetic to the CAC. She had not made these points earlier in our study; she felt that she was not really conscious of them when she first invited us to do the study.

The administrator discussed his initial reluctance to have the survey performed with the staff and the board, citing as one of his reasons that "knowledge can be power." The information that we obtained, even though objective, might be disruptive to the center at this time when the center had a number of serious problems.

The issue of our role suggests several points: (1) Citizen groups' interests may conflict with those of staff; (2) there is an equilibrium of power among staff, board, and CAC that might be upset by an objective assessment of citizen participation; and (3) despite our intentions to be impartial and to supply objective information, our role could easily be transformed in the political context, within which the CAC was attempting to establish a clearer defined role. These perceptions are consistent with the literature that notes differences in power between staff and citizen groups and the reluctance of mental health professionals to share power (e.g., Hunt, 1972, 1973; Morrison, Holdridge-Crane, & Smith, 1978).

Entry and a Systems Perspective

The issues surrounding role are closely related to the issue of entry and to a systems perspective. Our entry to the CAC was easy: We were invited. However, we soon found that the CAC did not function in a vacuum. Everything it did was related to the staff or board (e.g., its subcommittees specialized in examining programs of the center, and it received its mandate from the board). We therefore felt that to understand fully the functioning of the CAC, we had to obtain assessments of functioning from the staff and the board as well. The leader of the CAC agreed to ask the administration for cooperation. She later decided that because of frictions between herself and a high-ranking administrator regarding the role of citizen participation, it would hurt our chances if she presented the idea. When we asked permission, the high-ranking administrator was initially reluctant; he added that he would have liked to have been consulted earlier in the study so that he could have had more input into the questionnaire. (We found this request reasonable. However, the questionnaire was created before the decision to include the board and the staff in the survey; and since we did not have time to redesign the survey, we adapted it so that staff, board, and CAC responses could be compared on the same items.) He turned the decision of whether to allow the survey of the staff and the board over to the Board of Directors. He expressed support for the idea when he presented it to the board, and the board approved it.

This issue illustrates: (1) the importance of a system perspective in viewing citizen participation (e.g., the necessity of obtaining information from the board and the staff and the necessity of board approval for the survey); in addition, the need for board approval suggests that the CAC is a potentially hot potato and that the balance of power must be watched; and (2) that even administrators like the opportunity to participate (e.g., input into the questionnaire).

Turnover and Utilization of Information

Interesting changes occurred within the CAC over the course of the project. During the spring semester (while we were working on the literature review and developing the questionnaire), the CAC was working on several projects. It had several subcommittees that examined specific

programs of the center (e.g., elderly, adolescents). The CAC also sponsored a banquet to honor staff. During the summer, meetings were sporadic and a reorganization of the CAC was initiated because a new
center had opened in one of the three counties served by the center we
were studying. A center administrator ruled that, according to NIMH
guidelines, residents of that county could no longer serve on the CAC.
The individual nominated to be the next chairperson could not attain
the post because she lived in the new catchment area. In addition, the
CAC leader who had worked with us became disillusioned by the arbitrary and abrupt way she thought the situation was handled and re-
signed. Shortly thereafter she moved to take a job in another state.

The loss of key leaders of the CAC, and turnover in general, cast
doubt on the CAC's survival. The old leadership was gone, and there
was a vacuum of leaders and functions. The center director proposed
several possible functions for the CAC including sponsoring a banquet
honoring the staff member of the year, sponsoring a sports tournament
for support of the center, and helping to lobby local government for
funds. In this period, we completed a report on our study. Copies were
sent to previous and new members of the CAC, and we offered to review the report with them and to help with its use. Recently, a small
group (approximately six to eight members, who attend meetings) re-
formed as the CAC and decided to work on some of the projects
suggested by the center director. In fact, the charter of the purpose of
the CAC was amended to include "and to provide support and advocacy
for the Center and its programs in the community." The CAC recently
sponsored an awards banquet and is helping to obtain scholarships for
the children's summer therapeutic camp. Our report was read by some
members of the present CAC, but those who commissioned it had left.

A number of important issues are illustrated here. Turnover and
lack of continuity are key problems for the CAC. The loss of active
leaders because of disenchantment and abrupt, seemingly arbitrary decisions made it difficult for the CAC to survive. It also renders use of our
study less likely because the purpose of the CAC has changed and those
who were most interested in our report have left. All this makes our assessment a less rewarding experience for us. Realizing the need for the
CAC to have specific projects, the center director suggested a number of
possible projects. These have the conservative goals discussed earlier;
nevertheless, they were welcomed by members of the CAC because they
were concrete, practical, and would have visible results. This fact suggests that vague mandates to citizen groups to address unmet community needs and to review center policies and programs can be frustrating
and nonfunctional. However, supportive advocacy projects may not

serve the goal of community accountability, though it may be possible
to have concrete projects that have less conservative goals.

Conclusion

Our literature review suggested that a number of problems surround
citizen participation in community mental health centers. We studied the
four components in the framework (external relationships, organizational
characteristics, effects, and individual differences) and compared assessments of the CAC from the perspective of the CAC, the board, and the
staff. Our study found additional evidence about the problems. Ambigu-
ity of goals, lack of information, problems in communication, and
doubts about impact emerged as salient.

The phenomenon of citizen participation influenced the process of
our study (e.g., in terms of role, entry, turnover, and utilization), and
this interaction provided information that (1) confirmed some of our results, such as problems with a lack of clarity in the functions of the
CAC, and (2) provided additional insights about participation that were
not fully revealed in the questionnaires, such as the degree of concern
about potential changes in the distribution of power held by key leaders.
In addition, qualitative results (Campbell, 1974) should be given more
attention in community research. For example, the change in the CAC's
charter regarding its purpose provides important information about influences on participation that can be hard to quantify. These and other
issues clearly point to the importance of process in interpreting results
and of illuminating the phenomenon being investigated and the system
in which it operates. According to Kelly (1979), "the process of our work
is as fully important as the content" (p. 245). Kelly suggests that consideration of process is one of the strengths of community psychology. His
ideas are oriented toward studying process in interventions; we feel that
process should also be studied in nonintervention field research. (See
Rosenberg, Reppucci, & Linney, 1979; Sank, 1979; and Munoz, Snowden, & Kelly, 1979, for interesting examples of the process and problems
of developing interventions.) Discussions of process often appear to have
a nonscientific, simplistic ring of truism; that is unfortunate because
there is a great deal to be learned from the interaction of the research
process and its subject. What we need in community mental health and
community psychology is systematic study of the process of field research. It will be anything but simple and will require much more than
anecdotes of familiar woes encountered in field research. Cowen and
Gesten (1980) provide some informative highlights of the problems they

encountered in over 22 years of intervention research in the public schools. Although they suggest ameliorative steps that they have found useful, community field research will eventually need to investigate empirically some alternative procedures.

Citizen participation presents a mixed bag of potentials and pitfalls to an agency.

> On the one hand, citizen participation is a control mechanism when citizens perform a monitoring or "watchdog" function. On the other hand, citizen participation provides an assistance function regarding agency decisions. Ironically, citizen participation may represent either a threat or a way of reducing threats to an agency. (Langton, 1978, p. 7)

Langton concludes that it is not surprising that many agency administrators are ambivalent about citizen participation. We would add that it is not surprising that many citizens who participate in citizen advisory committees are ambivalent and confused about their purpose. Systematic research on citizen participation is needed, and social scientists should then give the research to the citizens in a useful form. This type of approach should enhance community accountability, which is the major purpose of citizen participation in community mental health centers.

ACKNOWLEDGMENTS

We would like to thank Lois Pall Wandersman, Karl Slaikeu, Lawrence McClure, and Karen Hansen for their valuable comments on earlier drafts of this chapter.

References

Bloom, B. L. *Community mental health: A historical and critical analysis.* Morristown, N.J.: General Learning Press, 1973.

Campbell, D. T. *Qualitative knowing in action research.* Kurt Lewin Address to the meeting of the American Psychological Association, New Orleans, August 1974.

Carifi, M., & Zinober, J. W. *Citizens' review of CMHCs evaluation data: Progress report and preliminary findings.* Tampa, Fla.: Florida Consortium, 1979.

Chu, F., & Trotter, S. *The madness establishment.* New York: Grossman, 1974.

Cowen, E. L., & Gesten, E. L. Evaluating community programs: Tough and tender perspectives. In M. S. Gibbs, J. R. Lachenmeyer, & J. Sigal (Eds.), *Community psychology: Theoretical and empirical perspectives.* New York: Gardner Press, 1980.

Greer, S., & Greer, A. L. *Governance by citizen's boards: The care of community mental health centers.* Unpublished manuscript, University of Wisconsin–Milwaukee, 1979.

Health Policy Advisory Center. *Evaluation of community involvement in community mental health centers* (NTIS No. PB 221-267). New York: Author, 1972.

Hunt, G. J., *Citizen involvement in mental health decision-making.* Baltimore: Maryland State Department of Health and Mental Hygiene, 1972.

Hunt, G. J. *Citizen participation in health and mental health programs: A review of the literature and state mental health acts.* Washington, D.C.: National Association for Mental Health, 1973.

Hunt, G. J. A process to close the gap. *Mental Health,* 1977, *61*(1), 9–11.

Kelly, J. G. T'aint what you do, it's the way you do it. *American Journal of Community Psychology,* 1979, *7*, 244–260.

Kupst, M. J., Reidda, P., & McGee, T. Community mental health boards: A comparison of their development, functions, and powers by board members and mental health center staff. *Community Mental Health Journal,* 1975, *11*, 249–255.

Langton, S. *Citizen participation in America.* Lexington, Mass.: D. C. Heath, 1978.

Morrison, J. K., & Cometa, M. S. The impact of a client advisory board on a community mental health clinic. In J. K. Morrison (Ed.), *A consumer approach to community psychology.* Chicago: Nelson-Hall, 1979.

Morrison, J. K., Holdridge-Crane, S., & Smith, J. E. Citizen participation in community mental health. *Community Mental Health Review,* 1978, *3*, 2–9.

Munoz, R. F., Snowden, L. R., & Kelly, J. G. *Social and psychological research in community settings.* San Francisco: Jossey-Bass, 1979.

Nassi, A. J. Community control or control of the community? The case of the community mental health center. *Journal of Community Psychology,* 1978, *6*, 3–15.

New, P., Hessler, R., & Cater, P. Consumer control and public accountability. *Anthropological Quarterly,* 1973, *46*, 196–213.

Rosenberg, M., Reppucci, N. D., & Linney, J. A. *Problems of implementation: Parent education for high risk families.* Paper presented at the meeting of the American Psychological Association, New York, September 1979.

Ruiz, P., & Behrens, M. Community control in mental health: How far can it go? *Psychiatric Quarterly,* 1973, *47*, 317–324.

Sank, L. I. Community disasters: Primary prevention and treatment in a health maintenance organization. *American Psychologist,* 1979, *34*, 334–338.

Smith, J. E., Morrison, J. K., & Brown, M. The citizen advisory board: Consumer token or consumer power? In J. K. Morrison (Ed.), *A consumer approach to community psychology.* Chicago: Nelson-Hall, 1979.

Wandersman, A. User participation in planning environments: A conceptual framework. *Environment and Behavior,* 1979, *11*, 465–482.

Wandersman, A. A framework of participation in community organizations. *Journal of Applied Behavioral Sciences,* 1981, *17*, 1, 27–58.

22

An Experimental Evaluation and Process Analysis of a Behavioral Consultation Program

ABRAHAM M. JEGER AND GARY McCLURE

The emerging field of behavioral community psychology is marked by an interface between the broader roles adopted by community psychologists (e.g., program designer, trainer, consultant, evaluator) and the incorporation of a behavioral technology within such roles (see Chapter 3; Glenwick & Jason, 1980; Martin & Osborne, 1980; Nietzel, Winett, MacDonald, & Davidson, 1977). One increasingly common role is that of the behavioral consultant (e.g., Jeger, 1980). A behavioral consultant may be defined as one who provides indirect services to a client system by offering his/her knowledge of social learning principles to direct interventionists who are to implement behavior change programs.

This study was part of a dissertation submitted by the first author to the State University of New York at Stony Brook in partial fulfillment of the requirements for the Ph.D. degree.

ABRAHAM M. JEGER • New York Institute of Technology, Old Westbury, New York 11568. GARY McCLURE • Department of Psychology, Georgia Southern College, Statesboro, Georgia 30458.

In reviewing the literature on the effectiveness of consultation, Mannino and Shore (1975) identify three levels at which outcome measures can be obtained: *consultees*—changes in knowledge, skills, and attitudes of consultees; *clients*—behavioral and attitudinal changes in clients of consultees; and *system*—changes in institutional structure or social environment. In line with the behavioral tradition, most behavioral consultation programs focused on changes in target *clients* (i.e., clients of consultees) in evaluating their efforts. Following our view of the behavioral consultant as a systems interventionist, assessing change at all three targets is clearly warranted, as changes in consultees and systems are likely to precede individual behavior change. Furthermore, recognizing the larger ecological context within which behavioral consultants operate, we wish to emphasize the necessity of a *process analysis* to complement quantitative measures and experimental evaluation.

This chapter presents a case study in the evaluation of a behavioral consultation program with the adolescent service of a state psychiatric facility. The project exemplifies the complementary use of a process analysis with a multilevel experimental evaluation, incorporating measures at the three targets cited above.

Overview of the Project

The senior author was invited by the chief of the adolescent service of a large psychiatric center in New York State to develop a behavioral program that will meet two needs: (1) providing training for nursing personnel, and (2) establishing a more systematic, wardwide treatment program. It was agreed that the consultant would serve as a collaborator with existing professional staff to implement a behavioral training program for the nursing personnel as well as a behavioral (i.e., token economy) program for residents. It was further decided that a major role of the consultant would be to conduct an experimental evaluation of the project.

Participants

A total of 21 nursing personnel participated in the project. Of these, 11 served as consultees and 10 as no-training controls. Thirteen subjects were male (six in experimental and seven in control group) and eight female (five in experimental and three in control group).

In addition, 22 males residing on the two state hospital adolescent wards participated in the project. Of these, 12 were in the experimental behavioral program, and 10 continued with the "milieu" approach on the second ward. Most (18) were diagnosed as psychotic.

Assessment Procedures

Three major categories of quantitative measures were obtained, corresponding to the three targets of the intervention: consultees (staff); clients (residents); and social environment (ward ecology). Experimental and comparison groups were subjected to the assessment procedures on a pre-post basis.

Consultees

The following variables were assessed by the instrument package completed by staff:

1. Knowledge Test. Knowledge of behavior modification was assessed by means of hypothetical behavior problems typically found on wards. Staff were requested to outline a behavior change plan for each situation; these were scored by a research assistant employing a variation of Ashbaugh's (1971) procedure.

2. Attitudes Toward Mental Illness. Morrison's (1975) Client Attitude Questionnaire (CAQ-B), a 20-item scale tapping the extent of one's endorsement of a "medical" versus a "social learning" model, served as a measure. In addition, Paul and McInnis's (1974) 9-item scale measuring "social learning" orientation was included.

3. Attitudes Toward Behavior Modification. A 20-item scale tapping favorable versus unfavorable attitudes toward behavior modification was incorporated into the assessment battery. Originally developed by Musgrove (1974) to assess teacher attitudes, this instrument was modified by Jeger and McClure (1979) for use with general populations.

4. Job Satisfaction. A 26-item Job Design Inventory previously employed with staff of human service settings (e.g., Reppucci, Dean, & Saunders, 1975; Chapter 9, this volume) was used to measure staff satisfaction with their jobs. This measure assesses nine factors: variety, autonomy, task identity, feedback, participation, information, learning, contact, and informal contact.

Clients

Pre-post behavior change in residents was measured in the following ways.

1. Behavior Checklist Ratings. All residents were rated by all staff on the 30-item Nurses Observation Scale for Inpatient Evaluation (NOSIE-30) developed by Honigfeld, Gillis, and Klett (1966). There are six subscales: social competence, social interest, personal neatness, irritability, manifest psychosis, and retardation. In addition, the first three subscales are summed to yield a "total positive factors" score, and the last three yield a "total negative factors" score. The difference between the two yields a "total patient assets" score.

2. Naturalistic Observation. A time-sampling instrument to tap in vivo client social interaction on the ward was developed specifically for this project. Eight mutually exclusive behavior class categories were devised: positive interaction with patients, negative interaction with patients, positive interaction with staff, negative interaction with staff, positive interaction with patients and staff, isolated positive, isolated negative, and isolated neutral. Categories can be summed across all positive and across all "interaction" categories to yield more general information. Residents were observed by a research assistant over a predetermined schedule of time blocks corresponding to periods when no formal activities were planned off the ward.

3. Social Environment. Pooled staff perceptions of ward social climate were tapped by the Moos (1974) Ward Atmosphere Scale (WAS). This 100-item instrument consists of the following 10 subscales, grouped according to three broader environmental dimensions: involvement, support, spontaneity (relationship dimensions); autonomy, practical orientation, personal problem orientation, anger/aggression (treatment program dimensions); and order/organization, program clarity, and staff control (system maintenance dimensions).

The Behavioral Consultation Program

Two interrelated components of the consultation effort were the behavioral training package offered to the nursing staff, and the wardwide "behavioral milieu" program developed for residents.

Training Program. Eight 2-hour weekly group training sessions were conducted by the senior author in conjunction with an M.A.-level psychologist employed by the psychiatric center. Training contents represented an adaptation of a standard behavioral package designed for training institutional staff (e.g., Brown & Presbie, 1974). Behavioral approaches geared to individual clients as well as to entire wards were incorporated. Briefly, staff were trained to define problems in behavioral terms; to pinpoint, observe, and record behavior; to identify reinforcers (material, activity, and social) and apply them contingently; to create new behaviors with such techniques as shaping, modeling, and prompting; to decrease behavior with differential reinforcement, reinforcing incompatible behaviors, response cost, and overcorrection; to employ individual and group behavioral contracting; and to work within a wardwide token economy/milieu program. Included were discussions of the theoretical underpinnings of the behavioral techniques and of some of the ethical and legal ramifications of specific procedures. The training sessions also served as a forum for the joint planning of a token economy for the ward on which staff trainees worked. Training procedures included formal presentations of material, group discussions, modeling, role playing, feedback, and social reinforcement. In addition, reading materials provided as handouts, a film, and field experiences with individual clients were incorporated into the training program.

Behavioral Milieu Program. With the culmination of staff training, a wardwide token economy program had evolved. Staff awarded points to residents onto a card by means of figured (e.g., heart shaped, diamond shaped) hole punches. Points were earned for engaging in self-help behaviors (e.g., grooming, making the bed), attending client government meetings, and performing designated work duties. Points were individualized according to a resident's capability. Earned points were spent for backup reinforcers at the "token shop" located in the building.

The client government and token economy provided the structure for expanding the already existing milieu program. For example, client government meetings served as a forum for developing additional activities during evening hours for which residents could earn tokens. As a result, current events discussions and problem-solving groups were developed. Extent of participation was rewarded with differential point earnings, as stipulated by the client government.

Procedure

Following pretesting, staff and residents were divided to form two equivalent groups based on assessment instrument scores and background variables. After the groups were assigned, staff (consultees and comparison group) completed the WAS to assess the ward social environment. Experimental staff participated in the eight-session behavioral training program and in development of the token economy for residents. Posttesting was conducted for staff and residents following 2 weeks of full token economy operation.

Experimental Evaluation

Between-group mean differences on all measures were analyzed by employing two-tailed tests on pre-post difference scores. The findings are grouped into the three levels of assessment.

Changes in Consultees

Between-group "change" scores were significant beyond the 0.01 level, t (19) = 8.34, favoring the experimental group, on the knowledge of behavioral applications test. Similarly, on the CAQ-B (tapping attitudes toward mental illness), the consultees changed in the direction away from the "medical" model, with between-group difference scores reaching significance, t (19) = 2.20, $p < 0.05$. No significant difference emerged on the social learning orientation scale. As for attitudes toward behavior modification, between-group change scores reached significance, t (19) = 2.15, $p < 0.05$, favoring the experimental group. No significant differences emerged on the Job Design Inventory, tapping job satisfaction.

Changes in Clients

No significant between-group difference emerged on any subscale of the NOSIE-30. However, naturalistic observations clearly favored the experimental group. When combining all the "positive" social interaction categories, experimental clients increased an average of 29%, whereas control clients decreased an average of 2%. Experimental clients also manifested a 30% reduction of neutral or negative solitary behaviors, compared to no change in the control clients.

Changes in Social Environment

Pre-post changes in perceived social climate favored the experimental program. Significant between-group differences emerged on the involvement subscale, t (18) = 2.18, $p < 0.05$, and the autonomy subscale, t (18) = 2.40, $p < 0.05$. The trend in the direction of change in the other subscales also favored the experimental program.

Discussion

Results of the experimental evaluation lend partial support for the effectiveness of the behavioral consultation program. They compare favorably with earlier evaluations of consultation efforts (nonbehavioral) that incorporated measures at three levels (i.e., Keutzer, Fosmire, Diller, & Smith, 1971; Schmuck, 1968). Our project extended this multilevel evaluation paradigm to the area of behavioral consultation, applied it to different consultee/client/environment targets, and incorporated diverse assessment criteria within each target.

Two general limitations of the research center around the timing of assessments, and research design. First, the study is weakened by a lack of follow-up. Administrative changes shortly after the consultant phased out precluded the attainment of such data. Second, an additional comparison group to control for the attention given staff and clients in the experimental (consultation) program would have strengthened the argument for the relative efficacy of the project. The latter issue is raised by Erickson (1975) in connection with earlier outcome studies in mental hospitals: "how can one control for the energy and enthusiasm that accompany the start of any new and experimental program?" (p. 529). Perhaps a solution might lie in concurrently initiating several programs. To determine the relative merits of a behavioral program, it would be advisable to compare it simultaneously with a milieu program as well as with the routine ongoing treatment. Unfortunately, it is rare when two experimental programs can be implemented in applied settings.

It is safe to conclude, however, that the short-term effects of the program are indeed favorable—especially when one considers that the program was not a typical well-funded demonstration project but took place with indigenous staff, limited resources, and under severe institutional constraints.

Process Analysis

As behavior modifiers have stepped out of their laboratories and private offices to apply behavioral technologies in large-scale natural settings (schools, hospitals, day care centers, etc.), they have become sensitized to the influences of the broader social system. These issues become even more salient when the behavior modifier serves as an outside consultant and is not in control of the setting in which a program is implemented. Furthermore, considering the limitations of experimental designs in mental health program evaluation, a process analysis to complement an experimental evaluation appeared timely (Jeger, 1980; see also "Introduction" to Part VI).

Effects of the System on the Program

Based on their long-term behavioral consultation with the Connecticut School for Boys (see Chapter 9), Reppucci and Saunders (1974) identify eight major social systems variables that behavioral innovators must consider:

1. *Institutional constraints*, such as competing reinforcers within the system that preclude making all reinforcers contingent on positive behavior, strained communication channels, and turnover in high-level administrative staff
2. *External pressure* or pressures from outside the institution resulting, for example, from a case of AWOL, which lead to increased emphasis on maximum security
3. *Language* or problems associated with such derogatory labels as "behavior modification"
4. *Two populations*, or problems centering around the fact that nonprofessional staff carry out the behavioral programs, and constraints imposed by union regulations prevent incorporating any differential rewards for staff who "perform" in a program
5. *Limited resources*, such as shortages or backup reinforcers and limitations of time and personpower
6. *Labeling* where indigenous staff object to the use of certain ongoing activities in a contingency program because of labels ("recreation," "educational trips")
7. *Perceived inflexibility* characterized by consultees' perception of the behavior modifier's desire to include all behavior into a contingency program
8. *Compromise*, that is, a warning to behavior modifiers that they will have to compromise on behavioral methodology after contact with a setting (e.g., program contents or evaluation aspects)

Institutional Constraints. Problems of competing reinforcers and intershift communications were prevalent in our project. For example, patients with access to outside cash resources were less dependent on the token program. Likewise, despite several attempts to maximize consistency of procedures among staff of three shifts, communication was virtually nonexistent. Another constraint related to frequent turnover of top-level administrators of the adolescent service. Furthermore, the timing of the project coincided with the implementation of a new recordkeeping system that placed heavy demands on staff time. Also, such concerns as when and where to hold the training sessions had to be overcome at the outset of the project, with some difficulty.

External Pressure. External accrediting bodies demanded extensive recordkeeping, which resulted in less time for staff interaction with residents. Furthermore, legal restrictions on client labor required close monitoring to ensure that resident activities included in the token program were part of a continually reviewed "treatment plan" for which there were legal provisions.

Language. Aside from concerns with the label "behavior modification" that several staff resented, difficulties were encountered in getting staff to define problems in behavioral terms, as opposed to the mentalistic constructs to which they were accustomed. In addition, the terms "research" and "evaluation" made staff uneasy—as research implies staff serving as guinea pigs in the investigation of new techniques, and evaluation raises more personal anxieties. We chose to emphasize "program" evaluation, which suggests that the program will be evaluated rather than any particular staff members.

Two Populations. A major concern in this area was the lack of control over staff reinforcers (e.g., salary, promotions) for purposes of motivating them to perform the extra tasks required by the consultation program. The civil service system prevents the allocation of any differential rewards. Relying on instructions alone to enhance staff performance is inefficient and largely ineffective. For example, data on staff reinforcement preferences show that 84% of attendants prefer "extra salary," and 71% prefer "more time off" (Watson, 1976)—both being factors that could not be manipulated under current regulations. (This situation contrasts with the staff motivation system employed by Goodson and Turner at the Huntsville Mental Health Center; see Chapter 19.)

Furthermore, it is our contention that more than *two* populations need to be considered. In offering a consultation program, the consultant is attempting to coordinate activities at various staff levels—nonprofessionals, professionals, administrators, support staff. For example, the consultant needs to be careful not to detract from the credibility of the existing professional staff who are primarily responsible for day-to-day program implementation, and to serve as a collaborator. In our program a conflict nearly arose when a professional staff member requested some "personal time" off duty from the unit administrator, who responded affirmatively, as long as it did not interfere with the "consultant's" program. Another showdown almost resulted because of inadequate coordination with the unit psychiatrists: When staff attempted to apply a behavioral technique to modify chair throwing by a resident, the team psychiatrist ordered that the client be medicated instead.

Limited Resources. Limited finances, time, and personpower are usually the norm in human service settings. Despite commitments made to the consultant during the entry phase, shortages impinged on the program throughout. For example, short staff on weekends made it difficult to open the token store as frequently as planned—curiously enough, weekends are times when the fewest activities are scheduled. Although supplies were sufficiently budgeted, they were often late in coming. Staff ingenuity was necessary to create emergency supplies (e.g., when running out of soda, homemade lemonade was substituted). Although seemingly mundane matters, these are the nuts and bolts of day-to-day token economy operations.

Labeling. Because of the labeling of certain activities as "recreation" (dances, trips), staff were resistant to incorporating them into the contingency plans. Thus clients obtained certain privileges on a noncontingent basis, and incorporation of all unit activities into the behavioral program was never realized.

Perceived Inflexibility. Our previously mentioned desire to include all activities into the program was seen as inflexibility. Furthermore, inflexibility arising from the demands of the evaluation design was manifested by many nonprofessional staff who were against employing a control group, arguing that everyone should receive the program at once. The importance of starting on a small scale and the need for evaluation were emphasized; support was received from the existing professional staff, who were committed to program evaluation.

Compromise. Compromises in behavioral procedures and in the consistency of the program had to occur because of many of the factors outlined above—lack of intershift communication, resistance to incorporating all activities into contingency management plans, and so on.

Other. Staff had a tendency to confront consultants with the most difficult clinical cases, raising the issue whether a "program" consultant can avoid falling into the trap of providing direct services. Since behavior modification is likely to be oversold, many staff expected miracles with their most difficult clients. Thus the behavioral consultant had to reduce the mystical aura surrounding the techniques.

The final issue was the continuation of the program following the consultant's departure, something we considered from the start of the consultation. In this case, it survived for approximately 9 months after the consultant left (and included staff and residents who were previously in the control groups), with ups and downs. Administrative shuffling of staff and residents from the original project finally led to the program's demise.

Effects of the Program on the System

The rehabilitation unit of the hospital intended to focus on the adolescents as the first group to enter the transitional living facilities that they were planning, and they saw our program as the necessary first step. Unfortunately, the transitional facility was never realized because of inefficiency and lack of coordination among the various hospital units. Thus our program did not contribute to the institutional change we thought we were working toward. Furthermore, professionals from other units visited the program from its early stages on, and indicated an interest in modeling after it. Although that gave both the program and the adolescent service positive visibility throughout the hospital, no replications were seriously attempted by any other unit. In addition, we observed that the program was used by hospital administrators as a showpiece for visitors from accrediting bodies. Indeed, the hospital had something to show for it—token shop, charts on the ward, client government system, and so on.

In retrospect, it may be that our program qualifies for what Graziano (1969) calls "innovation without change." Taking this point a step further, to the extent that the program appeared innovative, it helped maintain the status quo of the basic institution. By becoming enmeshed in the internal forces of the institution our project had, in some small way, contributed to maintaining the institution as such. We agree with Krasner (1976) who, following implementation of a token economy in a state hospital, found that

> to the extent that we were successful in developing a token economy on a hospital ward, we were helping maintain a social institution, the mental hospital, that in its current form, was no longer desirable in our society. We decided that based on our own value system, we would not develop further token economy programs in mental hospitals. (p. 635)

Similar observations were made by Baer (1970) in connection with school-directed behavioral consultation. He argues that despite its innovative features, consultation is an inadequate vehicle for institutional change. By continuing to offer consultation for purposes of remediation, attention is diverted from the basic need to revamp the entire teacher training curriculum in the first place. The analogy to the present situation is self-evident. A more viable target for behavioral consultation should be the basic institution (see, e.g., Chapter 9). Developing a program in one component of the institution is unlikely to induce significant change.

Conclusion

Process analyses must be incorporated into program evaluation efforts. It is clear that an incomplete picture of our project would have emerged had we presented only the experimental results.

It is the process analysis that makes one appreciate the complexity of behavioral consultation. It provides an antidote to the view that consultants can easily implement canned packages in any setting. Most significant, perhaps, is the fact that a process analysis raises such questions as, What is your program used for? and, Should you have offered consultation in the first place?

Whereas the experimental evaluation (which is the focus of most articles in professional journals) leads one to believe in the relative effectiveness of the program, the process analysis sheds some light on the larger social-political functions of the project. At the same time, however, by pointing to the constraints on the program, the positive gains achieved can be better appreciated.

ACKNOWLEDGMENTS

Appreciation is extended to Dr. Leonard Krasner, who served as chairman of the dissertation committee, State University of New York at Stony Brook, and to Dr. Sharon Rosen and Dr. Charles Hoffmann, members of the committee. Thanks are also due the staff and residents of Pilgrim Psychiatric Center's Adolescent Service, who served as participants in the study; and to Harold Bishop, who served as research assistant.

References

Ashbaugh, L. L. An evaluation of an attendant training program based on principles of behavior modification. *Dissertation Abstracts International*, 1971, *32*(5-A), 2510.

Baer, D. M. The consultation process model as an irrational state of affairs. *Psychology in the Schools*, 1970, *4*, 341–344.

Brown, P. L., & Presbie, R. J. *Behavior modification skills: A complete training program*. Hicksville, N.Y.: Research Media, 1974.

Erickson, R. C. Outcome studies in mental hospitals: A review. *Psychological Bulletin*, 1975, *82*, 519–540.

Glenwick, D. S., & Jason, L. A. (Eds.). *Behavioral community psychology: Progress and prospects*. New York: Praeger, 1980.

Graziano, A. M. Clinical innovation and the mental health power structure: A social case history. *American Psychologist*, 1969, *24*, 10–18.

Honigfeld, G., Gillis, R. D., & Klett, C. J. NOSIE-30: A treatment sensitive ward behavior scale. *Psychological Reports*, 1966, *19*, 180–182.

Jeger, A. M. Community mental health and environmental design. In L. Krasner (Ed.), *Environmental design and human behavior: A psychology of the individual in society*. Elmsford, N.Y.: Pergamon Press, 1980.

Jeger, A. M., & McClure, G. The attitudinal effects of undergraduate behavioral training. *Teaching of Psychology*, 1979, *6*, 226–229.

Keutzer, C. S., Fosmire, F. R., Diller, R., & Smith, M. D. Laboratory training in a new social system: Evaluation of a consulting relationship with a high school faculty. *Journal of Applied Behavioral Science*, 1971, *7*, 493–501.

Krasner, L. Behavior modification: Ethical issues and future trends. In H. Leitenberg (Ed.), *Handbook of behavior modification and behavior therapy*. Englewood Cliffs, N.J.: Prentice-Hall, 1976.

Mannino, F. V., & Shore, M. F. The effects of consultation. *American Journal of Community Psychology*, 1975, *3*, 1–21.

Martin, G. L., & Osborne, J. G. (Eds.). *Helping in the community: Behavioral applications*. New York: Plenum Press, 1980.

Moos, R. H. *Evaluating treatment environments: A social ecological approach*. New York: Wiley, 1974.

Morrison, J. K. *The client attitude questionnaire: A brief manual*. Unpublished manuscript, Department of Psychiatry, Albany Medical College, 1975.

Musgrove, W. J. A scale to measure attitudes toward behavior modification. *Psychology in the Schools*, 1974, *2*, 392–396.

Nietzel, M. T., Winett, R. A., MacDonald, M. & Davidson, W. S. *Behavioral approaches to community psychology*. Elmsford, N.Y.: Pergamon Press, 1977.

Paul, G. L., & McInnis, T. L. Attitudinal changes associated with two approaches to training mental health technicians in milieu and social learning programs. *Journal of Consulting and Clinical Psychology*, 1974, *42*, 21–33.

Reppucci, N. D., & Saunders, J. T. Social psychology of behavior modification: Problems of implementation in natural settings. *American Psychologist*, 1974, *29*, 649–660.

Reppucci, N. D., Dean, C. W., & Saunders, J. T. Job design variables as change measures in a correctional facility. *American Journal of Community Psychology*, 1975, *3*, 315–325.

Schmuck, R. A. Helping teachers improve classroom group processes. *Journal of Applied Behavioral Science*, 1968, *4*, 401–435.

Watson, L. K. Shaping and maintaining behavior modification skills in staff using contingent reinforcement techniques. In R. C. Patterson (Ed.), *Maintaining effective token economies*. Springfield, Ill.: Charles C Thomas, 1976.

23

A Structural Framework for Conceptualizing Ethical Issues in Behavioral-Ecological Practice

LEO R. EILBERT AND HENRY EILBIRT

It is an inevitable aspect of the human condition that we are intermittently faced with deciding what we *ought* to do. Ethical "problems" are matters of "correct" behavior, no easy thing to define. Perhaps unfortunately, ethical judgments cannot be made with scientifically precise or consistent criteria. Indeed, such judgments about what is right and what is wrong, what ought to be done and what ought not to be done, when punishment is warranted and when it is not—such judgments are, for most of us, relative rather than absolute and invariant. Different people do not necessarily arrive at the same conclusions even when they have the same data. The differences are heightened when the people viewing the same event or situation do not share the same percepts, assumptions, and values: Collisions of this sort are often passionate. Moreover, our judgments may manifest a "rubber yardstick," for we often apply stan-

LEO R. EILBERT ● Human Resources Development Center, New York Institute of Technology, Old Westbury, New York 11568. HENRY EILBIRT ● Bernard M. Baruch College, School of Business and Public Administration, New York, New York 10003.

dards somewhat more loosely to our own actions than to those of others, and make allowances for the actions of some people or some groups that we are unwilling to make for others.

Nevertheless, ethical issues are important. One gauge of their importance is provided by the attention they receive from different segments of our society. Ethical issues have been deliberated in the courts, government, professions, business, unions, and religious bodies (Welles, 1976). Thus questions about medical ethics date to antiquity. Integrity, wisdom, goodwill, joined perhaps with an ability to read the handwriting on the wall, led to the formulation of the Hippocratic oath. That a *Journal of Medical Ethics* exists suggests the topic is still considered important, current, and unresolved. One of the fuels that keep interest in this topic heated is the growing impact of malpractice suits. Nor is malpractice limited to the medical profession. Dentists, mental health providers, attorneys, accountants—even school systems are increasingly being sued for malpractice. The recent ABSCAM scandal on congressional corruption illustrates that the ethics of our politicians are not always above reproach. Questions about the ethics of various business practices have been raised over the centuries.

Professional ethics are also at issue in cases involving the theft of research ideas; the misrepresentation of data; and claims by students against instructors that the tests used in a course did not adequately measure what the students had learned (Sanders, 1979). Research ethics received some desultory treatment during the nineteenth century. But the first major code of research ethics, the Nuremberg code, as it came to be called, evolved in the late 1940s in response to the Nazi practice of performing high-risk experiments on nonconsenting subjects (Walters, 1978). Our federal government recently published a stringent set of guidelines for the ethical conduct of research when human subjects are involved.

Clearly, ethical dilemmas have received a huge amount of attention that has led to much discussion about guidelines and standards. Unfortunately, the guidelines or rules of conduct that have been developed are often difficult both to interpret and to enforce.

The primary purposes of this chapter are (1) to develop a useful morphology capable of supplying a framework for the study of ethical issues in mental health; and (2) to define what these issues in fact are, that is, to examine the range and complexity of ethical dilemmas encountered in mental health practice.

Ethical issues in mental health arise because of policies or practices that have created conflict or are subject to question. We present our morphology as a vehicle for conceptualizing such traditional ethical concerns as privacy, informed consent, and confidentiality as well as issues in behavioral-ecological practice. This morphology does not profess to be a code of ethics inasmuch as it makes no attempt to prescribe behavior. It includes behavioral categories even where it is uncertain just what policies or practices are right or wrong. For our purposes, simply the identification of an ethical issue warrants its inclusion in this morphology.

Derivation of Ethical Principles

Millennia ago, religious teachers and leaders laid down certain fundamental injunctions that were to be followed or observed (see, e.g., Exod. 20, 22, 23). In the era of what we think of as ancient Greece, philosophers began to review the fundamental meaning and nature of morals and ethics. Whereas religious teachers frequently relied on authority —the word of God—in their assertions as to what criteria should be followed, philosophers sought to employ reason and logic to determine what correct behavior should be and how it should be judged. In short, the regulation of human conduct has an ancient history.

Various professions and guilds have established codes of conduct and guidelines by which to police themselves. Thus codes of medical practice have existed for a long time. There is a published code of *Ethical Standards for Psychologists*. Lawyers have a *Code of Professional Responsibility*. Accountants have also developed standards of ethics. The administrative manuals of many police departments contain numerous references to ethical obligations. Various trade associations in advertising, real estate, and public relations have prepared codes of ethics to guide individual behavior. A number of professions and associations have established machinery for enforcing their codes, usually in the form of peer review committees.

The philosophical approach provides broad general principles that require more "processing" before they can serve as criteria of ethical conduct. By contrast, the codes of ethics of trades or professions, though still composed of general principles, are pertinent and responsive to the ethical issues likely to be encountered in that line of work. Of course, such codes frequently originate in charges of misbehavior by members of the trades or professions. The purpose of the code is to reduce the incidence of misbehaviors or at least to give the appearance of seeking to do so. Sometimes the wrongdoing is clear-cut and obvious. But not infrequently cases coming before peer review or ethics committees involve two or more conflicting general principles, and the merits of the case are determined not only by the complainee's conduct but by the particular set of circumstances, or contexts, in which this conduct occurred.

Promoting Mental Health

Mental health delivery takes many forms. At one end of the spectrum is the individual practitioner doing individual psychotherapy. Alternatively, we see group psychotherapy or sensitivity training conducted with small groups. Organizational involvement in mental health delivery occurs in community mental health centers or other types of community action programs. Finally, there are movements for social reform, federal laws governing abortion or drug abuse, and other *macrolevel* social interventions.

The term "mental health provider" covers a variety of roles. At one level it may refer to a patient's family physician, seen throughout the individual's life. The provider may be a licensed mental health specialist, for example, a psychiatrist or a clinical psychologist. Or the provider may be an advanced student in training working under a professional supervisor, a technician, a paraprofessional, or someone whom professionals would label a charlatan. The provider may also be an agency, a self-help group, or a social-political group seeking to change environmental conditions. Friends and relatives can also provide solace, for purposes of this chapter, however, we shall not regard them as mental health providers.

Alternative Strategies for Promoting Mental Health

By definition, mental health seeks to promote the public's health and welfare. One important way of promoting mental health is to focus on the intrapsychic problems of persons who do not fit readily into the existing social structure. Thus, either by removing impediments or by developing hitherto unidentified resources, the individual can be changed or improved to fit better into society.

A second way of promoting mental health accepts the individual as he/she is, either because of the viewpoint that people have the right to be different, or perhaps because of pragmatic difficulties involved in effecting change. Consequently, mental health is furthered by changing an individual's environment or context. Such environmental changes may simply involve establishing special classes for gifted children or allocating certain resources to meet the academic needs of handicapped children. Others call for more radical environmental modifications, including political activism and the social and political organization of communities, in order to bring about desirable changes for population segments lacking influence and power (Rappaport, 1977).

Therapy, regardless of whether it is individually oriented behavior modification or involves broader ecological change strategies, is a form of social intervention. As Kelman and Warwick (1978) point out,

There are four aspects of any social intervention that are likely to raise major ethical issues: (1) The choice of goals to which the effort is directed, (2) The definition of the target of the change, (3) The choice of means used to implement the intervention, and (4) The assessment of the consequences of the intervention. (p. 4)

The authors contend that in practice ethical issues seem always to involve conflicting values. These conflicts raise questions about which values are to be sacrificed in order to attain certain other values. Nor is it always clear just where the problem lies. For example, a change effort to improve the conditions of an economically disadvantaged group can have more than one target of change. If our strategy is aimed at changing or improving individuals, then we stress the reduction of the educational, social, or psychological deficiencies of the disadvantaged group members per se. If, on the other hand, we are ecologically oriented, we would focus more on modifying the milieu that led to the systematic exclusion of this group from the economic life of the community. In a similar vein, Kelman (1970) discusses the research significance of alternative concepts of deviant behavior. We can either decide that the appropriate goal is to change the behavior of persons whose behavior is deviant, or we can choose to view deviance as a social phenomenon that calls for reevaluating social policy. However, this goal-setting process is extremely important because once a goal is chosen, it governs the set of constructs to be employed and the courses of action to be followed in dealing with deviance.

A Framework for Ethical Issues in Mental Health

Ethical criteria are greatly influenced by the social contexts in which they appear. These might include the roles of different professionals involved in health care decisions; the education and participation of recipients of health care; the method of payment (including third-party payments) for health care; and an emphasis on prevention (the Chinese system), rather than on cure, of illness.

Our fundamental morphological approach to the relationships between ethics and mental health care is portrayed in Table 1, which focuses largely on the way provider practices (which may be a result of policies or even large-scale political action) affect the seeker of mental health services. The three column headings represent three contexts for ethical dilemmas: demand, supply, and quality of services. The five rows depict the provider–client relationship and the ethical issues that may arise between them. These relationships have a temporal sequence, which we divide into five main parts, namely: (1) the period preceding face-to-face contact between provider and client; (2) an assessment peri-

Table 1. A Structural Framework for Conceptualizing Ethical Issues: Contexts for Ethical Enigmas and Dilemmas

Temporal sequence of intervention	Demand for services	Creation and allocation of supply of services	Quality of services
Before contact with client	Type of public announcements concerning services	Socialized care versus a free enterprise system	Provision of information about services offered
	Information given about the cost and duration of treatment	Reform movements	How well physical plant is designed to handle the services offered
	"Educational" campaigns to teach the public about the value of periodic checkups	Policies of the profession with respect to training	Adequacy of staffing
	Coercion	Political action via licensing and certification to set qualifications for practice	Operation under multiple roles
	Professional referral	Policies with respect to utilization of trainees and paraprofessionals	
	Insurance coverage	Creation of community action or self-help networks	

Initial assessment period	Diagnosis, prognosis, and interpretation of findings in terms of "proving" the need for treatment	Allocation of resources for the prevention of mental illness	Crisis intervention resources used when needed
		Crisis intervention programs	
		Refusing treatment	
	Referral to a community action or self-help program	Waiting list dynamics	Adequacy of resources for diagnosis and prognosis
		Membership into an existing community action group	Availability of researched guidelines for appropriate care
	Professional referral		
	Insurance coverage		Informed consent
Course of therapy or intervention	Duration of treatment	Referral to another therapist or agency (either for simultaneous or alternative attendance)	Privacy/confidentiality
	Cost of treatment		Treatment or program assessment procedures

(Continued)

Table 1. (Continued)

Temporal sequence of intervention	Demand for services	Creation and allocation of supply of services	Quality of services
	Client testimonials about program or services		Premature publication
	Patient or client referrals		Whistle blowing on one's organization or colleagues when a serious breach of ethics has occurred
	Professional referral		Referral when indicated
	Insurance coverage		Informed consent to continue service
			Billing practices
			Client satisfaction with program or services
			Initiation of a sexual relationship

Termination of therapy or intervention	Termination viewed from the standpoint of the independence–dependence dimension	Termination because of inability to pay	Recognition that course of therapy has been completed
	Professional referral	Referral to another agency or program	Adequacy of preparation for termination
			Technical excellence of the results
			Candid reports of therapeutic or research failures
Follow-up period	Recommendation for follow-up	Creation and provision of follow-up services	Provision of follow-up for therapeutic reasons
			Provision of follow-up for research

od, which is the time required for completing a diagnostic work-up on the client, or, if the contact is nonprofessional, it might be the first few visits to a self-help group; (3) the time covered by the course of therapy or intervention; (4) termination; and (5) follow-up.

Enigmas and dilemmas are omnipresent in the mental health field. They arise to a large extent from manipulations inherent in demand and supply and from disagreements concerning the quality of care. They may be related to organizational membership and the constraints imposed by the organization.

Personal dilemmas, for example, result when the pros and cons for various courses of actions are inconclusive and enigmatic or when a course of action is personally unpleasant yet urgently called for. A doctor faced with the prospect of telling a patient that the diagnosis suggests either of two equally unpleasant alternatives may find it easy to postpone this discussion. He is not under specific organizational constraint. A salesman on the verge of receiving an order may be "asked" to do a (objectionable) favor for the prospective buyer; and although the organization examines sales records and rewards success, there is no specific organizational constraint to comply with the request. Nevertheless the intrapersonal dilemma is in each case quite real.

Personal dilemmas may also come about because of professional or organizational constraints. A psychiatrist may be torn between bearing witness in, say, a case of clearly incompetent care and enduring the disapproval of colleagues plus possible sanctions from medical establishment. Mirvis and Seashore (1979) vividly describe a number of situations encountered by research psychologists whose ethical dilemmas stem from becoming entangled in multiple, sometimes conflicting, roles that lead to unanticipated and unwanted consequences. These are instances of both intra- and interpersonal moral conflict. And yet sometimes a mental health provider may become confused as to whose agent he/she is—is he/she the patient's agent, an agent of the source of funding, an institutional representative, an agent of a profession, or of society at large? Nor are these role demands themselves always consistent.

Ethical Issues: The Demand Side

Table 1 presents the variables that influence the demand for mental health services. Since mental health care is largely deferrable, economics plays a substantial role in decisions about it. Crowell (1977) maintains that the demand for mental health services is income elastic in that increases in the consumer's income are accompanied by at least a proportional increase in the demand for the services. Under free market conditions the poor are less likely to be consumers of mental health services. However, there has been a trend in Western societies for government to subsidize service providers. As a result, prices have often been set administratively. Thus demand for services tends to be bolstered without an increase in supply (Buck & Hirschman, 1980). This situation, in turn, may lead to nonmarket means to reduce demand, such as refusing treatment, that is, curtailing supply to some clients and/or using waiting lists. Certain clients may remain forever near the end of the waiting list. Because of the prevalence of third-party payments, insurance companies are also capable of manipulating demand for services. The practice of readily reimbursing inpatient services, quite irrespective of client need so long as hospital beds are available, can lead to needless diagnostic hospitalizations. Other mental health needs, such as parent education, which insurance companies will not reimburse, receive little financial encouragement. According to Landsberg and Hammer (1977), such reimbursement policies on the part of insurance companies have damaged innovative programming in community mental health centers.

Client Solicitation. There are various ways in which an agency can present itself to the public—advertising, media information campaigns, lectures, publications. Clients also hear about certain agencies or programs by means of referral from a practitioner they know and trust, or referral from family or friends. Sometimes the prospective client will seek out listings of certified practitioners maintained by professional groups.

One very serious ethical abuse exploits the hopes of those in distress. Normally, a prospective seeker of mental health services is interested in learning how long a waiting period is required before service becomes available, the costs involved, the amount of time the service will take, and how long a period will be required before it is completed. Assurances of success are welcomed; virtually every mental health client focuses on one or two salient problems and wishes for some magic that will rid him/her of these problems quickly, economically, and effortlessly. In this vulnerable situation, hucksters appear to capitalize on clients' common and predictable fantasies: They promise all that could be hoped for, and offer to provide it quickly and relatively cheaply.

In general, professions have sought to regulate advertising to some extent and in some cases to prohibit it. A common distinction is made between, on the one hand, announcing the availability of services, specifying the kinds of services offered, and listing one's academic credentials and, on the other hand, openly soliciting business by extolling one's services, using tactics to generate urgency, and claiming great therapeutic success. Nonprofessionals, of course, are not even bound by such distinctions, and nobody monitors their claims.

Questionable advertising practices are not limited to any single profession. For example, Back (1978), in his ethical critique of encounter groups (which he views as a medical-religious movement) points out that encounter group leaders claim that their work is recreational or educational in the sense of providing an intense emotional experience. Nevertheless, encounter group advertisements have been produced that promise "cures for a whole range of ills" (Back, 1978, p. 114).

In summary, demand for mental health services is susceptible to many pressures. It rises to the seductive tones of hope (as some cancer clinics know well); it can be fomented by scare tactics. The ritual requirement of a periodic checkup creates demand; or demand can be set in motion by professional authority, as when a mental health client is referred to a specialist for further examination. In fact, Blue Cross/Blue Shield has run newspaper advertisements advising the public that half of all visits to physicians are unnecessary. Referrals have in some cases been intertwined with fee-splitting arrangements. Some forms of authority, for example, parents or courts, create demand by coercion.

Coercion and Informed Consent. As in other health care areas, there are persons who choose to come for therapy to rid themselves of mental health problems or habits that cause them distress. They select an agent or agency to help them overcome their problems; familiarize themselves with the goals of therapy, the approach to be used, and the costs; and with this information they agree to proceed with the therapy. In this sense they can be said to have given informed consent to the mental health provider. They may change their mind or regret the choice they made later, but that would not alter the fact that informed consent was initially given. Sometimes, however, therapeutic efforts may involve various degrees of coercion, particularly when these efforts "are directed at individuals who either have not consented to be treated or who, by virtue of their state or condition, are not in a position to engage in those rational operations required for a meaningful and valid consent" (D. N. Robinson, 1974, p. 233). At the extreme is the high-risk medical research done in Nazi concentration camps on unwilling, but helpless, inmates. Some forms of coercion are much more subtle. Prospective mental patients on the threshold of being committed to a mental hospital are often amiably invited to "come for a ride in the country." There are many points on the continuum from pure coercion to pure voluntarism.

Under what conditions can coercion (i.e., compulsory therapy) be justified? Robinson observes that there is a rationale for compulsion in the case of "individuals presented for treatment, for therapy, behavior modification, etc. [who] for reasons of having physically harmed others can lay no moral claim on the right not to be changed" (1974, p. 236). However, he rejects compulsory therapy as a way of changing ideology, or individuals whose behavior constitutes a "nuisance," or those who defy moral conventions, arguing that society with its laws and its great power of persuasion probably has all the influence it needs to cope with such problems.

One controversial form of compulsory therapy is the imposition of indefinite sentences. This practice is based on the concept that prisons should rehabilitate rather than simply punish. However, libertarians and others have challenged the right of the state to impose an indefinite sentence, maintaining that when, in the name of therapy, the state assumes the right to examine a person's mind until some vested authority pronounces the prisoner "cured," such mind control is a serious infringement on personal freedom (Kittrie, 1971).

The central tenet of informed consent is that mental health clients must play a primary role in decisions relating to their own health and welfare. But as Warwick (1971) points out, the ability truly to employ informed consent rests on having the capacity, the opportunity, and the incentive to make reflective choices and to act on them. Psychotics, mental defectives, children, and the comatose are considered unlikely to have the capacity for informed consent. Capron (1978) questions whether prisoners, because of their special status as captives of the state, are ever capable of giving informed consent.

Assuming that a practitioner has a duty to inform his patient, the scope of the disclosure is by no means clear. According to Judge Robinson (1978), full disclosure is both prohibitive and unrealistic. It would require a practitioner to discuss every risk with the patient no matter how small or remote. The issue then becomes: If not full disclosure, how much information should be imparted?

There are still further complications to the concept of informed consent. If a patient in a coronary care unit is comatose and thereby reduced to a state of abject dependence, he/she cannot be in a position to give informed consent. But as such patients recover they may at some point regain the executive function, that is, the ability to make decisions on their own behalf. When should the informed consent function be resumed by such a patient? The issue of informed consent is as vital as it is clouded.

Temporal Sequence. The bulk of ethical issues pertaining to demand for services occur early in the temporal sequence. Indeed, many surface before the initial assessment period has been completed. Some variables are primarily linked to a single temporal interval, for example, advertising is most important before contact with the client. Other variables pertain to practically the entire temporal sequence—as in the case of referrals, which can be made at any point of the treatment and even after treatment is terminated. Or, ethical issues pertaining to insurance coverage may figure most prominently early in the temporal sequence, but they may also emerge later in the sequence.

Ploys have been used in the offer of free diagnostic assessments, inevitably followed by using the findings to show a definite and urgent need for services (Eilbert & Spector, 1979). Sometimes individuals are accepted into treatment when referral to a self-help group might be an equally valid yet more economical alternative for them.

During the course of therapy, such demand variables, as the duration and cost of treatment can be manipulated. Some mental health providers continue to see patients for years and years. Perhaps some patients do require 15 years of therapy to reconstruct personalities that are near disintegration; but there are clearly instances where the practice of prolonging the need for services is not easily justified, and strong dependence needs are being selectively reinforced (and in some cases created). In short, the course of therapy and its termination are major variables in the morality of mental health services.

During and perhaps even after therapy, clients can be "encouraged" to refer friends, neighbors, or family. No doubt some clients feel a spontaneous gratitude for the help they have received and mention the services to friends; but in some instances clients are pressured into referring others in an ethically questionable manner.

Follow-up after the completion of therapy may also involve the manipulation of demand. Sometimes clients who need ongoing care or support are simply dumped; no referral or follow-up is offered. Conversely, some clients are scheduled for follow-up despite the fact that there is little to indicate a need for it. Either course of action gives rise to ethical issues.

Ethical Issues: The Supply Side

As shown in Table 1, there are many variables that pertain to the creation, allocation, and supply of mental health services. A large proportion of these variables are political and/or social in nature.

Sociopolitical Variables. Factors of this kind exert a powerful influence on supply, through control over the number of providers available, the types of services made available, as well as the costs of the services. For example, moving from our system toward socialized medical care would have a tremendous impact on all these factors, as would placing greater emphasis on the prevention of mental illness. Buck and Hirschman (1980) recommend increasing the supply of services by increasing the number of qualified providers. It is widely believed that the medical profession has traditionally restricted the number of medical school candidates accepted in order to prevent an oversupply of physicians. Because of its great wealth and political power, the medical profession has also been able to restrict the areas in which other mental health practitioners can perform.

When appropriately edified by the news media, the public can be sufficiently aroused to launch massive political reform movements that affect both the supply and nature of mental health services. Such movements are usually powered by noble, charitable sentiments and directed at removing serious injustices or great suffering. But sometimes the resulting reforms do not stand the test of time, primarily because of unforeseen circumstances. For example, when the Prohibition amendment was passed it was viewed as a milestone in social legislation. It was not foreseen at the time that this amendment would later be repealed, but not before it had been implicated as a major factor in the development of organized crime. When in the latter part of the nineteenth century Dorothea Dix led a reform movement for better care for our mentally ill, she helped create the state mental hospital system. At the time this hospital system was heralded as a cost-effective, humane means of caring for disturbed individuals. One hundred years later, however, state mental hospitals were no longer institutions to which we could point with pride. Bassuk and Gerson (1978) review the results of a recent massive reform in the delivery of mental health services. According to these authors, one of the major objectives of this reform was the deinstitutionalization of many disturbed people in the state hospitals. Indeed, this population has been reduced by about two-thirds. However, the authors question whether this new program has really been successful in that their bleak hospital existence is probably matched by their bleak existence as marginal members of the community. Such considerations demonstrate the need for periodic evaluations of institutional "reforms" that, over time, have generated new problems or failed to deal adequately with old ones.

A contemporary problem involves halfway houses. Although the community at large may accept the need for such a facility, there is usually considerable neighborhood resistance to having a halfway house set up in a specific neighborhood. The issues are: Who should have the right to decide where a halfway house can be located, and should immediate-area residents have a right of veto over setting up a halfway house in their neighborhood?

Economic Variables. Hammonds (1978), a physician, provides additional insight into the way demand and supply operate in a medical health delivery system. He notes that on a per capita basis, twice as much surgery is performed in the United States as in Great Britain. Also on a per capita basis, there are twice as many surgeons in the United States as in Great Britain. "This suggests the grim 'law' that the number of operations expands to meet the case-load needs of the available surgeons" (p. 49). The implied question is serious: Does the prevalence of surgery in the United States primarily benefit the patients or the practitioners?

Some view current certification and licensing procedures as a means of creating barriers to entry into status as a professional mental health provider, thereby restricting the supply of providers. The proposal to use paraprofessionals as a way of increasing the supply of services has been both strongly endorsed and strongly resisted. Some charge that the practice is an abrogation of the mental health profession's obligation to give the best possible care (Fink & Weinstein, 1979; Hopkinson & Hurley, 1976). In his review of outcome studies comparing the relative effectiveness of professionals and paraprofessionals, Durlak (1979) concludes that "the clinical outcomes paraprofessionals achieve are equal to or significantly better than those obtained by professionals" (p. 89) (see also Chapter 25, this volume, where he qualifies this conclusion).

The Role of Mental Health Facilities. In Chapter 7, Twardosz and Risley highlight the importance of the environment in the effectiveness of a day care center. Behavior problems may sometimes be largely attributable to the physical layout of the center, to a lack of appropriate facilities, or to unnecessary waiting periods. The authors call attention to ecological factors that have been studied extensively in industrial settings and that are also important in mental health facilities, where they have not received as much scrutiny. Appropriate attention to such impersonal variables as the utilization of space, the arrangement of equipment, and the flow of movement can result in more efficient utilization of personnel and a better allocation of services.

Temporal Sequence. On the supply side, as on the demand side, the bulk of the issues occur early in the temporal sequence. Of course, behavior that is ethical to begin with cannot guarantee ethical behavior throughout the entire sequence; still, the prospects are markedly better than if the beginnings contain unethical behavior.

Some complex issues may involve both demand and supply factors. For example, the setting of standards for the quality of services may act to curtail their supply. What mental health provider abilities, then, are essential for the provision of the various services? A definitive response to this important question is, of course, still lacking.

Ethical Issues: Quality of Care

Early in the temporal sequence, the quality of care involves the adequacy of the physical plant, the adequacy and ability of staff, the clarity of purpose, and the definition of organizational roles. Another part of the task is to provide accurate information about the services to those who request it, including, if necessary, information about crisis intervention or emergency services.

Quality-of-care issues during a course of therapy vary from the fully manifest to the barely perceptible. There are gross cases of client neglect, as in cases of Medicaid fraud, where clients may be scheduled for appointments but receive virtually no attention. Conversely, individuals with mental health problems can become cult members and for all practical purposes give up their individuality to a charismatic leader (as happened in Guyana). Less manifest, but perhaps more common, are instances where therapists or intervenors assume the responsibility for offering care that lies beyond their area of expertise. There are also instances where clients are exploited to satisfy a practitioner's personal (e.g., sexual) needs. Last, but not least, are those instances where excellent, conscientious care is provided and gratifying improvements are obtained.

An important variable is the merit of the methods employed in determining the quality of care. A growing literature on the politics of evaluation research (Gurel, 1975; Sjoberg, 1975) considers the choice of an appropriate yardstick for judging programmatic success. The criteria employed, for instance, to evaluate the effectiveness of paraprofessionals would presumably differ depending on whether the program designers were primarily professionals or paraprofessionals (or their advocates). The use of different criteria could easily cause one study to conclude that paraprofessionals are effective, whereas a comparable study finds they are not. The notion of experimenter bias is not new; however, Hilton and Lumsdaine (1975), in a review of the literature on family planning programs, found significant gaps between the data presented and the conclusions reached.

In Chapter 19, Goodson and Turner evaluate their own community mental health efforts from 1971 to 1973. We question neither the value of their work nor the need for evaluation studies; means of determining effectiveness or impact. But we do question the ability of an investigator to switch from being strongly identified with a program to becoming an unbiased evaluator of this same program. There are signs that Goodson and Turner's role reversal is difficult. For example, their Hypothesis 4 states "that behavior modification can reduce therapy time required to achieve goal attainment." Yet the data in their Table 2, which pertain to this hypothesis, are grossly incomplete because the results for more than one-third of the cells in the table which compare center averages with national or regional averages were not available. Still, the table is used to support the hypothesis.

Fawcett *et al.* (Chapter 16) describe a community information project that was developed in response to a neighborhood association's request for assistance in blocking the construction of a four-lane highway through the neighborhood. Fawcett *et al.* agreed to collaborate in this project and devised a consequence analysis guide to educate citizens about the possible effects of the planned roadway. In their words, the method for informing residents was "practical and unbiased." Although we can accept the practicality and perhaps the desirability of the approach, we cannot accept as "unbiased" any part of this study from its inception to its end. Here again the politics of evaluation may well be used to camouflage various aspects of experimenter bias.

Temporal Sequence. Ethical issues pertaining to quality of care appear throughout the temporal sequence. That is so because the quality of mental health care depends heavily not only on provider practices but also on the outcome of treatment. Also, it takes time for outcome data to become available, whether for the assessment of therapy or the assessment of programs.

Conclusion

Although we would like Table 1 to be a comprehensive morphology of ethical issues, we recognize that it is as yet incomplete. Even in its present form, however, it sheds light on a large number of issues by bringing them together in a scheme. Thus Table 1 permits some significant inferences to be drawn.

It illustrates, for example, that many ethical issues come into play before the client is seen. Such policy decisions as the way an agency presents itself to the public, its use of agencies that offer ancillary services, and its reliance on scientific evidence are likely to have powerful ethical implications.

Also, the table makes it easier to see why some cases simultaneously allow both cogent defense and strong prosecution. One of the great difficulties concerning the ethical aspects of mental health care is the uncertainty of moral imperatives. For example, how should we appraise the ethics of a case where a referral is made to another service provider who is known to give excellent service, when a number of equally proficient others are also available? Would full disclosure of the range of providers invariably serve a client's interests better than a single referral? Such ethical judgments are often more difficult than they seem at first glance.

Table 1 also has implications concerning the assessment of programs. We agree that mental health programs need to be evaluated; and clearly, the people who know the most about these programs—that is, those who have created and implemented them—must participate in any meaningful program evaluation. However, we believe that technically sound evaluation requires the ongoing services of a consultant who has (1) technical expertise as a program evaluator, and (2) full emotional detachment from the program to be evaluated.

Finally, training programs are all too often proposed as a tactic for fostering ethical behavior, and Table 1 may help suggest which variables are susceptible to change by means of training. Such training may have little influence over ethical dilemmas arising because of professional or organizational constraints; over sociopolitical variables; over individuals whose actions reflect a perceived threat to their livelihood or to their status as professionals; or over those who seek primarily to further their own interests. On the other hand, training programs may have considerable utility in sensitizing individuals at least to the possible ethical dilemmas in their own conduct.

On the whole, our morphology (Table 1) may assist in showing where and how potential ethical problems originate and may facilitate analysis of the conditions under which desired changes may be induced.

ACKNOWLEDGMENT

We gratefully acknowledge Abraham M. Jeger for his comments on earlier drafts of this chapter.

References

Back, K. W. An ethical critique of encounter groups. In G. Bermant, H. C. Kelman, & D. P. Warwick (Eds.), *The ethics of social intervention*. New York: Wiley, 1978.

Bassuk, E. L., & Gerson, S. Deinstitutionalization and mental health services. *Scientific American*, 1978, *238*, 46–53.

Buck, J. A., & Hirschman, R. Economics and mental health services: Enhancing the power of the consumer. *American Psychologist*, 1980, *35*, 653–661.

Capron, A. M. Medical research in prisons: Should a moratorium be called? In T. L. Beauchamp & L. Walters (Eds.), *Contemporary issues in bioethics*. Belmont, Calif.; Wadsworth, 1978.

Crowell, E. Redistributive aspects of psychotherapy's inclusion in national health insurance: A summary. *American Psychologist*, 1977, *32*, 731–737.

Durlak, J. A. Comparative effectiveness of paraprofessional and professional helpers. *Psychological Bulletin*, 1979, *86*, 80–92.

Eilbert, L. R., & Spector, B. The Moire Contourographic analysis controversy: A question of validity in present-day clinical practice. *Journal of Manipulative and Physiological Therapeutics*, 1979, *2*, 85–92.

Fink, P. J., & Weinstein, S. P. Whatever happened to psychiatry? The deprofessionalization of community mental health centers. *American Journal of Psychiatry*, 1979, *136*, 406–409.

Gurel, L. The human side of evaluating human services programs: Problems and prospects. In E. L. Struening & M. Guttentag (Eds.), *Handbook of evaluation research* (Vol. 2). Beverly Hills, Calif.: Sage, 1975.

Hammonds, W. D. Pain and surgery. In S. F. Brena (Ed.), *Chronic pain: America's hidden epidemic*. New York: Atheneum/SMI, 1978.

Hilton, E. T., & Lumsdaine, A. A. Field trial designs in gauging the impact of fertility planning programs. In C. A. Bennett & A. A. Lumsdaine (Eds.), *Evaluation and experiment*. New York: Academic Press, 1975.

Hopkinson, D., & Hurley, S. J. Helper ethics and the professional-paraprofessional gap. *Professional Psychology*, 1976, *7*, 319–322.

Kelman, H. C. The relevance of social research to social issues: Promises and pitfalls. In P. Halmos (Ed.), *The sociology of sociology* (*Sociological Review*, Monograph No. 16). Keele: University of Keele, 1970.

Kelman, H. C., & Warwick, D. P. The ethics of social intervention: Goals, means, and consequences. In G. Bermant, H. C. Kelman, & D. P. Warwick (Eds.), *The ethics of social intervention*. New York: Wiley, 1978.

Kittrie, N. N. *The right to be different: Deviance and enforced therapy*. Baltimore: Johns Hopkins University Press, 1971.

Landsberg, G., & Hammer, R. Possible programmatic consequences of community mental health center funding arrangements: Illustrations based on inpatient utilization data. *Community Mental Health Journal*, 1977, *13*, 63–67.

Mirvis, P. H., & Seashore, S. E. Being ethical in organizational research. *American Psychologist*, 1979, *34*, 766–780.

Rappaport, J. *Community psychology: Values, research, and action*. New York: Holt, Rinehart & Winston, 1977.

Robinson, D. N. Harm, offense, and nuisance: Some first steps in the establishment of an ethics of treatment. *American Psychologist*, 1974, *29*, 233–238.

Robinson, S. W., III. Comments on Canterbury v. Spence. In T. L. Beauchamp & L. Walters (Eds.), *Contemporary issues in bioethics*. Belmont, Calif.: Wadsworth, 1978.

Sanders, J. R. Complaints against psychologists adjudicated informally by APA's Committee on Scientific and Professional Ethics and Conduct. *American Psychologist*, 1979, *34*, 1139–1144.

Sjoberg, G. Politics, ethics and evaluation research. In E. L. Struening & M. Guttentag (Eds.), *Handbook of evaluation research* (Vol. 1). Beverly Hills, Calif.: Sage, 1975.

Walters, L. Bioethics as a field of ethics. In T. L. Beauchamp & L. Walters (Eds.), *Contemporary issues in bioethics*. Belmont, Calif.: Wadsworth, 1978.

Warwick, D. P. Freedom and population policy. In Population Task Force, *Ethics, population, and the American tradition*. Hastings-on-Hudson, N.Y.: Institute of Society, Ethics, and the Life Sciences, 1971.

Welles, C. Ethics in conflict: Yesterday's standards—outdated guide for tomorrow. *American Journal of Occupational Therapy*, 1976, *30*, 44–47.

VII
Mental Health Personpower
EDUCATION AND TRAINING

> We must choose between education and training. The choice is ours,
> the future is contingent on the decisions we make now. (Rappaport,
> 1978, p. 2)

Introduction

The three chapters in this part consider programs and issues pertaining
to the education of professionals and paraprofessionals for mental health
practice. Our focus here is on models of education that are compatible
with a behavioral-ecological perspective of community mental health.

Unfortunately, to date, programs in the traditional core mental
health disciplines (psychiatry, clinical psychology, social work, and psychiatric nursing) have for the most part failed to educate professionals to
meet the initial mandates of community mental health. It thus comes as
no surprise that clinical activities and direct treatment remain the most
common functions in community mental health centers (Bloom, 1977).
For community mental health goals to be realized, new education models
for new roles must be developed.

Educating behavioral-ecologists to function in community mental
health settings requires incorporation of the various theoretical, research,
and applied areas covered in this volume. These include specialized
knowledge and skills in designing community alternatives to institutionalization, offering consultation, developing prevention programs, enhancing social support networks, evaluating large-scale mental health
programs, and training nonprofessional mental health workers. It is pri-

marily these areas that distinguish behavioral-ecologists from traditional providers of direct clinical services (e.g., individual psychotherapy, clinical behavior therapy).

Although they have been used interchangeably in this volume, we wish to distinguish between the terms *education* and *training*. Training refers to a ·particular set of skills and technology applicable to specific problems by prescription. Such skills are perceived to be "packageable" and certifiable. Education refers to a way of thinking about problems by applying divergent reasoning. It implies such relatively nonspecific competences as sensitivity to how values inform action, maintaining flexibility and adaptability, and ability to apply cross-disciplinary knowledge to complex human problems. Education cannot be licensed; it is a continuously evolving process. It is more a condition of mind than a specific number of courses, examinations, degrees, and internship hours. In applying this distinction to the emerging field of community psychology, Rappaport (1978) argues that community psychologists should be educated rather than trained. Such education is characterized by such "special skills" as

> evaluation methodology, problem solving, social policy and value analysis, and the ability to listen to and represent diverse community groups. The skills are political as well as academic, social as well as psychological and they are not of the sort to be licensed. (p. 8)

A major issue relevant to educating for such broader roles is the *site* of training. In the area of psychology, one alternative calls for training practitioners in separate professional schools akin to medical, dental, and law schools (as opposed to departments of psychology within a larger graduate school). The rationale for such separate schools is considered by Albee and Loeffler (1971), who elaborate on role conflicts between the scientist and professional components of the "scientist–professional" model of training clinical psychologists. As such, they call for a stricter division of the field into scientific and applied components. As shown by the growing number of independent professional schools of psychology, this position is attracting many adherents within clinical psychology. However, it is our position that these schools are likely to train psychologists for even narrower roles than are programs within academic psychology departments (although these independent schools are clearly training *more* practitioners of the traditional types, generally with less of a research emphasis).

Although Hersch (1969) notes that the scientist–professional model was "never scientific enough to suit the scientist and never professional enough to suit the professional" (p. 911), we reject the basic rationale for dividing scientific and applied psychology. Instead, what is called for is a redefinition of the traditional research and service roles to permit a stronger synthesis between the two. That can be accomplished by training programs that are problem focused (rather than technique focused), interdisciplinary in nature, and that integrate research/evaluation into the delivery of mental health services. Such programs might best be housed in community-based centers that would be linked to universities and human service agencies. Unfortunately, universities are generally not ideal sites for such training because of their characteristic "disciplinary chauvinism" and poor community relations (Tornatzky, 1976).

As for training at subdoctoral levels, the behavioral-ecological perspective allows for the engagement of nonprofessionals in both direct and indirect service capacities. Nonprofessional staff who serve as "junior professionals" (e.g., psychotherapists) for less pay are likely to feel cheated and exploited. However, with professional behavioral-ecologists assuming such roles as trainer, supervisor, consultant, and evaluator, employing nonprofessionals in direct service roles is likely to complement rather than duplicate or conflict with professional roles. At the same time, in working with natural support systems and consulting with community agencies, nonprofessionals likewise assume indirect service roles alongside professionals. In such instances nonprofessionals must share the interdisciplinary and problem-focus orientation of professional behavioral-ecologists if their working relationships are to be compatible.

An interesting undergraduate training program with an interdisciplinary focus is the University of California (Irvine) Program in Social Ecology (Binder, 1972). Undergraduate specialities, covering course work integrated with field experiences, are offered in community psychology, urban and regional planning, environmental quality and environmental health, and criminal justice, among others. Another interesting model is described by Vidaver and Carson (1973), namely, the Maryland human services career "lattice." Three 2-year self-contained modules are offered leading to A.A., B.A., and M.A. degrees. Specializations include community mental health, child care/educator, and neighborhood center administration. Job descriptions and salary levels are designed by the state to correspond to the various points at which graduates can enter (i.e., after the A.A., B.A., or M.A.).

As we saw in Chapter 1, a major impediment to the development of effective paraprofessional careers has been the medical domination of community mental health centers (Chu & Trotter, 1974). Some support for a behavioral-ecological approach employing paraprofessionals comes from a study comparing staff utilization by Hurley and Tyler (1976). Briefly, they compared community mental health center teams that functioned within a "medical, illness/clinical" (MIC) paradigm with those that functioned within a "psychosocial, learning/community" (PSLC) paradigm. Results showed that the PSLC paraprofessionals had more flexible roles, rated themselves as having greater influence, reported greater team cohesiveness, and claimed greater satisfaction with work, supervision, and coworkers. As the authors conclude, merely introducing paraprofessionals into MIC systems is not sufficient to solve the personpower shortage in mental health. Since MIC systems are underutilizing their paraprofessional resources and are apparently alienating them, they are not likely to reach the indigenous community of which they are a part.

This research also provides support for Reiff's (1966) argument that meeting the mental health needs of the poor "is not primarily a problem of manpower but a problem of ideology" (p. 647). To Reiff, the ideological problem concerns endorsement of the medical model; the model is said to be at the root of the power struggle. The power struggle extends beyond *interprofessional* conflict, but also serves as a force to maintain existing institutional practices. Current institutional practices, in turn, prevent the utilization of new kinds of personpower since "effective" use of nonprofessionals (that they provide true links between professionals and the poor, underserved communities) demands the creation of new professionals.

This position is further supported by Bartels and Tyler's (1975) survey of paraprofessionals in community mental health centers. The problem category mentioned most frequently by paraprofessionals was "difficulty working with professional staff" (e.g., lack of acceptance, tension, and conflicts). It is hoped that the behavioral-ecological perspective espoused in this volume will provide a framework for developing new professional roles to permit more effective utilization of paraprofessionals.

In our view, a major source of the difficulty in integrating paraprofessional workers into mental health teams involves the culture and social class of paraprofessionals and their clients. For the most part, paraprofessionals are being trained to emulate a middle-class model of therapy and to apply it to indigenous clients. Thus both the content and the style of service delivery have remained the same, whereas the providers have changed. Perhaps such a lack of fit is at the root of professional–nonprofessional conflicts and questions of effectiveness. What is needed is an alternative technology and style of delivery based on *collaborative* relationships between professionals and paraprofessionals. It is hoped that compatible new roles for professionals and paraprofessionals alike will emerge from behavioral-ecological practice in community mental health.

Although the mental health literature, the chapters in this part, as well as our preceding comments employ the terms "paraprofessional" and "nonprofessional," we wish to emphasize that we remain uncomfortable with such labels. These terms define workers by who they are not, rather than by who they are and what they can do.

In Chapter 24 Tornatzky discusses the Ecological Psychology Doctoral Program at Michigan State University. The purpose of the program is to educate social change agents who will function as "experimental social innovators." Tornatzky considers the intellectual content of the program, the socialization processes involved in educating systems interventionists, as well as some barriers to such programs. We view this doctoral program as a "model" that will, we hope, be adopted now that dissemination efforts are under way.

In Chapter 25 Durlak reviews paraprofessional training programs based at the college level as well as those offering inservice training. He presents a series of guidelines for establishing successful paraprofessional training programs for various roles in community mental health. In addition, he discusses some barriers to effective utilization of paraprofessionals in mental health, and emphasizes the significance of professional, administrative, and financial supports.

Finally, in Chapter 26 Hoffnung and his colleagues present an exploratory case study employing the Community Mental Health ideology (CMHI) scale as a guide for catalyzing change in staff orientation within a community mental health center. Differences between various professional and paraprofessional groups in terms of their endorsement of a community mental health ideology are discussed. The authors suggest utilizing the CMHI scale for inservice education.

References

Albee, G. W., & Loeffler, E. Role conflicts in psychology and their implications for a reevaluation of training models. *The Canadian Psychologist*, 1971, *12*, 465–481.

Bartels, B. D., & Tyler, J. D. Paraprofessionals in the community mental health center. *Professional Psychology*, 1975, *6*, 442–452.

Binder, A. A new context for psychology: Social ecology. *American Psychologist*, 1972, *27*, 903–908.

Bloom, B. L. *Community mental health: A general introduction*. Monterey, Calif.: Brooks/Cole, 1977.

Chu, F., & Trotter, S. *The madness establishment*. New York: Grossman, 1974.

Hersch, C. From mental health to social action: Clinical psychology in historical perspective. *American Psychologist*, 1969, *24*, 909–916.

Hurley, D. J., Jr., & Tyler, F. B. *Relationship between systems' mental health paradigm and personpower utilization*. Paper presented at the meeting of the Eastern Psychological Association, New York, April 1976.

Rappaport, J. *Education, training, and dealing with the contingent future.* Paper presented at the meeting of the American Psychological Association, Montreal, August 1978.

Reiff, R. Mental health manpower and institutional change. *American Psychologist,* 1966, *21,* 540–548.

Tornatzky, L. G. How a Ph.D. program aimed at survival issues survived. *American Psychologist,* 1976, *31,* 189–192.

Vidaver, R. M., & Carson, J. E. A new framework for baccalaureate careers in the human services. *American Journal of Psychiatry,* 1973, *130,* 474–478.

24

Educating Professionals for Social Systems Intervention

A 10-Year Retrospective

LOUIS G. TORNATZKY

Twice in the past decade, I have put on paper my observations on the development of a novel Ph.D. training program, one that has been explicitly oriented toward social change and community research. These earlier thoughts encompassed, respectively, the initiation and ideological-conceptual underpinnings of the program (Tornatzky, Fairweather, & O'Kelly, 1970), and some of its adolescent crises and growing pains (Tornatzky, 1976). Now, after 9 1/2 years of association with the Ecological Psychology Program of Michigan State University, I once again feel compelled to share participant-observation data, and advice, on how to create and run such programs.

The analysis to follow will be fourfold. First of all, I shall describe what the final "product"—the trainee, if you will—of such programs ought to be like in terms of skills, professional repertoire, and outlook. Second, I shall discuss some of the essential intellectual content of the training program. Third will be a description of the socialization and

LOUIS G. TORNATZKY ● National Science Foundation, Division of Policy Research and Analysis, 1800 G St., N. W., Washington, D.C. 20550. The views expressed here should not be construed as representing official policy of the National Science Foundation, or of any other institution, but are entirely those of the author.

group process aspects of innovative training. Finally, I shall dwell on some of the institutional, organizational, and attitudinal impediments to training of this nature. Paradoxically, although we have done a fair amount of dissemination research (see Chapter 5), the diffusion of this mode of professional training, as an "innovation" in psychology or in related fields, has indeed been limited.

In contrast to several of the chapters in this volume, the title of this one includes no mention of mental health per se. The omission is explicit. One of the contentions of the Ecological Psychology Program has been that the intellectual baggage and ideology of mental health, however "progressive," are inevitably restrictive of the kind of social change that we hope to accomplish. As we shall see, social change encompasses far more than the content and methods of mental health sevices can capture.

The Experimental Social Innovator

At a recent conference on social program evaluation, I made the following rhetorical comments on that field, and on role incumbents in it:

> The principle goal of program evaluation ought to be the identification, development and advocacy of social programs that provide more effective services to the clientele of public bureaucracies. A corollary is that the program evaluator also ought to function as something akin to an institutionalized "hit man," performing the euthanasia of social programs that are ineffective, or harmful, or both. (Tornatzky, 1979)

Another set of professional expectations has been captured by Fairweather's (1967) description of Experimental Social Innovation. Equally grandiose, they approximate the following: (1) to find and/or develop innovative alternative solutions to pressing social problems; (2) empirically, preferably experimentally, to evaluate the effectiveness of these solutions; and (3) to achieve widespread adoption and implementation of solutions. These larger professional goals have important bearing on the goals, content, and format of the training experience.

Experimentalist/Researcher

In contrast to some of the neo-Luddite social movements of the 1960s, it is my contention that the training of professionals in systems intervention ought to be premised on science, and good science. Although a great amount of turgid prose has been written on the dire necessity to innovate, and to effect substantive change in social systems, there is unfortunately less of a commitment expressed in such literature to gaining *rational control* of that process. My reasons for being concerned about the need for rational and scientific input to change processes are straightforward: There is insufficient appreciation of how intellectually dishonest, morally bereft, and occasionally harmful many social programs often are. These are not the lamentations of a reactionary, but of someone who has grown skeptical after several years of field experience in developing and evaluating social programs. I believe in innovation, but innovation that works.

Fortunately, there is an armamentarium of scientific skills to assist the process of rationalizing change. Recent years have witnessed a rapid focusing of social science methods to field settings in general, and to the creation of innovative solutions to social problems in particular. These developments include design considerations (Campbell & Stanley, 1966), evaluation research techniques (Rossi, Freeman, & Wright, 1979), field experimentation (Fairweather & Tornatzky, 1977), and such novel analytic techniques as path analysis. Methodological developments have been paralleled by a significant increase in highly sophisticated social experiments (Boruch, McSweeney, & Soderstrom, 1977) and in field applications of program evaluation techniques (Struening & Guttentag, 1975).

In general, then, one set of skill expectations that need to be integrated into the core goals of training programs are empirical research skills. My own orientation is to emphasize especially one subset of these skills—field experimentation—a stance that has implications for other parts of the role set being described.

The Interventionist

One part of a student's repertoire is probably not trainable in any intellectual sense. As Goodstein and Sandler (1978) point out, the "process" of using psychology to promote human welfare can vary in related role expectations from that of the passive professional to the adversarial. It is inevitably a value choice, but a choice premised on epistemological grounds.

The behavioral essence of experimentation is to manipulate, to tinker. In this sense, a methodological stance has implications for a "political" choice. One can train people to observe passively, to sweep data out of the corners of social problems, or one can encourage students to attempt to *shape* these programs. My orientation has been unequivocal. I have always attempted to impart to students—if not already present—

the value of intervention. The way to change something is to change it; the way to find out if something works is to try it and see what happens.

Social Systems Change

The complete student should not only be experimentally oriented and interventionist, but should also be focused on a unit-of-analysis, and locus of intervention, of organizations, and of complex, interlocking networks of behavior. That is difficult given the intellectual traditions of psychology, which are largely individualistic rather than collectivistic. As Vallance (1976) points out, "most members of APA's Division 27 (Community) are clinicians, and virtually all of the leaders of the community psychology movement are variously reconstructed clinicians" (p. 193). Although many social problems can undoubtedly yield to one-to-one ministrations, most cannot. Whether we like it or not, most social problems—and solutions to these problems—are mediated by large, complex organizations. (And there is also considerable moral skepticism—which I share—about the practice of individual psychotherapy as constituting a "subsidy to the rich from the poor" [Albee, 1977].)

Psychologists in general, and mental health workers in particular, need to start looking at larger aggregations of behaviors. Many settings that have, from a psychological perspective, been assumed to consist at most of loosely joined dyadic interactions (e.g., teacher–student) can also often be profitably considered as *organizations* with group norms, expectations, and system incentives. An example is Brookover's work (Brookover, 1977) on the academic climate of urban elementary schools. He has found organizational norms and expectations to be highly predictive of student achievement across schools, and there is evidence suggesting that organizational interventions can change (Tornatzky, Brookover, Hathaway, Miller, & Passalacqua, 1979) those features in a manner likely to have a positive impact on student achievement. In a similar vein is Fairweather's (1964, 1967) work with the Community Lodge. Here an intervention was made—by field experimentation, no less—into the mental health *system,* and a community-based alternative to existing, individualistically oriented therapeutic practice was designed, implemented, and evaluated (see also Chapter 5, this volume).

The bottom line of the argument is that in contemporary America most things—services and products, good and bad—are delivered by large, organized systems. To ignore this fact, either intellectually or strategically, is quixotic. Interventions that rely on the concept of individual culpability or capability are usually doomed to failure.

Given the above general goals of a training program oriented toward system change, how do they translate into a specific curriculum and a set of training experiences?

Issues of Intellectual Content

There are certain curricular features that seem to me essential to a strong training program. Some of these features are translated directly from my experience with the Ecological Psychology Ph.D. program at Michigan State; others are logical extensions of that experience.

Interdisciplinary Focus: Methodology and Content

Not surprisingly, the disciplinary departmental structure of the university, formulated a few hundred years ago, does not yield a one-to-one correspondence with contemporary social problems. There are two areas in which an explicit interdisciplinary focus can yield benefits: (1) methodology, and (2) content knowledge.

As Kuhn (1962) points out, every field of knowledge develops a dominant paradigm in its inquiry. The paradigm consists of both the range of *content* covered, and the *method* of inquiry employed. Most disciplines could do well to push the limits of that paradigm further than they do.

In psychology, the dominant research paradigm has historically been laboratory experimentation. However, such an exclusive orientation is inherently limiting. As Atkinson (1977) points out:

> To be effective and to command a position of influence in interdisciplinary research, the psychologist needs a sound background in several other fields of science. Psychology departments are doing a disservice to students, if they do not encourage them to develop a broad range of mathematical and scientific skills in addition to training in psychology. (p. 209)

Despite this advice, much of psychology is still constrained by past practice. (See Helmreich, 1975, for a plaintive discussion of the limitations of laboratory experimentation in social psychology, and the continuing infatuation with it.) Largely ignored until recently have been multivariate correlational techniques, ethnography, survey research methodology, causal analysis, and the like. One feature of a viable training program must be a catholicity of methodological approaches. In the training program at Michigan State we actively encouraged students to partake of a wide range of course offerings. It was not unusual for a student's portfolio of methods course work to be predominantly *outside* the Department of Psychology, including excursions into statistics, education, sociology, anthropology, and so on.

Concurrently, any meaningful training program for social system interventionists cannot be bound to a single disciplinary orientation in *content* knowledge. As Vallance (1976) observes:

> Problems of society do not come packaged so as to be dealt with through the use of a set of analytic methods and action modes that are the property or the tradition of a single academic set of mind or "discipline." (p. 194)

The implication is that a *problem-focused* inquiry is likely to lead far astray, into a number of disciplines. Students need to acquire backgrounds and course work not only in psychology, but in economics, sociology (particularly organizational behavior), anthropology, law, and large portions of the physical and natural sciences.

Although the tremendous intellectual resources of the modern university at an *aggregate* level would seem congruent with such an approach, at an operational level there are indeed difficulties. Universities, incidentally, are quite nonchanging systems themselves. The organizational locus for training programs in the university is typically the academic department, and Ph.D. training programs of an explicitly interdisciplinary nature suffer greatly in terms of prestige, resources, and legitimacy. Although this problem has been discussed elsewhere (Fairweather & Tornatzky, 1977), the *organizational setting* for interdisciplinary training needs to be well scrutinized. Perhaps supraorganizational degree-granting centers, institutes, or similar academic anomalies would be more appropriate than the classical department as a training site. Our own experience is that the disciplinary-oriented department is too often beset with hardening of the paradigm. At any rate, it is important that a widely varied background—both in method and content—be offered by the training program.

People-Changing and Management Skills

Not only must students have wide disciplinary knowledge, they should also be conversant with the applied action extensions of that knowledge. For example, it is useless to understand theories of social learning without understanding behavior modification (Bandura, 1969) techniques. Knowledge of organizational theory is sterile without an acquaintance with organizational development techniques (Huse, 1975) and the prevailing practices of management. An important subspecies of the management literature is that dealing with research and development management. Macro- and microlevel economic theory should be coupled with knowledge as mundane as accounting, procurement practices, corporate legal structures, and the like. Quite simply, it is a disservice to nurture in students a fervor for change and intervention without the necessary practical skills. Some of these skills, and knowledge, *can* be acquired in course work.

One management technology of particular importance is program evaluation. Although some might consider it a purely methodological skill, it encompasses considerably more. As Wertheimer, Barclay, Cook, Kiesler, Koch, Riegel, Rover, Senders, Smith, and Sperling (1978) point out, program evaluation appears to be "the magic phrase for the future." If change, through intervention, is to be brought about, then the effects of that change must be determined. In addition, the logistics and management skills involved in fielding large-scale social program evaluation are considerable (see Fairweather & Tornatzky, 1977; Rossi & Williams, 1972) and go far beyond methodology qua methodology.

Some course work ought also to be provided in "solutions" to social problems. A systems intervention need not always be an idiosyncratic event; some social problems are recurrent across settings, locations, and populations. Moreover, we are moving closer to having a stockpile of reasonably well-validated programmatic solutions to recurrent needs. Change can often involve a prepackaged solution. There are a variety of source books describing innovative programs in education (Far West Laboratory, 1975), mental health (Arutunian, Kroll, & Murphy, 1976), and other service areas (Wilner, Greathouse, Wilton, Ershoff, Foster, & Hetherington, 1976); students should be familiar with such resources.

Some needs can be assuaged simply by transfusions of funds. Explicit course work, or at least readings, in the nuances of grantsmanship—public and private—is a must. A related set of professional skills is the ability of the interventionist to tap into the informal networks of these resource providers—that is, to be able to secure the dollars once an idea is developed. These skills usually come through the socialization/professional growth portion of the training experience (see the next section).

Finally, given the conviction that solutions are not, and moreover need not be, idiosyncratic, a prime course of study ought also to be in the dissemination/diffusion/implementation of innovations and of new technologies. The wide-ranging literature (Rogers & Shoemaker, 1971; Tornatzky, Fergus, Avellar, Fairweather, & Fleischer, 1980; Yin, 1978) in this area is invaluable. Unfortunately, many self-styled interventionists focus only on changing *one* system (one school, one community mental health center) without appreciating the potential for *national* transfer of knowledge. They should be more grandiose.

Issues of Socialization

So far I have focused on training goals and curriculum content, or on what skills and knowledge are transmitted. Yet a training program is itself a social organization with group processes and norms. We need to consider not only *what* gets done, but *how*.

Clear Expectations and Clear Rewards

It is best to be as explicit as possible to incoming students about core goals and expectations. For example, in the program at Michigan State we were distinctly interested in training field experimentalists. However, in some of the field research literature (e.g., Weiss, 1972) there is a prevailing belief that field experiments are difficult if not impossible to bring off. How then could relatively näive graduate students be asked to do them?

Simply, we told them they had to. From the initiation of the program (see Tornatzky *et al.*, 1970) it was *expected* that a Ph.D. dissertation would be a full-blown field experiment. The tactic paid off, and a wide range of topics (see Tornatzky, 1976) have been the subject of successful student experiments. Over time, this initial intellectual expectation has become a *norm* of the social system. As such, incoming students are rapidly socialized into its pervasiveness by both faculty and students. A related implicit norm has also grown over the years: Since the program's inception in 1970, no student or faculty member has, to my knowledge, ever engaged in traditional laboratory experimentation. Hull and Tolman would be aghast.

A somewhat more difficult norm to maintain is that research ought somehow to be interventionist, and oriented toward social change. It seems that although there is a clear distinction between field methodologies and laboratory methodologies, the distinctions among the various role postures of field research are more subtle. For example, when does the program evaluator's role become basically that of a passive data counselor, as opposed to a system intervener? What is the requisite amount of involvement that the interventionist researcher should have in system design decisions? The extremes are clear, but the fine distinctions are not.

A training program does have, and should have, values and norms, either articulate or ephemeral. My view is that they should be explicit and, if possible, reinforced by group processes and peer pressure. The training program director is well advised to establish the norms early, and loudly. A culture once established is doubly difficult to change in its core goals.

Opportunities for Group Maintenance

In recent years one of the stronger themes in writings on organizational behavior has been that of organizational contingency theory (Galbraith, 1973; Litwak, 1961; Thompson, 1967). The basic argument is that different types of organizational tasks demand different types of organizational structures and processes. To the extent that tasks are predictable, repetitive, and normative, they can be handled in a bureaucratic modality. To the extent that they are uncertain, nonuniform (Litwak, 1961), or idiosyncratic, they need to be handled by an organization that emphasizes interpersonal interaction, informality, shared decision making, and communication richness. These general concepts have important implications for the design and maintenance of innovative training programs.

It is my contention that much of what transpires in a training program such as I have been describing is inevitably "uncertainty arousing" in nature. Social change is an ill-defined enterprise, and the training of action researchers is itself such a process. As pointed out earlier, the norms are apt to be deviant from the larger academic culture and the expectations greater. Given these multiple sources of uncertainty and stress, the training program needs to function *as an organization* in those nonbureaucratic ways most congenial to nonuniform tasks.

It becomes doubly important to maintain cohesion among faculty and students in such a program, to maximize interaction, and, if possible, to promote participative decision making. For example, one of the practices that we were able to employ for many years in our program was the use of peer involvement in admissions decisions. We found that it gave students a stake in socializing incoming candidates to the prevailing norms.

Training programs of this nature need to be run explicitly as democratic systems. Operationally, that means: (1) Periodic, frequent meetings of the *entire* faculty–student group should be held; (2) if permissible, a one-person–one-vote system should be employed; (3) students need to be given significant delegated responsibilities in planning and operation of the program; and (4) no cult of leadership centering around a single person, or clique, should be allowed to develop or continue.

A research/change agent organization needs to be changeable, open, and flexible. Otherwise the stresses of the endeavor will break the program apart. Although, as suggested earlier, the core values are or should be stable over time, the mechanics and procedures of training programs do change. Decisions must be made, and for all of the maintenance reasons previously discussed, these decisions should be participative. Of course, it would also do well to distinguish between decisions that are trivial/administrative and real "policy" decisions. The former might be better handled by faculty, or by the program director alone. The trick is to make wise judgments about which decisions warrant democracy and which do not.

Finally, given the nature of social system intervention training, it is also necessary to maximize student–faculty *informal* contact. One of my colleagues formed a softball team named Truth and Justice, composed of both staff and students. Other opportunities for social interaction included parties, picnics, and the like. The point is not that partying and interaction per se build research competence, but that a complex social system such as a training program needs to attend to its own group maintenance issues.

Faculty Training Role

In most professional Ph.D.-level training programs, the role played by faculty is explicitly one of maintaining a certain decorous distance from students, reinforced by terms of deference, status differentials, and the like. But in any program designed to train system interventionists or community researchers, this situation is not feasible.

It seems that training in certain skills can only proceed by role modeling (i.e., hand holding on the part of faculty). It is fine to transmit the intellectual basis and ideological rationale of community intervention, but experiential learning also has its place. It may often be necessary for faculty to involve a student directly in their own community intervention research as a learning device. Similarly, it may be necessary for a faculty member to go into the community with a student and help with the finagling necessary for initiating an intervention research—meeting with political figures, bargaining with service program directors, addressing community organizations, writing explicit agreements of cooperation, formulating contracts, sharing of financial resources, and so on. Although many of these talents can be learned from books, they also constitute an art form sufficiently complex to warrant direct instruction.

Clearly, much of the skills repertoire of the community intervention researcher is primarily logistical and political. Such talents as the acquisition of resources and funding can prove critical. Similarly, the skills necessary for the management of other people working on a large, complex, longitudinal experiment can be enhanced by experiential learning. Such skills can best be learned by walking through a "real" exercise, and the training program is well advised to provide facilitative opportunities and structures.

There is one additional area in which faculty, in collaboration with students, need to reach out from their institutional setting. There is ample evidence that job seeking is significantly aided (see Solmon, 1978) by interpersonal "contacts." In turn, the jobs obtained by individuals trained in community research are of a wide variety, far beyond the mainstream academic positions. Thus it is incumbent on faculty members to nurture and maintain these opportunities, and faculty–student strategizing is called for.

Student–Faculty Relationships: Some Examples

Two dissertation projects completed at Michigan State during my tenure there will help illustrate the different types of roles that faculty may play in the implementation of community intervention research.

One project cast the faculty person in a role of coinvestigator—actually contractee—of the involved student. This individual occupied a position as a research administrator for a large state agency while attending graduate school. As part of his job responsibilities, he had the opportunity to promote the use of program evaluation methodology across a sample of local service agencies. Since these methodologies can be seen as a significant *innovation* for adopting agencies, the student had an opportunity for an action research to study the adoption and implementation of an innovation.

The student created a proposal for a 2 × 2 factorial experiment comparing various change tactics (basically differences in consultation approaches). It also turned out that the student had control over a small amount of contract money in his agency. In order to field the proposed research he needed to have experienced consultants to implement the experimental conditions. A rather novel solution was transacted in which contracts for consultation services were made with several faculty members. Since membership on the student's dissertation committee overlapped with these consultancies, a conflict-of-interest problem arose. The department chairman was sought out for advice, and a set of explicit agreements was struck among the involved parties. The intent of these agreements was to separate, in time and space, the faculty responsibilities from the consultant responsibilities. The arrangements worked, role differentiation was possible, and an outstanding research project was completed. Of course, such faculty involvements are not the norm in academic settings.

A second dissertation project epitomized the mentor–novitiate type of faculty–student relationship. In a major longitudinal study in organizational change with a national sample of mental hospitals (Tornatzky *et al.*, 1980), a number of issues worthy of research naturally developed. For example, as part of an inquiry into indigenously inspired innovation processes, a study of the effect of site visits on change seemed useful. A graduate student working for the project became interested in the area, and a research proposal was developed.

Subsequently, there was a two-stage review and fine-tuning process. First, given that the project was to be conducted under the auspices of an NIMH grant, the coinvestigators and the research staff had to review the proposal for compatibility with the overall project. Concurrently, the student had to have the proposal reviewed and approved by the normal dissertation committee. Afterward, resources were set aside from the larger project budget for completion of the research. During the research the faculty person involved (myself) wore two hats—dissertation chairperson and project director; occasionally these roles conflicted. Graduate students are known to be sluggish with dissertations; but in the context of a larger, time-limited, grant-funded project, such slackness is not feasible, and arm twisting was often in order—another example of the somewhat different kinds of roles that faculty need to play in this type of training.

Institutional Impediments to Innovative Training

Clearly, the intervention training that has been described is not within the mainstream of academic, or professional, practice. Thus there are some institutional impediments to such programs.

Resource Misallocations

The multidisciplinary, problem-focused nature of our endeavor at Michigan State naturally goes against the prevailing structure of most academic organizations. In most universities, disciplinary chauvinism reigns supreme, and the most influential organizational unit is the academic department. There are few interdisciplinary research efforts, much less training efforts. Generally, the ones that exist are low in prestige, and in resource allocation, compared to the traditional. For example, it is not unusual to see innovative research and training programs able to garner significant amounts of external research funds and successfully to place students in meaningful jobs, at a marked disadvantage in terms of commensurate resource commitments by the home institution. Other Ph.D. training programs, with only handfuls of students, a limited supply of jobs, but with a mainstream academic tradition, are often blessed with three to four times the faculty positions that they can fruitfully utilize.

These situations to some degree reflect the support by external funding agencies of traditional categories of training. Unfortunately, there are few ways for training monies to adjust to the support of problem-focused research. It is equally problematic for academic institutions to readjust their own structures.

Ultimately, there is a significant cultural lag in the resource allocations to various types of Ph.D.-level training. I know from experience that it is possible to combine a problem focus and scientific rigor; but the disciplinary and funding infrastructure of training remains unconvinced.

Premature and Inappropriate Professionalism

Although this chapter is primarily concerned with training issues in psychology, the comments in this section are applicable to many disciplines. One of the less rational ways to circumvent some of the disciplinary resource allocation problems just described is to have oneself "certified," or ligitimated as a *profession*. Using this device one can control access to the practice of an activity, and ostensibly control quality of training. This orientation has been increasingly common in clinical psychology (Gross, 1978; Hess, 1977), and it has many short-term attractions.

However, this development is quite disturbing. As we have seen, the successful performance of community intervention research demands a maximum or organizational flexibility. The thrust of most accrediting, licensing, and certifying efforts is to etch a set of activities into stone. For example, one of the fringe effects of accreditation/licensing in clinical psychology has been to perpetuate and reinforce a one-to-one psychotherapy model of clinical intervention. Yet as many researchers have pointed out, the efficacy of that approach is still suspect. It would be unfortunate if community training became similarly frozen in its current state of development.

How New Is the New?

As a historical footnote to the problem of institutional impediments to change, it might be useful to look at the current status of community psychology as a case example. This movement, begun 10 to 15 years ago, was ostensibly to be the salvation for psychologists concerned with social policy issues. It was to take the best of many traditions in psychology and mold them into an innovative composite. What has happened?

As for methodology and content, in an ongoing study by Lounsbury (Lounsbury, 1979; Lounsbury, Cook, Leader, Robeitz, & Meares, 1979) the output of community psychology research journals is being

content analyzed for research approaches used and the content of inquiry. In the majority (59%) of articles involving human resource subjects,
the subjects had some type of psychological problem (Lounsbury *et al.*,
1979). In addition, "only 5½ % of the articles tapped organizational variables." So much for altering the traditional content paradigm of the discipline. Additionally, Lounsbury (1979) reports that though the *research*
paradigm is shifted, it is shifted away from the methodological strengths
of psychology (true experimentation) and toward a preoccupation with
case studies and simple correlation studies. Lacking are longitudinal investigations, multivariate designs, and multiple operationism. Community psychology does not appear to be the salvation.

Summary

After nearly 10 years' experience in an innovative training program,
I remain convinced that such training, in the long run, will dramatically
change the face of psychology; however, in the short run I am moderately disillusioned. For me and for others, the institutional blocks and
disincentives to these programs have probably had a cumulative effect.
Change is tiring. In psychology, many of the more innovative training
programs were launched in the 1960s when there still was a feeling that
progress was possible, perhaps inevitable. Much has already been written on the narcissism of our age, the decline of idealism, and so on; all
in all, a groundswell of support for new training modalities is not likely.
The training programs that still exist will somehow have to sustain
themselves until some new burst of idealism.

However, it is hoped that something can be gained from our experience. The mere fact that an innovation such as the Ecological Psychology Program has survived for 10 years indicates that something must be
right; what we have learned may prove useful for those who begin similar programs.

References

Albee, G. W. Does including psychotherapy in health insurance represent a subsidy to the
    rich from the poor? *American Psychologist*, 1977, *32*, 719–721.
Arutunian, C., Kroll, J., & Murphy, S. *Source book of programs: community mental health centers.*
    Palo Alto, Calif.: American Institutes for Research, 1976.
Atkinson, R. C. Reflections on psychology's past and concerns about its future. *American
    Psychologist*, 1977, *32*, 205–209.

Bandura, A. *Principles of behavior modification.* New York: Holt, Rinehart & Winston, 1969.

Boruch, R., McSweeney, A. J., & Soderstrom, E. J. *Randomized field experiments for program development and evaluation: An illustrative bibliography* (Revised). Unpublished manuscript, Department of Psychology, Northwestern University, 1977.

Brookover, W. B. *Schools can make a difference.* East Lansing: College of Urban Development, Michigan State University, 1977.

Campbell, D. T., & Stanley, J. C. *Experimental and quasi-experimental designs for research.* Chicago: Rand McNally, 1966.

Fairweather, G. W. (Ed.). *Social psychology in treating mental illness: An experimental approach.* New York: Wiley, 1964.

Fairweather, G. W. *Methods for experimental social innovation.* New York: Wiley, 1967.

Fairweather, G. W., & Tornatzky, L. G. *Experimental methods for social policy research.* New York: Pergamon Press, 1977.

Far West Laboratory for Educational Research and Development. *Educational programs that work.* San Francisco: Author, 1975.

Galbraith, J. *Designing complex organizations.* Reading, Mass.: Addison-Wesley, 1973.

Goodstein, L. D., & Sandler, I. Using psychology to promote human welfare. *American Psychologist,* 1978, *33,* 882–892.

Gross, S. J. The myth of professional licensing. *American Psychologist,* 1978, *33,* 1009–1016.

Helmreich, R. Applied social psychology: The unfulfilled promise. *Personality and Social Psychology Bulletin,* 1975, *1*(4), 548–560.

Hess, H. F. Entry requirements for professional practice of psychology. *American Psychologist,* 1977, *32,* 365–368.

Huse, E. *Organization development and change.* St. Paul, Minn.: West, 1975.

Kuhn, T. S. *The structure of scientific revolutions.* Chicago: University of Chicago Press, 1962.

Litwak, E. Models of bureaucracy that permit conflict. *American Journal of Sociology,* 1961, *57,* 173–183.

Lounsbury, J. W. Personal communication, 1979.

Lounsbury, J. W., Cook, M. P., Leader, D. S., Robeitz, G., & Meares, E. P. Comment. Community psychology: Boundary problems, psychological perspectives, and an empirical overview of the field. *American Psychologist,* 1979, *34,* 554–557.

Rogers, E., & Shoemaker, F. *Communication of innovations.* New York: Free Press, 1971.

Rossi, P., & Williams, W. *Evaluating social programs.* New York: Seminar Press, 1972.

Rossi, P., Freeman, H., & Wright, S. *Program evaluation: A systematic approach.* Beverly Hills, Calif.: Sage, 1979.

Solmon, L. C. Attracting women to psychology. *American Psychologist,* 1978, *33,* 990–999.

Struening, E. L., & Guttentag, M. (Eds.). *Handbook of evaluation research* (2 vols.). Beverly Hills, Calif.: Sage, 1975.

Thompson, J. D. *Organizations in action.* New York: McGraw-Hill, 1967.

Tornatzky, L. G. How a Ph.D. program aimed at survival issues survived. *American Psychologist,* 1976, *31,* 189–192.

Tornatzky, L. G. The triple threat evaluator. *Evaluation and Program Planning,* 1979, *2,* 111–115.

Tornatzky, L. G., Fairweather, G. W., & O'Kelly, L. I. A Ph.D. program aimed at survival. *American Psychologist,* 1970, *25,* 884–888.

Tornatzky, L. G., Brookover, W. B., Hathaway, D. V., Miller, S. K., & Passalacqua, J. *Changing school climate: A case study in implementation.* Unpublished manuscript, Department of Urban and Metropolitan Studies, Michigan State University, 1979.

Tornatzky, L. G., Fergus, E., Avellar, J., Fairweather, G. W., & Fleischer, M. *Innovation and social process: A national experiment in implementing social technology.* Elmsford, N.Y.: Pergamon Press, 1980.

Vallance, T. The professional nonpsychology graduate program for psychologists. *American Psychologist*, 1976, *31*, 193–199.

Weiss, C. (Ed.). *Evaluating action programs: Readings in social action and education.* Boston: Allyn & Bacon, 1972.

Wertheimer, M., Barclay, A. G., Cook, S. W., Kiesler, C. A., Koch, S., Reigel, K. F., Rorer, L. G., Senders, V. L., Smith, M. B., & Sperling, S. E. Psychology and the future. *American Psychologist*, 1978, *33*, 631–647.

Wilner, D., Greathouse, V., Wilton, R., Ershoff, D., Foster, K., & Hetherington, R. Inside DOPE: The custom research databank in the analysis and transfer of information. *Evaluation*, 1976, *3*(1–2), 11–13.

Yin, R. *Changing urban bureaucracies: How new practices become routinized.* Santa Monica, Calif.: Rand Corporation, 1978.

25

Training Programs for Paraprofessionals
Guidelines and Issues

JOSEPH A. DURLAK

The importance of paraprofessionals within the mental health field can hardly be overestimated. Paraprofessionals constitute the single largest category of mental health staff; there are an estimated 145,000 paid paraprofessionals in all mental health facilities throughout the country including more than 10,000 in community mental health centers (James, 1979). These figures represent 50.4% and 29.6% of the full-time equivalent positions in these agencies, respectively. Moreover, the number of part-time volunteers participating in helping programs probably exceeds the number in permanent staff positions. Paraprofessionals have become so extensively and intimately involved in the mental health field that the effective delivery of services, particularly in community mental health centers, is often predicated on paraprofessional personpower. Indeed, many of the community projects described elsewhere in this volume rely heavily on paraprofessional change agents.

JOSEPH A. DURLAK • Applied Psychology Program, Water Tower Campus, Loyola University, 10 East Pearson St., Chicago, Illinois 60611.

Overview of the Paraprofessional Movement

Research data support the service value of paraprofessionals. By late 1979, over 1,000 outcome studies using paraprofessional therapists had appeared, with no more than 20 reporting negative results. The benefits of using paraprofessionals have been demonstrated for virtually all types of helping roles, treatment programs, target problems, and client populations (Gershon & Biller, 1977). In direct comparisons, data suggest that the clinical results paraprofessionals achieve are at least as good as, and in some cases, significantly better than those obtained by professionals (Durlak, 1979). Conclusions from outcome research must be made carefully, however, until more rigorously controlled investigations are conducted to examine the specific conditions and factors that affect paraprofessionals' helping abilities.

Despite generally positive outcome findings, several practical problems have been noted in the use of paraprofessionals. There have been reports of inadequate training and supervision, and professionals have expressed doubts about paraprofessionals' clinical performance, ethical behavior, and agency loyalty. Programs have often failed to use paraprofessionals' talents and resources wisely; some facilities have kept paraprofessionals in unchallenging, dead-end jobs with limited opportunities for advancement, or, alternatively, have overworked paraprofessionals, provided them with minimal administrative and social support, and expected too much from them. As one might expect, some paraprofessionals have become disenchanted and have left their positions prematurely. There have also been power struggles between professionals and paraprofessionals; in several cases, professionals have subverted the goals of paraprofessional programs by resisting the use of paraprofessionals for a variety of personal and professional reasons. Therefore, many political and administrative issues must be resolved to maximize paraprofessionals' service contributions (see Alley, Blanton, & Feldman, 1979; Field & Gatewood, 1976; Gershon & Biller, 1977; Maierle, 1973).

In this chapter I shall highlight the most successful or promising approaches in paraprofessional training and discuss several unresolved issues. Effective training is a necessary but far from sufficient condition for successful paraprofessional programs. However, it is possible here only to focus on programmatic issues that bear directly on training.

Professionals are usually identified on the basis of formal postbaccalaureate training and education in psychiatry, psychology, psychiatric nursing, or social work. Paraprofessionals do not have such advanced mental health training. Instead, they represent an extremely heterogeneous group in terms of characteristics, background, and job-related clinical activities. Paraprofessionals include full-time, salaried staff with training ranging from a grade school to a college education and such part-time, unpaid volunteers as homemakers, students, parents, and the elderly. Furthermore, at least a dozen different services ranging from intake interviewing to individual and group counseling to crisis intervention and community outreach work are provided by paraprofessionals. Therefore, the following recommendations and commentary must be tempered by the situational parameters of paraprofessional programs. The three primary factors affecting training include who the paraprofessionals are, the situations in which they work, and the services they will be asked to provide. Nevertheless, several prominent paraprofessional training issues cut across all these factors.

Preliminaries to Training

An "oral history" that has developed regarding the use of paraprofessionals contains several examples of paraprofessional programs being terminated prematurely when needed administrative, financial, and personal support dissolved or active professional resistance to the continued use of paraprofessionals arose. These examples suggest that programmers should develop a strong support base before implementing programs that involve paraprofessionals. Four preliminary tasks should be accomplished before beginning training:

1. Clearly establishing the need for the proposed services
2. Securing support and acceptance of paraprofessionals from existing agency staff
3. Developing clear role definitions and job descriptions for paraprofessionals
4. Making adequate arrangements for ongoing, posttraining supervision of paraprofessionals

The fourth point will be discussed later in this chapter; the others merit comment here.

Programmers must work to obtain a true commitment from agencies regarding the use of paraprofessionals. That may be possible only through extensive preliminary discussion, negotiation, and, at times, compromise. Clear role definitions and job descriptions for paraprofessionals are absolutely essential. Role definitions should include explanations of skills needed to perform each job as well as delineation of clinical and administrative responsibilities and limitations. Moreover, the paraprofessional's role vis-à-vis the professional should be clarified with respect to any changes in responsibility and behavior required of the latter. New role demands created by the influx of paraprofessionals should be carefully articulated, discussed, and accepted by all the relevant staff. A foot-in-the-door approach when advocating paraprofessional programs is risky. Plans to resolve professionals' philosophical, practical, and personal resistances to paraprofessionals should be formulated at the outset; otherwise, any ventures involving paraprofessionals will be open to continuous unwarranted scrutiny and criticism, if not outright sabotage by prejudiced parties. Invariably, social programs are not maintained because they "work," that is, because they are effective as determined by objective data, but because their procedures and goals are generally judged admirable and valuable.

In summary, before any efforts are expended on actual training, it is important that all personnel whose support and cooperation is essential agree on the need for and roles of new paraprofessionals within the agency.

Training Paraprofessionals: Guidelines

Training programs can be divided into four broad categories: preservice, inservice (on-the-job training), supervision, and college-level training. These categories are by no means mutually exclusive. Preservice and inservice programs are considered collectively here with an emphasis on specific skill development. Individualized job requirements will dictate the necessary timing of training.

Preservice and Inservice

Probably the best choice of a training model for developing helping skills in paraprofessionals is one that relies on social learning principles. Training programs using a social learning orientation have consistently produced the most effective results both in terms of posttraining levels of skills and trainees' subsequent impact on clients. The most prominent programs are Carkhuff's (1969) Systematic Human Relations Training, Danish and Hauer's (1973) Basic Helping Model, Ivey's (1971) Microcounseling Approach, and numerous behavior modification programs exemplified by the work of Carnine and Fink (1978) and Fabry and Reid (1978).

Training time in these programs ranges from 25 to 100 hours and has been used successfully to train teachers, parents, medical and college students, psychiatric aides, crisis workers, resident hall advisers, nurses, and various types of indigenous personnel. Gershon and Biller (1977) provide an extensive description of these successful programs (see also McCarthy, Danish, & D'Augelli, 1977; Stokes & Keys, 1978).

Although these training programs attempt to teach different types of clinical skills, they are in basic agreement about some fundamental properties of effective training procedures, including:

1. A breakdown of desired clinical competence into operationalized components
2. A step-by-step approach in which skills are taught and learned one at a time whenever possible
3. A pretraining assessment of trainees' competence in each skill
4. Brief didactic instruction on how each skill is performed
5. Modeling of effective skills by competent practitioners
6. Supervised trainee practice of modeled skills
7. Immediate performance feedback to trainees emphasizing positive reinforcement as much as possible
8. Repetition of Steps 4 to 7 until trainees meet or exceed clearly established criterion levels for each skill
9. A systematic posttraining evaluation of trainees' skills

Research has yet to tease out the relative contributions of different training components (e.g., instructions vs. modeling vs. feedback). Training elements probably assume differential importance depending on therapist, client, and treatment parameters. At this point, then, prospective trainers of paraprofessionals should recognize the following principle: Effective training consists of a step-by-step, didactic-experiential approach that involves continuous systematic evaluation of trainees' progress toward operationalized clinical goals using a carefully orchestrated combination of instructions, modeling, behavioral rehearsal, and feedback.

To date, social learning training models have been used to develop skills in interviewing and individual and group counseling or behavior modification, but similar programs can be adapted to train paraprofessionals for virtually any clinical role or function. For example, Fawcett and his colleagues have recently applied social learning techniques to train paraprofessionals in several community-oriented services such as referral making, neighborhood canvassing, and community education. The pioneering work of Fawcett and his colleagues (see Chapter 16; Fawcett, Fletcher, & Mathews, 1980) could be profitably emulated by others wishing to train paraprofessionals in community-oriented services.

Another successful preservice or inservice approach for training paraprofessionals has been to deemphasize training per se and instead to develop standardized treatment packages for specific target problems. These treatment packages consist of a series of carefully structured and sequenced helping procedures and often involve prerecorded video- or audiotapes (Durlak, 1979). Specific therapist behaviors are usually described in detailed treatment manuals. In such cases paraprofessionals offer services by following a manual; issues that arise in program implementation can be monitored through ongoing supervision.

Treatment manuals have also been developed for client use in self-help programs, but there are indications that minimal therapist contact is instrumental in maintaining client motivation and preventing premature termination from treatment (Glasgow & Rosen, 1978). However, researchers have successfully used paraprofessionals to offer this therapeutic contact (Glasgow, 1978; Moss & Arend, 1977).

Standardized treatment programs should not be undervalued. Although it is the professional who develops the structure and sequence of effective helping procedures, it is still the paraprofessional who implements procedures in the prescribed fashion and deals with the interpersonal dynamics of the helping situation. Furthermore, standardized treatment programs involving therapy manuals are highly efficient and cost effective in terms of training change agents. Currently, studies using standardized treatment packages have for the most part been those in which college-student therapists have assisted clients with target problems relating to test or speech anxiety, lack of assertiveness, or specific habit problems involving eating and smoking (Durlak, 1979). The ability of professionals to develop standardized treatments suitable for a wider range of therapists and clinical populations remains to be seen. Nevertheless, carefully structured treatment programs are an effective means to increase the range of services that paraprofessionals can offer with a relatively minimal time investment for training.

Finally, it must be emphasized that effective training should not be limited to specific clinical skills training. Training should also be directed at ethics, necessary record keeping and report writing, administrative and procedural rules and policies of the host agency, and relevant local, state, and federal laws and regulations.

Supervision

Ongoing supervision is often overlooked as an important training vehicle for paraprofessionals. Several authors believe that supervision may be the most important factor in paraprofessional staff development (Field & Gatewood, 1976; Thigpen, 1979). Therefore, it is disconcerting to learn that many paraprofessionals may receive infrequent or inadequate supervision (Doyle, Foreman, & Wales, 1977; Young, True, & Packard, 1976).

Whenever possible, supervision should be systematically related to the training that paraprofessionals have received. Supervision is one mechanism whereby individuals can consolidate previously acquired skills and develop new techniques. Therefore, it makes no sense for training to be highly systematic and for supervision to be diffuse and nonspecific. Supervisors should not only understand paraprofessionals' prior training, they should also model effective behavior and provide systematic positive feedback in much the same way as those who train paraprofessionals using a social learning format. Supervisory goals should be clearly established and mutual responsibilities discussed and clarified. Supervisors should recognize paraprofessionals' anxieties about being evaluated by providing emotional support through direct expressions of empathy, trust, and confidence in paraprofessionals' abilities. The importance of the supervisory relationship should not be underestimated. A recent survey involving 139 paraprofessionals suggests that the quality of the supervisory relationship (e.g., "My supervisor acknowledges my efforts") may play a critical role in the extent to which staff experience burnout on the job (Bruck & May, 1979).

Two caveats are in order about typical supervisory practices. First, the traditional clinical-analytic model of supervision does not seem appropriate for many paraprofessionals (Sobey, 1970; Thigpen, 1979). Clinical interpretation of paraprofessionals' personal style and personality makeup is probably best offered only after positive feedback about work performance and emotional support are first expressed. Second, supervision scheduled at weekly intervals may not be conducive to many paraprofessionals' personal needs. Temporal availability of supervision may assume critical importance in certain situations, particularly in the early stages of on-the-job activities. Supervisors may have to respond to the need for immediate supervision by rearranging their schedules to correspond with paraprofessionals' initial contacts with clients.

College-Level Training

The most ambitious endeavor to train paraprofessionals has been the development of 2-year, college-level associate of arts (A.A.) degree programs. Most of these programs train mental health generalists, that is, middle-level workers with a variety of basic skills who can eventually carry out many of the direct service functions traditionally performed by professionals. The curriculum of A.A. programs consists of both theoretical and applied (skill oriented) courses, including credits for extensive field work or practicum experience (Becker, 1978). Typical skill-oriented courses include interviewing, group process or dynamics, and crisis intervention, behavior modification, or some other specific therapeutic technique. Five A.A. programs began in 1966, and there are now at least 170 programs throughout the country producing an estimated 4,000 graduates each year (Young *et al.*, 1976). There are also numerous specialized 4-year baccalaureate programs that emphasize applied training in the human services.

Despite their popularity, A.A. programs seem to be a mixed blessing. On the positive side, these programs provide paraprofessionals with the necessary academic credentials for obtaining entry-level employment. Academic credentials rather than functional competences are still the rite of passage in our society for increased pay, status, and occupational responsibility. Therefore, A.A. programs serve a useful function by preparing large numbers of persons for possible entry into human service jobs.

On the negative side, however, there is little evidence concerning the breadth and quality of skills attained by graduates of college-level training programs for paraprofessionals. These programs do not usually follow systematic training procedures, so that it is assumed rather than documented that program graduates can function adequately as human service workers. Furthermore, as Becker (1978) notes, curricula are devised primarily to suit the background, interests, and expertise of the training faculty. However, an important consideration should be the needs of the local agencies who may employ program graduates. Surveys suggest that program graduates may not be prepared for the types of roles they eventually assume in different agencies (Baker, 1973; Young *et. al.*, 1976).

The curriculum committees of college programs are therefore in a quandary. In their attempt to train broadly so that graduates can potentially obtain jobs in many different types of agencies, they may not be offering sufficient training to enable workers to function well in specific programs. One useful recommendation is that the training faculty of college programs collaborate with local agencies who may hire paraprofessionals regarding the nature and depth of training for A.A. workers (McPheeters, 1979).

Training Professionals to Work with Paraprofessionals

Training programs cannot be effective without the presence of a competent training staff. Unfortunately, one cannot assume that the majority of professionals are willing or able to train and supervise paraprofessionals effectively. For example, only 38% of 385 advanced graduate students from 102 training programs in clinical and community psychology indicated the availability of field work experiences related to educating and training paraprofessionals; and over one-half of these students (53%) believed these field work experiences were not adequate to satisfy their professional needs and interests (Zolik, Sirbu, & Hopkinson, 1976).

Since many of our newer professional graduates are not being prepared to deal with paraprofessionals, one would expect still smaller numbers of already practicing professionals to be heavily involved in paraprofessional education, training, and supervision. This expectation seems confirmed by Bloom and Parad's (1977) survey of the job activities of 1,019 mental health professionals from 55 community mental health centers in 13 western states. These professionals devoted only approximately 3 hours of their total clinical activities per week to training and supervision, and this time was not necessarily exclusively directed at paraprofessionals. The modal number of hours devoted to training and supervision for the 211 psychologists in these centers was zero (Bloom & Parad, 1977)!

By and large, paraprofessionals have prospered because of the motivation, skill, and dedication of a small cadre of mental health professionals. However, for maximum benefit to be obtained from paraprofessionals, larger numbers of professionals must be prepared to work with paraprofessionals as trainers, supervisors, and collaborators. More opportunities must be established in professional training programs and continuing education workshops to assure that more professionals acquire the requisite skills to work with paraprofessionals. Wasserman, Messersmith, and Ferree (1975) stress that professional contact with and training of paraprofessionals should begin in graduate school so that the development of paraprofessional programs can become an important part of the professionals' subsequent work. Instructively, Moore (1974) recommends that training programs for professionals follow the same social learning principles described earlier for paraprofessional training, and offers an excellent example of just such a program. In his program, professionals develop competences as trainers and supervisors by participating in structured sessions that emphasize modeling, behavioral rehearsal, and feedback regarding target skills.

Training Paraprofessionals: Issues

Career Ladders

The use of paraprofessionals in the human services was greatly accelerated by the new-careers movement, a series of employment and training programs funded by the federal government beginning in the mid-1960s. By 1970 there were an estimated 250,000 to 400,000 paraprofessionals employed in the fields of education, probation, social service, and mental and physical health (Cohen, 1976). In many respects, the new-careers movement can be viewed as a social movement because of its idealistic and far-reaching aims: (1) to increase the *quantity* of service through additional personpower; (2) to increase the *quality* of service by redirecting agencies' priorities toward previously underserved populations; and (3) to provide meaningful careers for low-income and minority persons.

It was hoped that entry-level positions could be created along with carefully articulated career ladders permitting vertical and horizontal mobility between and within paraprofessional, preprofessional, and professional job levels. Furthermore, it was hoped that career advancement would be based on a flexible combination of formal education and training, job experience, and demonstrated competence.

Cohen (1976) provides an excellent but somber assessment of the impact of the new-careers movement. Although human services were increased in several areas, other accomplishments fell far short of expectations. Cohen observes that there was little evidence that the quality of human services was very drastically altered or that the development of true career ladders ever became widespread: "While many people have obtained paraprofessional *jobs*, a relatively small number have been given the opportunity to pursue viable *careers*" (p. 87). With a few exceptions, then, the career development of paraprofessionals in the mental health field is extremely restricted beyond the entry level; advancement within the mental health system is still very much dependent on obtaining traditional educational and training credentials. Unfortunately, it is unlikely that this situation will change appreciably in the near future.

Indigenous Workers

An aura of charisma and mystery has always surrounded indigenous paraprofessionals, that is, workers similar to clients in background, life style, and personal and demographic characteristics. Indigenous workers' charisma relates to their supposedly unique perspective and ability to understand and identify with local community groups. As a result, indigenous therapists are often cited as the treatment agents of choice for low-income or minority groups. The mystery behind the indigenous worker is exposed, however, when it is realized that the comparative effectiveness of indigenous and professional change agents working with nonmiddle-class populations has never been evaluated (Durlak, 1979). Furthermore, indigenous workers' supposedly unique knowledge and their seemingly effective interpersonal skills have not been defined in any systematic way.

Not all indigenous workers are effective, and some professionals have been very successful when working with socially disadvantaged groups. It is quite possible that paraprofessionals' success with clients is correlated with rather than caused by their indigenous status. Therefore, it is important to objectify indigenous workers' clinical and interpersonal behavior in an attempt to resolve some of the mystery underlying their job performance.

Dangers of Co-Optation

There is often concern that paraprofessionals will eventually become co-opted by professional agencies, that is, their involvement in traditional mental health agencies will "professionalize" the paraprofessionals in the negative sense of greatly eroding their natural helping skills and their commitment to and identification with the community. This concern is greatest with respect to indigenous workers who are recruited because of their unique relationship with certain populations. However, whether or not paraprofessionals become negatively co-opted by the system depends largely on the confidence, respect, and relative freedom they experience on the job. As long as some professional role models demonstrate a true commitment toward improving the quality of services and allow paraprofessionals flexibility in attaining agreed-on goals, the danger of negative co-optation of paraprofessionals is diminished. Furthermore, as Cohen (1976) points out, there actually is no research evidence that paraprofessional staff lose their commitment to community work over time.

ACKNOWLEDGMENTS

I express my appreciation to Chris Durlak and Pat McCarthy for their helpful comments.

References

Alley, S., Blanton, J., & Feldman, R. E. (Eds.). *Paraprofessionals in mental health: Theory and practice*. New York: Human Sciences Press, 1979.

Baker, E. J. The mental health associate: One year later. *Community Mental Health Journal*, 1973, *9*, 203–214.

Becker, H. J. Curricula of associate degree mental health/human-services training programs. *Community Mental Health Journal*, 1978, *14*, 133–146.

Bloom, B. L., & Parad, H. J. Professional activities and training needs of community mental health center staff. In I. Iscoe, B. L. Bloom, & C. D. Spielberger (Eds.), *Community psychology in transition: Proceedings of the National Conference on Training in Community Psychology*. Washington, D.C.: Hemisphere, 1977.

Bruck, B., & May, T. *Correlates and indicators of burn-out in mental health workers.* Paper presented at the meeting of the American Psychological Association, New York, September 1979.

Carkhuff, R. R. *Helping and human relations.* Vol. 1. *Selection and training.* New York: Holt, Rinehart & Winston, 1969.

Carnine, D. W., & Fink, W. T. Increasing the rate of presentation and use of signals in elementary classroom teachers. *Journal of Applied Behavior Analysis,* 1978, *11,* 35–46.

Cohen, R. *"New careers" grows older: A perspective on the paraprofessional experience, 1965–1975.* Baltimore: Johns Hopkins University Press, 1976.

Danish, S. J., & Hauer, A. L. *Helping skills: A basic training program.* New York: Human Sciences Press, 1973.

Doyle, W. W., Jr., Foreman, M. E., & Wales, E. Effects of supervision in the training of nonprofessional crisis-intervention counselors. *Journal of Counseling Psychology,* 1977, *24,* 72–78.

Durlak, J. A. Comparative effectiveness of paraprofessional and professional helpers. *Psychological Bulletin,* 1979, *86,* 80–92.

Fabry, P. L., & Reid, D. H. Teaching foster grandparents to train severely handicapped persons. *Journal of Applied Behavior Analysis,* 1978, *11,* 111–123.

Fawcett, S. B., Fletcher, R. K., & Mathews, R. M. Applications of behavior analysis in community education. In D. Glenwick & L. Jason (Eds.), *Behavioral community psychology: Progess and prospects.* New York: Praeger, 1980.

Field, H. S., & Gatewood, R. The paraprofessional and the organization: Some problems of mutual adjustment. *Personnel and Guidance Journal,* 1976, *55,* 181–185.

Gershon, M., & Biller, H. B. *The other helpers: Paraprofessionals and nonprofessionals in mental health.* Lexington, Mass.: D. C. Heath, 1977.

Glasgow, R. E. Effects of a self-control manual, rapid smoking, and amount of therapist contact on smoking reduction. *Journal of Consulting and Clinical Psychology,* 1978, *46,* 1439–1447.

Glasgow, R. E., & Rosen, G. M. Behavioral bibliotherapy: A review of self-help behavior therapy manuals. *Psychological Bulletin,* 1978, *85,* 1–23.

Ivey, A. E. *Microcounseling: Innovations in interview training.* Springfield, Ill.: Charles C Thomas, 1971.

James, V. Paraprofessionals in mental health: A framework for the facts. In S. Alley, J. Blanton, & R. E. Feldman (Eds.), *Paraprofessionals in mental health: Theory and practice.* New York: Human Sciences Press, 1979.

Maierle, J. P. The politics of supporting paraprofessionals. *Professional Psychology,* 1973, *4,* 313–320.

McCarthy, P. R., Danish, S. J., & D'Augelli, A. R. A follow-up evaluation of helping skills training. *Counselor Education and Supervision,* 1977, *17,* 29–35.

McPheeters, H. Training, supervision, and evaluation of paraprofessionals. In S. Alley, J. Blanton, & R. E. Feldman (Eds.), *Paraprofessionals in mental health: Theory and practice.* New York: Human Sciences Press, 1979.

Moore, M. Training professionals to work with paraprofessionals. *Personnel and Guidance Journal,* 1974, *53,* 308–312.

Moss, M. K., & Arend, R. A. Self-directed contact desensitization. *Journal of Consulting and Clinical Psychology,* 1977, *45,* 1234–1241.

Sobey, F. *The nonprofessional revolution in mental health.* New York: Columbia University Press, 1970.

Stokes, J. P., & Keys, C. B. Design and evaluation of a short-term paraprofessional-training program. *Counselor Education and Supervision,* 1978, *17,* 279–285.

Thigpen, J. D. Perceptual differences in the supervision of paraprofessional mental health workers. *Community Mental Health Journal*, 1979, *15*, 139–148.

Wasserman, C. W., Messersmith, C. E., & Ferree, E. H. Professional therapists, paraprofessional helpers, and graduate students: An uneasy alliance. *Professional Psychology*, 1975, *6*, 337–343.

Young, C. E., True, J. E., & Packard, M. E. A national study of associate degree mental health and human services workers. *Journal of Community Psychology*, 1976, *4*, 89–95.

Zolik, E., Sirbu, W., & Hopkinson, D. Perspective of clinical students on training in community mental health and community psychology. *American Journal of Community Psychology*, 1976, *4*, 339–349.

26
Endorsement of a Community Mental Health Ideology
A Guide for Inservice Staff Training

ROBERT A. HOFFNUNG, H. AUGUSTUS TAYLOR,
ISAAC TYLIM, AND MARTIN B. KORETZKY

The past two decades have witnessed substantial changes both in conceptualization and in service delivery systems within the area of mental health. Hard on the heels of the "tranquilizer revolution"—perhaps the crowning achievement to date of the medical model—has come the ideological shift to an emphasis on social factors in the etiology, prevention, and treatment of "mental disorders." This emphasis became embodied with the establishment of community mental health centers (CMHCs).

The staffs of CMHCs are made up of a wide variety of professionals, trained in the several traditional mental health disciplines, and of paraprofessionals at differing levels of training. Each of the traditional professions can be expected to impart to new professionals its characteristic set of attitudes and practices. Psychiatrists, psychologists, social

ROBERT A. HOFFNUNG, H. AUGUSTUS TAYLOR, AND ISAAC TYLIM • Elizabeth General Hospital, Community Mental Health Center, Elizabeth, New Jersey 07201. MARTIN B. KORETZKY • Veterans Administration Hospital, Northport, New York 11768.

workers, nurses, and others may differ in their approach to mental health issues, suggesting a need for inservice training programs at the CMHC to promote uniformity in the acceptance and implementation of the ideology of the CMHC movement. A major purpose of our study was to explore the usefulness of a particular instrument, the Community Mental Health Ideology (CMHI) scale, as a device for assessing attitudinal disparity and as a guide for training.

The CMHI scale was devised by Baker and Schulberg (1967), who specify five aspects of community mental health ideology: (1) responsibility of the mental health specialist for the entire population of the community; (2) primary prevention through counteraction of harmful social forces; (3) stress on social adjustment rather than reconstruction of personality as the aim of treatment; (4) the provision of an integrated network of caregiving services to provide for continuity of care; and (5) the extension of effectiveness of mental health specialists by working with and through other people. Their attitude measure, developed to assess the extent of endorsement of these ideas, was found to differentiate reliably among criterion groups of professionals. Baker and Schulberg's (1967) original data revealed the following rankings in degree of CMHI endorsement: (1) Harvard Medical School postdoctorals in community psychiatry, (2) Harvard visiting faculty, (3) community psychologists, (4) Columbia postdoctorals, (5) members of Division 12 (Clinical Psychology) of the American Psychological Association, (6) members of the American Occupational Therapy Association, (7) members of the Society for Biological Psychiatry, (8) members of the American Psychiatric Association, and (9) members of the American Psychoanalytic Association.

The present study focused on one CMHC, (a New Jersey CMHC) which was established around the nucleus of a general hospital by federation agreements with outside agencies, and on the creation of new service elements in-house to provide the five services originally required by federal legislation for funding eligibility. This organization juxtaposes traditional medical practitioners, a cadre of newly recruited staff drawn from nonmedical specialities, and staff of existing socially oriented agencies. It was predicted that CMHI scores would show a high degree of variance attributable to professional affiliation and to service element. Furthermore, it was conjectured that those areas of the center that served as points of interface between groups of differing ideology would be stress points, with possible negative consequences for staff morale and cooperation. Accordingly, the CMHI survey to be done was incorporated into an in-house workshop that would be a forum (1) to report on survey results to the staff, and (2) to provide for discussion that could lead to increased understanding and tolerance of differences, or even reduce such differences, with a consequent reduction of internal tensions. It was hoped that such a workshop approach would demonstrate the practical utility of the CMHI scale in focusing the entire interdisciplinary professional staff on the central issues of CMHC ideology.

Overview of the Literature

A number of studies have confirmed the reliability of CMHI differences among professional groups. For example, Baker and Howard (1975) found psychiatric nursing students to adhere closely to CMHI values. Penn, Baker, and Schulberg (1976) studied social workers and social work students and likewise found high CMHI scores for these groups. Baird (1976) found social workers to have homogeneously high scores, with no significant variation because of setting or demographic characteristics. Mangum and Mitchell (1973) found faculty and graduate student social workers to score higher on CMHI than did clinical psychology and law faculty and students at a large southeastern university. Robin and Wagenfeld (1976) found CMHC psychiatrists to score lower as a group than other CMHC professionals. However, the scores of psychiatrists varied significantly, with (1) those working at agency- or board-sponsored CMHC settings scoring higher than those employed at public- or government-sponsored CMHC settings; (2) those spending more time in indirect rather than direct service scoring higher; and (3) younger psychiatrists scoring higher than older ones. Block (1974) found physicians and psychiatrists to score lower than other professionals. Langston (1970) studied two CMHCs and reports similar differences relating to professional affiliation; he also reports positive correlations between CMHI scores and (1) years of liberal arts education, and (2) number of years working in a CMHC.

Intraprofessional differences have been studied as well with the CMHI scale. Del Gaudio, Stein, Ansley, and Carpenter (1975) found CMHI scores to be related to the socioeconomic background of the therapists within one CMHC. Brown (1974) found a significant correlation between CMHI score and nontraditional attitudes toward mental illness, with a rejection of mental illness stereotypes by high-CMHI licensed psychologists in Texas. Del Gaudio, Stein, Ansley, and Carpenter (1976) found therapists scoring high on the CMHI scale to be less influenced by the class background and degree of disturbance of patients when assigning ratings of likability and of favorable prognosis. In general, the high-CMHI therapists liked their patients more and assigned more favorable prognoses than did low-CMHI therapists; the CMHI scores were also found to correlate positively with a measure of democratic values. Penn *et al.* (1976) found CMHI scores of female graduate student social workers to be related to scores on the Edwards Personality Preference Scale. Higher CMHI scores were associated with lower needs for deference and order. Baker and Schulberg (1969) found CMHI scores to be correlated negatively with dogmatism and political-economic conservatism among members of citizen mental health boards.

The CMHI scale has also been employed as an instrument to study the nature of the CMHC as an institution. Wagenfeld, Robin, and Jones (1974) surveyed 20 CMHCs and reported the highest adherence to CMHI values within rural areas, under agency or board structures, among social workers and psychologists, and among those who saw their agencies as oriented more toward social than toward medical services. Robin and Wagenfeld (1976) conclude that CMHCs are staffed by workers heterogeneous with regard to CMHI and that the centers act neither as promulgators nor as repositories of CMHI values, calling into question the notion that the CMHC is the unique manifestation of the movement toward community ideology.

The Present Study

Setting

The setting of the study was a CMHC attached to a general hospital in urban New Jersey. The organizational structure of the CMHC has already been described; as for physical structure, most of the service elements were housed in a modern, two-story wing of the hospital building, located immediately contiguous to the inpatient psychiatric ward and to the hospital emergency room area.

Participants

The 179 participants included the entire professional and nonprofessional staff of the CMHC and its affiliates, plus staff of the nonaffiliated branch offices of the outpatient clinic. Included were psychiatrists and other physicians, psychologists and psychology students, psychiatric social workers and students, psychiatric and nonpsychiatric nurses, activities therapists, clerical and secretarial personnel, aides and technicians, paraprofessionals, and housekeeping, security, and administrative personnel.

Procedure

Each member of the survey population was sent a cover letter, which included an endorsement of the project by the CMHC administrator. With the letter went a questionnaire covering demographic information and areas of professional experience and responsibility, including age, sex, ethnicity, country of birth, non-English language fluency, marital status, number of children, years of experience in mental health areas, and weekly hours spent in various types of activity. Completing the mailing packet was the CMHI questionnaire, which consists of 38 items, each with six response alternatives. The items are scores from 1 to 7 in the direction of CMHI endorsement, with a score of 4 assigned only to unanswered items. The items are totaled, yielding a CMHI score ranging from 38 (low CMHI) to 266 (high CMHI).

The materials for each participant were labeled with a unique code number so that individual respondents would be able to learn their score. A reminder memo was distributed 1 week after the initial mailing.

Two months after the initial mailing, a 3-hour general meeting of the CMHC, attended predominantly by professional and paraprofessional staff, provided the setting for a program that consisted of (1) a formal presentation of the study and its results, (2) workshop groups of about 10 people each to discuss selected items from the CMHI scale for a 30-minute period, and (3) a talk by an outside expert discussing themes that had emerged from the workshops and placing them into a broader perspective.

Findings

Of the 179 questionnaires distributed, 105 (59%) were completed and returned. Chi-squares were calculated for frequency of return and nonreturn by discipline (16 disciplines) and by department (11 departments), in each case yielding a significance level from .10 to .05, so that neither of these variables proved a highly significant factor in return rate. A further analysis of return rate classified departments on two dichotomous variables: (1) whether the department was an integral part of the CMHC, and (2) whether the department was a pre-CMHC hospital unit. The chi-square computed for return and nonreturn frequencies over these four categories proved significant beyond the .05 level; inspection of the data suggests that existing hospital units that had been incorporated into the CMHC provided a disparately low rate of return.

The CMHI questionnaire data were subjected to a series of one-way analyses of variance on the several classification axes available; it must be borne in mind that multiple analyses raise the likelihood of encountering a "significant" result by chance, and also that many of these variables may be interdependent and confounded. The results of the analysis are presented in Table 1.

Since professional or occupational affiliation (discipline) proved a significant source of variation, the differences between all groups were analyzed by Sheffe's method (without correction for unequal *N*s). The two differences significant at the .05 level were that between psychiatrists and other physicians and that between psychiatrists and administrators.

Age likewise proved a highly significant factor. There was a consistent dropping off of CMHI score with increasing age beyond age 21. Perhaps surprisingly, years of experience is a variable that proved of marginal significance; inspection of the data suggests a tendency for those reporting 16 or more years of mental health experience to score lower on the CMHI than their less experienced colleagues.

For the analysis of CMHI scores by country of origin, the single Asian respondent was dropped; Sheffe's test indicates that each of the three remaining means differs significantly from the other two at the .05 level; ranging from highest to lowest. The order is presented as follows: U.S.; non-U.S. American; European.

Type of work is the remaining variable that proved highly significant. Respondents were assigned to one of the following classifications: supervisory, administrative, direct clinical, technical/paraprofessional, or clerical and other/nontechnical. Supervisory respondents had significantly higher CMHI scores than all others; administrators, the next highest scorers, differed significantly from all other groups except for the direct clinical respondents.

Finally, Table 2 compares the present results with findings from

Table 1. Analyses of Variance of CMHI Scores

Variable	F	df	p
Department	1.37	10.94	$> .05$
Discipline	5.18	15.88	$< .01$
Age	4.11	5.99	$< .01$
Sex	4.09	1.102	$< .05$
Ethnicity	0.27	2.100	$> .05$
Country of origin	3.32	2.101	$< .05$
Marital status	1.24	4.100	$> .05$
Years of experience	2.51	4.100	$\approx .05$
Type of work	3.97	5.99	$< .01$

Table 2. Mean CMHI Scores Compared with Previous Findings

	Rockland CMHC executives	Rockland CMHC staff	Two Texas CMHCs	University of Rochester CMHC	State hospital in Florida	Present Study
Psychiatrists	203	174	202	199	197	165
Psychologists	251	—	229	230	214	212
Social workers	240	235	236	230	212	209
Nurses	247	241	210	216	197	216
Secretaries	—	—	205	194	—	168

previous studies. With the exception of the scores from nursing, the means from our hospital-based, urban, northeastern CMHC appear more in line with those reported for a state hospital than with those found at CMHCs.

Discussion

Several aspects of these results are noteworthy. First, the study provides an additional validation of the power of the CMHI scale to discriminate meaningfully among professional and occupational subgroups. Among providers of clinical services, physicians and, to a lesser extent, psychiatrists are less likely to subscribe to the CMHI orientation than are nonmedically trained practitioners.

The notion that our hospital-based CMHC might have properties that could usefully be approached through the CMHI scale was confirmed in at least two ways. The easier of these to describe is the low range of scores obtained in comparison with other CMHCs: Staff scores from this study seem more comparable to those reported for a state mental hospital than for other CMHCs. This finding presumably reflects a relatively conservative orientation on the part of the parent hospital and either selective hiring practices to reinforce this orientation or an evolutionary process whereby new staff either adapt their views to the prevailing norms or, unwilling to do so, leave the organization. It would not be surprising to discover that hospital-based CMHCs tend to have less of a CMHI orientation than do other CMHCs, although obviously such a generalization calls for more extensive sampling for validation.

The second aspect of the data that is meaningful for our CMHC is the high degree of heterogeneity of staff with regard to CMHI orientation, in this case a confirmation of the expected. The implications are complex. On one hand, there may be a positive, helpful aspect: From an external point of view, an organization with varied staff orientation is likely to be less specialized and hence more capable of responding to a wide variety of environmental demands from potential service groups and from potential funding sources. From an internal perspective, ideological pluralism may foster a climate in which one's beliefs are broadened through exposure to others and deepened through challenge, a process we hoped to enhance with the staff workshop around ideological issues.

At the same time, however, each viewpoint reveals potentially problematic or troublesome aspects of such variety. From the external perspective, there is the danger that the community may be frustrated and perplexed by what appears to be an inconsistent or conflicting set of communications emanating from the CMHC (as when a family or an agency must deal with staff members of differing orientations involved in a particular treatment case). And from the internal perspective, more of a concern in our study, it seems likely that those who may believe they are approaching a common task may experience friction because of extensive and poorly understood ideological differences underlying their perception of the task and of the techniques to accomplish it. For example, nurses, who were the highest-scoring group in our study, consistently have been found to score higher in CMHI than physicians, particularly in the CMHC setting. Since nurses traditionally have functioned under the direction of physicians, one might wonder whether this measurable difference in orientation might not make for strained relationships between the two groups in mental health settings, with perhaps more stress entailed for the nurses as the formally subordinate members of the treatment team.

We have no direct measures of personal or occupational stress to report as part of this study. However, the units reporting the widest range of CMHI scores among service personnel were those preexisting hospital elements that became incorporated into the CMHC structure at its inception, and it is interesting that these are the units with the lowest rate of questionnaire return; informal data suggest that these units have experienced relatively high turnover in CMHC personnel, a likely indicator of job dissatisfaction.

A more general, pragmatic conclusion to be derived from this project is the degree of usefulness of the CMHI scale for management both as an assessment device for measuring relevant attitudes within a CMHC organization and identifying areas of likely conflict, and as a tool for staff development. The program of presentations and workshops was well received by those attending, who considered them helpful in the explication of important issues that had not previously been formalized or discussed. Indeed, the staff-development aspect of these workshops resulted in considerable intellectual ferment and discussion, serving to raise the educational level of all concerned regarding the function of the institution within which they worked. It also served as a catalyst for personal self-assessment of one's degree of commitment to CMHI and to traditional ideology. Whether there has resulted an enduring understanding and tolerance of the differences that emerged, one of the goals of the project, is a question that must await further research.

References

Baird, J. C. Social workers' orientations towards community mental health concepts. *Community Mental Health Journal*, 1976, *12*, 275–285.

Baker, F., & Howard, L. A. Mental health ideologies of psychiatric nurses. *Community Mental Health Journal*, 1975, *11*, 195–202.

Baker, F., & Schulberg, H. C. Development of a community mental health ideology scale. *Community Mental Health Journal*, 1967, *3*, 216–225.

Baker, F., & Schulberg, H. C. Community mental health ideology, dogmatism, and political-economic conservatism. *Community Mental Health Journal*, 1969, *5*, 433–436.

Block, W. E. The study of attitudes about mental health in the community mental health center. *Community Mental Health Journal*, 1974, *10*, 216–220.

Brown, P. M. Community mental health ideology and nontraditional attitudes toward mental illness. *American Journal of Community Psychology*, 1974, *2*, 255–263.

Del Gaudio, A. C., Stein, L. S., Ansley, M. Y., & Carpenter, P. J. Community mental health ideology as a function of professional affiliation and social class background. *Journal of Community Psychology*, 1975, *3*, 341–345.

Del Gaudio, A. C., Stein, L. S., Ansley, M. Y., & Carpenter, P. J. Attitudes of therapists varying in community mental health ideology and democratic values. *Journal of Consulting and Clinical Psychology*, 1976, *44*, 646–655.

Langston, R. D. Community mental health centers and community mental health ideology. *Community Mental Health Journal*, 1970, *6*, 387–392.

Mangum, P., & Mitchell, K. Attitudes toward the mentally ill and community care among professionals and their students. *Community Mental Health Journal*, 1973, *9*, 350–353.

Penn, N., Baker, F., & Schulberg, H. Community mental health ideology and personality preferences of social work students. *Journal of Community Psychology*, 1976, *4*, 292–297.

Robin, S., & Wagenfeld, M. The nature and correlates of community mental health ideology in community mental health centers. *Journal of Community Psychology*, 1976, *4*, 335–346.

Wagenfeld, M., Robin, S., & Jones, J. Structural and professional correlates of ideologies of community mental health workers. *Journal of Health and Social Behavior*, 1974, *15*, 199–210.

VIII
Epilogue
WHERE DO WE GO FROM HERE?

The goal for community development is to create opportunities for a community to plan for its own change. (Kelly, 1970, p. 197, cited in Chapter 27, this volume)

27

From Community Mental Health Centers to Community Resource Centers

ROBERT S. SLOTNICK AND ABRAHAM M. JEGER

What future directions are implied by a behavioral-ecological perspective? The theme that integrates our fantasies is a vision of future *community resource centers* (CRCs). These centers may provide bases for activities conducted at the local community level for purposes of enhancing the capacities of community residents to influence personal and community change (Jeger, 1980). Behavioral-ecologists can serve as collaborators with community groups to facilitate individual/community development.

CRCs differ from community mental health centers along two salient dimensions. First, these centers will be controlled by the community, as opposed to professional or other interest groups. Community residents will serve as the primary participants, policy directors, and leaders of all center programs. Professionals are likely to be involved as "technical" experts in consulting capacities or as providers of specific

ROBERT S. SLOTNICK AND ABRAHAM M. JEGER • Human Resources Development Center, New York Institute of Technology, Old Westbury, New York 11568.

services at the behest of the community. Professionals are more likely to be accountable to the community if they do not control policies and resources. Second, CRCs will be characterized by the intentional absence of any linkage to "mental illness." The point is not to downplay mental health, but that mental health problems should not be treated separately and should instead be integral parts of CRCs.

In their broadest function, CRCs will serve as *mediating structures* (Berger & Neuhaus, 1977; see also Chapter 2, section on "Enhancing the Psychological Sense of Community"), whose purpose is to strengthen the linkage between individuals and the larger megastructure (government, multinational corporations, etc.). Centers will offer programs that increase the capacities of such traditional mediating structures as family, church, neighborhood, and voluntary associations. When strengthening these traditional structures is not feasible (e.g., in the case of nonintact families), such centers will focus on developing alternative community support systems (e.g., single-parent support groups, cooperative day care).

Rather than a mental health model, we propose that specific center activities operate within an *educational model*. Educational programs will be directed to all constituencies of a community, and will cover the entire life span—children, adolescents, adults, and elderly. In addition, such frequently neglected groups as women, ethnic minorities, physically handicapped, and psychologically distressed are likely to be active participants. Thus the framework of comprehensive community educational programs enables the center to serve as a resource for the entire community.

Proposed Program Components

The following is an outline of some proposed activities for various populations of a "model" CRC.

The *adult education* program should continuously evolve to meet the changing needs of the community. Innovative courses will draw on the expertise of local community residents, health and human service agencies, schools, and universities. Classes will be offered for community adults (during days, evenings, and weekends) in three general areas: (1) physical health, (2) mental health, and (3) general enhancement.

Physical health will be viewed as a life style rather than a set of discrete activities. The emphasis will be on disease prevention, health maintenance, and health enhancement through courses on nutrition, exercise, weight control, dental care, and so on.

Mental health activities may fall into two broad categories: *instruction* in anxiety management, stress reduction, assertive training, smoking cessation, and so on; and *support groups* for single parents, new mothers, stepfamilies, widows, preretirees, and so on.

General enhancement will include courses on use of leisure time, household management, consumer awareness, job seeking, ethnic awareness, speed reading, crafts, hobbies, and so on.

In short, at the individual level programs will aim to activate citizens to become their own primary health care agents. The nature of the activities will help to demystify the helping enterprise. On a community level, the centers will serve advocacy functions to empower citizens by providing access to resources (e.g., media-based health enhancement programs such as the Stanford Heart Disease Prevention Project described in Chapter 14).

In the area of *children's services*, CRCs will focus on strengthening families through provision of comprehensive family supports. Full day care would emphasize social-emotional development, cognitive enhancement, and utilization of advanced technological instruction (videorecorders, computer games). For families who require only part-time child care, the flexibility of drop-in day care may be incorporated. In an attempt to replicate natural home environments and extended families, cross-generational activities with elderly and youth will be incorporated. Finally, the day care center may provide the locus for parent education, family support groups, and skills exchanges.

To provide supports for *adolescents*, preteen after-school programs may emphasize recreation and involvement in cross-age tutoring and child–aide activities. The teen program as a "place" for youth activities may include career exploration, rap groups, recreation, community service, or community beautification. Programs may be coordinated with school districts, community agencies, and business organizations.

Services for *elderly* may include a traditional day program for purposes of socialization, recreation, and maintaining independent living. Health maintenance groups can be built into the program to promote health skills, sensitize individuals to medical problems, and the like. Community resource groups—for example, consumer awareness, money management, food stamps, medical benefits, social security—may be included. Finally, mutual support groups where members meet on evenings, weekends, and holidays, utilizing each other as resources, can extend the availability of supports. This function is especially critical for elderly living alone and those without children in the community.

In the area of *women's services*, CRCs may offer career exploration and development—that is, seminars and workshops including skill training

for women returning to the work force. In addition, consciousness raising for women at different life stages may be included.

Special activities for the physically and mentally *handicapped* will be
developed in conjunction with existing health and human service agencies serving these populations. Particular attention will be given to families of the handicapped through development of mutual support groups
and educational programs to provide them with necessary coping skills
to maintain the independence of their handicapped family member.

Through a *cultural/ethnicity* unit within the CRC, it will be possible
to promote ethnic awareness. Community residents will be given opportunities to benefit from exposure to the cultural diversity in our pluralistic society. This aim will be accomplished through activities of art
leagues, theater guilds, music groups, literature readings, and exhibits. A
"community museum" will be developed as a particular community education project within the center.

Community needs will dictate the evolution of programs for additional groups, as the primary aim of the center is to provide access and
serve as a resource for all community members. Indeed, ongoing community assessments will determine the specific contents and activities of all
program components. The listing we have given is only one hypothetical
set of activities at a given time.

Proposed Organizational Structure

The organizational structure of CRCs should facilitate the integration of intracenter programs as well as coordination with extracenter
community resources. We draw on Sarason's (e.g., Sarason & Lorentz,
1979; Sarason, Carroll, Maton, Cohen, & Lorentz, 1977; see also Chapter
3, this volume) notion of the *resource exchange network* (REN) as the basis of
our proposed organizational structure.

To facilitate intracenter linkages among program components, a *resource exchange council*, made up of consumer and provider representatives
from all programs (e.g., children, elderly, women), will be formed. To
gain access to the larger community's resources, centers can become the
prime movers in catalyzing a *communitywide resource exchange network*, including representatives from universities, schools, hospitals, clinics, churches,
and other professional and lay agencies. The local CRC becomes one
member of the larger network, thereby permitting center–community interface. The purpose of these RENs is not just to facilitate coordination,
but to stimulate sharing and exchanging resources in barter style—in

contrast to the prevailing practice among human service agencies, which operate by the myth of unlimited resources and constantly compete for material and personal assets.

Intracenter Linkages

In order to consolidate resources within the center, coordinated activities can be planned across program components. For example, physical exercise can be planned jointly for day care children and senior citizens, providing opportunities for physical contact between elderly and children. The elderly can be involved in teaching the teen-agers cooking; teen-agers can do shopping for elderly and visit them at their homes. Similarly, teen-agers can assist in childcare with children and thereby learn about child development.

Center–Community Linkages

Since it is inconceivable that the proposed centers will ever be self-sufficient, they will require access to the larger educational and human service community. Centers will adopt as a priority activity the establishment of a communitywide REN (of which they will be one member). It will thus be possible to draw on available community resources to enhance center programs, and at the same time to offer the center as a resource to meet community needs. For example, hospital and university staff will be encouraged to interface with the adult education program; in return, teen-agers from the youth program will provide volunteer services in the hospital. Similarly, a local college may be permitted to offer courses at the center (thus generating tuition revenues) in return for giving community youth access to such campus facilities as the library, computer center, pool, and so on.

Community Participation

Active community participation is an overarching value of all CRC programs. This fact will be reflected in the governance of day-to-day program operations by the resource exchange council. Furthermore, community representatives will be engaged in carrying out the needs assessments to determine community priorities for specific activities. They will also be involved in program evaluation—both their processes and outcomes.

Summary and Conclusion

In summary, some of the unique features of the proposed centers include:

1. An emphasis on citizen participation in all programs
2. Development of the resource exchange council as a mechanism to promote linkages among center programs
3. Use of RENs to link the center with community programs, avoid duplication, and expand resources
4. Incorporation of an evaluation design into all center components
5. Integration of innovative technology (videotapes, microcomputers) to enhance community educational programs
6. Focus on prevention, health promotion, and fostering community supports

Although some of the specific components of such centers are our own fantasies, the general notion of CRCs is compatible with the visions of many others working within a behavioral and/or ecological framework. For example, Bandura (1967), a behavioral psychologist, makes the following prophecy:

> The day may not be far off when psychological disorders will be treated not in hospitals or mental hygiene clinics but in comprehensive "learning centers," when clients will be considered not patients suffering from hidden psychic pathologies but responsible people who participate actively in developing their own potentialities. (p. 86)

Our CRC would clearly encompass the kind of social learning program for (heretofore) "mental patients" called for by Bandura.

Similarly, Keller (1980) shares his dream of a community learning center for promoting competence in daily activities and fostering personal enhancement. Community residents may offer courses on topics from income tax to driver education to bicycle repair. Classes employ a behavioral education procedure, namely, personalized system of instruction (PSI), which permits each participant to progress through small, successive units at his/her own pace. Clearly, PSI is appropriate for the adult education component of our proposed center.

Rappaport (1977), an ecologically oriented community psychologist, proposes the development of human resource centers as alternatives to present community mental health centers. Each neighborhood would be granted a human services budget on a per capita basis; the funds could be allocated to any services that community members deem necessary.

Thus some communities may choose to emphasize traditional mental health programs, others may prefer crisis services, and yet others may develop social action centers focusing on employment, economic development, and so on. Professionals can be employed at the behest of the community, which maintains full control over program development. Again, our notion of CRCs is compatible with Rappaport's proposals.

In conclusion, we wish to speculate that as CRCs evolve in particular neighborhoods they will begin to interface with the larger governmental structures of the region (townships, county, city, etc.). In this way, centers may assume a better position to bring to bear the "utopian" streams of behavioral psychology (Krasner, 1980; Krasner & Ullmann, 1973; Skinner, 1948), social ecology (Moos & Browenstein, 1977), and community psychology (Klein, 1978) with their focus on planning entire living environments, influencing broader community institutions, and facilitating social change. For example, within the context of Krasner's (1980) notion of "environmental design," Jeger (1980) suggests that CRCs provide a base for participating in "new town" planning. Specific activities might include planning day care settings, schools, senior centers, recreational facilities, and housing design.

A role for behavioral-ecologists participating in town planning is to stimulate maximum input into the planning process to incorporate pluralistic interests—for example, numerous ethnic groups, political persuasions, religious denominations, and women. Furthermore, behavioral-ecologists can contribute their skills to building an evaluation process into the planning and functioning of the town in order to help guide community change. In the context of his ecological model, Kelly (1970) discusses some relevant longitudinal research designs to evaluate the extent to which citizens are involved in planning and implementing community change. He is particularly interested in looking at the diversity of citizens groups that participate in the community change process.

We conclude by reiterating the basic value that should guide the work of behavioral-ecologists in the proposed CRCs. As Kelly (1970) states, "the goal for community development is to create opportunities for a community to plan for its own change" (p. 197).

References

Bandura, A. Behavioral psychotherapy. *Scientific American*, 1967, *216*, 78–86.

Berger, P. L., & Neuhaus, R. *To empower people: The role of mediating structures in public policy.* Washington, D.C.: American Enterprise Institute for Public Policy Research, 1977.

Jeger, A. M. Community mental health and environmental design. In L. Krasner (Ed.), *Environmental design and human behavior: A psychology of the individual in society*. Elmsford, N.Y.: Pergamon Press, 1980.

Keller, F. S. A vision of community development. In G. L. Martin & J. G. Osborne (Eds.), *Helping in the community: Behavioral applications*. New York: Plenum Press, 1980.

Kelly, J. G. The quest for valid preventive interventions. In C. D. Spielberger (Ed.), *Current topics in clinical and community psychology* (Vol. 2). New York: Academic Press, 1970.

Klein, D. C. (Ed.). *Psychology of the planned community: The new town experience*. New York: Human Sciences Press, 1978.

Krasner, L. (Ed.). *Environmental design and human behavior: A psychology of the individual in society*. Elmsford, N.Y.: Pergamon Press, 1980.

Krasner, L., & Ullmann, L. P. *Behavior influence and personality: The social matrix of human action*. New York: Holt, Rinehart & Winston, 1973.

Moos, R. H., & Brownstein, R. *Environment and utopia*. New York: Plenum Press, 1977.

Rappaport, J. *Community psychology: Values, research, and action*. New York: Holt, Rinehart & Winston, 1977.

Sarason, S. B., & Lorentz, E. *The challenge of the resource exchange network*. San Francisco: Jossey-Bass, 1979.

Sarason, S. B., Carroll, C. F., Maton, K., Cohen, S., & Lorentz, E. *Human services and resource networks*. San Francisco: Jossey-Bass, 1977.

Skinner, B. F. *Walden two*. New York: Macmillan, 1948.

Appendix

Resources in Community Mental Health and Behavioral-Ecology

JUDITH A. JURMANN

The resources in this Appendix include professional societies, journals, newsletters, informal networks, clearinghouses, and other organizations. They were selected on the basis of their having useful information to offer on community mental health in general and behavioral-ecology in particular. Although the list is not exhaustive, an attempt was made to include mainstream as well as less known, specialized resources.

1. *American Association of Volunteer Service Coordinators,* 18 S. Michigan Chicago, Illinois 60603. The purpose of this organization is to stimulate, coordinate, and integrate community volunteer services.

2. *American Journal of Community Psychology,* Plenum Publishing Corporation, 233 Spring St., New York, New York 10013. Published in conjunction with the American Psychological Association's Division of Community Psychology, this journal is devoted to theory, research, and practice in the interaction between individuals and communities, organizations, and institutions.

3. *American Journal of Orthopsychiatry,* American Orthopsychiatric Association, 1775 Broadway, New York, New York 10019. A multidisciplinary journal in preventive and social psychiatry.

JUDITH A. JURMANN • Psychology Department, St. John's University, Jamaica, New York 11439.

4. *American Nurses Association,* 2420 Pershing Rd., Kansas City, Missouri 64108. The major national professional society of nurses. A newsletter and journals are published.

5. *American Psychiatric Association* (APA), 1700 18th St. N.W., Washington, D.C. 20009. The major national professional society of psychiatrists, the APA publishes *Psychiatric News* as well as several journals and special reports.

6. *American Psychological Association* (APA), 1200 17th St. N.W., Washington, D.C. 20036. The major national professional society of psychologists, the APA publishes *Psychological Abstracts* as well as its automated data base version, *Psych INFO.* Most mental health journals are indexed. The APA also serves as a general resource through publication of the *American Psychologist,* the *APA Monitor,* journals in many psychological specialities, and books on special topics. The APA recently organized a *Research Support Network* to keep individuals informed of funding programs in the psychological sciences. Of special interest to behavioral-ecology is Willo White's volume, *Resources in Environment and Behavior* (APA, 1979). APA divisions of particular interest to behavioral-ecology include: Experimental Analysis of Behavior (25), Community Psychology (27), Population and Environmental Psychology (34).

7. *American Public Health Association,* 1015 18th St. N.W., Washington, D.C. 20036. The association promotes personal and environmental health, conducts research, and establishes public health standards. Information regarding toxic substances is also disseminated, and a newsletter and journal are published.

8. *APA Division of Community Psychology Newsletter,* Raymond P. Lorion, Editor, Department of Psychology, University of Tennessee, Knoxville, Tennessee 37916. Published three times a year, this is the official newsletter of the APA's Division 27. The Summer 1980 issue was devoted to "Social Ecology in Community Psychology." It included conceptual essays, descriptions of ecologically oriented doctoral programs, and resource sections.

9. *Association for Advancement of Behavior Therapy* (AABT), 420 Lexington Ave., New York, New York 10017. An interdisciplinary society devoted to the promotion of behavior therapy, the AABT publishes the *Behavior Therapist* and *Behavior Therapy.* A special interest group within the AABT, *the Community Research Network,* includes individuals whose work is compatible with behavioral-ecology.

10. *Association for Behavior Analysis* (ABA), *International*, Department of Psychology, Western Michigan University, Kalamazoo, Michigan 49008. The ABA seeks to promote basic and applied work pertaining to operant analyses in such fields as behavioral medicine, teaching, retardation, mental health, and community psychology. A newsletter is published.

11. *Association for Rural Mental Health*, c/o Dr. Peter Keller, Department of Psychology, Mansfield State College, Mansfield, Pennsylvania 16933. The association, a national organization of professionals and citizens, is preparing a directory of programs that train mental health professionals for work in rural areas.

12. *Association for the Study of Man–Environment Relations*, P.O. Box 57, Orangeburg, New York 10962. The association seeks to advance understanding of the functional interaction between the environment and biological, psychological, and social activities. It publishes a journal, *Man–Environment Systems*.

13. *Association for Voluntary Action Scholars* (AVAS), Box G-55 McGuinn Hall, Boston College, Chestnut Hill, Massachusetts 02167. The AVAS is a professional society for those concerned with citizen involvement and volunteer participation. It publishes two journals (*Journal of Voluntary Action Research; Volunteer Administration*), a quarterly abstract series (*Citizen Participation and Voluntary Action Abstracts*), and a newsletter.

14. *Behavioral Assessment*, Pergamon Press, Maxwell House, Fairview Park, Elmsford, New York 10523. A new interdisciplinary journal focusing on assessment, design, methodology, statistics, dependent variables, and program evaluation.

15. *Community Research Network*. See No. 9.

16. *Behavioral Counseling Quarterly*, Human Sciences Press, 72 5th Ave., New York, New York 10011. This new journal combines an interdisciplinary forum and a social learning orientation for counseling and community-level interventions.

17. *Behaviorists for Social Action* (BFSA), c/o Saranne Oberman, Department of Human Development and Family life, University of Kansas, Lawrence, Kansas 66045. The society was initiated as a Special Interest Group of the Association for Behavior Analysis. The BFSA seeks to extend the role of behavioral psychology toward social change efforts. A journal is published.

18. *Behavior Modification*, Sage Publications, 275 S. Beverly Dr., Beverly Hills, California 90212. A journal focusing on behavioral techniques for a variety of settings and populations.

19. *Behavior Therapy*. See No. 9.

20. *Center for Community Change*, 1000 Wisconsin Ave. N.W., Washington, D.C. 20007. Concerned with broad-spectrum social change efforts, the center publishes a newsletter, a *Federal Program Monitor*, and Citizen Action Guides.

21. *Center for Human Environments*, CUNY Graduate School, 33 W. 42nd St., New York, New York 10036. Research and resources in environmental psychology. The center publishes the *Childhood City Newsletter* among other resources.

22. *Citizen Participation and Voluntary Action Abstracts*. See No. 13.

23. *Clearinghouse of Evaluation Training Materials*. See No. 38.

24. *Clearinghouse for Structured Group Programs*, c/o Office of Counseling and Student Development, Roosevelt Hall 222, University of Rhode Island, Kingston, Rhode Island 02881. Maintains information on group programs in three areas; life skills (e.g., stress management, self-improvement, parenting); life themes (e.g. sexuality, jealousy, self-esteem), and life transitions (e.g., grief, divorce, transitions to college).

25. *Community Mental Health Journal*, Human Sciences Press, 72 5th Ave., New York, New York 10011. An official publication of the National Council of Community Mental Health Centers, this journal focuses on theory, research, and practice in all areas of community mental health.

26. *Community Mental Health Legislative News*. See No. 72.

27. *Community Mental Health Review*, Haworth Press, 149 5th Ave., New York, New York 10010. A bimonthly newsletter containing general abstracts, and a review article on a topic in community mental health.

28. *Community Service Newsletter*, Community Service, Inc., P.O. Box 243, Yellow Springs, Ohio 45387. Devoted to promoting the "small community as a basic social institution involving organic units of economic, social, and spiritual development."

29. *Corrective and Social Psychiatry and Journal of Behavior Technology Methods and Therapy*, 122 N. Cooper, Olathe, Kansas 66061. An eclectic forum for papers on therapeutic communities and behavioral applications.

30. *Data Bank of Program Evaluation* (DOPE), School of Public Health, University of California at Los Angeles, 10833 LeConte Ave., Los Angeles, California 90024. A computerized field of reports of evaluations in mental health. Drawn from over 100 journals and from unpublished sources, since 1969.

31. *Diffusion Project*, P.O. Box 19367, Washington D.C. 20036. This project was established as a clearinghouse for new social experiments and public policy innovations. Information has been distributed on such social action programs as the *Tenant Resource and Advocacy Center* (TRAC) and the *Kansas Community Resources Act* (which provides state funding to local citizen organizations for establishing community resource programs following community needs assessments).

32. *Drug Abuse and Alcoholism Newsletter*, Vista Hill Foundation, 3420 Camino del Rio North, Suite 100, San Diego, California 92108.

33. *Eco/Community Psychology Newsletter*, Community Psychology Program, Psychology Department, University of Illinois at Urbana-Champaign, 603 East Daniel, Champaign, Illinois 61820. Newsletter containing resources and brief essays on ecological and community psychology.

34. *Environmental Design Research Association* (EDRA), P.O. Box 23129, L'Enfant Plaza Station, Washington, D.C. 20024. The association is committed to improvement in the quality of life through the proper design of physical and social environments. To that end, basic and applied research is promoted and information disseminated to designers, planners, and public policy makers. It publishes the *EDRA News* and the proceedings of its annual conventions.

35. *Environmental Sociology Newsletter*, c/o Professor A. R. Gillis, Department of Sociology, Erindale College, Mississauga, Ontario, Canada.

36. *Environment and Behavior*, Sage Publications, 275 S. Beverly Dr., Beverly Hills, California 90212. An interdisciplinary journal devoted to theory and research in the environment–behavior fields.

37. *Evaluation*. See No. 85.

38. *Evaluation and Program Planning*, Pergamon Press, Maxwell House, Fairview Park, Elmsford, New York 10523. An interdisciplinary forum for evaluators and program planners, offering innovative solutions to practical problems, different ways to analyze and interpret data, and improved methods of integrating practical evaluation with program planning.

39. *Evaluation Network*, c/o Phi Delta Kappa, Inc., P.O. Box 789, Bloomington, Indiana 47401. A professional organization for all individuals involved in evaluation efforts, this network publishes the *Evaluation News* (P.O. Box 64, Point Reves, California 94956). In addition, an evaluation training catalog (listing graduate programs in evaluation) and a Clearinghouse of evaluation training materials are maintained.

40. *Evaluation Research Society* (ERS), c/o Timothy C. Brock, Department of Psychology, Ohio State University, 1945 N. High St., Columbus, Ohio 43210. An international orgainzation committed to the improvement of the theory and practice of evaluation for public service.

41. *Futurist.* See No. 97.

42. *Health and Social Work*, National Association of Social Workers Publications Department, 2 Park Ave., New York, New York 10016. A journal committed to improving practice and extending knowledge in the field of physical and mental health.

43. *Health Policy Quarterly*, Human Sciences Press, 72 5th Ave., New York, New York 10011. This journal stimulates vital communication between program evaluators and policy makers in all phases of public health administration.

44. *Hispanic Journal of Behavioral Sciences*, Spanish Speaking Mental Health Research Center, Department of Psychology, University of California at Los Angeles, Los Angeles, California 90024. A quarterly journal of theoretical and empirical work.

45. *Hospital and Community Psychiatry*, American Psychiatric Association, 1700 18th St. N.W., Washington, D.C. 20009. A monthly journal focusing on programs and research in hospital and community treatment of psychiatric populations.

46 *Human Ecology*, Plenum Publishing Corporation, 233 Spring St., New York, New York 10013. A journal devoted to the study of interdependences between people and their environments.

47. *Innovations*, American Institutes for Research, P.O. Box 113, Palo Alto, California 94302. An experimental magazine to communicate information to mental health service personnel about innovative programs and techniques and how to implement them. Available free of charge to staff members of community mental health centers, state hospitals, other mental health agencies, and individuals interested in mental health services.

48. *Institute for Local Self-Reliance,* 1717 18th St. N.W., Washington, D.C. 20009. The primary purpose is to provide technical assistance to urban communities seeking to encourage community-controlled development. Publishes *Self-Reliance,* a newsletter.

49. *Institutions Etc.,* National Center on Institutions and Alternatives, Suite 1024, Dupont Circle Building, 1346 Connecticut Ave., Washington, D.C. 20036. A newsletter dealing with problems, strategies, research, politics, scandals, and debate surrounding institutions and community-based alternatives for the mentally ill, retarded, delinquents, aged, offenders, and dependent children.

50. *International Journal of Partial Hospitalization,* Plenum Publishing Corporation, 233 Spring St., New York, New York 10013. The primary intent of this journal is to stimulate and communicate research, programming, and administrative issues regarding all types of partial hospitalization programs and community-based rehabilitation settings.

51. *International Journal of Therapeutic Communities,* Human Sciences Press, 72 5th Ave., New York, New York 10011. An interdisciplinary journal that covers the field of therapeutic communities, therapy, and the psychodynamics of large groups, natural groups, and both small- and large-scale therapeutic institutions.

52. *International Network for Social Network Analysis,* c/o Barry Wellman, Center for Urban and Community Studies, University of Toronto, Toronto, Ontario, Canada M5S 1A1. This interdisciplinary society of network analysts publishes a bulletin *(Connections),* compiles a directory of its membership, sponsors conferences, and is associated with the new journal *Social Networks.*

53. *In Touch,* National Mental Health Association, 1800 N. Kent St., Arlington, Virginia 22209. Published six times a year for members and friends of the NMHA, resources on a separate topic are covered in each issue including pertinent articles, publications, audiovisual aids, hotlines, organizations, and clearinghouses.

54. *Journal of Applied Behavior Analysis,* Department of Human Development and Family Life, University of Kansas, Lawrence, Kansas 66045. Devoted to operant programs in applied settings.

55. *Journal of Behavorial Assessment,* Plenum Publishing Corporation, 233 Spring St., New York, New York 10013. A broad-based journal concerned with measurement of human behavior; contributions are from the fields of behavior therapy, behavioral medicine, biofeedback, and others.

56. *Journal of Community Psychology,* Clinical Psychology Publishing Company, 4 Conant Square, Brandon, Vermont 05733. Devoted to research, evaluation, assessment, and interventions that deal with human behavior in community settings. Emphasizes the community as meeting needs and supporting growth and development of its residents.

57. *Journal of Current Social Issues,* 10 Pelham Pkwy., Pelham Manor, New York, 10803. Devoted to various topics of social significance.

58. *Journal of Man–Environment Relations,* S-126 Henderson Building, Pennsylvania State University, University Park, Pennsylvania 16802. Devoted to basic and applied research on relationships between designed and natural environments and human behavior.

59. *Journal of Prevention,* Human Sciences Press, 72 5th Ave, New York, New York 10011. Emphasizes articles in the fields of primary prevention.

60. *Journal of Voluntary Action Research.* See No. 13.

61. *Knowledge: Creation, Diffusion, Utilization,* Sage Publications, P.O. Box 5024, Beverly Hills, California 90210. A forum for communication among individuals working in the fields of knowledge creation, knowledge diffusion, and knowledge utilization.

62. *La Red/The Net,* 5080 Institute for Social Research, University of Michigan, Ann Arbor, Michigan 48106. A monthly newsletter of the National Chicano Research Network.

63. *Learning Exchange,* P.O. Box 920, Evanston, Illinois 60204. A national organization to promote the development of educational networks, that is, bartering skill. It maintains a directory of learning networks in the United States, and publishes a newsletter as well as a manual on how to organize a learning exchange.

64. *Man–Environment Systems.* See No. 12.

65. *Mental Health Materials Center, Inc.,* 30 E. 29th St., New York, New York 10016. Disseminates mental health education program aids, publications, films, techniques, and ideas to mental health program planners. The MHMC publishes *a Selective Guide to Audio-Visuals for Mental Health and Family Life Education* and *Selective Guide to Publications for Mental Health and Family Life Education.* In addition, the MHMC publishes three newsletters: *In Depth Reports* (a bulletin covering innovative programs); *Sneak Previews* (a review of audiovisual materials); and *News, Notes, and Ideas* (includes conference announcements, seminars, research projects, etc.).

66. *Mental Hygiene Newsletter,* 4th Floor, O'Connor Building, 201 W. Preston St., Baltimore, Maryland 21201.

67. *National Alliance for the Mentally Ill,* 500 N. Broadway, Suite 2100, St. Louis, Missouri 63102. Advocates on behalf of persons with chronic mental illness. Published conference proceedings, *Advocacy for Persons with Chronic Mental Illness: Building a Nationwide Network.*

68. *National Association of Prevention Professionals,* c/o Gary Wapps, P.O. Box 3969, Eugene, Oregon 97403. A national organization of professionals interested in the prevention of mental illness and related problems.

69. *National Association of Social Workers.* (NASW), 1425 "H" St. N.W., Suite 600, Washington, D.C. 20050. The national professional society of social workers, the NASW publishes journals and books on special topics.

70. *National Center for Voluntary Action,* 1214 16th Ave. N.W., Washington, D.C. 20036. The NCVA's primary function is to enhance and broaden the volunteer community through its affiliation with a network of over 300 voluntary action centers. It publishes a quarterly journal, *Voluntary Action Leadership.*

71. *National Commission on Resources for Youth,* 36 W. 44th St., New York, New York 10036. Focusing on promoting youth participation the NCRY provides information, training, and other supports for interested individuals and organizations. It maintains a clearinghouse on youth participation programs and publishes a free newsletter, *Resources for Youth.*

72. *National Council of Community Mental Health Centers, Inc.,* 2233 Wisconsin Ave. N.W., Suite 322, Washington, D.C. 20007. Made up of 800 member organizations, the council is the only national organization representing community mental health centers. Its purpose is to promote the concept, funding, and delivery of community mental health services, and to provide technical guidance and support for its members. It publishes two monthly newsletters (focusing on general resources and legislative information), sponsors the *Community Mental Health Journal,* and conducts regional and national annual meetings.

73. *National Education Center for Paraprofessionals in Mental Health,* 18 Professional Center Pkwy., San Rafael, California 94903; also at New Careers Training Laboratory, CUNY Graduate Center, 33 W. 42nd St., New York, New York 10036. Serves as a resource center, gathering and disseminating information about the effective utilization of paraprofessionals in the delivery of mental health services.

74. *National Information Center on Voluntarism*(NICOV), P.O. Box 4179, Boulder, Colorado 80306. Among other functions, NICOV offers service plans including training, information, and organizational services. It also serves as a clearinghouse for information and materials on voluntarism.

75. *National Institute of Drug Abuse* (NIDA), 5600 Fishers La., Rockville, Maryland 20857. The institute is a branch of the federal Department of Health and Human Services devoted to promoting research, service, and training in the drug abuse field. It maintains the *National Clearinghouse on Drug Abuse Information.* It disseminates such information as the conference proceedings on *Nonresidential Self-Help Organizations and the Drug Abuse Problem,* as well as other reports.

76. *National Institute of Mental Health* (NIMH), 5600 Fishers La., Rockville, Maryland 20857. A branch of the federal Department of Health and Human Services the NIMH oversees the operation of community mental health centers. It also provides funding for research, service, and training in the mental health fields. It maintains a *National Clearinghouse for Mental Health Information,* providing computer-aided searches on specific topics. Specialized information is also available through the individual NIMH centers—for example, information on aging, community support, or rehabilitation. The NIMH publishes reports on specialized topics as well as an occasional-papers series, "New Dimensions in Mental Health." Resource materials are published and disseminated such as *Monitoring and Evaluating Mental Health Consultation and Education Services; A Working Manual of Simple Program Evaluation Techniques for Community Mental Health Centers; Resource Materials for Community Mental Health Program Evaluation;* and *Needs Assessment Approaches: Concepts and Methods.* Finally, the NIMH distributes free a *Directory of Federally Funded Community Mental Health Centers.*

77. *National Self-Help Clearinghouse,* CUNY Graduate School, 33 W. 42nd St., New York, New York 10036. Serves as a general resource on self-help activities. It provides referrals to self-help and mutual aid groups, assists in the formation of such groups, sponsors workshops and conferences for group leaders, and maintains bibliographic information on self-help. A newsletter, *the Self-Help Reporter,* is published.

78. *National Self-Help Resource Center,* 200 "S" St. N.W., Washington, D.C. 20009. A nonprofit technical assistance and information broker for local participation efforts. The center works with neighborhood organizations, consumer groups, service organizations, universities, libraries, and community colleges to develop citizen expertise in local planning, information networking, dialogue forums, skill banks, and

community organization. It developed the National Community Resource Center Network, a linkage among centers committed to improving the quality of citizen participation.

79. *Network Research, Inc.,* P.O. Box 18666, Denver, Colorado 80218. Publishes books, essays, and resource materials pertaining to networks.

80. *New Designs for Youth Development,* Associates for Youth Development, Inc., 5423 E. Fairmount Place, Tucson, Arizona 85712. A publication devoted to stimulating new ideas and methods for promoting the well-being of young people.

81. *Population and Environmental Psychology Newsletter,* Toni Falbo, Department of Educational Psychology, University of Texas, Austin, Texas 78712. The newsletter of the American Psychological Association, Division 34.

82. *Prevention in Human Services,* Haworth Press, 149 5th Ave., New York, New York 10010. This journal is devoted to the application of the philosophy of prevention in mental health and other human services. Three issues a year will be devoted to in-depth coverage of special themes, and the fourth will be nonthematic and publish significant work not related to the themes covered during the year.

83. *Primary Prevention Program Clearinghouse,* Department of Psychology, Dewey Hall, University of Vermont, Burlington, Vermont 05405. This clearinghouse has on file published and unpublished documents that describe primary prevention programs and/or discuss current issues in the field. Topics include drug abuse, alcoholism, rape, childrearing, sexism, the elderly, and social support systems. Many are available for sale.

84. *Professional Psychology,* American Psychological Association, 1200 17th St. N.W., Washington, D.C. 20036. A journal devoted to the various applied psychology specialities including clinical, counseling, school, community, and organizational.

85. *Program Evaluation Resource Center,* 501 S. Park Ave., Minneapolis, Minnesota 55415. General resources on program evaluation, including publication of a journal, *Evaluation.*

86. *Self-Help and Mutual Aid Association, International,* c/o Alfred Katz, School of Public Health, University of California at Los Angeles, Los Angeles, California 90024. A forum for research and information exchange on self-help/mutual support in the health and human service fields.

87. *Self-Help Reporter.* See No. 77.

88. *Self-Reliance.* See No. 48.

89. *Social Ecology Network* (SEN), c/o Abraham Jeger and Robert Slotnick, Human Resources Development Center, New York Institute of Technology, Old Westbury, New York 11568. A network within the American Psychological Association's Division of Community Psychology, SEN sponsors a resource exchange newsletter, symposia, and provides a vehicle for information sharing among ecologically oriented psychologists.

90. *Social Networks,* Journal Information Center, Elsevier's Science Division, 52 Vanderbilt Ave., New York, New York 10017. A journal focusing on network analysis, with special emphasis on relations between network structures and functions.

91. *Social Policy,* New Human Services Institute, CUNY Graduate Center, 33 W. 42nd St., New York, New York 10036. An interdisciplinary, broad-based social science journal that focuses on policy in the human services.

92. *Social Psychiatry Newsletter,* Social Psychiatry Research Institute, Inc., 150 E. 69th St., New York, New York 10021. Devoted to rational approaches to social and psychological problems in the modern world.

93. *Training/Research/Service Catalogue,* Clinical Research Center, Camarillo Neuro-Psychiatric Institute, P.O. Box A, Camarillo, California 93010. This Catalog lists training materials for professionals, paraprofessionals, and lay persons. Included are program guides for behavioral training for children, adults, and families for implementation in schools, clinics, and community mental health centers. Films depicting various therapeutic and self-enhancement skills are available for purchase or rental. Many of the materials were developed as part of the Behavior Analysis and Modification Project (see Chapter 4).

94. *Urban Alternatives Group,* 1740 Walnut St., Berkeley, California 94709. Seeks to promote community competence in health, education, and other areas as well as economic and political decentralization to enhance a sense of community. It publishes a newsletter and provides other resources for its national membership.

95. *Voluntary Action Leadership. See No. 70.*

96. *Women and Environments: International Newsletter,* c/o Faculty of Environmental Studies, 4700 Keele St., Downsview, Ontario, Canada M3J

2R2. Serves as an information network, publishing articles, abstracts, reviews, and comments in such areas as ecology, planning, architecture, space, and so on.

97. *World Future Society,* 4916 St. Elmo Ave. (Bethesda Branch), Washington, D.C. 20014. The society publishes the *Futurist,* a monthly popular journal of forecasts, trends, and ideas about the future. The society's free catalog is a resource of books, magazines, newsletters, and learning materials of interest to social ecologists.

Author Index

Subject Index